D1000200

MEDICAL CARE
IN DEVELOPING COUNTRIES

MEDICAL CARE IN DEVELOPING COUNTRIES

A Primer on the Medicine of Poverty
and
A Symposium from Makerere

Edited and Illustrated by
MAURICE KING, M.A. Cantab., M.R.C.P. Lond.

Based on a conference assisted by WHO/UNICEF, and an experimental edition assisted by UNICEF

Published with a grant from the Ford Foundation, through the 'East African Teaching Materials Fund'

Nairobi
OXFORD UNIVERSITY PRESS
Lusaka Addis Ababa London
1966

Oxford University Press, Ely House, London W. 1
GLASGOW NEW YORK TORONTO MELBOURNE WELLINGTON
CAPE TOWN SALISBURY IBADAN NAIROBI LUSAKA ADDIS ABABA
BOMBAY CALCUTTA MADRAS KARACHI LAHORE DACCA
KUALA LUMPUR HONG KONG TOKYO

Cover artwork prepared by
HILLARY CORREIA

Made and Printed in East Africa

To the reader and to our students, and through them to the common man and his family in developing countries everywhere.

FOREWORD

No conscientious doctor in Africa can afford to isolate himself from the special needs and circumstances of community medicine any more than he can afford to isolate himself from Africa as a whole. These needs and circumstances are very real and very compulsive in determining the general pattern of medical care and enforcing a logical solution to the problems of under-doctored countries, which are entirely different from those of the highly-doctored ones. The needs and conditions of the patient, and the diseases from which he suffers are different, and the types of subject on which he needs education and advice differ quite radically, though perhaps not in principle, from those which are put before practitioners in other countries. Moreover, the responsibility of the doctor is inevitably different. Whereas in the highly-doctored countries it is possible, and often reasonable, for him to accept responsibility for a limited group of people knowing well that others can seek and obtain equivalent advice and care elsewhere, in the under-doctored countries he must often accept responsibility for large numbers of people, often quite beyond the possibility of his own personal management, acknowledging that if he declines this responsibility he deprives them of all sources of medical help. He thus finds himself necessarily as the central unit of a group of people of varied training and origin whom he must himself manage, supervise and often train in order to meet his responsibilities.

Although these points are put as if they should be axiomatic, they have not always been recognized. Too much of tropical medical practice consists of a limited effort to repeat the activities which are appropriate to highly-doctored areas, to the advantage of a few but to the great deprivation of the majority, and, though there have been brilliant exceptions, many of the available textbooks have dealt with medicine exclusively from the point of view of the highly-developed areas. Admittedly the scientific basis of medicine must be the same in both, and the developing countries, whether tropical or not, deserve the same high standard of technical education for their doctors in this scientific basis, but the vocational aspect of medicine differs radically and different teachings and practices are more than justified, indeed they are essential.

This book is a leader amongst the brilliant exceptions in the teaching of the vocational aspect of medicine. The twelve axioms with which it starts epitomize the attitudes which run throughout the book and deserve very careful study in their fully amplified form. The authors regard the doctor as the essential unit in an organization, not as an isolated individual. Moreover, they develop that organization on the soundest of principles, ensuring accessibility to the public by due attention to distance, as well as to population/staff ratios within the organization.

The doctor needs urgently to retain his technical skill; moreover he needs to acquire new skills in some aspects of technology in the laboratory and elsewhere which were catered for separately in the more elaborate arrangements of the Medical School in which he was educated. The authors range over all of these subjects and have produced a manual which should itself go a long way to modifying patterns of medical care, and thereby hasten the advancement of health, which is a universal object of all developing countries.

Professor of Tropical Hygiene in the University of London and Director of the Ross Institute. GEORGE MACDONALD

PREFACE

The idea of writing this book came to the editor, a lecturer in microbiology at Makerere, while acting as locum for his friend Dr. Peter Cox, a missionary in Karamoja, one of the remoter provinces of Uganda. There he found himself faced with many problems that were new to him. But, though his ignorance of the answers was largely due to the deficiencies of his own training and experience, combined with the further atrophy of his clinical skills occasioned by many years at the laboratory bench, it seemed that they were perhaps not the whole cause of his inadequacy. In addition to the ordinary problems of medicine and surgery, to which there were well tried solutions, there was a further range for which there seemed to be no ready answers. How should a doctor spend his time under such circumstances? How should such a hospital be built? What drugs should the hospital stock? What should be the scope of the laboratory in a hospital of this kind? What form of record system is appropriate? How should blood transfusion be undertaken in a remote rural area? To a few of these questions ingenious solutions had been found, but many remained unanswered, and there appeared to be some that had not even been formulated. Why not collect them up and gather them into a handy paperback? It was with this idea in his mind that the editor returned to Kampala.

The project was well received at Makerere, for it seemed that by some strange chance the editor had stumbled into an empty space in the bookshelves of the world, and that it was one that particularly wanted filling. Nevertheless, the final decision to go ahead would never have been made without the continued encouragement and enthusiasm of Professor D. B. Jelliffe, nor would it have been possible had not Professor W. D. Foster kindly let his only senior lecturer wander so far from the narrow confines of the Petri dish. With the assistance of WHO/UNICEF a conference was held a year later on 'Health Centres and Hospitals in Africa', at the seventeen sessions of which many aspects of the work of these units were discussed. This book is largely the outcome of that conference, and many of the ideas recorded here were originally put forward by its delegates whose deliberations were recorded on tape for subsequent analysis.

From these tapes draft manuscript was prepared for submission to those whose names appear at the head of the chapters and to other interested people also, ideas and information being placed in whatever chapter they fitted best. A duplicated experimental edition of 200 copies was then prepared and circulated. This was favourably received and many readers were kind enough to send in criticisms and suggestions. These have been incorporated in the present edition, and such virtue as it may have thus lies to the credit of many contributors for whose ideas the editor has but provided paper and ink. But, as it grew, it seemed that the completed work might be more than a mere compendium of assorted information. Something seemed to be appearing, something which for want of any other term can perhaps best be called a 'primer on the medicine of poverty'. A distinct pattern of medical care, a particular attitude to medicine slowly seemed to define itself as each chapter was worked over and the final volume gradually took shape. The main feature determining this pattern of care and this attitude to medicine is poverty, and all that this means, but for a further analysis of it the reader must turn to the first chapter (1:4). He may be interested to know that the thesis that is developed there, and the axioms which follow it, were almost the last contribution to the book, not the first.

The main criticism made of the experimental edition was that the generalizations made in it were too categorical. To some extent this is perhaps inevitable, for the value of a generalization is apt to be lost if too many qualifications are inserted. Nevertheless, in preparing the present edition an attempt has been made to counter this criticism, but even so the reader is cautioned to be watchful.

The editor of a symposium has surely a right to use a few paragraphs of it as a platform. He would like to make the most of his opportunity to leave a message with his colleagues in the developed countries.

To doctors in developed countries — a spell of service abroad?

After a glance at the first figure and the opening pages of the introduction no more need be said about the need for doctors in developing countries. Eventually they will be produced in sufficient numbers by these countries themselves, but in the meanwhile, the highly-doctored parts of the world have a great responsibility to lend some of their skills to areas in greater need. 'We should like to see it widely accepted in this country that a professional career should normally include a period of work overseas in a developing country'. These were the words of the first British Minister of Overseas Development, and they surely hold true for other developed countries also.

Long service abroad with all that prolonged immersion in a strange culture implies, especially in the difficulties of rearing teen-age children, must make it the role of a tiny minority. But, although the opportunities for service of this kind are now more limited than they were, due to the promotion of local citizens to the most senior posts in all fields, the need for such service is likely to continue for a long time to come — provided that the expatriate is prepared not to get to the top. The continuity and experience that come with long service make it especially valuable, so it is to be hoped that there will always be some who are prepared to undertake it, particularly in mission hospitals and medical schools (especially their basic science departments). But long service has to be entered into on one condition only, this is with the full realization that it can last only for as long as a particular person is wanted, and no longer. Because it is difficult to lay down any further rules, and because it must inevitably remain the choice of the few, no more will be said about it here beyond the fact that the need for long-term service very definitely still exists.

The great opportunity is for short-term service, say for a period of from two to five years somewhere between the ages of twenty-five and thirty-five. When internships are over and before children require secondary schooling a doctor and his family are mobile: this is the time for a spell abroad. Until recently some of it would have been taken up by military service, but, now that in the United Kingdom at any rate, this is no longer required, a period of voluntary service overseas rightly, and much more pleasantly and profitably, fills its place. When the remainder of a professional life is to be spent caring for the affluent, a few years of it spent in the developing countries, where at least half of the world's peoples live, will provide a stimulating challenge and help in forming a balanced view of the world. As for the professional experience gained, the general practice of the tropics, which is the work of a district hospital, has much to commend it over the general practice of Europe or North America. The general practice of Africa is usually the total care of the sick with all that this means, that of England is so often only the treatment of minor ailments — in developing countries auxiliaries usually see to these (1:15) (7:1). Later on much is said of the difficulties of district hospital practice. This is the time to say what a very exhilarating and rewarding experience it can be, despite these difficulties, and when the time does come to return, the worries of the city commuter will probably seem a poor exchange for the zest and gaiety of the tropical villager.

There is space for only a few general hints. Following the practice of the rest of the book these will be summarized like this:

Method: Planning a period of service in the developing countries.

Start considering the possibility of it while still a student, as part of the general planning of a career.

Make the most of the opportunities provided by the years immediately after internships are completed.

Find out as much as you can about the job, the people, the place, and if possible your colleagues, before you go. It won't be possible to follow the golden rule of never taking a job before inspecting it, and the completely per-

fect post is unlikely to turn up. Perhaps in the end it may be best if it does not, but to be forewarned is to be forearmed, and it will be for a limited period only.

Make the most of your talents — if these be academic, look for a lectureship, or a post with one of the research organizations.

Don't be put off by the thought of surgical responsibilities for which you have never been trained. See to it that you spend your first few months abroad where there is someone at hand to teach you the essential surgery, and obstetrics. Be comforted by the thought that, though you may not be expert, it is likely to be either you or nobody, and most patients will still prefer you.

See if you can find somewhere to come back to before you go, and, if you can get a deferred or 'proleptic appointment' in a practice or with a hospital board, then so much the better. In higher professional circles, in Britain at any rate, there are signs that a period of service abroad is now increasingly counting in a candidate's favour, so be heartened.

For a time you will be leaving your own culture, and many of the influences which have produced and now maintain present standards and values will now no longer be operating, so be watchful. Try to go abroad married; the tropics are still not much of a place for the celibate, and they are in many ways suited to those with young families.

Be prepared to go where you are wanted most, this is more likely to be the rural areas than the capital city.

Remember that, at least as far as expatriates are concerned, the roads of developing countries are now more deadly than their microbes.

Insure everything you possess.

If there is the remotest possibility of your coming don't delay, but, if you are British, write to the Ministry of Overseas Development, Eland House, Stag Place, London, S.W.I.

What of the 'rat-race', the ladder of fierce competition for status and professional advancement? How will a period of service abroad affect this? Though the overseas universities are sometimes a good stepping stone to preferment for those who go abroad with higher qualifications and research hard while they are here, in general, it is for the many graduates who will later become general practitioners that a period of service overseas is so well adapted. Those who are uncertain as to whether or not to join this race are reminded that they already represent favoured minorities in favoured nations. By world standards they are already very lucky, there is a world shortage of doctors and they are unlikely ever to lack not only their daily bread, but, by these same standards, a lot of jam as well. To contract deliberately out of the race for the race's sake, and do the job for the job's sake, is likely to prove both a considerable liberation of the spirit and a source of the most uncommon content as well.

Having said this the editor would most particularly like to thank for their continued help and interest Dr. David Morley of the London School of Hygiene and the Institute of Child Health at Great Ormond Street; Dr. David Bradley of this department, Dr. Patrick Hamilton during his stay at Makerere, and Dr. N. R. E. Fendall, formerly Director of Medical Services in Kenya and presently with the Rockefeller Foundation. Especial gratitude is also due to Richard Jolly of the Department of Applied Economics in Cambridge and his wife Alison, not only for their great help and interest, but also for their most generous hospitality during two working Christmases spent in Zambia during which parts of this book were written.

These are but a few of the many to whom thanks are due for what may be found useful on the pages following, further names being listed in Appendix K. But before ending, thanks are due to an even larger and more anonymous number, who, by their taxes and their gifts have made possible the peace, facilities, and above all the leisure of this fine university, without which no venture of this kind is possible. Lastly, most sincere thanks are due to Joyce Bosa, Betty Eddy, Janet Volrath, Wynne Quanstrom and Enid Schram for their great efforts in the preparation of this manuscript.

But the end of one thing is only the beginning of another. In this symposium a certain body of knowledge has been tapped, and some ideas recorded. If readers like what has been provided for them here and this edition sells out, it is hoped to replace it by a second to follow hard upon the heels of the first. *The editor looks forward therefore to corresponding with any reader who feels he has anything to add (or detract)* and would like to point out that, with the notable exception of Chapter 20, on the village of Aro, almost all the ideas gathered here came from the minds of expatriates. It is to be hoped that in the future more and more of the new ideas and innovations will come from the citizens of the developing countries themselves, for whom this symposium was written.

University Hall,
Makerere University College.
(Box 2072, Kampala, Uganda.)

Maurice King
August 14th 1966

CONTENTS

APPENDICES

A LIST OF ILLUSTRATIONS

A NOTE TO THE READER

Reference are to chapters and section numbers. Thus the figures 1:2 refer to the second section of the first chapter. References to firms supplying equipment are given as a three letter code like this — (A&H), which refers to Allen & Hanbury Limited, and is to be found in Appendix A. References to journals are given thus — (1), and are to be found in Appendix B. References to books are given in this way — /1/, and are in Appendix C.

Notwithstanding the help that has kindly been given by The World Health Organization, particularly its regional office in Brazzaville, only the editor and those whose names are to be found in Appendix K are finally responsible for what is said here. This symposium does not therefore necessarily represent the decisions and the policy of either the World Health Organization, or any other body.

It is essential that a book of this nature should continually be kept up to date and although it is hoped that there will be a demand for a revised edition, this will take time to produce. In the meanwhile there be many items of new information relating to the contents of the current edition that readers will want to know as soon as they become available. To make this possible the Editor of the *East African Medical Journal* has kindly agreed to insert, when requested, amendment slips in the monthly issues of the *Journal*. In order to avoid confusion each amendment slip will carry a reference to the section number concerned and the slip can then be pasted over the relevant passage.

This arrangement with the *East African Medical Journal* will continue experimentally for a year, the first issue to contain the new material being that of January 1967.

The annual subscription to the *East African Medical Journal*, which is concerned mainly with tropical medicine, is 45/- inclusive of postage and inquiries should be addressed to The Editor, P.O. Box 1632, Nairobi, Kenya.

Chapter One

INTRODUCTION

Maurice King

:1 **Medical care and the condition of the common man in developing countries.** The cleavage of the world into rich nations and poor ones divides care in sickness quite as sharply as it does any other aspect of the human condition. In this, the great division of mankind, the rich have money and medical skills in comparative abundance, the poor have not.

These facts determine the nature of the entire practice of medicine in developing countries, and to show how wide the disparity is they have been illustrated diagrammatically in the first figure. On one scale the average number of patients per doctor is recorded for several countries rich and poor, and on the other, the average sum spent annually by these same countries on the health of their citizens. Because the nations differ so widely, both scales are logarithmic and cover three cycles. But although this makes a convenient diagram, such scales tend to hide the real difference between countries, unless it is realized that there is a thousandfold difference between the top of each scale and the bottom.

This figure shows that a developing country is fortunate if it has as few as 15,000 patients for each of its doctors, or can spend more than 7/- ($1.0) a year on the medical care of each of its people. This would be difficult enough, but the situation is usually made worse by the inequality with which doctors are distributed between town and country. In Kenya for instance, the overall doctor-patient ratio is 1 : 10,000, but in the rural areas the ratio rises as high as 1 : 50,000 (14). The situation is said to

---

Footnote. It may interest the reader to know that aid to the developing countries accounts for an average of no more than 0.7% of the Gross National Products of the industrial nations, despite the fact these have been increasing by about 5% annually. In this, the Development Decade, only France approaches the target set, which is 1%. The annual total has stayed the same for five years past, and, in real terms, has even been falling.

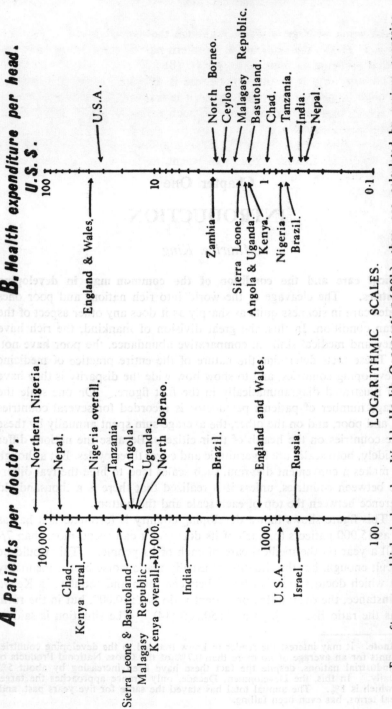

Fig. 1. **TWO MAJOR DETERMINANTS OF MEDICAL CARE —— DOCTORS AND MONEY.**

From figures published by the World Health Organisation (39b); they are calculated by various countries in different ways so these diagrams should be interpreted with caution. Also (8),(14).

be even worse in Nigeria where, although the overall doctor population ratio is 1:33,000, the ratio in the Northern part of the country has been reported as being as high as 1:140,000 (8).

The disparity in health expenditure is also seen to be even greater than might appear at first sight, when it is realized that industrial countries spend large additional sums on such essential health activities as drainage and sanitation.

Doctors are scarce; money is lacking, and so is all that goes with it in the form of buildings, drugs, equipment, and facilities of every kind. But this does not limit difficulties to be overcome in the provision of medical care.

Fig. 2. POPULATION RURALITY.

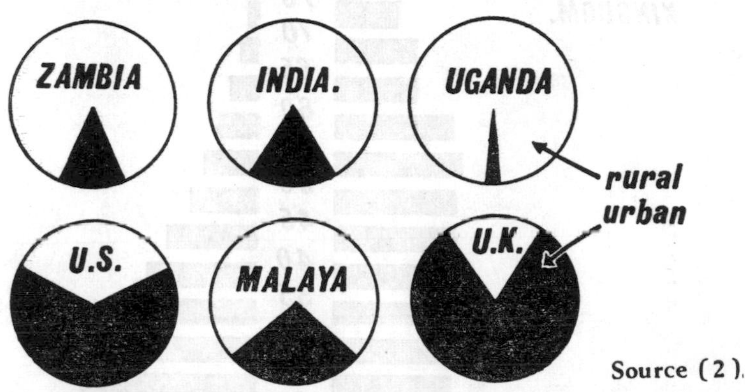

Source (2).

The patients themselves are poor with all that this means in terms of nutrition, education, transport and housing. Thus, for a typical developing country, the average value for the total goods and services produced per head, the Gross National Product or 'GNP per head' (18:2c), is about a twentieth of that for an industrial one, and the gap between them continues to widen. The developing countries not only contain half the world's people (1:5) but they also contain most of that half of them who are reckoned to be hungry or undernourished or both (30). In Uganda, and Uganda is comparatively fortunate, only about 40 per cent. of all children complete even their primary education, and only about 20 per cent. of the adult population have had four or more years of primary schooling. The peoples of most developing countries live in the rural areas where lack of transport imposes major difficulties in the provision of medical care. Though the amenities of an outdoor life may make up in large measure for the inadequacies of a villager's hut, the crowded conditions of urban 'shanty-towns' offer no compensation for poor housing there. Because modern agricultural technology permits one countryman to feed ten townsmen, the spread of improved farming methods promises to increase rural unemployment, to hasten townward migration and to make the urban slums of developing countries one of the major human problems in coming decades. Urbanization is already taking place at a formidable rate, as the slums of Lagos, Calcutta, Sao Paulo and Nairobi demonstrate only too well.

Fig. 3. **POPULATION AGE STRUCTURE.**

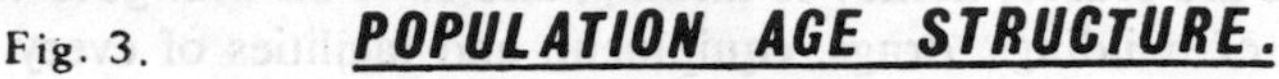

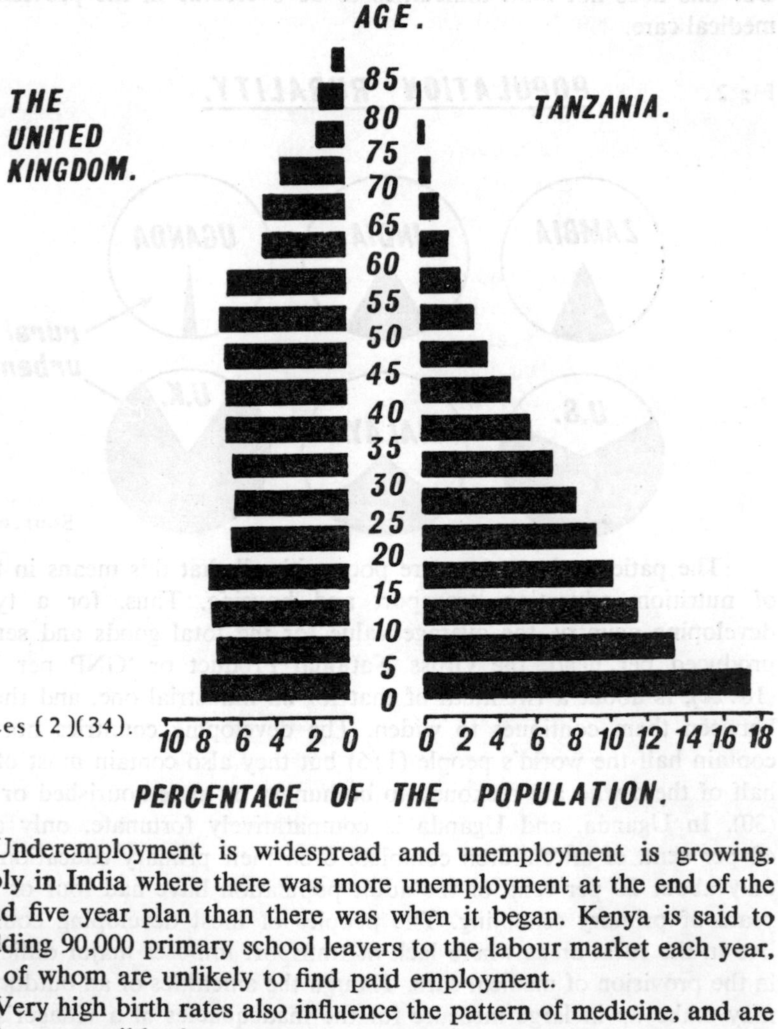

Sources (2)(34).

Underemployment is widespread and unemployment is growing, notably in India where there was more unemployment at the end of the second five year plan than there was when it began. Kenya is said to be adding 90,000 primary school leavers to the labour market each year, most of whom are unlikely to find paid employment.

Very high birth rates also influence the pattern of medicine, and are largely responsible for producing populations with the type of age structure shown in Figure 3 that is usual in developing countries. Death rates, especially those in early childhood, are also high: in one part of Western Nigeria, for example, half of all the children born die before they are five years old from infections and malnutrition, all of which are potentially preventable. Nevertheless, in spite of this, populations are growing rapidly. In Latin America the growth rate is 3 per cent. annually and in South East Asia it is only slightly less. In some countries it is as high as $3\frac{1}{2}$ per cent., which means a doubling of the population in about 20 years (Figure 39 (18:1)).

Lastly, there is the remoteness of pre-industrial cultures from the concepts of scientific medicine and the 'cross-cultural conflict' to which this leads (4:5).

Such a picture may seem too simple, for some nations are poorer than others; there are patches of under-development in Europe and North America, and affluent elites in Asia, Africa and South America. Nevertheless, the division of the world into rich nations and poor ones is generally a fairly clear one.

:2 **The central thesis.** The central thesis of this book is that the factors that have just been described not only provide a formidable challenge to the provision of 'medical care' in developing countries, but give it a very distinctive quality. But, before developing this thesis further something must be said about just what is meant by the term 'medical care'. A distinction can be made between finding out fundamental knowledge in the first place, and then finding out how best it can be applied in the community. *Medical care is the study of how the fundamental knowledge embodied in medicine and public health can best be applied to the benefit of a community*. One of its main attributes is its comprehensiveness, and, as this symposium will show, medical care has its own particular approach to very many subjects. In its present usage it is a term which appears to have originated in North America in connection with health insurance plans, but, in the United Kingdom, the concept of medical care is so bound up with the National Health Service, that, until recently, it has hardly emerged as a separate entity.

The thesis that, in developing countries, medical care not only provides a major challenge, but has a very distinctive quality, can be developed as the following four propositions.

1) That medical care in developing countries differs sharply from medical care in industrial ones.
2) That its main determinant is poverty rather than a warm climate.
3) That it is a subject of the greatest importance.
4) That it is possible to gather together a certain body of knowledge as to how this challenge is best met.

The main purpose of this symposium is to assemble the knowledge suggested by proposition four in a form useful to doctors working in developing countries, and to students preparing to work in them.

1:3 **Proposition one. That medical care in developing countries differs sharply from medical care in industrial ones.**

This is largely self-evident from what has been said in the opening paragraphs about the factors which determine the pattern of care in developing countries — a doctor has to approach his tasks in a different way when the doctor-patient ratio is 1:100,000 from the methods he is able to employ when it is only 1:1,000.

Although the first figure and what has already been said provide the basis for the distinction, it may be difficult for some readers to picture the conditions that actually exist without a specific example. This will be provided in the words of an able young Makerere graduate describing his experience in a district hospital in East Africa during the conference mentioned in the Preface. But before quoting him, it must be pointed out that the country where he worked is richer, better doctored and better administered medically than very many parts of Africa.

> 'The hospital had a hundred beds, and, although there was one other doctor, he mostly looked after the district and the administration. I would say that my problems were mainly these; overwork, lack of equipment, lack of staff, shortage of drugs, the absence of anyone to consult with, shortage of beds and the lack of diagnostic facilities. I had to look after the medical, surgical, maternity and children's wards. I used to see the outpatients; I had one major operating day each week; I had to collect blood for transfusions, do many police post-mortems and often attend court. In other words I was needed in several places at the same time, and this used to make life a little bit difficult ... Very few trained nurses and medical assistants were employed at the hospital. Only one medical assistant or certificated nurse was on duty each night for the whole hospital, with one ward maid or dresser in each ward. They did not know how to look after drips, so I used to visit the wards at night to do this myself ... We did not have any Balkan beams but I asked a carpenter to make one, he made two, but we did not have any pulleys so I asked the orthopaedic surgeon at the national hospital for some, but he could not spare any. I could not obtain any scalp vein needles, nor enough of the big ones for taking blood. There was a pressure lamp in the theatre which attracted flying arthopods; these frequently hit the lamp and fell into the operation

> wound . . . There was one laboratory assistant, but he could not do a blood urea, a blood sugar, test for urobilinogen in the urine, or count reticulocytes. He was also very busy and could not cope up with all the stools I wanted him to look at . . . We were very short of beds; there were lots of floor cases, and often two children in the same cot . . . The premature babies had to be nursed in the general ward . . . There was no physiotherapist or social worker, so it was difficult to look after paraplegics and impossible to discharge the homeless. There was no fence round the hospital, and visitors came in at any time.'

After such an account, which nobody at the conference thought out of the way or disputed, some at least of the distinctive features of medical care in a developing country need no further elaboration. There are some better district hospitals in the country concerned, and most do in fact have electricity, but the one described is not exceptional.

:4 **Second proposition. The main determinant of the pattern of medical care in developing countries is poverty, rather than a warm climate.**

Poverty directly determines the pattern of medical care; it is not easy to provide medical care of any kind when the money available per head may be only a fortieth of that available to an industrial nation.

In the account of medical care that has just been quoted it was poverty and what follows from it that was responsible for the lack of doctors, nurses, physiotherapists, social workers, drugs and equipment; for the lack of a proper transfusion service, for the overcrowding, and, through their lack of education, for the indiscipline of the patients. To a lesser extent the pattern of medical care in developing countries is determined by the diseases commonly found in them. Some of these are almost entirely due to poverty, and others are only found where there is a warm climate for their transmission. This is best understood historically.

In former times, apart from tiny elites, everyone in the world was poor, and the diseases that are mainly due to poverty were once seen everywhere. During the last century or so, many countries which happen to be in the temperate zone have undergone industrial revolutions which have enabled them to conquer poverty to a great extent and to apply modern methods of disease control. The diseases of poverty have thus retreated to the countries which remain poor, and which happen to be in the tropics. Thus cholera, smallpox, leprosy, plague, rabies, and probably kwashiorkor, were common in Europe but are now effectively confined to the tropics. More recently even tuberculosis has retreated to the poorer tropical countries, because poverty prevents the application of the knowledge which is fast banishing it from the industrial ones.

There is another group of diseases, which are spread by vectors that need a warm climate, and which are not usually transmitted in the colder parts of the world. These tropical diseases include yellow fever, trypanosomiasis, onchocerciasis, and schistosomiasis. Malaria is a special case, and fits into neither group exactly, because although transmission can take place in temperate regions, it occurs much more readily in the tropics. Wealth has helped to banish it from industrial countries, and could at least reduce its incidence in the many developing ones where it is still common, as it could other tropical diseases also.

Poverty thus has a double effect in determining the pattern of medical care; it directly effects the availability of equipment and skills, and indirectly it has an effect on the disease pattern of a community which may be greater than the specifically tropical location of most developing countries.

If this is so, then medical care in Uganda, India or Peru is different from that in Europe, not so much because Uganda is in the tropics, but because Uganda is poor. That the developing country pattern of medical care is independent of a specifically tropical location is well shown by central and southern Chile. These areas lie outside the tropics and resemble Uganda much more closely in the pattern of their medical care than they do the United States which lies at an equivalent latitude.

From this it follows that a doctor preparing for work in the developing countries must be taught the principles of medical care under conditions of poverty, as well as about the diseases of warm climates. It is the aim of this symposium to provide this knowledge, it is in effect, a 'primer on the medicine of poverty'.

1:5 **Third proposition. That medical care in developing countries is a subject of the greatest importance.**

Most doctors have been trained against the background of medical care as it is possible in industrial countries. It is therefore natural for there to be an attitude that this is the usual way in which the world's sick are, and should be, looked after, and medical care provided. This attitude is false, for such lavish standards of care are exceptional — most of the world's 3.3 billion people are probably lucky even if they can get the kind of care described in the first proposition. If China is included, then no less than two-thirds of the world's people live in developing countries, if she is excluded then only half of them do. Medical care under the circumstances of the developing countries is thus of the greatest importance from the global point of view — *it is medical care for the majority of mankind.*

1:6 **Fourth proposition. That it is possible to gather together a body of knowledge as to how this challenge is best met.**

As has already been stated, medical care is the study of how to make existing medical knowledge available to the community. In the special circumstances of the developing countries this study produces a certain body of knowledge. Inevitably, this knowledge is untidy, it has no clearly defined limits, it is closely interconnected, it has its own particular approach to many disciplines and there is no existing framework to build upon. The knowledge gathered here has been organized as twelve groups of rules or axioms, two particular attitudes of mind, one especially useful concept, and much minute practical detail. The first three are the major axioms on which the others depend. After these come three which should determine 'the pattern of a medical service'. Then come three which determine the role of the doctor and those who help him. The last two axioms deal with the adaptation of medical care to local conditions. Of the latter, one brings out the importance of adapting methods to the special needs of the developing countries — 'methodology'. The other emphasizes the links between medical care and the local culture, and the adaptations which this demands.

One of the two particular attitudes of mind that are required is that of the economist which permeates much of the book, the other, the sociological one, is implicit in Chapter Four on the 'cross-cultural outlook'. The especially useful concept is that of 'the community diagnosis' in Chapter Five and the minute detail occupies most of the rest of these pages. Sometimes the knowledge is entirely specific to developing countries, the maternity village (19:6), the mother's shelter (13:3) or the bicycle ambulance (28:4), for example. Often it is not. Thus the community diagnosis is relevant to medicine anywhere, but is particularly useful under the varied cultural circumstances of developing countries.

Very often the critical part of making knowledge available is merely knowing what is relevant to particular circumstances. Thus the mere selection of material can in itself be of great value. There have for instance been several enquiries for the contents of the chapter on laboratory services, not because its contents are original, but because the selection of techniques and the apparatus suited to them is a skilled and time-consuming task.

The reader will probably note the absence here of any special mention of medicine or surgery. This knowledge is already widely available in books discussed in Chapter Twenty-Nine on the library, and anyway our sister university in Ibadan has just prepared a symposium on surgery in Africa /50/.

TWELVE AXIOMS ON MEDICAL CARE

1:7 Medical care is so complex that such axioms as can be defined are inevitably linked to one another closely and it is not always possible to discuss them separately. Many apply generally, but are especially important in developing countries. The first is, in one sense, out of line with the others, for it is a forthright statement of values, yet it lies behind them all. Without it they would all be entirely irrelevant.

This page has been left blank so that all the axioms can be seen together.

TWELVE GROUPS OF AXIOMS ON MEDICAL CARE

MAJOR AXIOMS

One — The medical care of the common man is immensely worthwhile.

Two — Medical care must be approached with an objective attitude of mind which is as free as far as possible from preconceived notions exported from industrial countries.

Three — The maximum return in human welfare must be obtained from the limited money and skill available:

a) In estimating this return means must not be confused with ends.

b) Medical care must be adapted to the needs of an intermediate technology.

THE PATTERN OF A MEDICAL SERVICE

Four — A medical service must be organized to provide for steady growth in both the quantity and the quality of medical care.

Five — Patients should be treated as close to their homes as possible in the smallest, cheapest, most humbly staffed and most simply equipped unit that is capable of looking after them adequately.

Six — a) Some form of medical care should be supplied to all the people all the time.

b) In respect of most of the common conditions there is little relationship between the cost and size of a medical unit and its therapeutic efficiency.

c) Medical care can be effective without being comprehensive.

Seven — a) Medical services should be organized from the bottom up and not from the top down.

b) The health needs of a community must be related to their wants.

THE ROLE OF THE DOCTOR AND THOSE WHO HELP HIM

Eight — The role a doctor has to play in a developing country differs in many important respects from that he plays in a developed one.

Nine — The role played by auxiliaries is both different and more important in developing countries than in developed ones.

Ten — All medical workers have an educational role which is closely linked to their therapeutic one.

a) Skilled staff members have a duty to teach the less skilled ones.

b) All medical staff have a teaching vocation in the community they serve.

THE ADAPTATION OF MEDICAL CARE TO LOCAL CONDITIONS

Eleven — In developing countries medical care requires the adaptation and development of its own particular methodology.

Twelve — Medical care and the local culture are closely linked.

a) Medical care must be carefully adapted to the opportunities and limitations of the local culture.

b) Where possible medical services should do what they can to improve the non-medical aspects of a culture in the promotion of a 'better life' for the people.

THE MAJOR AXIOMS

1:8 **First axiom.** THE MEDICAL CARE OF THE COMMON MAN IS IMMENSELY WORTHWHILE.

This is not only of inestimable value to this man himself, to his family and his community, but as a human action it is also something of lasting value for its own sake. If this is admitted, then some support at least must be given to 'vocation' as distinct from 'profession'; support for the idea that the medical care of a district or a remote hospital has a value in the scheme of things independent of the personal advancement of the practitioner in terms of either seniority, wealth or even of technical expertise. Prestige however he will have, not that of wide professional acknowledgement, but something which is surely of even greater value, the status inherent in the affection and respect of a grateful district.

Several people who were so kind as to read this in draft urged the deletion of this section. It has been deliberately left in with the conviction that it is only this sense of values which makes possible that continued and dedicated toil which medicine so often demands. One reader even urged its deletion on the grounds that the intention to do good is now hardly even respectable. On the contrary, it is held that whatever may be its value as a science, and whatever the social and financial preferment that attend it, medicine is still a major vehicle of compassion, of charity in its true sense.

1:9 **Second axiom.** MEDICAL CARE MUST BE APPROACHED WITH AN OBJECTIVE ATTITUDE OF MIND WHICH IS FREE AS FAR AS POSSIBLE FROM PRECONCEIVED NOTIONS EXPORTED FROM INDUSTRIAL COUNTRIES.

So often, those whose earlier medical experience was obtained in Europe or North America feel that anything they do in the difficult circumstances of the tropics is only second best. In one sense so it may be, but they should overcome the feeling of guilt which the attainment of only the second best implies, and think out a fresh set of standards more closely related to the realities of the situation. For example, the European tradition that no patient coming to a hospital must ever be sent home without first seeing a doctor is obviously quite impracticable, when he may have only a minute or two to see each one, or possibly even less. Such an unreal standard has to be discarded, and an efficient sorting system organized using carefully trained and supervised auxiliaries (12:2).

A similar approach is required to hospital building. Apart from the operating theatre, what might be termed the 'white corridors' attitude to hospital construction is not only financially impossible, it is not even desirable, and cheap local methods of construction are quite adequate for many parts of a hospital (10:6, 12:3). For most doctors, medical administrators, architects and public works departments, this will mean a profound change in their present attitudes as to what a district hospital or a health centre should look like.

Professional co-operation with 'traditional healers' who are unqualified in the Western sense is another example of how an established professional ethic may have to be adapted to the needs of a developing country (3:10, 20:6).

The distinctive needs of medical care in developing countries are frequently forgotten, too often the wrong answers to its problems have been exported from the developed, industrial ones. We have been a long time in finding out that the village mother may be the best person to look after the clinic records of her children, and how many tropical hospitals are actually built with a hostel for the patients' relatives? (10:2).

0 **Third axiom.** THE MAXIMUM RETURN IN HUMAN WELFARE MUST BE OBTAINED FROM THE LIMITED MONEY AND SKILL AVAILABLE.

0a **In estimating this return means must not be confused with ends.** Human welfare is not easy to measure, and the resources of a country have to be spread between education, economic and social welfare as well as the provision of medical services. This is not the place to discuss the distribution of funds between these fields, but, within medicine, the aim must be to make the most of limited resources in the reduction of disease — this is the ultimate purpose, not the provision of doctors, hospitals or even health centres, for these are merely means that are easy to measure towards an end that is hard to measure. As planning aims they are the equivalent to a motor manufacturer trying to maximize, not his output of vehicles, but the number of his workers and the size of his factory. That doctors and hospital beds are so common a planning aim is due in large measure to the great practical difficulties of measuring the effect of medical endeavour in the reduction of disease — the necessary statistics just do not exist (5:5). But even in the absence of data which make it possible to estimate the reduction of disease with any precision, there are certain approaches to the problem, which, though crude, are certainly practical.

One of them is to ask how much benefit is likely to follow several roughly costly alternative aims. On a national or regional level a sum of money, say £100,000 ($280,000), might be spent in several different ways. Even though benefit is not an easy thing to measure, some measurement of it is possible in terms of life expectancy and morbidity, and a rough judgement can often be made of the general benefits that are likely to follow the spending of a given sum on such alternative ventures as the prevention of poliomyelitis by immunization, the control of malaria by such methods as spraying and draining of swamps, or the prolongation of life by the establishment of a radio-therapy department. Comparisons of the relative benefits of alternative programmes are also possible on a smaller scale in a single hospital or district.

Another possible approach to the problem is to try to calculate how much money is likely to be needed to reduce the incidence of several alternative diseases by a given amount. Sometimes, there is more than one way of achieving the same result; under these conditions it is obviously important to try to calculate the cheapest path to the same end. This is common practice in the economics of industry: it should also become common in the economics of medicine.

Despite these difficulties, even such simple studies as those in Chapter Twelve enable very useful information to be obtained about ways to reduce costs and increase efficiency. There are also some important generalizations in this field. Of great importance is the cheapness of health centre care compared with hospital care (3: 15), of outpatient as compared with inpatient care (12:6), of 'self-care' as compared with 'intermediate care' (9: 1), of care in a district hospital as compared with care in a national one (2:4), and the great return in human welfare to be obtained from the comparatively small cost of training and employing auxiliaries.

1:10b **Medical care must be adapted to the needs of an 'intermediate technology'.** Medical care is essentially a service that one human being, be he doctor, sister or dresser, performs for another. It may involve delivering a baby by Caesarian section, fetching a bed-pan, giving a health education talk or an anaesthetic, or even performing a post-mortem, taking a message or sluicing out the theatre floor. Because of the great importance of what can be called the service element in medical care, half or more of the annual budget of a hospital or health centre will be its wage bill. Thus, in the hospital studied in Chapter Twelve 52 per cent. of the annual budget was spent on wages (Figure 23B (12:3)),

Footnote. The reduction of disease is taken as the ultimate aim here, not the promotion of health. This is deliberate, because, though the reduction of disease is difficult enough to measure, 'health' as a positive entity is much more so. If the idea of health as something more than the mere absence of disease, is discarded as an immeasurable and thus unhelpful abstraction, then the idea of 'promotive' or health increasing medicine, as distinct from 'preventive', or disease preventing medicine has to be discarded also, despite what is said in section 3:1. The editor is grateful to Dr. David Bradley and Dr. Emil Rado for the ideas upon which much of the third axiom is based.

and the percentage would have been more had the capital cost of the buildings been less, and thus the sums included in the annual budget for depreciation and interest on capital.

Other things being equal, it follows therefore that the larger the number of people in medical employment, the greater the amount of medical care that can be provided. But, as well as needing training, each medical worker needs the tools of his trade and particularly the buildings in which to work. It is the cost of these buildings rather than the cost of training (1: 16) and equipment, which for medical auxiliaries is fairly cheap, that is so often the major factor limiting the provision of medical services. It will be shown later that, for the comparatively inexpensive standard type of hospital studied in Chapter Twelve, the cost of buildings and equipment amounted to £770 ($2,150) for an average hospital job, and much the same sum is also required for the provision of a job in a health centre (12:3, 3:15).

How does this sum relate to the economic resources of a developing country? Is it excessive? In answering this question some comparative figures are necessary for the cost of providing an average job under different types of technology. To take a modern or industrial technology first, it is found that the average cost of buildings, machinery and equipment is £2,000 ($5,600) or more for each worker. For a traditional or peasant technology it is only about £1 ($2.8). In a developing country the vast sums needed for the tools of modern technology are not available on a wide scale, nor are they likely to be for many years hence. The only level of capital that it is possible to provide is about £100 ($280), a so-called 'intermediate technology'. Thus, at the standards of the hospital in Chapter Twelve or the health centre in Chapter Three, the cost of creating a job in the medical service is extravagant when related to the level of the resources and income of a developing country. It might be said that more money should be spent on medical services, but to do this in one quarter usually involves cutting expenditure and employment in another. If £100 per job is the level of capital which it is practicable to finance, then the closer it is approached the more equitable will capital expenditure become and the larger the number of jobs created. In the medical sphere this means that, if the cost of providing the buildings and equipment for a medical worker can be halved, two can be employed for the capital sum that would otherwise have only employed one.

If an average sum of £700-£800 for a medical job is about the present level in the simpler existing units, and yet is extravagant in the light of the economic circumstances of a developing country, can this sum be lowered? It will be shown in a later chapter that most of the capital required for hospital services is needed for buildings (83 per cent. in the hospital in section 12: 3) and it can only be reduced by putting up really cheap ones (10:6). *In the medical sphere, cheap well-maintained buildings are an important key to higher levels of employment, the expansion of health services and the reduction of disease.*

How does this figure of £700-£800 compare with hospitals presently being built? At the time of writing a contract has just been signed in one developing country for nearly a dozen 100-bedded hospitals at a cost of £2,700 for an equipped bed. Assuming that a district hospital employs one worker for each of its beds, this being about the figure found in section 12:3, then this is also the approximate cost of providing a job in one of these hospitals — over three times the figure of £700-£800 calculated for simple existing hospitals of traditional construction and twenty-seven times that practicable in an intermediate technology.

This has been medical care looked at from the point of view of the demands of an intermediate technology. But, if these can be followed, an intermediate technology confers other benefits. Thus, because it is the most effective way of reducing unemployment, it makes the best use of the human capital of a country, it promotes a more equitable distribution of wealth by increasing the proportion of the people who are neither very rich nor very poor: it makes the best use of partly educated members of the community, and provides both more and cheaper labour with a certain degree of skill.

Closely related to the capital needed to provide a job is the money available to provide the worker's wages. *In this the developing countries have a choice, either they can employ a few lucky people on high wages and in the case of medicine produce little medical care, or they can employ many people on lower wages, provide more goods and services and reduce unemployment.* At present professional salaries are high and too closely tied to those current in developed countries through the example set by expatriates. Although the case for lower professional wage rates is more acute in education, where the salaries paid to teachers form a larger part of the recurrent budget of the education service than do those of doctors in the medical service, *the general case for all wage rates being low and levels of employment correspondingly higher is a very pressing one.* To bring this about a rigorously implemented incomes policy is one of the really major needs of most developing countries.

THE PATTERN OF HEALTH SERVICE

1:11 **Fourth axiom.** A MEDICAL SERVICE MUST BE ORGANIZED TO PROVIDE FOR STEADY GROWTH IN BOTH THE QUANTITY AND THE QUALITY OF MEDICAL CARE.

The very term 'developing country' implies the planned progression of a nation from one beset by poverty and disease to one capable of providing all its citizens with the means of a healthy and interesting life. Each aspect of a country's life takes part in this progression and each must keep in step with the others. Thus, the organization of health services must keep pace with the growing needs and resources of a country. If health services lag behind the whole community will suffer, but, if on the other hand the pattern of medical organization of a country is pushed ahead of its general economic development, standards will be set that can only be maintained in a small section of the country. If this happens a favoured few will have a very good service, but most people will have no service at all, or at least, an inadequate service available only at prohibitive distances. The general level of health of the people will then fall short of what it might have been, and the rest of development will suffer too, since the labour force (and those outside it) will lack the vigour and vitality needed for sustained effort. It is therefore essential for those planning or working in the medical services to have a very realistic sense of the most appropriate form of organization medically and economically for their particular time and place. *There is a great temptation to upgrade the standard, complexity and amenity of medical care before extending its coverage.*

In the very first stages of a health service cover is inevitably restricted, but as it develops, there is a common tendency to introduce a number of prestige-making changes which do little to increase the return in human welfare while involving large expenditures of money and skill. Behind such changes lies a fundamental misunderstanding of the process of development and the stage a country has reached. For example, the very latest in expensive operating theatres may be built to replace a still serviceable one when most children are still unvaccinated against smallpox, or when clinics are still short of syringes. Expensive multi-story hospitals may be planned in remote provinces before provision has been made to train a sufficient number of auxiliaries to run them. A thoracic surgeon may be recruited before an expert in health education. A service may spurn local methods of building (10:6) in favour of an inadequate volume of more expensive construction. From some points of view, and especially as far as building is concerned, it can truly be said of many developing country health services, not that their standards are too low, *but they are too high*! They make lavish provision for the few rather than some provision for the many. In this the minister of health is often in a real dilemma and has to resist the influence of those whose attitude is 'Our people deserve nothing but the best'. If he gives in, a few may well get the best — the many will get nothing.

A major cause of errors in health planning is the fluctuating economic fortunes of most developing countries which depend upon the export of a few main crops or products. As world prices fluctuate, so the

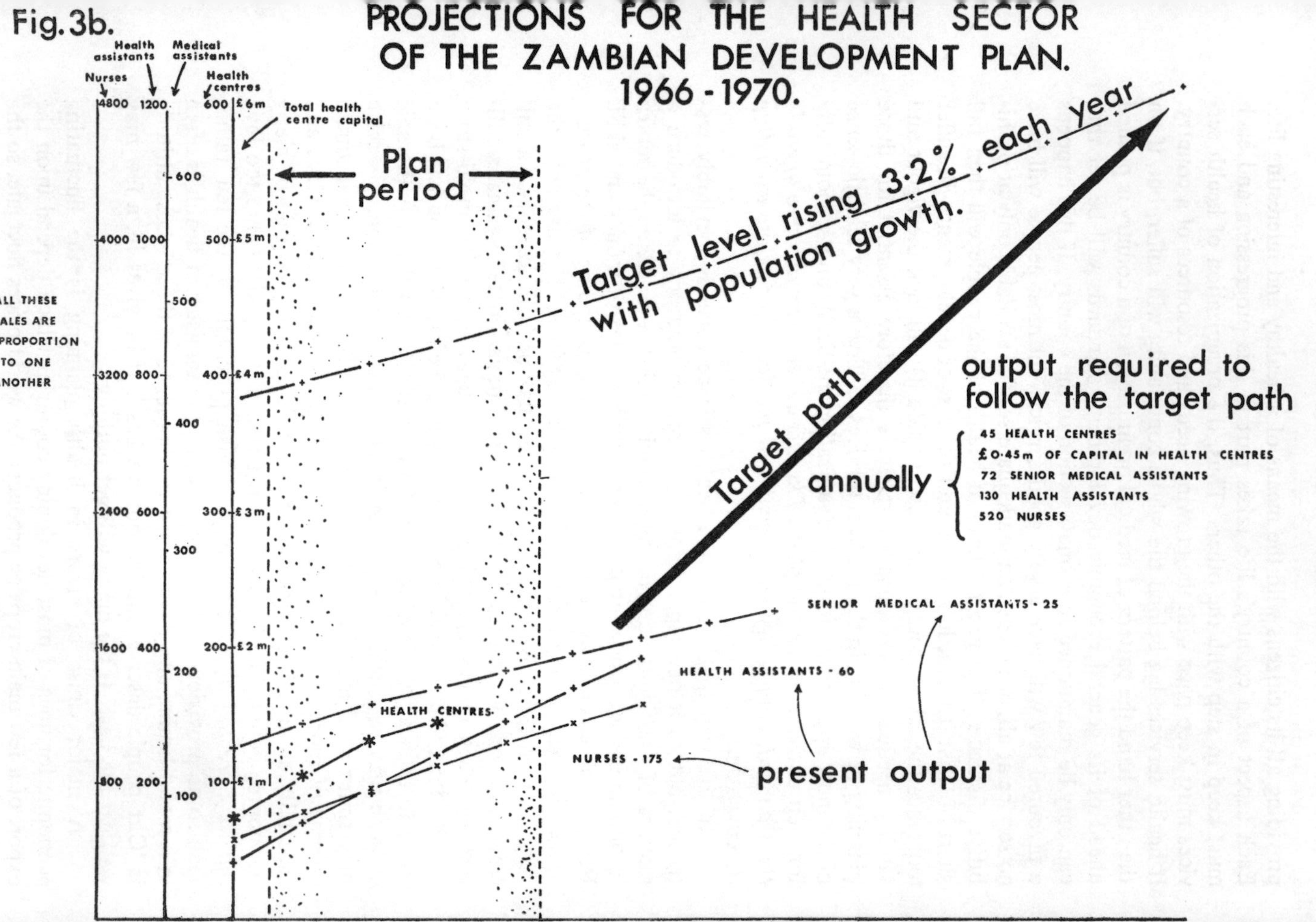

Fig. 3b. PROJECTIONS FOR THE HEALTH SECTOR OF THE ZAMBIAN DEVELOPMENT PLAN. 1966 - 1970.

economy of the country shifts from slump to boom and back again. Government revenues follow these cycles and in times of boom expensive building projects are started and salaries often raised. When the slump comes, projects have to continue because it is difficult to cut standards or salaries. Instead, the coverage and particularly the preventive work of a service suffers. The benefits of the boom are largely lost because the health services of the country have got out of step with its economy. The correct thing to do is to build up peripheral units first with the cheapest possible methods of construction, and so extend medical cover maximally particularly in the rural areas: to rely heavily on auxiliaries in the early stages of a service and only afterwards extend the number of expensive regional and national hospitals in the cities. *If a slump comes, then the administration may have to have the courage to explain the situation to the people and to cut their own salaries as well as those of the rest of the service.* There may well be no other way.

Not only should a whole health service progress in an orderly and dynamic manner, but each of its constituent parts should also. This is particularly true of hospitals where it should be a rule to develop them according to a carefully thought out 'master development plan' each stage in the unit's growth being carefully related to the next (10:1). Similarly, no dispensary should ever be put up without provision to turn it into a health centre (3.3). Among other things this means that every ministry must keep adequate site plans of all its medical installations.

Careful forethought needs to be given to staff structure. This implies forecasting the numbers of staff required in each category as far as *thirty years* ahead. Estimates need to be made of wastage and the output of training schools adjusted to take account of expected rates of population growth. Only in this long perspective can any real assessment be made of the staff position of a service. Provision should be made to phase out the senior auxiliary grade as the service matures so as to make a clear separation between the junior professional or 'para-medical' grade and the middle auxiliary grade (7:2).

An instructive illustration of the long-term staff position of a country has become available as this book goes to press. It comes from Zambia and concerns the health centre programme for that country's four year development plan 1966-1970 (Figure 3b). All the targets set are related to population growth and all are proportionate to one another. A health centre is reckoned to cost £10,000 ($28,000) and to serve 10,000 people (3:15). It is assumed to be staffed by a medical assistant (with 10 per cent. employed on non-health centre duties), two health assistants, and three comprehensive nurses (3:4). The scale for nurses in this diagram includes all types of nurse, and for every three nurses working in health centres there are assumed to be five more staffing the hospital service at the rate of one for every four beds and two beds per 1,000 of the population.

It will be seen that *projections for the present rate of staff output merely maintain the existing state of affairs at about a quarter of the target value*. Because of the time taken to build a training school and train the first intake, no increase in numbers can take place until the end of the planning period. It is for this reason that the 'target path' starts at the end of this period, ten years being chosen as a reasonable length of time by which the target might be achieved. The output needed to achieve it is calculated from the gradient of the 'target path' to which is added a figure for a 5 per cent. annual wastage. For convenience this wastage is averaged as being 5 per cent. of the staff at the mid-point of the path. A similar 5 per cent. wastage has been assumed for projections for the present output.

A graphical method such as this which sets targets related to population growth and which permits them to be followed over the years is held to be the most convenient way to form a true picture of the quantity of medical care needed by a country. Unless such a method is followed the true magnitude of the *scale* on which medical care is needed is apt to be lost.

1:12 **Fifth axiom.** PATIENTS SHOULD BE TREATED AS CLOSE TO THEIR HOMES AS POSSIBLE IN THE SMALLEST, CHEAPEST, MOST HUMBLY STAFFED AND MOST SIMPLY EQUIPPED UNIT THAT IS CAPABLE OF LOOKING AFTER THEM ADEQUATELY.

Health units form a chain of increasing size, cost, staff skill, level of equipment and rarity. This ranges from the health centres at the periphery of a health service through district and regional hospitals up to the national teaching hospital in the capital city of a developing country. Ideally, only when one unit cannot provide what a patient needs, should he be referred to the unit next higher up in the chain. This is the essence of the 'referral system' (N.R.E. Fendall). Patients are to be treated close to their homes because transport is such a major problem (2:6), and so that they can be visited and given health education in their homes. They are to be treated in lower rather than in higher units of the chain, mainly because these are the cheaper ones.

Where the population density is low and transport a problem to the patients, the units providing care of a given kind should be as small as are funcionally efficient and as widely scattered as possible. There is thus no place for a unit of say 40 beds staffed by medical assistants that some services favour — such a unit provides what amounts to health centre care, and two health centres of twenty beds in different places are a better alternative. Two small units are much more accessible to the patients than one large one. Such a division will increase the transport between units that a medical service has to provide, but it will reduce the travelling that the patients need to do.

This implies that there should be a clear gap in the range of size of the medical units in a service. This gap extends from the largest health centre with a maximum of about 20 beds to the smallest district hospital with a minimum of, say 80 beds and two doctors, an operating theatre, laboratory and X-ray plant, etc.

13 **Sixth axiom**. a) SOME FORM OF MEDICAL CARE SHOULD BE SUPPLIED TO ALL THE PEOPLE ALL THE TIME.
b) IN RESPECT OF MOST OF THE COMMON CONDITIONS THERE IS LITTLE RELATIONSHIP BETWEEN THE COST AND SIZE OF A MEDICAL UNIT AND ITS THERAPEUTIC EFFICIENCY.
c) MEDICAL CARE CAN BE EFFECTIVE WITHOUT BEING COMPREHENSIVE.

3a **Some form of medical care should be provided to all the people all the time.** This is based on the value judgement that it is more desirable for moral, political and other reasons to provide some form of medical care to many people rather than to provide a complete service to only a few.

3b **In respect of the common conditions there is often little relationship between the cost and size of a medical unit and its therapeutic efficiency.** Most patients with the common diseases of developing countries such as kwashiorkor, hookworm infestation, malaria, pneumonia and tuberculosis can be treated effectively from health centres, and for most of them the care provided by the health centre may be as effective as that provided by a district hospital. Similarly, there is a further range of common cases such as most of those due to trauma or the abnormalities of childbirth which are likely to be treated nearly if not quite as effectively in a good district hospital as they are in a regional or national one. There is thus a group of common conditions suited to each of these units which it is little point in referring higher up in the referral system. In respect therefore of most cases of these common conditions there is thus little relationship between the cost and size of a medical unit and its therapeutic efficiency. Important though this may be when contrasting district and regional or national hospitals, it is probably of the greater importance contrasting health centres and district hospitals. In effect this is merely a further argument in favour of developing health centre care.

1:13c **Medical care can be effective without being comprehensive.** What does 'some form of medical care' mean? Is it ever possible so to dilute medical care for it to be useless? In answering this question it should be realized that, even within regions which are often pictured as having comprehensive or complete medical services, levels of medical care vary greatly, and only in the most advanced institutions is it truly comprehensive. At one end of the chain or spectrum of scientific medical care come the best teaching hospitals of the industrial countries, which are capable between them of any medical procedure known to man; at the other end comes the bush midwife who has merely been given some sterile dressings to put on the umbilical cords of the babies she delivers (13:5). Between these two extremes fall the chain of health units that have just been mentioned in the fifth axiom — the national, regional and district hospitals, and the health centres of the developing countries. In all these units, even the humblest of them, the care given is invariably worth having, provided it is sound scientifically. Thus, although a patient may sometimes be better cared for in a unit higher up in the chain, some form of care is always better than none at all.

If medical care is not always to be even nominally comprehensive, what parts of it are to be supplied in preference to others? The third axiom answers this question — supply the kind of care that will give the maximum return in human welfare for the limited money and skill available. It is one of the main contentions of this symposium that health centres fulfil this axiom best, and, although hospital and health centre care is complementary, health centres are undeservedly neglected almost everywhere in favour of hospital services. Health centres give this high return because they are comparatively cheap to build and run (3:15), because they are staffed by auxiliaries and because their main function is preventive (3:1). Rigorously applied, this axiom would appear to demand the full provision of health centres in a region before any hospitals are built at all, but because health centres must have somewhere to refer their more difficult cases, and, because this is such a major break with tradition, some compromise is necessary. It is suggested therefore that, after the establishment of the minimum acceptable level of district hospital care, say one or perhaps two beds per 1,000 people, the next stage should be the widespread establishment of health centres. District hospitals should take priority over regional and national ones, because they are cheaper to run (2:4) and thus likely to give a greater return in human welfare for given expenditure in money and skill. To take an extreme case, the choice may well be between saving two mothers' lives by Caesarian section in a district hospital, or one by mitral valvotomy at a national one.

If medical care is not to be comprehensive, is it to be concentrated on particular diseases? To a large extent this question has already been answered, because the building of health centres in preference to district hospitals, or district hospitals in preference to regional ones, inevitably determines the kind of diseases that can be effectively treated. By demanding that money should be spent in providing this pattern of health unit, emphasis is automatically placed on the preventive aspects of medical care and on the more easily treatable medical and surgical conditions. Such a policy means that those patients are inadequately treated who suffer from diseases requiring highly specialized and expensive surgery, radiotherapy, or complex laboratory investigation and control — some treatment, if only with palliatives is however, always possible. Unhappily, such imperfect treatment is inevitable, for only in rich countries can diseases of this kind be treated in any but the smallest numbers.

Although the nature of a unit largely determines the diseases that can be treated, should there be any selective concentration on particular diseases within any one unit? Certainly. Thus the advice in section 13:4 that the only attitude possible to the occasional child with a congenital malformation or an inborn error of metabolism has to be one of palliation only, is in effect a plea to concentrate medical endeavour where it will be of the greatest value.

But this does not end the relationship between health centres and the selective concentration of resources on particular aspects of medical care. Health centres are often the best and sometimes the only place from which campaigns can be mounted against particular diseases. Among these diseases are tuberculosis, leprosy, yaws, whooping cough, measles, hookworm infection and kwashiorkor. These are some of the common killing diseases which it is often possible to prevent and treat comparatively cheaply from health centres, either as a continuous endeavour or as part of a widespread campaign against any particular one of them.

Thus, although health centres cannot provide comprehensive medical care, they can provide effective care in many critically important conditions. This axiom is in effect a plea for the paramount importance of health centres, their auxiliary staff and the services they provide. It is also a plea for training auxiliaries and charging or taxing the local community in order to provide health centre services (3:15). (The editor is grateful to Dr. N. R. E. Fendall and Dr. Richard Jolly for many of the ideas behind these last three axioms.)

:14 **Seventh axiom.** a) MEDICAL SERVICES SHOULD BE ORGANIZED FROM THE BOTTOM UP AND NOT FROM THE TOP DOWN. b) THE HEALTH 'NEEDS' OF A COMMUNITY MUST BE RELATED TO THEIR WANTS.

1:14a **Medical services should be organized from the bottom up and not from the top down.** This follows on closely from what has just been said. Greater benefit is likely to be obtained from large numbers of suitably trained and supervised auxiliaries working in health centres and district hospitals of carefully maintained 'mud-wattle-and-whitewash' (10:11b), than from huge expensive ill-staffed hospitals with glittering facades, particularly if they do not undertake any training. From this follows the principle that *the quality of medical care must never be judged either from the splendour or the humility of the buildings in which it is undertaken (see the Epilogue).*

In the ordering of priorities trained men and women come before bricks and mortar and multitudes of competent auxiliaries before a multiplicity of specialists. *The provision of training facilities for auxiliaries comes before all else.*

:14b **The health 'needs' of a people must be related to their 'wants'.** This is a highly contentious matter politically, for medical demands or 'wants' have a high priority in the minds of the electorate. The complete satisfaction of these wants is likely to be impossible with the resources available, and their partial satisfaction is not likely to be the best way of satisfying what the health planner considers to be the people's greatest medical 'need'. An electorate may insist on doctors, hospitals, and curative medicine. In terms of overall health strategy their 'needs' may be best met by giving them auxiliaries, health centres and preventive medicine.

This is perhaps a brutal overstatement, and politicians and medical administrators must live, but in practice it seems that the inevitable compromise too often favours the satisfaction of politically expressed 'wants' rather than the fulfilment of medically diagnosed 'needs'. Part of this compromise should be to make use of the opportunities presented by 'wants' to fulfil 'needs'. For example, the opportunities presented by hospital attendance in search of curative medicine can be used for the preventive purposes of immunization (16:5).

THE ROLE OF THE DOCTOR AND THOSE WHO HELP HIM

1:15 **Eighth axiom.** THE ROLE A DOCTOR HAS TO PLAY IN A DEVELOPING COUNTRY DIFFERS IN MANY IMPORTANT RESPECTS FROM THAT WHICH HE PLAYS IN A DEVELOPED ONE.

Because he has to spread his services thinly over so many patients, a doctor in a developing country has to play a different part from his colleague in an industrial one. This distinctive role is seldom fully appreciated, for, *in a developing country a doctor's main task must be to act as a teacher, organizer, supervisor and consultant to a team of auxiliaries.* Only when he and his helpers form a team will the best use be made of his very scarce skills. From this it follows that a doctor should not regularly undertake routine tasks that could be done by less skilled persons under his supervision. (It is desirable, however, that he does such tasks occasionally, but for this see section 8:2). An important consequence of this is that a doctor's work becomes much more interesting once he has deputed the monotonous routine to his auxiliaries. The supervision of child welfare clinics, the consultant role in an outpatient department, major surgery in a district hospital, or the direction of several health centres is both a more logical and a more satisfying role for a doctor than routine tasks in any of them. Because it is more satisfying, a doctor is more likely to remain in a service which accepts the fact that this is his proper role, rather than in one which requires that every outpatient be seen by a doctor, no matter for how short a time.

If a doctor's role is to be a leader of auxiliaries, and he is to depute jobs wherever possible, what tasks, other than the training, supervisory and creative ones, remain to him at the district hospital level? In practice, the only other tasks which are necessarily his amount to major surgery (12:6), the consultant role in the outpatient department (11:2), inpatient ward rounds and such time consuming and miscellaneous jobs as coroner's post-mortems and giving evidence in court. Compare this with a doctor's role in a developed country where doctors do the majority of child welfare clinics (16:3) and almost all the work done by medical assistants (7:1) (11:2).

Implicit in the idea of the doctor as organizer is that of the doctor as initiator and creator. So overwhelming is the 'need to get things done', and so great are the medical tasks to be accomplished, that initiative, the capacity to start things and carry them through to the end, is a quality of particular medical importance. In a developed country a doctor can often be content to be only a cog in an already efficient machine, but in a developing one the machine hardly exists, and if he does not do such things as initiating a training scheme for the dressers, organizing an immunization programme or persuading a chief to build a clinic, he can usually be sure that nobody else will. The capacity to 'get things done' is thus a highly desirable quality (8:11). It is not to be confused with the capacity to get through a vast quantity of work merely to keep things going and the wheels turning, though this is an admirable quality also. The capacity to get things done usually implies new creation and it may mean standing back a little from the routine labours, having a fresh look at them, and delegating some, so that time is made for building up a good machine rather than merely keeping a poor one running somehow. This is particularly important after some time in a post when the routine is well established.

There are always plenty of people to train, and if local materials are used for building, the doctor in charge of a district has at least some of the major requirements for creating medical facilities himself.

But there are two parts to the creative endeavour, one is the initiative, the creativity of the doctor himself, and the other the opportunities and constraints within which he works. Originality and enterprise are too often discouraged by those administering a service, but rightly directed such talents can be of great value and are thus to be encouraged by those in authority. Among other things this means that care must be taken to see that a doctor is allowed to stay in a given post long enough to be able to bring his endeavours to fruition.

Another aspect of the differing role of the doctor is the need for him to orientate his medical thinking more towards the community than towards the individual. There are so many patients that a doctor may be misusing his time if he devotes most of it to a very few and neglects the majority. If the alternatives for a given evening are planning an immunization programme or spending the time with a single case, it may be that the immunization programme is more important (31).

From this it follows that a doctor needs a clear understanding of what are to be the priorities in his endeavours, which must be adjusted so that the best balance is achieved. The attainment of this balance requires that he learn to budget both his time and the rest of his resources carefully. Because this requires considerable self-discipline, it is not uncommon to find that the balance has gone astray with undue emphasis in favour of such things as excessive major surgery, frantic building activity or an unwarranted preoccupation with paper work and accounts. Somehow, into this balance there must also come time for recreation, and, because the demands upon him are so exacting, a doctor should plan to have one completely free day each week, which is only to be disturbed by the gravest emergencies. Every so often a complete change of environment is beneficial, and one experienced director of medical services advised a long weekend away from the job once in six weeks. But overwork and staleness are not the only dangers, another is isolation from the stimulation and contact with colleagues, and lack of sufficient opportunity to exchange ideas. Besides regular reading this makes it important to take every chance of visiting other hospitals, to become aware of other standards, to talk to other people and see what they do. Medicine only prospers if the medical profession forms a community with active intellectual interchange between its members. No doctor is sufficient unto himself, and this applies to other members of the staff also, particularly nursing sisters.

If a doctor's job is different, it follows that his training must be different also, and set him different goals. Thus, it is likely to be difficult for a doctor to grasp his true role if he was trained in an academic environment where the height of professional endeavour was to work in a narrow and highly technical speciality. If, as a student, the pinnacle of achievement was to join the cardiac unit, a young doctor is unlikely to adapt easily to the role of leader of a team of auxiliaries treating large numbers of patients with common conditions.

.6 **Ninth axiom.** THE ROLE PLAYED BY THE AUXILIARIES IS BOTH DIFFERENT AND MORE IMPORTANT IN DEVELOPING COUNTRIES THAN IT IS IN DEVELOPED ONES.

When doctors are rare many tasks that would otherwise be done by them have either to be done by auxiliaries, or else not done at all. Among these tasks are even such complex ones as setting up a scalp vein transfusion, extracting a tooth, administering a general anaesthetic or repairing a hernia. *Thus, any task which has to be repeated many times, even though it is comparatively intricate, should if possible be taught to an auxiliary.* This implies the careful analysis of the tasks to be done, and the definition and selection of those suitable for delegation. This has then to be followed by appropriate training, the provision of the right apparatus, and continued supervision thereafter. Such fragmentation and delegation of the traditional tasks of a doctor is sometimes said to lower standards, but the answer to this criticism is that the choice is, either fragmentation and delegation, or the job cannot be done at all.

The auxiliary fits well into the economic structure of a developing country and the jobs that a health service can provide, particularly if capital is wisely used (Third axiom 1:10b), are largely jobs for auxiliaries. Their salaries are within the means of a health service (Table 2, 7:2), so is their training. Thus doctors cost about £6,000 to train, though this varies greatly (2:15), medical assistants about £600, and health assistants only about £200 (15).

.7 **Tenth axiom.** ALL MEDICAL WORKERS HAVE AN EDUCATIONAL ROLE WHICH IS CLOSELY LINKED TO AND ENHANCES THEIR THERAPEUTIC ONE.

a) SKILLED STAFF MEMBERS HAVE A DUTY TO TEACH THE LESS SKILLED ONES.

b) ALL MEDICAL STAFF HAVE A TEACHING VOCATION IN THE COMMUNITY THEY SERVE.

1:17a **Skilled staff members have a duty to teach the less skilled ones.** Within a medical unit skill is so short that the most skilled members of the staff have a duty to teach the less skilled ones. This is developed extensively in section 8:3 (Figure 14) where it is held that staff training is the most urgent call on a doctor's or a sister's time — the very *first* priority in their time budgets.

If the educational drive is to be active in the hospitals and health centres of the periphery, these units must in their turn be continually educated by the centre. If a country is fortunate enough to have a medical school at its national hospital then the staff of this hospital have a duty to teach not only medical students, but the doctors of the country also. This means conferences and refresher courses at the national hospital and regular visits by its staff to the peripheral ones. Even if there is no medical school, the consultant staff of a national hospital should still play a teaching role in the territory they serve.

But organizing this training and retraining requires the time and energy of an active person. A service cannot do better than to examine its ranks for the most suitable candidate, give him the post of 'training officer' and put him in charge of not only all regular staff training but also of the organization of refresher courses for doctors, para-medical staff and auxiliaries. The laboratory assistant or medical assistant whose practice has slowly deteriorated during many largely unsupervised years in a clinic is so common a phenomenon that these courses are of the greatest possible importance. They must follow the next axiom and be closely related to the work the auxiliary is expected to undertake.

The same principle holds for health centre as well as hospital staff and a National Reference Health Centre has, as one of its main functions, the training and retraining of health centre personnel (3:14).

There is also an economic side to teaching. The more skilled a man in a given salary grade becomes, the more useful and productive he is for the money spent on him. Though there will come a time when promotion is necessary and men need to be paid more, to increase the level of skill in each grade and in the unit as a whole, is to increase the return in human welfare for the same expenditure of money (Third axiom).

1:17b **All medical staff have a teaching vocation in the community they serve.** Every medical unit has some educational functions, but in developing countries this aspect of their work is especially needed, for health education is potentially capable of preventing so much disease. This is developed further in Chapter Six where it is stressed that health education should be carried out by all the staff of a unit from doctors to sweepers.

THE ADAPTATION OF MEDICAL CARE TO LOCAL CONDITIONS

18 **Eleventh axiom.** IN DEVELOPING COUNTRIES MEDICAL CARE REQUIRES THE ADAPTATION AND DEVELOPMENT OF ITS OWN PARTICULAR METHODOLOGY.

If the extreme scarcity of doctors means that many tasks which are their strict prerogative in industrial countries have to be deputed to auxiliaries as being the only way in which they can be done, then the challenge becomes one of training, organizing and supervising these auxiliaries and determining the methods they shall use. Much, for instance, is known about the scientific treatment of anaemia, kwashiorkor and tuberculosis, but what are auxiliaries to be taught, and how are they to apply this knowledge amid the milling crowds of a tropical outpatient department, or against the stark realities of a tropical children's ward? (13:2).

If this is granted, then 'methodological research' becomes a paramount need in developing countries (13:2). Routine methods for common conditions need to be worked out, adapted to local circumstances and taught to the auxiliaries who will have to carry them out. This is the duty of every doctor working with auxiliaries, and it is also one of the main functions of the National Reference Health Centre (3:14).

Methodology is not a part of the training of most medical students, and the attitude of mind is unusual in medicine which is continually asking such questions as — How could we do this more efficiently? or, How can I make the best possible use of such staff as I have? Such an attitude of mind is useful anywhere, it is particularly useful in the circumstances of developing countries.

19 **Twelfth axiom.** MEDICAL CARE AND THE LOCAL CULTURE ARE CLOSELY LINKED.

a) MEDICAL CARE MUST BE CAREFULLY ADAPTED TO THE OPPORTUNITIES AND LIMITATIONS OF THE LOCAL CULTURE.

b) WHERE POSSIBLE MEDICAL SERVICES SHOULD DO WHAT THEY CAN TO IMPROVE THE NON-MEDICAL ASPECTS OF A CULTURE IN THE PROMOTION OF A 'BETTER LIFE'.

19a **Medical care must be carefully adapted to the opportunities and limitations of the local culture.** The previous axioms apply to developing countries generally because these countries have so many features in common. Each country and each locality has however its own particular features, and no general advice can be given about them, other than they must be studied closely. This is implicit in the chapter on the 'cross-culture outlook' where a plea is made for a careful study of the local culture (4:1), in that on the 'community diagnosis' (5:1) where the local medical needs are discussed, and also in the account of health education (6:1). In section 19:1 the importance of adapting obstetric care to local needs is discussed, and the point made that this should be both an organizational adaptation as well as a strictly obstetric one.

Expressed in another way this means that in every local medical situation there will be particular medical needs as well as particular helps and hindrances in fulfilling them. The hindrances are likely to be only too obvious, but the helps may not be and need looking for and exploiting. Kwashiorkor may be common, but are there any local sources of protein that are not being used? (14:2). Most of the year the community may be pitifully poor, but in the season when they sell their cash crops they may have some money in their pockets. Can they be made to pay something, say 10/- ($1.4), to the hospital at this time of the year so as to act as a form of health insurance for the rest of it? It may be impossible to get the patients to keep a card bearing their hospital number, but will they wear a metal number tag among the beads around their necks? (26:3).

1:19b **Where possible medical services should do what they can to improve the non-medical aspects of a culture in the promotion of a 'better life' for the people**. In developing countries the major enemies are ignorance, poverty and disease, but, although doctors and medical services in general are of course mainly concerned with the third of these evils, disease, they must be watchful for opportunities to fight the other two. Thus the staff of a health centre, particularly the health inspector and his assistants, have opportunities to promote the better life of the community which extend beyond their strictly medical roles. They have a chance to promote improved building standards, to encourage the villagers to plant new crops in their gardens and to rebuild the roads. Though there is an obvious medical component to some of these endeavours, their effect on the general level of amenity and standards of living is important also. Similarly, when enrolled nurses are being trained at a hospital, they should have included in their curriculum, such instruction as will make them better wives and mothers, which will after all be the major work of the lives of most of them. A further example is the nutrition rehabilitation unit, when the opportunity is taken to teach mothers anything that might make them more effective members of the community (14:17e). In most communities there is so much that needs to be done in the interests of the better life, and the inertia, conservatism and ignorance of many peasant communities is so often so great, that no resource can be dispensed with in making a total attack on those aspects of a culture which need improving.

These then are the twelve axioms which tie together the detail in the pages that follow. They are not exhaustive, but they are held to be the main foundation upon which medical care in developing countries should rest.

Chapter Two

THE ORGANIZATION OF HEALTH SERVICES

Richard Jolly, Maurice King.

2:1 **Introduction.** In the developing countries disease will only be reduced to the fullest degree possible, when the twelve axioms of the first chapter are put into action. They must be applied to every aspect of medical care from the large issues of policy down to the smaller details of daily practice. Countries vary in their educational and economic resources, in the present organization of their health services as well as in other ways which affect health planning, but even so, it is only too obvious that the available resources of many of them are badly deployed, and that this is in part because some of the basic axioms have been given too little attention.

This chapter suggests how these axioms relate to the large scale organization and development of health services and makes some basic generalizations governing the provision of medical care in developing countries. But before considering organization, it is necessary to look at what scientific medicine has to offer in the way of preventive and curative services, the relationship between them and what the villager thinks about them.

2:2 **Prevention and cure.** The most important preventive measures in the rural areas are health education, particularly that directed towards improving environmental sanitation and modifying personal habits, immunization, and the routine examinations of the antenatal and underfives clinics. These form the main work of the health centre as it is described in the next chapter. But there are other preventive measures also, such as campaigns against specific infections, trypanosomiasis and malaria for example, as well as legislation concerning such things as alcoholism, building standards and accidents, particularly burns.

Curative services also take many forms: some patients come to hospitals or health centres to be cured of illness in a mild enough form for them to be treated as outpatients. Common among such conditions are minor trauma and sepsis, upper respiratory infections and malaria. Other patients present themselves when so ill as to need admission to a hospital ward under the supervision of a doctor, and at times, need also the services, both emergency and elective, of a surgeon as well as the facilities of an operating theatre, a laboratory and an X-ray plant. In the rural areas these are the practical limits of curative medicine.

Though it is useful to make a theoretical distinction in this way between prevention and cure, they are in practice closely interwoven in almost every part of the medical endeavour, and nowhere perhaps is this better shown than in the account of the under-fives clinic in Chapter Fifteen. It is for this reason that there is no special section devoted to organizing preventive medicine apart from curative medicine. Rather, it has seemed better to emphasize the health centre as a unit whose major function is prevention, and health education has been considered as an important part of the practice of both health centres and hospitals, which should be places for educating people and not only for curing them. All through these pages, as through medicine itself, prevention and cure are intimately linked.

Prevention and cure are also often linked in the way the tropical villager looks at scientific medicine. When a community is new to it — and this is becoming increasingly rare — some dramatic cures may be necessary to win the confidence of the people and to persuade them to come for medical attention of any kind. In other communities people will attend a hospital for the cure of their disease and then go to a traditional healer for the removal of its cause. Many villagers are sensibly pragmatic in what they accept, and soon come to know which illnesses a particular hospital or surgeon can cure, and what diseases it is useless to attend with. The same pragmatic attitude may extend to preventive medicine also, and there are even some indigenous systems of medicine with a decidedly preventive outlook. But with the passage of time, scientific medicine as a whole is coming to be held in ever higher esteem by the present communities of developing countries, and there is an ever-increasing popular demand for medical services — above all for the provision of doctors and hospitals.

These in brief are the preventive and curative services that medicine has to offer, and the staff and facilities that patients and politicians clamour for. The fundamental question is therefore this. *How, in the rural areas in particular, can preventive and curative services be planned so as to provide the maximum return in human welfare from limited resources of money and skill?*

Distance, population, finance and staff are the four main determinants of medical care, and, although other issues are often important, these four usually predominate. Before considering just how critical they are, it is necessary to consider very briefly the kind of units that have been devised to provide this care, the relationship between them, the dimensions and units in which medical care can be measured, and the sort of standards it should attain. Much of what is said applies to both urban and rural conditions, but it is rural services, particularly as they involve problems of distance and transport, that are mainly the concern of the next few sections.

2:3 **The units of medical care.** Ideally, the first and simplest 'unit' of medical care should be a person with some medical skill, however little, in each and every village. He or she should act as the local representative of the health services right at the periphery of the health service in the heart of the community itself. Such people need not be whole time employees, and can even be the indigenous midwives or the traditional circumcisers of the locality. Whatever their exact status, these local representatives must be visited regularly by mobile teams from the health centres, they must be given instruction and encouragement, and progressively upgraded with every visit. They need a few drugs and dressings so that they have something to give away, but their main function should be to spread health knowledge in their village. They are discussed further in section 2:7 where, for want of a better term, they are called 'station masters', as being the persons in medical charge of the 'station' where a mobile team stops to hold a clinic.

Unfortunately, these local representatives usually exist in theory rather than in practice. They are not part of the otherwise excellent Kenyan scheme of health centres described in the next chapter, and at present most health services omit the village worker altogether. Instead, health services usually start at the periphery with the 'aid post' which is followed up by the 'dispensary' and the 'one doctor hospital'. These units represent the initial attempt to provide medical care in the rural areas, and, though theoretically outmoded by 'health centres' and more substantial hospitals, they are still typical of many developing countries.

An 'aid post' is really no more than a rendezvous visited weekly by a medical assistant from a dispensary, a health centre or a hospital. He comes armed with a box of drugs, and is helped by a nurse who gives the injections. Between them they may see some hundred patients at each visit, but the treatment they offer is minimal, and any health education they can give is usually inadequate.

The dispensary is a small building staffed by a medical assistant, a nurse and also perhaps by a midwife. As many as three hundred outpatients may be seen daily, and a dozen or so inpatients treated during short illnesses or pending their transfer to hospital. Many dispensaries run aid posts in their vicinity, but apart from this, their work is restricted to the minor curative activities that can go on within their walls. Dispensaries have neither the staff nor the facilities to do anything more.

By contrast the ideal unit of medical care near the periphery of a health service is the 'health centre'. Because it is so important this unit is described separately in Chapter Three. There it is defined as a unit which provides a family with all the health services it requires, other than those which can only be provided by a hospital. Each health centre is responsible for a specified area, and, ideally, the whole country, urban and rural, should be divided up between health centres. Great emphasis is laid on the importance of health centres extending their influence throughout the territory they are responsible for, and on their role in health education. In the rural areas in particular, health centres should be the fundamental units providing both preventive and curative medical care. Their importance in a developing country can hardly be over-emphasized.

Dispensaries and health centres are often confused, but, though a poorly developed health centre may be little more than a good dispensary, these two units are really quite different. They are distinguished by the range of services they can provide, by their activity in the surrounding area and by the emphasis placed on health education. Dispensaries are not converted into health centres, as has been attempted in at least one country, merely by changing their names in order to keep up with the latest fashion. A true conversion from a dispensary to a health centre demands both the expansion, and the thorough retraining of existing staff, with increased emphasis on preventive activities, especially those outside the centre (3:9 & 11).

There is a wide measure of agreement on the theory and functions of a health centre, but there is some difference of opinion on the size of the unit for which the term should be used. In Chapter Three it is applied to a unit without a doctor led by a specially trained medical assistant and staffed by half a dozen other auxiliaries. In some countries a health centre refers to a larger unit run by a doctor who administers a number of smaller satellite clinics with the same functions. The term 'health sub-centre' is also used. These play the same role as health centres, but are smaller and not so fully staffed.

2:4 The relationship between units of medical care — the 'Referral System'. The concept of the health centre is closely bound up with that of the 'referral system'. This system is based on the idea that patients are to be treated as close to their homes as possible in the smallest, cheapest, most simply equipped, and most humbly staffed unit that will still look after them adequately (Fifth axiom 1:12). Only when a particular unit cannot care for a patient adequately is he to be referred to a unit higher up in the chain: the chain being the health centre, the district hospital, the regional hospital and the national hospital.

Treatment at the periphery of a service is much cheaper than that at the centre; this is the great advantage of the referral system. The following table from Kenya shows how greatly the cost of treating an illness increases, the closer it is referred to the centre of a service. Even when allowance is made for the longer stays in the regional and national hospitals, due largely to their treating different kinds of case, the difference in average cost is considerable (13).

Institution	Average Stay	Average cost per illness Shs	$	Average cost per day Shs	$
Health Centre		4/-	0.56		
District hospital	7 days	84/-	11.80	12/-	1.68
Regional hospital	10 days	170/-	24.00	17/-	2.40
National hospital	22 days	370/-	52.00	17/-	2.40

Does the referral system work? Only in part; it often fails peripherally because few hospitals have health centres close enough to them, after the manner shown in Figure 16 (10:4), to screen their general outpatients so that the hospital deals only with referred cases. Transport difficulties also greatly impede the efficiency of the system and inevitably regional and national hospitals have mainly to act as district ones. For example, about 80 per cent. of the patients admitted to the New Mulago Hospital, Uganda's national hospital, come from the neighbouring district of Mengo which contains only 20 per cent. of Uganda's people (20) (33). Even so, the referral system is very important, particularly at its lowest level in which health centres refer cases to the district hospitals.

2:5 **Dimensions and levels of care.** There are many dimensions to medical care. This is well shown by the wide range of services provided by the health centres, but, as convenient dimensions for measurement and as illustrating the points at issue, only two will be considered here — total outpatient attendances and the availability of hospital beds.

Before either of these can be discussed with profit they have to be seen against some level of reference; some level of outpatient care is required and likewise some level for the provision of hospital beds.

As a realistic, if somewhat arbitrary level of outpatient care, it has been suggested that two adult and three child attendances per person per year constitute a convenient basis for planning (1). To some readers this may seem unrealistically high, and it is certainly seldom achieved, but, when it is realized that this should include attendances at clinics for antenatal mothers and the under-fives, as well as repeated attendances for dressings and injections, it will not seem excessive, particularly when infectious diseases and malnutrition are usually so prevalent. The under-fives clinic in Chapter Sixteen requires more attendances than this, but, until more is known about the levels of outpatient care that should be attained by tropical communities, this figure will have to serve. If, as is usual, about half the population are under fifteen this level of attendance implies an average of roughly 2.5 attendances per person per year.

As a way of measuring the availability of hospital beds the total number per 1,000 people is chosen here. This is a well accepted dimension, gross national averages, ranging from 10.6 in the United Kingdom to 0.12 in Nepal — almost a hundredfold difference. Here again little is known about the number of beds which should be available to tropical communities.

It is to be noted that both outpatient attendances and hospital beds are merely means to an end — the reduction of disease (Third axiom — 1:10a). They are chosen here as convenient dimensions or parameters of medical care for discussion in the sections which follow, but increasing the availability of health facilities should never be confused with improving the health of the people.

OUTPATIENT CARE

6 **The inequality of access to outpatient care.** In a developing country distance is a critical determinant of medical care, and it is widely realized that only those close to a medical unit can derive the full benefit from its services. While this may seem obvious, it is not generally appreciated just how inequitable this way of distributing medical care really is. For example, it was found in Kenya that 40 per cent. of the outpatients attending a health centre lived within five miles of it, 30 per cent. lived between 5 and 10 miles from it, and a further 30 per cent. lived more than 10 miles away (14). What these figures imply about the distribution of medical services can best be appreciated by expressing them in terms of the areas from which patients were drawn. When this is done it will be seen that approximately four times as many people came from each square mile within the 0-5 mile zone as came from one in the 5-10 mile zone. The same grossly inequitable distribution of outpatient services has also been observed in Uganda in the study based on Mityana hospital described in Chapter Twelve. Here data were obtained from a

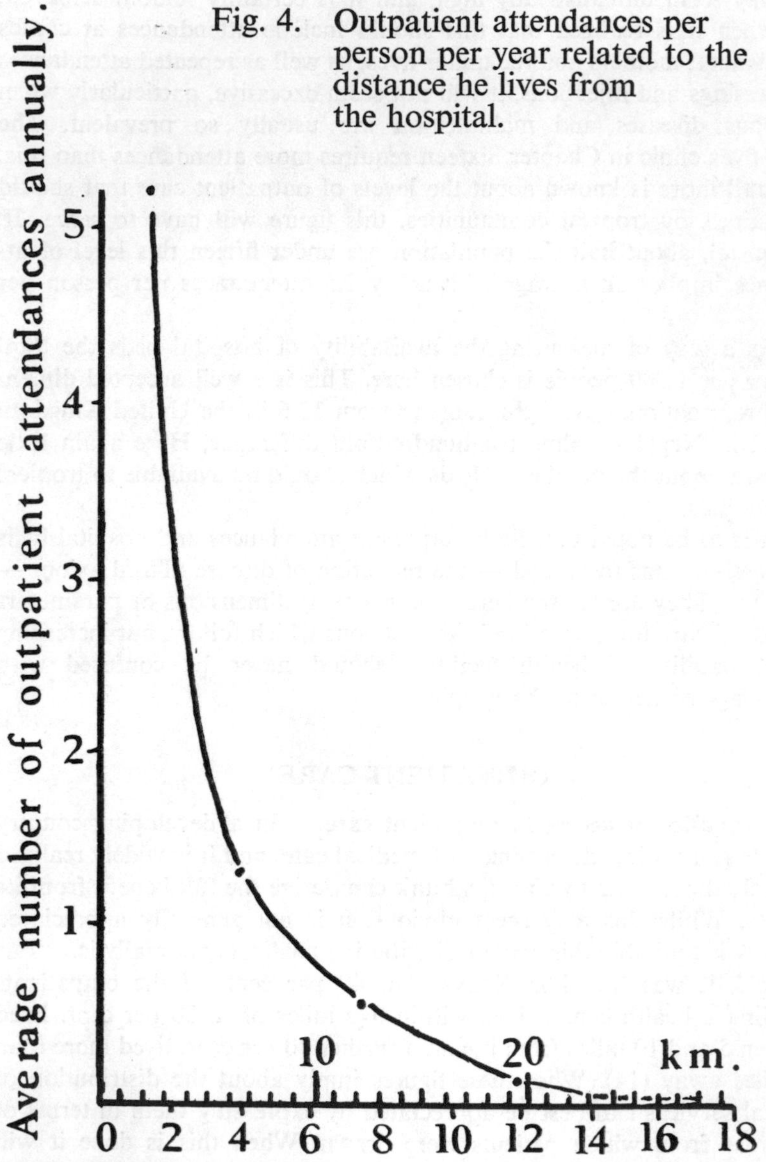
Fig. 4. Outpatient attendances per person per year related to the distance he lives from the hospital.
Average number of outpatient attendances annually.
5
4
3
2
1
10
20
km.
0
2
4
6
8
10
12
14
16
18
Distance of patient's home from the hospital in miles.

hospital, a dispensary and an aid post, and it was found that the same principles governed outpatient attendance at all three of these units.

Because distance and the difficulty of transport have such a profound effect on the availability of medical care, the purpose of the following sections is to present arguments for the importance of providing mobile services so as to take medical care closer to the homes of the people. Arguments are presented based on 'outpatient care gradients', on population density and on economy.

TAKING SERVICES TO THE PEOPLE

The argument from outpatient care gradients. Figure 4 shows how the average number of outpatient attendances per person per year falls precipitously the greater the distance that separates the patient's home from the hospital. The relationship is in fact exponential which means that attendance drops by a constant percentage with each additional mile that separates the patient's home from the hospital. If a graph is drawn showing distance and outpatient attendances on a logarithmic scale, the relationship between attendance and distance becomes a linear one, and the slope of the line measures the 'outpatient care gradient' for this hospital (Figure 5).

Outpatient care gradients have also been measured for a dispensary and an aid post. These have been plotted with that from the hospital in Figure 6. Comparative data obtained from a dispensary in India are also shown on the same graph (18). The slopes of the outpatient care gradients for the dispensary and the hospital differ slightly and are at different positions on the graph, because the number of outpatients seen by these two units differ widely (about 100,000 attendances annually for the hospital and 52,000 for the dispensary). The average number of outpatient attendances per person per year will be seen to halve itself about every 2 miles (3.2 km.) for the hospital and the dispensary, and every mile (1.6 km.) for the aid post. The slope of the gradient for the dispensary in India is the steepest of all — attendance there halves every half mile.

The factors determining the slopes of an outpatient care gradient are complex, but the distance that patients are prepared to walk appears to be a major factor. As Figure 24 (12:7) shows, few Ugandan patients were prepared to walk more than five miles. The cost and availability of different kinds of transport is another important factor and is well shown in the same figure. Perhaps the most important factors of all are the severity of the patient's disease, and the quality of the care available — the better the medicine the further will people be prepared to go for it.

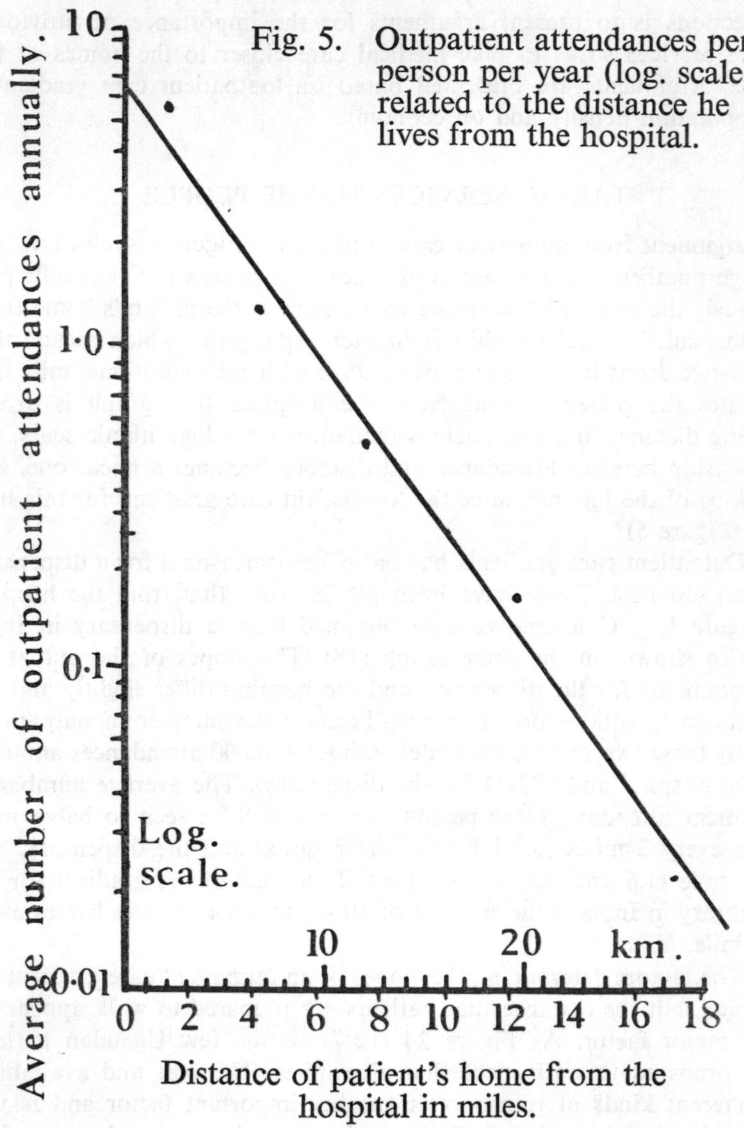

Fig. 5. Outpatient attendances per person per year (log. scale) related to the distance he lives from the hospital.

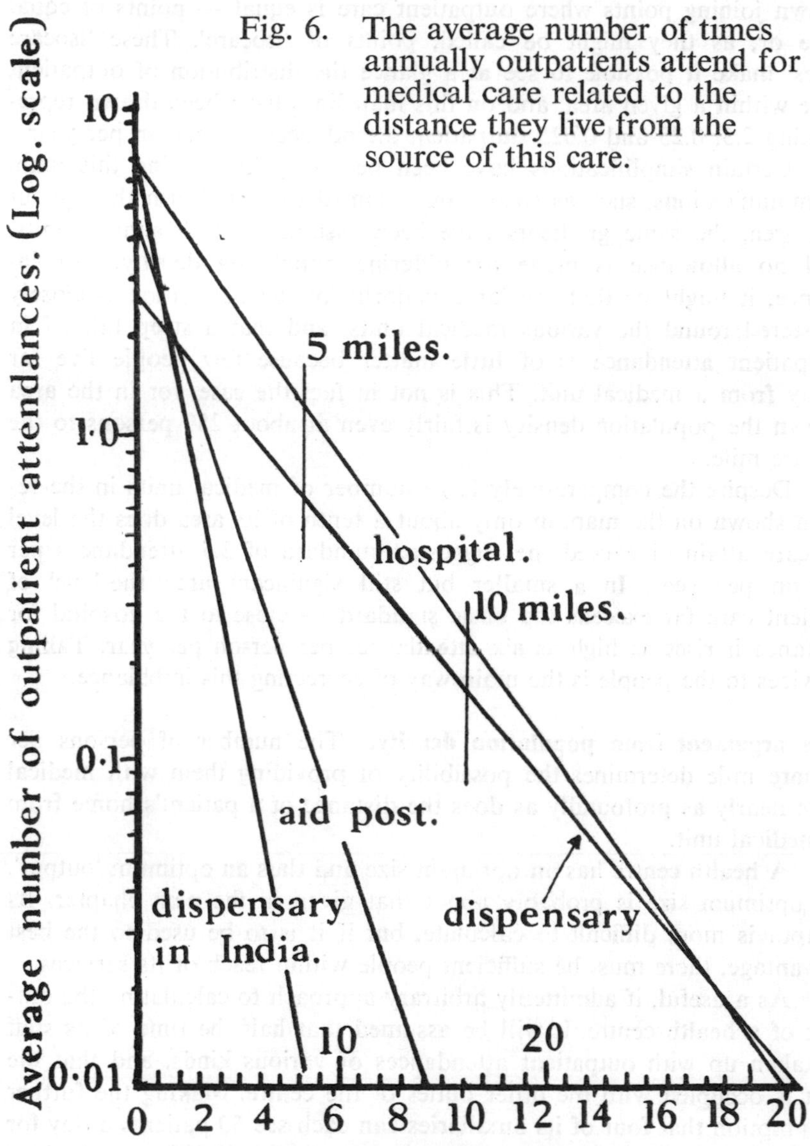
Fig. 6. The average number of times annually outpatients attend for medical care related to the distance they live from the source of this care.
Average number of outpatient attendances. (Log. scale)
10
1·0
0·1
0·01
5 miles.
hospital.
10 miles.
aid post.
dispensary in India.
dispensary
10
20
0
2
4
6
8
10
12
14
16
18
20
Distance of the patient's home from the source of care in miles.

The infoımation contained in the graphs can also be expressed as a map. Figure 7 is a map of the Mityana area on which lines have been drawn joining points where outpatient care is equal — points of equal care or, as they might be called, points of 'isocare'. These 'isocare lines' make it possible to see at a glance the distribution of outpatient care within a given area, and on this map lines have been drawn representing 2.5, 0.25 and 0.025 outpatient attendances per person per year.

Certain simplifications have been necessary in drawing this map. Communications, such as roads, are assumed to be uniform throughout the area, the same gradients have been assumed for all similar units, and no allowance is made for differing population density. For instance, it might be that the large majority of the population is closely clustered round the various medical units, and that a steep fall off in outpatient attendance is of little matter because few people live far away from a medical unit. This is not in fact the case, for in the area shown the population density is fairly even at about 250 persons to the square mile.

Despite the comparatively large number of medical units in the region shown on the map, in only about a tenth of its area does the level of care attain or exceed the suggested standard of 2.5 attendances per person per year. In a smaller but still significant area the level of patient care far exceeds the basic standard — close to the hospital for instance it rises as high as six attendances per person per year. Taking services to the people is the main way of correcting this imbalance.

2:8 **The argument from population density.** The number of persons per square mile determines the possibility of providing them with medical care nearly as profoundly as does the distance of a patient's home from a medical unit.

A health centre has an optimum size and thus an optimum 'output'. Its optimum size is probably about that given in the next chapter. Its output is more difficult to calculate, but if it is to be used to the best advantage, there must be sufficient people within reach of its services.

As a useful, if admittedly arbitrary approach to calculating the output of a health centre, it will be assumed that half the time of its staff is taken up with outpatient attendances of various kinds, and that the rest is occupied with the other duties of the centre. Making the further assumption that four of its auxiliaries can each see 50 patients a day for 250 days a year, their output will amount to some 50,000 consultations annually. Using the figure of 2.5 consultations per patient per year as a working optimum, this means that a centre can look after 20,000 people. This figure may well be too high and 10,000 people is considered by some to be the optimum size (3:1). In Figure 8 a graph has

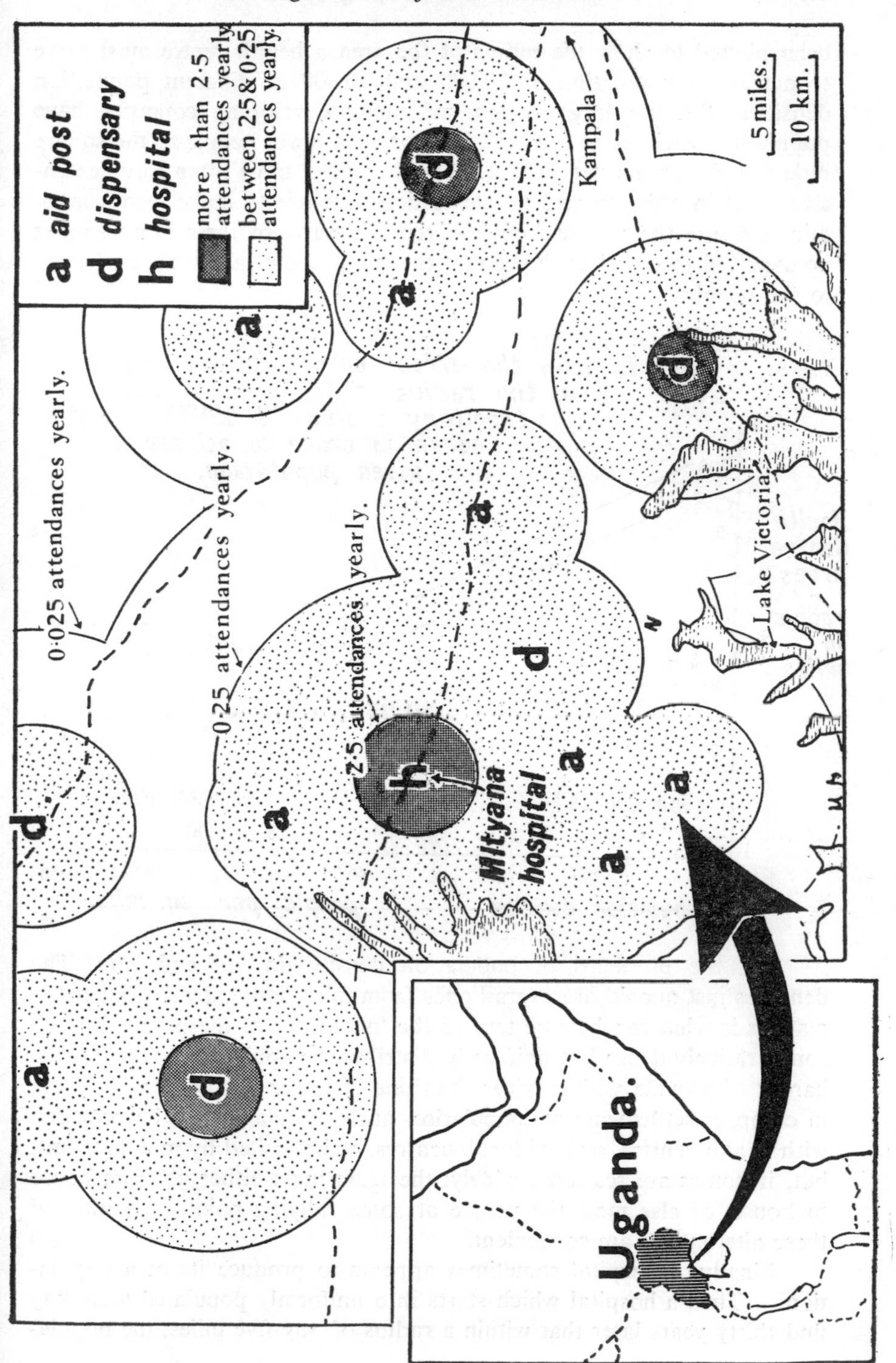
a aid post
d dispensary
h hospital
more than 2·5 attendances yearly
between 2·5 & 0·25 attendances yearly.
0·025 attendances yearly.
0·25 attendances yearly.
2·5 attendances yearly.
Mityana hospital
Kampala
Lake Victoria
5 miles.
10 km.
Uganda.

been plotted to show the radius of the area a health centre must serve to achieve a population of 20,000 and 10,000 at different population densities. Because large regions of many developing countries have population densities as low as 25, 10 or even fewer people to the square mile (10, 4 persons per sq. km.), health centres must often serve extensive areas in order to accumulate sufficient people to make them economic. Because the people from the remoter parts of these areas cannot be expected to travel to the centre, the centre must take mobile services to the people.

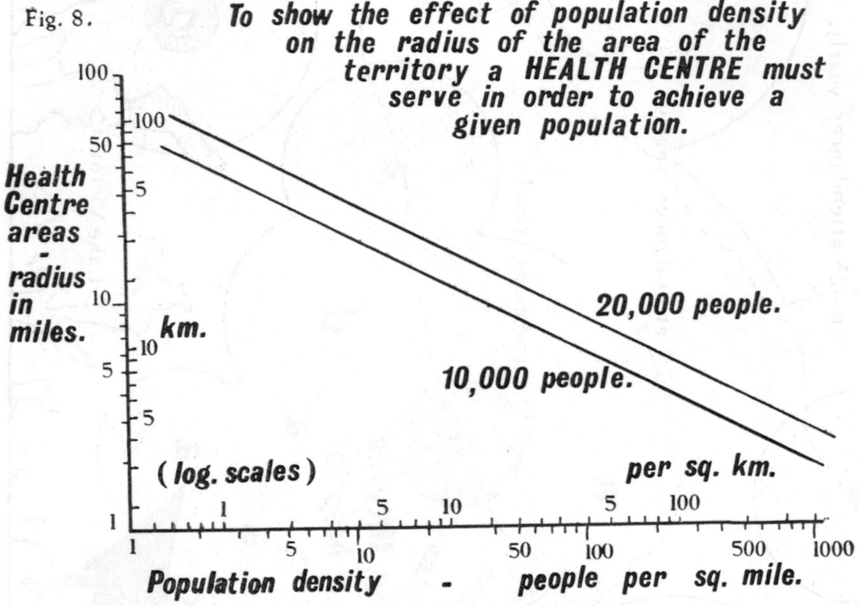

But the problems of population density do not end here. The densities just quoted are overall ones from fairly large areas; what really matters is what can best be termed the 'nuclearity of the population'. A comparatively dense but uniformly distributed population is likely to be harder to provide with services than one of lower overall density living in compact settlements or 'population nuclei'. Villages can be provided with health centres, or health sub-centres, or be visited by mobile teams, but, if homes are scattered widely, the team must either go from house to house, or else meet the people at some rallying point. Neither of these alternatives are convenient.

Finally, a hospital sometimes appears to produce its own population. Thus a hospital which starts in a uniformly populated area may find thirty years later that within a radius of, say five miles, the population is much denser than it is in the area beyond. In this both migration and the long-term effects of medical care play a part. In effect, patients have not only come to the source of care but they have stayed there.

:9 **The economic arguments.** At the hospital studied in Chapter Twelve, it was calculated that, each day three hundred patients travel collectively 1,900 miles (3,000 km) in order to benefit from the services of two medical assistants and a doctor half time. The average distance each patient travelled was over 6 miles (10 km.). Sheer economy demands that this travelling be minimized by making a few staff cover most of the distance so that many patients need travel less.

Chapter Twelve also shows this vividly in terms of money spent. In this study the average patient spent 2/50 ($0.35) in transport to the outpatient department to benefit from the -/81 ($0.11) worth of services that he received there. Together, the patients spent on transport the equivalent of more than half the total budget of this hospital.

But there is another factor to be taken into account besides the cost of transport. This is the value of the time spent waiting at the clinic and travelling to and from it. For adult Ugandans with skills this may in practice be an even more important hidden cost than that of the transport. The study in Chapter Twelve is about one place only, but it is probably repeated elsewhere, and points to the logic of taking services to the people, charging them what they save in transport, and using these funds to pay for the additional cost of the services provided.

The desirability of making a charge is further supported by the diagram depicting total health expenditure in Figure 1. Several developing countries spend as little as 7/- ($1) annually per head on all forms of medical care. This does not provide much, and it may be that some of the people might be able to pay the 1/- ($0.14) that the average health centre attendance costs. Considering that the annual per capita income (GNP per head) in many developing countries is of the order of £25 ($70) or more, this would appear to be possible.

Charges are beset with many administrative, political and educational difficulties. The collection of many small sums of cash has its problems, medical charges are keenly felt by the people and are thus politically distasteful, and patients need educating as to how a charge can actually be saving them money. If charges are difficult there are other alternatives; the additional expense can be met through a special local association, from employers (who will save their employees' working time), from the general revenue or from some simple health insurance scheme (1:19). But, in the last resort the choice is this: either some way is found to pay the cost of bringing services to the people or the people will pay their own way to hospital to receive treatment there. And in many cases — quite possibly the majority — the first alternative is the cheapest for everyone.

2:10a **Mobile outpatient services.** In general, mobile services can be of two kinds. The first is the complete mobile medical team that is away from its base many days bringing medical services to remote areas, and especially to nomadic people. Such teams require several vehicles and are expensive; they are not very manoeuverable and there is an enormous amount of packing and unpacking to be done every time they break camp. In some areas they are the only possible form of medical care, but, as their applications are limited, they are not considered further here.

The second type of mobile services are those provided by a health centre, or sometimes by a hospital within its own region (39), particularly in its extended area, and especially in regions of low population density. It is services of this kind that the steep outpatient gradients in Figure 6 show to be so necessary. It is fortunate therefore that, with the exception of the few holding beds and the labour ward, all the services of a health centre can be made mobile.

2:10b **Theory.** Mobile services are discussed from other points of view in the next chapter, but what is said here is complementary to what is said later. Mobile services should be based on health centres, for it is health centre services that they exist to provide: but, if there is no system of health centres in the area, then hospitals may have to provide them instead, and fulfil as much as they can of the health centre role in doing so (3:1).

Right at the start it must be made clear that mobile services have to be provided by auxiliaries, who must between them offer a range of skills and know how to organize themselves (3:4). Another important point is the multipurpose nature of the services that a team from a health centre or a hospital have to provide at any one visit. They will usually be able to visit each village only once a week, and, to be effective they must bring with them a wide range of facilities each time they come, including general outpatient services, antenatal and under-fives clinics as well as drugs for tubercular patients. The demand for these services is likely to be heavy, and there may well have to be a system of priorities in which such services as those for tuberculosis and the under-fives take preference. Visits must be regular and should make the most of the natural gatherings at markets or local government headquarters. It is best if the mobile clinics visit definite 'stations' in regular rotation, each of these stations having a local health representative or 'station master' of the kind suggested earlier in the chapter (2:3).

While the general arguments for mobile clinics are strong, two major objections are sometimes raised which it will be useful to deal with specifically. First it is argued that mobile services can at the most visit each centre once a week, and that this is insufficient, particularly for urgent cases. This is in fact a confusion over what the alternatives really are. The choice is likely to be between (a) a large daily clinic at the health centre, run by several staff; (b) the division of this into two smaller fixed clinics, one at the health centre and one somewhere else, at a health sub-centre for instance; or (c) one fixed clinic at the health centre with a mobile team serving different points in the area on each of the five working days of the week. Without mobile services, most villagers will have to travel considerable distances to reach treatment, and experience shows that only a few will do so. With mobile clinics, the medical care is likely to be available near at hand at least once a week. And, if it is not possible to wait, a patient can travel, either to the mobile clinic which is operating somewhere in the area, or to the health centre itself. For most people, this is no worse than before and — on one day a week at least — far better.

Second, it is argued that mobile clinics would make it impracticable to refer cases to a doctor and would thus lower the standard of medical care provided. But, if the mobile team is run by a health centre, patients are not going to see a doctor anyway, and they can if necessary be referred to a hospital for a doctor's opinion direct from a mobile clinic. If the mobile team is run from a hospital, and is in effect serving as its outpatient department, patients can still be referred to the hospital for a doctor's opinion. It may even be possible for the team to take one or two patients back to the hospital with them, depending on the size of the vehicle they are using.

There is another objection which, although not widely considered, may arise in the minds of those concerned with the economics of mobile clinics. In countries short of capital with much unemployed manpower, are not mobile clinics too 'capital-intensive', using too much capital and relatively too little labour? The short answer is that the real economic alternatives are not whether to run the health services with transport or without, but whether many forms of private transport should be used to bring patients to the clinics, or whether the health service should use its own transport to take the services to the people. From this overall point of view, mobile clinics may well use less transport than other forms of organization, Figure 24 (12:7) for example shows how many patients came in hired cars.

Practical detail. There are many practical points to make mobile clinics easier. One is the vehicle itself, and although an ordinary ambulance or Land Rover can be used, a specially fitted vehicle may well be worth the extra expense. Thus one group (28) propose to use a one ton 'pick-up' truck with side opening steel cabinets each side of its main load compartment (CHE). These trucks are made primarily as mobile workshops for such people as telephone linesmen and plumbers: they cost little more than the standard type of 'pick-up', and may prove to be the ideal vehicle for the provision of mobile services. The cabinets with which they are fitted are already water-proof and can be made dust-proof and lined with plastic foam to prevent their contents rattling. When the vehicle stops these are immediately available without lengthy unpacking. The cab seats three, or even four, and can be completely fitted and equipped with four wheel drive for £1,650 ($4,600). Such a vehicle could, it seems, do much to make mobile services practicable, and if their price seems excessive this should be compared with what some patients will spend on private transport (12:7), if services are not made mobile. A special mobile clinic conversion of the Land Rover is also available (PIL).

A major point of organization is the distance a mobile team has to travel. The less of their time the staff spend travelling the more of it will be available for treating patients. Thus, if a vehicle can travel at 20 miles an hour (32 km/hr), it can reach a village ten miles (16 km.) away in half an hour — mobility within this radius is thus highly practicable from the point of view of time. Transport needs to be economical if it is to be used on the necessary scale without becoming inordinately expensive, and is considered in further detail in sections 3:12 and 28:4.

Numerous minor details could also make mobile services easier. It may be found convenient to get the patients to keep their own records in polythene envelopes (26:5), though additional records may have to be kept for patients within the 'defined area' (3:2). Other useful points are to bring drugs prepacked in envelopes (21:18c) (30:5) and mixtures in plastic bottles which will not be broken in transit. If a microscope, a centrifuge or lighting are needed, the vehicle's own battery can be used. Only simple accommodation is required for the station; it can be borrowed for the occasion and need be little more than a roof of thatch or corrugated sheeting and a few cubicles of 'mud-wattle-and-whitewash' (10:6). Some tables and chairs will be wanted, a source of water and also latrines. If the local community cannot provide anything else they can usually provide these bare essentials.

Such mobile services are the key to outpatient care in the rural areas. Their organization provides a challenge that has been met in very few developing countries so far. While the detail and form of the service may have to vary considerably, there is little doubt that, in large areas of most developing countries, mobile clinics have an important part to play in bringing medical care to people who would otherwise have none.

INPATIENT CARE

1 **The need to concentrate inpatient care.** Figure 9 shows the inpatient care gradient for the same hospital in Uganda from which the outpatient care gradients were derived. It shows the decline in the use of hospital beds the greater the distance that patients live from hospital. The graph was plotted by calculating the average number of days spent in hospital each year by persons living in a number of concentric zones around it. As a hospital bed is able to provide 365 bed-days each year, this figure can readily be converted to the number of beds used per 1,000 of the population. The graph has the same exponential form as the outpatient gradients, but, compared with the outpatient care gradient for the same hospital, its slope is much less steep — the use of inpatient facilities halves every three miles (5 km.) while the average number of outpatient attendances halved every two miles (3 km.) .Inpaticnt carc is thus spread somewhat more equitably than outpatient care. Furthermore, because so many inpatients are selected directly from those who originally attend as outpatients, it is probable that inpatient facilities would become even more uniform if outpatient care could be distributed more evenly.

The comparatively flat slope of the inpatient care gradient, with its expected further flattening if outpatient care could be made more equitable, is a major reason for providing a few comparatively large hospitals rather than many small ones. But there are other good reasons for concentrating inpatient facilities at the same time as spreading outpatient services more widely. One is the support offered by health centres; a major advantage of an efficient network of health centres is that they permit hospitals to be large, fewer and more efficient. This they do by providing minor curative services to many outpatients, and some inpatients, by sorting patients generally, so that only those deserving hospital attention are referred there, and by helping to provide transport for such patients as are referred to hospital.

The concentration of inpatient services is also supported by the small part that transport plays in the total cost of a hospital admission — in the study in Chapter Twelve transport accounted for only 10 per cent. of an average inpatient admission, as against 75 per cent. of the cost of an average outpatient attendance (Figure 23 G & H (12:3)). Looked at in another way, only about one inpatient journey was made for every twenty outpatients journeys.

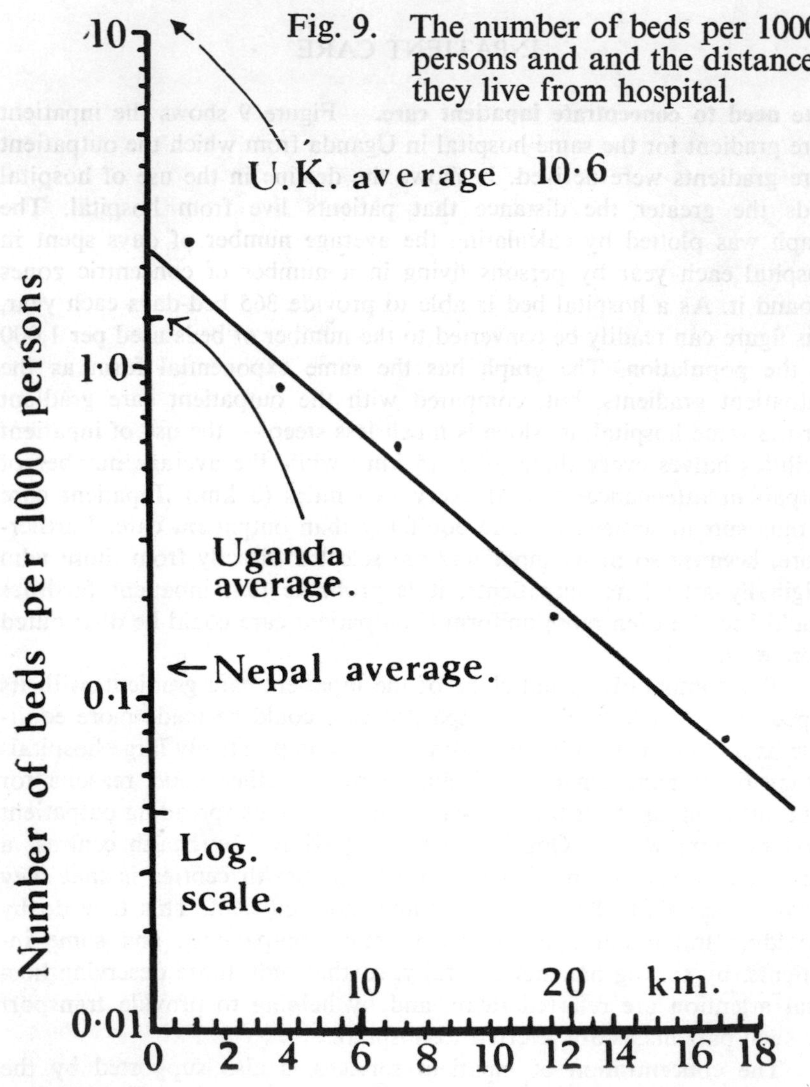

Fig. 9. The number of beds per 1000 persons and and the distance they live from hospital.

When contrasted with a hectic 80-bedded one-doctor hospital, a reasonably sized district hospital of 250 beds staffed by at least three doctors is a much more satisfactory place for a doctor to work in. When there are several doctors in a hospital, they can relieve and consult one another and specialize somewhat among themselves. A hospital of this size also makes better radiological and pathological facilities possible, and it reduces overheads as well as the time and money spent on administration. So great are the benefits to be drawn from having doctors working in units of more than one, that the one-doctor, 80 or 100-bedded hospital must now be considered an anachronism. The smallest practical size for a hospital is one with two doctors, and the 250 bed three or four doctor hospital should be the norm.

It is not possible to leave the subject of hospitals without defining just what a hospital is and what it is not. At its humblest a hospital is held to be a medical unit with beds, staffed by someone capable of doing at least some emergency surgery and equipped with a theatre, a laboratory and if possible an X-ray plant. Thus the use of the terms 'rural hospital', or even 'district hospital', for units staffed only by a medical assistant and devoid of a theatre is to be condemned, for a 'hospital' which cannot, for instance, provide a Caesarian section or a blood transfusion plainly is not one. Politically, it may be useful to call such units hospitals, functionally they are not so.

Such then are, or should be, the district hospitals which need to be backed up by regional hospitals, each with a range of specialist services which are in their turn supported by a national teaching hospital in the capital city.

SOME MAJOR ADMINISTRATIVE MATTERS

12 **The comparison of hospital and health centre costs.** Certain working estimates have to be made in attempting to compare hospital and health centre costs, and although they are considered individually elsewhere, it is convenient to bring them together here (1:10b, 3:15, 12:4).

As a working assumption a health centre is considered to cost £8,000 ($22,000) to build, £4,000 ($11,000) to run each year, and to provide an adequate level of service for 10,000 people (3:2) (3:15). Similarly, an equipped hospital bed is reckoned to cost £3,000; about the price at which they are currently being provided in several African countries. Once provided, such a bed is reckoned to cost £300 ($850) a year to service (12:4), and to be capable of being used for 68 inpatients a year (12:6).

Comparing the two units and considering capital costs, it will be seen that health centre facilities can be provided for 1,000 people for

£800 ($2,200), a sum that would only provide them with about a quarter of a hospital bed, that is one which could be used for an average of seventeen patients during a year.

Considering annual recurrent costs, health centre facilities can be provided for 1,000 people for an average sum of £400 ($1,100). This would service 1.3 hospital beds, in which about 100 inpatients could be treated in the course of a year.

Which is better? Is capital better invested in providing health centre services or an additional quarter of a hospital bed for every thousand people? Are recurrent expenses better used in providing health centre services or in servicing about one and a third additional beds for every thousand people? Strict calculations on the return in human welfare from these alternative forms of expenditure are not at present possible, but these figures for the comparative cheapness of health centre services tend to support what has been said under the sixth axiom (1:13c) that, once a certain minimal level of hospital services have been provided, then the next expenditure should be to provide adequate health centre services.

It may be argued that the provision of adequate health centre services will increase the demand for hospital beds because so many more cases will be referred for hospital care. This is likely to be true, and the exact relationship between the needs for these two kinds of service is certainly complex, and depends on such factors as the skill of the health centre staff in looking after patients who might otherwise have to be hospitalized, and the use that can be made of self-care facilities.

The comparison between the capital costs of hospital and health centre services is even more striking when they are considered on a national scale. Consider, for example, a country with 8 million people. At £3,000 a bed, to increase the average number of hospital beds by one per thousand would require a capital investment of £24 million, but to provide an adequate level of health centre services would require a capital outlay of only £6.4 million.

£24 million is a large sum to raise and it is instructive to consider what a more realistic sum, say £3 million, would do in such a country. This would provide 1,000 beds and increase the average number of beds per 1,000 people by one-eighth of a bed. Such a sum would have provided full health centre services for half the population on the basis of a centre to 10,000 people, or almost the entire population at the rate of one to 20,000 people.

It may be argued that an extreme case has been taken and the price of £3,000 for a hospital bed is an extreme one. It is however about the sum commonly being spent on district hospital beds in many African countries.

13 **A hospital in every constituency?** Medical services have a high priority in the minds of the electorate. The party that will promise the voter a hospital and a doctor in every constituency has an enormous advantage over the party that does not, because, even if it were possible, such a promise might not be the best health strategy. The dilemma is a real one. Most voters will know what dispensaries are but may not think much of them; they are unlikely to know what health centres are until they are well established — they have become very popular in Kenya. Voters well realize that money is short but will probably not appreciate the great difference between the costs of hospital and health centre services. In this situation there is a strong temptation to give the electorate what it wants instead of attempting to explain what is better. Too often this leads to many promises of little hospitals in numbers that make it impossible to staff and equip them properly, even if they were the most efficient unit.

Sometimes the electorate has a very firm idea that what it wants is doctors and will not be satisfied with medical assistants. Many voters do not understand the value of the work done by well trained medical assistants in health centres, the impossibility of producing doctors in sufficient numbers, the difficulties of paying them, and their reluctance to work in the rural areas.

In the long run the answers to the problems lie in a change of attitude and a new understanding from both voters and parliamentarians. Health education in schools should therefore include elementary ideas on the organization of health services as well as on the diseases themselves.

14 **The administration of hospital and health centre services.** So far hospital and health centre services have been considered as if they were entirely separate. They are however complementary parts of the same health service, and must work together. Patients are referred from health centre to hospital and vice versa; all levels of their staff should on occasion visit the other part of the service; some at least of their workers are interchangeable; both owe final allegiance to the same directorate, and it is often convenient for a hospital store to supply health centres with drugs and equipment. If this close integration is so necessary, how is it to be achieved, and how are these two sides of the service to be administered?

When trying to provide the best solution, one almost universal danger has to be borne in mind; it is that hospital services almost invariably come to take undue precedence over health centre ones. There are several obvious reasons why this should be so. Prevention is never so dramatic as cure, and its results, though enormous, are not very easily measured. As has already been said, electorates and their politicians are well aware of hospitals but usually know little of health centres. Added to this most doctors prefer hospital work and few enjoy continued travelling that the supervision of health centres requires. Furthermore, in preparing plans for development, the emphasis is too often on large prestigious capital projects which lead to preoccupation with two or three large hospitals rather than with many humbler health centres. All these factors combine against the health centre and it is thus little wonder that among developing countries so few have established them effectively, the great exception being Kenya.

Because of the likelihood of erosion of health centre services in favour of those of the hospitals, the first administrative principle should be to support the health centre wherever possible. Some have said that this is best done by separating them administratively, while others equally eminent and experienced hold exactly the opposite view!

The writers are hardly in a position to mediate, but wonder if the answer may be for hospitals and health centres to be administratively separate on the district level, but under the same direction at provincial level? This is implied in Figure 16 (10:4) where a regional hospital and health centre are drawn close to one another but separate, one supervised by the district medical officer and the other by the medical superintendent. It has been pointed out that the possibility of rivalry and disputes in the district can be minimized if it is made quite clear who is the senior of the two officers in the service, the district medical officer or the medical superintendent. This would vary from time to time, depending upon the seniority of the officers who happened to be occupying these posts. The provincial medical officer would on the other hand be in charge of both parts of the service.

2:15 **The place of the private authority hospital and the private practitioner.** The health scheme that has been described is an organization to which a variety of medical units may adapt themselves. It is but a historical accident that missions, or 'voluntary agencies' as some prefer to call them, have usually provided only hospitals, while governments have sometimes organized health centres as well. Provided some member of their staff has public health training, missions might well supervise a group of health centres and so complete their medical service to the area. To help them in this, it should be the aim of the state to supply funds to the limit of its capacity, and, if need be, auxiliary staff also, so as to make the best use of the medical skills that a mission has to offer.

So far the private practitioner has not been mentioned, and health services have been described here as being staffed entirely by salaried employees of the community through their agent, the State. It is one of the main themes of this symposium, that, in the developing countries, a doctor is at his most efficient in the service of the sick as a teacher, organizer and consultant to a team of auxiliaries, and that this is the best way in which his skills can be used when doctor-patient ratios approach those at the top of scale A in Figure 1 (1 : 1).

It should be a doctor's role to see those outpatients referred to him by auxiliary staff, to bring his skills to the bedside of the sick, to undertake major operations and to supervise, administer, encourage and teach his many helpers. Working like this a doctor fulfils the third axiom '... obtain the maximum return in human welfare from the limited ... skill available'. It is his skills that are short, and only by working with a team of auxiliaries does he make the most of them.

In his urban consulting room the private practitioner is without the help auxiliaries provide in the building of an efficient team, and he is usually also denied the beds, services and equipment needed for the most effective use of his skills. Too often he is but a provider of expensive palliatives to the few with the money to pay his fees. Though he will enjoy the amenities of the urban life, and is apt to grow rich, he will be of much greater value to the community, who provided the means of his education, if he serves them from a district health centre or in a district hospital.

If a doctor in a developing country leaves the government medical service, which is in effect the community's medical service, where he is of the greatest value, and starts to practise privately, it is only fair that he should refund to the community the complete sum that it spent in training him. This is reported to vary between £3,000 and £20,000 ($8,500) and ($56,000) and may sometimes be even more (15). To introduce such a payment would not only be fair, but it would provide a major incentive for working within the government health service, thus leading to a more efficient allocation of a country's medical resources.

If a government finds it difficult to persuade doctors to work in the rural areas, it is well entitled to bond those to whom it has given a scholarship to a period of service in these areas. It can also give a salary differential for up-country work, and there is something to be said for tying an unpopular post to a very popular house.

Chapter Three

THE HEALTH CENTRE

Based on the papers of Rex Fendall (11) (12) (13)

3:1 **Definition.** The word 'health centre' means different things to different people. When used here it is *a unit which provides a family with all the health services it requires, other than those which can only be provided in a hospital.* Fundamental to the nature of a health centre is that it takes its services and exerts its influence outside its own precincts right in the very homes of the people themselves. Once it fails to do this, and its staff stop visiting the surrounding villages, it is no longer a health centre. Its functions are promotive in that it promotes healthy living conditions, 'preventive' in that it seeks to prevent disease in the population by immunization, better environmental sanitation, better child feeding practices and early diagnosis; and curative in that minor ailments are treated in the centre and do not need to be referred to hospital.

When well developed a health centre provides general outpatient services and limited domiciliary care of the sick; it provides clinics for antenatal and postnatal mothers, school children and the 'under-fives', while, in addition to these there is usually a midwifery unit within the centre itself. It also provides environmental health services and gives advice and guidance on home living conditions, water supplies and sanitation. Simple dental care is also provided; at present this is mostly confined to tooth extraction, the relief of pain and the recognition of more serious oral pathology. Above all, and at every possible opportunity, a health centre educates the individual, the family and through them the community it serves. It strives also to obtain the active participation of the community in its health promoting activities (5:6 — community directed health action).

Because the health centre is *the* important unit of rural medical health in its area, all other health activities must be channelled through it. It is not to be regarded as an embryo district hospital, but as an entirely separate entity with different and complementary functions. Health centres are complementary because they enable hospitals to be fewer, larger and more efficient (2:11) and so make the building of multiple little hospitals unnecessary (2:13).

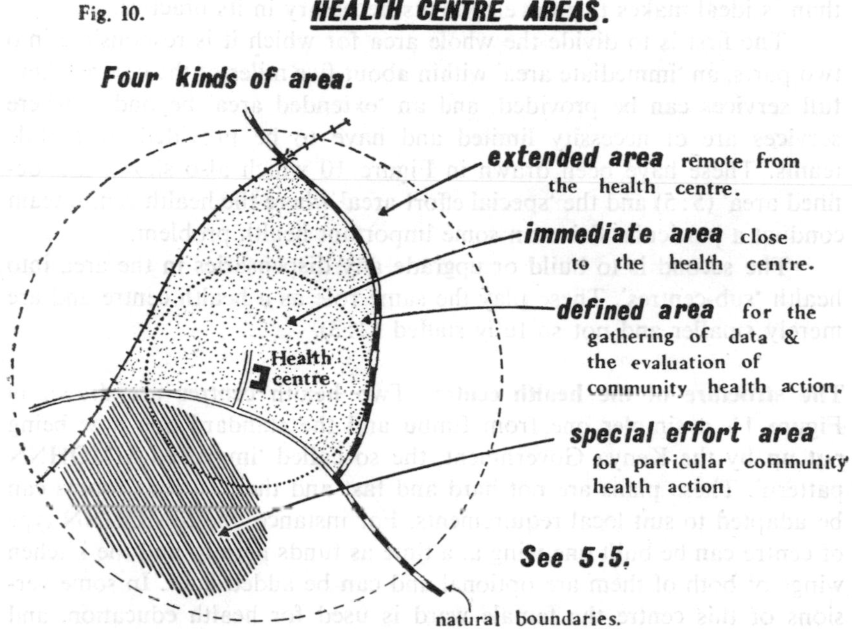

Health centres do not exist in isolation, their staff co-operate with other workers, especially agricultural extension officers, community development workers and schoolmasters. Co-operation must be mutual. This means for instance, that the medical assistant in charge of a centre must try to enlist the help of the local schoolmasters in the health education of their pupils. It also means that, if veterinary officers want the co-operation of the health centres in spreading information about such things as cattle diseases, then the health assistant should do his best to help them as he goes round the villages.

Health centres areas. In Kenya, from whence this account is derived, and where more than 150 health centres have been built in recent years, the ultimate objective is to have a health centre for every 10,000 persons. This is a somewhat arbitrary target, but if it can be achieved it permits a very satisfactory level of health centre services to be attained. In the more densely populated regions these centres need only serve an area with a radius of about five miles, but in other areas this has to be extended (Figure 8 (2:8)). Because of a lack of sufficient capital and trained auxiliaries, 1:10,000 is not a practical immediate objective, so, for the time being at any rate, the target is to try to achieve a health centre for every 20,000 persons serving an area which may have to be ten miles and more in radius. The need for a health centre to serve a larger area than is ideal makes two developments necessary in its practice.

The first is to divide the whole area for which it is responsible into two parts, an 'immediate area' within about five miles of the centre where full services can be provided, and an 'extended area' beyond it where services are of necessity limited and have to be provided by mobile teams. These have been drawn in Figure 10 which also shows the 'defined area' (5:5) and the 'special effort area' where the health centre team conduct a particular drive on some important health problem.

The second is to build or upgrade any dispensaries in the area into health 'sub-centres'. These play the same role as a health centre and are merely smaller and not so fully staffed (2:3).

3:3 **The structure of the health centre.** Two health centres are drawn in Figure 11, a simpler one from Embu and the standard one now being put up by the Kenya Government, the so called 'improved SIMOHNN pattern'. These plans are not hard and fast and their various rooms can be adapted to suit local requirements. For instance, the SIMOHNN type of centre can be built one wing at a time as funds permit, and the kitchen wings of both of them are optional and can be added later. In some versions of this centre the female ward is used for health education, and the male ward as the health office. On the whole, a separate health education room has not been found generally successful, and health education is more conveniently undertaken in the clinics themselves, or in the waiting space where a blank wall is provided for the projection of slides and films after dark.

One point is quite clear: it is that no dispensary should ever be put up except with the intention of converting it later into a health centre. This means that there must be a rudimentary 'master development plan' like that for a hospital (10:1).

STAFF

3:4 **The value of auxiliary staff.** In most developing countries professional staff, especially doctors, are so scarce that health centres have to be staffed by auxiliaries, and preferably by auxiliaries indigenous to the region. But this is no disadvantage, for they are at the same time more

Fig.11. **TWO HEALTH CENTRE PLANS.**

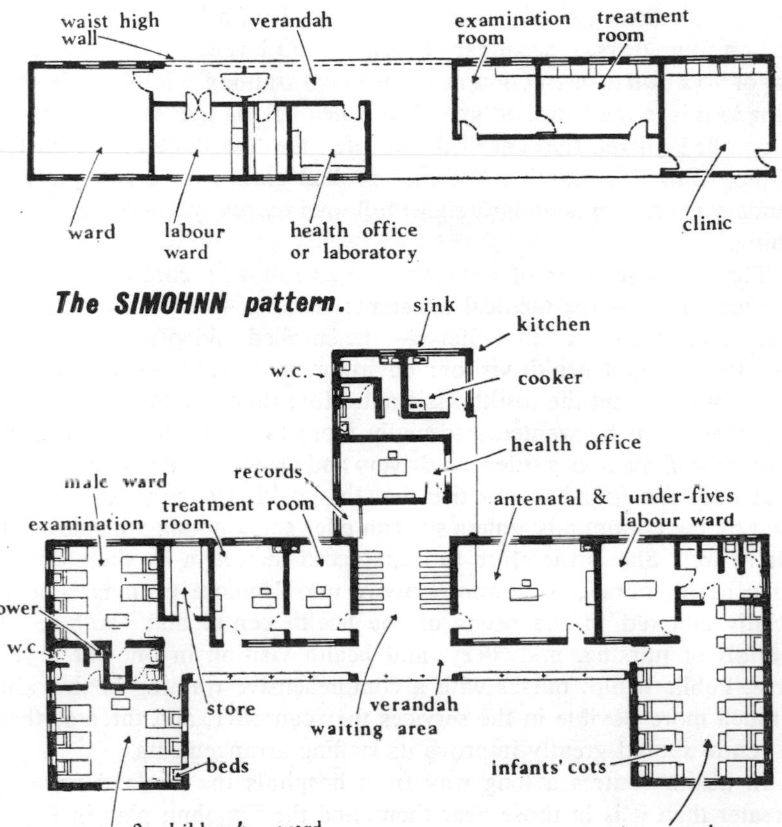

This is the latest Kenyan pattern, plans being obtainable from the Ministry of Health (KEY). Minor buildings, such as staff housing, are also needed. This building need not be completed all at one time; one wing can be built first & the rest built later.

economical and are generally more closely in touch with the local inhabitants than are doctors, and, very important indeed, they are also much more content to remain in the rural areas. In Kenya auxiliaries have proved to be effective substitutes for fully qualified professional people, be these doctors, midwives or health inspectors, and, when carefully selected and adequately trained, they develop that real sense of vocation and responsibility which is the true hallmark of the professions.

There are at present no less than five categories of trained auxiliary staff at the centres and usually two grades in each category. This is complex, and some simplification is planned in future. The senior grade to which the medical assistant and the assistant health inspector belong is based on four years of secondary education ('O level') plus three or four years of vocational instruction at the medical training school in Nairobi. Junior to this is the 'enrolled grade' to which belong the 'graded dresser', the 'enrolled nurse', the 'enrolled midwife', the 'assistant health visitor' and the 'health assistant'. All these enrolled grades have two years of secondary education (standard eight) followed by two years of vocational training.

The five categories of auxiliary are as follows: curative medicine and paediatrics — the medical assistant: nursing — the enrolled nurse and the graded dresser: midwifery — the enrolled midwife: health visiting — the assistant health visitor: environmental health — the assistant health inspector and the health assistant. More than one member of each group may often be wanted, especially more than one health assistant, and other staff such as gardeners, drivers and cleaners are also employed.

It has been found in practice that the health visitor is not well accepted by the community unless she can offer some nursing or midwifery skills as well. She is therefore to be replaced in Kenya by the auxiliary 'public health nurse', or 'comprehensive nurse' whose training is to be specially adapted to the needs of the health centre and combine the essentials of nursing, midwifery, and health visiting in one three year course. Public health nurses with a comprehensive training of this kind are much more flexible in the services they can offer, and three of them in a centre should greatly improve its staffing arrangements.

In health centres a long way from hospitals the demand for beds is greater than it is in those near them, and the Simohnn plan in Figure 11 shows a health centre with about as many beds as it is practicable to have. When there are as many beds as this there must be enough staff to look after them without calling on those who should be out visiting in the surrounding villages. Additional public health nurses, or their enrolled nurse, midwife and health visitor components, are thus required whenever the beds exceed a certain minimum number. Looking after the patients in the wards does not occupy much of a medical assistant's time, and of course none at all of that of the health inspector and his assistants, so the demand for these grades of staff is largely independent of the number of beds in the centre.

All members of the staff, particularly ambulance drivers, are instructed in first aid and emergency medical treatment, for the failure of any member to cope with a crisis may discredit the whole team.

At a health sub-centre there are only two or three staff members, all of the junior grade, a health assistant, an enrolled midwife and a male enrolled nurse.

Careful staff training in a central school, and continued supervision are the key to a good system of health centres. Because the staff will have to learn to work with one another as a team, and, as a good team spirit is vital, it is desirable to let the staff select their own teams and to train these teams together. This training and retraining of health centre staff both auxiliary and professional, for the district medical officer needs instruction too, is one of the main functions of the National Reference Health Centre (3:14).

If standards and morale are to be maintained, centres must be regularly visited and supervised, both by the district medical officers who are in direct command, and by other professional personnel, especially by the tutors responsible for training health centre staff.

The medical assistant. A medical assistant is in administrative charge of each centre; he diagnoses and treats the sick and visits patients in their homes — he is in fact the general practitioner of the area. He gives health education talks and sees that the other members of the staff do so too. Health centres provide valuable opportunities for health education, for this starts with the premise that the sick are much more susceptible to advice about preventive action than are the healthy (6:4). Medical assistants also give health education talks to the elders and chiefs, they co-opt members of other departments to help in this field and they co-ordinate their work with community activities as a whole, including community development workers and homecraft centres.

The medical assistant organizes the work of the centre and tries to see that the health assistants correlate their work to take account of the diseases shown to be prevalent by the outpatient clinics. He also conducts regular staff discussions that do much to maintain the interest and morale of the team (8:2). One half day each week is reserved for such meetings when all the staff of the centre can discuss cases and exchange information. The medical assistant is also responsible for record keeping and sends in returns to the district medical officer, whose duty it is to supervise a group of centres (5:8).

The health staff. In Kenya the assistant health inspector is of similar status to the medical or hospital assistant, and the health assistant is the equivalent of the dresser. Thus the assistant health inspector at each centre has several assistants to help him, one posted to each large village or location, and preferably centred on a dispensary or health sub-centre. They are responsible for providing safe water by digging wells and protecting springs, and often have a mason to help them in these tasks. These health assistants also provide latrines and see that these are used, they advise on improvements in indigenous housing, they assist in measures against diseases such as malaria, and they help to trace the contacts of infectious cases. They inspect meat and supervise markets. Like other members of the staff, assistant health inspectors and health assistants go into the patients' homes where their work is particularly valuable in times of epidemic, because it is then that the villager is most susceptible to advice and instruction.

All the health staff are taught to be active workers with their *hands* as well as their heads, and are encouraged not to be afraid of getting their hands dirty.

3:7 **Graded dressers and enrolled nurses.** Dressers and enrolled nurses apply all dressings, and give all the treatments and injections ordered, but, though they may give antibiotics, they are not allowed to prescribe them. In Kenya they act as a filter (11:2) to the medical assistant, for they are capable of dealing with most minor complaints and need only refer the more seriously ill patients for his opinion. Dressers and nurses do not normally leave the centre and may even take temporary charge of it when the medical assistant is out in the district. If patients come up meanwhile, these dressers treat what patients they can and either save any perplexing ones until the medical assistant returns, or else send them on to hospital.

3:8 **The enrolled midwife and enrolled health visitor.** Enrolled midwives are able to handle normal deliveries and recognize complications which they refer to hospital. They hold antenatal and postnatal clinics at the centre and in the villages, they deliver mothers in the centre and in their homes, and they assist the health visitor with under-fives clinics. A midwife pays one postnatal visit to each case during the postnatal period, after which the health visitor takes over the care of that family.

Kenya cannot afford institutional delivery for all mothers, so, in order to encourage confinement at home, mothers are charged a fee for hospital delivery, and half fees for health centre delivery, while domiciliary delivery is free. The policy is to send abnormal cases to hospital, and to restrict health centre delivery to 'primips' and cases where the home conditions are particularly bad.

Kenya has a high birth rate, so the midwives are busy, most of them managing to deliver about 20 babies a month, half of these at home.

Antenatal clinics are popular, and once mothers are assured that their pregnancy is normal, most of them are content to have their babies at home, even if it is not possible for them to be attended by a midwife. The most important aspect of this work is, however, the opportunity it gives these midwives to instruct mothers in domestic and personal hygiene.

The enrolled health visitor holds under-fives clinics in the centre and in selected villages, she visits as many families as she can in their homes, she helps the midwife and she undertakes health education and schools visits. In future her tasks will be taken over by the auxiliary public health nurse or comprehensive nurse (3:4).

THE WORK OF THE HEALTH CENTRE

The services of the health centre classified. The activities of a health centre can be summarized like this:

Personal services

General curative outpatients services.
Maternity care (19:1).
The care of the under-fives (16:1) — immunization (17:1).
The care of school children.
Consultative clinics.
Clinics for special diseases, e.g. tuberculosis (21:18a) and malnutrition (14:1).
Dental care.
Mental care.
Home visiting.
Case work.
Limited inpatient care.

Community services

Health education (6:1).
The improvement of water supplies.
The improvement of excreta disposal.
The supervision of housing conditions.
The regulation of food shops and markets.
Campaigns against communicable diseases (1:13).
The collection of statistics (5:5).

This list does not claim to be complete, nor is it always mutually exclusive, but one thing in particular is missing from it. No mention has been made of family planning which should become one of the more important health centre services in many developing countries in the years ahead (18:1). At the time of going to press there are reports that this is causing considerable concern in Kenya.

These services are provided both within the health centre itself, its 'internal services', and outside it, particularly in the extended area, its 'external services'.

3:10 **Internal services.** Large numbers of general outpatients are seen in the centre itself. Inpatient facilities are limited, but they are not so greatly needed, for many acute illnesses when treated early respond to two days or so of modern treatment, and require only a short admission followed by outpatient treatment if necessary. Accidents, particularly head injuries, often need observation for a day or two, so these few beds are very useful.

General outpatient clinics are held at the centre daily, but emergencies are seen at any time. Clinics for particular categories of persons, such as antenatal mothers or the under-fives are held on appointed days when there is usually more time to see and deal adequately with each person. These clinics are often finished in the morning which leaves the staff time to visit villages nearby in the afternoons. Care is taken to hold under-fives clinics on the same day as antenatal clinics, thus saving mothers a second visit. These clinics have not, however, reached the peak of development described in Chapter Sixteen, selected children only being encouraged to attend according to their need.

Though clinics for particular disease are sometimes held, special records are more important for they make it unnecessary for members of the same family to come up on separate occasions. Thus, if a tuberculous father brings up his child with a cut knee, father and son are both attended to at the same time, and the general policy is to treat such diseases as tuberculosis and leprosy along with the general outpatients. Consultative clinics by visiting doctors are routine, and the equivalent of such consultations by visiting experts in environmental sanitation, public health nursing or health education are *just as important as the strictly clinical ones* in maintaining the standards of the centres. *The real purpose of such consultations is to teach the staff who must be present whenever these visiting consultants are at work.* This is just one example of the teaching opportunities of clinical consultations (11:2 & 16:3). In planning these clinics efforts are made to hold the general ones at the times most convenient to the patients and the consultative ones at times that suit the consultants.

Health centres are also expected to co-operate with 'traditional practitioners', whether these be 'witch doctors' (20:6) whose assistance may be useful in treating the mentally disturbed, or indigenous midwives

(19:2) among whom the health centre can play a very useful educational role. If it starts by supplying these women with cotton wool, umbilical tape, and razor blades to cut the umbilical cord, goodwill is rapidly established and a spirit of co-operation is soon built up.

3:11 **External services.** Because the staff only hold full clinics at the centre once a week they are able to hold a regular programme of clinics in the villages nearby on the four other days. A very real attempt is thus made to take the services to the people — even within the immediate area — and to make the 'care gradient' (2:7) as fair as possible. Multipurpose clinics are held after the pattern described in section 2:10, and are staffed by two or more auxiliaries working together, usually the medical assistant and an enrolled midwife.

In the immediate area auxiliaries are able to visit the sick at home, deliver mothers at home, find cases, trace contacts, and keep a close watch on environmental sanitation — in other words to provide complete health centre care. The immediate area is mostly served by individuals working on foot, bicycle or scooter, though when occasion demands two or more members may visit together in a motor vehicle (28:4).

The extended area is visited by teams consisting of the medical assistant and the assistant health inspector, or one of his assistants, who are often assisted by a midwife or a health visitor. By working together, they gain a better understanding of each other's work and are able to look at the community as a whole. This team holds multipurpose clinics in the villages all over the extended area in a regular fortnightly rotation. While they are away, a nurse or dresser remains at the centre to cope with the daily flow of sick. The schedule is arranged by the medical assistant in consultation with his team and the local authority councils, and is adhered to until sufficient progress has been made to warrant their moving to a fresh series of villages. Thus, although the team cannot visit every village in the extended area every fortnight, they are in turn able to extend their influence over the whole territory assigned to their centre.

On arriving at a village in the extended area the team select a spot to hold their clinic. It may be held in a building loaned for the purpose, in a specially built mud-and-wattle hut or 'station' (2:10b), or even under a tree. Clinics are preceded by a health talk in simple language given by the medical assistant or the assistant health inspector. A subject of topical interest is chosen, such as typhoid fever for example; the villagers are told what it is, how it spreads and the measures that the community should take to avoid it. At the end of the talk questions are invited. Clinics are then held, while the assistant health inspector tours the village inspecting and giving assistance and advice on general sanitation, water supplies, latrines, building standards and the food shops. He also investigates any special problems that the elders bring to his notice. The staff confer on the results and each member of the team talks for five minutes on a subject that needs particular attention by the community. The four members are able to cover the subject fairly well between them. For example, if malaria is found to be prevalent the talk would cover its cause and treatment, the harm it does to children, why it is afflicting the villagers and what steps they should take to protect themselves.

Local elders and headmen are co-opted to see that the preventive measures are put into effect and to be certain of their support.

Progress is checked when the team next visit the village. If there are any local health personnel in the village, they are automatically made part of the health centre team and carry on with its work until its next visit.

One of the most valuable results of teamwork is, that when there are outbreaks of infectious disease, the whole team can go into action together in an all-out community effort.

Attention has to be paid to the special needs of certain groups of people, and to places of particular need; schools for example, should be visited regularly. As an example of the value of school work, the prevalence of scabies in certain schools in one district was as high as 70 per cent., but, by repeated visits it was reduced to almost nothing (16:9). Veterinary and agricultural workers should be called upon for assistance in areas where malnutrition is rife.

These teams are very popular in the districts, they enable the centres to attack disease and ignorance and promote a better standard of living.

3:12 **Mobility**. Mobility is of critical importance, so health centres are equipped with bicycles, motor-cycles and a motor vehicle which also functions as an ambulance. While the team is using their vehicle, emergency cases arriving at the centre are transported in an ambulance from the district hospital, in a hired vehicle, or by public transport.

The cost of motor transport is discussed in section 28:4, where the principle of using the cheapest vehicle capable of doing the job is emphasized. This is particularly true of mobility in the extended area, where an expensive four wheel drive Land Rover is not always required and can often be replaced by a cheaper vehicle.

There is a tendency to save on transport now that many health centres in Kenya are run by the local authorities who find it difficult to raise sufficient money for them. This is a pity because it means that the influence of the health centre team is diminished, particularly in the extended area. Transport costs form a significant fraction of the health centre budget, and detailed studies of the economics of health centre mobility are much needed.

There are areas where water-borne units are practical, the Nile and Lake Victoria, for example.

In nomadic areas with vast distances of inhospitable terrain the mobile health unit has to be much more self-contained, and undertakes sorties lasting ten days or more. In such areas a forward timetable is essential if faith is to be kept with the people. The movements of nomadic tribesmen must therefore be studied, and efforts made to meet them on specified dates at such points as their cattle watering places.

3 **Drugs and equipment.** A standard list of drugs is issued to all health centres. All centres are given drugs for the routine treatment of the more important diseases such as tuberculosis, leprosy and syphilis, for which standard treatment programmes are laid down. Sulphonamides, penicillin and chloramphenicol are issued routinely, a little morphia is also supplied, as are drugs for such conditions as trypanosomiasis, kala-azar and onchocerciasis, where these diseases are prevalent in the area. The general policy is in effect to be liberal, and to supply what is needed under the discretion of the district medical officer. Carefully constructed circulars on management routines for the more important illnesses are sent round to the health centres, both to simplify procedures and to economize in the use of drugs (Eleventh axiom 1: 18).

One of the present weaknesses of the health centres is the difficulty their staff have in making a definite aetiological diagnosis, that is, in actually confirming the presence of malarial parasites, tubercle bacilli or schistosome ova, etc. Their staff need further elementary laboratory training, a carefully selected outfit of laboratory apparatus (Appendix F) and a suitable manual (24: 1).

4 **The National Reference Health Centre.** Careful training and *retraining* of the several grades of auxiliaries is the key to a good system of health centres. In Kenya this is undertaken at the Medical Training School in Nairobi, but something is required to support the health centres in addition to the traditional type of school.

This supporting unit is the 'National Reference Health Centre' which has the following functions.

1. It acts as a model working health centre serving a population living in a typical rural African setting and is thus an example on which other centres can be built.
2. It serves as a unit for training and retraining all categories of staff who have anything to do with health centres, whether they be as senior as provincial medical officers or as junior as enrolled nurses. Whenever possible training is *team* training.

3. It serves as a 'community health laboratory' for detailed investigations into community health, and as a centre of operational or methodological research into health centre practice. On the outcome of this research can be based plans to be carried out on a national scale in other centres (1:18).

The World Health Organization advise the establishment of a series of Primary Reference Health Centres, one for each province, supported by a National Reference Health Centre (47). Because this is not possible in Kenya at the present time, a single reference centre has been started at Karuri near Nairobi to combine both the functions of a Primary and a National Reference Health Centre.

A 'community health laboratory' is also discussed in connection with these centres and is apt to be considered as something distinct from them; it is not, and is inherent in the third or research function of both types of reference centre, and indeed of any health centre where a community diagnosis is made followed by carefully planned and evaluated health action (5:1).

3:15 **Health centre economics.** These are not easy to calculate exactly, but an approximation is that a centre costing £8,000 ($22,000) to build and £4,000 ($11,000) to run each year can provide about 50,000 outpatient attendances annually (15). This makes each attendance cost about Shs. 1/60 ($0.23) but takes no account of the fact that the staff spend about half their time rendering services of other kinds. Reckoning that an illness at a health centre involves 2-3 attendances, each illness costs about Shs. 4/- ($0.56) (2:4).

Serving a population of 20,000 such a centre might provide an average of 2.5 outpatient attendances per person per year, which is the same as the somewhat arbitrary figure used as a basis for calculation in section 2:5.

There are about ten staff employed at a health centre, so each job requires a capital outlay of about £800, a figure which closely resembles that for the district hospital in section 12:3. These costs are based on standard methods of construction, and what has been said about cheap hospital buildings applies equally to cheap ones for health centres (10:6, Third axiom 1:10b).

If the annual running cost of £4,000 is spread over the 20,000 people that a typical health centre is intended to serve, then the average cost per person per year also works out at Shs. 4/-. It is instructive to compare this figure with two others.

The first is with the amount spent on health services by developing countries as shown in Figure 1 (1:1). Here it will be seen that many developing countries spend about Shs. 7/- ($1) per head per year on medical services. Four shillings amounts to about half of this sum and might seem a just proportion to spend on health centre services. In practice, however, hospital services are incomparably more expensive (2:12), and in Kenya, where health centres have a very high priority, the amount spent directly on health centres in 1961 was only about £600,000 ($1,170,000), or about 13 per cent. of the £4.7 million ($13 million) health budget that year. The demands for hospital medicine are so strong that in practice it is difficult to allocate health centre services a larger fraction of the health budget (2:13).

The second revealing comparison is that of the cost of health centre services with the GNP per head per year (1:1) (18:2c). For a typical developing country this is of the order of £25 ($70). The annual cost of health centre services (4/-, $0.56) amounts to less than 1 per cent. of this. Admittedly, this figure only covers the running costs of the centres and it is difficult to estimate how much more should be added to cover training. supervision and administration, nor is it easy to take account of the capital costs of the centres themselves, but if simple building methods are followed this should not be excessive (10:6). Even if the proportion of 1 per cent. of the GNP is doubled to account for these other costs, the sum is still only half the figure of 4 per cent. which is approximately the fraction of the GNP which the United Kingdom and the USA spend on health services (29). This can for convenience be considered as being not more than the just fraction of its GNP that a country should spend on health services. In practice, Kenya only spent 2.1 per cent. of its GNP on health in 1961, and even this figure was twice what it had been only five years previously.

Looked at in this way, as a percentage of the GNP, health centre services manned by auxiliaries are cheap. They represent a substantial return in human welfare for comparatively little expenditure of money and skill. If this is granted they must be a high priority in a health service budget and money must somehow be raised for them, either by taxation or direct charges (1:13) (2:12).

So convincing are the economic arguments, that a very strong case indeed can be made out for restricting further hospital expansion in a country until efficient health centre services have been built up (1:13c).

Chapter Four

THE CROSS-CULTURAL OUTLOOK IN MEDICINE

Maurice King

4:1 **'Culture'.** Though it is all around us the most important parts of our 'culture' remain invisible to us. As we slowly reach our full thoughtfulness and maturity inside it we inevitably absorb it unawares; whether we like it or not we are the product of it. Only when we have reached a high level of education, and obtained something of the insight of the comparative sociologist or social anthropologist, can we see our own culture for what it is, and understand where it differs from those of other communities.

But what is this abstraction 'culture'? It is the sum total of the customs, beliefs, attitudes, values, goals, laws, traditions and moral codes of a people. It includes their language and their art as well as everything they make, be it a stone axe or a spacecraft. It includes their corporate view of the universe and also their attitudes to health and disease. In all these dimensions does the culture of a people like the pygmies of the Ituri forest differ from the culture of the commuters of New York city. The reader will say that this is obvious, and in a limited sense so it is. The American doctor practising among the pygmies will immediately see that in such things as language, dress and education his patients differ from those he looked after in North America. But these are only the obvious and visible parts of a culture. Its values, attitudes, traditions and morals are invisible and not nearly so obvious.

The almost inevitable human tendency is to accept the visible parts of a strange culture, and unconsciously graft on to them invisible elements from the observer's own culture, albeit in a very incomplete and haphazard way. A real understanding of the invisible elements of another culture, and even more so of one's own, requires training, effort and great openness of mind. Unless he is watchful the doctor will tend to assume that his tropical patients know about the spread of infectious diseases and put the same value on the possession of money or cows as he does. He may know that witchcraft exists, but disregard it, because it plays such a small part in his own culture. This compounded view of a strange culture — 'the visibles of the strange culture plus some of the invisible elements of the observer's own culture' — is the common view of the educated but sociologically untrained person contemplating a culture new to him.

The value of a 'cross-cultural' outlook. Few doctors, even in developed countries, practise among patients who are culturally similar to themselves, and this is even more so in developing ones which typically contain so many varied tribes. If this cultural difference between a doctor and his patients is granted, how necessary is it that he understands their culture, and obtains what might be called 'a cross-cultural outlook'? It may be argued that penicillin works similarly whatever the culture of the patient, that a post-partum haemorrhage requires the same treatment anywhere in the world, and that the signs of mitral stenosis depend only on disordered physiology. This is true, and it must be admitted that many doctors have practised with some success, and even achieved academic eminence with hardly the faintest understanding of the way their patients look at the world. But their success is partial and perhaps their eminence is undeserved. If medicine is to be more than just the application of technique, and indeed even if it is to be merely the efficient application of technique, then the patient's culture must be understood as it relates to their health, and in practice it is found to relate at a great many points. Why will they not give their blood for transfusion? (23:2) Why, when their children are malnourished, will they not use the protein sources that seem readily available? (14:2) Why are they so loath to accept family planning? (18:5) Why is it so difficult to persuade them that tuberculosis is infectious? (6:12) Why is gonorrhoea so prevalent in the area? All these questions and a great many others may only be explicable in their cultural setting.

Obtaining a 'cross-cultural' outlook. If it is granted that a cross-cultural outlook is necessary, how can it be obtained? How can a doctor, as it were, get inside his patient's culture and see the world as they see it?

The first step is to realize that the cross-cultural problem exists, and that active measures are needed to discover and understand a strange culture.

The next is to observe the culture closely. Why does a child patient wear such a peculiar necklace of skin and bits of hair? Has it been supplied by the traditional healer, and, if so, what is the system of beliefs on which it depends? What are those peculiar herbs the patient's relatives are cooking so busily in that pot? Why do the women wear dresses which bear such a remarkable resemblance to those fashionable in Europe in 1890? Why is this adult literacy class composed mostly of women? Is it because by learning to read these women seek to gain influence over their illiterate husbands? Why are the words 'Sea never dry' written on the tailboard of that 'Mammy wagon'? These are just some of the visible starting points from which the invisible aspects of a culture can be built up by careful question and enquiry. Some of them have no obvious relation to health, yet they are well worth following because an overall view of the culture is necessary if those parts of it which are relevant to health are to be seen in their true context.

Those about to practise in a strange culture should make a point of reading whatever published work is available on the local community. Thus, Southall and Gutkind's book *Townsmen in the Making* /124/, is a classical and easily readable study of the sociology of urban Uganda and *Igbo-ora, a Town in Transition*, is a more recent account of a somewhat similar kind from Nigeria /19/. Oscar Lewis's book *Children of Sanchez* /93a/, will provide vivid insight into the culture of the common man in Mexico. Though they have wider application, these are only local studies, and a textbook of medical anthropology for developing countries is greatly needed. In its absence the popular works of Margaret Mead will provide some background knowledge /96/. In a few developing countries, the local novelists and playwrights provide useful insight into the culture. This is especially true of Nigeria where the works of Chinua Achebe and Wole Soyinka will be found very instructive.

Thanks to endeavours of anthropologists, many of the world's cultures have now been fairly adequately studied, and if a particular tribe has not been examined, there is likely to be an account available of a closely similar one. Hitherto, the readership of works in this field has been small and some accounts may be hard to obtain, but if local studies can be found they may well make interesting reading.

Similarly, if there are anthropologists working in the area they may have much to tell doctors working with the same tribes. Once they have learnt the local language and been accepted by the people, they are likely to be a good source of information on customs relevant to health. They are unlikely to have the information available in a very accessible form, but it should not be too difficult to elicit from them.

Educated members of the community, particularly the hospital staff, are another source of information on the local culture and here again careful questioning will be needed. Care must be taken to account for the bias of the informant, who may try to cover up what he feels ashamed of, be ignorant of what actually happens, or be incapable of conveying the true state of affairs, even if he knows it.

Lastly, but most important of all, there are the patients themselves. Besides observing them carefully, the critically important step is to learn their language, but time is short, languages are diverse, postings from one part of the country to another are often frequent, and few doctors acquire new languages with sufficient facility to enable effective two-way communication to take place. Sometimes there is a language like the Nigerian 'Pidgin' which makes communication at a certain level very easy, but interpreters have usually to be used. But working through an interpreter is time-consuming, and it is convenient to know a few clinical questions in the vernacular to which the expected answer is 'yes' or 'no', such as 'Have you got a cough?' or 'Is there blood in your sputum?' Even more useful are what might be called the clinical imperatives, such as 'Take a deep breath' or, 'Say aaah'. A few dozen phrases of this kind, and especially the local greetings, must be considered the minimum knowledge of the local language for clinical efficiency. On being posted to a place where the language is strange it is well worth making a list of the phrases and learning them. The reader could hardly do better than translate into his local vernacular the phrases compiled by Strover and Mazorodze in their *Shona Phrase Book* which is published as a supplement to the December 1965 issue (Vol 11, No. 12) of the *Central African Journal of Medicine*. Here at least is the basis for a planned interview, and a foundation upon which a working knowledge of a language can be built.

Even so, there will be many occasions when interpreters will have to be used, and sometimes, if the language is a very unusual one, two of them will be needed working together, one interpreting to the other. Try to make sure that the interpreter himself understands the question and that he does his best to make sure that the patient does so too. Get in the habit of insisting on being given the answer to the question asked and not the answer to a different one. Once the answer to a different question is accepted further logical interrogation becomes impossible.

But this has been a digression. The important point, as far as this chapter is concerned, is, that when histories are being taken, some questions should be asked which relate to the patient's general culture. This will enable a clear picture of their society to be built up steadily over the years. In every community the doctor is in a uniquely favourable position to study his fellow men, because, with due care, he can ask almost any question he likes in the name of medicine.

Some early steps in the study of a culture. Even the simplest human society is enormously complex and the novice can be pardoned for not knowing where to begin. Large numbers of individuals play many different roles, they interact with one another, with their physical environment and with other societies in intricate and ever changing ways. The following list contains just a few of the things that have to be known in the description of every human community. They are the sort of questions to begin by asking and form some of the more obvious dimensions of a culture. Further lists are recorded in connection with health education and malnutrition in sections 6:9 and 14:2.

Method: A start in the study of a strange culture.

The Family. What are the common patterns of family composition? What is the age of marriage and how stable is it? What are the strongest emotional ties within it? What are the obligations towards the extended family of uncles, aunts, and cousins? What is the status of women?

After the family, what other important associations are there? Political parties? Guilds? Agricultural co-operatives? Initiation groups? Religious communities?

Who are the influential members of the community? Chiefs? Party officials? School teachers? Ministers? Hospital assistants?

What accords status in the community? Cattle? Wives? Children? Land? Money? Education?

What are the values of a community? Leisure? Conformity? Happiness? Fulfilment of the personality?

What are the customs of the community over the use and ownership of land and money? How is the land inherited? What is the income of the average family? Is money the common property of the family? Is there money available in the community for medical expenses?

What are the attitudes and practices of the community in matters of health and disease? What is the traditional system of medicine? Do people consult their healers first, or only after scientific medicine has failed? What are the concepts of causation of the common diseases? Does the indigenous system of medicine include the idea of prevention? What are the local names for the common diseases?

The practices of the community on matters of health can be divided into three groups, those which are beneficial to health, those which have no effect and those which are positively harmful. It is their effect on health that matters, not their strangeness to the observer nor their remoteness to his own culture. Some practices may seem very odd indeed and yet be either harmless or even actually helpful. Thus, the habit that mothers in some cultures have of prechewing their infant's food and giving him the masticated material straight from their own mouths is not to be discouraged; it is likely to be harmless and may even be beneficial. Mother and child share the same bacterial flora anyway, and part of the child's digesting will already have been done for him.

Some useful sociological concepts. This is no place to go deeply into the structure of human communities, but here are certain ideas that are well worth bearing in mind.

A culture is a logically integrated dynamic whole and is not merely an accidental collection of customs. Looked at overall it makes sense, and, unless great changes are taking place, most cultures are fairly harmonious. But, because a culture is in equilibrium, a major change in one part of it is likely to cause multiple changes elsewhere, for the old balance will now be changed. For example, the assumption of professional or middle class standards of life is at variance with the traditional idea that many cultures have of the obligations to an extended family. The desire for a higher standard of living may lead to the limitation of family obligations, and this in turn may produce further changes, such as less security in sickness and old age, and lessened responsibility for the education of nephews and cousins.

A culture makes it possible for the members of a society to interact with one another in a more or less automatic manner. As they grow up its members learn the behaviour expected of them in the innumerable roles they will have to play in life, whether as sons, fathers, employees, lovers, buyers, students or professors, etc. This stereotyped activity of a stable culture is a great convenience, for it makes interaction between one individual and another so very much simpler. In an unstable or changing culture these roles will be changing too, and its members will be without the security of knowing the exact behaviour that is expected of them in each social situation.

All culture is learned by one member from another. For many individuals the learning process is complete once childhood is past, and it is only the minority of adults who are likely to learn new forms of behaviour. But this minority is of great importance, because, if we can only identify the few people who are susceptible to being taught and teach them, then the society can in time be introduced to new patterns of behaviour.

In most communities there are a few individuals to whom the rest look up. These are often, but not always, the natural leaders of the group such as chiefs, priests, schoolmasters and doctors. If these can be identified, and it may be more difficult to identify the women leaders in communities where their status is relatively low, they are the people who are most likely to be effective in spreading a change in behaviour through the group.

Every society has a few individual members who are inventors or discoverers and their activities are one of the reasons for the fact that no culture is ever quite static. But the main reason for cultural change is not a community's own inventors, but its power of absorbing the inventions of other cultures. Thus the scientific industrial culture of developed countries has in the past absorbed an immense wealth of invention from the civilizations which preceded it, coinage and the wheel to mention only two. It in its turn is now being absorbed by the traditional cultures of the pre-industrial countries at a very rapid rate. This meeting of the two cultures, the scientific and the traditional, is so extensive, and they are so profoundly opposed on so many issues, that the stress resulting can best be described as 'cross-cultural conflict' (13:1).

In this cross-cultural conflict, in which the indigenous doctor is likely to be involved quite as much as any of his patients, it is natural that the health aspects of the clash should be uppermost in his mind. Nevertheless, a doctor is well placed to observe the whole process of social change, and, though there may be little any individual can do to modify it, a doctor has a uniquely influential position in the local community.

It is suggested that he be guided by the following principles which determine whether a change in the culture is to be encouraged or discouraged. Inevitably, any attitude in this matter is deeply influenced by the observer's own values. Too often, the individual is powerless and principles often conflict, but despite this some guidance may be useful.

Other things being equal, any social change is likely to be beneficial which does the following:

(a) Promotes harmonious social interaction and cohesion of any lawful kind between individuals; that is, anything which promotes 'togetherness' or 'community'. Thus, unless there are compelling reasons against them, clans and societies, rites and rituals, etc. are all to be fostered.

(b) Enables the individual to realize his innate potentialities; this includes any kind of education.

(c) Preserves or enhances the uniqueness and creativity of the group. Thus, art, in any form, folk tales, local languages and customs are to be preserved as valuable components of the total achievement of our species.

When two cultures meet it is unusual for one to displace the other completely, a more common result is for elements of the two to fuse in some way, the process being given the name of 'syncretism'. For example, in societies where scarification or tatooing is done with non-medical intent, it is possible for the populace to interpret the scientific process of vaccination merely as an addition to their present beliefs and not as an entirely different concept. Should such a process of integrating scientific medicine with the local beliefs be encouraged or discouraged? Opinions differ, but most workers would probably agree that it is better to get a desirable practice adopted by this means than not to get it adopted at all.

Summary. Before summing up there is one final message to leave with the reader. This is the importance of learning from the culture being studied. One thing that compels admiration in so many tropical societies is their intense sense of community (20:2). This is surely *the* critical ingredient in human happiness, and how far removed from, and how infinitely preferable it is to the loneliness and social fragmentation of the industrial suburbs of Europe and America. The incorporation of deep and vigorous community life in a technological society is widely held to be one of the major problems of our age.

Method: Obtaining a 'cross-cultural outlook' in medicine.

Observe the society closely. Use what is visible to lead to what is invisible in terms of attitudes, values and goals etc.

Read some anthropology.

Read what novels and plays may be relevant.

See if there have been any specific studies of the tribes in the area and read them.

Make the acquaintance of any anthropologist working in the vicinity.

Obtain an insight into the local culture by carefully questioning some of the more educated members of the local community.

Follow this up by obtaining more information in routine case histories taken from the patients.

Take at least some steps to learn a local language, even if it is only the greetings and the necessary clinical questions and imperatives.

Lastly, all the world's cultures are equally fit for study, be they those of affluent technocracies or pygmy aborigines. Anthropology is the study of man in all his variety, and is in no sense limited merely to the study of remote and barbarous tribes. It has been rightly said that anthropology is not merely 'barbarology'.

Chapter Five

AN APPROACH TO PUBLIC HEALTH

Based on a talk given by Professor Sidney Kark

5:1 **The community diagnosis.** The diagnosis of an individual patient is a fundamental idea in medicine, but applied to the community, it is a public health concept that will be new to many readers. The meaning of 'community diagnosis' is, however, well worth grasping, for it provides fresh insight into the disease pattern of a population and makes it possible to take more efficient action to improve the health of the group. The easiest way to describe the community diagnosis is to compare it with the individual diagnosis.

In caring for a sick individual the first step is to look for signs and symptoms, the next is to infer causation from them — to make the diagnosis. After this comes treatment and then follow-up to see whether this treatment has been effective. There are similar stages in caring for a sick community.

The first stage is to gather epidemiological data, the next is to make inferences from it — to make the 'community diagnosis'. The third is to prescribe community treatment, or as it is usually called, 'community health action' as part of a 'community health action programme'. Finally, the effect of this health action is followed up and evaluated.

With the individual, the term diagnosis is usually used to cover both the eliciting of signs and symptoms and the making of inferences from them. The same is true of community diagnosis which includes both the collection of data and the deductions to be drawn from them.

The community diagnosis may be defined as the pattern of disease in a community described in terms of the important factors which influence this pattern. When this definition is examined it is seen to incorporate *the* essential feature of the community diagnosis. This is the inferences to be drawn from the data, because, unless such inferences have been drawn, the factors responsible cannot be described nor can their relative importance be assessed.

In gathering his data and making inferences from them, the public health worker is merely applying the scientific method termed 'induction'. This is to gather data, to make inferences from them as to why things happen and then to construct experiments with which to test the truth of these inferences. Hypothesis is the term more often used instead of

Fig. 12. **AN AID TO UNDERSTANDING THE COMMUNITY DIAGNOSIS OF KWASHIORKOR.**

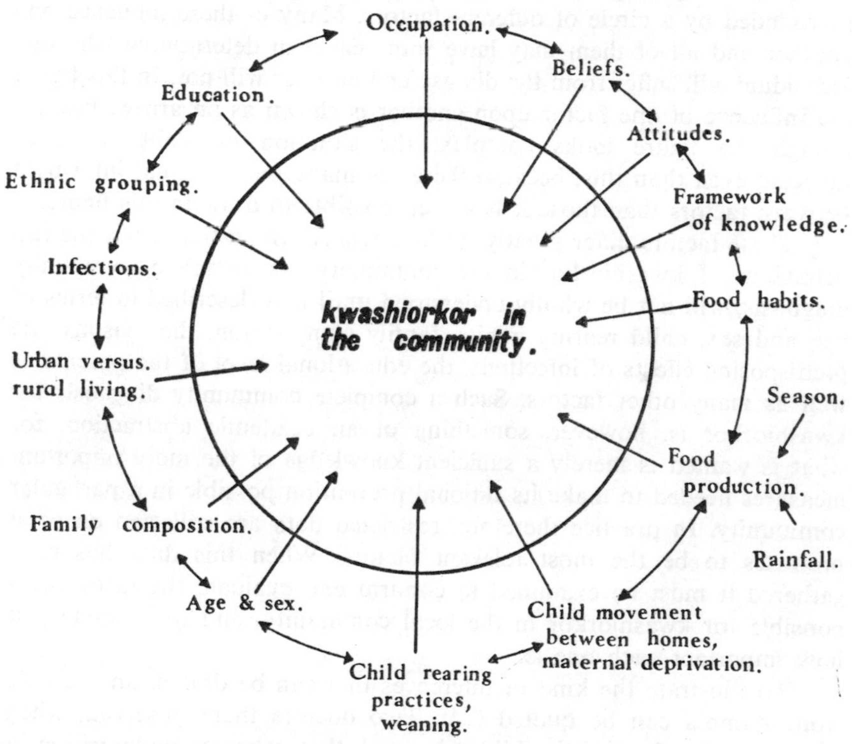

This is an attempt to describe in diagrammatic form the relation of kwashiorkor in a community to some of the factors which are responsible for it, and to give some idea of their intricate relation to one another. All the factors in this diagram have an effect on the prevalence of kwashiorkor in a community, and most of them also influence one another.

inference, but in this context they mean the same thing. The critical part of the process is the 'inference', which is really an intuitive guess, but what distinguishes science from mere guesswork is the ability to design experiments to test the truth of the guess.

The public health worker makes inferences about the disease producing factors at work in a community, he takes action to modify them, and then he evaluates the effect of this action. Failure to 'cure' the community may be due, either to making the wrong inferences leading to the wrong action, or to taking logically correct but inadequate action following from the right inferences.

The process will perhaps become clearer if kwashiorkor is taken as an example.

5:2 **The community diagnosis of kwashiorkor.** Figure 12 shows kwashiorkor surrounded by a circle of different factors. Many of these influence one another and all of them may have some effect in determining why one individual will suffer from the disease and another will not. In this figure the influence of one factor upon another is shown as an arrow, but, although the figure looks complex, the situation in reality is more intricate even than this, because there are many more mutual influences between factors than those it has been possible to draw in this figure.

These factors differ greatly in their relative importance, but the full behaviour of kwashiorkor in the community, its complete community diagnosis, will not be wholly understood until it is described in terms of age and sex, child rearing habits, family composition, the seasons, the predisposing effects of infections, the educational level of the parents as well as many other factors. Such a complete community diagnosis for kwashiorkor is, however, something of an academic abstraction, for what is wanted is merely a sufficient knowledge of the more important measures needed to make its rational prevention possible in a particular community. In practice therefore, restricted data are collected on what promises to be the most relevant factors. When this data has been gathered it must be examined to confirm and evaluate the factors responsible for kwashiorkor in the local community, and to estimate just how important each one is.

To illustrate the kind of inferences that can be drawn, an example from Zambia can be quoted (24). Two doctors there observed, when analysing data from their children's ward, that, whereas malnutrition in all its forms was more common in the heat of October, in the cold of June cases of kwashiorkor comprised a much larger fraction of all the malnourished children. From this they inferred that cold might be an important factor in precipitating the oedema which is such a striking feature of this form of malnutrition. The 'health action' that this led to concerned therapy more than prevention and, with other observations, has done much to emphasize the importance of keeping these children warm, of leaving them close to the heat of their mother's bodies and of nursing them in a warm room.

TABLE 1

AN EVALUATION OF THE EFFECT OF HEALTH ACTION ON A GROUP OF MALNOURISHED CHILDREN

The health action taken was that involved in starting an under-fives clinic (16:1), Data from Sierra Leone (39),

	The Average Weight of the Children		
	6 *months*	12 *months*	18 *months*
Initial data	lb. oz.	lb. oz.	lb. oz.
Before starting the clinic	14 2	16 8	18 4
Evaluation data			
One year after starting the clinic	14 6	18 6	19 2
Two years after starting the clinic ..	14 8	18 8	20 8
Three years after starting the clinic ..	14 10	18 2	20 10

In a disease influenced by as many factors as kwashiorkor, a sudden dramatic drop in incidence must not be expected to follow even the most vigorous community health action. Slow steady improvement is all that can be hoped for. This is evaluated in Table 1 where the average weights of children in an under-fives clinic in Sierra Leone are shown, both before and after the starting of this clinic (38). The health action taken was of various kinds of which health education was the most important. It will be seen to have caused a progressive rise in the average weight of the children towards the optimum described in section 26:5 and illustrated in Figure 64. Before the clinic was instituted children between 9 and 18 months were conspicuously underweight with many cases of frank kwashiorkor, but, as their average weight increased, this became less common.

Both these examples have been criticized as much less than ideal, the first one in particular because the writers did not rule out all the other factors that might have precipitated kwashiorkor, such for instance as a winter increase in infections, or a seasonal alteration in the foods available. These provisos further illustrate the complexity of the community diagnosis of this disease, and the editor can find no better examples.

3 **'Hard' and 'soft' points in the culture.** Having collected the data and made the inferences from them, a community diagnosis is still incomplete, for 'community health action' tries to alter peoples' practices in relation to their health. The community diagnosis must therefore contain information on just how susceptible to change these practices are. Some alterations involve 'soft' points in the culture that are easily changed, while

others are so deeply established, so 'hard' as to be quite unchangeable. Often, there are alternative approaches to the eradication of a particular disease, and, whereas one will involve a 'hard' point another may involve a 'soft' one. The first is likely to fail, the second may succeed. Thus, most people are very 'hard' on the point that their particular staple is the best of foods and nobody would be advised to try to make them live on anything else. However, such people can often be persuaded to *add* other acceptable foods to this staple — a 'soft' cultural point and, in trying to make the change like this, food habits can often be improved and the incidence of kwashiorkor reduced. Community diagnosis is therefore completed by the inclusion in it of information on the capacity for change by a community at the critical points in its cultural pattern. In such community studies social scientists can make a very useful contribution.

5:4 **The community diagnosis need not be complete.** Kwashiorkor has been taken as an example, and it has been shown that, even with this one disease, a complete community diagnosis is impracticable. But kwashiorkor is only one of many diseases that afflict the human group. What then of the total community diagnosis — all the diseases in terms of all the relevant factors? This is an impossibly complex entity. Nevertheless, as an idea and in a limited form applied to some of the major factors influencing the more important diseases, community diagnosis is at the same time useful, straightforward, and intimately related to the daily practice of hospitals and health centres. In the tropics the community diagnosis is of special value, for the common tropical conditions of malnutrition and infection are particularly susceptible to control by the established methods of public health.

It may be argued that such an apparently complicated process of data collection and analysis is not required and that clinical impressions alone suffice. This is not true, although clinical impressions do provide valuable leads in suggesting what data might usefully be collected. By themselves they are usually inadequate, and they are sometimes entirely wrong.

5:5 **The defined area.** In the second two chapters much was said about the extent of territory for which a health centre can be responsible — about 'the immediate area', the 'extended area', and 'special effort' areas (Figure 10, 3:2). A fourth area is also needed — the 'defined area'. *This is an area of intensive study from which is gathered the data for community diagnosis and in which health action is most easily evaluated.* In well staffed health centres responsible for comparatively small areas it can be the whole territory served by the centre, but, in developing countries where resources are extended, it is usually better if it is less than the total area assigned to a centre. In general, it should be in this area alone that data should be gathered and health action evaluated, because unless it is limited and defined in this way, it may be difficult to gather data that are complete enough to be useful. The general work of a centre must of course go on throughout the territory assigned to it. To avoid confusion the records of patients from the defined area should be distinguished carefully from the rest.

A recent report emphasized the great value of carefully collected data and contained the following passage:

> 'Irrespective of whether one is dealing with disease in the urban or the rural areas of Africa, the outstanding obstacle to a rational approach to disease control is the complete lack of valid statistical data relating to the African population, and describing its distribution, birth rates, death rates and incidence of disease in terms of mortality and morbidity ... Before any plan for the control of disease in Africa can be soundly formulated, it will be necessary to establish studies to secure substantial data on the actual incidence of disease ... in both rural and urban areas.' (21)

Clearly, *valid* data from defined areas have a value which transcends their usefulness to an individual hospital or health centre, and thus deserve publication so that they can be fitted into the overall public health picture of the continent.

:6 **Community health action.** This is the sum of the steps decided upon to remedy the critical features revealed by the community diagnosis. Action takes various forms; health education is the most important and is described in Chapter Six. Immunization is perhaps the next and is described in Chapter Seventeen. Other forms of health action are legislation, especially that relevant to such things as motor accidents and alcoholism, the issue of health-promoting foods such as dried skim milk (14:14), the improvement of water supplies and campaigns against specific infectious agents. These are all different forms of community health action and in almost all instances simultaneous action of several different kinds is required. This action must be co-ordinated as a 'community health action programme' and, though it is only possible to give a few general ideas about it here, further details will be found in section 6:9 where the educational side of such a programme is discussed in some detail.

Action should be directed towards the particularly susceptible groups in the community and to those aspects of the environment that have been found to be related to their health. Action is taken at three levels, at the level of the individual patient himself, at the level of the family and at the level of the community as a whole.

Individually directed action is taken at the various clinics, curative and preventive, in the midwifery unit, and in the domiciliary care of the sick. At this level hospitals and health centres function in the same way and should work together, especially in the follow-up of hospital patients, a task which is often best done by health centre staff.

Home and family directed action seeks to modify and improve home and family living and is carried out in the home itself by any workers who visit it, be they public health nurses, health visitors or midwives. But action directed at the home and family can also be taken at clinics or in community groups such as women's clubs.

Community directed action involves the community as a whole through its leaders, formal and informal, and its various natural groups. Here, it is important to realize that community directed action is not merely action directed at the community at large by professional health workers of various kinds, but, that it seeks to promote health action by groups within the community *led by the community's own natural leaders*. In a developing country, schoolmasters, especially primary schoolmasters, are among the most important natural leaders in this respect.

Because the resources for health action vary so much from one society to another, the local society should be studied very carefully before any community health action programme is planned. Close liaison needs to be established with organizations of various kinds, such for instance as tribal chiefs and community development workers.

The way in which these different types of health action can work together is best illustrated by an example taken from a boys' club in Israel which involved a community that was not well advanced. Shigella dysentery and infantile gastroenteritis were endemic in the area and very difficult to counter with public health measures. A Health Educator therefore approached the leader of the club, explained the problem to him and spoke to the boys, telling them of the disease, how it is spread and how it could be countered. Thereafter, the boys under their own leadership carried out a survey of sanitation and refuse disposal in their area, tabulated their own data and did much to educate their friends and families in fighting it. The whole project lasted several months, and is a good example of community directed health action *led and organized by members of the community themselves* with the help of a trained Health Educator. At the same time as it was being carried out, individually directed health action was intensified in the various clinics, and public health nurses and others stressed the same problems in the families they visited.

5:7 **Evaluation.** All health action has to be evaluated. This means that data must be gathered to measure the improvement in the health of the community by methods similar to those originally used in making the community diagnosis. This evaluation has to be thought about before any action is taken so that methods of doing it can become *an integral part of the health action programme itself*. This is shown in Table I (5:2) where the clinic weight charts were used for this evaluation.

8 **The role of the health centre.** So much for the public health sequence of data collection, inference making, community health action and evaluation — who is responsible for it and in what units does it take place?

Though it must also operate on a national and a district scale, it is at the health centre that the process is most relevant, for public health work of this kind is the main purpose of a district medical officer in his role as supervisor of a group of health centres. Medical assistants are not usually capable of making the relevant deductions themselves, but they can at least gather the data for him and put into effect most of the health action he plans.

9 **The role of the hospital.** Though the full public health sequence of community diagnosis, followed by a wide range of different forms of community health action is properly the responsibility of the health centre, limited health action, notably health education and immunization, must be undertaken by hospitals. If this health action is to be planned wisely, community diagnosis is essential. Added to this, circumstances often compel a hospital to assume the health centre role, however imperfectly. Community diagnosis and some community health action thus have a real part to play in the thinking and practice of a hospital.

10 **Some practical suggestions.** So much for theory, but what are the first steps in actually making the community diagnosis?

The first thing to realize is that some at least of the data needed for community diagnosis are usually present in the records that are already being kept by most hospitals and health centres. As an example of how useful such ordinary hospital data can be, though in this case it was not used for community diagnosis, much of that required for the plotting of the 'care gradients' in Figure 6 (2:7) was easily extracted from the ledgers of the hospital and dispensary concerned. Hospital data have however to be interpreted with caution, and information is usually more accurate if it is collected prospectively for a specific purpose. With little extra effort clerks can readily be trained to extract additional information from the patients they see and record it in a suitable form for analysis.

Hospitals and health centres are therefore encouraged to make good use of their opportunity for data collection, and, having done so, to use it creatively in planning community health action, particularly health education.

Method: Making a community diagnosis.

Choose a defined area limited by convenient natural boundaries from which data can be collected. This area should include the hospital or health centre itself and not be too big — say 2-4,000 people.

Mark out this defined area on a map with a 'felt pen', fasten it to a piece of 'softboard' that easily takes pins and hang this up on the wall.

See if any basic data on the population of the villages in the defined area is available from the records of the provincial administration or the tribal headquarters.

Make arrangements to add to this information by recording births and deaths within the defined area, and, if possible, encourage the population to come up and register these events themselves.

Distinguish the records of patients from within the defined area by the use of cards of a special colour, some distinguishing mark or a special prefix to their record numbers.

Choose one or two diseases of particular interest or importance, think about them and decide what data would be of greatest value in studying their behaviour in the community, or might most usefully point the way to effective community health action.

Explain the idea to the record clerks, and get them to collect the required information by questioning the patients, and recording their data for analysis, preferably after the manner suggested in 26:12. Where relevant, record the location of the cases being studied by sticking coloured pins into the map.

Plot the data obtained in graphical or tabular form and pin it on the wall.

When sufficient data has been collected, analyse it carefully, form some judgement as to its accuracy, see if it needs amplifying or extending, and see what conclusions it leads to.

Then plan the necessary health action accordingly.

Data that have been carefully gathered and analysed have a value that extends beyond that to the health centre or hospital where they were originally collected (5:5). A place must be found where they can be made available to others, and one of the functions of a local medical journal should be to record data of this kind. It is advisable, however, not to waste time writing an article until the advice of the editor has been sought as to the general suitability of the material for publication.

Such a study of community health and the effect a health centre or hospital is having on it adds greatly to the interest of medical work. But in studies of this kind, look upon what the textbooks say should happen with a certain caution, because diseases behave differently in different areas, and an open mind is required if interesting local variations are not to be passed over.

Chapter Six

HEALTH EDUCATION

John Bennett

6:1 **The aims of health education.** If a disease can be prevented by an alteration in behaviour, then the achievement of this altered behaviour enables its incidence in the community to be reduced. To alter behaviour where it causes disease is the aim of health education. Some of the behaviour alterations that may be required in appropriate circumstances are the adoption of locally appropriate and correct feeding practices (kwashiorkor), careful driving (road accidents), not smoking (cancer of the lung), defaecating and urinating only in a latrine (many diseases, especially ancylostomiasis), having one's children immunized and seeing that they take antimalarial drugs (16:1). The achievement of these altered behaviour patterns on a really wide scale would reduce the incidence of many of the major diseases which now beset the developing countries. The problem looks simple and health education may seem dull, yet it remains a formidable challenge and a fascinating exercise in psychology and sociology.

Lest it be thought, that health education is merely the removal of ignorance, it is pointed out that it involves four things:

Firstly, and most easily, it supplies a person with enough new and correct knowledge about a disease to make the preventive measures required by scientific medicine seem reasonable.

Secondly, it makes a person feel sufficiently keenly about the importance of his own health to make him alter his behaviour and adopt these preventive measures.

Thirdly, it makes him concerned for the health of others.

Fourthly, and much the hardest, it tries to make him feel so strongly about the first three that he supports and even initiates preventive action by the community.

Health education is a many-sided endeavour of such importance that it must be furthered by every possible means. The newspapers, the radio, the television, and particularly the schools all have their part, so also do hospitals and health centres. The health education that can be undertaken by a health centre has already been discussed in section 3:1, so it remains to this chapter to explain the theory and practice of the subject, and to describe the great scope for health education that hospitals provide. The first point to realize is that *all* the staff, from doctor to sweeper, have a part to play in health education, both during the course of their work and in their other activities, both within the walls of the hospital and in the community outside it. *Although a doctor can do much health education himself, one of his more important duties is to see that other people do it too.*

Health education — a function of all the staff. 'All medical workers have an educational role which is closely linked to and enhances their therapeutic one.' This is the Tenth axiom (1:17), part of which is concerned with the importance of the more skilled members of a medical community continually teaching the less skilled ones, and part with the need for all the staff of hospitals and health centres, be they doctors, sisters, ward maids or even cleaners (6:6b) to be actively teaching the patients and their visitors. From this several things follow. One of them is that, from doctors downwards, all trained members of the medical community, must, during their training period, be both impressed with the teaching side of their work and given some skills in it. Because the unskilled staff members have no formal training period in which they can be taught about the importance of health education, the best way to incorporate them (and the other members of the hospital staff also) in the educational side of the hospital's work is to gather them together from time to time for a talk about the health problems of the community, and the part they can play in teaching the patients.

Many hospitals and wards have found it useful to have a special person who devotes a substantial part of his or her time to health education. Such a person is particularly valuable if this entails time-consuming demonstrations such as those required for nutrition education. Provided that the rest of the staff do not consider themselves relieved of this side of their duties, the appointment and training of such a person is often justified, although it must be pointed out that this is contrary to WHO policy which emphasizes very strongly that health education is the role of everyone. Because health education is the duty of all members of the medical staff, *health education is to be looked upon as a team activity.*

The health education specialist. Although health education is part of every medical worker's job at the local level, a specialist in this field should be available at the regional or national level. He is the key person in planning and co-ordinating health education in an area, and is also concerned with ensuring that health education is included in the training of the many grades of hospital and health centre staff. He should see that instruction in health education forms part of the basic training, the refresher courses and the 'in-service training' of all the relevant staff. One of his tasks is to direct the production, and specially the evaluation of posters and pamphlets, as well as radio and television programmes. A specialist is required because this is a skilled task and an important one, both from the point of view of the end to be achieved and desirability of not wasting time and money. To be able to fulfil his duties satisfactorily he needs a 'Health Education Unit' and the support of several sub-ordinate staff, including an artist.

6:4 **A hospital's opportunity.** Among the patients coming up to a hospital many are already suffering from the diseases that health education tries to prevent, and it might at first seem too late to try to educate these patients as to how they might have kept well. This is true as far as it goes, but it neglects the opportunity that health education has in preventing a second attack of the same disease, and also the effect that such education may have on the patient's local community when he is eventually cured and goes home. It is this last effect which is so useful, because the patient in hospital, who has actually succumbed to a disease, is the representative of a 'target group' of people in the community outside who resemble him in being especially vulnerable, and exposed to the same disease producing factors. If such a patient can be educated while in hospital, he will take the knowledge he has acquired back with him into the community; here it will spread in this specially vulnerable group just where it is needed most. The spread of this knowledge is assisted because a newly discharged patient is of particular interest to his community. Its members are therefore likely to be influenced by what he has learnt in hospital, and should he be influential, his effect may be profound.

In the case of a child patient health education is of even greater importance, because, by educating his parents we improve not only his own future, but that of his brothers and sisters also. It is for this reason that the education of mothers is emphasized so repeatedly in these pages (13:3, 14:17d, 16:4).

6:5 **The complexity of the education process.** Health education does not start in a vacuum. The right health knowledge and practice has usually to displace at least part of what the patient already believes and practices. Therefore, the first step must be to study the health relevant beliefs and practices of the local community in their true cultural setting. This is so important that it is one of the main reasons why an entire chapter has been devoted to the cross-cultural outlook in medicine (Chapter Four). From the practical point of view health practices are what matter, and beliefs matter only in so far as they determine practice and make it difficult to change a harmful practice into a beneficial one. Following the advice given in section 4:4, the health relevant practices are to be divided into the harmful, the harmless and the beneficial.

We will therefore assume that, when health education begins, it does so against a background of belief and practice that is at least partly incorrect. When finally it is complete the individual is not only properly informed and carrying out the correct health practices, but he feels so strongly about matters of health that he is even prepared to initiate health action by the community (5:6). Many subtle intermediate states of mind lie between these two extremes of ignorance or the wrong ideas on the one hand, and active conviction on the other. Though the four aims of health education in the opening section of this chapter suggest their existence, the educational process is more complex even than this, and the successive changes it involves at various levels in the mind can be summarized in the following way by taking dysentery as an example.

A change in knowledge — this is the first stage, such for instance as knowing that dysentery is an infectious disease.

A change in attitude follows this; the patient is not only able to repeat what he has been told, but now has a greater regard for the possible spread of the disease.

A change in behaviour is seen next; the patient begins to act on his belief and no longer disposes of his excreta indiscriminately.

A change in habit follows; the patient now disposes of his excreta in a latrine as an unthinking habit that requires no conscious decision.

A change in custom is the last stage, when care in disposal of excreta has become one of the cultural characteristics of the group to be handed on to the children of the next generation.

It should not be thought that these changes always proceed in an orderly manner from above downwards — they may do so, but it is common for a person to believe in something which he does not practise, or for him to practise something in which he does not believe. This divorce of practice from belief — this 'cognitive dissonance' as it is called — produces a certain psychological tension which is only relieved by the adjustment of practice to belief or vice versa. Thus, having once instilled the belief that dysentery is infectious, it is important to strive to relieve the dissonance and complete the educational process by establishing the practice of careful excreta disposal. Dissonance may be relieved equally well by the loss of belief, in which case the educator is back where he began, but while it lasts he has an advantage and is nearer to completing the education of his patient than when it does not.

This account of the variety of the changes involved in health education should encourage the educator when great efforts fail to bring the success he expects. Health education is a slow process and proceeds in stages — part of the process may well be established and a little persistence may be all that is required to make it at least partly effective if not finally complete.

6:6a **Personal methods.** This sequence of a change in knowledge, attitude, behaviour, habit and custom can, broadly speaking, be brought about by groups of methods of two kinds, or more effectively by methods of both groups acting together. These two groups are the impersonal methods and the personal ones. But, though impersonal methods are simpler and less time-consuming, it is the personal ones which are especially convincing. Both groups of methods need the same careful tailoring to the mind of the patient, and the same continued assessment of their effectiveness.

6:6b **In the hospital.** Whether it be undertaken in a school, a health centre or a hospital, personal health education depends upon the relationships between people. In a hospital some of these relationships are obvious, such as those between the patients and the doctors and nurses looking after them. Not so obvious but very important also are those between the patients and their visitors, and between old patients and new ones. Less obvious still, but probably of even greater significance are the relationships between the patients and the cleaners and maids in their wards.

It is natural to suppose that the most significant channel of communication would be that from the doctor direct to his patient, but study has shown that it is frequently not so. A doctor is busy, he has little time to talk and listen and he may often not speak the patient's language. But, even if he is a good linguist, he is unlikely to be effective in communicating with the patient in the short time available across the wide cultural barrier that probably separates them. Often, as he proceeds down the ward to the next bed, the patient will turn to the nurse with the words 'What did he say?' She then may be in closer communication with the patients than he is, but closer still may be the ward-maids, for it seems that it is often the more leisurely conversations with maids and cleaners that leave the most lasting impression — a circumstance that has its drawbacks in view of their lack of knowledge. It does however point to the importance of instilling the correct health knowledge into all levels of the hospital staff, especially the lowlier ones, for, like maids and cleaners, junior nurses may have more leisure to talk to the patients.

The first thing for a doctor to realize, if he wants to increase his own effectiveness in communicating his ideas to the patients, is just how little he may be getting across. The direct transfer of an item of information is only part of the teaching process, and, if it is to be acted upon, a doctor must be aware of the framework of knowledge in the patient's mind into which this item of information is supposed to fit. A good way for him to find this out is to question his patients carefully on their knowledge and attitudes to a particular disease; he will then be able to adjust his teaching accordingly. This is implicit in what has already been said about the cross-cultural outlook (4:6), and what is about to be said about teaching junior staff (27:1).

Individual health education of this kind, as part of a consultation during a ward round or outpatient clinic, is just one of several personal methods, but personal methods can also be applied to a family or to larger groups. In general, the more people who hear a given piece of health education the better, for not only is this more economical of the instructor's time, but an individual patient may find it easier to change a long standing habit if others in the group are being asked to do so too. As far as mothers are concerned this is well brought out in the section on 'learning by overhearing' (16:4).

In the community. A doctor and his staff are reminded that they too are members of the community, and that their personal role in the educational drive does not end within the hospital. A doctor is one of the 'big men' of the district, and he can have a profound influence with politicians, chiefs and elders, with village councils, and district or provincial development committees and especially with women's clubs. In Zambia, for instance, the district medical officer should try to see that the 'Resident Minister' for the province knows what its health problems are and what he can do to encourage the people to adopt better health practices. In Tanzania his place is taken by the 'Area Commissioner' and in that country such organizations as the 'TANU Women's League' and the 'Ten House Committees 'also have their part to play in health education.

There are other important leaders in the community. One is the primary schoolmaster — the secondary schoolmaster is so comparatively rare in developing countries as to be of less importance, except in blood transfusion (23:4). Primary schoolmasters have a useful level of education themselves, they are likely to react favourably when a doctor tells them how very valuable they can be, they have a big hold over large numbers of children and through them great potential influence with their mothers and fathers. Because of this, one of the first duties of a doctor in a district should be to see that the schoolmasters know the local problems that are amenable to health education, that they know what locally relevant knowledge to impart and really understand the value of what they are doing. In Uganda 'health science' is soon to be taught in all primary schools and should contain all the necessary health education. Until a suitable manual is available the instruction of these schoolmasters will have to depend on duplicated 'handouts', lectures at meetings and refresher courses, and personal contact with interested doctors. Not only can schoolmasters be valuable but the schools can be a very convenient way of gathering groups of mothers *and fathers* together for health education. This need not necessarily be confined to the problems of schoolchildren but can extend to the health of younger children also.

Another important group of leaders are the priests. They reach adult audiences directly where they are in a great position of influence, they are highly motivated and they visit patient's homes. If a priest recognizes kwashiorkor, especially in its mild stages, and knows even the value of eggs and beans, he can be very useful.

Traditional healers (1:9, 3:10) can also be used to impart the correct health knowledge. They need to be treated with respect and approached very carefully, for they may feel that their livelihood is threatened. They should be asked what they advise for various conditions and gently persuaded to abandon harmful health practices for beneficial ones. Most of their rituals are likely to be without any great significance for health, so these they can persist with.

6:6d **Community development.** In some areas active 'community development' will be going on. This is a form of social activity, in part spontaneous and in part led by special 'community development workers', in which members of an unsophisticated village community meet to discuss their individual and joint needs. They establish priorities, make plans to the best of their ability and resources, seek help from outside and proceed to undertake a variety of different projects. These may involve such things as providing a well, or building a market or a clinic. Community development is essentially self-development at the village level; wherever it exists or can be started, it is a social activity of the greatest importance, both in its own right and as a means for spreading health knowledge and providing better health facilities, be these merely improved latrines or complete health centres (10:6). It is thus a process in which a district medical officer should take the greatest interest. In approaching a development group of this kind he should try to make the villagers themselves see the problem and propose answers to it. After enough discussion and by careful suggestion he should be able to make them bring forward the right questions and some possible answers to them. If he is skilful the final course of action proposed should appear to be the result of their initiative rather than his own.

Impersonal methods. These are the leaflets, slogans, pamphlets, posters, tape recordings, films and film strips which all have a part in the educational process. Posters should be large, colourful, strategically sited and changed from time to time.

Pamphlets for the patients to take home with them are especially useful because they can be used for reference when certain points have been forgotten and they are also usually shown to friends and neighbours. At a certain stage in the educational progress of a community, there is an enormous thirst for reading matter of almost any kind, and, under these circumstances, plenty of printed material in the vernacular and possibly even a story may be the best way of conveying the educational message.

The really important point about pictures is that conventions that are taken for granted by the educator may be quite meaningless to the peasant. Thus, throughout the Western world there is a convention that the diminishing size of an object in a picture implies its increasing distance from the observer. A cow in the foreground is therefore drawn large, one in the middle distance is shown a little smaller while one far away is made smaller still. To those unfamiliar with this convention the smaller cow may look like a calf, while the smallest one may be taken for a dog. In another drawing what to the educated looks like an eye may be interpreted by the villager as a fish or a rising sun. The same sort of difficulty is likely to be experienced by the reader in interpreting Figure 20 (11:3a), which is an axonometric projection with which he is unlikely to be familiar, but, once he is used to it, this will seem a very good way of representing a three dimensional object. Because of these difficulties the health education specialist (6:3) should be asked to give advice on the kind of pictures that are likely to be most useful. He will also have been trained to evaluate their effect.

The same misunderstanding is even more true of films and film strips which are readily misinterpreted if they run too fast. Like posters they should also depict the local people (27:2) and must be shown slowly enough to be easily understood. They should be explained to the audience who should be given an opportunity to ask questions afterwards.

Reinforcing knowledge with practice. Health education does not end with merely talking or sticking up posters, it starts there. If the educational sequence is to be completed and proceed from a change in knowledge through one in attitude, behaviour and habit, to end finally in a change of custom, then instruction must be followed by demonstration, and demonstration by practice.

Wherever possible, therefore, a talk should be followed by showing the patient what to do, and when this is over he must be encouraged to try out what has been taught him. The Chinese have an aphorism — 'If I do it I know' — it is this *doing a thing* which really advances the educational process.

Thus, education on infant feeding might start with a talk using whatever aids were available, go on to discussion, be followed by a demonstration and finally end with the mother herself making a feed and giving it to her child. For this to be possible the right apparatus has to be built into the hospital itself, so this means cooking places for relatives, good latrines, protected water supplies, and even perhaps a hospital garden where a mother can see growing the right foods she could herself produce for her own family (10:13, 14:13, Figure 16 (10:4)).

Because mothers are the most important target for health education, it is vital for them actually to practise what they have been taught. A suitably equipped 'mothers' shelter' is thus an invaluable educational facility (10:4, 13:3). The actual care of the patient provides another good opportunity to reinforce knowledge with practice, and relatives particularly mothers, should where possible be invited to help look after their children. Here, as always, a mother should be taught not only what to do but *why* she is to do it.

It might seem that the obvious teaching example to use might on some occasions be a child suffering from the disease in question, say kwashiorkor. But to demonstrate before a class a child who is sick because of his mother's ignorance or negligence must be considered unethical.

6:9 **The educational side of a community health action programme.** Section 5:6 made it clear that health education is but one side of a community health programme, whether this be a large-scale one originating at a high level in the Ministry of Health, or a small-scale one planned by a health centre or hospital. A carefully made community diagnosis will demonstrate the health problems of a community, and among the various types of health action that will be wanted, health education is likely to be only one, albeit often the most important one. Because this is a chapter on health education, and because the community health action programme has as a whole already been dealt with, this section will be confined to the health education side of such a programme.

The health education component of a programme is compounded of two closely linked parts: one is its *content,* or *what* is to be taught; the other is its *strategy,* or *how* the teaching is to be done. Content follows naturally from what has already been said about the community diagnosis and strategy follows from the Third axiom, 'the importance of obtaining the greatest return in human welfare from the least expenditure in money and skill' (1:10).

Though the aim of getting the maximum return for the effort expended must be the dominant principle in planning a programme, there are some others which are also important and which are best considered in the form of questions concerning both content and strategy. Some are implicit in the idea of the community diagnosis while others are closely linked together.

What are the most important diseases that can be countered by achieving alterations in behaviour? These must be looked at both from the point of view of the individual sufferer and from that of the community.

What are the chances of success? The major health problems are sometimes too deeply embedded in the culture, too 'hard' (5:3), to be amenable to change by educational means. Some food taboos may be problems of this kind and the failure of an early project may prejudice the success of later ones; there will however be other issues on which the attitude of the community is likely to be 'softer'.

What are the values and goals of a people? What do they want? What incentives are there? If a community want nothing it is difficult for them to see any change as one for the better. If, however, there are things the people want, education for example, it may be possible to link their wants with the need for changes in their health practices. They may be persuaded by the reasoning that, if they do not use latrines, their children will not be healthy and will thus be unable to go to school.

Can the people be made to see that some benefit is likely to follow from a change in their health practices? This is closely linked with the previous question; if they can be made to see that benefits are to be expected, then they are much more likely to change their habits.

What resources are available to the hospital for personal health education? These may be doctors, nurses, community health educators, health assistants, midwives, maids and cleaners.

What impersonal resources are available? These include pamphlets, posters, tape recorders, flannelgraphs, films, radio, television and newspapers.

How is the effort of the hospital to be balanced between prevention and cure? What proportion of the facilities available is to go to one and what to the other?

The content of a programme is closely bound up with the resources available to carry it out, and, as with all human decisions based on inadequate information, the informed judgement needed to make them amounts to an art.

6:10 **The strategy of a health education programme.** Having decided what to teach — it is next necessary to decided how it is to be taught — the strategy of the programme. All the methods available, personal and impersonal, should be used to the best advantage, but in deciding how this is to be done two principles must be borne in mind. They are closely associated, the first is that *all efforts must be carefully linked with one another* and the second that *health education be planned at as high a level as possible.*

It is not easy to link together every side of the educational effort when it may involve several different kinds of workers and a variety of different administrative units. A good example of what can be done to link the educational efforts of a hospital and various community services is provided by the nutrition rehabilitation unit of Mulago Hospital which is described in more detail in section 14:17. Here mothers of children with kwashiorkor are taken into a special residential hostel and taught how to prepare the correct food for their children. They are then given opportunities to teach men and women from the community development clubs of villages which may be as far as 30 miles away. Workers from the rehabilitation unit visit and follow up discharged cases and teach groups of neighbours who have been brought together by the patient's family. Agricultural workers and school teachers are also invited to the unit to ensure that they will be teaching the same knowledge of improved nutrition.

At the district level planned health education means that hospitals and health centres must work together. On the more limited scale of a single hospital, concentration for a short period on one problem at a time can be very effective — say an hour a day, part of a day every week or perhaps a day a month.

Health problems can often be attacked successfully by different methods using the same figures and slogans at the same time, for in this way they reinforce one another. When national campaigns can be organized to deal with selected topics using several different communication media, such as television, radio and newspapers, then hospitals dispensaries and health centres should all back them up with individual and small group teaching.

6:11 **An instructive comparison.** The methods used by the mission hospitals to impart religious knowledge and religious practice could well be followed by all hospitals in their efforts to impart health knowledge and health practice. In the outpatient department of a mission hospital this starts with texts on the walls, and a morning's clinic may pause for a period of verbal instruction by a staff member, a visiting speaker or a suitable patient. In the wards tracts are distributed, both the staff and the patients take part in religious services much of which are primarily instructional in nature. These services are repeated at a set time each day and on set days each week. Radio programmes, films and tape recordings are used for reinforcement, and a special staff of religious educators is employed who run a programme planned on a careful time budget and co-ordinated at highest level for the whole calender year. Lastly, but perhaps most significant of all — no member of a mission staff is ever too busy for this form of communication which is regarded as of supreme importance to the purpose of the hospital.

2 **Tuberculosis as a specific example.** As an illustration of the kind of approach needed, tuberculosis can be taken as an example. Careful questioning will have shown how the community look upon the disease, its cultural setting, and will have suggested ways in which the preventive measures can best be explained. As has been said in the opening paragraph, the targets for education will not only be the patient himself but also all his contacts in the community. He must be taught the infectious nature of his complaint, the hazards of inadequate treatment, the possible side effects of the drug, the value of BCG for his children and especially how long treament is likely to take. All this can be imparted by talks to individual patients, discussions each month with a group of tuberculous patients, demonstrations of BCG in clinics, talks from the nurses about the importance of sputum disposal, and very conveniently indeed, by the preparation of carefully made and evaluated tape recordings (27:6).

This may sound excessive effort for just one disease, and if so, it may be found convenient to concentrate most of it into a particular period of the year—say four months and to keep only a part of it running continuously .

3 **Some practical suggestions.** At present few hospitals do any effective health education. The following advice is offered therefore to the many who as yet do none, and whose tasks already seem to stretch their resources to the limit.

Method: A start with health education.

Resolve to undertake some health education, however little may be possible at first, and plan what is done. See that some interested person is in charge of the educational drive.

Try to base the content of the programme on a careful community diagnosis.

Obtain the help of a health education specialist if this is available.

Begin with the problem which is likely to show the highest dividend for the least effort. Some workers advise starting in a village which has already begun to show some signs of change and readiness to progress. If there is a choice of villages in which to work, choose that with the most co-operative headman. Approach the most senior man in the area first, the 'Area Commissioner' for instance, and, having secured his co-operation, then seek the aid of his subordinates.

Endeavour to follow these seven points:

(1) Decide how much of the available knowledge on a particular subject should be passed on to the community and to specific groups within it, mothers and adolescents for instance.
(2) See how these ideas can best be expressed in the vernacular.
(3) Determine which beliefs, customs and attitudes, are likely either to help or hinder the acceptance of this knowledge. See what can be done to circumvent any hindrances.
(4) Try to discover which individuals or groups of people in the community are in a position to help or hinder the acceptance of this knowledge. See if it is possible to minimize the effect of the potential hinderers.
(5) Make the most of a variety of teaching methods.
(6) Make the most of teaching aids, having first determined that they are understood.
(7) Endeavour to measure success or failure and make this evaluation an integral part of the educational programme.

What is to be expected as the result of such effort? There can be no getting away from it that health education requires subtlety in its application; it is gradual in its effect and is difficult to evaluate. But in spite of this, it is also immensely worthwhile, for gains, however, small, are apt to be lasting, and health education is likely to be the main way in which many devastating diseases will ultimately be conquered.

Chapter Seven
THE AUXILIARY

Maurice King
largely from the papers of Rex Fendall

The auxiliary defined. People differ in what they mean by auxiliaries and confuse them with other kinds of medical staff. The World Health Organization defines them like this: 'An auxiliary is a technical worker in a certain field with less than the full professional qualifications' (49). Auxiliaries are to be distinguished from professional workers who have attained the generally accepted level for their discipline in a particular country. These professional workers are of two kinds, a senior grade whose training has been based on a university degree and almost all of whom are doctors, and a junior professional or 'para-medical' grade, whose training is usually based on 'O-level' education and includes nurses, pharmacists and laboratory technicians. The standards, status, and training of both these two professional grades are widely recognized internationally, those of auxiliaries are not.

Enough has already been said about the shortage of doctors in developing countries, but members of the junior professional or para-medical grade are usually just as scarce. It is as substitutes for members of both professional grades that the auxiliary is so very important. Although auxiliaries are often called 'assistants', they are in practice more often a substitute for a professional person, than an assistant to him. But the distinction is far from absolute, thus, at one moment, an orthopaedic assistant may be substituting for an orthopaedic surgeon and at the next merely assisting him. Because the main function of auxiliaries is to take the place of professional people, it is a pity that they are so often called 'assistants', and the sooner this low status term can be discarded the better.

Before discussing auxiliaries further there is another distinction to be made; this is that between single purpose and general purpose auxiliaries. The single purpose auxiliary is of minimal education, or possibly even none at all, who is taught either a single skill, or at the most a limited range of skills. The auxiliaries used by Waddy in his sleeping sickness campaigns in West Africa were of this kind, and were merely trained to undertake only such techniques as lymph node aspiration and intravenous injection, as were particularly required for his campaigns (35). Though single purpose auxiliaries have a valuable part to play, particularly in rural health teams of this kind, it is with auxiliaries of the second kind that this chapter is concerned. These are the general purpose auxiliaries who are trained in a variety of skills.

It must not be thought that auxiliaries are only for developing countries. In Europe and North America educational facilities are comparatively abundant, and many people attain the basic education that would qualify them at least for junior professional or para-medical training. But, because of the competition with other vocations, there is a shortage of volunteers for training in these grades. To fill this gap there is an increasing tendency to look to those with less education and train them to auxiliary levels of skill. This is especially true of nursing, and the 'enrolled' or 'practical nurse' with lower qualifications than the 'State Registered Nurse' or 'SRN' is becoming increasingly common. It is unlikely therefore that the auxiliary will ever become redundant in a developing country, though his role may change.

7:2 **The auxiliary classified.** The classification of auxiliaries is often complex and reflects the history of a medical service, the changes in outlook of its policy makers, and educational progress in the country concerned. If the classification which follows looks complicated, the reader is reminded that it is even worse in Indonesia where there are as many as forty-four kinds of auxiliary. Auxiliaries are classified according to three main factors, the level of their basic education, the specialities within medicine and the length of their vocational training. Something must first be said about basic education.

Many readers will be only too familiar with Figure 13 as being similar to the ladder they themselves have climbed, for it is a summary of the educational structure as it exists in many developing countries. There are numerous local modifications to it, and the system is already about to be modified in some areas by including standard seven in primary education, and abolishing standard eight altogether. When this happens, junior secondary education will no longer exist as a separate entity. In other areas university admission to a preparatory course takes place at standard twelve. The figures for those succeeding to the grade above are from Uganda; a country which is better served educationally than many in Africa; but Figure 13 illustrates the typical features of the educational system of a developing country, it demonstrates the great narrowness of the educational pyramid and shows just how exceptional a junior secondary certificate really is. It is easy for the medical graduate to look down on such a qualification as an educational attainment of no

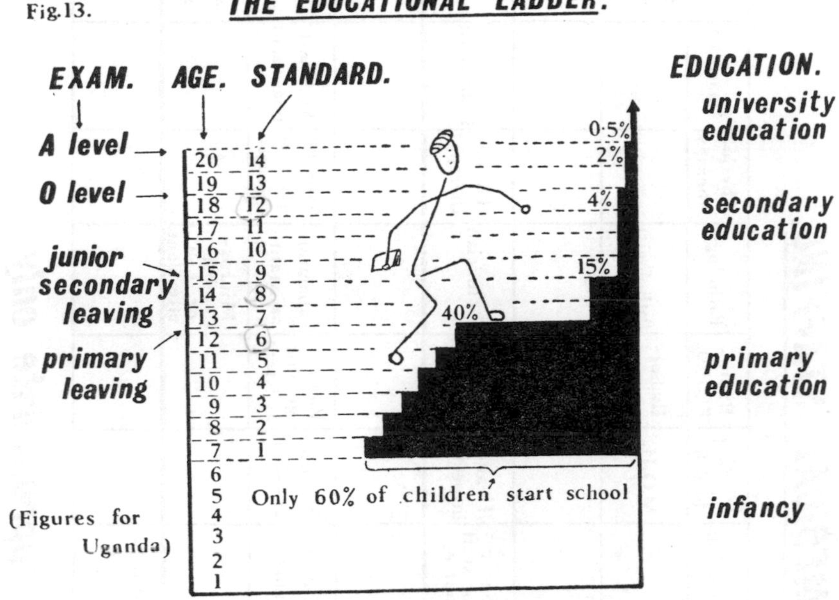

value, but in Uganda at any rate, it is an achievement that sets its owner apart from 85 per cent. of his fellows. Most auxiliaries are recruited at standard eight, some at standard six and a few at standard twelve. But, with the passage of time and the spread of education, it is increasingly possible to recruit at the higher rather than the lower of these levels.

Using these educational levels, and cross-classifying them with the specialties in medicine Table 2 is produced. For convenience and completeness staff have been divided into four groups A. B, C and D. Group A are the senior professional grade, Group B the junior professional or para-medical grade, Group C the auxiliaries and Group D the unskilled cleaners, etc. However, as is mentioned elsewhere, cleaners are sometimes called upon to do some very skilled tasks (22:1).

Auxiliaries are divided into three levels, senior, middle and junior, depending upon their basic education and the duration and quality of the vocational education they have received. Classification as to level is somewhat arbitrary, and there is little general agreement as to where a given auxiliary should be. In effect there is a continuous spectrum of skill extending from the top of the table to the bottom, the best medical

Table 2.

A TABLE OF MEDICAL STAFFING.

	Grade.	Years school.	Starting salary in Uganda. £	$	Medicine.	Nursing.	Environ-mental health.	Radio-graphy	Pathology.	Physio-therapy	Pharmacy	Ortho-paedics	Admin-istration
A. University education, international status.	Specialist.	14	2,375	6,700	Specialist physician.		M.O.H.	Radiologist	Pathologist			Ortho-paedic surgeon	Hospital super-intendent
	Medical Officer.		1,128	3,200	Medical officer.								
B. Secondary education international status.	Professional, para-medical.	12	687	1,900	X	Sister or staff nurse.	Health inspector	Radio-grapher	Technician	Physio-therapist	Pharmacist		
C. Secondary education. Produced to meet demand.	(Auxiliary) Senior.	10–12	473	1,300	Clinical assistant. ↑								Assistant super-intendent
	(Auxiliary) Middle.	8–10	190	530	Medical or hospital assistant.	Enrolled nurse.	Health assistant	Radio-graphic assistant	Laboratory assistant.	Assistant physio-therapist	Assistant pharmacist	Ortho-paedic assistant.	Storeman & clerk.
	(Auxiliary) Junior.	6–8	130	370	Graded dresser.				Micros-copist or Lab. attendant.			Appliance maker.	
D. Primary education or none at all.	Unskilled.	0–6	90	250	Ungraded dresser.	Ward-maid.							Cleaner.

Salaries are approximate only.

assistants being more skilled, but much more poorly paid, than the worst doctors. This is a common source of friction, and it has been suggested that, as a country develops, and professional people become more abundant, their senior auxiliary grade be increasingly left empty. Either a recruit is good enough for professional training, or he remains a middle auxiliary. This leaves a clear gap in the skill spectrum with a wide salary jump across it.

'The enrolled grade' has already been mentioned in discussing health centre staff. This is a junior or middle auxiliary grade and is mainly used to distinguish auxiliary nurses and midwives from their fully trained para-medical 'SRN' or 'SCM' counterparts.

It will be seen in Table 2 that the box in grade B, the para-medical category, has been crossed out under the specialty medicine. This is because there is no such person as a 'sub-doctor' of internationally recognized professional status, even though the skill spectrum is in practice continuous from doctor to medical assistant. The nearest approach to such a person is the 'clinical assistant' or 'rural health practitioner', grades which some services have created to promote and reward their abler medical assistants.

The example of the theatre cleaner who found himself acting as anaesthetist (22:1) has already been mentioned. This is an extreme, though hardly commendable, example of the way in which a nominally unskilled and untrained person can sometimes do a very useful job — presumably there was nobody else in this hospital to look after the anaesthetic machine while the surgeon operated. It illustrates the fact that it may sometimes be necessary to look beyond the recognized categories of auxiliary and teach any suitable person to do some essential task. If, for instance, one of the dressers can be taught to do a few laboratory tests with sufficient reliability, even though he is not a laboratory assistant, then this may be justified as the only way of getting these tests done.

Certificates. When teaching is considered in other chapters, it is thought of as being something that everyone with greater skill should do for everyone with lesser skill, and nothing is said about grades and certificates. But most people like to feel that they are getting somewhere, and it should be a principle to teach to some sort of syllabus, examine the candidates, issue a certificate to the successful ones, and, if possible, give them a salary increment. Certificates are prized by their owners, so the smarter they are the better. They are also used in obtaining jobs in other hospitals, so they should state the *exact* level of skill attained, preferably in some detail on the reverse side. Individual hospitals have often to issue their own certificates, but nationally recognized ones are better, for they raise standards and enable auxiliaries to move from one hospital to another more easily.

7:3b **A training school in every district hospital.** The grades that as many hospitals as possible should train for are those of the 'enrolled nurse', the 'public health nurse' and the 'enrolled midwife', or, better still, the 'comprehensive nurse' who is all these three rolled into one (3:4). There is a huge demand for such people in hospitals, child welfare clinics, and health centres. They are an inexpensive, if somewhat inefficient form of labour while training, and the benefit these girls derive from a few years of disciplined instruction is a priceless asset to themselves, their families and their communities. Most of them will soon get married, and only a proportion will return to work afterwards, yet despite this, the training endeavour expended on them is one of the most useful sides of a hospital's work. So great is the demand for these nurses, that a district hospital must be considered incomplete if it has not got a training school. Many sister tutors will be required, and thus a sister tutor's training school is a national priority of the greatest importance.

7:4 **Maintaining standards.** Every developing country faces the problem as to whether or not professional standards are to be maintained. The demand for professional services is so great, and suitable recruits and training facilities so limited, that the pressures to lower standards are very real.

The principle adopted in Kenya, and by some other developing countries, is to maintain the professional standards of Groups A and B and to limit output in these grades to the recruits and training facilities available (14). The output of auxiliaries in Group C is, however, expanded to suit local demands, and facilities and standards are adjusted as required. This may seem an admirable arrangement, but there are certain difficulties.

Standards and salaries are closely linked, and the maintenance of international standards requires that the salaries paid to the professional grades shall at least approach those that their members can earn in other parts of the world. These are more than developing countries can afford, and are out of all proportion to the wages of the 'common man', thus the Ugandan doctor starts on about thirteen times the minimum wage for his country. But, if these wages are not paid, and yet qualifications are recognized internationally, there is a tendency for professional people to leave the developing country to which they belong, and to obtain more lucrative employment in an industrial one. This danger can be guarded against by following the practice of some countries and refusing to issue passports to nationals with badly needed skills. This prohibition of emigration is well justified, especially when the persons concerned have obtained their education and training at the public expense. If this is thought too strong an infringement of individual rights, the prohibition can be enforced for a specified period, say an equivalent number of years to that spent in education and vocational training. Some developing countries are said to have deliberately chosen not to have had their qualifications recognized overseas, so as to keep their graduates at home on wage rates in keeping with the realities of the economy.

Another difficulty is that professional standards, particularly those in such subjects as laboratory technology, are rising so fast in industrial countries that trainees in developing ones cannot keep up. Thus, candidates from Uganda, who would have passed the intermediate examination of the Institute of Laboratory Technology of the United Kingdom five years ago, now fail it because its standards are beyond them.

The scope of an auxiliary's work. As a specific example of just what an auxiliary can do, the orthopaedic assistant will be described as he is being trained at Mulago Hospital under the direction of Mr. Ronald Huckstep. These assistants are now being trained in quantity so as to supply all the up-country hospitals with at least one if not several auxiliaries of this kind. As Figure 23 E & F (12:3) show, trauma is a common cause of admission to a rural hospital, and it has also been found in Uganda that orthopaedic cases may fill up to two-thirds of all surgical beds. A well trained orthopaedic assistant can thus be of the greatest help in the running of a busy district hospital, and, like many auxiliaries with long practice, he often becomes much more adept at practical procedures than the average doctor.

The following curriculum is based on a book, *A Simple Guide to Fractures* /83/ and emphasizes the usefulness of integrating a course for auxiliaries with a really suitable manual. The lack of such books for other types of auxiliary is one of the most acute medical needs in developing countries. In order to become orthopaedic assistants Grade 1, senior nursing assistants must master the following skills.

Plaster of Paris technique. Assistants must be capable of all the plasters in *A Simple Guide to Fractures;* they must also know the indications for them and the dangers associated with their use.

Fractures. Assistants must know the principles of elevation of patient's limbs, and of balanced traction; they must know how to put up all types of traction apparatus accurately.

Physiotherapy. Assistants must know the principles of physiotherapy, the use of radiant heat and massage. They must know in detail how to teach a patient exercises for his quadriceps, his hip, knee, ankle or back.

Poliomyelitis. Assistants must know the principles of the disease and of the muscle chart, they must know the main muscles acting and how to assess their power. They must know which patients require calipers and how to measure, make, fit and adjust them.

Orthopaedics. They must know the important aspects of tuberculosis of the bones and joints, osteomyelitis, arthritis, talipes, etc., as well as the principles of treatment of such things as low back pain, sciatica, nerve injuries and minor muscle tears. They must know the common operations for straightening contractures of the lower limbs, and the names and use of the more important orthopaedic instruments.

This list is a good example of the way in which it is possible to analyse the tasks that have to be repeated many times and then select those that are suitable for delegation to assistants (Ninth axiom 1:16). There is no need to point out the value of adequate numbers of assistants trained in these skills, when the ravages of poliomyelitis have left 25,000 of Uganda's seven million citizens crippled, and she has only two fully trained whole time orthopaedic surgeons, who have also to deal with the increasing havoc wrought by cars and scooters. When suitable assistants are available they can form a theatre team with an orthopaedic surgeon, and, by doing most of the simpler manipulative procedures themselves, they enable his skilled attention to become available to many more patients than would be possible otherwise.

7:6 **Justice for the auxiliary.** To many patients auxiliaries mean more than doctors; they work long hours in lonely places and, as shown in Table 2, their salaries need no further comment. It is not surprising, therefore, that they are often dissatisfied. Above all they need a proper career structure. Like the private soldier who feels that he has a field marshal's baton in his haversack, the medical assistant should feel that he has potentially a doctor's stethoscope in his pocket. He must feel that there is a career structure ahead of him, and, if he is not to get to the top, then he should at least feel able to get part of the way there.

Rewards, especially salaries, should as far as possible be based on merit and not depend too much on basic education. This means that it must on occasion be possible to waive the necessity for a particular level of education in promoting a man from one grade to another.

The widely recognized principle that senior non-commissioned grades should earn more than junior commissioned ones should also apply to medical assistants and doctors. Senior sergeants earn more than lieutenants and senior technicians more than junior lecturers; it is thus only fair that senior medical assistants should earn more than junior doctors.

In keeping with what has been said above, every encouragement and assistance should be given to the auxiliary to reach the professional grades. For this certain levels of basic education are usually essential. If an auxiliary attains part of this himself, by such means as night school and correspondence courses, he should where possible be released on pay to attain the rest of it as full time education. This means that a medical service should not only provide continued vocational training for its auxiliaries, but do what it can for their basic education as well.

Besides there being just opportunity for advancement, the status of auxiliary grades and their salary scales should be carefully related within a medical service, within a civil service and, where possible, within the community as a whole. In effect, the status of the auxiliary needs to be defined, legislated for and protected; especially is this true of the medical assistant.

Working with auxiliaries. The doctor who has been trained in a developing country, and who has had the opportunity of working in district hospitals during his vacations, adapts his practice to fit in with auxiliaries more naturally than does one who trained in Europe, and who meets his first medical assistants on coming to Africa. The most important fact that such a doctor should realize is that the skills of auxiliaries differ very greatly. Due to varied and often inadequate standards of training, it is seldom possible to be sure quite what a particular auxiliary knows, or what he can do. Doctors are thus often surprised by both the skill and ignorance of the auxiliaries they meet. The first essential therefore, in starting to work with an auxiliary, is to assess what he can do, what he cannot, and what he must be taught. The doctor who has trained his auxiliaries ever since they were schoolboys is in a very good position, for he knows inevitably the exact limits of their capacity.

After assessing the capacity of his auxiliaries the doctor must next adjust his own practice to fit in with their skills, and be flexible in what he allows them to do. After this he must continue to train them, a vitally important matter that is discussed in great detail in the next chapter and also in Chapter Twenty-Seven. He must also continually supervise them, for few auxiliaries are capable of maintaining their standards indefinitely without having their work inspected and checked fairly often.

Wherever possible things must be made foolproof for them. A very good example of this occurred in one hospital where the laboratory assistant added fourteen times too much sodium citrate to the blood culture medium he was making, with the result that few organisms would grow. He had once been told how much to add, but it had never been written down. But, had exact directions been recorded for him on a card, this would probably never have happened. The details for the dilution of drugs described in section 13:14 are a further example of the importance of making instructions as straightforward as possible, and in particular, of the need to circumvent any kind of calculation, no matter how simple.

One of the difficulties of working with auxiliaries, especially the junior ones, is the problem of communicating instructions to them. They appear to understand when they do not, and much trouble and confusion results. Some help in this respect is to be had by saying to someone to whom instructions have just been given, 'Now, tell me what I have told you' or, 'Now, what are you going to do?' Much depends on how this is said, but it is unlikely to cause offence, except with those with whom it is unnecessary anyway.

Everybody has a 'morale', auxiliaries included, and they require to be told what splendid people they are, and congratulated whenever possible. And, needless to say, all of them, including even the humblest cleaner, need to be treated with courtesy and respect, and acknowledged as a person of value in the medical community.

Chapter Eight

ADMINISTRATION AND TEACHING

Richard Manche

The role of the administrator. To its administrator a hospital or a district is a machine, a piece of mechanism that must run smoothly with the least attention possible, its parts, human and material, meshing harmoniously in the healing of the sick. Such an analogy implies the idea of the administrator as a mechanic above and outside an engine that he had first laboriously to build, but now need only watch, service, and occasionally repair; its wheels turning independently of him and continuing to run when he is no longer there. This is a good analogy, for an administrative machine, whether it has the complexity of a substantial health service or amounts to no more than a few dozen junior staff, takes much recruiting, training and organizing, but, once it is created, it should continue to run with comparatively little detailed supervision from above.

Very often, the parts of the machine have not merely to be put together, they have first to be made. As the most important parts of the machine are the human ones, and, as making men implies teaching them, it is inevitable that the administrator shall also be a teacher. Wherever a new unit has to be created from scratch, or an existing one improved, the first duty of the man in charge of it must therefore be to teach. It is for this reason that administration and teaching are considered together here.

Administrative methods will vary with the size of the hospital or district, and with the nature of the organization of which it forms part; but even so, there are certain principles which remain the same and certain rules which make it easier to run a hospital or a district well. Because the tasks of 'superintendent' and 'district medical officer' have often to be thrust upon very inexperienced shoulders, an attempt will be made to discuss some of the more troublesome problems that beset these two important organizers. The superintendent administering a hospital may be one of several doctors on the staff, or he may be just part of the one doctor who has to do everything himself. When therefore he is referred to in the pages following, such a reference is to superintendents of both these kinds.

The opening pages of this symposium stressed the general organizing role of doctors in developing countries, and it must not be thought from what has just been said that the only organizers are those in charge of districts or hospitals (Eighth axiom 1:15). Experienced supervisory staff are almost always scarce and doctors have often to run their own wards and departments. Small-scale organization can therefore be very important.

8:2 **Leadership, morale and communication.** The staff of a hospital are a team, and as a team they have a 'morale' — at its best a mutual sense of zest, industry and dedication; at its worst a corporate feeling of sloth, futility and frustration. Such feelings are catching and depend mainly on the leader of the group, for the staff will tend to take on his ideals and his enthusiasm — or his lack of them. High morale makes so much difference to the productivity of any human group that it is worth taking pains to foster it. Mostly, morale depends upon the simple rules of human relationships, courtesy, justice and real concern for the well-being of the junior, but there remain a few points worthy of special mention.

Example. The first is the example set to the junior staff, particularly during the critical period of their training, for it is at this time that attitudes become established, especially attitudes to work. If their superior devotes the first half hour of the day to the newspaper, they too will come to consider that as the norm. If it is his habit to stay until the work is done, it is likely that they will come to follow his example. Attitudes and traditions, that have once been learnt during training under close supervision, tend to persist afterwards when close supervision may no longer be possible.

The dignity of honest labour. This is perhaps the best place to stress what might be called the dignity of all honest labour, no matter how menial it may seem. Too often there is a tendency to think that because a task involves physical labour or dirty hands it is somehow degrading. Whatever may be the ethical faults of such an outlook, it has a very bad effect on the morale of the junior staff. A doctor's time is too valuable to do humble jobs routinely, but, if he himself occasionally shows mothers how to feed their children by cup-and-spoon in the under-fives clinic (16:8), or the washers up in his laboratory how to clean bottles, then the status of the work and the morale of the worker are both likely to improve. The tradition that manual labour does *not* degrade is one of those which particularly needs establishing in developing countries. If the reader wants an example, he is reminded that the late Sir Winston Churchill, when out of office, was wont to amuse himself by building brick walls.

An interest in the work of the junior. Another principle is the importance of taking an interest in the work of subordinate staff, however humble. This should be a continuing concern, but it is very useful if a superintendent makes a habit of going all round his hospital once a week, be it large or small, having a look at everything, a word with everybody, and commending all those found to be doing their job well. Such regular interest and congratulation of the industrious does more to improve performance than many reprimands and much cajoling of the indolent. Not only should he make this regular and predictable visitation, but the staff should never be quite sure when they may not see him — it does a dresser asleep in his ward no harm to be rudely awakened in the middle of the night.

Meetings. The huge leaps in development that are necessary in so many countries require the utmost endeavour from everyone. Such universal effort springs only from high morale. In trying to promote it other developing countries may have something to learn from the Cubans, whose enthusiasm is so great and whose advance has been so spectacular. One of their practices is to have regular meetings of all the members of a unit, be it a hospital, a factory, or a school, where ideas can be brought forward, resolutions made and plans discussed. From these gatherings representatives are elected to attend area meetings where the same process is repeated. Such arrangements seem strange against the background of most civil service traditions, but they appear to succeed in engendering a fine corporate spirit as well as producing astonishing practical results.

Whatever may be the limitations of such meetings on a national scale, they are of the greatest value on a local one, even down to units as small as a ward, a laboratory or an outpatient department (16:6). The members of every unit should make a habit of gathering together once a week for the discussion of plans and problems. What a group decides to do its members are more likely to carry out with a will than they are commands from above, and with skill the leader can make his own will that of the group. Whether this meeting should include all its members, or only its more senior ones will depend upon the circumstances. Above a dozen a meeting becomes cumbersome, and there is little point in including those so humble that they do not understand the significance of what is said. But, within these limits, the larger the fraction of a unit attending these meetings the better. They must be as informal as possible; some form of refreshment is often desirable and they should be carefully fitted into the week's routine.

The effect of such meetings can be augmented, though not replaced, by regular daily meetings at the morning refreshment break. The larger the number of people who are able to meet one another at this time the better, for these occasions do much to promote the harmonious social relationships on which the smooth running of a unit depends; they provide a time for business to be transacted and ideas exchanged. The morning break should therefore be made the most of.

'A medical assistant in chief'. Free communication with the leader is important, not only within a hospital, but also within a service, for it minimizes frustration and reduces ill feeling. To further this communication and facilitate command through a nursing service, it has long been standard practice for the senior nursing sister to have an office in the medical directorate. The same practice can be usefully extended to the medical assistant cadre also. If the senior medical assistant also has an office in the medical directorate together with the salary and esteem that go with it, then the director will have a close link with his medical assistants and they with him; their profession will gain in status and their own career prospects will improve. One director claimed this to be one of the most useful moves he had ever made, so great was its effect on the morale of the assistants in his service.

8:3 **Delegation and teaching.** (Eighth axiom 1:15, Eleventh axiom 1:18). In theory, a medical superintendent, be he the only doctor in the hospital or merely one of several, is responsible for everything that goes on in it. He cannot do everything himself and must delegate most of his tasks. Delegation is thus the key to administrative success and makes the best use of skilled staff at all levels. The rule to work on is this:— **'Delegate every task to the humblest member of the team capable of doing it satisfactorily'.** So often, there is nobody who can do the job satisfactorily — delegation therefore inevitably implies teaching people so that jobs can be delegated to them. Thus, if a lay administrator can be taught to make out the annual returns, the time instructing him will be well spent, for next year the superintendent will not have to spend so long on this job himself; if a medical assistant can be taught to do a lumbar puncture with safety, this will free a doctor to do something else; if giving a tube feed can be safely delegated to a junior nurse, then a staff nurse can spend more of her time on something requiring greater skill. Delegation and training are thus inextricably linked.

The skill pyramid. The staff of a hospital form a pyramid with a few skilled people at its apex and many pairs of unskilled hands at its base. The composition of this 'staff pyramid' is critically important, and, ideally, each of its layers should be properly proportioned and carefully related, both in quality and quantity, to the work the unit is expected to do. The 'skill gradient' of this staff pyramid, which at its simplest passes from the doctor through medical assistants and dressers down to the

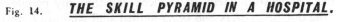

Fig. 14. 

This is the hospital in Chapter Twelve.

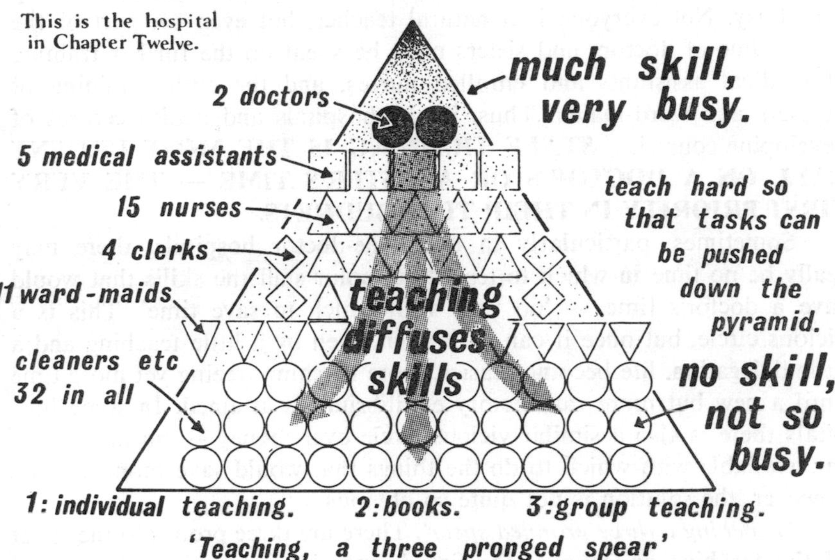

sweepers at the bottom, is often top heavy — a few grossly overworked skilled people at the top and many untrained and comparatively idle hands at the bottom. To make the most of the human resources available, this skill gradient must become more even, and only continued teaching will achieve it. There has to be a constant striving to 'push tasks down the pyramid', so leaving the staff at the top free to make the most of those skills which, by their very complexity, they cannot pass on. This has been drawn diagramatically in Figure 14 which is held to be *much the most important of any in these pages.* The numbers and kinds of staff involved were taken from the hospital at Mityana in Uganda described in Chapter Twelve. It so happened that, at the time the survey was done, no nursing sister or matron was employed at this hospital, but she could be readily fitted into this diagram. A doctor must be continually teaching his sisters and medical assistants, though there will often be much that he can learn from them, particularly if he is new. They in their turn must teach the ward-maids and dressers, and the whole staff must do all they can to teach the patients (6:2).

Most hospitals can expect to receive at least some skilled staff from the training schools of the region, be they those for enrolled nurses, medical assistants or other grades, but in practice this input of skills is seldom enough, either in volume, or in ability. The shortfall has to be made up, and these nurses and medical assistants diluted with locally recruited dressers and ward-maids. Such people need training; the only way to train them is to train them 'in service', and the only people to train them are the doctors, sisters and other skilled staff who are already very busy. Not everyone is a natural teacher, but even so, part of the scarce time of doctors and sisters must be spent on the further training of medical assistants and enrolled nurses, and the entire training of dressers and ward-maids. Thus, in the hospitals and health centres of developing countries, **STAFF TRAINING IS THE MOST URGENT CALL ON A DOCTOR'S OR A SISTER'S TIME — THE VERY FIRST PRIORITY IN THEIR TIME BUDGETS.**

Sometimes, particularly in busy one-doctor hospitals, there may really be no time in which to teach the junior staff the skills that would save a doctor's time — 'no time with which to save time'. This is a vicious circle, but once it can be broken, even by a little teaching and a little delegation, life becomes easier, more teaching freeing yet more time until a new but more satisfactory equilibrium is attained. In some hospitals there is also a similar vicious circle over money — no money being available with which to do the things that would save money. Here, however, the solution is not quite so obvious.

'Teaching a three pronged spear'. There are three prongs to the spear of the teaching endeavour; the first is individual teaching, the second group teaching, and the third provision for the staff to teach themselves. Much training is a continual individual process — correcting a dresser's sterile technique, teaching a clerk how to set out a letter properly, a storeman how to keep his ledgers, a laboratory attendant how to measure the blood urea, a medical assistant how to recognize the earlier stages of kwashiorkor, a cleaner how to sweep a corridor or clean a window, and perhaps even a mortuary attendant how to sew up a corpse or open a skull. Such teaching depends very largely on having the correct attitude of mind. Some people seem to spend a large part of their time teaching their subordinates, others either do the job themselves, or get it done by somebody who has previously been taught by another person, or don't do the job at all. The value of these 'habitual teachers' to their society needs no further stressing, as also does the value of trying to emulate them.

This continued individual teaching is immensely valuable, but it is also very time-consuming, and it has to be complemented wherever possible by regular periods of formal group instruction which make full use of teaching aids (27:1). In terms of knowledge imparted per hour of the instructor's time, these formal sessions are very valuable, and somehow enough time must be found to make them a regular part of the hospital routine. These two approaches must be assisted by the third prong of the teaching spear — seeing that all junior staff have access to such books as might help them. Really suitable ones are sadly lacking, but such as have been found are listed in Appendix C and are discussed in Chapter Twenty-Nine.

The 'culture gap' in teaching. Teaching has its agonies, staff cannot be paid enough and leave; once partly trained they tend to consider their former tasks beneath them, and grave deficiencies in basic education come to light. The expatriate in particular finds it difficult to adjust to the differences between his culture and that of his clerks and dressers. He tends too often to take it for granted that everyone knows how to wrap up a parcel, rule a straight line, open a tin, answer the telephone, or take a message. He forgets that there are people who have to be taught these things. However, despite all these difficulties, continued teaching is still the key to a really good hospital or district.

'Doctor=Teacher'. If all this fails to convince the medical student in a developing country that when he qualifies he is to be a teacher as well as a doctor, he is reminded that 'doctor' does in fact mean 'teacher'. The word doctor is derived from the Latin, *docere,* to teach, and, of the ten usages of the word given by a standard dictionary, the first five refer to learning or teaching, and the medical use of the word comes only sixth on the list.

The selection and deployment of staff. Hospitals in developing countries have one great advantage — they have a huge pool of labour from which to recruit staff at the primary, junior secondary or even school certificate level. Only a small fraction will have been selected for further education, and the selection process is unlikely to have been very efficient in removing the brightest members of society from the labour pool. How is a hospital to find the best trainees when there are so many to choose from? Some form of intelligence test is required and the best appears to be the Standard Progressive Matrices, Sets A-E (Revised Order 1956) by J. C. Raven (LEW). These do not depend on a knowledge of English and a good score is said always to mean a trainable recruit. These matrices are supplied in a packet complete with a book of instructions for 25/- ($3.5), and anyone faced with the selection of junior staff is advised to make use of them (36). Another method that is recommended is to use the puzzles that are sold by toyshops, such as getting beads into holes, or a ball bearing up a helix.

Once a little experience is gained in the use of such tests, the selector is likely to find himself relying on them more and more and putting correspondingly less reliance on the traditional methods of the testimonial, the interview and the 'personal hunch'. Nevertheless, the critical point is to make it quite clear to selected candidates that they are on probation only, and at an early stage to dismiss all but those who prove themselves really satisfactory. If the hospital and the trainee part company after a fortnight, a month, or even six months, neither has lost very much. If an unsatisfactory man is given permanent terms of service a great wrong has been done to the hospital, which may be indefinitely denied the services of a good typist, a good gardener, a good dresser, or even, let it be said, a good doctor. Excellent people exist in every community to fill these roles — **the trouble spent in looking for really good staff will be repaid many times.**

It should be a rule in the deployment of staff that nobody is indispensable — not even the superintendent — that is to say, there should be no jobs in the hospital which only one man can do. This entails making careful provision for each man to learn something about the job of the next one. Thus, one of the laboratory assistants should learn just enough about X-rays to be able to replace the radiographer and vice versa. This is not difficult, for it is largely a matter of rotating staff round a bit and encouraging them to teach one another — a highly economical process.

'The job expands to fill the time available for it.' So said Professor Parkinson in one of his laws, and it is certainly well demonstrated in some hospitals where the junior staff are sometimes conspicuously under-employed. It is therefore worth having a critical look at what many of them are up to — a rudimentary 'job analysis' and 'time and motion study' of their tasks. They can often be shown how to do things more effectively and rapidly, two jobs can sometimes be combined, and it may help in getting more work out of some with more indolence than initiative, if a timetable of their daily, weekly and monthly duties is posted up for them — if they cannot read it themselves someone else can do this for them.

8:5 **The lay administrator.** Lay administrators are perhaps more valuable even than doctors, for wherever they exist, they relieve a doctor to perform the proper tasks for which he was trained. But even in some industrial countries they are relatively new as a professional cadre, and it is time that the need for this grade was more widely recognized and its training and examinations better organized. In some places these men are recruited from among senior laboratory technicians, pharmacists or clerks who have learnt some aspects of the job as part of their previous experience in these professions. This has much to commend it, though it is often impracticable because these grades are usually in equally short supply. Under such conditions, and where no training course exists, there is nothing for it but to find the most suitable person and train him in service as intensively as possible. The trainee administrator should spend at least a few weeks in each department of the hospital, and receive the rest of his training at the hands of the superintendent himself, who cannot spend his time better than in teaching someone to pay out salaries, 'keep the books', order the stores, fill in the returns and deal with the numerous smaller problems of the hospital. Provision for the recruitment, training and salary of such a person has thus a very high priority.

Where there is a lay administrator the superintendent must learn to work with him. As many as possible of the routine tasks should be delegated to him, and it ought to be possible for a superintendent to do his part of the administration in as little as half an hour each day. Needless to say, the superintendent must make all the major decisions himself and back up his lay administrator firmly on all matters of discipline.

Overspending. This is a common trap for the unwary and the inexperienced medical superintendent all too often finds that he has spent his whole year's vote in the first nine months of it. This can be a very embarrassing situation, both professionally for the superintendent and politically for his minister. The best way to prevent it is to plot a line on a graph representing what the cumulative monthly expenditure should be — the months of the year along the bottom of the graph, the money spent up the side. The actual expenditure is then superimposed on the graph and entered in month by month.

Theft. Theft is often a major annoyance, for the material possessions of a hospital can be a real temptation to the local people. Security precautions are a nuisance and take up much time that would be better spent in other ways. Clearly, a balance has to be struck between the extent of the theft and the effort worth spending to stop it — the measures to be taken must be adjusted to the severity of the loss.

A campaign against theft must start with the senior staff themselves, who must maintain, and be seen to maintain, an attitude of scrupulous rectitude towards the hospital's property — it is so easy to 'borrow' things and so important not to. In larger hospitals there may have to be a system of signed 'chits' for borrowed articles, and if there is, the senior staff must stick by it, especially when the equipment is in the charge of a junior. Further, it is a very good rule that nothing can ever be borrowed from the hospital, or from one department to another, for more than a month without its being returned or 'taken on charge' in the inventory. 'Spot checks' of the departmental inventories are advisable from time to time, while it is good practice for a superintendent never to go into the store without asking to see the ledgers and checking some item at random. He should get into the habit of doing this often, and pay particular attention to antibiotics and any items which have a domestic use, such as soap or fabrics. Crates in a store may not always contain what they should, so all crates should be opened.

Keys are a source of great frustration, and the early acquisition of the appropriate duplicate or master-key will save much annoyance when something is wanted urgently, and 'somebody has gone off duty with the keys'.

A useful alternative in some situations, particularly where portable tools are concerned, is to have a board, preferably a 'pegboard', fixed to the wall where each piece of equipment hangs on a hook. If a 'shadow' is painted behind each of the items on this board, the missing ones will be obvious immediately.

Syringes are often a very tempting item, but an absent syringe is soon spotted when a ward is equipped with a box made with pigeon holes to fit its whole syringe stock. If all syringes have to be placed in their pigeon holes at the end of every shift, theft is again obvious and potential thieves are deterred. 'Private practice' by junior hospital staff is so common and potentially so dangerous that there is much to be said for making the unauthorized possession of syringes and antibiotics illegal in developing countries.

Antibiotics frequently go astray and are very difficult to check. Vials should if possible be printed by the supplier with the name of the medical service. If the pharmacist can be trusted, empty bottles can be recalled and replaced with fresh supplies 'one-for-one'. Sometimes, it may be possible to trace them through the hospital by putting surreptitious marks on a batch. If tablets disappear they can be crushed and made into a mixture which is not quite so saleable.

Some hospitals have found that, whereas cheap enamel buckets disappear very rapidly, expensive stainless steel ones do not, and are less expensive in the long run. In general, it seems that the closer that items like blankets or sheets are to those in local domestic use, the more likely are they to be stolen, conversely, the more distinctive they are the less likely are they to disappear.

Linen has problems of its own, but, if boldly marked it is less of an attraction. The best way of doing this is to paint the name of the hospital in the centre of the sheet with 1% silver nitrate and a large paint brush. If this is either ironed, or allowed to stand for some days before washing, the marks become a dense indelible black. If dirty linen disappears from the wards, make tall bins of wood, so high that it is not possible to remove their contents by reaching down with an arm from the top, removal being only possible though a padlocked door at the bottom.

There is a useful cross-check that can be made on the issue of rations from the stores to the kitchen. It depends upon there being a standard ration per patient per day which is issued in quantities depending on the daily bed state, and prices of food supplies fixed by tender for the whole year. The price of a daily ration can then be calculated exactly. When this is multiplied by the number of patient days for the year, the product should approximate closely to the total sum spent on food by the hospital. If this does not agree to within, say 5 per cent. then food is going astray somewhere. This does not of course prove that all the food issued is being eaten by the patients, but it is some check on the honesty of the storekeeper.

It may be too late to alter the geography of a hospital, but if theft is really severe, the only answer may be a perimeter fence and a guard on the gate with a right to search all passers — particularly all cars. Visitors can be asked to leave their cars outside the perimeter and the fewer the staff houses inside the wire the better.

Stores and indents. The frustration of running out of essential drugs, equipment, or spares is one of the more exasperating experiences of a day's work. There is little to be done when this is due to lack of the money to buy them, but more often the administrative machine is at fault.

The first measure to be taken is to see that a record is kept of all expendable items, and of all anticipated calls for spares. These should either be in a loose-leaf ledger, or on filing cards — a different card or a different page for each item. These cards or pages should be headed with the exact details of the item, the catalogue number and the supplier. This is a detail of great convenience when making out an indent, because the ledger or a pile of cards can be handed to a clerk who has then only to copy out the required specifications from the head of each page or card. These should be ruled with columns for the date and the quantity of material ordered, delivered, used, and in stock. Such cards may not always be filled in very meticulously but they are valuable even so. Another useful storekeeping tip is to have the items on the shelves in the same order as the cards in the file or the pages in the ledger — a great convenience when taking stock. Some storekeepers prefer to leave the cards on the shelves by the items they represent.

How much of an item should be stocked? This will depend on the frequency at which indents are sent in, and the time taken for their delivery. It is a good storekeeping rule always to keep enough stock in hand for one indent to go astray without disaster. This allows enough latitude for something to be overlooked once, for an item to be out of stock in the stores, or for an unexpected increase in demand to occur.

8:9 **'The right tool for the job'.** Poverty and theft are not the only reasons why a ward may be without its essential equipment — a common, if unexpected one, is that nobody has ever had the energy to indent. If therefore, something is wanted, try ordering it. But, should the item be an unusual one, take great care to supply full details as to cost, catalogue number and maker, for stores officers are more likely to place an unusual indent if they have these details to go on. If the item does not appear the first time, keep on trying.

A doctor is readily aware of the possible short-comings of the equipment he himself has to use, but may tend to forget that his subordinates, be they dressers or laboratory assistants, also need 'the right tool for the job'. Often, they do not even know what they could or should have, and, as their needs are frequently both simple and inexpensive, a certain awareness of how the right tool might help him can be well repaid in the improved output that may result when it is provided.

The correct tool for a particular task is specified on many occasions in the following chapters — they are all well worth the effort needed to obtain them. Among them are such things as a Heaf gun (21:3), a low reading thermometer (13:16), a special needle for transvaginal pudendal blocks (19:10), a heat sealer for plastic film (30:5), scalp vein needles (15:11), the apparatus for a very simple blood urea (24:26), and the EEL colorimeter (24:6).

The comparative insignificance of the cost of the right tool for the job is brought out in the economic analysis of a hospital's budget in Chapter Twelve. Equipment forms such a small fraction of the total budget that it is tragic to be without the correct tools unnecessarily, particularly if they are ones with a long life, such as weighing scales for example. It follows, therefore, that *economy should never be quoted as being the reason for the absence of necessary articles of minor equipment.* Such economy is indeed false economy.

It often happens that a medical stores does not know the use of some of the items they hold in stock, and, because these are not in the catalogue, nobody ever asks for them. There may be all sorts of useful equipment to be had, if not for the asking, often at least in return for an indent. For this reason, and in accordance with the general principle of endeavouring to meet people who would otherwise only be known from their signatures on letters or forms, a visit to the medical stores can be well repaid.

A stock of equipment is more readily assessed than a stock of drugs. A suggested check list of routine and emergency drugs is therefore supplied as Appendix J. When first arriving at a hospital this list can be used to see that the essential drugs are available. The dispenser should be asked to check it through, and an indent placed for whatever is missing.

On taking charge of a new unit. When the newcomer first comes to a strange place he has one great advantage — he sees things to which he will be oblivious once a few days have passed. He may notice that the hospital or the staff look dirty, that the paint is peeling off the walls or the sign outside the gate, that the drains need immediate attention or that items of equipment which he had previously considered essential were missing, or had never been ordered. A few days later all these things and many more he will take for granted. Let him therefore not waste these valuable first impressions, but note them down with the firm resolution to see them changed rapidly.

On getting things done. When the role of the doctor was discussed in the Eighth axiom (1:15) much emphasis was laid on the value of the 'ability to get things done', because there is in developing countries so much that needs doing. It is an ability which some seem to have and others not, but, like other abilities, it can be increased with practice.

The first step is to define exactly the task to be undertaken — what is to be done and to form some estimate of its value. The next is to list what is required for the task in terms of men, money, material, land, permission, or whatever else may be required. After this comes the stage of finding out in whose power the desired things lie. This is followed by the attempt to obtain them, and it is at this stage that skill is required, for this usually involves obtaining something that the owner is not keen to part with. The guile required to do this is one of the oldest human arts, and careful study of the personality holding the power will be well repaid. Nevertheless, there are certain general rules that make success more likely. The plan should be carefully worked out, where money is involved this should be calculated, as exactly as possible and the whole project must be neatly written out. It should be presented at the right time, when the person holding power is well disposed, and, where relevant, at the right time of the financial year. The person to whom the request is made should appear in a good light and any possible benefit to him pointed out. The closer the relationship between the person placing the request and the person granting it, the more likely it is to be answered, and, if this is remote, and particularly if there is antipathy, it may be better to work through a third party.

All this is but the beginning, next comes the *massive hard work* which is largely the means by which all those who have ever done anything have attained their end. With it must go the resolution that *any* task may have to be undertaken personally in order to see the job through. The attitude of mind which refuses to do something because someone else should be there to do it, and is not, never accomplishes anything. If the thing to get done is the organizing of a conference, then the organizer must not be put off by the possibility of having to write all the letters himself. If it is editing a book, and the person who should draw the diagrams will not draw them as he should, then the editor must learn to do them himself. If it is opening a clinic, then this must be expected to involve the doctor personally in teaching the nurses.

Lastly, neither the magnitude of the labour, nor the value of the final achievement, must ever be underestimated — it *is* worth it, and this value is totally independent of any recognition or thanks that may, or may not, attend it.

Chapter Nine

PROGRESSIVE PATIENT CARE

Edward and Peter Williams

The spectrum of health and sickness. Extreme sickness and perfect health can be looked upon as forming the opposite ends of an evenly graded continuum. Between the full vigour of life on the one hand and the final agonies of the dying on the other, there falls an even spectrum of progressively poorer health and steadily increasing illness and disability.

The individuals of which this spectrum is composed can for convenience be divided into a number of groups which have been shown diagrammatically in Figure 15. Here, the many healthy members of a community have been drawn as a plain white column at the left of the page, and the small number of individuals who are very sick at any one time have been drawn as a short black column on the extreme right. These few patients are so ill as to require very intensive looking after, and are therefore classified as needing 'intensive care'. Between these two extremes three further groups can be distinguished; one is a group of ambulant mildly sick persons who form the bulk of the ordinary outpatients of every hospital, while the other two are both of them inside the hospital itself. The members of one of these groups are ambulant like the outpatients, and many of them might in fact be outpatients if they did not live so far away. Even though they are in hospital, patients in this group are all well enough to look after themselves and are therefore classified as being capable of 'self-care'. Members of the next group are intermediate between these self-care patients and the desperately ill ones needing intensive care; they are the average patients who need the ordinary services of a hospital ward and are thus classified as requiring 'intermediate care'.

In most hospitals *all* the patients deemed ill enough to be admitted to the wards enjoy the *same* facilities, no matter how nearly well or how gravely ill they are.

Fig. 15.

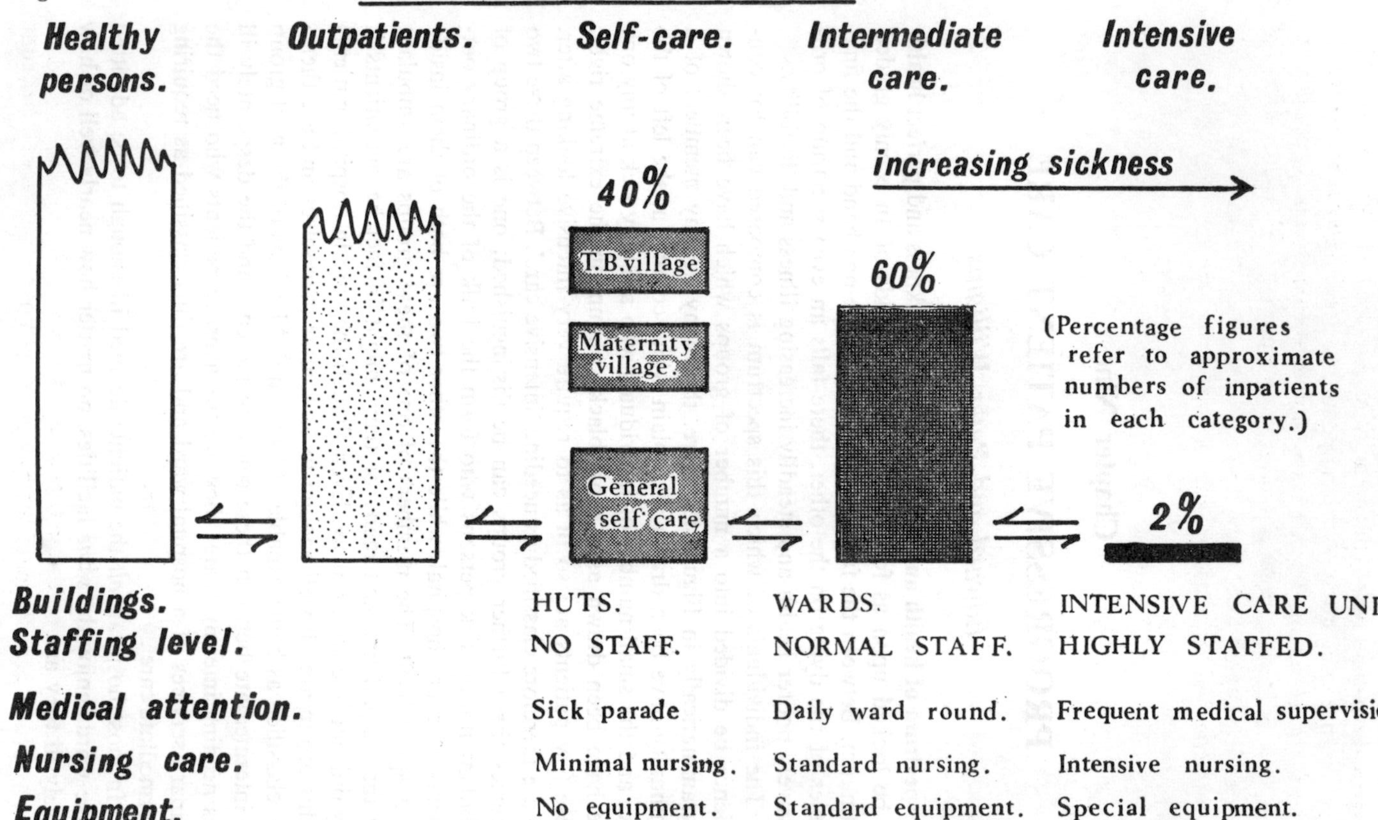
PROGRESSIVE PATIENT CARE.
Healthy persons.
Outpatients.
Self-care.
Intermediate care.
Intensive care.
increasing sickness
40%
T.B.village
Maternity village.
General self care
60%
(Percentage figures refer to approximate numbers of inpatients in each category.)
2%
Buildings.
Staffing level.
Medical attention.
Nursing care.
Equipment.
HUTS.
NO STAFF.
Sick parade
Minimal nursing.
No equipment.
WARDS.
NORMAL STAFF.
Daily ward round.
Standard nursing.
Standard equipment.
INTENSIVE CARE UNIT.
HIGHLY STAFFED.
Frequent medical supervision.
Intensive nursing.
Special equipment.

2 **'Progressive patient care'** This is the term given to the system which seeks to rationalize this situation by according to these several categories of patients the standards of care most suited to their needs. In its present form it is a modern concept, though the tradition of looking after any gravely ill patient close to the sister's desk that was started by Florence Nightingale, was an early attempt to match the needs of the patients to the care they are given.

This method of looking after the hospitalized sick separates them into the three groups that have already been described — the patients requiring 'self-care', 'intermediate care' and 'intensive care'. A fourth group is sometimes also defined, though it is not shown in Figure 15. These are the patients who need long-term or 'continuous care' for some permanent disability. The severely handicapped lepers in a leprosy settlement require care of this kind.

Figure 15 has been drawn with arrows which lead from one category of patient to another, but these inevitably simplify the true nature of things. Thus, a patient suffering a severe motor accident might go from the healthy to the intensive care group almost instantaneously, and, as he recovered, he might slowly progress through the intermediate to the self-care group.

Such a system offers two major advantages over the traditional way of looking after hospital patients. Firstly, it gives the very sick ones a much better chance of survival. Secondly, it is highly economical to the hospital authorities, for the scarce staff and facilities that are saved on the self-care patients can be used to look after a greater total number of patients as well as to give a better service to the gravely ill.

Progressive patient care originated in North America and is being slowly introduced in Europe. In industrial countries it appears to commend itself to the more enterprising hospital with a comparative staff shortage. Thus, whereas a teaching hospital with abundant nurses can afford to provide a 'special' nurse for each gravely ill patient, less well staffed hospitals find it better to group their very sick patients together in an 'intensive care' unit. What applies to the less well staffed hospitals in Europe applies even more to the hospitals of Africa and Asia. Thus the Titmuss report advised its adoption in Tanzania (32). But in an incomplete form and under another name it has been practised in some tropical hospitals for many years. This has particularly been the case in French-speaking Africa, where hospitals are commonly provided with 'village' accommodation for their ambulant sick.

3 **Care requirements classified.** In more detail the type of patients and the care they need can be summarized as follows:—

Intensive care. Patients needing intensive care form about 2 per cent.

of the whole and include those with acute illnesses, disturbances of consciousness, severe metabolic upsets, grave injury and respiratory failure. Trained staff must be on constant watch for these patients may need oxygen, suction, intubation, intravenous therapy or even a respirator. They are confined to bed and have to be washed, fed and turned, and have their pulse, temperature and respirations charted at frequent intervals.

Patients are too ill to need segregating by age or sex, and are looked after together in a special 'intensive care unit'. These have usually only about 3 beds, patients stay but a few hours or days and are admitted to one, either direct from their homes, from the theatre or from other units.

Intermediate care. This is the largest group and contains about two-thirds of all cases. These are the average hospital patients who can feed themselves, wash their hands and faces, perhaps go to the toilet, sit out of bed, need no special equipment and require only daily charting of their pulse, temperature and respiration.

Self-care. About one-third of all patients are fully ambulant and are either convalescent or undergoing investigation or simple treatment — they therefore need no normal nursing and can be housed in huts or a hostel. They include convalescents from intensive or intermediate care, chronic tropical ulcers, patients awaiting operation, cases of anaemia, minor injury and trivial infection. They can usually either cook for themselves or else have a relative who can do this for them.

9:4 **Some particular features of progressive patient care in developing countries.** The study in Chapter Twelve showed that in one hospital as many as 40 per cent. of the patients fell into the self-care category. In view of the great cost of standard ward accommodation as compared with cheap self-care huts (12:3) (10:6), *self-care facilities offer a major economy in the initial capital outlay on a hospital.*

Where a hospital of the standard pattern already exists, *the addition of self-care facilities enables the total number of its effective beds to be increased at minimal further cost.* This is of course subject to one important proviso; it is that the limiting factor in the care of the patients is buildings, not staff.

Outpatients are a complex group, but among them are some who should be seen several days running in need of such things as dressings for the treatment of minor sepsis or trauma, or a series of daily injections, etc. If they live close by they can come up to the outpatient department daily and their management presents no difficulties. But, if they come from further away, the choice may either be to admit them or else to let them fend for themselves with friends or relatives. They may have none in the vicinity, so these patients may be put to considerable discomfort and hardship and often do not stay in the neighbourhood to re-attend as they should. There may be too much pressure on the general or 'intermediate case' wards to admit them there, but if self-care facilities are readily available, this kind of outpatient will be saved much unnecessary inconvenience. Where transport is difficult and outpatient care gradients steep (2:7), the availability of such self-care facilities may in practice decide whether patients of this kind are going to be treated at all.

Hitherto, all self-care patients have been considered together, but there are really several categories of them; these are, the general self-care patients suffering from such conditions as anaemia and the milder degrees of malnutrition; there are also several specialized groups, such as the tuberculous, the leprous and the antenatal mothers. Apart from those with infectious diseases, and perhaps the antenatal mothers, all the rest of the self-care patients can be housed together in the same self-care or hospital village which can also house the relatives of those in the wards (Figure 16 (10:4)).

The importance of providing such self-care facilities is often overlooked, thus the relatives and some of the outpatients attending one of the most famous hospitals in Africa live in and around one tiny hut that was added as an afterthought.

Though the 'self-care' part of the system offers the greatest economic returns, an intensive care unit saves many lives in the circumstances of a developing country. Here many patients and few staff make it especially difficult to look after the occasional very sick patient adequately in the midst of a large general ward. The comparatively few really sick patients are thus much better segregated and looked after together in an intensive care unit.

Practical advice based on experience in East Africa. For some years the writers, who run a mission hospital at Kuluva in Western Uganda, have made use of progressive patient care and found it of the greatest value. When bringing it into use in an existing hospital a few beds should be separated off as an 'intensive care unit', and hostel or hutted accommodation provided for such patients as are capable of looking after themselves. The remaining beds of the hospital are then used by patients requiring intermediate care.

Method: The self-care village.

Most of the detailed management of such a village is either obvious or has been mentioned already. Some suitable person has to be deputed to look after it, and the patients should parade daily to be seen by a doctor, either in the outpatient department

or at the end of a ward round. They may require treatment several times daily which can be given either in the outpatient department or in the wards. One difficulty in management of such a village is that patients may be inclined to stay in it indefinitely and may later be difficult to discharge. Feeding these patients is no problem. They cook their own food.

Method: The intensive care unit.

If a special building cannot be built, adapt a small ward or partition off a large one to hold two or three beds and cots; curtain them off, leave plenty of space to move around them and provide good lighting, both in emergency and for minor procedures; provide oxygen if possible, a sucker, drip stands, intravenous equipment and sterile packs for cut-down infusions and minor procedures. See that such skilled staff as can possibly be spared take special care of this unit, that it is manned day and night when need be, and that it always contains the most gravely ill patients, regardless of their age, sex or specialty.

In a large hospital the number gravely ill at any one time will be fairly constant, in smaller hospitals it will vary widely. Sometimes there will be nobody requiring intensive care, while at others several cases will require it simultaneously. An intensive care unit should always be available, but staff deployment needs to be flexible.

Chapter Ten

THE ARCHITECTURE OF HOSPITALS AND HEALTH CENTRES

David Church A.R.I.B.A.

1 **The organic nature of a hospital.** Like its patients, a hospital is alive. In Africa some begin as tiny dispensaries and eventually grow to become thriving institutions of several hundred beds. New departments are added, others are adapted and sometimes old wards are pulled down to make room for new. The flux of continued alteration thus complicates the simplicity of mere growth.

Few doctors and not many architects create a whole hospital from scratch. Many however alter and add to them — a new kitchen here, a new mortuary there and an isolation ward somewhere else. But unless this continued creative activity proceeds to some plan, it ends in that untidy and inefficient chaos which so many hospitals demonstrate too well.

The cardinal principle for those planning to build or enlarge a hospital progressively over the years, is to ask an architect with experience in hospital planning to draw out a 'master development plan' — early in the hospital's life. This will make it possible for such expensive and basic services as drainage to be planned with cheapness and efficiency. A master plan is not expensive and saves money in the long run because, by his training, an architect is aware of many subtleties that a layman is not.

Although hospitals are the subject of most of this chapter, much of what is said here, particularly that pertaining to cheap methods of construction, applies equally to health centres. Plans for these units are supplied as Figure 11 (3:3).

10:2 **The adaptation of structure to function.** Essentially, the fabric of a hospital is but a box to protect and support the human activities that go on inside it. It must thus be intimately adapted to the needs of both the patients and the staff. What does the tropical villager require when he comes into hospital? This must be uppermost in the mind of the designer, and, had it been better understood, there would not be hospitals in Africa costing millions of pounds where relatives have to sleep on the stairs, because nobody thought about building a hostel for them when the place was built.

The following pages describe some important adaptations to the requirements of the tropical peasant — a mothers' shelter, a hospital garden, benches at the height local people like, the maternity village — these are all adaptations to specific human needs. As they will vary in detail from country to country, careful enquiry into the local preferences must precede any attempt to draw up a plan (Twelfth axiom 1:19).

10:3 **Space for expansion.** No restriction is finally so absolute as a shortage of space. A health centre requires about 3 hectares (7 acres), and a 250 bedded hospital not less than 16 hectares (40 acres). All medical units must thus have a site on which they can grow. Later on the only alternative may be an entirely new structure in another place. This may sometimes be the best course, but so much money is likely to have been invested already that it may be cheaper to go on adding than to rebuild completely on another site.

Not only must all new units have adequate space, but they must also be laid out so that each further addition completes a pre-arranged plan, and be so zoned that shell buildings are kept apart to allow the ordered growth of the central nucleus — it is a pity to have later to pull down a solid, useful, but badly sited house to make way for a ward. One point is quite clear in this regard. It is, that, provided the size of a site is adequate and there are no overwhelming objections as far as the position of the hospital is concerned, it is usually more economical to pull down some of the existing buildings and replan the same site than it would be to build a new hospital of a *similar kind* on another site. If a single story pavilion style hospital is to be replaced by a multi-storied one this is another matter, but to replace a pavilion style hospital by one of the same kind, albeit better laid out, is likely to be a major waste of resources.

If a new hospital is to be built, it should be put up close to the old, for it is certain not to be long before they will both be in use, the new one for the general care of the sick and the old one for a wide variety of other purposes. This is what has happened at Mulago where the new hospital was erected close to the old. The buildings of the latter now form the nutrition rehabilitation unit (14:17), the orthopaedic workshops, the psychiatric outpatient department besides serving many other functions also. The value of making use of old buildings in this way is as great in a district hospital as it is in a national one.

A building can serve a succession of functions during a hospital's life — for example, one which serves both for outpatients and inpatients when the unit is still small can later be adapted for outpatients alone. This flexibility is all important in hospital planning, and is made easier by building to a 'module', such as the commonly accepted one of 100 cms. (40 ins). If the design is drawn wherever possible in units of this length, subsequent alteration will be easier, particularly if the roof is supported on posts and the walls made of panelling which can be modified as required.

Money is often so short that a new building is not put up until it is long overdue, but when eventually it is built, it must be adapted not only to the needs of the present but also to those of the future. It must, as it were, 'leap-frog' today's requirements and be ready for those of tomorrow.

Earlier in the book it was stressed that a health centre is not to be looked upon as an embryo hospital and that these are two distinct units with separate and complementary functions (3:1). The prospect of a health centre growing to become a hospital should not therefore be a common one, but there will be some occasions when a health centre will ultimately be replaced by a hospital, so building must be planned accordingly. An ingenious way of making this possible has been devised by G. Ferrand entitled *Le Centre Medical Rural dans les pays en voie de dévélopment* (16). It is based on experience in French-speaking Africa and deserves to be better known, for each stage in the development of a small health centre to a hospital of more than a hundred beds is carefully planned and the progressive adaptation of the outpatient department is particularly ingenious (11:4). (In the French usage a *'Centre Medical'* means a district hospital).

The 'nucleus' and the 'shell'. When land is plentiful and the site reasonably level, a single storied structure is the cheapest one. When it is not quite so abundant and there is a little more money available, a two story hospital with a ramp to provide access to the upper one may be a useful intermediate between single story construction and that involving three or more. Two stories are cheaper than three because there is no need to increase the strength of most standard types of walling merely to add one more floor. A ramp is also much cheaper than a lift and is without the operating difficulties that may beset the latter in a remote place.

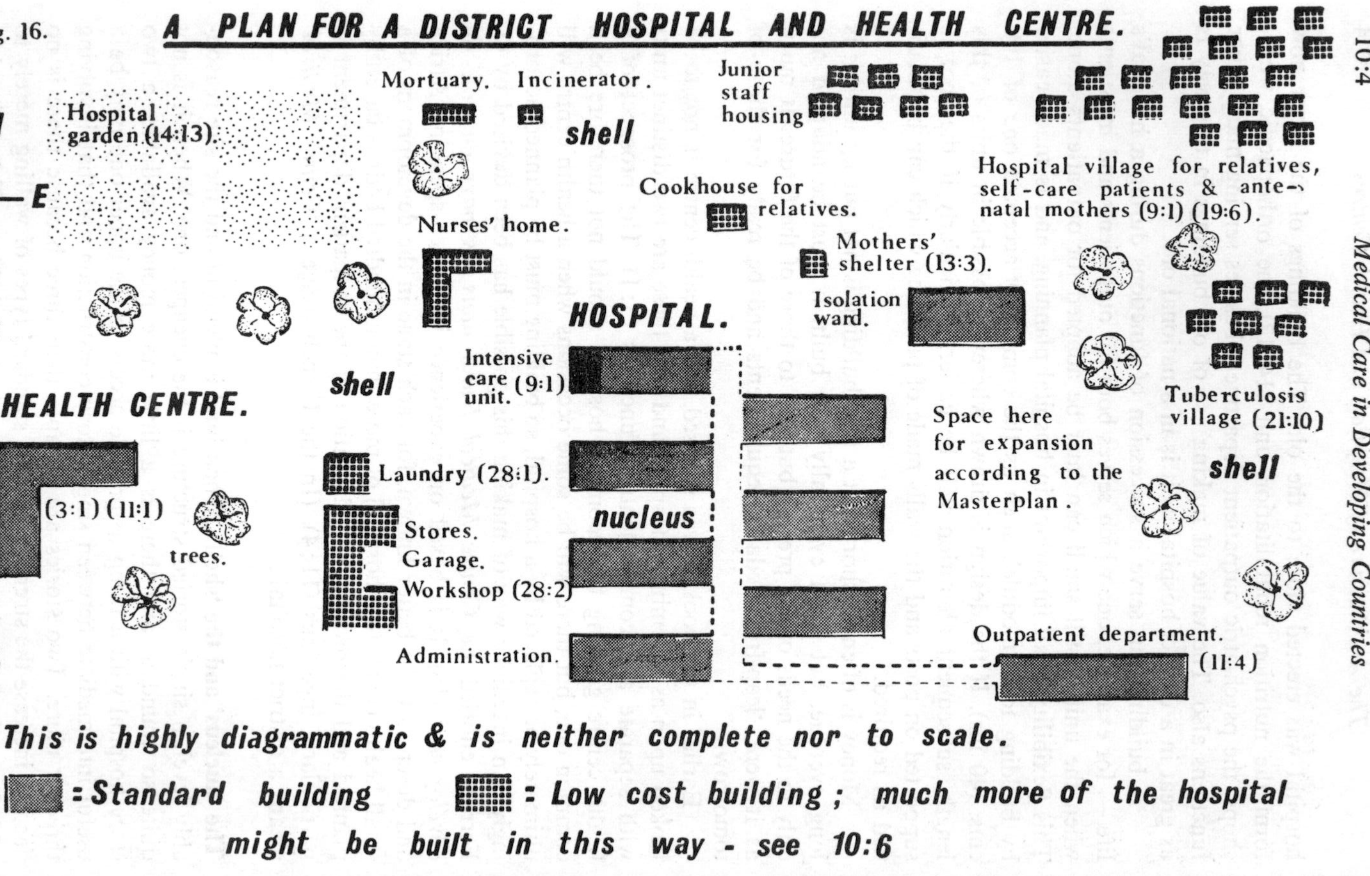
Fig. 16.
A PLAN FOR A DISTRICT HOSPITAL AND HEALTH CENTRE.
N
W
E
S
Hospital garden (14:13).
Mortuary. Incinerator.
shell
Junior staff housing
Cookhouse for relatives.
Hospital village for relatives, self-care patients & ante-natal mothers (9:1) (19:6).
Nurses' home.
Mothers' shelter (13:3).
Isolation ward.
HOSPITAL.
Intensive care (9:1) unit.
shell
HEALTH CENTRE.
Tuberculosis village (21:10)
Space here for expansion according to the Masterplan.
shell
Laundry (28:1).
(3:1) (11:1)
nucleus
trees.
Stores. Garage. Workshop (28:2)
Administration.
Outpatient department. (11:4)
This is highly diagrammatic & is neither complete nor to scale.
:Standard building
: Low cost building; much more of the hospital might be built in this way - see 10:6

Functionally, such a hospital, whether it has one floor or two, has a closely integrated central 'nucleus' supported by a shell of lesser buildings, and is shown diagrammatically in Figure 16. In the nucleus are the wards, the outpatient department, the office, the theatre, the laboratory and records department, the X-ray department and the intensive care unit. Scarce highly paid staff are continually moving from one part of the nucleus to another, and the further apart its buildings are, the more time they waste. It is thus a useful exercise when laying out a new hospital, to measure the distance between important places, and to adjust the plans to minimize the distance travelled, yet without compressing the plan too much and so destroying the general amenity of the site. In none of the 'shell' buildings do senior staff work very much, so little precious time is wasted if they are not close by, and as some are noxious in one way or another, they should be kept well apart.

The buildings of the nucleus are best laid out down each side of a central covered corridor open at both sides. This forms a 'spine' to the building, and another can be added later parallel to the first, so converting the plan into that of an 'H'. Such a system is cheap, compact and easily extended; it also allows the buildings forming the 'ribs' of the spine the same optimal orientation to the sun. Other plans, the 'courtyard', the 'cross' and the 'spider', do not offer these advantages.

At differing distances from the nucleus and separated from one another come the lesser buildings of the 'shell'. These are the isolation ward, the kitchen, the laundry, the mortuary, the stores, the garage, the workshop, the incinerator, the nurses' hostel, housing for the junior staff, the mothers' shelter and the self-care or hospital village (9:4). This village houses the relatives of the sick, those patients capable of self-care and includes the maternity village (19:6). If there is a village or a hostel for tuberculous patients, or a settlement for lepers, these should be separate again. One hospital has even built a profitable motel for the relatives of its richer patients. If the relatives are expected to cook for the patients, a cookhouse for them has also to be provided among the shell buildings.

There is some difference of opinion on the best position for the outpatient department. If it is too close to the wards it may be difficult to control visitors, yet if it is too far away it is inconvenient for the outpatients to make use of such services as the laboratory and the X-ray department.

The site of the doctor's house is critical. If a doctor visits the hospital four times a day, and many visit it more often, he will travel an additional 165 miles each year for every extra hundred yards that separates his home from the hospital. Close proximity thus saves much time.

10:5 **Orientation.** In the tropics east facing windows get the morning sun and those facing west get it in the afternoon; those looking either north or south get almost none. To make the most of this and keep them cool, buildings should therefore be sited with their long axis running east and west letting their corridors, particularly the axial spine, run north and south.

In hot wet cloudy regions, where air movement may be more important than protection from the sun's rays, buildings will be more comfortable if they are turned to catch the breeze as suitable sun screens can always be provided if necessary. Under other conditions there may have to be a compromise between the orientation demanded by the sun, and that best for the prevailing wind; this must however always be used to blow away smoke and smells from the kitchen, the mortuary and the incinerator.

10:6 **Building methods** (the editor). The need for really cheap ways of building hospitals and health centres is a recurrent theme in this symposium, for cheap building is one of the keys to making medical care more widely available in developing countries where capital is so critically scarce. This has been discussed under the Third axiom (1:10b) where medical care was considered in the light of the demands of an intermediate technology. It was pointed out that the amount of medical care that can be provided is determined by the number of medical workers that can be employed, and, that in addition to needing training, each needs the tools of his trade and the buildings in which to work. As far as auxiliaries are concerned training costs are comparatively cheap (1:16), so also is equipment (12:9). Buildings are the really expensive item in the provision of a medical job, and thus of medical care. Just how important building costs are is shown in section 12:3, where they amounted to as much as 83 per cent. of the capital cost of one district hospital.

If the need for cheap buildings is great, how is the cost of buildings compared and what order of difference separates a cheap building from a costly one?

Building costs vary considerably from country to country, and also from one region to another depending on availability of materials and the cost of labour and transport. Also, with the rising standards of living in the developing countries, the cost of building rises steadily, but the present average costs in Uganda are as follows. Expensive buildings cost about 60/- or more a square foot ($72 a sq. metre), and average ones of conventional pattern about 40/- a square foot ($48 a sq. metre). Some mission hospitals manage to build in burnt brick for as little as 10/- a square foot ($12 a sq. metre). When unburnt bricks, '*pisé de terre*', or 'mud-and-wattle-and-whitewash', are used even cheaper buildings can be constructed. Satisfactory structures of this kind can sometimes be built even for as little as 5/- a square foot ($6 a sq. metre). These then are the sort of savings that can be made in building costs, but in being asked to make them the reader must first be convinced that cheap buildings need result in no material diminution in the quality of the medical care going on inside them. What effect does the quality of a building have on the outcome of a patient's illness, either directly or indirectly through its effect on the staff?

There are several misconceptions to be cleared away in attempting to answer this. One is that there are some parts of any hospital which should perhaps be of accepted construction; these include the theatre and possibly the intensive care unit. But cheaper methods can be used for much of the rest of it, especially for the self-care unit (9:5), and there is no reason why a hospital or even a building should be constructed to the same standards throughout. A hospital built in several different ways is a break with tradition, but, as the second axiom (1:9) implies, breaks with tradition may sometimes be necessary.

Another is that cheap buildings should necessarily be badly laid out, for cheap building methods need have little effect on the general plan of a single story district hospital, and the conveniences of an efficient and logical arrangement are likely to be obtainable just as easily with cheap building techniques as they are expensive ones. Although short spans are cheaper to build than wide ones, cheap methods of construction are without any great effect on such matters as the closeness with which patients are packed in a ward, or with the width of verandahs and passages, etc. In effect, cheap buildings do not imply lack of space; the necessary number of square feet of floor area can be provided quite as easily in a mud walled building as in one of standard construction.

In most areas the local mud-built buildings have tiny windows, or sometimes none at all, so there is a natural tendency to associate buildings of this kind with a dim interior. Though window frames are more expensive than an equivalent expanse of wall, a mud-built ward can readily be equipped with as much window space as required. This is likely to be cheaper if window frames are of wood rather than metal. Although mosquito gauze may have medical advantages in a warm climate, there is no medical reason for putting glass in a window, providing it can be closed with wooden shutters. If the eaves of the building are wide, as is necessary with mud walls, these will seldom have to be closed except in very windy weather. The idea that glazed windows are medically necessary in the tropics is a convention imported from cold countries where they are needed to retain heat.

The reader will have been thinking about the walls and the floor. A floor that can be sluiced out is essential in many parts of a hospital, but a mud-built ward can well have a concrete floor, though a mud floor may serve the office or the stores quite satisfactorily. Staff housing forms such a large part of a hospital's cost that it may well be justified to reduce the cost of a dresser's house by building it in mud, after all, this is likely to be what he is used to and it will help in making it possible to employ more of them. Mud walls can be plastered with cement and cement can be painted, they can also be plastered with mud, and white-washed as often as monthly if necessary.

Lastly, there is the morale of the staff, it benefits nobody to work under conditions of squalor. But mud buildings do not imply squalor, nor do they imply dirt; they can well mean trim wards, frequently scrubbed, patched and whitewashed, and carefully kept in good repair by someone whose special task this is. At the mission hospital from which this section is written there are tin-roofed, unburnt mud brick buildings which look as tidy as they presumably did when they were built fifty years before. Admittedly the squalid tumbledown houses seen in most tropical villages are built by some of the very methods that are being advocated, but the reason for their untidiness is that they were probably badly built anyway, even according to their own standards of construction, and have certainly been badly maintained ever since. Buildings well constructed in unburnt brick, '*pisé de terre*', 'mud-wattle-and-whitewash', or whatever other cheap method is used, and roofed with corrugated sheeting, need not be squalid, provided they are well planned, properly put together, and kept in good repair. When this is so they are difficult to tell from brick ones. Maintenance is critical, and it may mean employing extra staff. But there is no difficutly about this, because suitable artisans need not be highly paid. Reckoning that one of them will earn £100 ($280) a year, this sum represents the 5 per cent. interest that might be expected on a capital investment of £2,000 ($5,600). Thus, if this sum can be saved on the capital costs of a hospital, one man can be hired indefinitely whole time to look after it. Even a 7 per cent. reduction in the cost of the hospital building in Chapter Twelve would have freed enough capital to provide one man's wages to maintain it. Considering that a 50 per cent reduction may be possible (20/- instead of 40/- a square foot), it will be seen that cheap building methods can both provide for a substantial net saving and take account of increased maintenance costs. When health centres have to be maintained, the staff could well be both expected and taught to do at least the simpler aspects of this themselves.

It is for health centres and district hospitals, rather than for regional and national ones, that cheap methods of construction are so greatly needed and so very appropriate. Regional and particularly national hospitals become inconveniently spread out if not built in several stories, and therefore they have to be of standard construction. Following from this, it is thus rural rather than urban building that is suited to these methods. Looked at overall, health centres and district hospitals should in aggregate form the largest fraction of the total buildings of a health service. Thus Uganda has one national teaching hospital, four regional ones, about 25 district hospitals (excluding missions), and she should have no less than 400 health centres, even at the rate of one for 20,000 people (3:2). But, even allowing for the differing sizes of the units considered, a large fraction of the total volume of building in a health service is suitable for construction by cheap methods.

There is another side of cheap buildings — they can be built by the people themselves, mostly from readily available local materials. In Zambia for instance the local co-operatives are regularly entrusted with minor health building in the rural areas. If the local authority want a health centre or a district hospital they could be given plans and manuals /6/ and told to build to a good standard, either all of it, or their share of it, after which the health department would be prepared to complete, equip, and staff it. If the local labour can be voluntary, this will be of great assistance in creating capital in the form of building where there was none before.

With the exception of certain mission hospitals, which have of necessity led the way, the medical profession and the educated public in developing countries are deeply committed psychologically to the 'white corridors' attitude to hospital construction, and any different approach requires radical rethinking. This is an enormous impediment to the expansion of district hospital and health centre services in developing countries, to the provision of some services for everyone rather than unnecessarily lavish accommodation for the few.

The cheap buildings that are being advocated so strongly are in one sense the very negation of architecture, which is the reason why this section is written by the editor and not by an architect. Yet they are in another sense completely in line with its true spirit — the creation of buildings perfectly adapted to their purpose, which in this case is the housing of medical facilities under conditions of poverty.

A hospital or health centre is often judged on its looks, and, though smart buildings may reassure an anxious minister or placate a clamoring electorate, they do not always mean good medicine — this book ends with some better criteria for judging these units than the elegance of their architecture.

7 **Prefabrication.** Because prefabricated buildings do little to raise employment, especially if they are imported, and because they are likely to be

less economical than the methods that have just been advocated, buildings of this kind should be thought of as being primarily for emergency

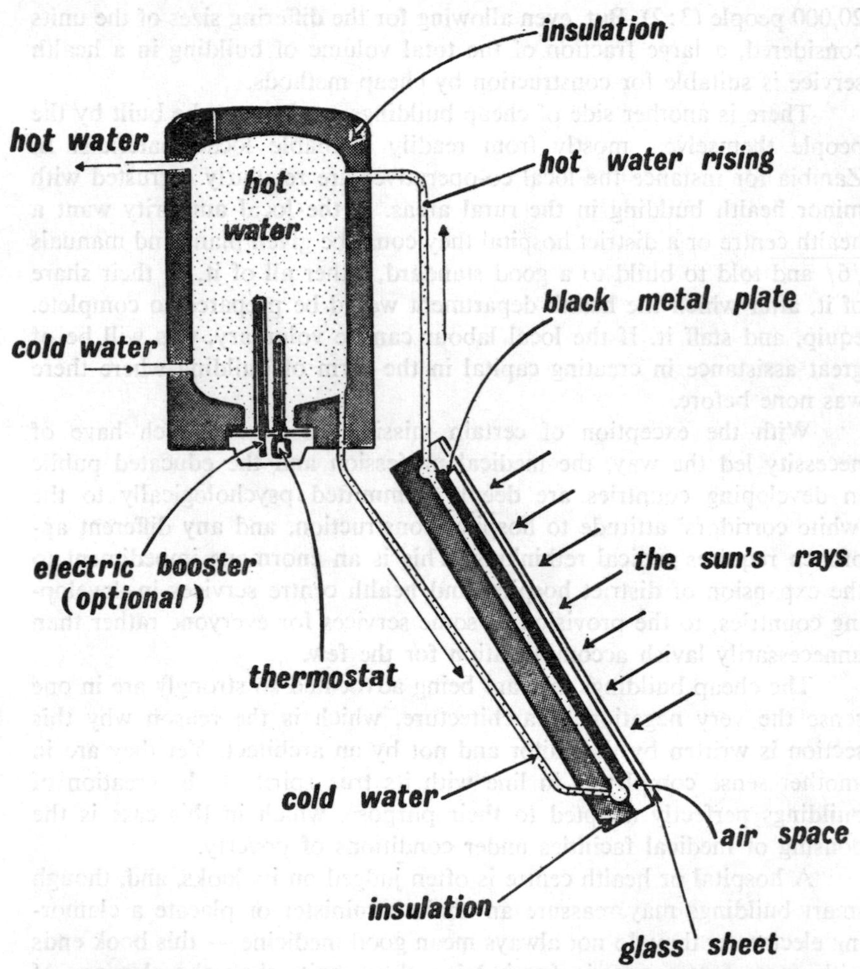

use, or for places where local building materials are not available. Prefabricated buildings are made by many manufacturers, but those supplied by one of them (COS) arrive packed in flat crates complete with all fittings and a book of easy instructions. They are of heavy gauge aluminium sheets with straight sided 4 cm. corrugations. Such sheets are rigid enough to support the roof without the need for a separate framework, and in the middle of Africa buildings of this type have been erected for as little as 20/- a square foot ($24 a sq. metre) — less than the cost of much traditional construction. A whole hospital can be bought complete.

Only a really solid building will keep out noise, but aluminium is a good heat reflector and its thermal qualities can be improved further by lining the building with sheets of expanded polystyrene or other insulation.

8 **Solar water heating.** Hot water is perhaps a luxury, but if the sun's rays can be used to provide the heat, it becomes more economic because there are no running costs. Techniques have recently become much more efficient and Figure 17 shows how a black-painted metal plate on the roof of a building can, in suitable climates, collect enough heat to provide a useful quantity of hot water (MIR). Such a plate is set at a slight slope, covered by a glass sheet and backed by an insulator. To it is brazed a small bore brass pipe; the water in this pipe collects heat from the plate and rises by convection to be stored in a tank. This device is satisfactory in a wide range of tropical climates and collects heat radiated from the clouds as well as that direct from the sun. Where dull weather might mean a period of cold water an electric booster can be fitted, but this is a luxury. Initial expenses are comparatively low, and a domestic plant costs only about £100 ($280). In Kenya such a plant pays for itself in as little as two years.

The rural doctor his own architect.

9 **'Do it yourself'.** Most buildings, particularly of those of the nucleus are jobs for an architect, but there are others which need not be, and it may be a choice between not having a building at all or having something which will do. The rural doctor is therefore encouraged to get permission from his superiors, to enlist the help of the local chief, to obtain some money from the local authority and to construct the cheap accommodation that his hospital or health centres need. Volunteers can build very useful structures, and all sorts of buildings will probably be required. Housing for relatives or the junior staff, a mothers' shelter and under-fives clinics are some of the buildings that are so often in short supply.

One of the glories of practice in the rural areas is this 'factotum' quality and a little building is an important part of it. Not all doctors are 'handy', but many of the older hospitals, particularly those of the missions, would not exist at all but for the ingenuity of their staff. In its proper proportion, the 'do-it-yourself' tradition is thus a valuable one.

The doctor's role in it is that of architect or 'clerk of works' and, as in other spheres, it is his task to initiate and organize the work of his helpers.

10:10 **Methods and manuals for the amateur.** There is an admirable series of cheap, well illustrated manuals for the amateur builder in the tropics /6/. These are designed for the villager, and, with the classic volume by R. F. Longland /94/, they should enable the novice to start work.

Mud-and-wattle and sun dried brick are both well known constructional methods, but some other simple techniques also be useful.

'Pisé de terre' is carefully selected earth mixed to a stiff paste with a little chopped straw and water. This is then firmly rammed between strong temporary wooden shuttering, like that used for reinforced concrete, and left to solidify before this shuttering is removed. Because no cement is employed, a wall of this kind must, like unburnt brick, be well protected from driving rains by verandahs or deeply overhanging eaves. Both the top and the bottom of these walls also need protection with good damp proof courses.

'Stabilized earth' employs soil mixed to a paste with water and 5-10 per cent. of cement. This mixture is then cast into blocks on the site, either by hand or machine, in the same way as concrete blocks. The common East African 'murram' and West African 'swish' both serve well, and if well made with sufficient cement, they will support a three story building for many years.

Precast concrete post construction is another useful building method. The posts are used to support the roof, and the panels between them filled in with any of a variety of cheap local materials, such as mud-and-wattle, thatch, 'tin', or asbestos sheeting. Such a building is cheap, the roof stays up, and the panels can be renewed as required.

Not only can several constructional techniques be used in the same hospital, but several can with advantage be used in the same building. Thus, the lower courses and the arches of a wall can be burnt brick set in cement mortar, while the rest of it can be sun dried brick set in mud.

10:11a **Termites.** This is an important and complex problem, particularly in cheaper buildings and it is difficult to provide detailed advice. The local pest control firm will probably be the best source of information, but there are some general principles that may be useful.

Termites like moisture and only work in the dark — see therefore that no unnecessary water lies around the building, that waste water is discharged some way away, that there are no leaking pipes, and that the lower walling is so solid that it is difficult for termites to enter. Don't let the builders leave bits of wood lying around in the soil which may attract termites to the building above.

If possible, provide a termite proof layer right through the building just above the ground level; a good barrier is made by an 8 cm. (3 inch) layer of good concrete which forms the floor of the building and extends across the foundation to project outside them an inch all round. The walls are later built on top of this layer, taking care that they are *exactly* positioned over the foundations.

In areas where the termite is well established, and some of the precautions above are too expensive, treat the foundation trenches, and all the ground on which the building is to stand, with 4½ litres (1 gallon) of 0.3% Dieldrin emulsion per square metre and rake this in to a depth of 15 cms. (6 ins.). To make this even more secure, dig a trench 40 cms. (15 ins.) deep and the same width all round the building, and apply the same solution to the trench at the rate of 2 litres (½ gallon) to each metre (3 ft.) of its length. Replace the soil and treat this with the emulsion in the same way.

1b **'Mud-wattle-Dieldrin-and-whitewash'.** Even when untreated good mud walled buildings can last fifteen years and more. Nobody yet knows how long they will last if they are protected from termites by the incorporation of a residual insecticide actually in the mud of the walls and the foundations beneath them. It is likely however that insecticides like Dieldrin have completely changed the economics of cheap buildings, which can now be expected to last very much longer. Not only can Dieldrin be used with mud-and-wattle, it can also be used with *'pisé de terre'*, and stabilized earth, etc. The local pest control firm will provide the necessary Dieldrin for these operations, its cost on a new building being only -/30 per square foot ($.36 per sq. metre). As it is underneath the floor and the foundations no harm can come from its toxic effects, while it is so stable that it protects the building above indefinitely. Such danger as does occur from its use arises while it is being applied so Dieldrin solutions should be treated with care.

A recent suggestion from Australia for termite proofing concrete with Dieldrin may prove of great practical value in the construction of low-cost housing. It has been shown by the Division of Entomology, Canberra, that a durable barrier is made when the mixing water in both normal and 'no-fines' concrete is replaced by 0.5% emulsion of Dieldrin (i.e. 2½ lbs. of 20% emulsifiable concentrate in 10 gallons of water). It is not yet known how long this will remain effective, but it allows the use of less well compacted concrete for slabs and checks the movement of termites upwards through small cracks.

Not only can new buildings be treated, but old infested ones can also, and their life prolonged indefinitely by piercing holes through the floor and injecting Dieldrin solution into the ground underneath.

10:12 **Some constructional hints.** Use arches to support the roof, for they are both elegant and economical, and can even be incorporated in a mud wall if the arch itself is mortared with cement or, as in West Africa, reinforced with lengths of timber from the fan-palm.

Use tiles for small spans only and make sure that any roof of asbestos sheet is firmly supported, because if this moves, these sheets will crack. Because roof spans are more expensive than mud walls, small buildings of this kind are likely to be cheaper than larger ones.

Be careful about the quality of timber, sheeting and bricks. Timber must be seasoned, free from termites and preferably pressure impregnated. Sheeting should be of a good gauge (e.g. 26 or 29) — if it is too thin it bends easily and if badly galvanized it soon rusts. In default of more refined testing methods, leave sample bricks and blocks in the sun all day, and in a bucket of water all night for at least a week. Accept the batch as fit for the building only if these specimens retain their shape and weight.

Mud walls should be finished with whitewash, either straight on the mud, or on top of a mud and sand or cowdung and sand plaster, which are the best cheap surfacings for these walls. Paint soon flakes off a mud surface. A cement plaster does too, unless it is bonded to the walls, either with a mesh of fine wire netting or, as is commonly done in Buganda, with a layer of reeds. The external corners of mud or cowdung plastered walls need protection, so do places where they might be rubbed by furniture, such as hospital beds for example.

Hang cupboards, shelves, equipment and working surfaces on the walls themselves, so leaving the floor underneath free to be swept more easily. This will be simpler if provision is made for their support while the wall is actually being built. Build benches into the brickwork during its construction, by incorporating battens going right through the wall to which planks can later be screwed and form a bench either side of the wall. Make these benches 40 cms. (16 ins.) from the floor, the height most villagers prefer, and incorporate them in every suitable wall, particularly those of the outpatient department.

10:13 **Grace and amenity.** Though it is difficult to achieve beauty, it should always be possible to achieve amenity — many small points contribute to the comfort of the patients and none are too small to be forgotten.

Provide outpatients with shade in which to wait, something to sit on, a supply of drinking water and convenient latrines. If the hospital is a reasonable size, see if someone cannot be persuaded to open a teashop or canteen to serve them.

Children appreciate amenities as well as adults, so see if space can be found for a playground with a swing and a climbing frame. Such a playground will require a latrine, and it may be best to provide one of the deep trench kind specially built for children. This will need a squatting plate containing a hole small enough for there to be no danger of anybody falling through, say 20 x 12 cms.

The graciousness of a building depends as much on the proportions and layout of the spaces enclosed, as it does on the structures which do the enclosing. This 'sculpturing of space' is one of the architectural arts, and while planning, it is well to think carefully about the proportions of any spaces enclosed, be they rooms, courtyards, or merely the spaces between buildings. When laying out a hospital give it some focal point, such as an entrance arch, a waiting hall, or an avenue.

The 'hospital garden' and its usefulness in health education has been stressed elsewhere (6:8). It should be planted with the crops that patients can grow in their own fields or *shambas* to improve their nutrition, as well as that of their families. Because such a garden is an agricultural as well as a medical endeavour, the Agricultural Department may be prepared to help with it as part of their own extension drive. Plant flowers, grow trees for shade and ornament, and so that they may be mature when needed, plant them where the 'master development plan' shows that they will later be wanted. A hospital should be a gay and pleasant place, so obtain educational posters, hang pictures and get someone to paint murals. There may be no money for these extras in the ordinary vote, but it may be possible to find a benefactor. Try approaching a few of the rich shopkeepers of the area, and remind them that their names will not be forgotten.

In the quest for functional efficiency don't forget that a hospital is more than a place in which to cure and be cured, it is also a human habitation — somewhere to be secure, comfortable and content. Hospitals differ greatly in the feeling they impart, their ambience, their general atmosphere, this almost intangible 'something'. Such an emanation is the sum of many things; the loyalty and devotion of *all* the staff contribute most of it, but every little detail plays its part. Neat notices, flowers, tidy grounds, clean wards and passages all have an effect and are worth striving after, for they add to the lives of those who heal and are healed within a hospital.

Chapter Eleven

THE OUTPATIENT DEPARTMENT

Maurice King

11:1 **The work of the outpatient department.** When the pattern of illness in a community is looked at as a whole, it will be seen that comparatively few diseases are severe enough to confine the sufferer to his bed. Most of them permit him to walk about, and, if given the choice, many patients prefer to be up and around. In addition to this bed rest is now coming to be considered of less value in some diseases than was formerly the case (21:10). Because of the great volume of ambulant disease in most communities, an efficient outpatient department is clearly of critical importance. This is increased by the cheapness of outpatient as compared with inpatient care (12:6). But besides treating outpatients of the traditional type, this department also serves another useful purpose; it is the place where 'self-care' patients are often best given their daily treatment (9:5).

An outpatient department is usually thought of as being part of a hospital, but general outpatients are also seen by health centres. There are thus many aspects of outpatient care which apply equally to both institutions. But one important difference between them is the differing scale of their activities; so many more outpatients are apt to seek attention from a hospital. It is this problem of scale, the vast numbers of patients to be seen, that is the critical determinant of outpatient practice. But before considering this in more detail, it should be mentioned that a health centre has been defined as a unit which supplies all the medical needs of a family other than those which can only be supplied by a hospital (3:1). Health centres should therefore provide all the ordinary outpatient services, and be so sited that they can relieve hospital outpatient departments of all but their most specialized functions. Ideally therefore, outpatient departments should only see patients referred to them by health centres; but in practice the ideal seldom happens, and most outpatient departments have to see anyone who comes to them. Health centre outpatient practice has already been considered in detail in Chapter Three and will not therefore be considered any further here.

The numbers of people seeking outpatient care would not matter so much if there were staff and facilities in proportion to the demand. Usually, there are not, and doctors in particular are almost always critically scarce. Not only this, but the services that outpatients require are both complex and varied. There are 'general outpatients' with a multitude of different conditions, there are children as well as antenatal and postnatal mothers. There are also cases with diseases of particular frequency and importance, such as tuberculosis and malnutrition. Several special clinics may therefore be required which have often to be organized in buildings of poor design.

The key to making the best of the facilities available is a proper appreciation of the role of the doctor and the auxiliary. Nowhere is *the doctor's role as organizer, teacher and consultant to a team of auxiliaries* more important than it is in the outpatient department (Eighth axiom 1:15). The only way in which huge numbers of patients can be seen is for medical assistants, and even dressers, to see most of them. Some means must be found whereby the common, mild and easily recognizable complaints can be dealt with by these auxiliaries, without their wasting the scarce time of a doctor.

There are medical services which require that all patients be seen by a doctor no matter for how short a time. Pressure must be exerted to try to get such regulations altered and a sorting system instituted. This should make it possible for a doctor to spend not less than a minimum of, say, ten minutes on each previously screened or sorted case. Depending on his experience he will of course be able to see cases much more rapidly, but this should not generally be his job.

Before considering sorting systems in more detail there are two things to be stressed. The first is the value of separating children from adults and organizing an under-fives clinic after the manner described in section 16:6. This incidentally serves as a fine example of the general principles of organizing outpatient services. The right use of auxiliaries, the principle of sorting and the value of simple standardized regimes of treatment are all well demonstrated, as too is the importance of carefully designed records.

The second is to see if it is possible to reduce the load on the outpatient department. Thus there is a general impression that those living near a hospital are seen there rather more frequently than perhaps they should be. This is supported by the outpatient care gradient in Figure 6 (2:7). There it will be seen that, at zero distance from the hospital the average outpatient attends about six times yearly, or about once in two months. Quite apart from the question as to whether or not this is excessive, it is certainly fairer to discourage those living in the vicinity by first attending to those who come from a distance. Where record clerks ask for the patients' address, this is easily arranged.

In some hospitals the same excessive attendance is also true of policemen, prison officers and other government employees as well as schoolboys, all of whom frequently attend with only minor complaints. Many want light duty or time off work, and there are departments where they form as much as a third or even half of the entire outpatient load. Their employers and teachers complain about the hours spent at the hospital, and doctors about their wasted time. This unnecessary work can be reduced by restricting routine cases in these categories to special clinics that are held only once a week, say government employees on Wednesdays between 2 and 3 p.m., and schoolboys from 3 p.m. onwards. Urgent cases have to be seen at any time, but if they turn out not to be quite so urgent, they can be referred to this clinic (3).

11:2 **Sorting systems.** There are several ways in which patients can be sorted or screened, and the particular method adopted will have to depend upon the staff available and the way in which the building is designed.

The simplest situation is that where no suitable auxiliary staff are available whatever. Under these conditions the best thing a doctor can do is to stand his patients in a queue, and quickly screen or sort them himself. He can then rapidly prescribe treatment for the straightforward ones, and examine the others in more detail afterwards.

When suitable dressers are available they should be made the most of, for many patients attend with such common and obvious conditions that dressers can readily diagnose and treat them. These diseases will vary from area to area and from time to time and include such things as tropical ulcers, guinea worms, minor cuts and sepsis, scabies etc. Because of this regional variation, it will be necessary to analyse the disease pattern of the department, to work out rule-of-thumb diagnoses and treatments for the diseases dressers can deal with, and to teach these dressers accordingly. They will then be able to select suitable cases from waiting queues and treat them on their own. Figure 18 shows them acting in this way and diverting cases from a queue, though in this case the queue is that waiting to see a medical assistant and not a doctor. When a dresser, a medical assistant and a doctor all work together in this way, sorting proceeds in the three stages shown in this figure.

When there is a medical assistant available there are two ways in which he can work. One is for him to work with a clerk to form a 'sorting centre' as shown in Figures 19 and 20. He can also work on his own in

Fig. 18.

A THREE STAGE SORTING SYSTEM.

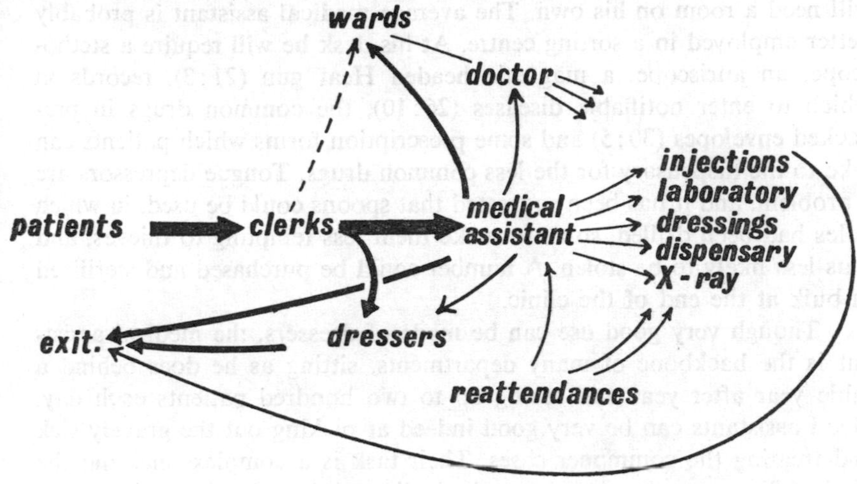
wards
doctor
injections
laboratory
dressings
dispensary
X - ray
patients
clerks
medical assistant
exit.
dressers
reattendances

Fig. 19.

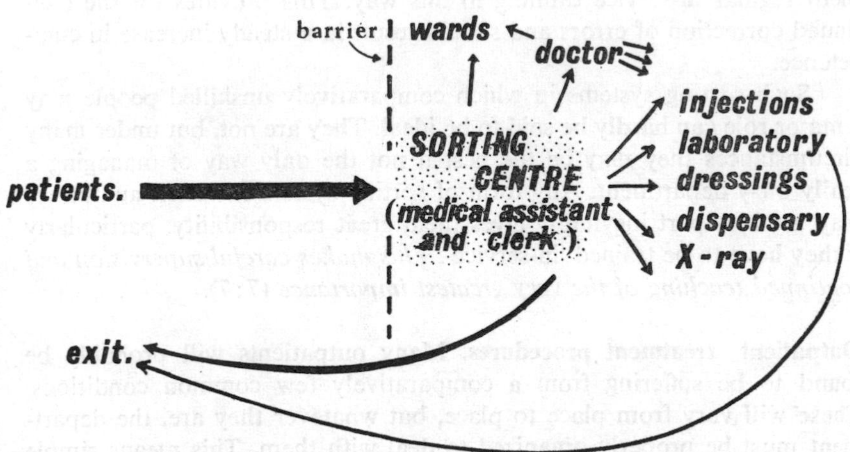
THE SORTING CENTRE.
barrier
wards
doctor
injections
laboratory
dressings
dispensary
X - ray
patients.
SORTING CENTRE
(medical assistant and clerk).
exit.

an office like the doctor. This has been shown diagramatically in Figure 18. No firm answer can be given about which is the best arrangement; but the closer a medical assistant approaches a doctor in skill the more use will he make of the facilities of an examination couch, and the more he will need a room on his own. The average medical assistant is probably better employed in a sorting centre. At his desk he will require a stethoscope, an auriscope, a magnetic headed Heaf gun (21:3), records on which to enter notifiable diseases (26:10), the common drugs in prepacked envelopes (30:5) and some prescription forms which patients can take to the dispensary for the less common drugs. Tongue depressors are a problem, and it has been suggested that spoons could be used, in which holes had been drilled, so as to make them less tempting to thieves, and thus less likely to be stolen. A number could be purchased and sterilized in bulk at the end of the clinic.

Though very good use can be made of dressers, the medical assistant is the backbone of many departments, sitting as he does behind a table year after year and seeing up to two hundred patients each day. Good assistants can be very good indeed at picking out the gravely sick and treating the commoner cases. Their task is a complex one, and the kind of diagnoses they have to make is discussed further in section 12:5. Considerable diagnostic ability is required of medical assistants, but where are they to learn it? Unfortunately, no really suitable books have yet been written, nor has anybody invented a workable rule-of-thumb diagnostic scheme. The only practical method of teaching them is for the doctor seeing the referred patients to let his medical assistants, and perhaps his dressers also, sit in on some of his consultations, and so give them regular in-service training in this way. This provides for the continued correction of errors and should result in a steady increase in competence.

Such sorting systems in which comparatively unskilled people play a major role can hardly be said to be ideal. They are not, but under many circumstances they may be the best if not the only way of managing a really busy department. Any form of sorting system in which auxiliaries play a major part inevitably gives them great responsibility, particularly if they have to be trained 'in-service'. *This makes careful supervision and continued teaching of the very greatest importance* (7:7).

11:3a **Outpatient treatment procedures.** Many outpatients will probably be found to be suffering from a comparatively few common conditions. These will vary from place to place, but whatever they are, the department must be properly organized to deal with them. This means simple standardized treatments, appropriately trained staff, readily available drugs and apparatus, suitable records and stationery, and if need be a

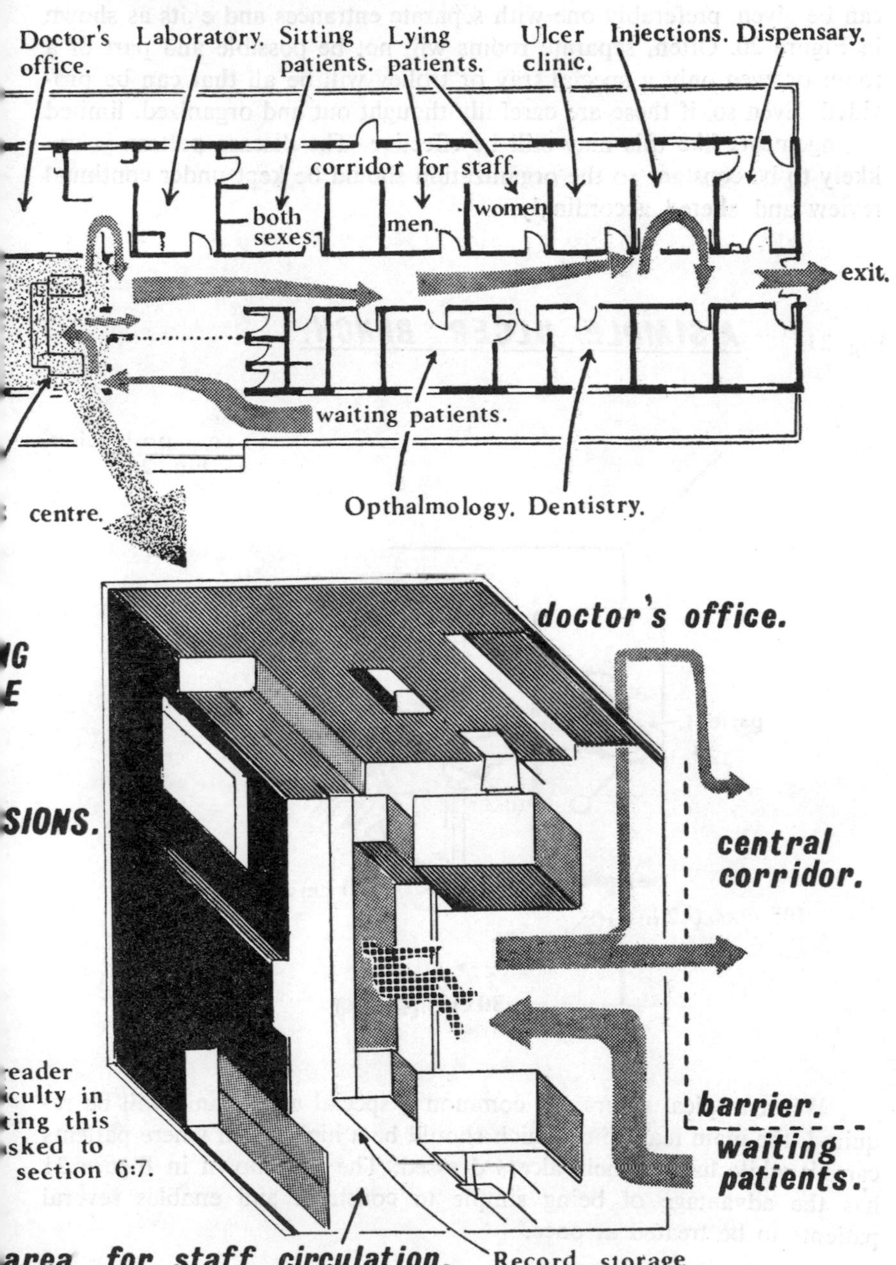
AN OUTPATIENT DEPARTMENT.
E PLAN. (after G. Ferrand)
Doctor's office.
Laboratory.
Sitting patients.
Lying patients.
Ulcer clinic.
Injections.
Dispensary.
corridor for staff.
both sexes.
men.
women.
exit.
waiting patients.
Opthalmology.
Dentistry.
centre.
doctor's office.
G
E
SIONS.
central corridor.
barrier.
waiting patients.
reader
iculty in
ting this
sked to
section 6:7.
area for staff circulation.
Record storage

separate room for each condition. Some departments will need a 'scabies room', others a special place for dealing with guinea worms. If children are being seen, then rehydration (15:15) and immunization rooms will be wanted (17:5). A room will also be wanted where penicillin injections can be given, preferably one with separate entrances and exits as shown in Figure 20. Often, separate rooms will not be possible and part of a room or even only a special tray or trolley will be all that can be provided. Even so, if these are carefully thought out and organized, limited arrangements like this may still be effective. The disease pattern is unlikely to be constant so the organization should be kept under continual review and altered accordingly.

Fig. 21. **A SIMPLE ULCER BENCH.**

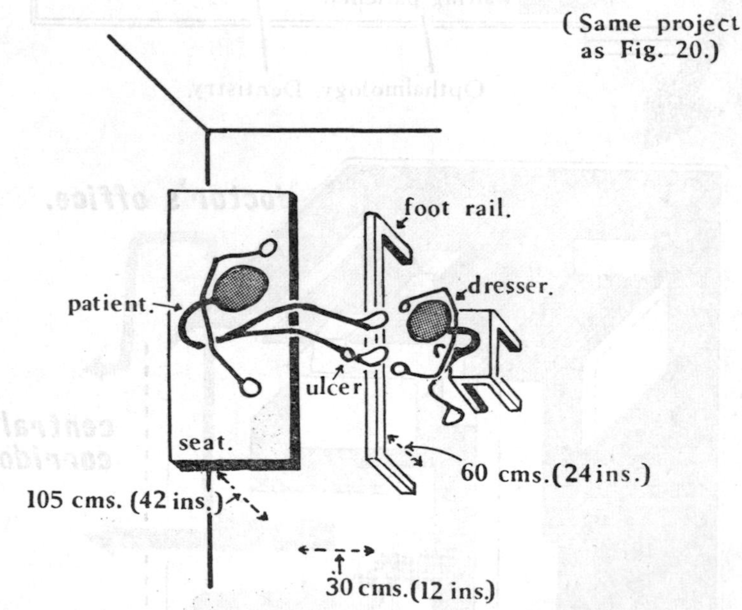

When tropical ulcers are common a special ulcer clinic will be required, the main feature of which should be a high bench where patients can sit while having their ulcers dressed. The one shown in Figure 21 has the advantage of being simple to construct and enables several patients to be treated at once.

Some dressings, examinations and treatments have to be given while the patient is lying down, but most of them can be given while patients sit. Sitting patients of both sexes can be attended to in the same room, but lying patients have to be separated. Because of this, big departments may find it practicable to have one big room for the seated patients of both sexes, and two separate smaller ones for the recumbent men and women. This arrangement is shown in Figure 20.

No hard and fast rules decide what can be done in an outpatient department and what can only be done in the wards. Some procedures, lumbar puncture for example, are normally thought of as only being done on inpatients, yet it may be very inconvenient to admit the patient for this procedure. When this is so it is very useful to be able to do a lumbar puncture in the outpatient department on young children who might have meningitis (13:10). If the fluid is purulent the diagnosis is likely to be straightforward and can be confirmed with a film stained by Gram's method (24:13). When the fluid is not purulent Pandy's test (24:29) and a quick cell count only take a moment and can, if necessary, easily be done by the doctor himself.

Even a rudimentary outpatient laboratory or side room will be found very convenient. Many of the techniques in Chapter Twenty-four are likely to be required, and it may be easier to do them on the spot rather than have the patient wait at the main laboratory.

The patient's time. A patient's time is valuable to him, so that anything which will speed the flow of patients through the department is well worth the effort. The importance of reducing the work of the records clerk is discussed in section 26:10, the usefulness of patients keeping their own records in polythene envelopes in section 26:5, the use of rubber stamps in section 24:4, albeit in another connection, and the value of a recognized system of shorthand clinical symbols in section 26:11. All these points can save time in the outpatient department, as can the use of prepacked drugs and medicines on the assistant's table, for this makes it unnecessary for patients to queue at the dispensary. If fees have to be collected, a cash register is another valuable time saver. A common cause of wasted time is for medical assistants to keep their own record ledgers. As they see so many patients in a day this unnecessary clerical work adds up to a significant proportion of their time. This writing should be done by clerks, so that medical assistants can use their scarce skills more profitably.

It is often difficult to get patients to reattend on the correct day. When this is so the use of a set of rubber stamps with the days of the week in the vernacular may be useful, the patients being handed a slip of paper with the appropriate day of reattendance stamped upon it.

11:4 **Buildings.** Because an outpatient department is usually crowded with people who flow all round it and so impede the smooth running of the hospital, it is best sited a little apart from the wards. There are two general approaches to planning it, but both depend on the need to separate the staff from milling crowds of patients.

The first is to let the patients wait on wide verandahs outside the building while the staff remain inside. Under this system patients present at hatches for such things as records and drugs, and are allowed to circulate through limited parts of the building only, preferably through adjacent doors for their easy entry and exit. Such an arrangement is cheap, it is possibly the best system for comparatively small units, and has been termed the 'Fort Plan'. In Figure 22 it is shown in two sizes, one, a very small department indeed (A) and the other, a department large enough to provide a central courtyard in which the staff may circulate (B).

The second and more usual method is to keep both patients and staff inside the building, to provide them with separate means of circulation, and to erect some form of barrier to control patient entry. The control point in this barrier is the sorting centre. This system can be arranged in several different ways. One of these is that used in the under-fives clinic in Chapter Sixteen (Figure 34, 16:12). Here the clerks sit behind a desk and let mothers through gates in a barrier. This gives them access to a passage along which they pass to the nurses' rooms. The clerks supervise the mothers and weigh the children, but real sorting is done by the nurses.

The relationship of the barrier and the sorting centre to the building as a whole is planned differently in the outpatient department shown in Figure 20. This is derived from French experience in West Africa and is very ingenious (10:3). The patients arrive, queue on the verandah, and are seen by a medical assistant in a sorting centre. They then pass through a barrier into the central corridor. Some are directed to see the doctor whose consulting room closely adjoins the sorting centre; most, however, pass to the several clinics which run the length of the building. Staff access is provided down one side of the department by an interconnecting passage between the clinics, and provision is made for it to grow by the addition of more rooms at one end.

A type of outpatient department which should be mentioned is that built at Bikumbi in Tanzania and shown in Figure 22c. Here a long linear building has, as it were, been snapped in half and its two halves put together to form an 'A'. This 'A' has then been roofed over, a records department placed at its apex and sliding doors provided along its base. The waiting hall thus formed is of interesting and elegant proportion, it can be blacked out for educational lantern shows and, since no additional walling was required, it was cheap to construct. A feature that is not

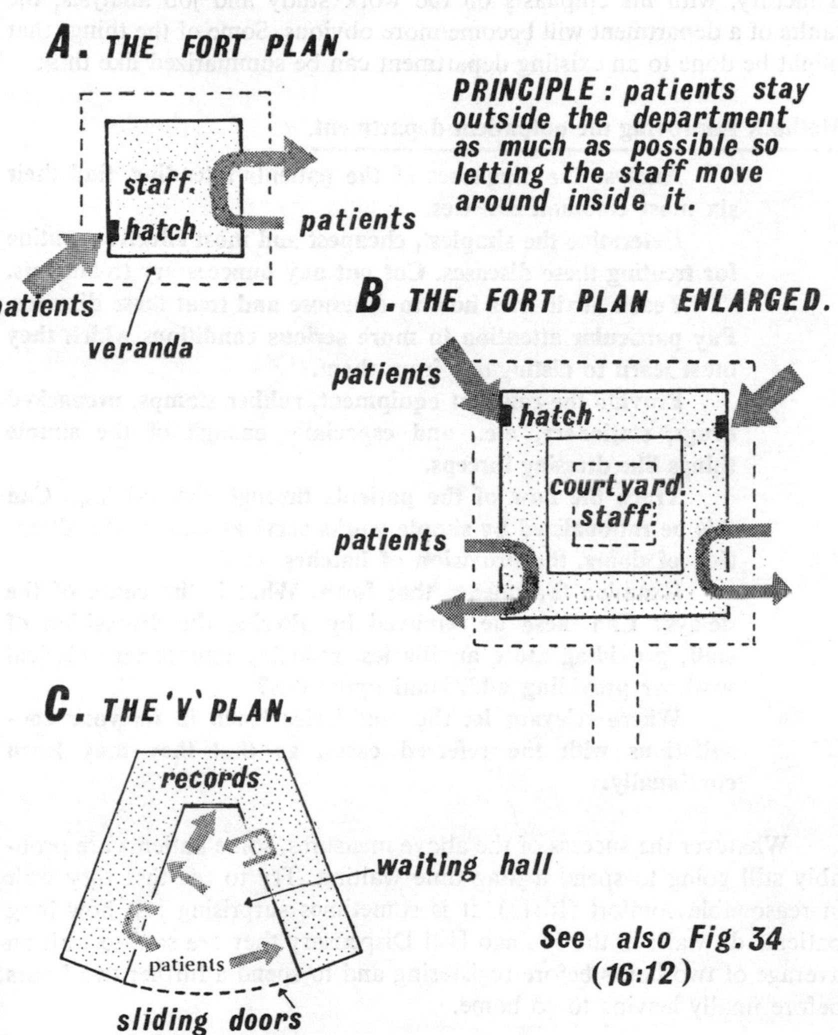

shown in this diagram is the provision made to post the patients' records from one room to another by slots made in the walls. No final conclusion can be given as to which is the best system, but that shown in Figure 20 is the most carefully worked out. Its great disadvantage is the large numbers of patients who tend to crowd the central corridor of the building.

11:5 **Improving an outpatient department.** An outpatient department can be likened to a factory or production line for making cured outpatients. Looked at like this, from the point of view of the production manager in a factory, with his emphasis on the work study and job analysis, the faults of a department will become more obvious. Some of the things that might be done to an existing department can be summarized like this:

Method: Improving the outpatient department.

Analyse the diagnoses of the patients attending, find their six most common diseases.

Determine the simplest, cheapest and most effective routine for treating these diseases. Cut out any unnecessary treatments.

Teach auxiliaries how to diagnose and treat these diseases. Pay particular attention to more serious conditions which they must learn to distinguish from them.

Provide the relevant equipment, rubber stamps, prepacked drugs, stationery, etc., and especially enough of the simple things like dressing forceps.

Trace the flow of the patients through the building. Can this be rationalized by simple works services such as the alteration of doors, the provision of hatches, etc.?

Examine the queues that form. What is the cause of the delays? Can these be removed by altering the disposition of staff, providing more auxiliaries, reducing unnecessary clerical work or providing additional apparatus?

Where relevant let the auxiliaries listen in on your consultations with the referred cases, so that they may learn continually.

Whatever the success of the above measures, some patients are probably still going to spend a long time waiting. Try to see that they wait in reasonable comfort (10:13). It is sometimes surprising just how long patients do wait; in the Mulago Hill Dispensary they are said to wait an average of two hours before registering and to spend a further two hours before finally leaving to go home.

Chapter Twelve

THE ECONOMY OF A DISTRICT HOSPITAL

Richard Jolly, Fabian Kamunvi, Maurice King, Paul Sebuliba

1 **The value of economic surveys.** 'The greatest return in human welfare from the least expense in money and skill' — this is one of the major themes of a book whose every page is dedicated to extracting the most services from the least resources (Third axiom 1:10). It would thus hardly be complete without an analysis of just how money and skills are actually being used in at least one district hospital. If therefore the following pages seem cluttered with detail, it can only be pointed out that money and resources are the ultimate determinants of medical care, and that the economic habit of thought is thus a valuable one.

The hospital chosen for study was that run by the Buganda Government at Mityana in Uganda. No fees are collected at this hospital and it was deliberately selected as representing the simplest possible unit that still provides the essential features of a hospital. Data were collected so as to give answers to the following questions:

Just where is the money going?

How much of the total medical expenses are provided by the state, and how much by the patients?

Where is the staff effort going?

If more resources could be provided, how could they best be used?

How equitably are the services provided by the hospital distributed among the surrounding community?

Most of these questions are answered here but the last one has already been considered in the second chapter (2:7-11). The answers to these questions are not so obvious as might at first appear. Indeed, one of the most important conclusions from this study is that quite small investigations on these lines might pay large dividends in other places.

Some of the data were collected from the files, inventories and stores catalogues of the Medical Department, while that about individual patients was gathered on extensive proformas by a final year Muganda medical student. A random sample of the outpatients (217) and almost all the inpatients (202) attending the hospital in June 1964 were interviewed individually, the data about them being recorded on proformas and subsequently transferred to punched cards for mechanical analysis (26:12). Some of the data are contained in the text, the rest of it is in Figures 4, 5, 6, 7 (2:7), 23 and 24.

12:2 **The background to the survey.** Mityana lies 42 miles (67 km) to the west of Kampala, and is a straggling village hardly more than a few houses deep which line half a mile of the main road. Within 30 miles of the hospital the average population density is about 200 per square mile (77 per sq. km.). Distribution is comparatively even for the Baganda live, not in large settlements, but scattered among their coffee bushes and banana plantations. Communications are relatively good, the main road is tarred, and cars are common, most of them also acting as taxis.

12:3 **Capital costs.** The hospital has 83 beds, has about 10,000 outpatient attendances a year, and is staffed by two doctors, five medical assistants and 62 supporting staff — about one member of staff for every bed. Built in stages over the last twenty years as a single storied structure of concrete blocks, the buildings comprise an outpatient department, a children's ward, a maternity ward, and a block with ward accommodation for men and women as well as a theatre. There is also an administrative building with a dispensary, a laboratory and offices. The lack of running water, even in the theatre, and of corridors between the buildings against the rain indicate the general simplicity of this hospital's construction.

The cost of replacing the hospital buildings is calculated at the rate of £2 a sq. ft. of floor area ($48 per sq. metre) to be £28,000 ($78,000) or £340 ($950) per bed. Staff housing, stores, and other equipment bring the total capital cost to about £53,000 ($148,000). The breakdown of this total is shown in Figure 23A. Here it will be seen that buildings account for no less than 83 per cent. of the capital costs of the hospital. Another feature of these building costs is that 30 per cent. of them are accounted for by staff housing — almost a third of the hospital's total cost.

At Mityana the capital cost 'per equipped bed' is £650 ($1,820), a figure which not only includes the capital costs of the equipment but also includes staff housing. About four-fifths of this sum is building. What then of those hospitals costing £3,000 ($8,400) or even £5,000 ($14,000)

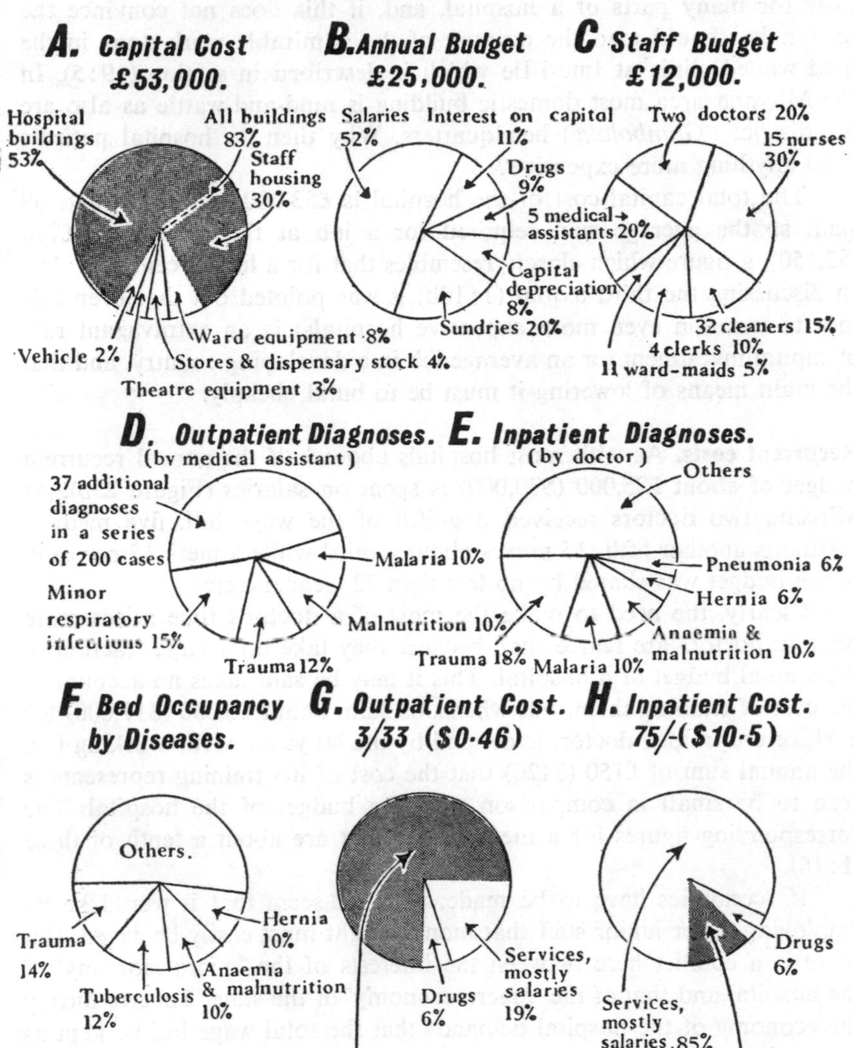

per bed that are currently proposed and indeed built in Africa? (1:10b) (2:12a). The capital cost, even of hospitals like Mityana, could be further reduced by employing methods of construction cheaper than £2 per square foot for part at least of their fabric — see section 10:6. In terms of economics it may well be a choice between either one hospital of conventional style or two of cheaper construction. Properly protected mud-and-wattle buildings last many years; they are perfectly satisfactory medically for many parts of a hospital, and, if this does not convince the reader, he should read the account of the admirable work done in the mud walled clinic at Imesi-Ile which is described in section (19:5). In the Mityana area most domestic building is mud-and-wattle as also are the district ('*Gombolola*') headquarters. Why then do hospital patients need anything more expensive?

The total capital cost of the hospital is £53,000 and it employs 69 staff, so the average sum required for a job at the hospital is £770 ($2,150), a figure which closely resembles that for a health centre (3:15). In discussing the third axiom (1:10b) it was pointed out that even this (not to mention even more expensive hospitals) is an extravagant rate of capital investment for an average job in a developing country, and that the main means of lowering it must be to build cheaply.

12:4 **Recurrent costs.** As with most hospitals about half the annual recurrent budget of about £25,000 ($70,000) is spent on salaries (Figure 23b). At Mityana two doctors received one-fifth of the wage bill, five medical assistants another fifth, 15 nurses about a third while a mere 15 per cent. of the budget was shared by no less than 32 cleaners, etc.

Clearly, the need to make the most of a doctor's time arises more because doctors are scarce than because they take up a large fraction of the annual budget of a hospital. This it may be said takes no account of the cost of training them, but when this sum, about £6,000 ($17,000) for a Makerere trained doctor, is divided by the 40 years of his working life, the annual sum of £150 ($420) that the cost of his training represents is seen to be small in comparison with the budget of the hospital. The corresponding figures for a medical assistant are about a tenth of these (1:16).

If economies have to be made, it might seem that it would be by employing fewer junior staff that money might most easily be saved. But there is a conflict here between the interests of the 'micro-economy' of the hospital and that of the 'macro-economy' of the state. To save money the economy of the hospital demands that the total wage bill be kept as low as possible. At the same time most developing countries urgently need to raise employment (1:10b). Both objects can only be obtained if increases in the wage bill are used to employ more staff rather than increase the wages of existing staff. This in turn means that all wage scales should be related to the level of development and economic production in the country as a whole. The great disparity in current wage scales is shown in Table 2 (7:2) and some of the difficulties inherent in adjusting them are discussed in section 7:4.

But economy is not the only scale of values, and the great cultural and educational benefits of employing and training many junior staff must not be forgotten, especially many junior nurses (7:3).

An interesting conclusion from an analysis of these annual costs is that about ten times the cost of a doctor's salary is required to provide him with the hospital services with which to work under the sort of circumstances described at Mityana. Thus, a service which hopes to employ a given number of doctors must expect to have to find ten times their salary to be able to put them to work effectively.

In strict accounting terms provision should be made in the annual budget for the interest on the capital value of the hospital; but from the point of view of a health department, once capital has been raised for hospital buildings, the interest on it does not usually occur in the annual budget in subsequent years. Nevertheless, a figure representing a 5 per cent. interest in capital is included. The figure for maintenance is a small one, 1 per cent. of the budget being allowed by the Buganda Government for this purpose. It is included in Figure 23B as sundries, along with such items as the cost of electricity, the depreciation of transport, petrol and oil, various stores and hospital food (where this is not provided by the patients). Individually, these items are small, collectively they add up to 20 per cent. of the annual budget.

Outpatients. The allocation of overhead costs between outpatients and inpatients must to some extent be arbitrary, but as a basis for calculation it has been reckoned that, at Mityana, the outpatient department is staffed by two medical assistants, five other staff and a doctor half time. Excluding drugs, the staff accounted for 90 per cent. of the total budget of the department. Its total cost when divided between the 100,000 outpatients seen annually (about 300 daily) gives an average cost of -/62 ($0.088) per outpatient attendance. The average cost of the drugs issued was -/21 ($0.03) making the average total cost to the hospital of an individual outpatient -/83 ($0.118) — a figure somewhat less than that costed for a health centre attendance in section 3:15 from Kenya.

There was no separate under-fives clinic and outpatients were first seen all together by a medical assistant who subsequently referred about one in twenty to a doctor. About half of the outpatients were made up of approximately equal numbers of cases of malaria, protein-calorie malnutrition, minor respiratory infections, and minor trauma (Figure 23D). The remaining patients were distributed among 37 further diagnoses, and, had the sample analysed been larger, the diagnoses required of the medical assistants would probably have been shown to be greater. Thus, the diagnostic skills required of a medical assistant are comparatively extensive and his task is more than merely a matter of recognizing a few common disorders. For his part, the doctor looking after the outpatient department made 113 different diagnoses on 430 patients referred to him during the month of the study, 58 of these diagnoses only once. If Mityana is anything to go by, diagnostic monotony is not so characteristic of rural practice as it is sometimes supposed to be.

12:6 **Inpatients.** Medical assistants were found to be more important than the doctors in determining who was admitted to the wards, thus in this series, they admitted two and a half times as many patients as did the doctors.

Trauma in all its forms was responsible for nearly a fifth of all admissions, with malaria, protein-calorie malnutrition (PCM) plus anaemia each responsible for about a tenth (Figure 23E). PCM and 'anaemia' — mostly hookworm anaemia — are considered together here for precise diagnoses were not reached by the hospital and they are often associated. When bed occupancy is considered tuberculosis in all its forms jumps to second place, malaria, the second commonest cause of admission disappears, and hernias are seen to fill a tenth of all beds. This however is an exceptional feature, for inguinal hernia is a condition that is unusually common in the region. Among the causes of short-term admissions malaria and diarrhoea were conspicuous, while the important causes of long-term admissions were tuberculosis, particularly spinal tuberculosis, and hernias.

Outpatient treatment is known to be much cheaper than admission to a ward; this is well shown by Mityana where the average cost to the hospital of an inpatient bedweek is 94/- ($13.2) and the average cost of an inpatient admission 74/- ($10.2), the average stay in hospital being 5.4 days. Thus, this hospital can provide 112 outpatient attendances for the cost of treating one inpatient for a week. This is somewhat biased in favour of the outpatients, since such charges as the laboratory and dispensary are all attributed to the inpatients, no satisfactory breakdown of them being possible. The difference in the drug costs of inpatients and outpatients is great, 5/- ($0.7) compared with -/21 ($0.03), more than a twenty-fold difference. However, at 5/- an inpatient, the cost of drugs still only represents 7 per cent. of the average cost to the hospital of admitting one inpatient.

It is instructive to contrast these figures with those from Kenya where the average cost of admission to a district hospital for one week was 84/-, a figure close to that of 94/- already quoted for Mityana. The figures for both a regional and the national hospital in Kenya were found to be the same, about 120/- per bed week (13). The costs per bed week at the New Mulago Hospital, the national hospital for Uganda, are 260/- or more than twice as much, a figure which does not include the salaries of the university staff employed there.

The Mityana figure of 5.4 days for the average length of stay in hospital also resembles the Kenya figure. There the average patient was found to stay in a district hospital for a week, a stay which was significantly shorter than the 10 days he spent in a regional hospital and the period of 22 days which was the average length of admission to the Kenyatta National Hospital (2:4).

One of the doctors at Mityana was an able and enthusiastic surgeon, but although he did all the major surgery himself, he was relieved of four-fifths of the minor operations which were done by a medical assistant.

Transport to hospital and its cost. Patients were carefully questioned about the sum they had spent on transport to hospital. On average each outpatient spent no less than 2/50 ($0.35) and each inpatient 7/80 ($1.09). The aggregate sums spent by 100,000 outpatients and 5,500 inpatients amounted to £14,000 ($39,000) — more than half the annual budget of the hospital. Eighty-four per cent. of this transport burden was borne by the outpatients. The means of transport and the sum spent on it are further analysed in Figure 24A and B. Here it will be seen that cost rises sharply with distance and the proportion of the different types of transport alters progressively the further away the patients live.

These costs have been questioned, but if the figure of 4/50 is taken as the average amount spent by an outpatient travelling a double journey of 15 miles each way, this will be seen to amount to no more than -/15 a mile, a sum of the same order as that commonly demanded from fare paying passengers in the Mityana area. Cars are comparatively common in Uganda and all but the richest owners obtain part of their running costs by taking fare paying passengers. The greater sum spent by inpatients is taken as being due to their wanting vehicles to come to their homes, by their needing vehicles in a hurry, and by their having less opportunity to share travelling expenses. A cost which was not examined was the transport cost born by the relatives.

The effect this has on the availability of medical care and its significance for the overall planning of health services is discussed in section 2:9.

Progressive patient care. This is described in detail in Chapter Nine. It was not practised at Mityana, yet an analysis of the patients showed that 40 per cent. of those in the wards could have been treated under 'self-care' facilities, had these been available. As the cost of such self-care facilities would be only a fraction of the cost of conventional ward accommodation ('Intermediate care') the savings it would bring might well be the equivalent of almost doubling the accommodation of the hospital for the

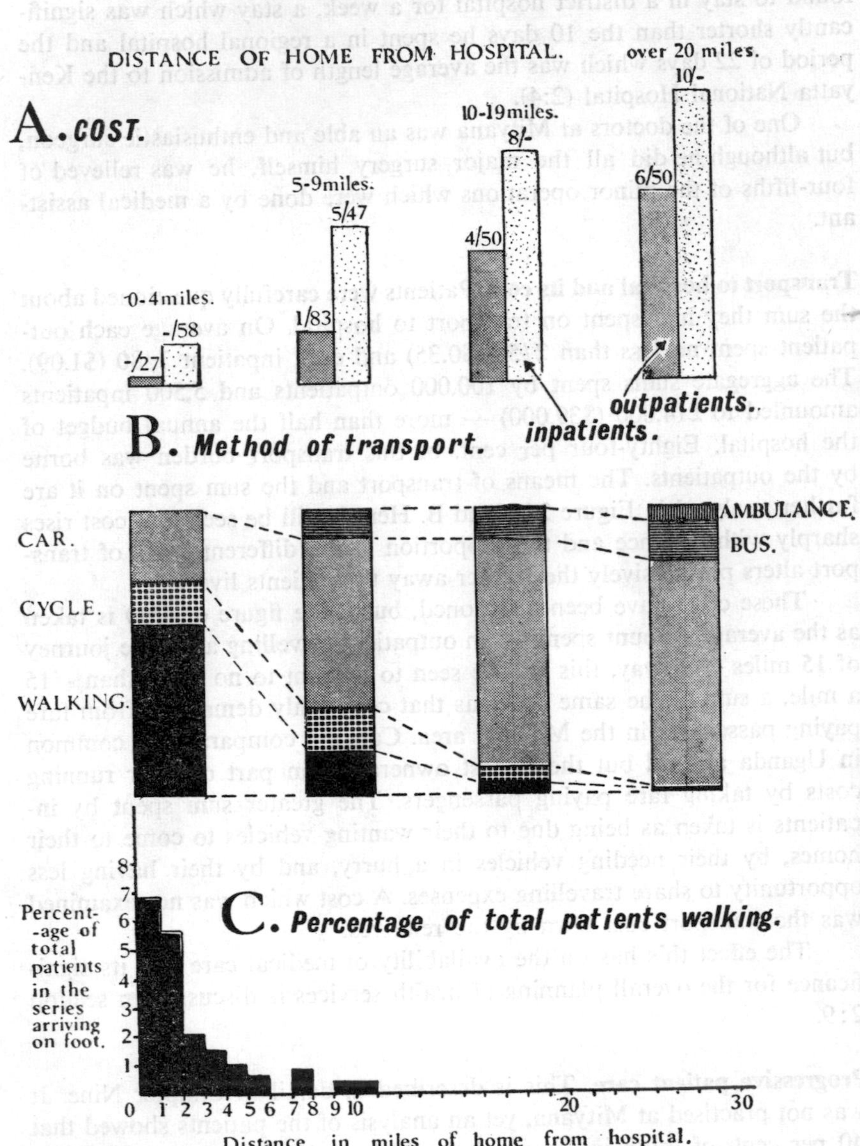

same capital outlay. About 4 per cent. of patients would have benefited from an 'intensive care unit' had this been available.

Conclusion. The most important conclusions from this study have already been incorporated in the second chapter. Some of the others can be summarized here.

Where is the money going? An overwhelming part of the capital cost of the hospital is accounted for by buildings. Even a small fractional saving here would be an appreciable economy. Comparatively little money is spent on drugs and to skimp here would be a false economy. Likewise equipment of all kinds, provided it has a reasonably long life, represents such a minute fraction of total costs as to make the apparatus needed for efficient medicine a top economic priority. In this class come such things as weighing scales, a Heaf gun, an efficient haemoglobinometer, and even such simple things as enough syringes or sufficient dressing forceps for good sterile techniques (8:9).

How much of the total medical expenditure is provided by the state and how much by the patients? In this study the equivalent of about half the entire hospital's annual budget was being paid in transport charges by the patients.

Where is the staff effort going? The analysis was not complete here, however, no health education or formal staff teaching was done and major surgery appeared to take a disproportionate part of the doctor's time.

If more resources could be provided how should they best be spent? Health education, a separate under-fives clinic, blood transfusion facilities, a 'self-care village' (9:5) and, above all, mobile clinics (2:10) are obvious urgent needs.

How fairly are the services provided distributed among the community? Just how unfairly they are in fact distributed is well shown by the 'iso-care map' in Figure 7 (2:7).

Chapter Thirteen

PAEDIATRICS

Professor Derrick Jelliffe

13:1 **The paediatric challenge.** In many developing countries infant mortality is about four times as high as it is in more privileged parts of the world, and between the ages of one and four it may be as much as forty times as great. The diseases responsible for this mortality are not only severe, monotonous and cumulative, but they are also largely preventable. This formidable challenge is made even more overwhelming by the huge numbers of children in most tropical communities. Thus three million of Uganda's seven million people are under fifteen and no less than a million and a half of them are of pre-school age.

To tackle such a burden, staff are short, money is scarce, buildings are inadequate and communications are poor — all these difficulties being aggravated by a variety of cross-cultural conflicts, such that the scientifically minded staff and the local community misinterpret one another's motives and behaviour only too frequently (4:5).

Not only are there too few staff at all levels, but their paediatric training has often been defective both in quality and in quantity. Even now, most doctors working in many parts of the tropics have been trained in Europe and North America where paediatrics is very different, and it is not easy for them to adapt to altered conditions. Not only are they themselves often undertrained in this field, but their nursing and junior staff usually are also. It is against this background that vast numbers of sick children must be cured rapidly, effectively and cheaply, with junior staff carrying out most of the work, and everything possible being done to introduce prevention.

The 'Big Three' among the killing diseases are the complex group of childhood diarrhoeas, pneumonia and protein-calorie malnutrition of early childhood — 'PCM'. Thus, the first of these was responsible for 21 per cent. of the admissions to the New Mulago Hospital last year

(1963), the second for 18 per cent. and the third for 14 per cent. The pattern is much the same in Madras, Lagos and elsewhere. Seven other groups of diseases also dominate, though not so grossly; they are tuberculosis, anaemia, intestinal helminth infections, measles, whooping cough, malaria and lastly accidents, particularly burns.

These diseases — the 'Top Ten' — have to be attacked not only in the hospital itself, but also in health centres and ultimately in the very homes of the people themselves. Everywhere, prevention must be combined with cure. This could hardly be demonstrated better than in the under-fives clinic that Dr. Morley describes so well, for the subtle gradation between sickness and health makes it quite impossible to divide such a clinic into two, one half for the healthy children, and other half for the sick ones.

'Practical methodology' — the key to medicine in the developing countries (Eleventh axiom 1:18). So much for the problem, the next step is to apply scientific principles to its solution. 'Time and motion study' and 'business management' provide at least part of the answer, for these are the sciences that examine how resources are best deployed. They can be applied in the same way, whether the gain is to be defined as money, or, as with health services, as disease prevented and sickness cured. How are we to get the very utmost from the limited resources we have — the greatest return in human welfare for least expenditure of money and skill? (Third axiom 1:10). Once again Dr. Morley's under-fives clinic is one model to go by, and a good example of the way to apply a completely logical and intensely practical methodology to a particular situation in tropical practice. The use of locally trained village girls, the weight chart he developed, its possession by the mother, the way in which the nurse herself dispenses the medicines, the use of ladle, the use of sulphadimidine — all the details of this very successful clinic, be they minutiae or not — this is what is meant by practical methodology adapted to this particular situation. It is just this kind of approach that must extend through every part of medicine in developing countries.

Applied to the children's ward there is one particular item of methodology that is worth aiming for, it is to keep all the cases of the same kind together. This is especially useful if they require skilled attention, cases of neonatal tetanus for example. It also enables a group of mothers, whose children have the same diseases, to be given health education together without the disadvantage of having to call them from different parts of the ward.

Mothers in hospital. Sick children in hospital need a ward to themselves, for their numbers alone demand it, and mothers must come into the hospital with their young children. Here, tropical practice is often in advance of that in Europe, for, though mothers may be untidy, ill disciplined, interfere with treatment, and often misunderstand when things go wrong, these disadvantages are small compared with the great benefits they confer.

Mothers provide psychological support for a child over a frightening and often painful illness in the unfamiliar atmosphere of a hospital ward. When guided, they can carry out much of the routine care and simpler nursing that would otherwise have to be done by paid staff — a critically important factor where nurses are scarce, as they usually are. They provide valuable opportunities for health education at a psychologically appropriate time, and they are the only source of that readily available, cheap, sterile, perfectly adapted, high protein infant food — human milk. Most useful of all, their presence in the ward enables young babies to be sent out of hospital while feeding at the breast — an absolute necessity if they are to survive long outside.

Some nursing sisters do not appreciate the presence of mothers in their wards, but it is essential that they co-operate, understand and not merely submit. Much gentle and steady persuasion may therefore be needed. Here the example of the great Sir James Spence should be remembered. He is said to have waited as long as six years before one of the sisters in his wards came round to the idea.

When they are admitted mothers have to be catered for. They want somewhere to sleep, sit, cook, wash themselves, their clothes and their children, as well as somewhere to store their possessions. They also want food, water and latrines; but, paradoxically perhaps, all these facilities are more easily provided in a small rural hospital, than they are in a larger urban one.

Mothers like the comfort and support of their friends, and a compromise between the dangers of cross-infection in a large ward and the solitude and isolation of single cubicles, is to provide rooms for two mothers at a time. These are often better placed round a courtyard which gives ready access to the open air than they are along a corridor. To care for their children's excreta they will want a sluice to themselves, separate from that of the nurses, while the rest of their needs are often best provided for in a 'mothers' shelter', a little apart from the hospital itself.

Such a building need not be elaborate for all that is wanted is a roof, cooking places, water, and preferably some lockers to which mothers may fit their own padlocks. Here they may go about their sundry tasks in peace, except for some all-important health education, which is conveniently given in the shelter.

The best sleeping arrangements for mothers are still debated. Are there to be beds and cots? mats and cots? cots and camp beds? or merely beds alone? In Mulago Hospital we are increasingly coming to the opinion that a tropical children's ward should be equipped with adult beds in which mothers can sleep with their young children. This however is a break with tradition and is likely to be unpopular with some nursing sisters. One hospital advocates the use of mattresses of plastic foam with a plastic and calico cover, for these are light, washable and easily stacked away during the day. But whatever sleeping arrangements are made, one thing must be expected; it is that a mother and her child are likely to end up sleeping in the same bed to their mutual benefit.

Mothers have many uses, and one which should not be forgotten is their function as the safest and most natural of hot-water bottles. A good way to warm a cold child is close against the warmth of his mother's body. Hypothermia can be almost as much of a menace in the tropics, especially during the night, as it is in colder climates, and it is often forgotten, especially in PCM (14:12). Low reading thermometers—down to 30°C (85°F) — are therefore important items of ward equipment (A & H). A specially warmed room must now be considered a highly desirable feature in all tropical hospitals, except those in the very hottest places.

The 'Top Ten' diseases. The 'Top Ten' diseases have all to be treated rapidly, simply and economically. The only attitude possible to the rare metabolic anomaly, or incurable malformation, must be to give minimal symptomatic treatment only — no other course is logical (1:13).

Therapeutic regimes for the major diseases are now becoming increasingly standard, particularly such methods as tube feeding for kwashiorkor, and it is tragic to see them still so little used outside the major paediatric centres (30:7).

Some conditions are so important as to deserve whole chapters to themselves. Protein-calorie malnutrition is the subject of Chapter Fourteen, diarrhoea of Chapter Fifteen, and tuberculosis in childhood is discussed in section 21:20. Immunization is the answer to several of the severe diseases of childhood and is described in Chapter Seventeen. Here it is only possible to mention a few key points about the remaining members of the 'Top Ten'.

Pneumonia. Many of the less severe cases of pneumonia can be treated as outpatients and respond to a three days' course of procaine penicillin (100,000 units I.M. daily). But penicillin preparations, such as 'Triplopen' (GLA) deserve special mention. Given as a single dose of 600,000 — 1,200,000 units, these are usually mixtures of crystaline, procaine and benethamine penicillin which produce a therapeutic level for four or five days at almost the same cost as an equivalent course of the simple procaine variety (30:1). A major point in their favour is that they make daily attendances unnecessary and so reduce the load on the outpatient department, and the number of journeys that a mother need make to a hospital or health centre. Another useful alternative is a large initial dose of procaine penicillin followed by a course of sulphadimidine at home. Therapeutic methods such as these can be very useful when a mobile clinic visits an outlying station only once or twice a week.

13:6 **Malaria.** Most cases of malaria in childhood can be treated with a three day course of oral chloroquine, one dose being given each day. When using tablets — 150 mg. *base,* give children 0 — 1 year a ¼ tablet, children 1 — 5 years a ½ tablet 5 — 10 years 1 tablet, and children over 10 years 2 tablets. Some form of parenteral chloroquine is often required and it must be stressed that the dangers of intramuscular chloroquine are being increasingly recognized. It it perhaps *the* commonly used drug where an accurately calculated dose for weight is really important. — 5 mg./kg. of chloroquine base (2.5 mg./lb.) being the dose advised, though even this will produce an occasional case of chloroquine enephalopathy.

As a useful middle of the road alternative between the intramuscular and oral routes, subcutaneous chloroquine is well worth bearing in mind. By this route absorption is sufficiently slow for toxic symptoms to be rare, the likelihood of entering a vein is slight, and risk of 'fixation poliomyelitis' is reduced. It has been found that, in the same dose as by the intramuscular route, it clears a parasitaemia towards the end of the second day, and no toxic symptoms have yet been observed. If the patient is vomiting, some form of parenteral chloroquine is essential, and, unsupervised at the dispensaries, it is safer by the sub-cutaneous route than it is by the intramuscular one. To lessen possible confusion in the minds of the junior staff, make out a table relating the weight of the child to the dose in ml. of the particular brand of chloroquine being used.

Cerebral malaria. This is one of the most important clinical emergencies where failure to diagnose and treat a patient correctly may cost him his life. It is seen in endemic areas, and almost always in the non-immune, that is, in the expatriate, the young indigenous child, or in the indigenous adult who has recently come from a non-malarious area, such as the mountains. Under these circumstances, and in the absence of any obvious cause, the combination of all or some of the following symptoms suggest the diagnosis: fever which is usually (but not always) high, convulsions, coma, and a variety of signs in the central nervous system, such as neck stiffness, and pareses. *P. falciparum* is almost always to be found in a blood film, usually in very large numbers, and late schizonts may be present. To the naked eye, the CSF is clear, although there may be a slight increase in pressure, cells, and protein. The differential diagnosis includes 'febrile convulsions' which may be due to the fever of malaria itself without cerebral involvement (a difficult distinction) and various forms of meningitis, encephalitis and poisoning, especially poisoning by indigenous medicines. The precise mechanism responsible for these symptoms remains obscure, as does the final cause of the patient's death, but obstruction of the small cerebral vessels is probably mainly responsible, while anaemia, anoxia, hyperpyrexia, and dehydration may also contribute.

The first principle is to give *immediate and adequate chemotherapy*. After this comes the correction of any dehydration present by the methods described in Chapter Fifteen, and any severe anaemia (haemoglobin less than 7g.%) by blood transfusion as described in Chapter Twenty-Three. Also important is the control of convulsions with either paraldehyde or phenobarbitone (dosage in Appendix I). So urgent is adequate chemotherapy, that, in endemic malarial regions, *the drug must be given immediately the clinical diagnoses is suspected*, without waiting for the result of a blood film, or a lumbar puncture, although, as is stressed elsewhere (11 : 3a), these can be available very rapidly. A potent schizonticide is wanted which will rapidly stop the multiplication of the plasmodia in the red cells, particularly those in the cerebral capillaries. There are two main drugs available — chloroquine and quinine.

There are three routes by which antimalarial drugs can be given, the oral (including the use of an intragastric tube), the intramuscular and the intravenous. The oral route is too slow to be relied upon in such an emergency as cerebral malaria, for it may take up to two hours for chloroquine to reach a therapeutic level in the blood. The intramuscular route enables such a level to be built up in about 15 minutes, but the intravenous one enables it to be achieved immediately. Against this rapidity of action must be set the virtual absence of side effects by the oral route, the possibility of abscesses and muscle necrosis with intramuscular quinine, and the danger of convulsions, collapse, hypotension and even death with both chloroquine and quinine when drugs are given intravenously. Especially is this true when they are given too rapidly or insufficiently diluted. As has been mentioned in the preceding section, chloroquine sometimes produces these symptoms even when given by the intramuscular route, particularly in children if the dose has been miscalculated.

Clearly, a compromise has to be reached, and a satisfactory one seems to be to give chloroquine in a 5 mg./kg. dose by intramuscular injection, and to repeat this if necessary six hours later, giving the second dose also intramuscularly, or by mouth or intragastric tube, depending upon the condition of the patient. The maximum *daily* dose must not be more than 10 mg./kg.

Cases of cerebral malaria are sometimes resistant to intramuscular therapy, a phenomenon which seems to be more common in some regions than in others. In these areas it may be desirable therefore to give one-tenth of the calculated first dose (0.5 mg./kg.) by *very slow intravenous injection,* using either a syringe or a drip and a concentration which must not be greater than 1 mg./ml. The remaining nine-tenths of the dose can be given intramuscularly immediately thereafter. *All calculations of chloroquine dosage are made using only the base content of the tablet or solution.*

With quinine the corresponding quantities are, 15 mg./kg. for the inital dose, the maximum daily dose being 20 mg./kg. Here again one-tenth of the initial dose can be given intravenously by syringe or drip, and, once more, the strength of 1 mg./ml. should not be exceeded. In order to avoid the danger of muscle necroses the remaining nine-tenths of the dose can be given by intragastric tube.

Chloroquine resistance. In late 1965 it is not possible to write a section on the use of chloroquine in treating malaria without a mention of chloroquine insensitivity and resistance. The drug has been in use for about 15 years and chloroquine resistance has now been reported from Colombia and South East Asia. It has not been confirmed as being present in Africa or shown for any species other than *P. falciparum.* Very specialized studies are needed to prove the existence of chloroquine resistance and it is not to be diagnosed lightly. When it does occur quinine may well be the drug of choice. If the parasite is merely insensitive, but not completely resistant, chloroquine may be effective in higher dosage.

13:7 **Ancylostomiasis.** The toxic effects of tetrachlorethylene — 'TCE' — have been overestimated in the past. In practice these are uncommon, and it is certainly the most effective drug in *Necator americanus* infections, while at -/05 ($0.007) an adult dose is also much the cheapest treatment available. But, when *Ancylostoma duodenale* is the cause of the infection, bephenium ('Alcopar') is reported as being more effective, though, at its present high price of 1/10 ($0.15) for a 5 gram cachet, it is beyond the range of most budgets. Being a bitter powder it is also very unpleasant to take. No purgative is required whichever drug is used. If very many *Ascaris* ova are also present we treat this species first, or both parasites can be treated simultaneously.

Though ferrous sulphate tablets, or an iron containing mixture can be used in treating older children and adults, intramuscular iron is a very valuable drug in younger children, despite its cost (30:1). Its great virtue is that it can be given as a depot injection free from any of the uncertainty that attends the issue of either tablets or mixtures. One of the major difficulties in using intramuscular iron is the calculation of its dose, for this varies with both the weight of the patient and his haemoglobin deficit. As the nomogram in Figure 25 shows, the iron required

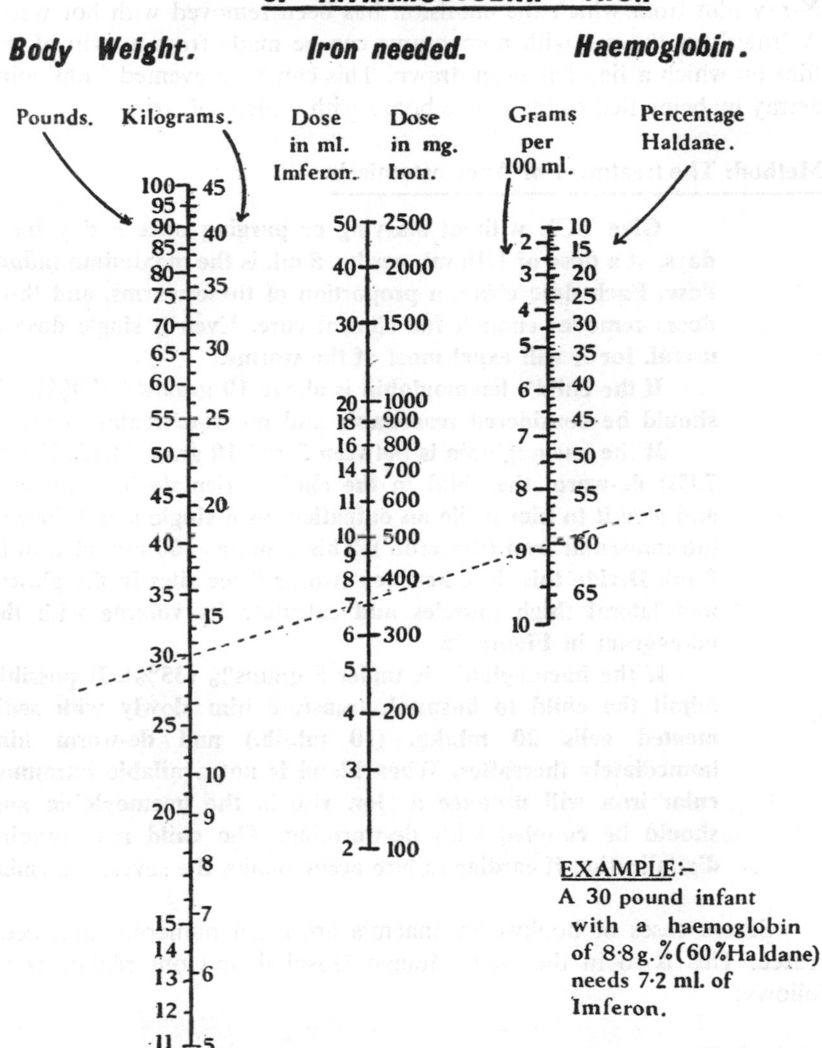
Fig. 25 A NOMOGRAM FOR THE USE OF INTRAMUSCULAR IRON
Body Weight.
Iron needed.
Haemoglobin.
Pounds.
Kilograms.
Dose in ml. Imferon.
Dose in mg. Iron.
Grams per 100 ml.
Percentage Haldane.
EXAMPLE:–
A 30 pound infant with a haemoglobin of 8·8 g. % (60 % Haldane) needs 7·2 ml. of Imferon.
Weigh the child & measure his haemoglobin. Find these values on the scales & join them up with a ruler. The point where it cuts the central scale gives the dose of iron required. The dose in ml. refers ONLY to those iron solutions containing 50 mg. of iron in each ml., Imferon for example.

varies widely. This nomogram will be found easier than a formula and is printed again at the end of the book. This spare copy can be torn out and pinned up in a ward or outpatient department. A useful way to protect these and other tables, which are designed to be pinned up on a notice board for frequent reference, is to cover them with a sheet of X-ray film from which the emulsion has been removed with hot water. A 'ruler' for the use with nomograms can be made from a strip of this film on which a line has been drawn. This can be prevented from going astray by being tied to the notice board with a piece of string.

Method: The treatment of Ancylostomiasis.

Give TCE without starving or purging once a day for 3 days, at a dose of 1/10 ml. per kg. 5 ml. is the maximium (adult) dose. Each dose clears a proportion of these worms, and three doses removes enough for clinical cure. Even a single dose is useful, for it will expel most of the worms.

If the child's haemoglobin is above 10 grams% (70%) this should be considered reasonable and no iron treatment given.

If the haemoglobin is between 5 and 10 grams% (35% and 70%) de-worm the child in the clinic, calculate his iron lack and give it to him while an outpatient as a single depot dose of intramuscular iron ('Imferon'). This contains 100 mg. of iron in 2 ml. Divide this dose between two or three sites in the gluteal and lateral thigh muscles and calculate its volume with the nomogram in Figure 25.

If the haemoglobin is under 5 grams% (35%). If possible admit the child to hospital, transfuse him slowly with sedimented cells 20 ml./kg. (10 ml./lb.) and de-worm him immediately thereafter. When blood is not available intramuscular iron will produce a slow rise in the haemoglobin and should be coupled with de-worming. The child may require digitalization if cardiac failure accompanies the severe anaemia.

Severe cases of hookworm anaemia are often numerous and beds scarce. This is so in the New Mulago Hospital and our régime is as follows:

Method: The management of severe hookworm anaemia when beds are scarce.

1st. day: Admit the child, measure his haemoglobin on the ward (24:17). Examine his stool (24:47), collected if necessary by anal tube

(15:3). Transfuse him with sedimented cells, and as soon as the transfusion is finished, de-worm him with TCE. If *Ascaris* ova are also seen in the stool give piperazine at the same time as TCE — for dosage see Appendix I.

2nd day: Give the second dose of TCE and, if necessary, more piperazine. Discharge the child.

3rd day: See the child in the outpatient department. Give the third dose of TCE with more piperazine if needed. If the family live too far away to make outpatient attendance easy, this dose can be given to the mother in a bottle to give to her child on the following day.

Two weeks later, or whenever is convenient, see the child again and check his stool and haemoglobin. Repeat the régime if a positive stool is found.

8 **Measles.** The importance of this disease in the tropics has long been misjudged, and its full gravity as a cause of death is only just being realized.

Measles is at its most infectious in its earliest stages, before the rash has appeared, but, once this is 48 hours old, and possibly even only 24 hours old, cases can be safely admitted to a hospital ward. Some hold that the measles child is a greater menace to himself from the secondary infection to which he is exposed in hospital than he is a danger to his neighbours by infecting them. However, no matter what view is taken, it is logical either to make every effort to keep measles out of a hospital, or to decide that the trouble is not worthwhile and thus to treat it in the general wards. If it is to be excluded, all admissions must be searched for Koplik's spots, and some kind of isolation facility will be needed. Even so, the outpatient department is the place where measles really spreads and the clinic nurse or the person doing the initial screening can attempt the isolation of patients who are considered to be potentially infectious.

In tropical countries the measles rash starts in the same way as it does elsewhere, but in the severer cases it darkens within a few days, scaling is conspicuous and it sometimes goes on to widespread desquamation. In cases of this kind the mouth is sore, and the larynx, the bronchi and also the bowel are probably affected in much the same way as the skin. The classical complications of measles are common, especially diarrhoea, pneumonia and subsequent malnutrition.

Method: The treatment of measles.

Treat any dehydration present, feed these children well, give them extra protein such as the reinforced skim milk diet (14:6), use 'golden eye' ointment routinely (yellow mercury oxide ointment), and, if vitamin A deficiency is common in the area, give severe cases an intramuscular injection of vitamin A (100,000 units).

The diarrhoea of measles is usually very resistant to antibiotics, and the value of prescribing them routinely is doubtful. The best advice is probably to give a sulphonamide to all children severely ill with measles, not so much as treatment for the diarrhoea, but as a general prophylactic against secondary infection, and to give an antibiotic such as penicillin or chloramphenicol only if there is a definite bronchopneumonia.

13:9 **Pertussis.** Though now one of the less important diseases of temperate countries, whooping cough still causes as much death and disability in tropical children as once it did in Europe. Little if any maternal immunity is transmitted across the placenta, and, in areas where children are carried about on their mother's back, they often catch whooping cough when they are still only a few weeks old. The disease is frequently unrecognized, for under the age of a year children do not 'whoop', and it is only the persistent nature of a cough, often with cyanotic attacks which suggests the diagnosis. Some sticky sputum is produced and this, their mothers often say, they have to pick from the child's mouth. In older children some help may be had from the general course of symptoms and the association of vomiting with the cough. Initially there is a catarrhal stage; this is followed by a rapid spasmodic cough often accompanied by choking or vomiting. After this follows the true whoop.

Diagnosis is not easy, and for this reason the true mortality from whooping cough is still not known, nor is it easy to tell which child is going to die, for a child may be sleeping peacefully on its mother's back between attacks only to die in the next paroxysm of coughing. Convulsions in an infant with whooping cough are a serious prognostic sign and justify immediate admission to hospital.

Early diagnosis is essential, for, in the first five days of the cough, chloramphenicol or tetracycline in a dose of 50-200 mg./kg./day (25-100 mg./lb./day) will often banish the disease, but after the first week chemotherapy is of no avail in stopping the 'whoop', though procaine penicillin may be useful in reducing secondary infection.

Like measles, pertussis readily precipitates a child into kwashiorkor or nutritional marasmus, particularly in the first year of its life, but this can usually be prevented by encouraging mothers to feed their children well during the illness. They should be persuaded to give another feed half an hour after a vomit, to give extra milk by cup-and-spoon and to modify the spasms with a sedative (tab. phenobarb. 5-10 kg. (10-20 lb.) 30 mg. (½gr.) twice daily; over 10 kg. (20 lb.) 60 mg. (1 gr.) twice daily) Mothers should be warned about these tablets, lest they are all given at once. Codein preparations should never be used.

Whenever an older child is seen with pertussis, enquiries should be made for any young babies in the family with coughs. These should be examined and treated with chloramphenicol or tetracycline on the assumption that they also probably have pertussis.

The real answer to pertussis is the *early* routine immunization of all children under five following the procedure described in section 17:12.

a **Meningitis.** This is not a public health problem of the magnitude of PCM, but it is common in young children and responds well to the correct chemotherapy, while the results of late or inadequate treatment are so tragic as to make early diagnosis vital. Fever, which is not otherwise explained, a convulsion, drowsiness, or the failure of a small child to suckle — these should all prompt an examination for a bulging fontanelle as well as a search for Kernig's sign or stiffness of the neck. If there is any doubt whatever, a lumbar puncture must be undertaken, if necessary in the outpatient department (11:3a) (24:27). A low threshold to the performance of this essential investigation is one of the attributes of the good paediatrician, and facilities for examining the CSF after the manner described in Chapter Twenty-Four must be made available in every hospital.

b **Tuberculous meningitis.** Suspect this whenever there is meningeal irritation of slow onset and obtain more evidence with a Heaf test, which is usually, but not always, strongly positive. Perform a lumbar puncture wherever there is the slightest possibility of tuberculous meningitis, the typical findings being a raised protein and a pleocytosis, usually lymphocytic but not always so.

The normal CSF sugar is about 10-20 mg.% lower than that in the blood. Because the blood sugars of some sick children, particularly malnourished ones, are apt to be low it is advisable to estimate the blood sugar at the same time as the CSF sugar and to attribute a low CSF sugar to a bacterial infection only if it is significantly lower than that of the blood. In interpreting these figures the reliability of the laboratory should be borne in mind.

On the occasions when there is still real doubt as to whether a case is a tuberculous or a suppurative meningitis, it is justified to give streptomycin, INH and thiacetazone, as well as ten days of penicillin, sulphadiazine, and chloramphenicol. If the patient is completely well at the end of ten days, and has a clear or almost clear CSF, the meningitis was probably suppurative, but if not, it is probably tuberculous and the full anti-tuberculous regime must be continued. A not uncommon cause of diagnostic difficulty is the inadequately treated case of suppurative meningitis. It is cases of this kind in which this quintuple therapy may be so useful. For cases with very thick purulent spinal fluid and for cases with classical tuberculous meningitis prednisone (2-3 mg./kg.) should be added to the drugs stated.

In the rural hospital the dangers of daily intrathecal streptomycin outweigh its possible benefits, but it must be given intramuscularly for three or four months, together with INH and thiacetazone by mouth for two years (see also 21:20).

13:11 **Prematurity.** Though many of the small children born in the tropics are 'premature' in that they are below the internationally accepted standard weight of 2,500 g. ($5\frac{1}{2}$ lb.), some are not premature in the sense that they have not been long enough in the womb. The 'low birth weight neonate' is thus a mixed group. In some tropical countries 40 per cent. of all children born may weigh less than $5\frac{1}{2}$ lb., and, though technically premature, when judged by their activity they are plainly not so. A local standard of 'special care' has therefore to be decided on. At Mulago Hospital 2000 g. (4 lbs. 6 oz.) is taken as the 'special care' level, and all children below this receive the care accorded to the premature. The prevention of a low birth weight depends on good antenatal care, which should include advice on diet, especially in relation to vegetable protein, the early correction of abnormalities and infections, and routine malarial chemoprophylaxis.

The main principle must be to send all premature infants out of hospital breast fed — anything else is certain death. Accommodation is thus essential for their mothers, for these children need expressed breast milk by intragastric tube. They should be put to the breast as soon as possible and it is surprising how well many of the very small ones suckle. (For further information on the management of prematurity see /89/).

13:12 **Sickle cell disease.** This will still be with many tropical communities when the 'Top Ten' diseases have all been conquered, but there is little specific that can be done for these children at present. However, trials have shown that chemoprophylaxis with long acting penicillins and chloroquine will reduce the number of dactylitic and aplastic crises and raise the haemoglobin levels of these patients. Such treatment is expensive, and these trials are not yet sufficiently complete to enable this régime to be advised on a wide scale. Other units have found that malarial prophylaxis combined with long-term folic acid therapy (5 mg. daily) is the best way of treating these children, and it now seems certain that, in malarious areas, routine chemoprophylaxis with antimalarials is indicated.

Initially there is little to be done for children with dactylitis, apart from giving them rest and aspirin, and observing them carefully. Older children with bone pain are often hard to diagnose on account of the difficulty in distinguishing whether this pain is due to an early osteomyelitis, often with Salmonella organisms, or is merely the result of a local infarction. Chloramphenicol or tetracycline should be given in case it is the former, and the child observed carefully meanwhile. When a chronic case of sickle cell osteomyelitis refuses to heal, raising the haemoglobin level by transfusion often succeeds after other methods have failed. Osteomyelitis due to Salmonella infections frequently relapses, so it is a good rule to keep all cases on chloramphenicol or tetracycline for as long as six weeks.

Poliomyelitis. Of all the causes of chronic disability none is more important than poliomyelitis. In some societies it may even be necessary to persuade the relatives that a child is merely diseased and not bewitched. They need to be told that no injections, pills or medicines are of any use, and that for the time being they have a very important task to do in trying to prevent contractures. The rehabilitation of such cripples is an overwhelming task and, as a practical guide to such things as the making of cheap calipers the booklets entitled 'Rehabilitating the Disabled in Africa' published twice yearly in French and English will be found valuable (NRP). A book that promises to be very useful is that by Huckstep /84/. Here again the ultimate solution inevitably lies in the routine immunization of all children with oral live vaccine of the Sabin type after the manner described in section 17:13.

Neonatal sepsis and septicaemia. This is an important cause of death in the neonatal period, and is easily overlooked, for at this age the response of an infant to a range of infections is limited, stereotyped, generalized and insidious. Experienced sisters know almost by second nature when a small baby is very sick and points to be aware of are poor feeding, lethargy, an unstable temperature (rather than pyrexia), jaundice, diarrhoea and fits. When a very young baby shows all or a number of these signs, he is probably septicaemic, whether or not there is an obvious primary focus, such as an infected umbilicus or a 'sticky eye'.

Ideally, every such baby should have his blood cultured and his CSF examined. These are both paediatric special investigations of critical importance, and, though blood cultures may be impossible, it should always be possible to examine the CSF. Staphylococci or enterobacteria are the common invading organisms and the following therapeutic regime will prove useful.

Method: Suspected septicaemia in young babies.

Give neonates penicillin in a dose of 10-20,000 units/kg./day (5-10,000/lb./day) and streptomycin 40 mg./kg./day (20 mg./lb./day), both drugs being split into two doses and given intramuscularly at 12 hour intervals. If the baby improves, well and good. If no improvement is evident in 48 hours, switch to chloramphenicol and give full term babies 25 mg./kg./day (12½mg./lb./day). Give premature babies half this dose — 12½mg./kg./day (6 mg./lb./day). The doses are somewhat more cautious than those in Appendix I.

Small doses are important, particularly with chloramphenicol, for too much of it may well kill the baby. But how are such doses to be measured by partly trained nurses when ampoules are so inconveniently large? The dilutions required should be worked out by the doctor and written down for the nursing staff, preferably on the ward notice board. Oral chloramphenicol is conveniently diluted with syrup to two different dilutions such that one contains 12½ mg. per teaspoonful and the other 50 mg. per teaspoonful. This is easily done and saves much trouble and error. When the smallest vials contain 500.000 units of penicillin or a gram of streptomycin the following scheme of dilution may be found useful, volumes being measured with a 1 ml. or 'minim' syringe.

Penicillin: Dissolve 500,000 units with 2½ ml. of water
½ ml. contains 100,000 units
¼ ml. contains 50,000 units
1/10 ml. contains 20,000 units
1 minim contains 10,000 units

Streptomycin: Dissolve 1 gram in 5 ml. of water
1 ml. contains 200 mg.
¼ ml. contains 50 mg.
1/10 ml. contains 20 mg.
1 minim contains 10 mg.

The last figure in each of these is approximated for convenience on the basis that 1 ml. is the equivalent of 20, not 16 minims.

13:15 **Neonatal tetanus.** The aetiology of neonatal tetanus presents few mysteries. It is common in all countries where practices concerned with the care of the umbilical cord allow contamination with dirt or dung containing tetanus spores.

The diagnosis is rarely difficult. The disease usually begins between the fifth and the tenth day of life, and the clinical picture is dramatic and characteristic. The first symptom noticed by the mother is failure to suckle, followed within 36 hours by the typical spasms.

In many hospitals, 90 per cent. of all afflicted infants die, but with careful treatment the mortality can be reduced to as little as 40 per cent. The principles of management are to neutralize the toxin, to prevent spasms by adequate sedation, to maintain ventilation and so prevent pneumonia, and to see that the child is adequately fed.

It is standard practice to give tetanus antitoxin in all forms of tetanus, but in neonatal tetanus there is no absolute proof that it is of value. Nevertheless, until more data are available antitoxin should be given.

The important therapeutic principle is to steer a course between too light sedation, which will fail to control the spasms, and too heavy sedation which will increase the dangers from pneumonia and may kill the baby. To achieve this babies need observing frequently by the ward staff and the drugs given them adjusted accordingly. The doctor is unlikely to be able to visit the ward very often, and for this reason it is essential that the nurse should participate with the fullest possible understanding of the care of the patient. In particular, she should appreciate the importance of preventing spasms and maintaining a good airway. She must take observations at least half-hourly, and chart these, together with the number of spasms and the treatment given on a special form. She must have a routine to work by; for observing, feeding, handling, aspirating and administering drugs, and she should practise these necessary techniques under supervision. It is a good idea to write instructions on a blackboard, or set them out clearly on a big chart, under headings. Others prefer to keep them in a plastic (X-ray film) jacket in the ward. As well as a basic routine, there must be a routine for extra therapy if the spasms become more frequent. Practical management may be easier if all the cases are kept together and put in charge of the same person. Nursing skill is likely to be scarce, and it may be possible to let someone less skilled watch over these babies. Such a person should be instructed in the emergency procedures and told to call a nurse when in difficulty.

The doctor should discuss the progress of the patient with the nurses, and keep them aware of their responsibility. It is probable that the good results reported for some small series are due, at least in part, to the drive and enthusiasm of a doctor lifting the feeling of hopelessness and apathy which often appears to surround a case of neonatal tetanus. The mortality rate is certainly going to be high, but it will be lower where a definite régime of management is carefully prepared and hopefully practised.

Method: The treatment of neonatal tetanus.

On admission give the baby intramuscular paraldehyde (0.2 ml./kg. 0.1 ml./lb.). 20 minutes later give 50,000 units of ATS intravenously via a scalp vein (15:11) or a jugular vein. If this is not possible, give it intramuscularly.

Pass a 1 mm polythene or nylon intragastric tube and leave it in place.

Swab the umbilicus with 'Savlon' ('Certrimide' with 'Hibitane') and if still moist apply a clean dressing.

Give chlorpromazine ('Largactil') (2-4 mg./kg: 1-2 mg./lb.) and phenobarbitone (5 mg./kg: 2-5 mg./lb.) six-hourly through the tube. If this fails to control the spasms, either add paraldehyde at the dosage rate above, or increase the dose of phenobarbitone and chlorpromazine. Another alternative is to give these drugs more frequently than once in six hours, say four-hourly. Though we use chlorpromazine, others prefer sodium amytal 3-4 hourly. Continue this sedation until the spasms are well controlled and then gradually lighten it. As soon as there have been no spasms for three days, stop all sedation.

Give 15,000 units (½ml.) of procaine penicillin intramuscularly once or twice daily for as long as sedation is continued. Some use oral penicillin down the tube instead, and give 62.5 mg. 6 hourly (usually 4 ml., or one teaspoonful).

Give expressed breast milk through the intragastric tube and calculate the amount required on the basis of 150 ml./kg./day (75 ml./lb./day). Avoid feeds during the night when regurgitation may easily pass unnoticed. Keep milk secretion going in the mother, because unless this is done, the baby may recover from tetanus only to die of starvation.

Keep a mouth or foot operated sucker beside the cot, and see that it is used to keep the mouth and larynx clear of mucus and regurgitated gastric contents.

Change the position of the baby every two hours, but otherwise disturb him as little as possible. Try to do all nursing procedures together so as to leave the child undisturbed in between whiles.

Health education and the training of indigenous midwives are the answers to neonatal tetanus. Among the measures that have been used successfully are the issue to mothers and indigenous midwives (3:10) of special cord packs containing a cord tape, one new razor blade, 2 small squares of lint, one of which is slit to encircle the cord stump, and a bandage (19:2). These can be obtained commercially (SNP) for -/75 ($0.1) or made up by the hospital, preferably in a plastic envelope (30:8). Points to stress to the mothers are the importance of hand cleanliness, and dressing the cord as early as possible to avoid contamination with dust. No further dressing is required until the cord finally falls off about 5 days after birth.

Other measures that have been successfully employed are the immunization of the mother during pregnancy with three injections of tetanus toxoid at monthly intervals, the last of which must be given not later than 18 days before delivery if it is to be effective. If alum precipitated toxoid is used — 'APT' — two injections at a month's interval are sufficient. Such régimes are difficult administratively, and another alternative where neonatal tetanus is common is to give 0.5 ml. of antiserum (1500 units) to every child seen before the fourth day of life. After this time it will be too late.

6 **Drugs and equipment.** All children must be routinely weighed and Heaf tested on admission to the ward (21:3). The sooner all hospitals convert to the metric system the better, and for this polythene metric measuring cylinders will be found inexpensive and very convenient for determining the volumes of fluids. All new weighing scales should be of the metric pattern and makers may be able to provide conversion kits that will convert existing imperial scales to the metric system.

Finally, the reader is reminded that in so-called tropical paediatrics there are few really vital pieces of equipment, and few indispensable drugs but that these few must be available. The drugs are listed in Appendix I, the equipment is as follows.

Polythene tubing (POR) (Table 17, 30:6).
A Heaf gun, preferably magnetic headed (A&H) as well as 'PPD' (A&H) for it (21:3).
One weighing scales for children in the ward itself (CMO) and another for their food in the ward kitchens.
Scalp vein needles (A&H) (POR) 3/- ($0.4).
Lumbar puncture needles for children (A&H).
Low reading thermometers (A&H) 3/60 ($0.5).
Some way of keeping children warm.

Chapter Fourteen

PROTEIN CALORIE MALNUTRITION

For authorship see 14:18

PREVENTION

14:1 **The critical importance of health education.** Malnutrition in early childhood is one of the dominant problems in most developing countries. Though easily recognized in its gross forms, it is often missed in mild cases and the prevalence of undernutrition in a community is apt to be grossly underestimated. The extent to which the child population conforms to the means plotted in Figure 64 (26:5) gives a useful indication of its nutrition; but the nutritional state of a population is a difficult thing to assess and the interested reader is advised to study a recent WHO publication on the subject /87/. Good accounts of the diagnosis of the grosser forms of malnutrition are readily available /86/, /132/, so this chapter is concerned only with prevention and treatment.

The many factors determining the incidence of kwashiorkor have already been discussed briefly in defining the concept of community diagnosis (Figure 12, (5:2)). Some were also mentioned in describing the principles of health education (6:8) and deeply relevant to malnutrition is what has been said about the cross-cultural outlook in Chapter Four. But although these have prepared the way for what follows, they are in no way adequate as they stand, because, *in many regions of the world, malnutrition would largely disappear if only tropical mothers would feed their young children with foods that are readily available*. This is certainly true for most parts of East Africa, although there are of course circumstances where a general lack of food production is the main factor, as has happened in the Congo where kwashiorkor became epidemic following the political unrest there. There are also further areas, parts of the Middle and Far East for example, where nutritional marasmus due to lack of breast milk is the major syndrome of PCM. Nevertheless, in spite of these provisos, this is a critically important generalization. In the many regions where it applies, the challenge of PCM becomes one of health education.

The principles of this subject have already been discussed, so the following sections will be confined only to certain particular aspects of this challenge. They are the community diagnosis of malnutrition in early childhood, and the right content of programmes of 'nutrition education'.

:2 **The community diagnosis of malnutrition in early childhood.** Before any health education programme can be planned it is imperative that the community diagnosis be as complete as possible. In childhood, malnutrition never occurs only for dietary reasons — it is due to a variety of factors, social, economic, cultural and infective, of which diet is merely the 'final common path'.

As amplifying what has already been said about the data needed to make this community diagnosis, detailed local information will be required in answer to the following questions.

What are the local methods of child feeding? The following matters are of particular importance: the usual length of lactation: the methods of breast feeding and the reasons for stopping it: the time solid foods are first given to children and their nature: whether milk, milk products or other protein foods such as legumes, eggs, meal or fish are ever given to children and in what quantities: the prevalence of such deleterious new prestige practices as bottle feeding, 'aerated beverages' and the use of white flours and sugar: and lastly, the methods of feeding mothers in pregnancy, the puerperium and lactation.

What is the local pattern of malnutrition? Is kwashiorkor the main problem or is it nutritional marasmus? Are infantile beri-beri or avitaminosis-A seen?

How important are other childhood diseases in 'conditioning' the occurrence of malnutrition? Among these are diarrhoea (15:2), measles (13:8), pertussis (13:9), tuberculosis (21:10) and hookworm disease (13:7).

What are the locally available foods? These include both those a family grows and those it purchases. The potential sources of both animal and vegetable protein are important as well as their cost and seasonal availability.

What is the local cultural pattern in regard to food? Customs and beliefs about food must be ascertained, and especially the presence of any 'cultural blocks' that prevent the use of any of the protein foods that could otherwise be given to these children. Thus some cultures have taboos about the use of eggs, milk or fish.

Traditional feeding practices are frequently relevant, such as the numbers of meals daily and the order of feeding within a family. Other aspects of general child rearing may bear on nutrition, such as the tradition of sending children away to be cared for by their grandmothers as soon as they have reached a certain age.

What are the local home economics? These include the type of kitchens, fuel, utensils and the use of any measures of weight or volume. On these will depend the range and complexity of the dishes that can be prepared in the villages. Inquiry should also be made about the money available to the family and its typical budget.

What is the status and activity of the local women? The type of work expected of the local women determines whether mothers can care for their toddlers adequately themselves, or whether they have to leave them alone with other members of the family while they go and work in the fields. Very important also is the independence women have in trying new methods of child rearing, and their freedom to spend the money belonging to the household.

When data have been obtained on such questions as these a community diagnosis can be made and health education planned on the lines that have already been discussed (6:9 and 10). There are however several points that deserve special mention. One is the existence of two sub-groups in most tropical communities. Although there may be a large number of different ethnic, religious, dietary and economic sub-groups in a country, there are usually only two main ones as far as the feeding of young children is concerned.

The first of these, 'the privileged group', consists of a small well-to-do minority who have a house with an adequate kitchen and running water, storage space, and occasionally a refrigerator. They earn sufficient money to be able to buy enough expensive protein foods, such as meat or milk. They are able to feed their young children well and they have received enough education to be able to cook using weights and measures. They usually understand the need for cleanliness and can feed their children on the European or North American pattern with only minor modifications.

The second group are the 'underprivileged'. They are the vast majority of the population who live either in villages or scattered homesteads, or else flock to the towns. There they form the slum dwellers of the 'septic fringe', or, if they are lucky, they find houses on urban housing estates. They have little or no education, and they are poor; they have dirty fly-ridden kitchens, few cooking pots, limited fuel, poor storage facilities and an inadequate water supply. These are the people whose children are malnourished and who require practical advice on how best to look after them. This therefore is the group with which this chapter is concerned. **The message to be brought home to these mothers by every possible means is that they must breast feed their children.**

3 **Breast feeding versus bottle feeding.** Breast milk is the mainstay of protein nutrition for the first six months of life and is usually all that is needed during this period. It is also the cheapest, cleanest, most easily available protein source. Any other food considered during this early period must be either nutritionally necessary, or of real cultural significance, and its alleged advantages must be weighed against the chances of its producing infective diarrhoea. Orange juice, for example, is not usually needed by tropical children in whom scurvy is rare.

After the first six months of life breast feeding is rarely nutritionally adequate by itself and usually amounts in effect to 'breast starvation'. However, lactation is of assistance to the child as a protein supplement even when prolonged into the second year of life, and is a useful partial prophylactic against malnutrition. But, from his mother's point of view, this prolonged or 'late lactation' represents a significant nutritional drain on her resources, especially when pregnancy is frequently repeated. If she is to make good these losses, her own diet must be adequate.

Unsophisticated village mothers are the world's experts on practical breast feeding with whom it is as natural a physiological function as swallowing. They are completely unaware that there is such a thing as the 'technique' of breast feeding, and their success follows from the unconscious imitation of their female relatives, whom they have observed ever since their own childhoods.

Unfortunately, the failure of breast feeding, which has become so prominent a feature of the Western world in the present century, has recently invaded the tropics, where it afflicts urban communities in particular. The reasons for this, and for the rise in bottle feeding with which it is associated are complex, but they are mostly related to the coming of towns and industry. Bottle feeding has come to be associated with 'prestige' and modernness. A sense of 'modesty' has appeared regarding breast feeding. Milk foods are over-advertised, and the successful use of bottle feeding by the well-to-do makes, the underprivileged feel that they are being denied the rights of modern living if they too cannot follow suit.

In tropical towns therefore, bottle feeding is ousting breast feeding with increasing success. However, most tropical mothers have neither the money, the education, nor the kitchen facilities with which to prepare a safe bottle feed. Their children thus receive a dilute, contaminated mixture, low in nutrients and teeming with bacteria. The resulting triad of infective diarrhoea, nutritional marasmus and oral moniliasis is often fatal.

Difficulties have arisen as a result of numerous reputable, but highly competitive, tinned milk firms marketing their costly, high grade wares in tropical countries and using the same pattern of advertising that they use for the educated populations of their affluent homelands. The results are excellent for the privileged minority, but are disastrous for the infants of the uneducated poor, who are increasingly impelled by the glossy glamour of this type of advertising towards ill-advised, impossibly expensive and frequently fatal attempts at prestige bottle feeding. There is little doubt that what is most needed is a reorientation of commercial thinking about infant feeding products marketed in developing tropical regions. For the poorer segment of the population two items are needed.

The first is a cheap or subsidized full cream milk, which is best given via a cup-and-spoon or a feeding cup. This is for the *occasional* baby whose mother is dead or not available (See 14:16).

The second is an inexpensive high protein food, which could be dried skimmed milk, or a mixture containing skimmed milk and vegetable protein ingredients, or a variety of other possibilities. This is wanted for infants over six months of age and need never be reconstituted as a liquid. It could be used either in powder form mixed in with the rest of the diet, or else made into a gruel. It is not a liquid milk, nor a 'milk' substitute' that is needed, but a high protein food, which can be both a true supplement to breast milk and a readily available toddler diet. Though it is possible to make these foods, it is not easy to persuade the people who need them most to use them as they should, particularly if they are marketed specially for the poor. For this reason such foods should be marketed in a form that is acceptable to the rich, they will then acquire 'status' in the eyes of the poor.

14:4 **Transitional diets.** One of the main principles in preventing kwashiorkor and similar less clear cut syndromes is the gradual introduction of the full mixed diet of the community, especially its protein foods, during the second six months of life. Failure to do this satisfactorily is a common defect of traditional feeding practices. **Kwashiorkor is usually seen in the second year of life and its prevention depends mainly upon breast feeding alone for the first six months, followed by the introduction of the local mixed diet, especially its animal and vegetable proteins, from the beginning of the second six month period onwards, combined with continued breast feeding.**

From the beginning of the second six months of its life a child needs gradually increasing quantities of soft, easily chewed, digestible foods, not less than four times daily. On some occasions at least it is desirable that these should be specially cooked for him. Only too often the first foods given to a child are merely portions of the adult diet from the one or two meals which are all most families have each day. These are insufficient for the growing infant who needs to be fed more often. It may be difficult to persuade a mother to prepare a separate meal for her youngest child at the same time as she prepares that for the rest of her family, and it is often inevitable that he has to share whatever they eat. But, when this has to be so, he should have priority as far as protein foods are concerned, and this meal should be supplemented by others specially cooked for him at other times in the day.

If a mother is to take the advice she is given, it has to be adapted to what is practical in her own culture. Thus, among the Baganda it is possible to make use of the traditional practice of steaming plantains in their own leaves to make suitable infant foods — the so-called 'ettu pastes'.

Protein is usually the critical nutrient in infant foods so those concerned with the prevention of kwashiorkor should make a 'protein sources list' of the various kinds of protein available in the region. This should list both animal and vegetable foods, those cultivated and those on sale; it should also include those available at welfare clinics as well as information on seasonal variations in supply and cost. In Kampala for example the cost of 100g. of various forms of protein is as follows: beans -/34, groundnuts -/57, meat 1/75, fresh milk 3/89 and eggs 5/36 (for further details see Appendix H). There is also a very considerable variation in cost between different brands of the same products in the shops. Again taking Kampala as an example, the cheapest brand of dried skim milk costs -/25 a pint, the most expensive 1/50, the cheapest dried whole milk -/70 and the most expensive 1/50, the cheapest sweetened condensed milk -/55 and the most expensive 1/25. Mothers at welfare clinics should be made aware of facts such as these in terms they can understand; they should also be dissuaded from wasting their money on such things as 'aerated beverages'.

In most tropical communities protein food for the young growing child is usually available, but is so comparatively costly that it is vital that what little there is be used to the best advantage. As a way of ensuring this 'triple foods' are very useful as being the most economical and nutritionally advantageous way of using what is available. The local carbohydrate staple is mixed with vegetable proteins and a little animal protein is added. The calories of the staple ensure that the protein is not burnt to produce energy and the vegetable protein ensures that the scarce essential amino acids of the animal protein are used to the best advantage (See what is said in section 14:6 about the addition of calories to milk diets for the same purpose). These triple foods should be soft, digestible, well cooked mixtures containing ingredients from each of the following three groups.

A local staple. If there is an alternative, it should be that with the higher protein content and preferably the local cultural 'superfood'. This may be a cereal, a tuber or something else, the plantain for instance.

A local legume. These should be peas, beans, groundnuts or lentils selected for their digestibility, protein content and acceptance by mothers.

A little animal protein. This may be egg, fish, meat or milk in any form, and should be mixed with the other ingredients before or after cooking depending on its nature.

One example from India is soft boiled rice with toasted Bengal gram flour and a little milk. Another, from Buganda, is steamed plantain with steamed beans to which is added an egg or some dried skim milk. Vegetable oils are not in common use in East Africa, so we have no direct experience of them, but in West Africa it is advised that they be added to infant foods as a useful source of calories and vitamins, particularly where the local staple is a poor one.

Fig. 26. THE THREE PLANK PROTEIN BRIDGE.

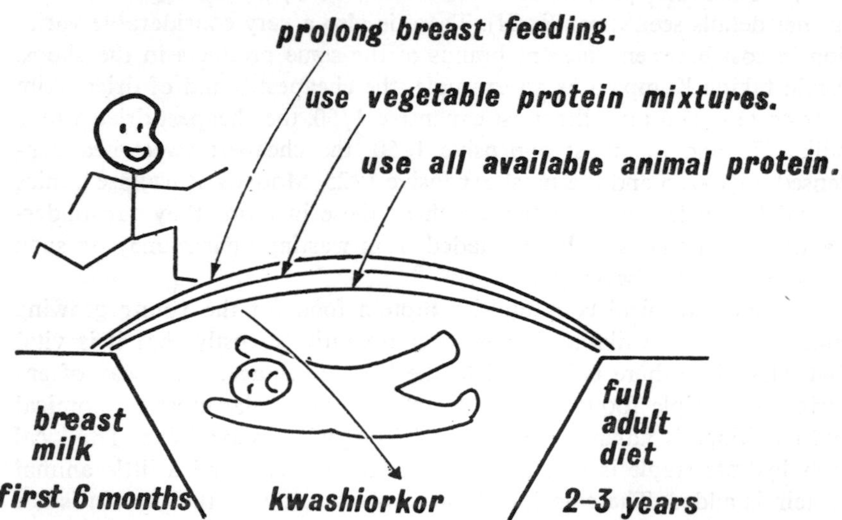

A useful aid in teaching this concept to auxiliary staff is the 'three plank protein bridge' which is illustrated in Figure 26. If the child is not to fall into the river of kwashiorkor in its second and third year, it must cross from breast feeding alone to a full diet on the three planks of prolonged breast feeding, animal protein and vegetable protein. Mothers have no idea what a protein is so this is no use as a teaching aid for them; it does, however, help to establish the idea in the minds of the junior staff. Some of them may not understand its symbolism, so, as with all pictorial teaching aids, ask them a few questions, just to make sure (6:7).

The essence of what has just been said can best be summarized in this way:

:5 **Method: A summary of infant feeding.**

Maternal nutrition. **Persuade mothers to feed themselves better, both on locally available foods, especially legumes, and if possible, on such high protein supplements as dried skim milk. This is especially important during pregnancy and lactation.**

The first six months of life. **Breast feed alone, unless there is definite nutritional need or strong cultural pressure. This implies the avoidance of unnecessary fruit juices or dangerous bottle feeds which so readily produce diarrhoea.**

When the child is six months old. **Continue breast feeding until the age of 18 months and preferably two years. Look upon this as a small but useful protein supplement. If pregnancy supervenes the child should be gradually weaned.**

'The first food'. **From the age of six months onwards gradually introduce a transitional diet of semisolid food. Encourage mothers to start their children with a 'first food' which should be a gruel or soft paste, or a boiled portion of some local staple i.e. maize gruel, soft boiled rice, porridge, the soft outer part of a baked yam, or some steamed plantain. Wherever possible persuade them to enrich this 'first food' with milk or eggs.**

'Triple foods'. **As soon as the child is well established on his first food instruct mothers to introduce gradually a triple food based on locally available products and their limited culinary facilities. Ask them to give small portions once a day at first and then gradually increase this up to four times daily. As dishes of this kind usually need special preparation, cheap small cooking pots with lids may be required, and it may be necessary to make these available at low cost at child welfare centres.**

Where mothers cannot prepare special dishes for their children, and, as a routine towards the end of the first year of life, persuade the parents to give them suitable protein rich portions of their own meals.

CURE

14:6 **Powdered milks and calcium caseinate.** Malnutrition in childhood is a complex clinical problem, but the two major syndromes, kwashiorkor and nutritional marasmus, are both due to lack of protein and calories in varying proportions. When this is made good, most children recover.

Mild cases of kwashiorkor, and cases of 'prekwashiorkor', whose only obvious abnormality is their low weight, can often be treated as outpatients. But, once oedema has appeared, children should be admitted for supplementary feeding and the health education of their mothers.

Mothers of the mild cases should be taught to use the sources of protein already available to the community, eggs and beans for example, and these should be included in the treatment. But suitable foods may not be easily available, and, until an effective system of health education has been built up, it may be difficult for the individual doctor to persuade mothers to use them. Some form of high protein supplement will therefore be required for outpatient use, and the most readily available one is likely to be dried skim milk. This, or its derivative calcium caseinate ('Casilan' (GLA)), is also likely to be the most practical way of treating moderate and severe cases of kwashiorkor in hospital. Dried skim milk is distributed free by UNICEF throughout the tropical world, and all hospitals or clinics are entitled to apply for it, through the medical departments of their governments. Even when it has to be bought, dried skim milk is likely to be the cheapest source of milk protein, but it is not always available and so diets are also given here using full cream milk.

Though invaluable as a source of first class protein, dried skim milk has two disadvantages as a method of treating the severer cases of PCM.

Firstly, it contains very few calories in relation to its protein content, so that, if it is given alone, much valuable and comparatively expensive protein is wasted by being burnt to produce energy.

Secondly, some of the calories it does have are in the form of lactose. This is unfortunate, because intestinal lactase is often deficient in PCM. Some lactose may therefore remain undigested and be broken down by bacteria to produce lactic acid which causes a mild diarrheoa and thus impairs the absorption of protein. But, in spite of this diarrhoea, some protein is still absorbed and a milk diet should never be stopped merely because it causes loose stools full of milk curds.

For these reasons it is therefore often the practice to alter dried skim milk in one of the following two ways.

One is to enrich it with calories in the form of sugar and vegetable oil to make 'calorie-reinforced-milk'. The most convenient way of adding these calories is to mix the dried milk with cane sugar and any local edible vegetable oil, palm oil, or cotton seed oil for example. This is easily done, for the oil can be mixed with the dried milk and the sugar to form a powder which mixes easily with water to make a liquid closely resembling natural milk (4) (7) (23).

Formulae for making these calorie reinforced milks are given in Tables 3A and 3B, one using dried milk and the other dried full cream milk. These look complicated because so many alternative measures are given. They are in fact very simple, as a moment's study will show. As a further convenience two other ways of making calorie reinforced dried skim milk are given in section 30:3. One which is suitable for the smallest hospital or a single ward, uses nothing more elaborate than a wooden spoon and a mixing bowl. The other is a medium sized plant that can make and pack this mixture for distribution over a wide area. The reader may say that he understands why skim milk needs calorie reinforcement, but why add calories when the cream is still there? The answer of course, is that calories are not really so important as with skim milk, but, even so, added calories are necessary. They are given as sugar only in diet 3B and as sugar and oil in diet 3D.

The other way in which milk can be altered is to remove the lactose from it commercially and market the bulk of the milk protein as calcium caseinate. The main use of calcium caseinate is as a replacement for some of the dried skim milk or full cream milk in a diet. This makes it possible to prepare a diet containing the same amount of protein, but proportionately less lactose. These are the diets called 'Casilan-calorie-dried-skim-milk', Table 3C, and 'Casilan-calorie-full-cream-milk', Table 3D. It is also possible to make a lactose-free high protein diet using only calcium caseinate as a protein source. This is the 'Casilan-glucose diet' described below in section 14:7. When mixed the dry ingredients pack to a slightly smaller volume. The number of *rounded dessert-spoonfuls* (Dsp.) of each dry *mixed* diet that are required to make 2 pints (1100 ml.) is indicated in each table. For example, in Table 3A 14 Dsp. are needed.

TABLE 3A

CALORIE—DRIED—SKIM—MILK **THE STANDARD ROUTINE**

14 Dsp.	**2 PINT, 1100 ml. QUANTITY**					**BULK**			
	Rounded Dessert Spoonfuls	Imperial Fl. oz.	Imperial oz.	Metric ml.	Metric g.	Weight %	Weight Parts	Volume %	Volume Parts
Dried skim milk	9	7	4¼	194	120	65	4	72	19
Sugar	2	1¼	1	36	30	16	1	13	3½
Oil	5	1½	1¼	39	35	19	1	15	4

TABLE 3B

CALORIE—FULL—CREAM—MILK

24 Dsp.		2 PINT, 1100 ml. QUANTITY				BULK			
	Rounded Dessert Spoonfuls	Imperial		Metric		Weight		Volume	
		Fl. oz.	oz.	ml.	g.	%	Parts	%	Parts
Full cream milk	22	19	6	543	170	85	17	95	19
Sugar	2	1	1	36	30	15	3	5	1

TABLE 3C

CASILAN—CALORIE—DRIED—SKIM—MILK

15 Dsp.		2 PINT 1100 ml. QUANTITY				BULK			
	Rounded Dessert Spoonfuls	Imperial		Metric		Weight		Volume	
		Fl. oz.	oz.	ml.	g.	%	Parts	%	Parts
Dried skim milk	3	2	1¼	57	35	20	1	16	3
Casilan	8	7	1¼	190	35	20	1	52	10
Sugar	2	1½	1¼	42	35	20	1	11	2
Oil	9	3	2½	77	70	40	2	21	4

TABLE 3D

CASILAN—CALORIE—FULL—CREAM—MILK

19 Dsp.		2 PINT 1100 ml. QUANTITY				BULK			
	Rounded Dessert Spoonfuls	Imperial		Metric		Weight		Volume	
		Fl. oz.	oz.	ml.	g.	%	Parts	%	Parts
Full cream milk	8	7	2	192	60	36	4	44	19
Casilan	7	6	1	163	30	18	2	37	16
Sugar	2	1¼	1	36	30	18	2	8	3½
Oil	6	2	1½	50	45	28	3	11	5

The exact place of calcium caseinate and the diets made with it has yet to be found, but three things are certain. Firstly, it is comparatively expensive and thus beyond the means of many hospitals, secondly, most children are easily cured with reinforced dried skim milk, thirdly, recovery often takes place more quickly with calcium caseinate than it does without it. Further, it is probable that in severe cases of PCM, especially when diarrhoea is conspicuous, calcium caseinate may sometimes be life saving. The 'Casilan-glucose diet' is particularly useful for cases of this kind. If funds permit, some calcium caseinate should therefore always be available. As calcium caseinate is normally only given to severe cases, and as these children have to be tube-fed, it is important that the brand used is one which easily flows down a tube. Casilan and other refined fine mesh preparations mix readily to form a smooth fluid which easily passes down a narrow polythene intragastric tube, but some other brands may not.

Diets A, B, C, and D are made up with the intention of giving between four and five grams of protein per kg. body weight per day. This is the quantity in 125 ml. of diet. It is thus given at the rate of 125 ml./kg./day or 2 fl. oz. lb./day. With the protein there is approximately one calorie in each ml. of diet (4).

What is the place of so many confusing diets?

Diets based on full cream milk are only included in case hospitals have no dried skim milk. Diets based on full cream milk appear to be equally good, but dried skim milk is cheaper. Full cream milk can be given plain, but it is better calorie reinforced with added sugar for the protein sparing effect described above. Calcium caseinate makes possible diets which are much better for curing severe cases of PCM, but their use is largely determined by cost. So much for the raw materials, the next consideration in the use of these diets is the severity of the cases treated.

Mild and recovering cases. These children will be treated as out-patients, and *health education in good feeding methods is what their mothers need most* (14:17). If necessary it must be supplemented, and unhappily sometimes even entirely supplanted by the issue of dried milk. This is best issued as 'milk packets' (14:14) and is most conveniently mixed in with the food dry (14:11).

Moderate and severe cases.

a) *When no calcium caseinate is available.* Use either calorie reinforced dried skim milk (Table 3A), or calorie reinforced full cream milk (Table 3B), whichever is easiest both for moderate and for severe cases.

b) *When calcium caseinate is available.* Use a protein and calorie reinforced diet, either that based on dried skim milk (Table 3C) or full cream milk (Table 3D).

The 'Casilan-glucose diet'. This is not in the tables; it is a high protein diet devoid of lactose and is thus the best diet to use for occasional cases which do not do well and have *a severe persistent diarrhoea on diets 3C and 3D. It is a diet to be used only by the particularly interested doctor under good nursing conditions.* Because it is vitamin and electrolyte free, the vitamin and electrolyte supplements mentioned below are absolutely essential (14:12). It is made by mixing 43 g. of calcium caseinate. 31 g. of sugar, 16 g. of glucose and 60 ml. of oil and making up to 1000 ml.

More than one reader who was so kind as to read this section in draft urged the deletion of this diet. It has, however, been retained in the conviction that there will be some readers who can make use of it and circumstances that justify its use.

14:7b **A note on fresh cow's milk.** Fresh cow's milk has not been mentioned, because, in areas where it is readily available, cases of PCM are unlikely to be common, and because most hospitals have to rely on powdered milk. However, if it is available, it can readily be used, either by making up diet 3B using cow's milk to replace both the milk powder and the water and merely adding sugar in the quantity advised, or by replacing half the water and all the milk powder in diet 3D by a pint of cow's milk.

14:8 **General notes for all diets.** There are certain general notes about all diets which are best summarized like this.

Method: General notes for milk diets.

Weigh the child and determine the quantity of feed to be given over 24 hours from Figure 27.

When making diets, mix the dry ingredients, add the oil, add the cold boiled water and mix again. If the ingredients are added in the wrong order, or the water is too hot, the mixture will go lumpy.

Where possible make up the dry powdered diet in bulk and mix small quantities at a time, adding the required number of rounded dessert spoonfuls to 2 pints (1100 ml.). This is best done by adding the powdered diet to a jug of cold water and mixing with a fork or egg whisk.

Try to use a metric scale for all solids and a metric measuring cylinder for all liquids.

Where possible measure solids by weight and liquids by volume because the density of powdered solids varies so greatly.

Do not keep unrefrigerated liquid diet more than six hours, or it will sour, and if possible, provide a refrigerator in the ward kitchen where made-up diet may be kept between one feed and the next. Otherwise, only make up the quantity of feed required at the time. In a refrigerator feed will keep for 24 hours.

There is no need to sterilize diets. Instead, make up the liquid diet with cold boiled water. Keep a stock of cold boiled water for this purpose.

There is no need to warm feeds because, even straight out of the refrigerator, the feed soon warms up to room temperature. If oil-containing diets are heated for any length of time,

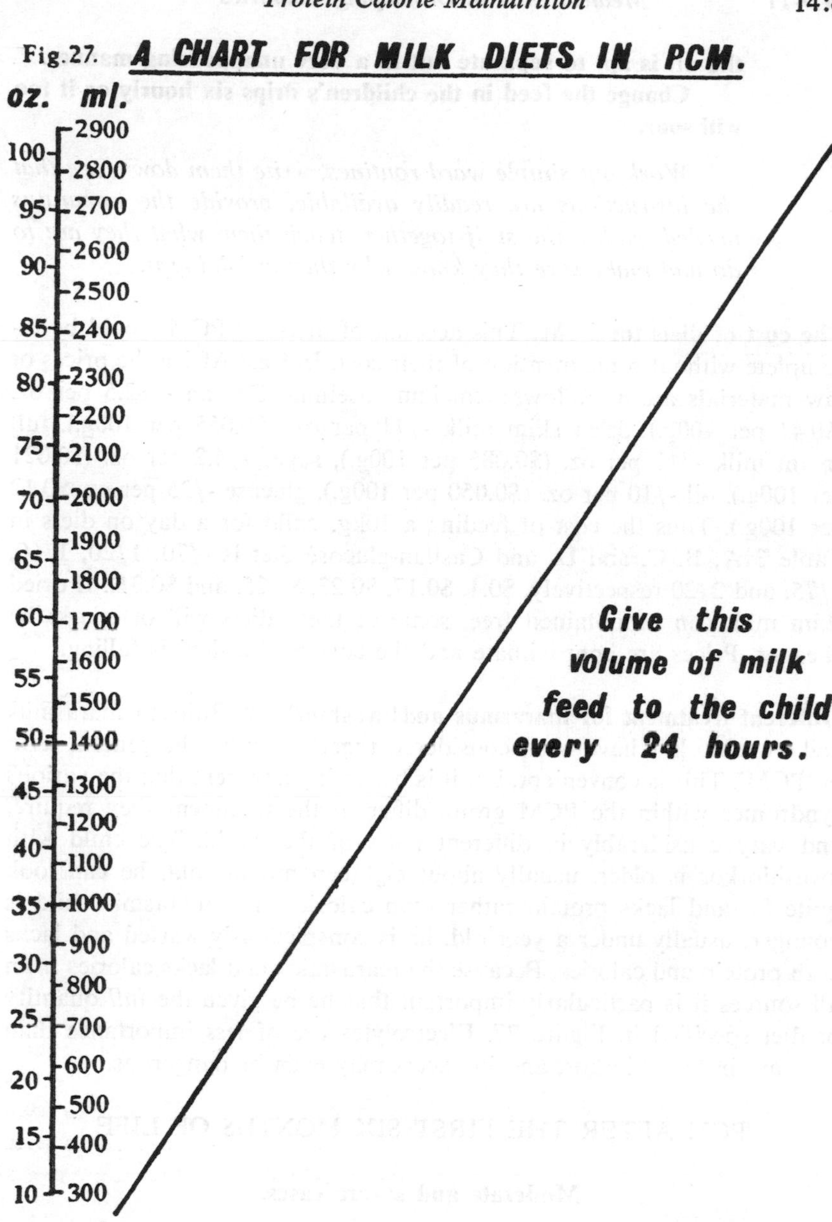

Fig.27. **A CHART FOR MILK DIETS IN PCM.**

the oil is apt to separate out in a very unappetising manner.

Change the feed in the children's drips six hourly or it too will sour.

Work out simple ward routines, write them down, see that the instructions are readily available, provide the apparatus needed, gather the staff together, teach them what they are to do and make sure they know why they are doing it.

14:9 **The cost of diets for PCM.** This account of diets for PCM would be incomplete without some mention of their cost. In East Africa the prices of raw materials are as follows: calcium caseinate Casilan -/82.5 per oz. ($0.41 per 100g.), dried skim milk -/11 per oz. ($0.055 per 100g.), full cream milk -/17 per oz. ($0.085 per 100g.), sugar -/4.2 per oz. ($0.021 per 100g.), oil -/10 per oz. ($0.050 per 100g.), glucose -/25 per oz. $0.12 per 100g.). Thus the cost of feeding a 10kg. child for a day on diets in Table 3 A, B, C, and D, and Casilan-glucose diet is -/70, 1/20, 1/60, 1/75, and 2/20 respectively, $0.1, $0.17, $0.23, $0.25, and $0.31). If dried skim milk can be obtained free, some of these diets will of course be cheaper. Prices are approximate and the cost of 'Casilan' is falling.

14:10 **Different treatment for marasmus and kwashiorkor?** Hitherto marasmus and kwashiorkor have been considered together under the general term of 'PCM'. This is convenient, but it is becoming apparent that the various syndromes within the PCM group differ in the treatment they require, and vary considerably in different parts of the world. The child with kwashiorkor is older, usually about eighteen months old, he can look quite fat and lacks protein rather than calories. The marasmic child is younger, usually under a year old, he is conspicuously wasted and lacks both protein and calories. Because the marasmic child lacks calories from all sources it is particularly important that he be given the *full* quantity of diet specified in Figure 27. Electrolytes are of less importance than they are in kwashiorkor, and in excess may even be dangerous.

PCM AFTER THE FIRST SIX MONTHS OF LIFE

Moderate and severe cases.

14:11 **General treatment.** The first few days of a child's admission are the really critical ones. **The main principle is to get enough high protein food into the child, be it the reinforced dried skim milk or one of the other diets.** The quantity required is given in Figure 27 and should be given continuously by tube, or as small frequent feeds, say six times daily. **Like** similar figures for other doses it is printed again later in the book so that it can be torn out and stuck up on the ward noticeboard. Milk diets can either be given by mouth or through a nylon or polythene nasal intragastric tube (30:7). When they are first admitted, the mother should try feeding these children by mouth, but if the feed is not taken, as it may not be in severe cases, use an intragastric tube. This overcomes the anorexia which is so important a feature of this condition. These tubes can either be used with a continuous drip of milk, or the feed can be given through them intermittently with a syringe. They have been one of the greatest advances in paediatrics in recent years, and it is a pity that they are not more widely used. If they are not already in use, their introduction must be an early priority.

The severe case needs a liquid diet, but as the child recovers solid food may be given as well. If this is so bulky that the child will not take its milk, then the milk must take priority.

When using dried skim milk to increase the protein intake of any patient, be he adult or child, the dry milk powder may be more acceptable if mixed in with the sauces or relishes that the patient normally eats than when given in the form of liquid milk. If the patient is able to take the calories he needs as the staple foods of his ordinary diet, there is of course no need to reinforce the dried skim milk with added calories, and it can be given as the plain powder mixed in with the diet. The calorific value of local diets vary greatly and in West Africa the abundant palm oil usually provides enough calories for added protein to be the only supplement required.

In some communities the small, thin, apathetic, anorexic, grossly underweight two or three year old child is a common clinical problem. Such children are usually without the other stigmata of kwashiorkor and are apt to vomit immediately they are fed, an excuse their mothers often give for not feeding them further, so producing a vicious circle. Sometimes the answer is to tube feed such children, others prefer to give them solid food, but great strength of will, and perseverance, may be required to get these children to take and retain their feed; some even advise refeeding them their vomit. But, if they can be made to retain sufficient food, even for a few days, vomiting may cease and appetite and activity reappear, often in a rapid, heartening and dramatic manner. When staff are insufficient for the much tedious spoonfeeding which is likely to be required, it may be possible to hire one of the local village mothers specially for this task.

Other treatment. PCM is always associated with some degree of electrolyte deficiency, and, though dried milk contains adequate electrolytes and some vitamins, its complete replacement by calcium caseinate makes the diet virtually vitamin and electrolyte free. An electrolyte mixture, such as 'PCM mixture' (30:4), is thus usually unnecessary with diets where all the protein is derived from powdered milk (Table 3A and B); it is a desirable addition to diets where part of the protein is in the form of calcium caseinate (Table 3 C and D), but it is an *essential* addition to the 'Casilan-glucose diet'.

One of the electrolytes these children lack is magnesium, and though there is some magnesium in PCM mixture, there is increasing evidence to suggest that parenteral magnesium therapy *may* be of critical importance in severe cases. Because magnesium is excreted by the kidney, dangerously high levels might follow parenteral therapy in a child whose powers of excreting it are impaired from dehydration or hypotension. Any dehydration present must therefore be corrected by one of the methods described in the next chapter, before parenteral magnesium therapy is given to a child with kwashiorkor, who is often dehydrated from diarrhoea, sometimes accompanied by vomiting. It is to be noted that this paragraph about magnesium applies to kwashiorkor only; marasmic cases are generally less electrolyte deficient.

A vitamin supplement is a desirable addition to diets where part of the protein is in the form of calcium caseinate (diets 3C and 3D), it is an *essential* addition to the 'Casilan-glucose diet'. Folic acid is probably the most important vitamin (5 mg. daily). A compound vitamin preparation such as 'Multivite' may be given for a few days until a mixed diet is started.

The metabolism of these children is such that they may show no febrile response to infection and even malaria may pass unnoticed — in malarial areas give three days oral chloroquine treatment as soon as the child is admitted. To all severe cases give a 5 day prophylactic course of procaine penicillin (2-400,000 units IM). Body temperature may not be maintained, even in quite warm weather, so take care that hypothermia does not occur for it may prove lethal (13:3). In a series at Mulago Hospital about 20 per cent. of children with kwashiorkor were found to have a rectal temperature of under 96°F on admission, or soon after. It

---

Footnote. One recent worker on the subject advises that, as soon as the child's dehydration has been corrected, all **severe** cases of kwashiorkor should be given sterile 50% magnesium sulphate ($MgSO_4.7H_2O$, the common 'Mag. Sulph.') by intramuscular injection (5). She advises that the following doses be given daily for a week, or until such time as the child recovers his normal appetite. When this happens, he can take his magnesium as 'PCM mixture'.

Daily intramuscular dose of sterile 50% Magnesium Sulphate.

5-7 Kg.	(10-15 lbs.)	—	½ ml.
7-10 Kg.	(15-20 lbs.)	—	1 ml.
10-15 Kg.	(20-30 lbs.)	—	1½ ml.
over 15 Kg.	(Over 30 lbs.)	—	2 ml.

seems that their temperature is particularly likely to be low the morning after admission.

When a gravely ill child is admitted, not only may he be very cold, but it seems that he may sometimes be hypoglycaemic also, without showing the typical signs of restlessness, shivering and sweating. In such cases it may be worth trying to correct this hypoglycaemia. Those seeing such children are therefore advised to pass an intragastric tube, which will be needed to give the milk diet anyway, and to start by giving the child some intragastric glucose, say 50ml. of 50% glucose followed by about 10ml. each hour thereafter until he responds. If the child is desperately ill, and suitable veins can be found and staff and skill are available, then, intravenous glucose should be given (10ml. of sterile 50% glucose). Too often, alas, these measures are of no avail.

Tuberculosis is very commonly associated with PCM and is often difficult to diagnose, for severely malnourished children are often Heaf negative (21:3). This makes it important both to Heaf test all children on admission to the ward and to retest any Heaf-negative children as soon as they are over the acute phase of their malnutrition. Because of the inadequacy of the Heaf test in these circumstances, radiology plays a major role in diagnosis.

Finally, no form of diuretic has *any* place in the treatment of PCM.

After-care. The after-care of PCM by correct feeding at home is just as important as the cure of the disease itself. Vigorous health education is therefore essential, and for this to be effective, the same foods that the mother is to give at home must be prepared in the wards. She must be shown how to prepare both the specially cooked dishes and how to improve the average family diet. While in hospital the mother should not only see them prepared but help to prepare them herself — 'If I do it I know' (6:8). It is for this purpose that a 'mothers' shelter' is so useful (13:3). Wherever possible a mother should actually help to grow the foods that have been used to cure her child in hospital, and which she should be growing for him at home. If it is desirable to introduce new strains of such things as legumes into the area, she should be given the seeds to take home with her. The purpose of a hospital garden is to make this kind of health education possible (10:13, 14:17). (See also the 'Mulanda Project' (20b)).

Try to convince a mother that these improvements in her child's diet are not merely for curing the child's illness, but must be continued indefinitely thereafter, if possible as part of the diet of the whole family. The 'triple foods' described earlier are the basis of after-care at Mulago Hospital and eggs are being used increasingly as their first class protein component.

When treating PCM in hospital see that the ward staff are thoroughly incorporated in the educational side of the therapeutic regime and become fully convinced that PCM really is a nutritional disease. Some feel so strongly about this that they do without any form of injection treatment in an attempt to demonstrate that kwashiorkor can be treated with food alone.

Mild cases

14:14 **The outpatient treatment of PCM.** Health education after the manner of the preceding section should play the largest part here, but mothers are often unwilling to come to a clinic merely to receive it. Nevertheless, they will often come if they can take something away with them, and dried skim milk is often the obvious supplement to issue. It must, however, be combined with health education, and to issue it alone must be considered very poor practice.

Unless dried skim milk is packed in some way its issue is both wasteful and messy, and for this purpose polythene bags make the most convenient package. At Mulago Hospital it is either issued plain in bags of 900 g. (2 lbs.) or reinforced with additional calories in bags of about 90 g. (3 oz.) — 'reinforced milk packets' as they are called (30:3 and 5). Each of the latter are the equivalent of a pint of milk. They are not expensive for they only cost -/29 ($0.04) inclusive of the cost of the milk itself, or -/09 ($0.01) without it. They are convenient and portable, and when given in the quantity advised are sufficient to cure PCM even though no other food is taken.

The decision as to whether the milk powder supplement should be given plain or calorie reinforced must be based upon the calories available in a child's diet. When these are adequate it should be issued plain, but, where it is likely that calories are deficient as well as protein, then the reinforced milk packets should be provided. Some workers feel that these children are so frequently short of calories that reinforced milk packets should always be issued, if available, as their oil content supplies low bulk calories. Directions for making both kinds of packets are described, and, though best made in bulk and distributed in drums, they can easily be made locally on a small scale.

One of the difficulties in the use of any kind of packaged milk powder, is that of getting mothers to give it to their children in a regular and ordered manner, in quantities that are both adequate and economical. There is a useful rule for the issue of 'reinforced milk packets'; this is to issue one packet per day for a child up to 10 lbs. (5 kg.), two packets a day for a child up to 20 lbs. (10 kg.) and three packets a day for one up to 30 lbs. (15 kg.). In the outpatient department supply the child's mother with enough of these packets to last her until she next comes up, and, rather than asking her to dissolve the milk powder in water of doubtful safety, ask her to add it to the sauce that she would normally give her sick child, or to other items of his diet. Try to persuade her that this supplement is for him and not for the other members of her family. It is less likely that the slightly oily reinforced milk diet will find its way into his father's tea than will plain dried skim milk.

Although these small reinforced milk packets are probably the best way of using dried skim milk in the outpatient department, there will be those who have to issue dried skim milk or full cream milk in larger quantities, either in the 2 kg. (4½ lb.) cardboard boxes in which UNICEF dried skim milk is often supplied, or distributed into smaller packages.

How are mothers to give it adequately and economically when it has to be given them in such comparatively large packs? In advising a mother how much to give her child it is helpful to know that one *heaped* dessertspoonful (with a fluid volume of 12 ml.) of dried skim milk weighs 15 g. (½ oz.), and that, because dried milk is one-third protein, two such spoonfuls, or 30 g. (1 oz.), contain 10 g. of protein (and 100 calories). Try to give outpatients 3 g. of dried milk protein per kg. per day rather than the higher dose of between 4 and 5 g. that is used to treat more severe cases in the wards. For example, a 10 kg. (20 lb.) child would need 30 g. of protein daily which would be supplied by 6 heaped dessertspoonfuls daily, given two or three times a day, mixed with the rest of the diet, especially the protein containing items such as beans, groundnuts, etc. The standard 2 kg. (4½ lbs.) package of dried milk contains 660 g. protein and would therefore last this child for 22 days.

As assisting a mother to use dried skim milk properly it is customary in Mulago to issue a leaflet with it like that shown in Figure 28. This has an outline of the kind of spoon the mother should use and the quantity of milk it should contain — because there is so much confusion about spoons she should also be shown one as is advised in section 16:8. Though the present Mulago leaflets are printed with a fixed dose (2 or 3 spoonfuls 3 times daily), it seems logical to leave a space for the dose to be filled in as has been done in this figure. Freely translated, the instructions on this leaflet read as follows:

> **'Give your child . . . spoonfuls of dried milk this size three times a day (on the packet a dessert spoon is represented life size). FOOD WHICH MAKES THE CHILD GROW WELL. This powder is to be mixed with the sauces or other foods the child is given. Suckle your child until he is one and a half years old. In addition, from the age of six months onwards, give him some solid food such as eggs, beans, peas, groundnuts or green vegetables, also if possible some meat or fish. All water for drinking**

Fig. 28. **A LABEL FOR MILK PACKETS.**

Note: This is a pudding or dessert spoon, it holds 15 g. of dried milk. (1/2 oz.)

EBIJIKO .... NGA KINO
BIWE OMWANA EMIRUNDI ESATU OLUNAKU.

EMMERE Y'OMWANA

EMMERE EKUZA OMWANA OBULUNGI

EMMERE ENO ETABULIBWA MUBUUGI MU NVA, ERA NE MU MMERE ENDALA YONNA.

YONSA OMWANAWO OKUTUUSA NGA AWEZEZZA OMWAKA GUMU N'EKITUNDU MUGATIREKO EBY'OKULYA EBIRALA NGA AWEZEZZA EMYEZI MUKAAGA NGA EMMERE ENO: AMATA, EBIJANJAALO, KAWO, EBINNYEBWA, ENVA ENDIIRWA ERA OBA KIYINZIKA AMAGGI, ENNYAMA, N'EBYENYANJA.

AMAZZI GONNA AG'OKUNYWA OBA AGATABULA EMMERE GATEEKWA KUBA MAFUMBE.

CHILD HEALTH DEPARTMENT
MULAGO HOSPITAL

DRIED SKIM MILK
DONATED BY AMERICA
THROUGH UNICEF

or mixing with food must first be boiled'. (The note in English in Figure 28 about the size of the spoon is not, of course, printed on the leaflet).

There is one further point in the use of dried skim milk as the main food for babies — it is not only low in calories, but, more important, it is virtually free of vitamins A & D, so if a young child is fed largely on this for any length of time, he runs a grave risk of irreversible blindness due to vitamin A deficiency (keratomalacia). For this reason, all UNICEF dried skim milk is now fortified with these vitamins, but users of brands of unfortified skim milk, both dried and condensed, must provide vitamin A, either orally in the form of fish liver oil or vitamin concentrate, or by a single intramuscular repository dose of 100,000 units, which will probably be sufficient for three months. The baby should also be exposed to sunlight to enable his skin to synthesize vitamin D.

PCM BEFORE THE AGE OF SIX MONTHS

The restoration of breast feeding. In the first six months of life nutritional marasmus is the commonest form of PCM. The cardinal principle in treating it is to restore breast feeding — the younger the child the more important this is. It is not as difficult as it may sound, for induced lactation is common in many communities — sometimes even by grandmothers — and it is a valuable traditional practice for the orphaned as well as the marasmic. It is usually quite easy and the first essential is confidence, for a mother must catch from the staff the feeling that plenty of milk is sure to appear. She is given milk by mouth, not usually for any direct nutritional effect, but rather for its psychological role, the idea in her mind being 'milk-in-therefore-milk-out', a useful reinforcement of her confidence. If need be, the child's dehydration is corrected, he is put to the breast frequently, and the mother is given a course of chlorpromazine (50-100 mgm. three times daily for 7-10 days), for its probable effect on the hypothalamus and hence on the pituitary gland in producing the milk secreting hormone, prolactin.

Nutritional marasmus often follows failed breast feeding, and as has been said before, the importance of encouraging lactation cannot be overstressed. As a food, breast milk is cheap, sterile, and perfectly adapted to the needs of the baby.

Artificial feeding. Only among the most affluent and educated is artificial feeding practicable — a tiny fraction of the world's people. Earlier this century the dangers of bottle feeding were well shown by the ten-fold greater mortality among the bottle fed infants of Europe and North America. It is almost impossible to prepare a satisfactory artificial feed in a villager's hut and the combination of nutritional marasmus and frequent diarrhoea merit the definition of a separate syndrome — 'feeding bottle disease'. The ubiquity of these dirty plastic bottles, which are so difficult for a villager to keep clean, and the misery they cause is one of the newer nutritional problems of the tropics.

Occasionally it will be necessary for a mother to feed her child artificially — how is she to do it? Firstly, it should be by cup and spoon, and not by bottle. At Mulago Hospital feeding bottles are barred from the wards as positively furthering 'ill-health-education'. Feeding by cup and spoon takes longer and is not popular with the staff, but in hospital a child's mother usually has plenty of time for it. Nevertheless, it must be admitted that in some hospitals sheer staff shortage compels the use of feeding bottles.

A 'home feeding kit' has recently been tried out in Uganda for those children needing some form of artificial feeding at home (37). This takes the form of an artificial feeding vessel with a spout for the child to drink from (Figure 29). With it goes a tin of dried milk and a packet of soap, these being contained in a larger tin which is used as a saucepan in which to boil water. With this boiling water a mother sterilizes the feeding vessel, and when it has cooled she uses the rest of it to make up the child's feed. These kits seem effective, but, until some enterprising manufacturer makes cheap aluminium or plastic feeding vessels of this kind, they will not be practicable. Until this happens a domestic teacup and teaspoon will have to be used; this is a pity, because feeding vessels are faster, and are washed quite as easily as teacups.

Fig. 29. **A FEEDING VESSEL.**

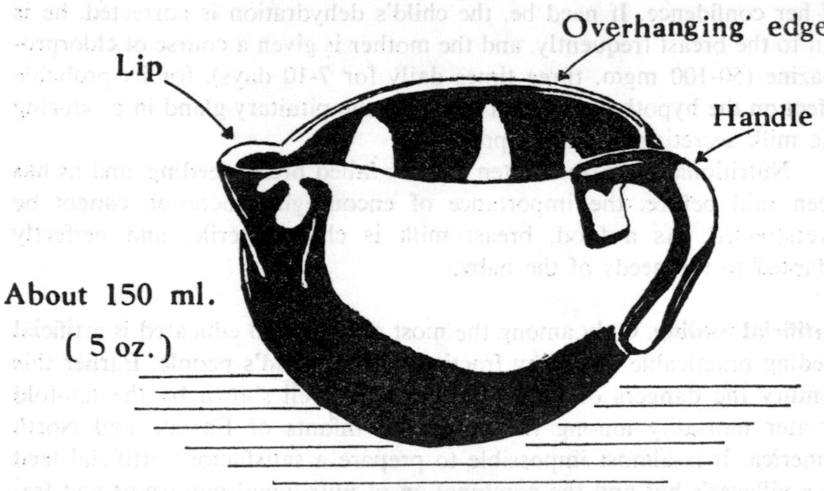

What is a mother to give her child? Sometimes fresh cow's milk from a reliable source will be the most practical artificial feed. Ask the mother to boil it, both to sterilize it and to render it more easily digested, to dilute it — 3 parts of cow's milk to one of water, and to add sugar 1 oz. (30 g. or 4 *heaped* teaspoonfuls) to a pint (568 ml. or about 3 teacups). If she adds one heaped spoonful of sugar to a cup of diluted milk she will not be far out. Spoons and cups vary, and these figures are for a cup of 200 ml. and a teaspoon with a liquid capacity of 5 ml. This holds about 7.5 g. of sugar when heaped and about 2.5 g. of milk powder when level. Heaped measures of sugar are fairly constant for a given size spoon, because an excess of sugar readily runs off the spoon and limits the amount which can be heaped upon it. This is not so with milk powder, a large quantity can readily be heaped on a spoon, so heaped spoonfuls of milk powder thus vary greatly; even so, heaped dessert-spoonfuls of milk powder (15 g.) are often sufficiently accurate and more convenient in use than level ones (6 g.).

Opinions differ as to how much cow's milk should be diluted, but within limits, the degree of dilution is not important, and if the mother is very unsophisticated, and unlikely to follow any but the simplest instructions (if those), then the best advice may be to ask her to give her child plain boiled cow's milk, undiluted and without added sugar.

See that the mother feeds her child at the rate of 2½ oz./lb./day or 150 ml./kg./day — *this rate applies to all the feeds in the following sections* and is a very convenient figure to remember — see the note under Table 5 (15:6).

If dried milk has to be used this should be the cheapest local brand of full cream milk (14:4) diluted, either one level teaspoon to the ounce; or seven level teaspoonfuls to the teacup (200 ml.); or 2 oz., 60 g., 4 heaped dessertspoonfuls or ten level ones to the pint (568 ml.) The dessertspoon here is one of 12 ml. liquid capacity. All these various alternatives produce a mixture that is equivalent to the diluted cow's milk that is described above (3 parts of milk to one of water) and approximate closely to a 10% solution of milk powder in water. To this mixture a mother should add sugar, one ounce to the pint, or approximately one heaped teaspoonful to the teacup, as above. The formula 'seven level teaspoonfuls of milk powder and one heaped one of sugar for every teacup' may be a convenient one for her to remember. Calculate the number of teacups the child needs daily on the basis of a 200 ml. (7 oz.) teacup, the child's weight and the 150 ml./kg./day formula given above.

Sometimes there will be occasions where dried *skim* milk *has* to be used. If so used it should be of the vitamin fortified variety (14:14) prepared, preferably with added sugar, in exactly the same manner as full cream milk. One thing has to be stressed, it is that dried skim milk, and particularly UNICEF distributed dried skim milk, is intended as a protein supplement in cases of PCM—it is *not* a substitute for breast feeding *except in the rare and particular case* when neither cow's milk nor full cream milk are available. If it is not properly managed, the distribution of free dried skim milk may tempt mothers to abandon breast feeding and replace it with dried skim milk from a bottle — *this is a disaster!*

There are two main kinds of liquid milk in tins, one is unsweetened, the so-called 'evaporated milk', of which 'Carnation' and 'Ideal' are two well known brands. The other is sweetened condensed milk which contains a large quantity of added sugar. The common form of sweetened condensed milk is the full cream variety, but sweetened condensed *skim* milk is also available. Neither kind of sweetened condensed milk is satisfactory as an infant food for they contain too much sugar in relation to their protein content — much more than that advised in the feeds above. Although, like powdered milk, they have the advantage of keeping once the tin is opened, mothers must be discouraged from using them, especially the condensed skimmed variety.

If tinned milk is to be used, the unsweetened evaporated variety is quite satisfactory, but, because it is more concentrated than fresh cow's milk, dilute it, not three parts of milk to one of water, as with fresh cow's milk, but two parts of milk to one of water. It will then be similar in concentration to the other feeds that have already been described. Add sugar to the diluted mixtures at the rate advised above — for convenience one heaped teaspoonful to the cup. Evaporated milk contains sufficient vitamins A and D, the important supplement being vitamin C, of which the child under one year of age needs 25 mg. daily, which it is sometimes most convenient to give as a tablet added to the milk feed for the day. It is also needed with *all* other artificial feeds.

Something must be said about the water with which the child's feeds are made up — encourage mothers to boil the day's supply and put it aside in a clean covered jug or in covered bottles.

THE NUTRITION REHABILITATION UNIT

14:17a **The nutrition rehabilitation unit.** Nothing is quite so important in the care of children with kwashiorkor as effective health education, yet few things are more difficult to provide on a large scale in a busy hospital. It was to fulfil this need that a nutrition rehabilitation unit was organized at Mulago Hospital. It is the first of its kind in Africa, and, though it is set up in a teaching hospital and staffed by a specialist paediatrician, there seems no reason why similar ones should not be equally effective on a more modest scale in district hospitals, for it is here that the need is greatest.

14:17b **Buildings.** The buildings of the unit are simple. There is a 'residential centre' consisting of a dormitory and a kitchen where mothers can prepare their own meals. There is an outpatient hall and several minor but very important educational structures in the grounds nearby, such as a simple rural kitchen. The unit is housed in single story buildings some way from the hospital itself. At Mulago some of these are of 'mud-wattle and-whitewash', but there is no reason why the whole unit should not be of the cheap local pattern advocated so strongly in sections 1:10 and 10:6, and used so successfully in section 19:5.

7c **Outpatients.** At Mulago all children with kwashiorkor come to the unit; mild ones are sent straight from the outpatient department, severe ones come to it after their discharge from the wards. Outpatient mothers in small groups are given health education talks, and are shown how to prepare a lunch for their children using the locally available foods and the dried skim milk powder that is issued to them in packets, either plain or calorie reinforced (14:14). They are taught the importance of breast feeding, and the value of boiling water and milk. There is an immunization programme (17:1) and antimalarial drugs are prescribed (16:10).

7d **The residential centre.** From the outpatient group, twenty mothers with their children are selected for admission to the residential centre for from four to six weeks. Great emphasis is placed on this period of residence so that a mother can actually see her child getting better without it being given anything more than the correct food. In this way she becomes convinced that the disease is due to faulty feeding alone (14:13). A mother learns that the training she is given is to help her to teach her neighbours the dietary principles involved in the prevention and cure of kwashiorkor. The programme in the unit is mother oriented rather than child oriented and mothers are taught general homecraft as well as good nutrition.

But residence probably has another effect. Mothers are in the unit long enough for them to form a community and, if the general attitude of this community is that kwashiorkor is a nutritional disease, then new mothers are likely to be converted to this way of thinking by those who have already been convinced. It is likely that a useful part of the unit's teaching is done for it automatically in this way. Working in pairs, two mothers from the residential centre, a more experienced and a less experienced one, are selected to teach the outpatient mothers. They show them how to prepare meals in the simple demonstration kitchen near the outpatient hall and, by working in pairs in this way, not only do both teach the outpatients, but the senior mother teaches the junior one how to teach. In this way a pair of mothers needs less supervision from the staff than they would otherwise.

On their discharge from the unit mother and child are taken home by a member of the staff. A meeting is arranged at which are present the mother and her child, who is now much better, the father, some neighbours and any chiefs or local authorities who can be persuaded to attend. The mother and staff member demonstrate the child to this group, and the mother tells them the dietary principles that she has learnt (6:4).

14:17e **Some important details.** This is the essence of what the unit does, but there are many other points which contribute to success. Fathers for instance are considered very important. Every week there is a 'Fathers' Day' at the unit when fathers visit, particularly the fathers of children who have been admitted with their mothers. They are shown the work of the unit and how they can assist their wives when they return home.

In the grounds around the unit there are several demonstrations of how families can improve their own homes and diets. There is a local pattern hut with its cooking facilities incorporating various improvements that are within the means of the family. Thus, there is a raised fireplace to keep pots of boiling water away from small children, the hut has a high shelf to keep the family's paraffin bottle out of the children's reach; there is also an improved local pattern larder, and tables, etc. In the hut are two large local pattern pots with lids. In one of these a mother can keep boiled water, and in the other unboiled water. Outside the hut is a proper soak pit, a drying stand and a compost heap. There is also a vegetable garden (10:13, 14:13), an improved chicken coop on the deep litter system and some rabbit hutches. Mothers are also taught sewing and anything else that is likely to make them more effective wives and mothers (Twelfth axiom (1:19b)).

14:17f **Staff.** The Mulago unit is directed by one doctor and employs a staff of sixteen. There are twenty mothers in residence at any one time and the outpatient department sees up to fifty mothers a morning. This may seem a luxurious level of staffing, but the unit is a prototype and has research functions; it also trains medical assistants, medical students, nurses and community development workers. On a district hospital scale it could probably work under the supervision of a visiting doctor with a medical assistant, a health educator (6:2), a staff nurse and three or four cleaners, gardeners, etc.

This is an experimental unit, and at the time of writing it has only been working nine months. It attempts to deal with an enormous problem and deserves to be tried out in other places. Some of its principles are general, some relate only to the residential part of it. They can best be summarized like this:

14:17g **Method: Running a nutrition rehabilitation unit.**

Relevant to the unit generally.

Adapt practice and particularly feeding methods to the local culture (Twelfth axiom 1:19a).

Take every possible advantage of any medical and social facilities that may be available, be these health centres, community development workers, etc.

Train suitable auxiliaries to do most of the work (Ninth axiom 1:16). In the absence of more suitable staff, these may have to be anybody who is available, staff wives for instance.

Constantly supervise the staff.

Make every possible attempt to evaluate what is done. How effective are the measures being taken?

Relevant to the residential centre.

Arrange to have some mothers in residence.

Get the trained mothers in residence to teach the untrained ones in the outpatient department.

Let mothers do all they possibly can themselves under supervision, especially their own cooking.

Co-operate with fathers as much as possible.

Secure the assistance of chiefs and local authorities.

Visit mothers at home, both with the intention of helping them and evaluating the effect of the training they have been given.

See that residential training is oriented towards the mother rather than the child, and take every opportunity to increase her general education and skill.

The work of the unit can be expressed in another way. Baganda mothers variously attribute *omusana-obwosi*, the disease recognized as kwashiorkor, to the sun, to the seeds of a certain plant entering a child's body, to air entering him if he is not properly covered at night, and to heat from his mother's womb. The unit aims to send mothers back to their villages convinced that all these notions are wrong, and vigorous protagonists of the idea that incorrect feeding is the major cause of *omusana-obwosi*. If they really are convinced, they will, it is hoped, convince their friends and spread correct knowledge through the community. Properly instilled, the knowledge imparted by the unit in the minds of a few mothers can multiply many times (6:4).

8 **Acknowledgements.** This chapter has been compiled from the practice of Mulago Hospital and the Infantile Malnutrition Research Unit in Kampala, financed and staffed by the Medical Research Council of the United Kingdom. It draws on the ideas and experience of many people, notably those of Professor D. B. Jelliffe, Dr. F. J. Bennett, Dr. P. S. E. G. Harland, Dr. D. C. Morley, Dr. and Mrs. H. J. L. Burgess and Miss I. Rutishauser. Section 14:17 describes the work of Dr. I. Schneideman at the Nutrition Rehabilitation Unit, a Freedom from Hunger Campaign project, assisted both by the Save the Children Fund (U.K.) and by OXFAM, and housed in buildings on loan from the Uganda Ministry of Health.

Chapter Fifteen

DIARRHOEA IN CHILDHOOD

Professor Derrick Jelliffe

15:1 **The prevalence of diarrhoea.** With malnutrition and pneumonia, diarrhoea is one of the three major causes of sickness and death in tropical children everywhere. Statistics are hard to come by, but, while it is certain that it has become less common in Europe and North America, diarrhoea seems to be increasing in frequency in many tropical countries, especially in young children who readily develop fluid and electrolyte imbalance, and who are often precipitated into marasmus or kwashiorkor.

As tropical towns grow and their slums extend, diarrhoea will probably become even more prevalent, for it is notoriously a disease of poor crowded communities, especially when children are no longer fed from the breast but from a bottle whose contents are not only nutritionally inadequate, but usually bacteriologically dangerous also.

15:2 **The principles of diagnosis and treatment.** The diarrhoeas of childhood are a complex of syndromes. Their pattern is determined by their varied aetiology, their severity and the acuteness of their onset, as well as the age of the children affected and their nutritional state.

The first step to be taken when seeing any child with diarrhoea is to make a guided 'guess' as to its probable aetiology, and the next is to estimate the severity of his dehydration. After this there are certain simple, safe and approximate therapeutic principles to be followed in regard to Dehydration, Drugs and Diet — the three 'Ds'. But, of these three, dehydration is much the most important.

15:3 **Aetiology.** The diarrhoeas caused by the Shigellae, the Salmonellae, the Enteroviruses, the amoebae, the enteropathic Escherichiae and malignant tertian malaria are all well known. But, though the absence of laboratory facilities makes it difficult to estimate their prevalence, they still appear to leave many cases unexplained. As part of the explanation, the concept of 'weanling diarrhoea' is becoming increasingly popular; for, in the second semester, when solid food is being taken for the first time, a child's gut is susceptible to bacteria that would be harmless later on. Weanling diarrhoea is thought to be produced by the ingestion of organisms that are not usually pathogenic, especially in the large numbers to which a child is exposed in an insanitary environment.

There is often a vicious circle, for the resulting diarrhoea lowers the nutrition of the child and makes him even more susceptible to infection. Such diarrhoea shades off into that from uncomplicated PCM, and, both in kwashiorkor and in nutritional marasmus, the general shortage of protein reduces the production of digestive enzymes and diarrhoea may result.

Diet alone can also cause diarrhoea, particularly when the child is fed with large quantities of indigestible legumes, or the coarse, ill cooked foods of many tropical countries.

Bacteria are probably the commonest cause of severe acute diarrhoea in the tropics. The stools of a bacterial diarrhoea are either watery with streaks of blood; frankly dysenteric with pus cells, red cells and shreds of mucosa; or often at least have red cells and pus cells visible microscopically. The malaria stool on the other hand is loose, watery and devoid of either pus or red cells. Malaria is so easily overlooked that it is always wise to examine a thick blood film in all cases of severe diarrhoea. In indigenous communities the importance of malaria as a cause of *mild* diarrhoea is now being questioned. How often in fact are the malaria parasites that may be seen in a child's blood the real cause of his diarrhoea?

In infants, other parenteral infections, such as otitis media and furunculosis, are also believed to result in diarrhoea, but this is probably uncommon and is seldom either severe or prolonged. In such parenteral diarrhoeas the stools are usually loose, greenish and devoid of either pus or red cells.

Amoebiasis is usually subacute or chronic with mucus and red cells, but few pus cells to be found in the stools. Giardiasis often produces characteristic pale, bulky, offensive, frothy, 'beaten egg' stools containing large numbers of Giardia trophozoites that are easily seen microscopically in a wet preparation of the faeces. It is important to recognize this syndrome, for it readily responds to a 5 day course of mepacrine (0-2 years, 25 mg. b.d.; over 5 years, 50 mg. b.d.).

Often the aetiology of a particular case is complex. Sometimes it is partly due to infection, partly due to malnutrition, partly to indigestible foods and perhaps also to misguided attemps at herbal cure.

Laboratory facilities are seldom available to confirm the aetiology of childhood diarrhoeas, and in practice the precise cause of most of them must usually remain speculative. Nevertheless, it is always worth looking at the stool in search of blood and mucus, and having those of the severer cases examined microscopically. Napkins are uncommon and there may be nothing to see, but, a useful sample of stool can be obtained, particularly if it is a liquid one, by inserting a smooth ended open glass tube 8 cm. long and 75 mm in bore (3 in. x ¼ in.) into the rectum, when liquid faeces will trickle out. Keep a supply of such tubes available, for they are readily washed and boiled and the appearance of the stool may provide useful clues to suggest the possible aetiology of the diarrhoea.

DEHYDRATION

15:4 **Half strength Darrow's solution in 2.5% glucose.** In a busy children's ward a single fluid that will suffice for the majority of cases is a major convenience. The solution advised is half strength Darrow's solution in 2.5% glucose. This contains, in each litre of water, 60 MEq of sodium, 18 MEq of potassium, 52 MEq of chloride, 25 MEq of lactate and also some calories. Its virtue is that it supplies the missing substances in quantities which are sufficient for the majority of cases, but not in dangerous concentration. Although it is better purchased it can be made up in any hospital, and directions are given in section 30:2. Liquid sodium lactate will be required and the effort of obtaining it, and teaching someone to make this solution will be well repaid, for this is one of the best routine solutions for the treatment of dehydrated children. If it is not available it should be replaced temporarily with 1/3 physiological saline in 5% glucose.

15:5 **Assessing the severity of dehydration.** It is impossible to assess a child's electrolyte state accurately, particularly if he is also malnourished. But an accurate assessment is of much less importance than might be expected, and dehydrated children can easily be divided into three grades, mild, moderate and severe, using the five key signs listed in Table 4.

TABLE 4

THE ASSESSMENT OF DEHYDRATION BY FIVE CLINICAL SIGNS

Stage	*Appearance*	*Skin Elasticity*	*Anterior Fontanelle*	*Eyes*	*Mouth*
MILD	Fretful	Normal or slightly reduced	Normal or slightly depressed	Normal or slightly sunken	Dry, red
MODERATE	Restless	Moderately impaired	Moderately sunken	Sunken	Very dry, slight cyanosis
SEVERE	Semi-coma	Severely impaired	Deeply sunken	Deeply sunken, 'staring'	Very dry, cyanosed

Note: Do not rely on skin elasticity in the presence of malnutrition.

A sign which is not listed there is a child's weight loss. If a child has a weight chart, such as that described in section 26:5, it is easy to estimate the extent of his dehydration, because the rapid loss even of 250 g. (½lb.) can be taken as evidence for it. If he has mild diarrhoea and is being treated as an outpatient, a daily record of his weight is a good indication of his response to treatment or the lack of it.

The three grades of diarrhoea are not all equally common and many mild cases will be seen for every severe one. The table describes the signs to be seen in the average child with diarrhoea. He will probably also have vomited a little and will thus be mildly acidotic as well as lacking water, sodium and potassium.

6 **The volume of fluid required and the speed of its administration.** There are many complex ways of estimating the fluid lost, and thus the volume required to replace it, but they are most of them quite impractical. The following method is therefore given as a useful approximation, its great virtue being not only that it is simple, but also that it works.

Method: The rehydration of dehydrated children.

Using Table 4 classify the dehydration as mild, moderate, or severe.

Weigh the child and estimate the fluid needed in the first 24 hours using either Table 5 or the graph in Figure 30.

Replace the whole of this calculated volume in the first 24 hours.

Thereafter, supply the normal daily requirements PLUS any further loss by diarrhoea and vomiting.

TABLE 5

THE FLUID REQUIREMENTS OF DEHYDRATED CHILDREN

FIRST 24 HOURS		
Degree of dehydration		*Fluid requirement*
Mild	—	200 ml. per kg.
	or	90 ml. per lb.
	or	3¼ oz. per lb.
Moderate	—	240 ml. per kg.
	or	110 ml. per lb.
	or	4 oz. per lb.
Severe	—	280 ml. per kg.
	or	130 ml. per lb.
EACH DAY THEREAFTER	or	4¾ oz. per lb.

To cover normal daily requirements give all cases—150 ml. per kg. or 70 ml. per lb. or 2½ oz. per lb. PLUS THE REPLACEMENT FOR ANY FURTHER LOSS BY DIARRHOEA AND VOMITING.

Note:—The figure of 150 ml./kg./day or 2½ oz./lb./day is a useful one to remember. It is the standard figure for fluid requirements in children, and is thus the feed requirement in babies (14:16). Dehydrated children obviously require more on their first day—200, 240 or 280 ml. according to the severity of their dehydration. The diet requirements in PCM have been worked out, somewhat arbitrarily, at a slightly lower fluid requirement—125 ml./kg./day, which is the basis of Figure 27. The child's weight in these cases is his weight on admission to the ward.

The normal daily requirements are those needed to make good the loss through the lungs, skin and kidneys and amount to about 150 ml./kg./day. This is shown in Table 5 and indicated by the dotted line on the graph in Figure 30.

Fig. 30

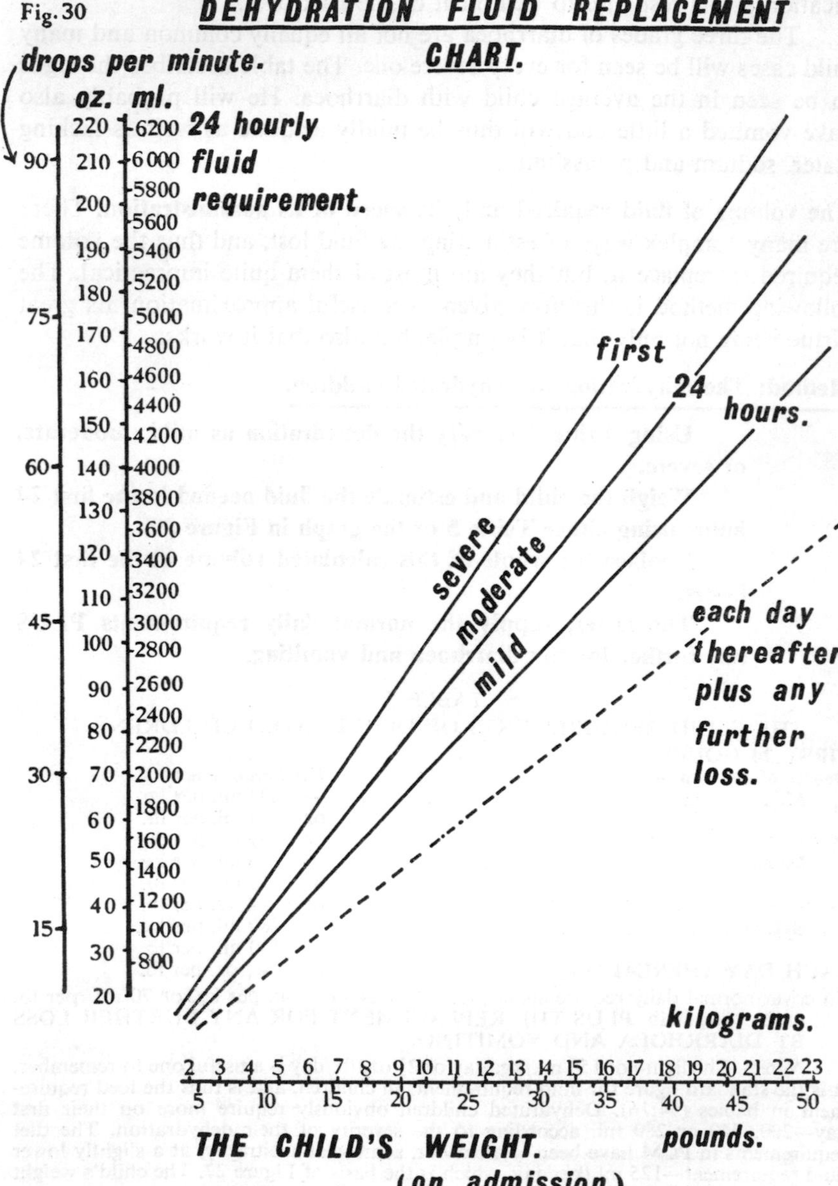

It is not easy to estimate the further loss by diarrhoea and vomiting, and a guess is the only thing that can be made in the circumstances, but all fluids given and lost should be charted and totalled each day.

The same volume of fluid is required whatever the route chosen to give it. The speed at which it is given will vary with the route by which it is administered and with the severity of the dehydration. Except when using the intraperitoneal route, where a rapidly administered fluid 'depot' is more slowly absorbed, and the subcutaneous route with a syringe, spread the fluid required by mild and moderate cases over 24 hours. With the oral and subcutaneous routes (by drip) this should not be difficult, but with the intravenous route it may be. One of the difficulties is, that with small children and thus a comparatively small volume of fluid, the drip has to run so slowly that it may cease to flow. To make it easier spread out the fluid over 24 hours. Figure 30 includes a scale showing the number of drops per minute at which the drip should run. The drops are those delivered by the MRC drop counter specified in section 23:7. At 15 drops a minute one litre of fluid is delivered in approximately 24 hours. Another way of spreading out the fluid is to stick a strip of adhesive tape down the side of the bottle and write on it the level the fluid must reach at specified times.

When a child is desperately ill and shocked some fluid must be given rapidly for he will be severely dehydrated. His whole body will be short of fluid, but its absence is most critically felt in the vascular compartment. It is essential therefore that this fluid be replaced and his blood volume restored without delay. Therefore, *in severe dehydration with peripheral vascular failure, always give some fluid intravenously*. Give 25% of the total fluid calculated for the first 24 hours intravenously with the drip wide open as fast as it will go, and, when this has been given, spread the remaining 75% over the rest of the first 24 hours.

Figure 30 is printed twice: this enables the spare copy printed at the end of the book to be cut out and pasted up for easy reference in a children's ward or outpatient department.

:7 **The routes by which fluid can be given.** There are several routes by which fluid may be given:

Mild dehydration: Fluid can be given by mouth either

i) by cup and spoon
or ii) intragastric tube.

Moderate dehydration: Fluid can be given parenterally either

i) intraperitoneally
or ii) subcutaneously either by a) a 'drip or
b) with a syringe

Severe dehydration: Some of the fluid has to be given intravenously either

i) by scalp vein infusion

or ii) by cutting down on an ankle vein.

There is general agreement that the oral route is best for mild cases and that in severe cases the intravenous route must be used. Opinions differ, however, about the best way of giving fluid in the intermediate situation, when a child is only moderately dehydrated, yet still too ill for complete reliance to be placed on fluids by mouth. Some give fluids intravenously, but for many paediatricians in tropical circumstances, the choice is between the subcutaneous and the intraperitoneal routes and, though both work well in different hands, the intraperitoneal route is preferred at Mulago Hospital. When staff are reasonably skilled and supervised, it is probably the best one, but where they are not so skilled, many think that the subcutaneous route is safer.

15:8 **The oral route.** This is the best route in mild cases, and in children who have diarrhoea but are not yet dehydrated — the 'pre-dehydration stage'. Such children deserve treatment and it is good practice to encourage the mothers of all children with mild diarrhoea to give them an electrolyte solution by mouth, whether they are dehydrated or not. In this way they may remain in a good state of electrolyte balance, and will be much better placed should severe diarrhoea subsequently supervene.

Method: <u>'Cup-and-spoon'.</u>

Use 'saline mixture' — a gram of sodium chloride and a gram of potassium chloride in each 15 ml. (½ oz.), diluted to 500 ml. (1 pint) in water or milk. Another alternative is Darrow's solution in 2.5% glucose, but it is extravagant to open a bottle carefully prepared for intravenous use when a simple salt solution will serve just as well. A mother can also make her own solution with ½ a teaspoonful of salt and 4 teaspoonfuls of sugar dissolved in 500 ml. (1 pint) of water.

Give a mother a cupful of diluted saline, show her how to feed her child by cup-and-spoon, and see that a nurse supervises her over the next few hours in some quiet corner of the clinic. Only when she understands what she is to do, should she be given a bottle of concentrated saline mixture to take away and dilute with boiled water at home.

Method: <u>Intragastric tube.</u>

Pass a nasal intragastric polythene tube as described in section 30:7 and, either give the fluid intermittently with a

syringe, or continuously as a drip. The intragastric method requires less attention from the staff which is a great advantage when nurses are scarce and a child's mother is not available; it is also less likely to lead to vomiting. If vomiting is already present it may be treated with intramuscular chlorpromazine (½ mg./kg.).

Even when a severely dehydrated child is being given fluid intravenously, it is useful to let a mother feed her child by cup-and-spoon; he will obtain some of the fluid he needs in this way, and a mother's anxiety is relieved for she now has something to do.

:9 **The subcutaneous route.** A convenient way of using the subcutaneous route is to give a drip from plastic bags containing a litre of half strength Darrow's solution in 2.5% glucose: the only disadvantage of this apparatus being its cost — 7/- ($1.0) (A&H). It is supplied complete with a needle, tubing, a drop counter and two pieces of string. One of these attaches the bag to a drip-stand, the other measures a distance of 45 cms. (18 ins.) which is the height of the bag above the bed that secures the best rate of flow for a subcutaneous drip without hyalase, and so enables it to be left more or less unattended. Hyalase is expensive, but fortunately it is unnecessary, for even without it, a drip gathers speed in time, though it may be slow at first.

Method: By 'drip'.

Clean the skin of the thigh or pectoral region, let out the air from the tube, pierce the skin obliquely until the needle has gone in about an inch, and then fix it there with strapping. Hang the bottle or bag at the limit of the tube until the fluid is dripping well. As soon as this happens lower it to about 18 inches.

When no 'drip-sets' are available it is possible to give a moderately dehydrated child of small size some fluid with a large syringe. Such a method is however decidedly second best in view of the large number of separate injections that have to be given.

Method: By syringe:

Obtain the largest syringe available, fill it with half strength Darrow's solution, and, using a stout needle give half the fluid required over 12 hours into the subcutaneous tissues of the axillae, the anterior abdominal wall and the thighs. Give the other half twelve hours later.

15:10 **The intraperitoneal route.** In effect this amounts to giving the child an artificial electrolyte ascites which forms a 'depot' of fluid that is steadily absorbed over the next few hours to the great benefit of the child's hydration.

As a route the intraperitoneal one has many advantages in the moderately dehydrated child; it needs much less skill than the intravenous one and can thus be carried out more easily by semi-trained staff; it is more rapid and therefore better suited to outpatient use; further, there is no need for the prolonged and skilled supervision that is so necessary if an intravenous drip is not either to stop or else run wild at night and overload the circulation in doing so. Fluid is absorbed rapidly enough from the peritoneal cavity to revive a moderately dehydrated child without being so rapid as to cause pulmonary oedema. The use of the intraperitoneal route is shown in Figure 31.

The dangers of the intraperitoneal route, those of infection, haemorrhage and the puncture of an enlarged abdominal organ appear to be more theoretical than real. In more than a thousand intraperitoneal infusions given at Mulago in recent years, we are not aware of a single case of either. The intraperitoneal route is contraindicated by skin sepsis, or ascites, or when the bowel is distended from any cause.

Method: Intraperitoneal infusion.

Send the mother out of the room to wait. Lay the child naked, unsedated, transversely across a couch. Warm a bottle of half strength Darrow's solution in 2.5% glucose to blood heat by putting it in hot water. Hang it on the drip stand and let out the air from the tube. Feel the abdomen of the child to make quite sure that the spleen or liver are not grossly enlarged and thus in danger from the needle. Clean the skin with an antiseptic solution. A local anaesthetic is unnecessary. Push the needle of a standard intravenous drip set through the skin horizontally in line with the outer border of the rectus muscle, level with the umbilicus. (Some prefer to give it midway between the umbilicus and the xiphisternum, as in Figure 31, but, in practice, an infusion can be given almost anywhere, provided the liver, the spleen and the bladder are not injured).

Once through the skin, open the pinchcock fully, and, holding the needle vertically, push it gradually and firmly straight into the abdominal cavity. As soon as it has gone in, fluid will flow, the stream of fluid pushing the viscera out of the way of the sharp end of the needle. Once it is flowing well, fix the needle with adhesive tape and run in the volume of fluid required over the space of ten minutes.

Fig.31.

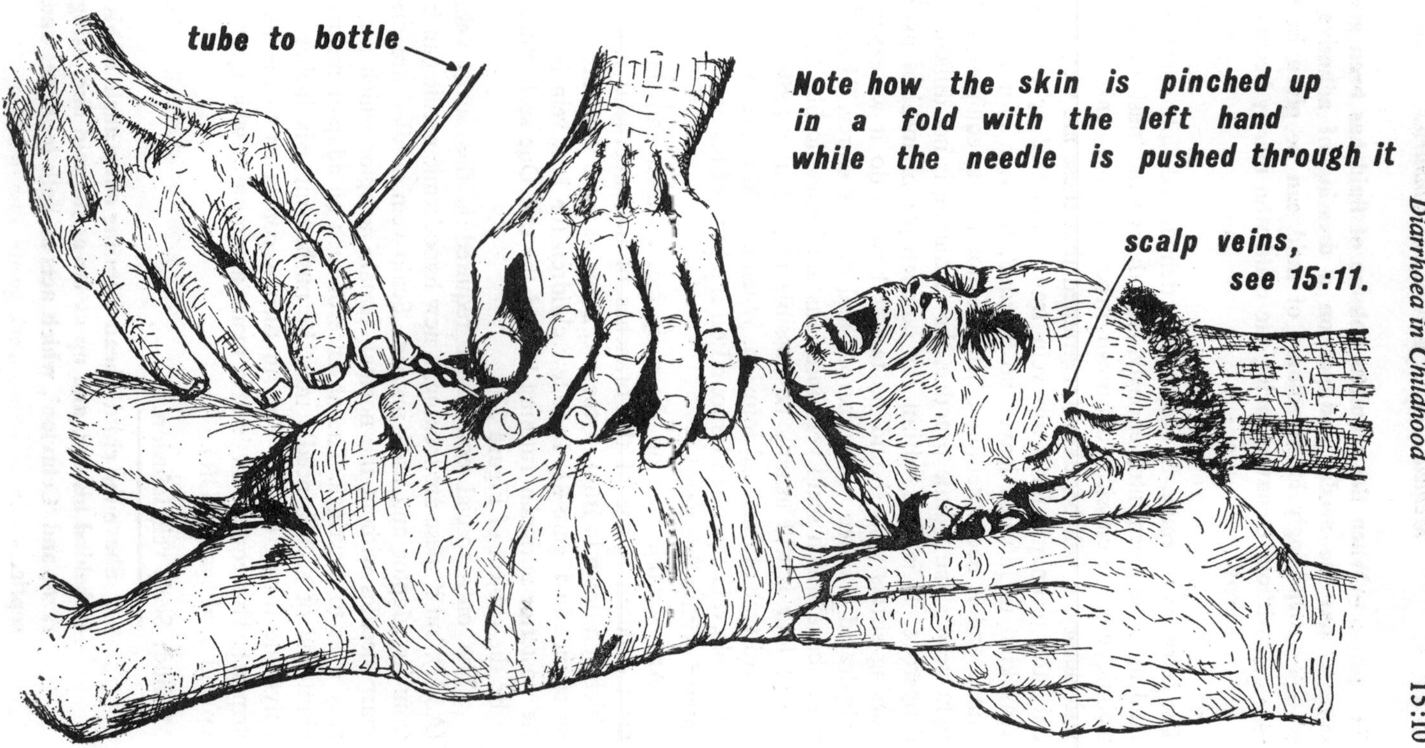
INTRAPERITONEAL INFUSION.
tube to bottle
Note how the skin is pinched up
in a fold with the left hand
while the needle is pushed through it
scalp veins,
see 15:11.

When the required volume of fluid has been given, take out the needle and put on a dressing of adhesive tape. A surprisingly large volume of fluid can be given in this way without inconveniencing the child who merely becomes a little sleepy.

15:11 **The intravenous route.** In the severely dehydrated child some part of the fluid must be given intravenously, and, though the 'push in' intravenous technique or the classical 'cut-down' procedure on an ankle vein are both satisfactory, it will be taken for granted that these are well known, and only the technique for scalp vein transfusion will be described here. This kind of infusion leaves no 'wound', the vein is not permanently ruined and it needs neither expensive nor fragile equipment. With the right needle and a little practice, the technique is not difficult, nor is it dangerous. It is thus within the competence of medical assistants or nursing sisters who should be taught how to do it wherever severely dehydrated children are numerous and doctors scarce. There is no age limit above which scalp vein infusions are impracticable, but above the age of four it will usually be possible to find a suitable vein for the standard type of 'push in' infusion. When a child is over six months old, a suitable vein can often be found on the back of his hand which can be entered with a fine needle.

Any suitable vein on the scalp can be used and the best one in most children is one of the branches of the superficial temporal vein which run down in front of the ear. Some of these veins are shown quite by chance in Figure 31. In a few children the best vein is a branch of the posterior auricular running behind the ear. One such child happens to be the subject of Figure 32.

The only special equipment required is the 'scalp vein needle' (A&H), but if these are lacking, a new hypodermic needle can be broken from its adaptor and used instead. 'Scalp vein needles' are merely fine sharp needles without the normal 'female' adaptor which fits the ordinary ones to a syringe. The absence of such an adaptor means that the blunt end of such a needle must be pushed into six inches of 1.0mm. polythene tubing (30:6). This in turn is connected to the needle of a drip set. This equipment is also made as an outfit which can be boiled up and used again (POR).

Method: Scalp vein infusion.

Shave the child's head from the outer angle of his eyebrow to behind his ear, and up as far as the mid line, using a safety razor and 'Cetavlon', which acts as both lubricant and an antiseptic.

32. **SCALP VEIN INFUSION.**

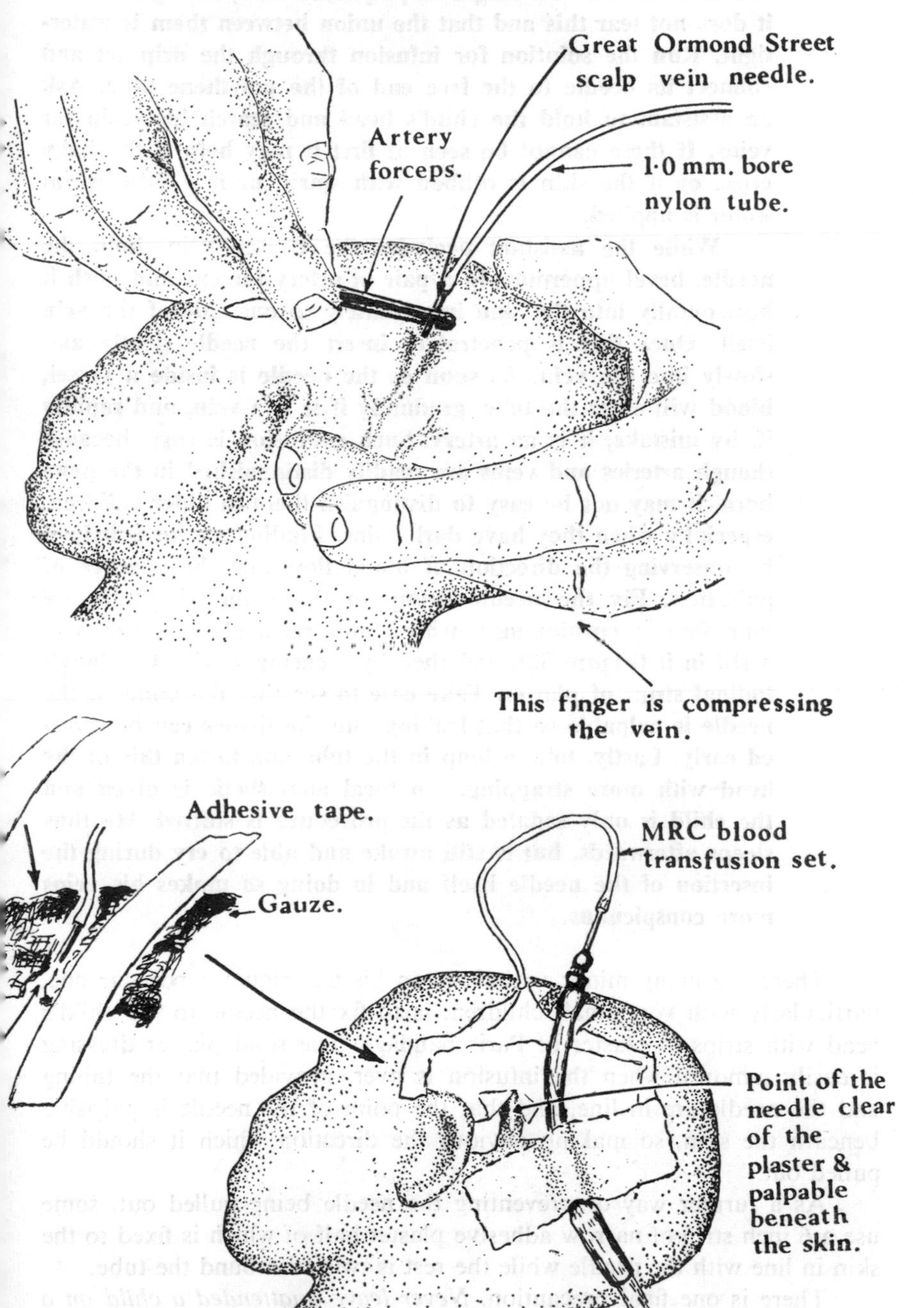
Great Ormond Street
scalp vein needle.
Artery
forceps.
1·0 mm. bore
nylon tube.
This finger is compressing
the vein.
Adhesive tape.
MRC blood
transfusion set.
Gauze.
Point of the
needle clear
of the
plaster &
palpable
beneath
the skin.

Hold the scalp vein needle firmly in gauze and push its hilt into the end of a length of polythene tube, taking care that it does not tear this and that the union between them is water-tight. Run the solution for infusion through the drip set and connect its needle to the free end of the polythene tube. Ask an assistant to hold the child's head and search his scalp for veins. If these cannot be seen at first it may help if the baby cries, or if the skin is rubbed with spirit, or if a little warm water is applied.

While the assistant occludes the chosen vein, hold the needle, bevel uppermost in a pair of artery forceps and push it horizontally into the skin immediately to one side of the vein itself. Once this is penetrated, insert the needle gently and slowly into the vein. As soon as the needle is inside a vessel, blood will enter the tube, gradually if it is a vein, and rapidly if, by mistake, it is an artery. Such confusion is easy, because though arteries and veins are readily distinguished in the new-born, it may not be easy to distinguish them in older children, especially when they have dark skins. Finding a vein is helped by observing the direction of blood flow and the absence of pulsation. Fix the needle firmly to the scalp with adhesive tape, first by cushioning it with a little rectangle of gauze with a slit in it (Figure 32), and then by securing it with two longi-tudinal strips of plaster. Take care to see that the point of the needle is palpable so that leaking into the tissues can be spott-ed early. Lastly, take a loop in the tube and fasten this to the head with more strapping. No local anaesthetic is given and the child is only sedated as the procedure is started. He thus sleeps afterwards, but is still awake and able to cry during the insertion of the needle itself and in doing so makes his veins more conspicuous.

There are many minor variations on his technique; a popular one, particularly with very small children, is to fix the needle to the child's head with strips of plaster of Paris bandage. The solid plaster dressing is easily removed when the infusion is over, provided that the tubing and the needle are in line, and that the point of the needle is palpable beneath the skin, so making obvious the direction which it should be pulled out.

As a further way of preventing the needle being pulled out, some use a 6 inch strip of narrow adhesive plaster half of which is fixed to the skin in line with the needle while the rest is twisted around the tube.

There is one final precaution. *Never leave unattended a child on a drip with so much fluid in the bottle that it would kill him if it all went in suddenly while nobody was looking.*

DIET AND DRUGS

2 **Diet.** If a child is starved his diarrhoea may diminish, but if food is given, part of this food is absorbed, even though most of it does appear in the stools. Because the fraction absorbed may be critically important to the malnourished child, he must not be starved, and an increasing number of paediatricians now hold that neither starvation nor dilution of feeds has any place in the treatment of diarrhoea in childhood.

Never stop breast feeding, because human milk is quite as bland as any of the electrolyte solutions that might be given instead. If a child fails to suckle, express his mother's breast milk and feed him this, for, unless her milk is expressed in this way, its supply will cease and the child will be in peril from nutritional marasmus.

When a child is vomiting get the mother to feed him continually with 'saline mixture' and change to milk feeds as soon as possible.

3 **Drugs.** Most diarrhoeas get well without drugs, an exception being that of malignant tertian malaria — give these cases a single dose of parenteral chloroquine (5 mgm./kg.) followed by two days' oral treatment. Apart from this, and the specific syndromes of amoebiasis and giardiasis, drugs are coming to be considered of less importance than was previously the case.

Only three chemotherapeutic drugs are usually within the economic reach of tropical patients with diarrhoea — the sulphonamides, streptomycin and chloramphenicol, and all of them are only effective in bacterial diarrhoeas, when they are effective at all. The Shigellae, which were formerly so well treated by the sulphonamides, are in many areas now resistant, while these drugs have never been of great value in Escherichia infections and none at all in the Salmonella diarrhoeas. It may thus be sound advice to abandon routine sulphonamides in diarrhoea for a trial period and to see what happens — their absence may well make no difference.

The ineffectiveness of sulphonamides, and the readiness with which streptomycin resistance develops, makes chloramphenicol the drug of choice in severe bacterial diarrhoea. Give it as chloramphenicol syrup 50-200 mg./kg. day (25-100 mg./lb.) four times daily. As it is comparatively expensive, and is also complicated by the possibility of agranulocytosis it should be reserved for the occasional severe case only.

In young children there is never any indication for the use of the stool solidifying agents kaolin or chalk, nor is there one for the use of opiates, purgatives or enemas. However, chlorpromazine ($\frac{1}{2}$ mg./kg.) by intramuscular injection is valuable in reducing vomiting.

SPECIAL SITUATIONS

15:14 **Protein-calorie malnutrition.** Diarrhoea is common in protein calorie malnutrition which produces clinical signs that obscure the assessment of dehydration by means of the signs listed in Table 4. Thus malnutrition itself impairs the elasticity of the skin, makes the eyeballs recede in the orbits, and may even make the anterior fontanelle appear depressed. This means that most reliance has to be placed on the fifth sign in this table, the dryness of the mucous membranes. The calculation of fluid requirements is complicated by the fact that a marasmic infant is grossly underweight, whereas the oedema of a case of kwashiorkor masks the child's true weight. The best advice that can probably be given is to forget these complexities and calculate fluid requirements on the basis of Table 4 or Figure 30.

It is common for a case of kwashiorkor to become dehydrated from diarrhoea, even in the presence of oedema. Such cases are usually also severely depleted of electrolyte. This means that half strength Darrow's solution in 2.5% glucose may be required parenterally, *even while such children are still oedematous.*

Continued moderate or mild diarrhoea may produce severe electrolyte depletion, even in cases of kwashiorkor which are not clinically dehydrated. Such electrolyte depletion is best treated orally with 'PCM mixture' (30:4). As the full replacement of this electrolyte loss may not be complete for some days, this treatment should be continued for at least a week.

The malnutrition may be just as important as the dehydration, so continue to give full strength milk feeds all the time.

THE REHYDRATION UNIT

15:15 **The need for rehydration units.** Dehydrated children are often so numerous, particularly in tropical slums, that it is not possible to admit them all to hospital and they have to be treated as outpatients. It is for this purpose that rehydration units are so valuable. They enable these children to be given simple, standardized short term rehydration, as well as providing valuable opportunities for educating their mothers, both in the prevention of diarrhoea itself and in better practices of infant feeding. They thus fill a great need in view of what has already been said about the rising incidence of diarrhoea, and its relation to the increasing use of badly managed bottle feeding.

In large towns they can be independent units in their own right, but under other circumstances they are better attached to health centres, to under-fives clinics or to hospital outpatient departments.

The methods employed. The whole range of rehydration techniques are used in one unit or another, but most of them rely on the intragastric drip or use the intraperitoneal or subcutaneous routes. The intravenous route is not commonly used for moderately dehydrated children, except in South Africa.

In some countries the rules of the local nursing council forbid nurses to give intravenous infusions. Where it is important that they do, it may be feasible to interpret such a rule so as to mean that they are not allowed to prescribe the type of fluid given, but that they may set up an infusion after it has been prescribed by a doctor.

Some units use the intragastric drip for mild or even moderate cases of dehydration, and oral fluids can be given by the mothers themselves under suitable supervision. The intraperitoneal route is, however, one which is particularly well adapted to the needs of the rehydration unit, for it is rapid, ten minutes being all that is needed for an infusion of this kind.

Many fluids can be used, but half strength Darrow's solution in 2.5% glucose is the one advised, and was originally adopted at Mulago Hospital from the practice of the large rehydration unit at the Baragwanath Hospital in Johannesburg.

Method: Rehydration unit procedure.

> **Examine the child on admission, take a history from the mother and prescribe in writing the fluid to be given — its type, its quantity and the rate at which it is to be administered. Ask a trained assistant to give this fluid, and see that the mother stays with her child to comfort him. At the same time she should be taught about the prevention of diarrhoea and the general welfare of her children.**

In large units where many intravenous infusions are given, it is convenient for these to be set up in a small room equipped with all the apparatus required, and for the child to be subsequently carried to a larger one with special accommodation for a number of children. If the drip is being given intravenously, the correct rate in drops per minute should be written on the bottle, and checked two-hourly from a large clock on the wall of the unit. Under these circumstances it is convenient to house the mothers with their other children in an adjoining building, and for them to visit and feed their dehydrated infant three-hourly during his intravenous infusion. The child's napkin is changed after each of these feeds and the intravenous bottle is looked at by the nurses who record the volume of fluid given.

When a child is only moderately dehydrated, he can be sent out shortly after his intraperitoneal infusion is complete, especially if he lives near by. In other cases a child's condition should be assessed twice daily and the decision taken as to whether he is to be discharged, admitted for a further period, or sent into hospital. Rehydration units are for short-term treatment only, and it is the exceptional child who should stay there for more than 24 hours. These units can be very effective indeed and good ones have a mortality of less than 10 per cent., death being most common in neonates and children with PCM, especially in those who are grossly underweight for their age.

Many rehydration units are large, but they are also practicable on a more modest scale. Rehydration does so much to save life, and the intraperitoneal infusion in particular is so simple that rehydration facilities should be readily available in all health centres, outpatient departments and mobile clinics (2:10). If this is to be possible, auxiliary staff must be trained to recognize dehydration and to treat it by the methods described in previous sections.

Rehydration units provide admirable opportunities for health education. Mothers must be told the reason why their children are suffering from diarrhoea and they must be taught what to do when further attacks occur. They will require an 'oral repair solution' like the 'saline mixture' already described (15:8); which should be readily available as a concentrated solution or in tablet form. If children are given this whenever they have diarrhoea, they will be likely to require the services of a rehydration unit much less frequently than they otherwise would. Mothers must also be taught to avoid violent indigenous treatments, such as purges or enemas.

Chapter Sixteen

THE UNDER-FIVES CLINIC

David Morley

The aims of an 'under-fives clinic'. The clinic described here was developed over several years to meet the paediatric challenge presented by the younger children of an area in Western Nigeria (26). This challenge is inherent in a birthrate of over 40 per thousand that is common to the whole of this region, and which is combined with a childhood mortality of 50 per cent., no less than half of all the children born there dying before they are five.

TABLE 6

THE MAJOR CAUSES OF DEATH AMONG CHILDREN IN THE WEST AFRICAN VILLAGE OF IMESI (26)

Diarrhoeal disease	12%
Pneumonia	12%
Protein-calorie malnutrition	12%
Malaria	8%
Pertussis	8%
Measles	8%
Tuberculosis	5%
Smallpox	5%
Other conditions (mostly neonatal)	30%

Note:—All the conditions in bold type can now be prevented in an under-fives clinic. Health education and early diagnosis can reduce mortality from the others.

The Wesley Guild Hospital where the clinic evolved serves Ilesha, a town of 100,000 people. This meant that had none of them died, there would have been no less than 20,000 children under five in the town, a figure that death did in practice reduce to the hardly more manageable number of about 15,000 — still a formidable task for one mission hospital. Though the main clinic is in Ilesha itself, it was developed from the findings of an intensive study of child health that was carried out in the nearby 'research village' of Imesi. Tables 6 and 7 come from this

TABLE 7

THE EFFECT OF AN UNDER-FIVES CLINIC IN REDUCING DEATH IN CHILDHOOD (26)

DEATHS	1957 *No Under-Fives Clinic*	1962 *Under-Fives Clinic established*
Neonatal deaths per 1,000 live births	78	20
Deaths in the first year per 1,000 live births . .	295	72
Deaths each year between the ages of one and four per 1,000 living children in these age groups . .	69	43*

Note:—* 16 of these 43 deaths were due to measles. All children now receive measles vaccine which has since proved effective in preventing almost all the deaths from measles in this clinic. The mortality in the first five years which was probably over 500 per 1000 births is now, in the absence of measles, approximately 180 per 1000 births.

village, and, besides confirming the importance of diarrhoea, pneumonia and malnutrition, they show that the starting of an under-fives clinic there coincided with the reduction of all deaths in the first five years of life to about a quarter of their previous value. Curative services alone can cut such gross mortality by half, among them being sulphadimidine or penicillin for broncho-pneumonia, and chloramphenicol for early whooping cough, but its further reduction to a quarter will only follow the introduction of preventive paediatrics. These are the whole purpose of an under-fives clinic, and the enormous number of lives they save are the entire justification for what follows.

An under-fives clinic aims to do three things: (1) it supervises the health of all children up to the age of five years; (2) it prevents malnutrition, malaria, measles, pertussis, tuberculosis and smallpox; (3) it also provides simple treatment for diarrhoea, pneumonia and the common skin conditions.

16:2 **A vicious circle in the children's ward.** In the tropics there is often a vicious circle in a children's ward, whereby children are only admitted when they are so gravely ill that many die. This further discourages mothers from bringing in their remaining children before these too are moribund, so perpetuating this sorry state of affairs. The under-fives clinic, or the young child clinic as some prefer to call it, is designed to break this vicious circle, for, through frequent visits, mothers come to rely on the clinic and readily bring their children up to hospital. They soon learn to bring them in early enough for treatment to be given while they are still only mildly ill, so that their lives can be saved, the circle broken and confidence in the hospital restored.

The main purpose of the clinic is to promote general welfare and good nutrition but, through vaccination, it prevents smallpox, whooping cough, tuberculosis, tetanus and diphtheria, while, now that measles vaccines are becoming available, it can prevent measles also — a scourge of the greatest magnitude in so many areas. Through chemoprophylaxis it reduces the severity of malaria, and with simple measures treats diarrhoea, broncho-pneumonia and the common skin conditions. No attempt is made to divide healthy children from the sick, nor to separate preventive measures from curative ones, the whole practice of the clinic being to integrate prevention with cure.

The role of the doctor and the nurses. As there is only a single part time doctor and so many children come to the clinic, they have to be seen by nurses who can only refer the occasional gravely ill or especially perplexing child for a medical opinion. But such an arrangement suits the doctor, for all the dull monotonous straightforward diseases, such as mild diarrhoea and bronchitis, are seen by the nurses. He knows that most of the common major diseases will have been prevented, and the cases he is asked to see thus form a group of particular interest and fascination (Eighth axiom, 1:15).

To the mothers of sick children the nurses inevitably become much the most important people they meet at the hospital. The great importance of the nurse is the really critical factor in the whole psychology of the clinic, and is something that the doctor does all he can to promote. Professor Spence of Newcastle held that consultation is the quintessence of the medical art, and in the under-fives clinic this is certainly true, except that here it is consultation not between mother and doctor, but between mother and nurse. He maintained that the true purpose of consultation is to give explanation and advice, and that diagnosis is usually but a means to achieve this, and must never become an end in itself. Such explanation and advice leads to the correct action by the mother in matters concerning the health of her child: this action is much more likely to follow careful and sympathetic explanation than it would an ill understood and peremptory command. Because she comes from the same culture as the patient, a nurse is the best person to explain and give advice in this way.

This mother-nurse relationship is so crucial that it must be strengthened wherever possible. Thus, every time a mother comes to the clinic it should be to see the same nurse, and each time she consults a doctor, this nurse must be present at the consultation also, pains being taken to see that in all he does or says the doctor always supports her in the eyes of her patient. If the child has to come into hospital, he should return to this same nurse on discharge. This vital continuity is easily maintained in practice, if the child's card bears upon it the number of the table where sits the nurse assigned to that family, or if these tables are distinguished by some special colour.

To a nurse 50-70 mothers are a morning's work, so many children mean several nurses, but this need be no discouragement, for in most areas suitable primary school leavers are readily available. They like the job, and the salaries they need are within the budget of the hospital. By virtue of their own home experience they make admirable nurses, for they will have carried their younger sisters about on their backs, and they may perhaps have already seen several children die. They therefore know a sick child when they see one. Thus, the training these nurses get in hospital is built upon an experience of child care which reaches far back into their own childhood to the time when they looked after the members of their own extended families.

After primary education, followed if possible by two or three years of secondary schooling, pupil nurses need a further two or three years of general hospital training as nursing aids or enrolled midwives. After this, to complete their instruction and to fit them for work in the clinic, they need some specialized training. This is best given to them by a doctor experienced in seeing children, and completed by their sitting beside him in the clinic, while he sees the cases that have been referred for his opinion.

In other places under-fives clinics are staffed by enrolled midwives, who also hold antenatal clinics in the same building, often on the same day, so saving the mothers the need for a second visit (19:5).

Boys with primary education and little chance of a better job may be as numerous as girls, so clerks need not be short either, and, like their sisters, they are better usefully employed on a humble salary than loafing about for nothing. They register mothers and children, weigh babies, fetch and carry, direct mothers around the clinic, and generally make themselves so useful that it is well to employ one of them for every nurse.

16:4 **Learning by overhearing:** This is one of the principles of the clinic, for in a Nigerian village few things are private, least of all the affairs of babies. Several mothers waiting their turn are therefore encouraged to sit near the nurse's desk and overhear her talking to their friends, for a mother learns much in this way and what she learns is reinforced by frequent repetition. Such an arrangement makes it possible for a whole group of mothers to be taught simultaneously, a nurse's teaching time is used to the best advantage, and a mother finds it easier to change her own practices if she knows that her friends are being asked to change theirs also.

16:5 **Prevention in the guise of cure.** Before they have been educated village housewives know little of prevention and care less. But there are signs that things are changing, for in Ibadan recently no less than 40,000 mothers attended clinics for poliomyelitis vaccination. Even so, in an unsophisticated community, a clinic which is essentially preventive in the eyes of its staff, must be curative in the eyes of its patients. Thus, a child brought up with the common but harmless complaint of 'noises in the stomach' is given the innocuous 'welfare mixture', while at the same time the younger infant on his mother's back is vaccinated with BCG, and the nurses, when taught that 'ten children vaccinated mean one child saved', soon learn to promote vaccination with enthusiasm.

Management. Besides few doctors and many children, several compelling circumstances determine the general pattern of the clinic; these are the need for stringent economy, the monotony of the diseases seen, the abundance of cheap intelligent labour at primary level, and the low cost of the clinic compared with the hospital wards which thus make it imperative to treat as many children as possible as outpatients (12:5).

The more patients a hospital outpatient department sees, the more specialized can it become, and one of its earliest divisions must be the separation of children from the adult sick. Children may form as many as 50 per cent. of all outpatients, and, at Ilesha, more than four hundred under-fives come to the clinic with their mothers each day. Their attendance is much assisted by the free treatment policy adopted by the regional government. Ideally, the whole family should be present at every visit, but this seldom happens; however, the Nigerian mother readily brings up her newest baby and, when doing so, she can often be persuaded to bring along the next oldest child also — a useful compromise for he is the one at particular risk, both to malnutrition and infection.

The clinic must be held on six if not seven days each week, because mothers should feel that its services are always available. Thus, it is better for one nurse to work daily rather than many less regularly, for to infrequent clinics come moribund children. As a daily routine the clinic should start at seven, the first mothers be out by eight, and the place clear by midday, the staff being encouraged to work through the lunch hour when business is brisk.

A whole day wasted waiting in the clinic can ill be spared by the African mother who is a busy woman with no domestic amenities, a large family, food to grow, a husband to cook for and only too often her own living to earn. Neither is it necessary, because, if she keeps her own record card, she need not waste time waiting for a clerk to find it each time she comes up, nor need she wait at the dispensary if the nurses keep medicines on their tables.

All the staff of the clinic, right down to the sweepers, meet together regularly once a week for half an hour. This is an opportunity for comment and discussion, for teaching and for the demonstration of cases.

Mutual co-operation and harmony are promoted and any tensions there might be between the staff are reduced: anyone who has anything which particularly needs discussion being invited to stay behind afterwards. This is just one example of the regular meetings that the staff of every unit should have and which are discussed further in section 8:2.

16:7 **Records.** The robust weight chart in its polythene envelope which is used by the clinic is described more fully in section 26:5 (Figure 64) and illustrated in Figure 33. These charts are fundamental to the practice of the clinic, and provide at a glance the essentials of a child's medical and nutritional history. They are kept by his mother.

The nurses require a card for their own use. This is a simple coloured card 8″ x 4¼″ (21 cms. x 11 cms.) on which the clerks stamp the date of attendance and also write in the child's weight. The nurses use it to record the nature and duration of such symptoms as there may be, and any further notes that they may wish to make. They are also asked to record any treatment they prescribe and any immunizations that need to be given. This card is a place where minor ailments can be recorded for which there is no room on the weight chart itself; it remains with this chart inside the polythene envelope and so stays in a mother's possession.

There is also a third card, the doctor's card, and this is the only one that is actually filed in the clinic. It is for his personal use and need only be removed from the files when a child is sufficiently ill to need seeing by him.

There are several advantages to a system of three cards. The main one is that neither the weight chart nor the doctor's card become cluttered with the trivialities recorded by the nurses. The system may seem complex, but it is used at Ilesha, cards are cheap and it does mean that the doctor always has a card to himself.

16:8 **Medicines.** Of the medicines used by the nurse none has been more criticized than 'welfare mixture', the coloured water so liberally dispensed at Ilesha. Flavoured with peppermint, and pink with cheap colour from the grocers rather than an expensive one from the chemists, it is surely defensible, for it displaces the ubiquitous and possibly toxic herbal brews with which so many mothers dose their babies, and which are common to all cultures in one form or another. Such a mixture ensures that no mother returns empty to a circle of enquiring friends wondering to what profit she has spent that morning. Finally, it supplies a psychological prop which even the affluent seem to require, if the contents of their bathroom cupboards are anything to go by. At a few pence a gallon it is both cheap and harmless.

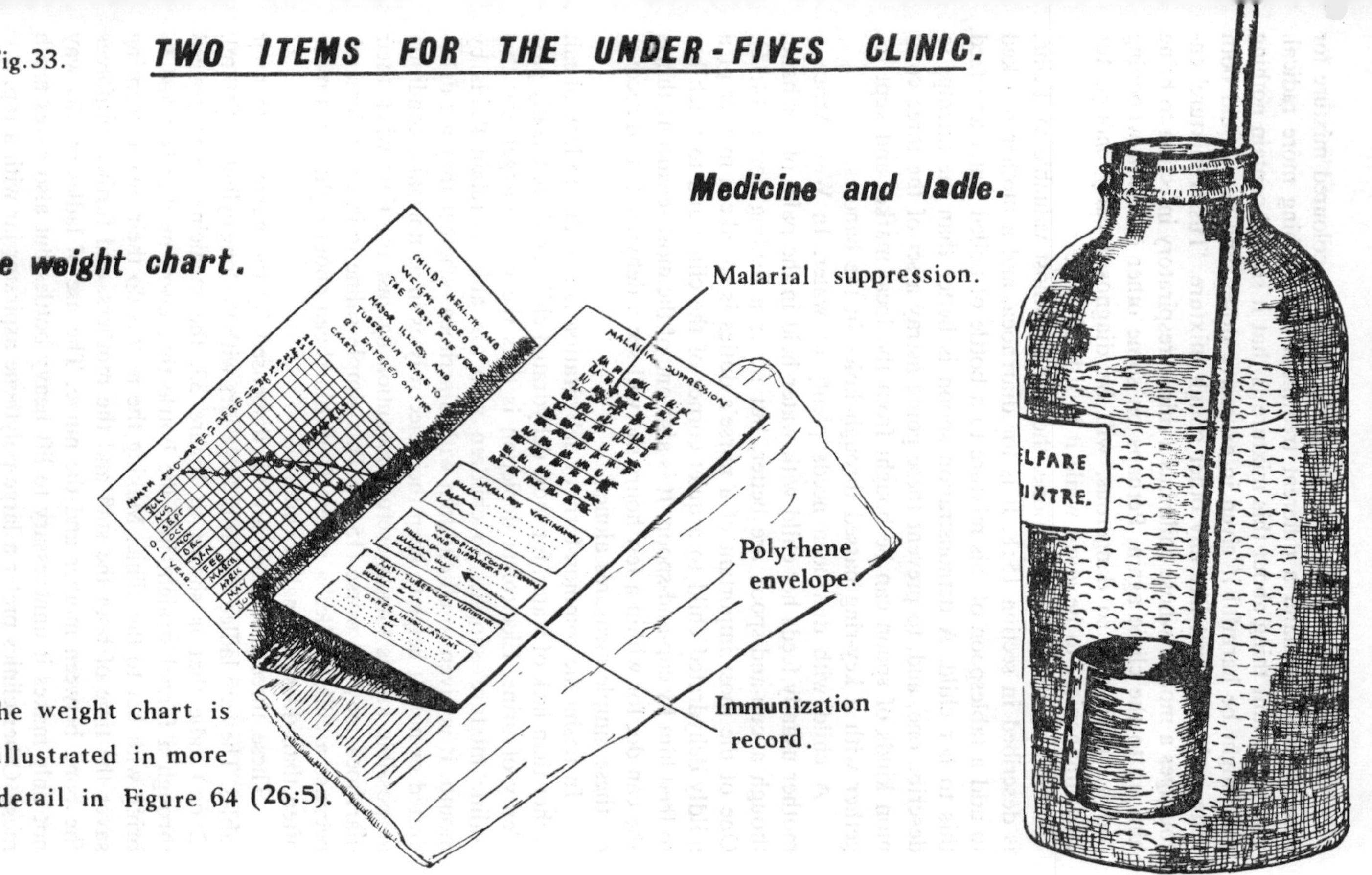

Fig. 33. TWO ITEMS FOR THE UNDER-FIVES CLINIC.

'Tussis mixture' is next on the table, a simple coloured mixture for coughs which demand a different treatment but nothing more radical. The important thing about this mixture is that it should contain nothing that might be harmful if given in excessive doses, and yet should both taste and smell just like any other cough mixture. 'Tussis mixture' encourages a mother whose child has a minor respiratory infection to bring him up to the clinic again. Perhaps on some other occasion whooping cough, potentially so dangerous, will be diagnosed early enough for chloramphenicol to be given while it is still effective.

'Saline mixture', a green one, the last and most valuable medicine, is described in section 15:8. It is for diarrhoea, and a mother is asked to add a tablespoon of this mixture to a bottle of boiled water and feed this to her child. A demonstration spoon is better than the attempt to describe one, and, to prevent these going astray a set of the three common kinds of spoon can be bought from the local market and kept together with a key-ring passed through holes in the handles.

A child with diarrhoea needs plenty of water. In West Africa a mother usually feeds her child with water held in the palm of her hand, though a cup-and-spoon are better, but never a feeding bottle (14:16). One of the most important of a nurse's duties is to take a mother of a mildly dehydrated child to a quiet corner of the clinic and to teach her to feed him by cup-and-spoon. It is also one of the most rewarding things she can do, for within a few hours she will see a dehyrated child recover on these simple measures alone.

In Ilesha the common form of dehydration is that due to lack of salt rather than lack of water, for most dehydrated children there usually pass plenty of urine. Electrolyte depletion is thus the main danger and this 'saline mixture' supplies to children who are able to retain fluids by mouth. It is given to all children with diarrhoea, whether they are dehydrated or not. It helps to keep their electrolytes in as normal a condition as possible and is thus a useful precaution against the time when their diarrhoea may get worse (15:8). This simple saline is in great demand, because a child in Ilesha suffers from diarrhoea about eight times more often than does an English child.

These three medicines are all dispensed by the nurses from their tables. They are ladled out from large jars with the long cylindrical 60 ml. (2 oz.) ladle that is shown in Figure 33, the medicine being poured through a funnel straight into the bottle that every mother is asked to bring with her to the clinic. Making the nurses do their own dispensing saves the time of both the staff and the mothers, and further reinforces the bond between mother and the nurse. The use of ladles in this way not only makes it unnecessary to lift heavy bottles but also saves much mess. Other clinics prefer a large polythene aspirator jar with a tap.

Tablets and local treatment. Three tablets accompany the three liquid medicines on the nurse's table. They are, pyrimethamine ('Daraprim') 25 mg., chloroquine 150 mg., and sulphadimidine 0.5g. At -/20 ($0.03) for a dozen tablets sulphadimidine is cheap, safe and mostly used for mild respiratory infections. Since sulphadimidine does not need to be given by injection, it is much more convenient than penicillin for routine use. The dangerous urinary complications have never been seen at Ilesha, despite the employment of sulphadimidine on the widest scale. As it is only issued in envelopes of 12 tablets for children over 7 kg. (15 lbs) and 6 tablets for children under this weight, little harm can result if by mistake all these tablets are eaten at once, while so small a number offers little incentive to the mothers to sell them for ready cash (30:5).

Of local treatments, dithranol is for the ubiquitous ringworm, while for scabies 5% tetmosol in rubbing oil at a few cents a time is cheaper, more effective and more acceptable than its rival benzyl benzoate. In Ilesha rubbing oils are part of the culture so the addition of tetmosol is an easy step; it is also a particularly useful one, since like scabies itself, these oils become the property of the whole family. 0.5% aqueous crystal violet is used for impetigo, infected sores, thrush and stomatitis.

Malaria suppression. Pyrimethamine for malarial suppression is a regular monthly routine at the under-fives clinic. Its value was proved in a double blind trial in which two groups of children were compared over a five year period. One group was given chloroquine for any attack of fever as well as a monthly prophylactic 25 mg., tablet of pyrimethamine. The second group of children received the same chloroquine treatment for their fevers, but were given a monthly lactose placebo instead of the pyrimethamine. The group receiving pyrimethamine had half as many unexplained convulsions, fewer attacks of fever, and higher haemoglobin levels than did the controls receiving only lactose. Further, when the pyrimethamine was eventually discontinued at the end of the five year period, they did not appear to suffer from malaria any more frequently than did the previously unprotected controls.

Pyrimethamine resistance seemed to be no problem in the area, for a survey team subsequently found that almost all the schoolchildren with a positive malarial blood film rapidly became film negative after a tablet of this drug. The absence of pyrimethamine resistance may have depended in part on the extensive use of chloroquine for the treatment of all children with clinical fever, for chloroquine would have cut short such pyrimethamine resistant infections as might have appeared, and thus reduced the likelihood of any pyrimethamine resistant strains of plasmodia being spread to other members of the community.

In this age group it is the purpose of prophylaxis to reduce the grave effects of malaria by partly suppressing it, yet without eradicating the parasite completely and so destroying the partial immunity that accompanies its continuing presence. A monthly tablet of pyrimethamine appears to achieve this desirable state of 'semi-suppression' very satisfactorily. Though a monthly chloroquine tablet is preferred by some workers and is significantly cheaper (30:1), it is sometimes difficult to persuade mothers to give their children such an intensely bitter a tablet as chloroquine with sufficient regularity. Further, and more important, should chloroquine resistant strains of plasmodia appear, the most effective schizontocide would then be lost (13:6).

Whatever is said about the differing merits of these two drugs, children in highly malarious areas should receive either pyrimethamine or chloroquine routinely during the first five years of their life, particularly in their second and third years. Lastly, if trivially, the association of a silver paper wrapped pyrimethamine tablet with the silvery moon is a useful reminder in the mind of the village mothers who are always aware of the phase of the moon. (Note. The same 25 mg. pyrimethamine tablet is given to all children irrespective of age.)

16:11 **The economics of the clinic.** The cost of a visit to the clinic is approximately the same as that calculated for a health centre attendance (3:15), and amounts to about 1/50 ($0.21). In arriving at this figure salaries were costed at the local Nigerian rate, and the annual budget of about £6,000 ($17,000) was divided between the 80,000 patients attending the clinic at the research village of Imesi during the year. These figures include many adults who take longer to see than children and makes no allowance for the research activities of the clinic staff. The true cost of a visit to an under-fives clinic may well be less than 1/- ($0.14).

16:12 **Buildings.** Figure 34 shows a plan of the clinic. It is a rectangular building two-thirds of which has walls that are only waist high, this part of its roof being supported on pillars. Such a design makes it possible to control the flow of patients and still secures the maximum ventilation that is so important in a hot climate. It is also very cheap to construct.

The largest part of the clinic is a waiting area with low benches on which mothers sit. This is separated from a passage that runs the length of the building by a low barrier in which there are several wicket gates. This passage allows staff to circulate unimpeded by a crowd of waiting mothers, while the gates, which are controlled by the clerks, allow mothers to proceed through to see the nurses in an orderly manner.

The clerks form what amounts to a 'sorting centre' after the manner described in section 11:2. But all they do in the under-fives clinic, in addition to issuing new mothers with charts, filing the doctors' cards and

Fig.34. **THE UNDER-FIVES CLINIC.**

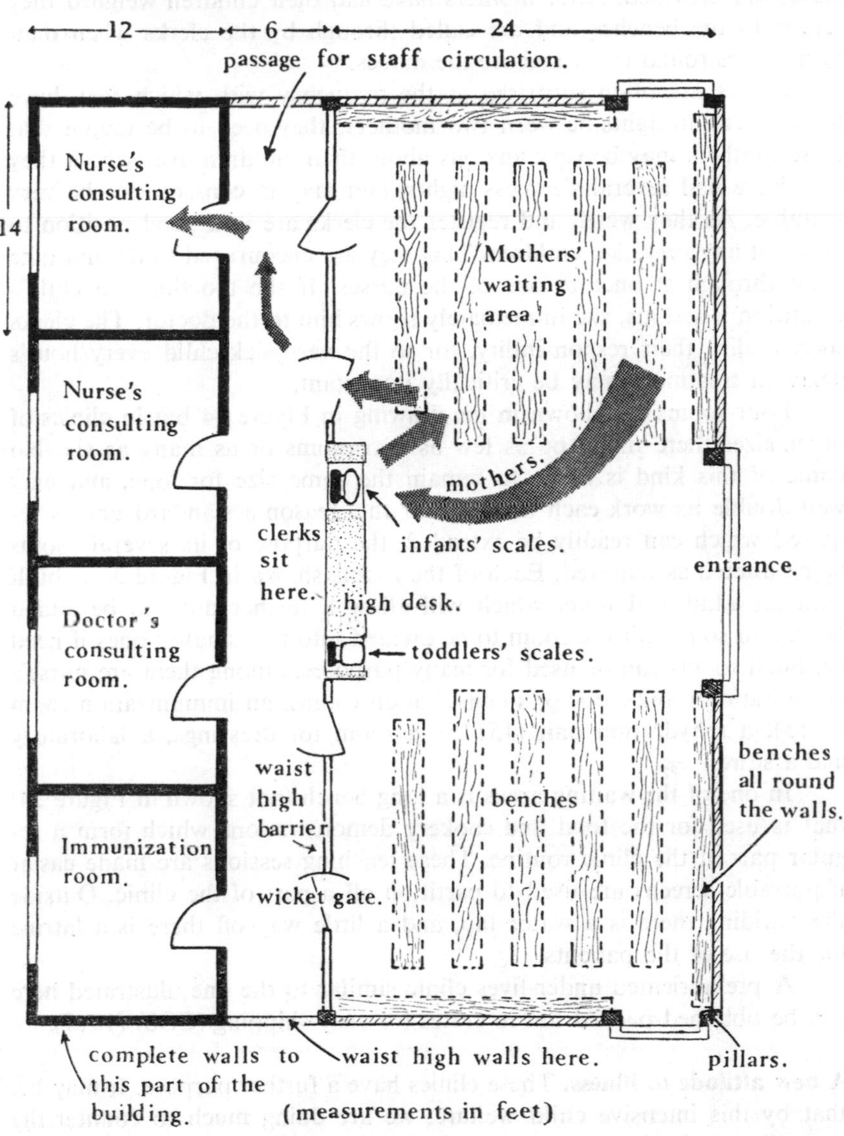

generally keeping order, is to weigh all children and enter up their weights. They sit on stools in the central corridor behind a high desk and are thus at the same level as the mothers standing opposite to them. At the desk there are two weighing stations, one is for infants, the scales

(CMO) ('Waylux Supreme') for them being so recessed that they are flush with the top of the desk. The other is for toddlers for whom separate scales are provided. After mothers have had their children weighed they return to the benches and are called through by the clerks when their turn comes round to go and see the nurses.

Clerks are often surprised at the frequency with which they have to intervene in fights between two mothers; they need to be taught that these mothers may be very anxious about their children over whom they may have had several sleepless nights, and may in consequence be very irritable. As they weigh and register the clerks are in a good position to pick out any very sick children. This they are encouraged to do and take them through at once to one of the nurses. If she too thinks a child's condition is serious, she immediately shows him to the doctor. The clerks soon realize their responsibility, for to the very sick child every hour's delay in treatment may be critically important.

Four rooms are shown in the drawing in Figure 34 but in clinics of other sizes there might be as few as two rooms or as many as six. No clinic of this kind is likely to remain the same size for long, and may well double its work each decade. For this reason a standard unit is required which can readily be extended, the purpose of its several rooms being altered as required. Each of the rooms shown in Figure 34 is built with an additional lintel which will allow a further door to be added later, and so permit the room to be divided into two smaller ones if need be. Such rooms can be used for many purposes, among them are nurse's consultation rooms, doctor's consultation rooms, an immunization room (17:5), a rehydration unit (15:15), a room for dressings, a laboratory and a store.

In one of the waiting areas is a long bench (not shown in Figure 34) that is used for the food and cookery demonstrations which form a regular part of the clinic routine. These teaching sessions are made easier if portable screens are used to partition off a part of the clinic. Outside the building there is a water tap, and a little way off there is a latrine for the use of the patients.

A prefabricated under-fives clinic similar to the one illustrated here can be obtained packed flat in crates for easy shipping (COS) (10:7).

16:13 **A new attitude to illness.** These clinics have a further purpose. It may be, that by this intensive child welfare, we are doing much to counter the prevailing attitude in peasant communities which sees in illness, not 'what' is the cause but 'who' is the cause, and, in every misfortune imagines some magic, 'bad medicine', or witchcraft. Even the clinic nurses will consult a witchdoctor on occasion, while the stories of the magistrate who closed his court because there was a spell on it, or the bishop's son who bought a talisman, are all too real for the importance of these practices to be underestimated. These beliefs are established in early life when a mother takes her sick child to the witchdoctor: it is his belief and his practice which make such a deep impression on the young child. The situation was much the same in Europe and America before the Industrial Revolution, and it is possible that in the pre-industrial countries only scientific infant welfare in early life will eventually see an end of these beliefs. They are deeply ingrained in the culture; it has taken more than a century to counter them in industrial communities and their removal there is still not complete.

Finale. Lastly, I would like to counter a criticism that has been raised by some whom I greatly respect against the clinic that I have described. This is that it is suited to the conditions of a particular mission hospital and to no others, for only there, it is said, is to be found the combination of staff continuity and high motivation that are required for success. I have never believed this, and am glad to be able to say that similar clinics have recently been started in Sierra Leone and elsewhere. There are thus signs that they are spreading, and so making it possible for the lives now being saved at Ilesha to be saved in other countries also.

Chapter Seventeen

IMMUNIZING THE UNDER-FIVES

Paget Stanfield

GENERAL PRINCIPLES

17:1 **The value of comprehensive immunization.** After what just has been said in the previous chapter, the need for comprehensive immunization requires no further stressing. In most of the countries for which this book is intended tuberculosis, pertussis, measles, poliomyelitis and tetanus will all be common; smallpox will be endemic and diphtheria may also be seen. Immunization can greatly reduce the incidence and severity of every one of seven diseases which are together responsible for between a quarter and a half of all deaths in children under the age of five (16:1) (Tables 6 and 7). Not only this, but prevention is likely to be much cheaper than cure.

Not only can the individual child be protected, but the community can be also, because, if a sufficient proportion of the susceptible population can be made immune, an infection will not spread among the remainder nearly so easily. The protection of a sufficient proportion of the population confers a kind of 'bonus'. Thus, when only a low percentage of susceptibles are immunized, only those immunized are protected; but, when a high percentage (70-80 per cent.) are immunized, considerable protection is given to everyone. The percentage of the population that needs immunizing to confer this 'bonus' cannot be defined exactly, and depends on many complex factors, but it is not likely to be substantial until at least 50 per cent. are immune. From this it follows that the usual intention of an immunization programme is not to get 100 per cent. of the population vaccinated, but to vaccinate merely a sufficient fraction to control the disease.

The practice of immunization is developing rapidly at the present time (1966). A wide range of new vaccines are being prepared and extensive trials are in progress. It is difficult therefore to provide hard and fast advice in a subject that is changing so actively, a task that is made no easier by the frequent absence of adequate data from field studies. Nevertheless, the immunization regime in Table 8 will probably be accepted as being practical under tropical circumstances.

TABLE 8

AN IMMUNIZATION REGIME

Age	*Vaccine*	*Opportunity*
Birth	BCG + Vaccinia sometimes	The maternity wards, the maternity village or the first visit to the under-fives clinic.
1 month	Triple antigen + polio + vaccinia usually	The under-fives clinic.
2 months	Triple antigen + polio	The under-fives clinic.
9 months	Triple antigen + polio + measles	The under-fives clinic.

Note: Ideally, this course should be completed by booster doses of triple antigen at school entry. Vaccination against smallpox needs to be repeated at 5-yearly intervals in endemic areas.

The real crux of vaccination is not the technicalities of the vaccines, nor the ages at which to give them; it is the administrative problem of organizing under-fives clinics, training and paying auxiliary staff to work in them, and persuading mothers to bring up their children with sufficient regularity for satisfactory courses of immunization to be given. The previous chapter shows how very rewarding such endeavour can be in terms of the lives it saves. Because most villagers are not prepared to come a long way for preventive medicine, successful community immunization in the rural areas depends upon taking services to the people (2:10). The more comprehensive the programme, the more protection it provides, and the greater is likely to be the return for the effort expended.

Immunization is just one side of 'community health action' (5:6) and, like all such health action, it needs to be evaluated, both in terms of the incidence of the diseases in question and in terms of the percentage of the vulnerable age groups immunized. Hospitals and health centres must therefore try to collect this data.

2 **Some immunological considerations.** For convenience, a complete immunization regime is provided in Table 8 against all the seven diseases just mentioned, but it is easily adapted to suit local circumstances. Though it is not possible to discuss all the factors upon which this regime or any modification to it depends, something must be said about the more important factors which determine its pattern.

In the neonatal period an infant's ability to form antibodies is poor; it is thus little use giving him vaccines in the hope of producing the sort of immunity that largely depends upon the level of circulating antibodies — the immunity to diphtheria, pertussis and tetanus is of this kind. But immunity of a cellular rather than a humoral nature is more easily established in the neonate, and BCG, for instance, is best given at birth. Vaccinia is also effective when given at this time, though it is usually given at the age of one month.

A child is born with many circulating antibodies which he acquires passively from his mother during his last months in the womb. These antibodies gradually disappear, until, at the age of about six months they have gone, but, while they last, they protect a child against several diseases among which measles is perhaps the most important. But as long as they last, they make it impossible for the live attenuated type of measles vaccine to multiply in a child's tissues and so provide him with the long active immunity which this vaccine is capable of conferring on the older child. A compromise has to be reached between giving the vaccine too early when it will fail to take, and giving it so late as to be useless because many children will already have had the disease. Nine months is the best compromise, but in some communities perhaps a quarter of the children will already have had the disease by the time they are this age. Ideally, it should be given at six months and again at nine months.

The age incidence of a particular disease in relation to the antibody forming power of the child is a major factor in deciding the best time at which a vaccine should be given. Because pertussis is at its most deadly during the second six months of life, pertussis vaccine must be given earlier than this if it is to be of any value. But if it is given too early, the antibody forming capacity of the child is so poor as seriously to reduce

TABLE 9

FIVE VACCINES

	Vaccinia	*Poliomyelitis (Sabin vaccine)*	*Measles*	*BCG*	*Triple Vaccine*
Nature	Live virus	Live virus	Live virus	Live bacteria	Diphtheria toxoid Tetanus toxoid Killed Pertussis bacteria.
Storage life at 2-10°C	2 weeks	6 months	6 months(?)	Freeze dried 1 year	2-3 years
Freeze dried preparation available	Yes	No	Yes	Yes	Not relevant
Dose	One drop	Three drops	0.1-1 ml.	(*a*) Intradermal 0.1 ml. (*b*) Multiple puncture one drop	0.5-1 ml.
Cost per dose Shillings E.A.	-/07	-/21	4/50	-/42	-/63
U.S.A.	$0.01	$0.03	$0.6	$0.06	$0.09
Dose per child	One	Three	One	One	Three
Route	Epidermal	Oral	Intra—muscular	(*a*) Intradermal (*b*) Multiple puncture	Deep subcutaneous or Intramuscular

Note:—Costs are approximate only, the dose of some vaccines varies with the manufacturer. The cost of measles vaccine for use with the Dermojet is likely to fall to about 1/-.

its effectiveness. The best compromise is to give a child his first dose of pertussis vaccine when he is about a month old.

Measles vaccine has a great advantage in that a single dose confers a major degree of protection for many years, and BCG is usually considered to do the same. Vaccinia is almost as convenient in that it only requires readministering at five yearly intervals under ordinary circumstances, although in highly endemic areas it should be readministered at intervals of 2-3 years. But triple vaccine and live poliomyelitis vaccine both require three administrations, which should not be given at intervals closer than a month. Triple vaccine has to be given three times because this is the only way in which a satisfactory antibody level can be built up to the dead antigens of which it is composed. Live virus poliomyelitis vaccine has also to be given three times, but the purpose here is to give each of the three strains of virus of which it is made a sufficient chance of multiplying in the child and so making him immune. With both triple vaccine and poliomyelitis vaccine one dose gives some immunity, but substantial immunity only follows the whole course of three doses.

3 **Variations upon a basic regime.** All the factors just discussed have been balanced with one another to produce the regime summarized in Table 8 which begins at birth, the best time to start. Not only is this good immunological practice, but it is also a good time to introduce mothers to the concept of immunization and it encourages their subsequent attendance at the under-fives clinic.

Should it not be possible to start the regime at birth it can be started at any time afterwards, but when this happens it should be modified by giving the birth and one month immunizations at the same time. The child thus gets BCG, poliomyelitis vaccine, vaccinia and triple vaccine at the same time. In this way a child catches up with his regime and can proceed with his second and third doses of poliomyelitis vaccine and triple vaccine at monthly intervals thereafter. Measles vaccine can be given him at any time from the age of nine months onwards and, if immunization does not start until this age, all five vaccines can be given together.

Immunization is not for outpatients only, and the opportunity that admission to the wards provides should be used to complete a child's immunization programme. This must be the responsibility of the doctor in charge of the children's ward.

4 **New vaccines and new instruments.** Even in hospitals where measles is ruled out by cost, the routine described in Table 8 may seem a formidable one. The complete course contains no less than nine different immunizations with five separate vaccines on five different occasions for a total cost of about 7/50 ($1.1) (3/- ($0.43) without measles). Efforts are being

made to reduce both the cost and the complexity of this regime, the ultimate aim being a cheap, 'one shot', general purpose vaccine mixture effective against all the relevant diseases. Triple vaccine is a step towards it, and a 'quadruple vaccine' containing Salk type killed poliomyelitis vaccine as well has been available for some years, but is too expensive for routine use. A 'quintuple vaccine' which is essentially quadruple vaccine to which a killed measles vaccine has been added is now being developed, but the difficulty with preparations containing killed viruses of any kind is their cost, for they have to contain much more viral material than do attenuated live virus vaccines. The latter need only contain just sufficient infective particles to establish an infection in the subject, and give him a mild or subclinical attack of the disease in question. Because they are so dilute they are cheap to make. Sabin live virus poliomyelitis vaccines are thus the only practicable ones in tropical circumstances, and Salk killed virus vaccines receive no further mention. The same applies to measles vaccines and only the live type of vaccine is considered here (GLA).

Syringes and needles are a nuisance. A busy clinic needs many of them, they are readily stolen, cumbersome to sterilize, and, if technique is poor, there is always the danger of serum hepatitis. These defects have stimulated the search for alternatives to the syringe and needle. Several devices have recently been developed which use a high speed jet of the fluid to pierce the skin, and so dispense with a hollow needle. The Dermojet, the Porton Injector, and the Ped-o-jet all work on this principle. For completeness, all the alternatives to the traditional syringe and hypodermic needle are listed below.

The Heaf gun. (A&H). This uses multiple short solid needles which are capable of introducing about 0.002 ml. of material into the skin. It can be used for tuberculin testing, as well as for immunizing with vaccinia and BCG: it is illustrated in Figure 46 (21:3) and discussed further in adjacent sections.

The Dermojet. (WRI) (SCH). This resembles a large steel fountain pen and was originally developed for anaesthetizing the gums in dentistry. Two versions are illustrated in Figure 35, an older one on the right and a newer one, Mark 3, on the left. Inside the instrument are a vaccine container and a piston arrangement driven by a powerful spring. This drives a fine jet of fluid into the skin, approximately 0.05 ml. entering the tissues. The whole instrument can be sterilized by boiling, and, since no vaccine-containing part of it comes into contact with the patient's tissues, it can be used for many patients and only needs sterilizing at the beginning of each clinic. A Dermojet costs about £22 and can be used for measles and BCG vaccine as described in section 17:7. A Dermojet that will deliver 0.1 ml. is now being developed (6b) (19).

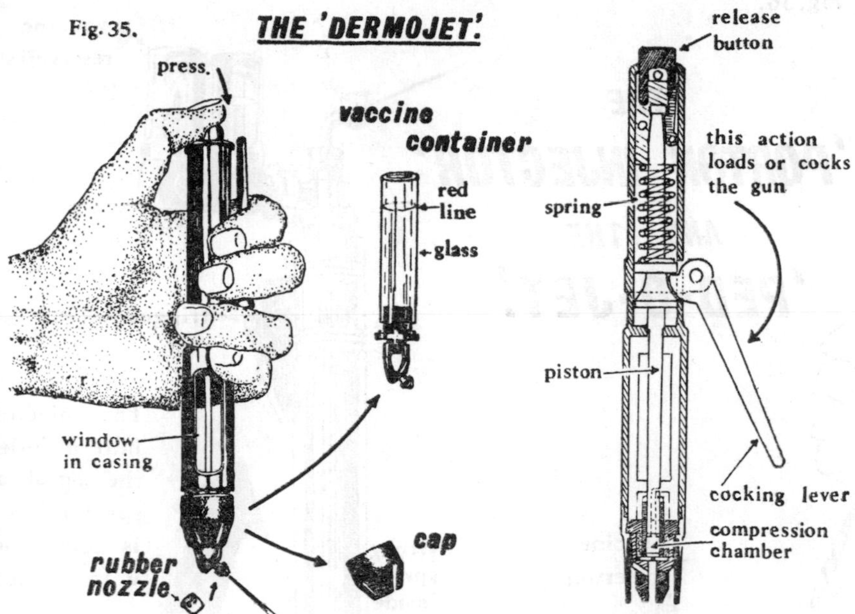

The Porton Injector. (A&H). At the time of going to press this is still in process of development. It works on the same principle as the Dermojet, except that the spring operating it is too strong to be compressed by hand, so foot power has to be used. The handle of the injector is placed in a recess on the top of a special box-like stand and its spring compressed by treading on a pedal inside the box. A volume of from 0.5 to 1 ml. is injected, so this device is suitable for triple vaccine and tetanus toxoid, etc.

The Ped-o-Jet. (SCI). This resembles the Porton Injector in that foot power has to be used to compress a spring that is too strong to compress by hand. But, in this instrument, the foot pedal remains permanently connected to the gun with hydraulic hoses. From 0.1 to 1.0 ml. of fluid can be injected, and the instrument has been in production for several years. Its disadvantages are its cost — £215 ($600), and the skill required to maintain and service it.

A notable feature of these devices is that their cost rises sharply with the volume of vaccine they inject, £5, £22 and £215, being the approximate cost of the instruments required to deliver 1/500, 1/10 and 1 ml. of vaccine respectively.

Apart from the Heaf gun, and to a lesser extent the Dermojet there has been little opportunity to try out these instruments under developing country conditions. Nevertheless, in section 17:7 a method is described for giving BCG with the Dermojet, but it is to be noted that it has not

Fig. 36.

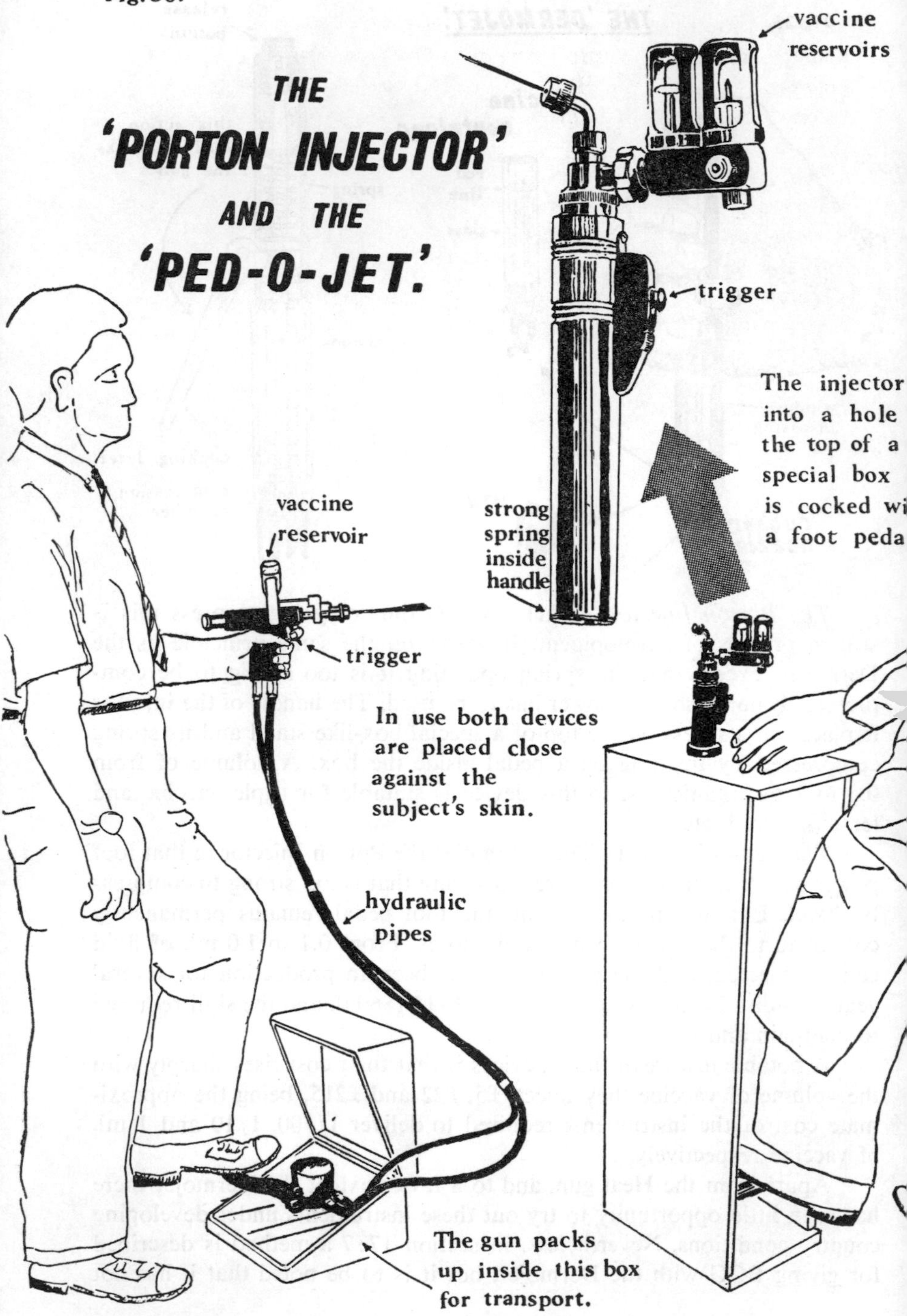
THE
'PORTON INJECTOR'
AND THE
'PED-O-JET.'
vaccine reservoirs
trigger
The injector into a hole the top of a special box is cocked wi a foot peda
strong spring inside handle
vaccine reservoir
trigger
In use both devices are placed close against the subject's skin.
hydraulic pipes
The gun packs up inside this box for transport.

yet been accorded the widespread acceptance given to the intradermal and the multiple puncture methods. There appears to be little to choose between them, and the Heaf gun is cheaper than the Dermojet. The real value of the Dermojet is in the administration of measles vaccine (6b).

7:5 **Clinic practice.** Try to persuade mothers to bring their children to the under-fives clinic each month and, so that the optimum time for a given immunization is not missed, try to make the whole range of vaccines available every time the clinic is held.

Immunization plays such a large part in the practice of the clinic that it is useful to keep an 'immunizing room' for this purpose alone (16:12). Here the apparatus for each vaccine should be put out on a separate enamel tray and a nurse deputed to see to the immunizing. Immunizing can be a useful teaching opportunity, so get the nurse to gather a group of mothers together and ask them to give their family experience of the diseases. In the ensuing discussion she can settle their fears, and make sure they understand the advantages of what is being done.

Syringes present a great problem. Ideally a fresh sterile syringe and needle should be used for each injection, for to use the same syringe and merely to change the needle is still to risk transmitting serum hepatitis. However, in most clinics the use of a separate syringe for each patient is quite impracticable. The only possible compromise is to use a fresh sterile needle for every patient and fresh syringes as often as possible, endeavouring to do so not less often than every ten or twelve patients.

Under many circumstances, and particularly if an immunization clinic is held out in a village, a domestic pressure cooker is very useful. At the rate of one syringe and 10 needles for every ten children, enough syringes can be both sterilized and stored in one pressure cooker to supply a clinic lasting a whole day and immunize 300-400 children. Operate the cooker at 15 lbs. per sq. in., or its maximum setting, for 15 mins.

The above is probably the best system under most circumstances, provided care is taken to avoid contaminating the sterile stock in the cooker. When boiling water is employed, the unsatisfactory kidney dishes that are usually used are better replaced by the needle racks shown in Figure 37. These are used in sets of three and are marked X, Y and Z in this diagram. One (X) contains the sterile needles ready for use, the next (Y), which is initially empty holds the dirty needles after use, while the third (Z) is in the sterilizer full of needles being boiled up (shown in Figure 37 as a charcoal stove and a saucepan). These racks of needles are moved round in a circle, and are quicker and safer than the usual method. No forceps are required to pick up needles from the pool of questionably sterile water at the bottom of a kidney dish: all that has to be done is to apply the syringe nozzle directly to the needle adaptor as it stands in the

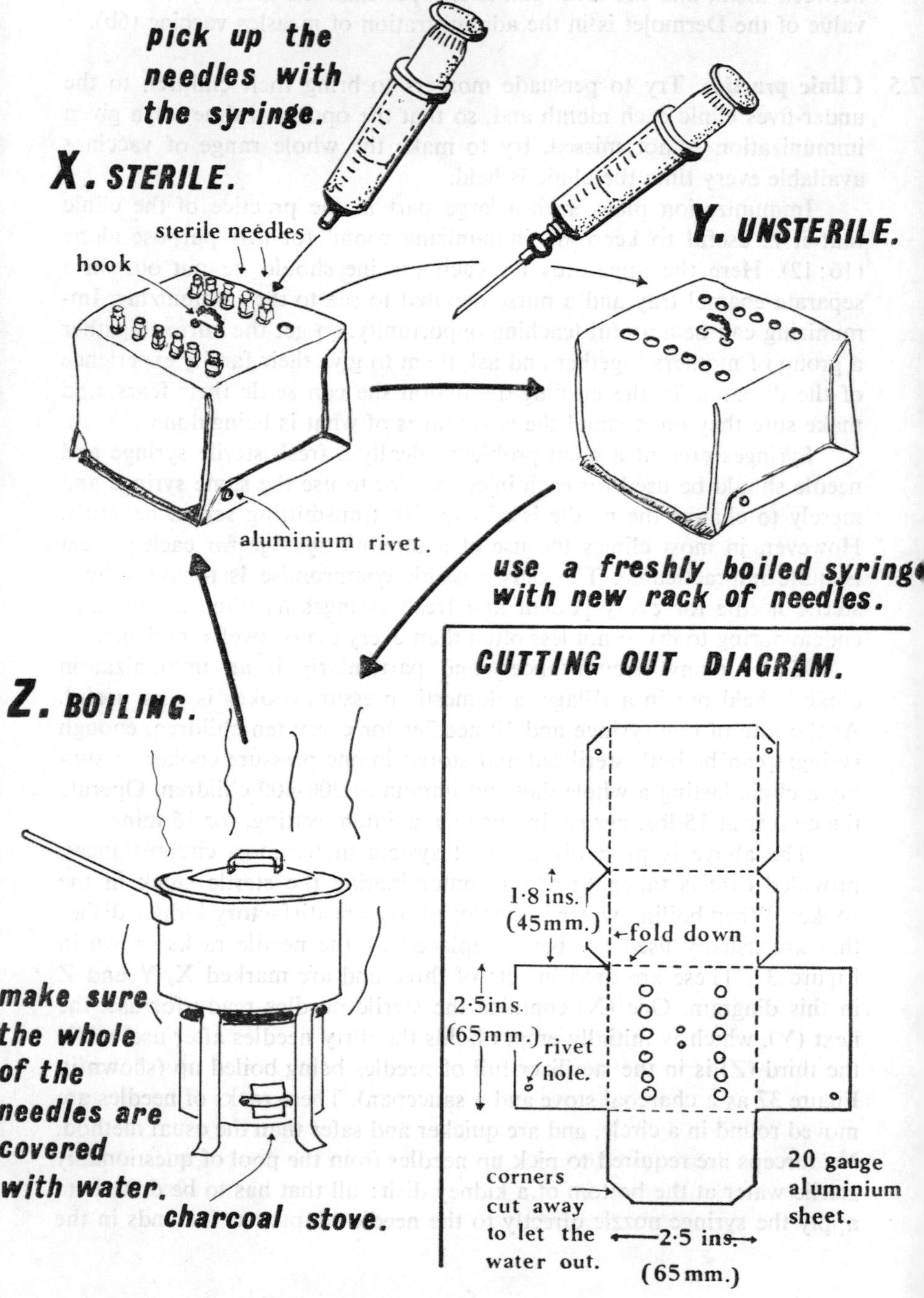
Fig. 37.
STERILIZING NEEDLES.
pick up the needles with the syringe.
X. STERILE.
sterile needles
hook
aluminium rivet.
Y. UNSTERILE.
use a freshly boiled syringe with new rack of needles.
Z. BOILING.
make sure the whole of the needles are covered with water.
charcoal stove.
CUTTING OUT DIAGRAM.
1·8 ins. (45mm.)
←fold down
2·5ins. (65mm.)
rivet hole.
corners cut away to let the water out.
←2·5 ins.→ (65mm.)
20 gauge aluminium sheet.

rack. The adaptors of the needles must be covered with water while they are boiling, the rack being lifted out of the water with a simple wire hook when sterilization is complete. To wash the dirty needles the whole rack is held under a tap, where, as they are in a vertical position, water runs through them readily.

These racks are illustrated in Figure 37 and have been made to contain only twelve needles though they could hold many more. The idea to be instilled in the mind of their user is that a separate syringe is to be associated with each rack, and boiled up with it when the twelve needles it contains have all been used.

This technique does not remove the danger of syringe jaundice but it should diminish it, and, used in this way, such racks represent a substantial improvement on the present syringe practice of many clinics. They are easily made according to the cutting-out diagram provided from 20 gauge aluminium.

17:6 **Some important technical and administrative points.** Because the immunization of the majority of children is the ultimate aim, immunization must become part of the routine practice of all dispensaries, health centres and hospitals. Such a resolve has many practical consequences, among them are the following:

Method: <u>Technical and administrative points in immunization.</u>

All medical assistants and nursing staff must be trained in immunization methods.

Immunization has to be stressed in the health education programmes of hospitals and health centres.

All dispensaries and health centres must have a refrigerator in which to store vaccines — paraffin refrigerators serve adequately.

Boxes to record the vaccinations given must be printed on the weight charts used in the under-fives clinic or on special record cards.

Store all vaccines between 2°C and 10°C; don't freeze them solid and don't let the storage temperature rise to above 10°C. Transport live liquid vaccines in thermos flasks on ice; vaccinia is better transported this way but can be sent by post. Freeze dried BCG, vaccinia and triple vaccine travel well by post, but refrigerate them as soon as possible on their arrival.

Never expose any live vaccine to strong sunlight — this is critically important with BCG. Don't keep open ampoules of live vaccine from one day to another.

The detailed use of a vaccine may vary from one maker to another, so read the instructions supplied with each brand.

Never give any living vaccine with a syringe that has been preserved with an antiseptic fluid — the antiseptic fluid remaining in the syringe may kill the vaccine.

METHODS

17:7 IMMUNIZATION AGAINST TUBERCULOSIS.

BCG vaccine. This is one of the cheapest and most useful vaccines and should be given to all children as soon as possible after birth, the only exception being the child of the sputum positive mother whose management is described in section 21:21.

Prior tuberculin testing is not required at any age: it is usually simpler to waste cheap vaccine on those already tuberculin positive than it is to try to exclude them by prior tuberculin testing. Ideally, children should be tuberculin tested 6-8 weeks after BCG vaccination to confirm that tuberculin conversion has taken place; however, this is quite impracticable in most clinics, nor is it strictly necessary.

Two forms of freeze dried vaccine are available. One is given intradermally with a 1 ml. tuberculin syringe; the other is given by multiple puncture with a special 'gun' (see below). These vaccines are prepared differently and strictly speaking they are not interchangeable. They are made up in different concentrations, that for the multiple puncture method usually containing 40 mg./ml., and that for the intradermal one only 0.5 — 1.0 mg./ml. Nevertheless, by adding less than the stated quantity of diluent, vaccine intended for the intradermal method can be given by multiple puncture. Thus an ampoule containing 5 mg. of vaccine that is normally diluted with 10 ml. of diluent for the intradermal method can be diluted with 0.125 ml. of diluent and given by multiple puncture. This quantity of vaccine is enough for 10 children, but, by the intradermal route, it would have been enough for 100 children (10 ml $\div$ 0.1). This is not therefore the best way to use this vaccine, and the correct kind should be ordered where possible.

If many patients are to be immunized at the same time the multiple puncture technique is best, even though it is perhaps not quite so effective. Its great advantage is that it is simpler technically — an intradermal injection requires some skill, whether it be for Mantoux testing or for giving BCG; firing a 'gun' requires very little (21:3).

The traditional instrument for multiple puncture BCG, is a modified Heaf gun with 20 needle points instead of only six, which is 'fired' into the skin twice only. It is economical however, to use the same standard six needled gun for both Heaf testing and for giving BCG. This is perfectly possible, for all that need be done is to 'fire' the gun repeatedly, 6 'firings' at 2 mm. being the method advised. With both types of gun about 40 punctures are required, either 2 x 20 or 6 x 6. Neither method is painful and both are equally effective.

Once a Heaf gun has been used for tuberculin testing it is very difficult to clean and render completely free from the tuberculin which would complicate its use in other procedures. Therefore, either use separate guns for Heaf testing and giving BCG or use the same gun with different magnetic heads (Figure 46. (21:3)). Magnetic headed guns of this type (A&H) are the best ones, and, if several heads are available, the same gun can be used for Heaf testing, giving BCG and even for vaccinating against smallpox, a technique which some people prefer to the traditional methods.

It is a good plan to teach auxiliaries in the under-fives clinic to give BCG to all children on the point of their *left* shoulder, and to revaccinate any child without a scar in this region. A scar on this shoulder is thus good evidence that a child has been given BCG. It is also useful to reserve the point of the *right* shoulder for vaccinia. Thus, a scar on the right shoulder is evidence that a child has been vaccinated against smallpox.

Unhappily, there is no general agreement about the site at which to give these vaccines — in Uganda, for instance, it is customary to give vaccinia on the left and BCG on the right. Though the position of a scar can be useful, scars can fade, particularly with multiple puncture BCG in infants, and good records are more important. It should thus become an invariable rule to give the mother some form of record for her child's immunizations, preferably in a polythene envelope, and if possible on the back of his weight chart.

BCG is the most light sensitive of all the common vaccines — even a minute or two's exposure to sunlight or direct skyshine will cause a significant decrease in its potency. Don't therefore vaccinate out of doors, and keep ampoules and vaccine-filled syringes covered with a sheet of black paper. Make sure that BCG vaccine is freshly made up, and discard any that remains unused once it is a few hours old.

With all three methods clean the surface of the skin with soap and water and wipe it firmly with cottonwool.

Method: <u>Intradermal BCG.</u>

Ideally, use a dry sterilized 1 ml. tuberculin-type syringe. Failing this, use one that has been sterilized by boiling. Add normal saline or water for injection to the contents of the

ampoule and allow it to stand for a minute, without shaking; then, using a stout intramuscular needle draw the mixture into the syringe. Replace this stout needle with a fine hypodermic one for the immunization itself, placing the needle on the syringe so that its bevel or 'eye' faces the graduations on the syringe barrel thus making it easier to measure the amount of vaccine given. Pass this needle through the flame of a spirit lamp for just long enough for a spitting sound to be heard — don't heat it so much that it becomes red hot. If the needle is carefully flamed in this way every time, there is no need to use a different one for each patient.

When immunizing adults, use the dorsum of the right forearm at the junction of its upper and middle third. When immunizing babies or children, use the left deltoid region. Select a clear site on the arm, stretch the skin over it between the thumb and index finger of the left hand. Discard a few drops of vaccine from the needle — this both cools it and removes the heated vaccine. Push the needle, bevel uppermost, into the skin, not into the subcutaneous tissues. Keep it as flat as possible, because a flat or acute angle of entry assures a superficial injection. Inject slowly and try to produce a small wheal in the skin about 5 mm. in diameter. This will contain about 0.1 ml. of vaccine.

Many syringes leak, and it may be easier to judge the size of the wheal than to measure the volume of vaccine delivered by the syringe. If no wheal appears and there is no leak of vaccine, the needle is probably too deep and the vaccine is probably being given subcutaneously rather than intradermally. When this happens, pull out the needle and try again.

Method: <u>Multiple puncture BCG.</u>

If possible use the special vaccine made for multiple puncture use (see above) and follow the precautions described above with regard to light and care in opening and filling the ampoules. Apply a thin film of the vaccine to the skin of the deltoid region with a short glass rod or a wire loop dipped into the reconstituted vaccine. Sterilize the multiple puncture apparatus by holding its needles against a cotton wool pad soaked in spirit and then flaming them rapidly (21:3). Set the gun to 2 mm., both for adults and children, and allow its plate to cool. Apply it to the vaccine-covered area and press the trigger — twice if the 20 needle device is being used and six times if

an ordinary Heaf gun is being employed. No dressing is necessary.

Method: Dermojet BCG.

Sterilize both the body and the vaccine container of the Dermojet by boiling. Reconstitute the vaccine to twice the concentration advised for intradermal use with the traditional hollow needle — approximately 0.05 ml. will enter the tissues so make up the vaccine to contain 1-2 mg./ml. (rather than the 0.5 — 1.0 m. per ml. recommended for intradermal administration). Shake the vaccine container as dry as possible. When cool fill it with the volume of vaccine required, but do not exceed the volume indicated by the red line on the vaccine container. Assemble the Dermojet, and, holding it vertically downwards, cock or load it by depressing the cocking lever as shown in Figure 35. Press the release button, the Dermojet will 'fire'. Load and fire again, and do this three times in all to clear any water from the compression chamber of the instrument. It is then ready for the patient.

Place the left forefinger and thumb about an inch and a half apart on the patient's left deltoid region and draw them together slightly — this takes the tension off the skin without causing it to bunch up. With the rubber nozzle (Figure 35) over the jet apply the Dermojet to the skin and fire. A small wheal will be raised. No dressing will be needed.

At the end of the clinic wash the Dermojet and fire it once or twice with water to clear the compression chamber.

The reader may wonder if it is possible to dilute the concentrated vaccine (40 mg. per ml.) intended for the multiple puncture procedure, and use it in the Dermojet. It is reported to be unsatisfactory for this purpose as it clumps if used in this way — use the vaccine prepared for intradermal administration.

:8 **The normal course of a BCG lesion.** The wheal left by an intradermal injection disappears in about half an hour. Two or three weeks later a small red, indurated slightly tender nodule forms and grows slowly during the following week. Sometimes, this nodule appears earlier, and when it does so this usually means that the person had a slight degree of allergy before vaccination was given — this is the 'accelerated reaction'. In most cases the nodule becomes a small superficial abscess which ulcerates and then rapidly crusts. Later, this crust separates to leave a small scar. The process is usually complete twelve weeks from the vaccination date and only the scar remains to provide permanent evidence that vaccination has been performed.

Leave the abscess or the ulcer untreated, and apply a dressing only when there is a profuse discharge. If some form of dressing is required, see that it is light and porous — otherwise the lesion will become soggy and take longer to heal. Six weeks after immunization with BCG the Heaf test should be positive. The lesion and the scar from multiple puncture BCG is very much less than that following intradermal administration.

17:9 **Complications.** Complications are occasionally seen, but they are much less common with the multiple puncture method.

Koch's phenomenon. This is an acute inflammatory reaction which appears within 2-4 days of vaccination — it is not serious and heals rapidly.

Deep abscesses at the vaccination site. These are almost invariably due to injecting the vaccine too deeply into the skin.

Excessive ulceration. An ulcer which is still present more than 12 weeks after vaccination or one which is more than 1 cm. across is usually a complication of one of the deep abscess already mentioned.

Lymph node enlargement. The epitrochlear or axillary lymph nodes draining the injection site sometimes enlarge. This seldom matters but watch these nodes carefully.

Treat all these complications with INH, and either thiacetazone or PAS (21:7). Very occasionally deep abscesses or glands need aspirating. When they do, inject 10-20 mg of streptomycin into the abscess cavity. Treat ulcers with PAS powder and 0.5% crystal violet locally as well as giving the above drugs by mouth.

17:10

VACCINATION AGAINST SMALLPOX.

The best age to vaccinate. Under average circumstances the best time for vaccination is at the under-fives clinic when children are about one month old. When there is much smallpox about, vaccinate at birth.

Complications are particularly likely in the presence of eczema, scabies, a bullous or vesicular eruption, any scaling skin disease or severe malnutrition — don't vaccinate therefore when any of these are particularly widespread, unless absolutely forced to.

Vaccine is supplied in glass capillary tubes containing 1-4 doses, in collapsible miniature 'toothpaste tubes', liquid in multidose ampoules or in the freeze dried state.

Method: Vaccination.

Don't clean the skin with spirit, but wash the right shoulder with soap and water and then wipe it firmly with cotton wool.

Place a drop of vaccine on the skin. Use a short glass rod or a wire loop if the vaccine is in a multidose ampoule. If it is in a glass capillary tube, either use one of the special rubber devices made for the purpose, or prick an ordinary rubber teat with a hot needle and insert the capillary tube into the hole thus made. If the open end of the teat is then closed, and its bulb gently squeezed, vaccine can be delivered from the capillary tube in a controlled manner.

Pass a straight sharp triangular sectioned Hagedorn needle quickly through the flame of a spirit lamp and let it cool a moment. Don't let it get red hot, or its tip will get blunt. Place this needle flat on the skin, its tip in the vaccine drop. Lift it up and down rapidly 30-40 times so that the tip stays in the area of the vaccine and just marks the skin but does not draw blood. The aim is to get the vaccine into contact with the cells of the deeper layers of the epidermis where the vaccinia virus can multiply — a good 'take' is less likely if the dermis is entered and blood drawn.

Don't apply a dressing, but tell the mother to let the vaccination site dry and ask her not to wash that shoulder until the following day.

The subsequent progress of a vaccine lesion. Three days after a successful vaccination the site becomes raised and red, and progresses through the stages of macule, papule, vesicle, pustule, crust and scar. A little fever is normal at the time of the vesicle, the area around the pustule may inflame, and the axillary lymph nodes often enlarge slightly. Secondary infection sometimes makes the blister break down and ulcerate — apply gentian violet to such a lesion. Successful primary vaccination leaves a small scar behind it, and, if at the next visit no such scar or scab is present, repeat the vaccination because the absence of a scar means that the initial vaccination was unsuccessful.

Vaccination against smallpox is not something to be forgotten as soon as a child is five, and in endemic areas he should be revaccinated at not less than five yearly intervals thereafter.

TRIPLE IMMUNIZATION AGAINST DIPHTHERIA, PERTUSSIS AND TETANUS.

Two types of vaccine. This 'triple' vaccine contains killed bacteria and toxoids preserved with an antiseptic and is therefore less labile than the living vaccines that have just been considered. Protection from light is thus less important and partly used ampoules can be kept up to three days in the refrigerator —not longer.

There are two kinds of triple vaccine, one of which is made with alum — 'mineral carrier vaccine'. This is the best kind to give to children a month old.

There is little or no immune response to a single injection of this vaccine, so make every attempt to give at least two and if possible three injections at monthly intervals.

Method: Triple vaccination.

Sterilize the skin with spirit and give 0.5 ml. or 1 ml. (according to the makers' instructions) of vaccine by deep subcutaneous injection into the lateral or anterior part of the thigh. This leaves the shoulders free for BCG and smallpox. Under the age of six months give half the standard dose.

Complications are rare, sometimes there is slight fever after about 24 hours, and very occasionally an injection abscess. Some workers advise the giving of an aspirin tablet on the day the vaccine is given.

17:13

SABIN LIVE VIRUS IMMUNIZATION AGAINST POLIOMYELITIS

'Oral polio' — a cheap vaccine. The Sabin type of live vaccine is the cheapest one, and now that the price has fallen to about -/20 ($0.03) a dose, it deserves to be used on the widest scale. It is labile and has a short storage life, limitations which make it difficult to stock regularly in the more remote hospitals and health centres. Due to its possibly being in competition with other entero-viruses, do not give it if the child is ill; this is especially important when there is diarrhoea or vomiting.

Method: Oral polio vaccination.

Place 3 drops of the water-like vaccine in the child's mouth and make sure that he swallows it. Give the remaining two doses at 4-6 week intervals.

17:14

IMMUNIZATION AGAINST MEASLES

Measles — still an expensive vaccine. This is the newest vaccine, it is a live virus and is still not in general use. At 4/50 ($0.6) a dose it is expensive, but in time its cost will surely fall. Because of its cost, measles vaccine is likely to be beyond the range of those who need it most, but those who are able to provide it should do so, because measles is such a lethal disease in so many tropical communities. As a general rule immunize all children at the age of 9 months (17:2). The vaccine must be stored carefully, and, because it is very sensitive to traces of metal, use the special diluent provided by the makers, or failing this use commercially prepared ampoules of 'water for injection'. Even the metal in an ordinary syringe may be deleterious, so preferably use disposable syringes, or, if these are not available, use all-glass ones.

Method: Measles vaccination.

Reconstitute the vaccine with metal free distilled water and inject it intramuscularly into the thigh in the dose stated on the pamphlet supplied with the ampoule. This is usually 0.5-1.0 ml.

At about the 8th or 9th day after the injection there may be short fever which is usually innocuous, but which may sometimes be quite high. Warn mothers about this and let them take home an aspirin tablet so that they can give it to the child when he is feverish. These reactions have been studied intensively and are no worse than those from vaccinia or triple vaccine.

For measles immunization with the Dermojet see (6b) (GLA).

Chapter Eighteen

FAMILY PLANNING

Based on material provided by George and Anne Saxton

THE CASE FOR FAMILY PLANNING.

18:1 **World opinion and the revolution in man's biological position.** In no part of man's affairs is a more profound change of both attitude and practice now taking place than in family planning. More and more thoughtful people are becoming aware of the consequences of the explosive population increase that is now occurring in so many parts of the world. One organization after another concerned with human welfare is recognizing the need for limiting the rate of population growth if their purposes are to be achieved. OXFAM now supports family planning schemes, the World Health Organization can now provide countries with expert advice when asked for it, and the 'Save the Children Fund' can employ doctors and nurses to give advice and practical assistance in family planning in the course of their normal work. Even in the most conservative churches there are signs that a more liberal attitude is not far away. Not only is the world opinion changing, but it is happily coming at a time when technical advances are making family planning possible to those who need it most, and who were previously denied it.

Population increase and the need for family planning has to be seen in its biological setting. Man is but one of a myriad of species competing on this planet. Until very recently his success has depended in large measure on his capacity to reproduce, and so make good his losses from war, famine and disease. Now, due mostly to the scientific developments of the last century, the situation has changed completely. Although there are usually a few small-scale wars somewhere in the world, they now

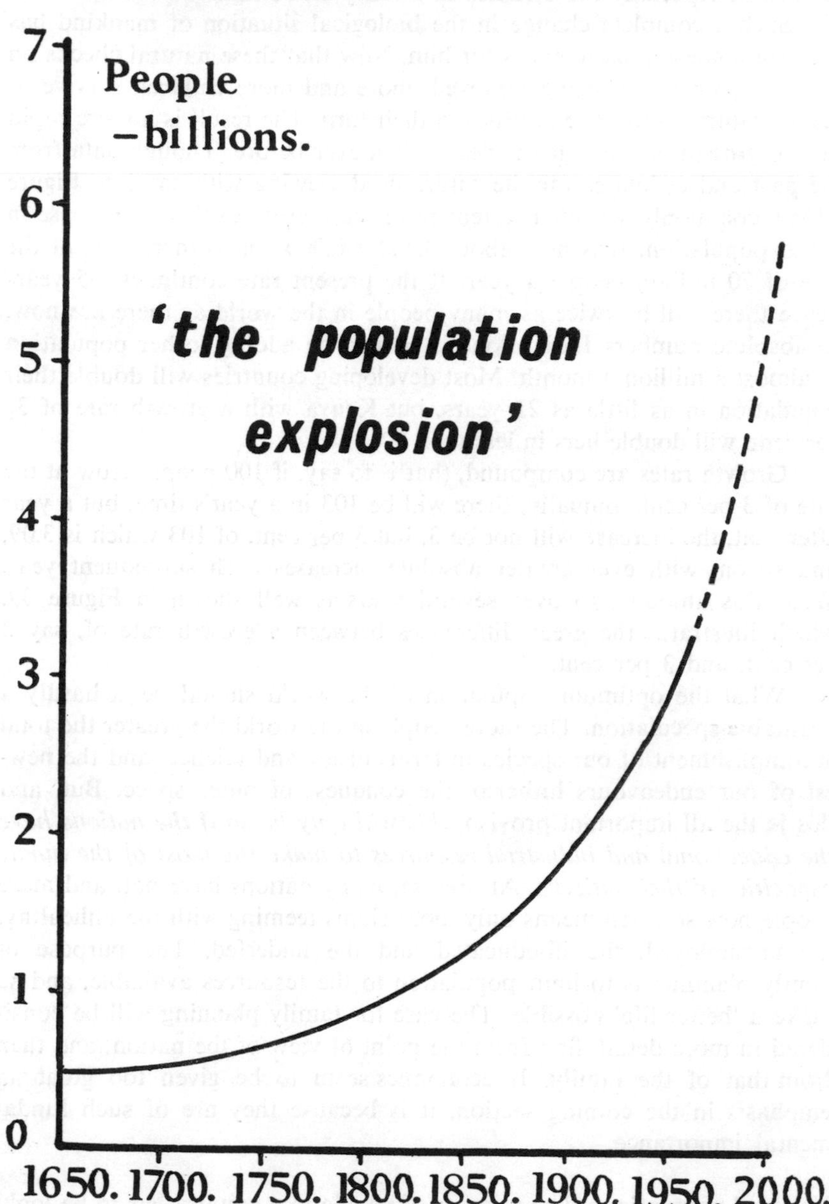
Fig. 38. The number of people in the world – actual & projected.
People –billions.
'the population explosion'
7
6
5
4
3
2
1
0
1650. 1700. 1750. 1800. 1850. 1900. 1950. 2000.

make little difference to population numbers. Food surpluses on one side of the globe can do something to allay famine on the other and man need no longer die from the diseases that have decimated his species until now, especially the diseases of infancy and childhood (16:1).

Such a complete change in the biological situation of mankind has the profoundest consequences for him. Now that these natural checks on human numbers are being removed, more and more children survive to reach maturity and have families in their turn. The result is a more rapid rate of growth of the human species than ever before. Though data from the past and estimates for the future need viewing with caution, Figure 38 is a commonly accepted statement of the present explosive increase in world population. It is now about 3,300,000,000 and is increasing at the rate of 70 million people a year. If the present rate continues, 35 years hence there will be twice as many people in the world as there are now. In absolute numbers India alone is said to be adding to her population at almost a million a month. Most developing countries will double their population in as little as 25 years, but Kenya with a growth rate of 3½ per cent. will double hers in less than 20.

Growth rates are compound, that is to say, if 100 people grow at the rate of 3 per cent. annually, there will be 103 in a year's time, but a year after that, the increase will not be 3, but 3 per cent. of 103 which is 3.09, and so on, with ever greater absolute increases each subsequent year. What this amounts to over several years is well shown in Figure 39, which illustrates the great differences between a growth rate of, say 2 per cent. and 3 per cent.

What the optimum population of the world should be is hardly a profitable speculation. The more people in the world the greater the total accomplishment of our species in terms of art and science, and the newest of our endeavours hitherto, the conquest of outer space. But, and this is the all important proviso, *this will only be so if the nations have the educational and industrial resources to make the most of the innate capacities of their citizens.* At present, many nations have not, and more people now so often means only more slums teeming with the unhealthy, the unemployed, the ill-educated and the underfed. The purpose of family planning is to limit population to the resources available, and so make a 'better life' possible. The case for family planning will be considered in more detail, first from the point of view of the nation, and then from that of the family. If economics seem to be given too great an emphasis in the coming section, it is because they are of such fundamental importance.

18:2a **National populations.** The number of people in a country has to be looked at in several different ways.

Fig. 39. To show the effect of several annual rates of increase on population growth.

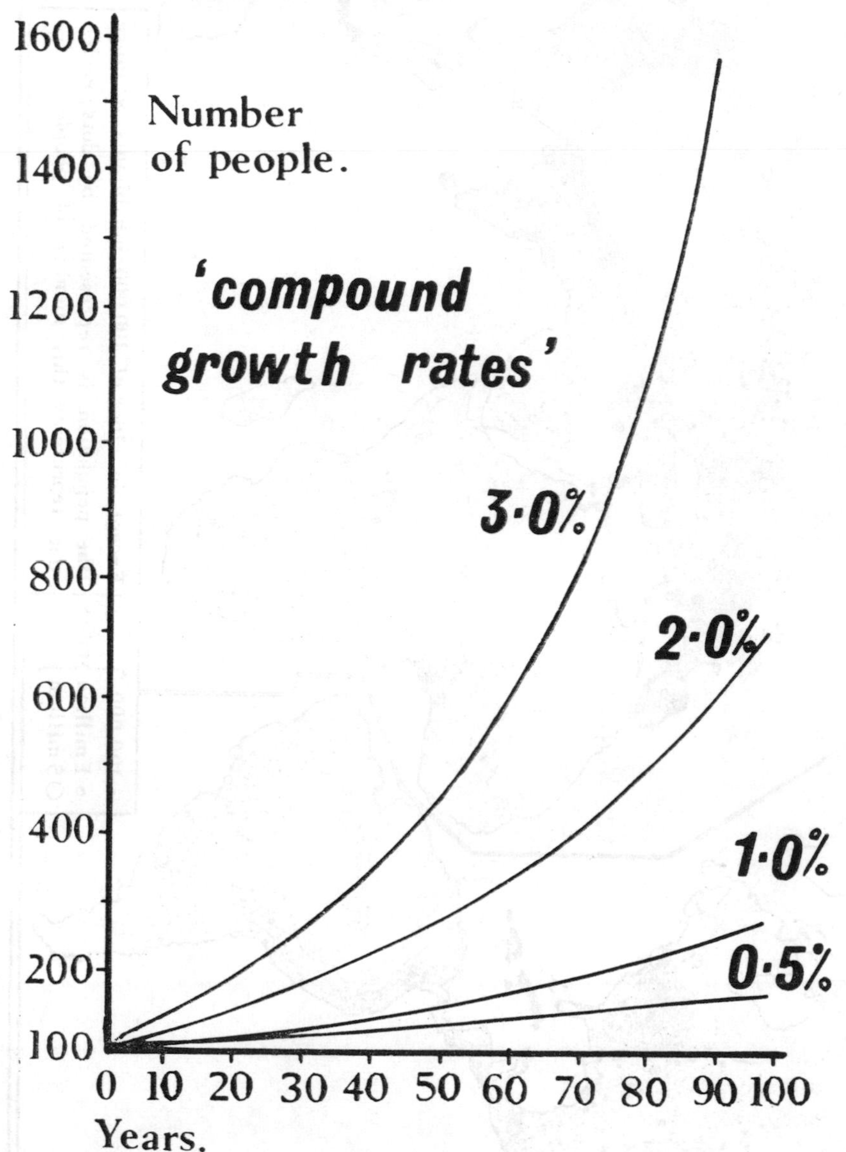

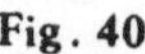

Fig. 40.

WORLD POPULATION.

• 100,000
○ 1 million
○ 5 million
cities
Except in cities of 100.000 inhabitants & more the population is represented by dots; each dot represents this number of people.

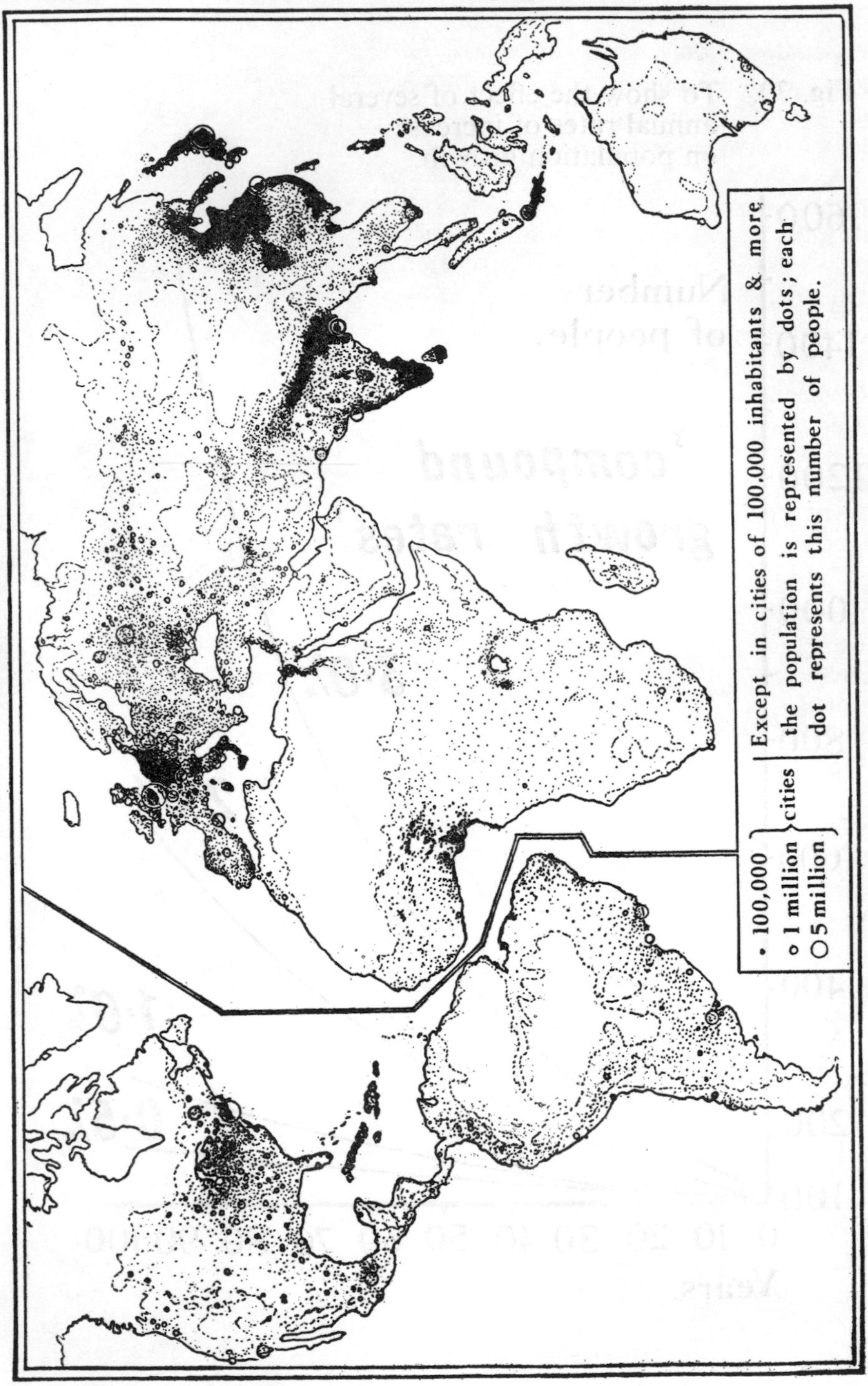

Population density. This will be discussed first only to be dismissed as being of comparatively little importance. Figure 40 supports the contention that a high standard of living is possible in both a sparsely populated country and in a densely populated one. Dense population may reduce the amenities of the citizen, but, by itself, it is compatible with a high standard of living. Maintaining low population densities is not therefore the purpose of family planning.

The GNP per head. The really critical issue is that in many developing countries populations are growing faster than it is possible to provide jobs or social services, in effect they are growing faster than their economies. Countries vary in the rate of their economic growth. For many of them it is about the same as the growth rate of their populations, sometimes it is a little more, sometimes a little less. The consequences of this can best be understood by considering its effect on what is termed the 'GNP per head'.

The GNP of a country is its 'Gross National Product', and is the sum of all the goods and services produced. When this is divided by the number of people in the country, the result, the 'GNP per head', gives a useful index of the wealth, standard of living or quality of life of the average citizen. On it depends the prospects he has for a job, education, medical care and social services of all kinds — it is thus a valuable index of the economic and social well-being of the people of a country. When the GNP and the population grow at the same rate, the GNP per head remains the same; when the GNP grows faster than the population, the GNP per head increases and the average citizen is better off; when the population grows faster than the GNP, the GNP per head falls, and the average citizen becomes poorer. The quicker the population expands, the higher must be the rate of economic growth that must be achieved merely to prevent a decrease in living standards, let alone increase them.

Among the rich, developed, industrial nations the GNP per head is not only already very high, being for many of them about £500 ($1,400), but it is in many cases rising at an average rate of about 2-4 per cent. annually. On the other hand, the GNP per head of the developing countries is not only very low, often as low as £25 ($70), the current figure for Uganda, but it by no means always shows this steady rise. For some it is rising slowly, for many others it is virtually stationary, while in some countries it is actually falling.

Nevertheless, **even should the GNP per head rise at the same rate for two countries rich and poor, the absolute gap between them will widen.** This can best be illustrated by considering what happens if the GNP per head of two countries just mentioned rise by 5 per cent.. A 5 per cent. rise for the first country will bring its figure to £525, while the same rise for the second country only brings its figure to £26.25. The *absolute* gap between has widened for it is now £498.75, whereas it was only £475 before. The *relative* gap between them is of course the same, £500 and £25 having the same twenty-fold relationship between them as do £525 and £26.25.

This in fact is what is happening. Even if a developing country can achieve the same rate of economic growth as an industrial one, and many of them are in fact far from achieving it, the absolute gap between the two countries will continue to widen. Because of this, the already vast distance between rich nations and poor ones grows wider every year throughout the world. **If the gap is ever to be closed, and the poor to catch up with the rich, then the developing countries will have to grow faster than the developed ones — an impossible feat at the rate their populations are now growing.**

Because the 'GNP per head' is such a good composite index of the economic, social, medical and educational opportunities of the citizens of a country, to 'maximize the GNP per head' should be the most important economic goal of every government. The obvious way to achieve this is to increase the Gross National Prouct itself; but, though this is critically important, there is a limit to what a government can do to raise it. This is mainly because the GNP is largely dependent on capital resources, and the skills needed to make use of them, and developing countries are short of both capital and skills of every kind. The limited amount that an individual government can do to raise the GNP makes the remaining factor, the population of a country, the critical determinant of its economic well-being. This must be limited if the quality of the life of the average citizen is to improve.

The governments of some developing countries realize this only too well, as do the industrial nations who see that the economic aid they give is of no avail when its benefit to the citizens of a developing country is immediately dissipated by population increase. **Therefore, though massive aid from the developed to the undeveloped nations is one of the keys towards progress, it is however only one of them, and it must be combined with a reduced rate of population growth in the countries receiving this aid.**

'Limit the size of our nations?' the reader will say. No, the idea is not to limit their ultimate size, *but to limit their present rate of increase.* The concept of the ultimate population of a nation, like that of the world, is a controversial abstraction which it will not be possible to discuss here, but, whatever it may be, it is not the intention that it ultimately be less than the country can support at a reasonable standard of living. The vital point is that growth to this size must take place more slowly than at present — slower growth will be of great benefit to the lives of a country's present citizens. This slow growth, if it can be achieved, will make it possible for a country to achieve, not *quantity* in its citizens, but *quality.*

d **Food supplies.** The economic argument is the main one, but it is supported by the relationship between population and the availability of food and land. Although the food producing potential of the world is great, the present situation is tragic. **In spite of there having been an overall increase in world agricultural production in the years from 1960 to 1965, there has been no significant change in the world agricultural production per head of population. Estimates indicate that for the years 1961-1963 food production per head has actually declined in many already undernourished countries in the Far East, the Near East, Africa and Latin America.** Only in Western Europe, North America and Oceania have there been increases in both the quality and quantity of food supplies. In effect, this means that the already large gap between the nutrition of the fat countries and the thin ones has grown even wider over these years. The need to match population growth to the growth in food production is thus further support for the need for family planning.

e **Productive acres per head.** When a nation is mainly pastoral, and depends for its livelihood on the export of agricultural products, the number of productive acres per person is critically important to its welfare. Figure 41 shows these for a number of developing countries, as they are at present and as they will be in future if existing rates of population increase continue. As with Figure 38 for the world population, Figure 41 should be viewed with caution, but it shows what some developing countries can expect if their populations continue to grow at their present rates. In terms of the map in Figure 40 it means that by the end of the century Kenya will look much as India does now (9).

3 **Family size.** What has been argued from national growth rates can be supported by arguments from the family. Here two things matter. One is its total size, the other is the interval between one pregnancy and the next and the effect this has on the health of both a mother and her children.

Except on farms, where many children may sometimes even be an asset, too large a family over-extends its financial resources and the care of too many children is a burden on their mother. Increasing parity increases her dangers in childbirth, and rapidly repeated pregnancies deplete her reserves of iron and protein. The best size for a family is not easy to determine, but here at least are some good reasons why it should not be too large.

The length of time between one pregnancy and the next is of great importance to a mother and her children. The ideal interval is one which permits the first infant to be both independent of breast milk, and able to walk, before the next one arrives. When the interval is shorter than

Fig. 41. The number of potentially productive acres per head forecast until the end of the century for several developing countries.

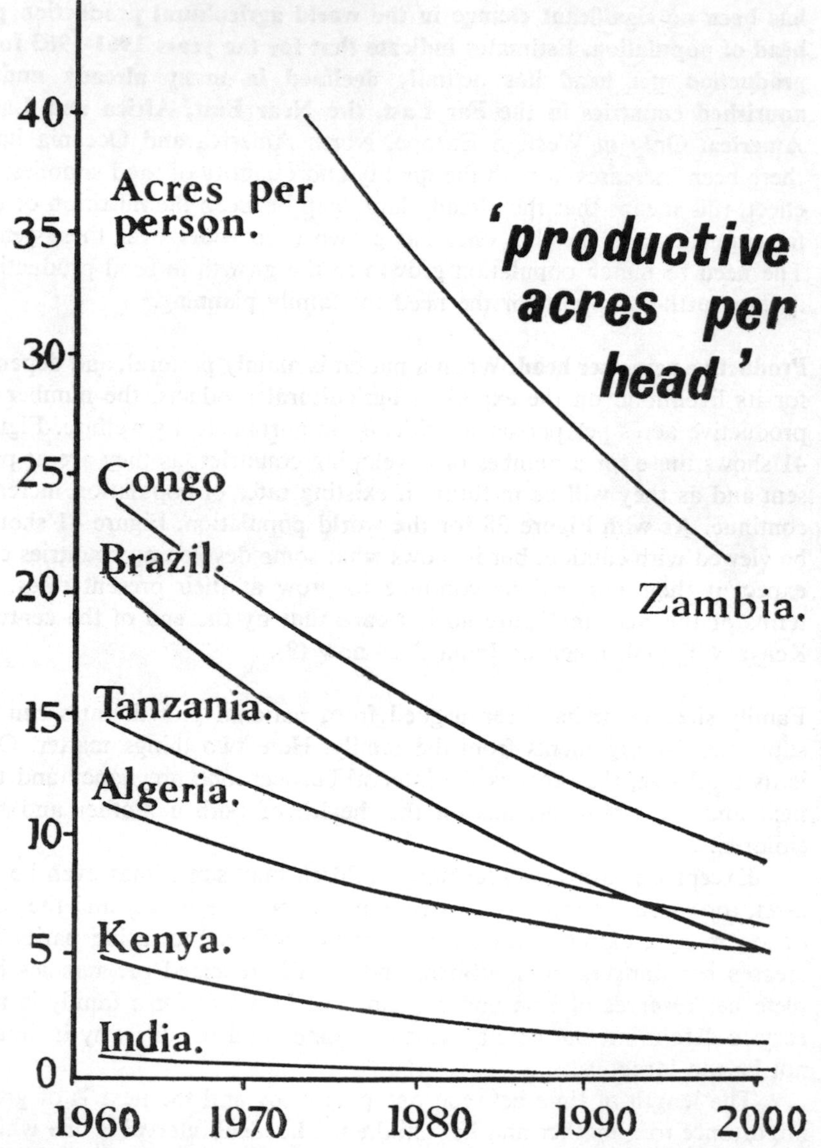

this, children in many societies are at great risk from protein calorie malnutrition and, if a child cannot walk before his mother is pregnant again, she has the added burden of carrying two children about with her at once; one on her back and the other in her womb.

The only logical conclusion. From what has been said it follows that, although the utimate ideal may be a highly populated world with each nation contributing maximally to the total accomplishment of our species, it is of the utmost importance to the well-being of many of the world's present citizens, that this dense population be achieved much more slowly than it is at present.

Rising standards of living are almost invariably associated with a falling of birth rate, and the developed countries now have birth rates which produce only a moderate annual increase in their populations. The reasons for this association are complex, and are not always clear, but the really significant fact is, that unless the birth rates of many developing countries can be reduced, their standards of living cannot begin to rise rapidly in the way they must. Once standards have risen to a certain degree, a further and automatic fall in the birth rate can be expected, so making possible yet a further rise in living standards. This is a highly desirable cycle, but it cannot begin without an initial reduction in the birth rate.

This means family planning. It is used for two purposes; the first is to space pregnancies for the reasons already described, and the second is to limit a family once its desired size has been reached, whether this be two, three, four, or possibly even more children. These are the reasons that will commend family planning to the millions of individual couples which will have to make use of it, if national birth rates are to fall to the required degree.

Ways and means. The duty of a doctor. Though man has long limited the size of his family in one way or another, it is only recently that an efficient method has become available which is really suited to the needs of the tropical villager. This is the intrauterine device or 'IUD' and much of this chapter will be devoted to describing it. Though, at the time of writing, it has only been in existence in its present form for about five years, the IUD promises to be a major break-through in the control of human populations, and could well bring about immense improvements in the well-being of mankind.

The IUD is only one method among many, but, now that it has become available, doctors in the developing nations have an added duty to their countries and their countrymen. They alone have both the understanding and the influence to diffuse knowledge of modern methods of family planning through their communities. The best way for them to do this is to seek to integrate it with existing maternal and child health — 'MCH' — services. Before introducing family planning in an area, it is important to find out how it is likely to fit into the local culture and what alterations may be necessary in the attitudes of the community.

18:6 **The integration of family planning with existing MCH services.** Doctors will almost invariably be too busy to instruct mothers themselves, so they should do their best to see that instruction in family planning not only becomes part of the regular training of all midwives and nurses, but also that those midwives who are already trained receive adequate postgraduate training in this subject. In most circumstances this means that the individual doctor will have to instruct these midwives himself.

In the grossly overpopulated type of developing country, population pressure has often forced governments to take active steps to limit it, and so family planning has become national policy. More and more nations are now doing this.

In the less populated developing countries official opinion is often still hostile to family planning, because those in high authority do not always appreciate the importance of increasing the 'GNP per head' as the most important goal. Under these circumstances the doctor who is concerned with this critical issue has a difficult task, for not only may such a government refuse to adopt family planning as its policy, but family planning may even be forbidden in the hospitals for which the government is responsible. When this happens family planning facilities have to be provided outside government health services. This can sometimes be done through the municipal health departments of large towns, for this is the place where population pressure is often first felt. In other areas doctors in independent hospitals will have to take the initiative.

18:7 **Voluntary organizations.** When the above methods fail it may be necessary for a voluntary organization to be formed. This will usually be a group of educated women encouraged by a doctor. They will have to find a site for a clinic, obtain regular medical assistance and supervision, and collect funds to pay for the part-time assistance of midwives and nurses. Such a voluntary organization can obtain financial assistance, as well as supplies of literature and apparatus, from various international organizations, such as the 'International Planned Parenthood Federation' — the 'IPPF' (IPP) or the Pathfinder Fund (PAF). These foundations may well be able to assist a family planning clinic in its early stages, but as far as the cost of the supplies is concerned, most clinics usually find it possible to cover this by selling them to the patients.

Family planning has often first been introduced by voluntary clinics serving only a few sophisticated families in the cities. But as time has gone by, more and more people have heard about it, and sought similar services in the places where they live. The local or national government may then take over this responsibilty, and incorporate family planning as part of their regular MCH services.

3 **Clinic practice.** Family planning should be introduced very carefully and fully explained to mothers in the antenatal clinics. This will be much easier, as well as much more necessary, if an under-fives clinic has been going some years, and has already produced a dramatic reduction in child deaths. Here, as in other situations, it is important that a doctor understands the beliefs and attitudes of the local people in this matter, after the manner advocated in Chapter Four.

TABLE 10

FAMILY PLANNING METHODS COMPARED

Non-Medical Methods	*Sex*	*Effectiveness*	*Annual Cost* Shs. E.A.	$
Disposable condom	Male	Very effective	100/-	14.40
Reusable rubber sheath	Male	Good	100/-	14.40
Vaginal cream (and applicator)	Female	Fair	90/-	12.50
Vaginal foam tablets, etc.	Female	Poor.	46/-	6.50
The Rhythm method	Variable effectiveness, depends upon menstrual regularity, careful record keeping and self-discipline		Nil	
Coitus interruptus	Male	Unreliable	Nil	
Medical Methods				
Diaphragm plus spermatocidal cream	Female	Very effective	diaphragm 11/50	1.50
			cream 90/-	12.50
'The Pill' or oral anovulatory tablet	Female	Very effective	84/6	12.00
The 'IUD'	Female	Very effective	1/-	0.14

Note:—Medical methods require the advice of a doctor or a midwife and some need fitting, non-medical methods do not.

Mothers and fathers, as well as many doctors, are much more likely to be impressed by the personal reasons for family planning than they are by such abstractions as the GNP per head. They are also likely to be very concerned about the increasing number of mouths to be fed from a small farm, or the many school fees and school books to be paid for out of a small income.

Couples who want to plan their families need some simple instruction, and a little inexpensive equipment. This is easily given if family planning forms part of the routine MCH services. When this is so, mothers can learn about family planning methods as part of the ordinary health education they receive in the antenatal clinic. It gives them a chance to discuss the subject with their husbands before they have to use their knowledge. Later, in the postnatal clinic, a mother can be fitted with the device of her choice and told where she can obtain the necessary devices and supplies.

If a husband accompanies his wife to the postnatal clinic, plans can be discussed jointly and misunderstanding prevented. This system has its difficulties in that few women ever return to the postnatal clinic; it is however a start, and, as the knowledge of family planning extends, it becomes increasingly the best way of providing instruction.

The choice of a particular method will depend on the culture of the couple, their religious beliefs, their marital habits, their income and their understanding. There is no one method for every pair. Early in married life the sheath or the 'pill' may be preferable, after a mother has borne a number of children she may be unable to retain a diaphragm, and an IUD may suit her best. The frequency of intercourse, and the family's ability to pay for some of the more expensive methods are other factors. When there is both privacy and some running water in the home, a diaphragm may be practical, but quite different methods may have to be used when there are neither. The availability of running water also determines the methods which can be employed in a clinic — those that require fitting inevitably require running water. All these factors have to be considered by a midwife as she advises a mother.

The methods which require fitting by a doctor or qualified midwife are usually termed 'medical methods', while those patients can obtain from shops and use for themselves are termed 'non-medical methods'. In general, the medical methods are the best, and the non-medical methods should be thought of as being temporary ones that are to be used only until a medical method can be employed.

The various methods available have been tabulated in Table 10 and their cost calculated on the basis of intercourse only twelve times monthly — an underestimate in many communities. Costs are approximate only, and take no account of the cost of running the clinic itself .The cheapness of the IUD is well shown, and this device has the added advantage that its cost does not rise with the frequency of intercourse.

When family planning is being started in an area, one of the local shops should be encouraged to stock the supplies that patients should be able to buy.

THE IUD

18:9 **The IUD described.** If a plastic coil like those shown in Figure 42 is introduced into the uterus, it reduces the likelihood of pregnancy to about 2.6 conceptions for every 100 women at risk for a year — approximately an eighteenth of the number of children those mothers would have borne had they not been so protected. The precise way in which these devices work is not yet clearly understood, but they appear to prevent implantation of the fertilized ovum in the uterine wall. One thing, however, is quite certain — it is that they do not act by causing a succession of abortions.

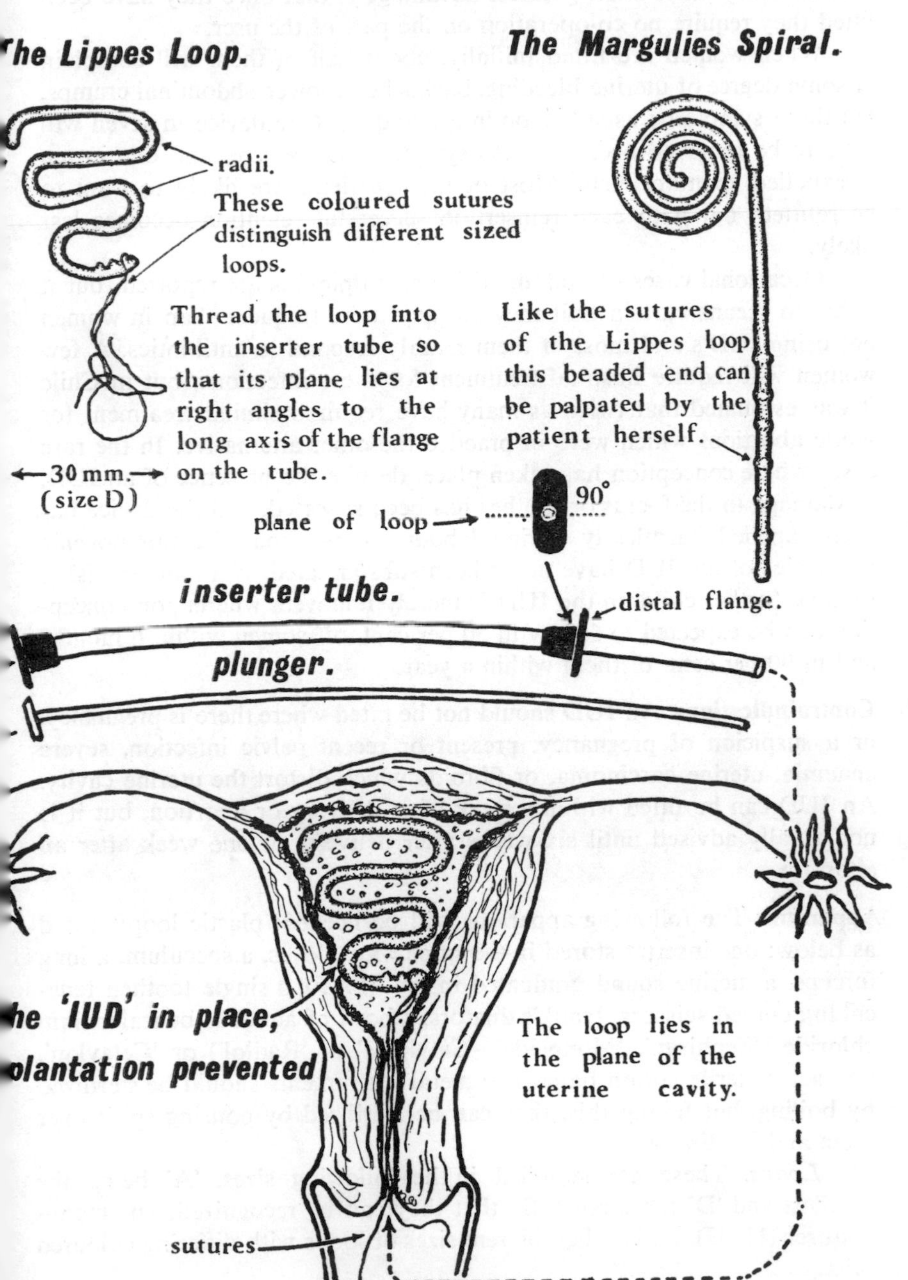
Fig.42.
THE INTRAUTERINE DEVICE.
The Lippes Loop.
The Margulies Spiral.
radii.
These coloured sutures distinguish different sized loops.
Thread the loop into the inserter tube so that its plane lies at right angles to the long axis of the flange on the tube.
Like the sutures of the Lippes loop this beaded end can be palpated by the patient herself.
30 mm.
(size D)
90°
plane of loop
inserter tube.
distal flange.
plunger.
he 'IUD' in place,
plantation prevented
The loop lies in the plane of the uterine cavity.
sutures

Not only are they cheap, but they require neither privacy nor the use of running water, as does a diaphragm which has to be removed and washed every time. Their greatest advantage is that once they have been fitted they require no co-operation on the part of the user.

When women are fitted initially, about half of them will complain of some degree of uterine bleeding, backache or lower abdominal cramps, but these symptoms usually stop in a few days. One device in seven will have to be removed because these symptoms are severe, and one in ten is expelled spontaneously. Most of these patients are likely to want to be refitted, but with each reinsertion successful retention becomes less likely.

Occasional cases of endometritis and salpingitis are reported, but it is by no means certain that they are any more frequent than in women not using IUD's and most of them readily respond to antibiotics. A few women will require hospital treatment for these infections, but in Chile it was estimated that twice as many have required similar treatment for septic abortions which were in practice the other alternative. In the rare cases where conception has taken place, despite the presence of an IUD, no damage to the foetus or mother has been reported, and the device has been expelled harmlessly during labour. Fears about the carcinogenic properties of the IUD have never been substantiated. If a mother wishes to have further children the IUD is merely removed, whereupon conception can be expected to follow in 50 per cent. of women within 6 months and in 90 per cent. of them within a year.

18:10 **Contraindications.** An IUD should not be fitted where there is pregnancy, or a suspicion of pregnancy, present or recent pelvic infection, severe anaemia, uterine carcinoma, or fibroids which distort the uterine cavity. An IUD can be fitted within a week after delivery or abortion, but it is not usually advised until six weeks after delivery, or one week after an abortion.

18:11 **Apparatus.** The following apparatus will be needed: plastic loops stored as below; one inserter stored in the same way, gloves, a speculum, a long forceps, a uterine sound graduated in cm. (PAF), a single toothed tenaculum, curved scissors, Hank's dilators, a bowl of aqueous benzalconium chloride ('Zephiran', 'Monocide', 'Cetylcide' or 'Radiol') or 'Cetavlon', and some sterile cotton balls. The metal instruments should be sterilized by boiling, but failing this, they can be sterilized by pouring spirit over them and lighting it.

Loops. These are supplied in the following sizes, 'A' being the smallest and 'D' the largest. So that they can be recognized, one manufacturer (HOH), makes the different sizes of loops with differing coloured tails.

Loop A. 22.5 mm. This has a blue tail and is for childless women only.

Loop B. 27.5 mm. This has a black tail and its most curved portions, or radii, are slightly thinner than the rest of the loop. Use it for women who have had miscarriages, for multips whose uteri are less than 5.5 cm. ($2\frac{1}{4}$ inches) on sounding, and in cases where loop C has had to be removed for bleeding or pain.

Loop C. 30 mm. This has a yellow tail, it also has reduced radii, and is suitable for almost all multips; it is thus the loop of first choice.

Loop D. 30 mm. This has a white tail, and normal radii, and is useful when loop C has been expelled.

When purchasing, size C should comprise the bulk of the order with a few of the others. Store a supply of loops, inserter tubes and plungers, either in 1/750 benzalconium chloride, or in 0.75% 'Cetrimide' plus 0.075 'Hibitane' in 70% surgical spirit for not less than 24 hours. If these are not available, 1:5000 aqueous iodine for five minutes can be used instead. Don't ever boil or autoclave an IUD.

2 **Method: The insertion of a 'Lippes loop'.**

Place the mother in the lithotomy position, palpate her uterus and adnexae to make sure they are normal. Expose the cervix with a vaginal speculum and swab it with Cetavlon or a similar antiseptic.

Pass a sterile uterine sound to determine the depth and direction of the uterine canal. If the canal is very narrow it may very occasionally be necessary to dilate it to the same diameter as the inserter tube.

With well scrubbed hands, and using a pair of forceps, remove from the storage solution a loop of the required size, an inserter tube and a plunger. Thread the suture-free end of the loop into the proximal end of the inserter tube, push it right down this tube until only the sutures are left protruding (Figure 42). Make sure in doing this that the plane of the loop is at right angles to the axis of the flanges, and don't thread the loop into the inserter tube until just before it is to be used. Further storage inside this tube will destroy the curved shape of the loop and thus its likelihood of being retained in the uterus satisfactorily. Push the end of the loaded inserter tube into the external os until the distal flange rests against it. The tip of the inserter should then be through the internal os and lie in the uterine cavity.

Make sure that the flanges are in the antero-posterior position. Insert the plunger and push it into the inserter tube as far as it will go. Pull out the plunger to make sure it is not entangled with the sutures. Pull out the empty inserter tube.

Teach the mother to feel for the presence of the sutures regularly once a week, especially after menstruation, so as to make sure that the loop has not been discharged accidently. It is sometimes said that mothers cannot do this, but it is the experience of the writers that they can, and that it is easier for women to feel the sutures than it is for them to fit themselves with a diaphragm.

Warn the mother that she may have cramps for the first few days, and that her next two or three menstrual periods may be excessive.

Ask her to report two months after fitting and again annually thereafter. The main purpose of these follow-up visits is to make sure that the loop is in place.

When a mother desires more children she merely comes up to the clinic and the loop is removed with suitable forceps.

The fitting procedure is not difficult, it requires only careful attention to the details mentioned above and the avoidance of force at any time. The main point to watch is the plane in which the loop is inserted, for this should be such that it lies in the plane of the uterine cavity. This is readily accomplished if the loop is threaded into the inserter tube at right angles to the long axis of its flanges which are then lined up in the antero-posterior (sagittal) plane of the patient. A useful tip is to hold the loaded inserter tube up to the light whereupon the plane of the loop will be easily visible, its relations to the flanges can be checked and their position in the patient adjusted accordingly.

Further methods including those employing home-made vaginal pads and domestic spermicides are fully described in the IPPF Handbook (IPP).

Chapter Nineteen

MATERNITY CARE

Professor Richard R. Trussell

:1 **The Twelfth axiom applied to maternity care.** In many industrial countries the chances of a live normal baby being delivered to a live uninjured mother have increased greatly in recent years. Many factors have contributed to this happy state of affairs; they include a rise in the general standards of living, better professional and lay education for childbirth and improved antenatal facilities. A major reason for the advance has been the detailed analyses that have been undertaken of the obstetric and perinatal problems of particular communities, and the exact knowledge that these analyses have provided has made it possible to direct existing resources to solve them in an economical manner.

An outstanding example of such an analysis is the 'Enquiry into maternal deaths in England and Wales' that was carried out between 1952 and 1954. This report showed that avoidable factors were present in no less than 40 per cent of the maternal deaths due directly to pregnancy and childbirth. The value of this study is reflected in the improvement in the survival rates of mothers. This was shown by a similar study some years later, after action had been taken to improve those parts of the general obstetric services which the earlier analysis had shown to be defective.

It is not possible to apply the recommendations of such analyses as these directly to the very different circumstances of the developing countries. Thus, a recent conference in the U.S.A. listed haemorrhage, toxaemia and infection as the major causes of maternal mortality in that country. This would certainly not be true in many parts of Africa. The commonest cause of maternal death in Mulago Hospital is rupture of the uterus, and this in turn differs from the situation in neighbouring territories. The same is true for the causes of death in the perinatal period; these too differ greatly from one region to another.

Before existing staff and facilities can be used to the best advantage, and before any useful plans can be made to improve the maternity care in the area, the local obstetric pattern has to be analysed. This inevitably places great emphasis on the value of good records as well as on their regular and frequent review. Only if this is done can maternity care follow the Twelfth axiom (1:19), be closely adapted to the local needs and facilities of a community and be a live and growing service sensitive to the obstetric pattern as it changes over the years. This adaptation to local circumstances must be both an organizational one concerning the general arrangement of maternity services, and an obstetric one concerning detailed obstetric care.

The care of a mother from the time of conception until she returns to her family responsibilities after delivery falls naturally into two parts. Firstly, a series of visits must be arranged during the antenatal period when supervision, advice and treatment can be given to her. At this time a decision has to be made as to the best place for her to be delivered (if indeed a choice exists) and recommendations made about the conduct of delivery should any abnormality present itself. Secondly, plans must be made to look after a mother during her labour and puerperium. Under the circumstances described in the first chapter (1 : 1), it is difficult to provide all, or even most, village mothers with either supervision during pregnancy or care during labour.

In rural areas success in the provision of antenatal care depends in large measure upon the provision of health centres in adequate numbers (3 : 2), the extent to which it is possible to provide mobile services (2 : 10), and the efficiency with which auxiliary staff (7:1) can be trained and deployed. Health centres and mobile services have already been discussed, so this chapter will be devoted to making the most of the various levels of maternity care that exist in a developing country, to some general principles of antenatal care, and to considering one specific example of a particularly successful adaptation to local circumstances — that at Ilesha in Western Nigeria. An important organizational adaptation of maternity care to the needs of the rural areas is also considered; this is the maternity village. Certain techniques are then discussed which are not described in all textbooks, and yet which are of particular value under the circumstances of developing countries. These are vacuum extraction, symphysiotomy, and pudendal block anaesthesia by the transvaginal route.

19:2 **Levels of maternity care.** Several levels of maternity care are likely to exist at the same time in a developing country. They are best considered from the point of view of the staff who provide this care. In addition to a very few specialist obstetricians and a larger number of ordinary doctors maternity care is provided by the following kinds of persons.

The state certified midwife. The State Certified Midwife, or SCM, is the equivalent to that of the State Registered Nurse, or SRN, and is of junior professional or para-medical status (7:2). These qualifications are often combined and persons holding them are employed training and supervising less skilled staff. Midwives of this kind are often so scarce as to be confined to national and regional hospitals. In the latter there may well be only one SCM who will be in charge of the obstetric department, and be responsible for teaching midwives and running refresher courses for the maternity staff of the region. She should visit the district hospitals nearby and be in touch with the enrolled nurses practising privately and with the indigenous midwives. With the doctor she should be responsible for a continuous review of services in her area made in the light of the local maternity and perinatal statistics.

As the numbers of these midwives increase, so will they become available in the district hospitals also.

The certificated or enrolled midwife. It will be a long time before girls with sufficient education ('O level' (7:1)) to enable them to train as SCMs will be available in sufficient numbers to staff the district hospitals and health centres. In the meanwhile these units have to be staffed by enrolled midwives who have had a three year training based on only two years of secondary education or sometimes on primary education alone.

Indigenous midwives. At present even enrolled midwives are not available in the numbers in which they are wanted, and many mothers have either to be delivered by a member of the family, or by a 'traditional birth attendant' or 'indigenous midwife'. Until such time as trained midwives are available these indigenous midwives are valuable members of the medical community. They specialize in delivering babies and their standards vary widely. If their traditions and practices can only be improved, or merely some of their worse habits removed, this can have a profound effect on the care of their patients. Later, they can be gradually replaced by scientifically trained midwives as these become available in adequate numbers. One of the functions of the health centre should be to take an interest in and to supervise these local midwives (3:10) (13:15). They should be encouraged to bring their difficult patients into hospital and welcomed when they do so.

Few countries appear to have been so successful in making the most of midwives of this kind as has been the Sudan. There, most indigenous midwives have already been given 'post-graduate' training and a certificate, and are now being steadily replaced by midwives of the modern type. Ideally such a programme should be administered on a national scale, but, failing this, individual hospitals may be able to undertake it in a modified form in their own districts.

19:3 **Private practice.** Many midwives, both certified and enrolled, marry and leave the hospital where they trained. Their skills are too scarce to be lost and, if there is no hospital or health centre near their homes in which they can work, they should be encouraged to set up in private practice, registered, supervised and regularly instructed in refresher courses. It should be made easy for them to refer difficult cases to a district hospital and be able to call upon transport to do so.

19:4 **Antenatal services.** The aim here must be to supervise the pregnancies of as large a fraction of mothers as possible, to ensure that abnormalities are diagnosed and treated appropriately, and to see that a mother starts labour in the condition which is most likely to result in the birth of a live normal child and leave her uninjured.

Antenatal clinics are inevitably overcrowded, and if abnormalities are not to be missed, an attempt must be made to distinguish and separate those who are at greater than average obstetric risk. This implies that, at an early visit, mothers should be seen by the most skilled person available, so that this high risk group can be distinguished from the majority whose labour is likely to be straightforward. Once distinguished this group should be given a card which is easily recognizable by its colour, or by some other feature such as a red star. These patients can either be asked to attend a 'special clinic' held on a particular day, or they can be seen in a special part of the general clinic. They will include the very young, the elderly, the very small, those with bad obstetric histories, and those who have undergone previous Caesarian section or other uterine operations.

Regular attendance is very important and should ideally be monthly until the 28th week of pregnancy, fortnightly thereafter until the 36th week, and from then on weekly until term. Sometimes, attendance actually improves when mothers are asked to attend fortnightly instead of monthly. Another way to improve attendance is to try to associate in the patient's mind the time for her next antenatal visit with some particular period in the lunar month. Fortunately however, the number of patients who can appreciate a given date seems to be growing in most antenatal clinics.

A general physical examination must be undertaken at one antenatal visit and should include a record of the patient's height. This is particularly useful in areas where disproportion is common and engagement of the foetal head unusual before the onset of labour. A height of under five feet, or its local equivalent, may be a reliable index of possible obstetric difficulty and may be especially valuable when the antenatal attendant is of limited skill. As a convenient way of distinguishing this group of patients, a bar five feet from the ground can be installed in the clinic — any patient capable of walking underneath it will be at greater risk in labour.

The examinations undertaken at the clinic must be related to the obstetric pattern of the area. Thus, if severe anaemia is more common than toxaemia, it may be more important to estimate the haemoglobin at a particular visit than it would be to measure the blood pressure.

When working at a peripheral clinic unsupervised by a doctor, midwives must know which cases they should refer for a further opinion. The criteria for deciding which these cases are should be decided on the basis of local obstetric experience and written down for them.

The writer is a firm believer in the practice of recording on the patient's notes a definite prognosis on the expected outcome of labour sometime between the 36th and 38th week. This is a useful discipline, and if it is subsequently reviewed when delivery takes place, much valuable experience may be acquired in a short time. This practice is of particular use in localities where the foetal head is not commonly engaged at 36 weeks and prognosis has to be based on factors other than this simple clinical sign.

Like the weight chart in the under-fives clinic, a mother's antenatal card is a record which she can well keep herself in a polythene envelope (Figure 33 (16:7)) (26:8). But, again following the practice of this clinic, a hospital must also keep its own records, preferably on punched cards for easier analysis (COP) (Figure 67 (26:12)). If full use is to be made of these records the data they contain must be reviewed regularly. The data on these cards will have to be taken by a midwife who must not only know what questions to ask but why she is asking them. She should ask, not for a history of tuberculosis but for that of a persistent cough, and for vulval sores rather than for venereal diseases.

:5 **The maternity services at Ilesha.** The under-fives clinic at the Methodist Mission Hospital at Ilesha has already been described in Chapter Sixteen, but besides pioneering in the care of children, it has been no less effective in the development of its maternity services (6).

This hospital, which serves a densely populated area, found that the demands on its limited maternity beds were imposing an impossible strain on them. Its authorities decided therefore that the best thing that they could do was to co-operate with the certified midwives who had recently started to run private nursing homes in the town, many of whom had originally been trained at the hospital. A booking clinic was therefore organized. so that the 50 or so new patients seeking antenatal care each week could be screened, and those considered suitable referred to such maternity homes in the town as were regularly inspected and supervised by the hospital staff. Following the starting of this arrangement the number of hospital confinements fell sharply and it became possible to give better care to those mothers in the greatest need (the 'high risk group', 19:4).

This hospital also runs a maternity and child welfare clinic at Imesi-Ile, a village of 5,000 people about 25 miles away. Almost all the children in the village are now born in this clinic which is a four-roomed mud walled building like those advocated in section 10:6, and most mothers are regular attenders at the antenatal clinics which are held there. Mothers are delivered in one of its rooms which is adapted as a labour ward, and return home a few hours later if their condition is satisfactory. In the period 1957-1961 no less than 1,032 births were supervised at this clinic; 54 cases were referred to the hospital at Ilesha, no mothers died and the stillbirth rate was only 36 per 1000 — figures which speak for themselves. The establishment of this centre has had a profound effect on the health and standard of living of the whole village and is run entirely by one sister and her enrolled midwives. Those responsible for this outstanding work have the following conclusions to make. Some apply to obstetrics in any developing country, some only to the densely populated areas like those in Eastern Nigeria.

Method. Some practical points in obstetric organization.

Use only the most efficient staff for the supervision of labour, which is the time of the greatest danger to mother and child.

Use less efficient staff for other purposes (8:3).

At an antenatal clinic get the orderlies to do such routine tasks as testing urines.

Make use of the antenatal clinics for instructing mothers in hygiene and child care. The best teacher is the midwife herself, and educational talks should precede each clinic.

Integrate antenatal, postnatal and child welfare clinics whenever possible (16:3).

Make all midwives, particularly those in the villages, feel part of this team and invite them back to the district hospital for refresher courses, seminars and social events.

19:6 **The 'maternity village' or 'maternity hostel'.** In few rural areas are there enough midwives to deliver many village mothers at home, or enough beds for these mothers to be in hospital for more than a few hours. Such mothers have therefore only two alternatives before them. Either they have to deliver themselves at home without a midwife to help them, or some means must be found whereby they can be in a hospital or health centre maternity unit only for the few critical hours of their delivery. A maternity village makes the latter alternative possible by combining the cheap conveniences of village housing with the safety of a supervised delivery at a hospital or health centre. A hospital with its more extensive facilities offers many advantages over a health centre as a site for a maternity village, and so further discussions will be confined to the type of maternity village which is associated with a hospital.

Maternity villages are far from being the final answer to the problems of rural midwifery, but they are valuable institutions and deserve to be used on a wider scale, particularly in regions where distances are great and populations sparse. The maternity village is to be looked upon as a 'self-care' addition to an ordinary maternity ward, the intermediate care facilities of which can thus be saved to treat only complicated cases. (Figure 15 (9:2), Figure 16 (10:4)). Sometimes huts are the best way of providing this self-care accommodation, at other times it is best provided as an annexe, hostel, or 'waiting area.' No firm figure can be given as to what the expected ratio between these two forms of accommodation should be, but it is probably about two 'self-care' beds for every one in the ordinary maternity ward.

At its simplest the maternity village is but a group of huts where mothers lodge, and with the assistance of a relative look after themselves until the time of their delivery. The huts in which they stay can be of the local pattern or of the 'mud-wattle-and-whitewash' variety described in section 10:6. A simple arrangement of this kind will often be the only practicable form of maternity village, and when such a village is referred to this is the sort of institution that should come to mind. As such a village hardly needs any further description the rest of this account is devoted to a village of a slightly more elaborate kind which provides mothers with more extensive services. The example of this more complex and thus more expensive type of maternity village that is chosen for detailed description is the one run by the Methodist Hospital at Ituk Mbang in Western Nigeria. For the following description the editor is grateful to Dr. H. Haigh, who developed it.

This hospital serves a highly populated area, there being, 200,000 people within ten miles of it. When compared with many other parts of the continent, the region is relatively prosperous. It is therefore possible for the accommodation provided to be comparatively good and its costs may thus seem high.

Mothers are housed in permanent dormitories and provided with a wooden bed, a mattress, sheets and a blanket. 'Village' may therefore not be quite the right word and perhaps the term maternity hostel would be better.

The village is a separate unit and is built on two acres of land on the other side of the main road from the hospital itself, but it is still close enough to enjoy all the hospital's services. There are two twenty-bedded dormitory blocks each with a central dining room, a bathroom and a store; a large room is available for health education and there are also kitchens for the patients and an antenatal examination room.

Two doctors from the hospital, a sister and the matron supervise the village which has its own full time staff of two midwives, two ward-maids, a labourer and a watchman. Such a staff may seem excessive, and in the simpler type of village the whole time staff need amount to no more than a porter, all other services being provided from the hospital itself. No food is provided and mothers are expected to bring with them a servant to do their cooking; in Nigeria she is usually a small girl from the family.

Except when abnormalities are found at the antenatal clinic, mothers are encouraged to come to the village two weeks before term. They are admitted via the hospital outpatient department and, if they have not been given an antenatal examination before, they are given one at the first convenient moment after their arrival. When abnormalities are found at the routine antenatal clinics mothers are advised to come to the village earlier than usual. Mothers coming up late in labour or with some serious disease are admitted to the ordinary maternity wards immediately.

A maternity village increases the number of patients attending for delivery and two more labour beds were required when the forty extra beds of the village were added to the 50 maternity beds already in the hospital.

Mothers staying in the village pay a total sum of 25/- ($3.5); this sum covers the upkeep of the buildings, the salaries of the village staff as well as the cost of the delivery itself. Small grants amounting to £300 ($850) each year are also contributed by neighbouring local authorities.

A maternity village can also serve another useful purpose. In it can be one of the typical dwellings of the region where pupil midwives can be trained under the conditions that will be found later in the homes where they will have to work. To the rural midwife a hut of this kind is a more realistic place in which to be taught than a hospital labour ward.

Though conclusive statistics are not available, there are reasons for thinking that both a mother and her child fare better if she spends the last days of her pregnancy under careful supervision in a maternity village of this kind, where a midwife can attend her labour in a clean environment with an obstetrician and a theatre nearby. It is not easy to provide the village mother with these blessings but the maternity village or maternity hostel is some help towards doing so.

TECHNIQUES

The Vacuum Extractor

19:7 **The place of this instrument.** Ever since the early attempts of James Young, obstetricians have been intrigued with the possibility of aiding the delivery of the human foetus by applying suction to its scalp; but it was not until Malmstrom invented his vacuum extractor that the technique became practicable.

In some units the extractor has replaced the forceps entirely and, although in our own case we were at first doubtful of its value as a substitute for what was so often a difficult manual rotation and forceps extraction, experience has shown that it is often the ideal instrument for this purpose.

It is of especial value to those doctors whose obstetrical practice is small and to whom the techniques of midwifery are but a part of the total skills with which they must be familiar. Further experience may well show that under these circumstances, vacuum extraction or Caesarian section are the only two wise alternatives in an obstructed labour when the head presents.

The use of this instrument by senior midwives is much more open to question, but in capable hands it may be much safer to both mother and child than either procrastination or a long journey to a larger delivery unit.

A vacuum extractor costs £45 ($126) (ABV) but it lasts indefinitely and should now be considered standard equipment on the stores list of every medical service. If this sum seems excessive it should be considered in the light of what has been said on the cost of equipment in section 12:9.

Advantages. Its application undoubtedly requires less skill than that required for the manual rotation of an occipito-transverse or occipito-posterior position followed by forceps delivery, or for the use of Keilland's forceps. Other advantages are that in severe cases of disproportion no valuable space between the head and the pelvic wall is taken up by forceps blades, and that the dangers of excessive force are avoided by the spontaneous detachment of the cup.

Whereas manual rotation of the head usually requires inhalation anaesthesia, the extractor is ideally applied in association with pudendal block. Its main value lies in the termination of the second stage of labour for either maternal or foetal indications, or where this stage has exceeded 1½ hours in a primigravida or three-quarters of an hour in a multigravida. It may be applied to any vertex presentation and suitable precautions may enable the correction of a brow presentation to take place.

Fig. 43. **THE VACUUM EXTRACTOR.**

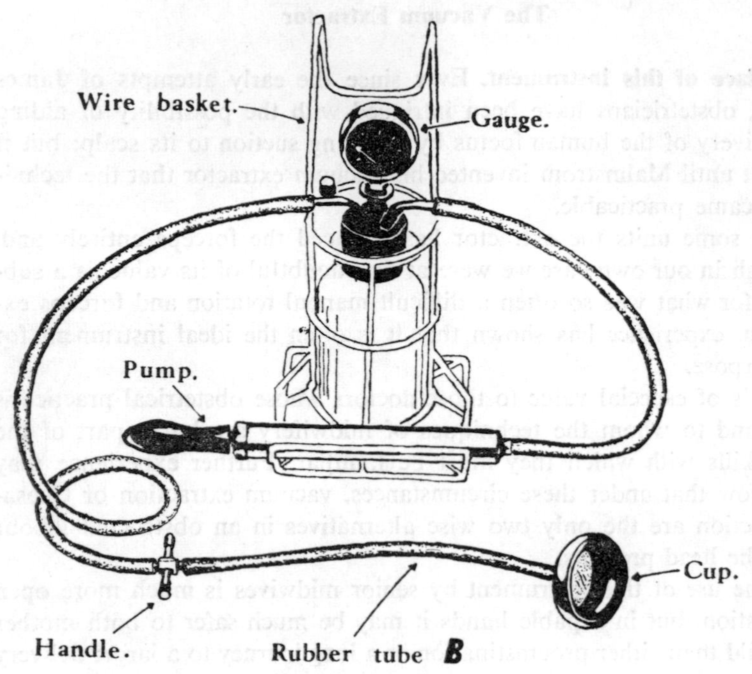

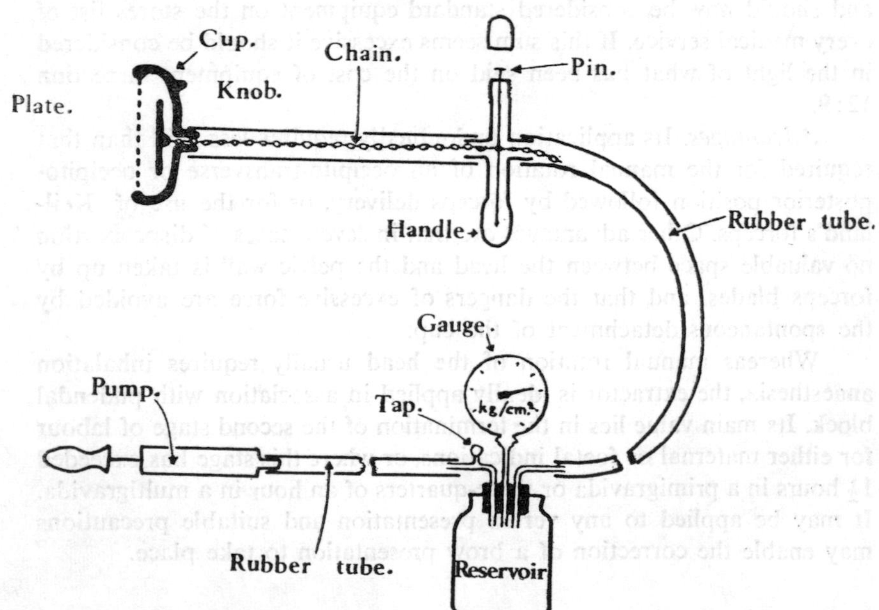

Although it was at first thought that the vacuum extractor would have great value in cases of disordered uterine action where delay in the first stage of labour is common and dilatation of the cervix delayed, its value has proved to be limited in these patients. It is probably wise to limit its application to cases where the cervix has reached at least $\frac{3}{4}$ dilatation and never to apply it for more than 20 minutes.

Disadvantages. These are nearly all due to bad selection of cases or unwise persistence after an initial failure.

The writer is convinced that repeated applications are dangerous and that not more than two attempts should ever be made at delivery when the cup pulls away from the scalp. Further, if delivery has proved impossible and the extractor itself is not at fault, forceps should not be applied, even if it seems they might succeed, for the dangers to the baby are too great. Few babies will survive failed vacuum extraction followed by a forceps delivery.

There is as a good case for the trial of vacuum extraction, as there is for trial of forceps, but this should take place in the operating theatre where Caesarian section can be undertaken if necessary.

Complications are sometimes seen in the baby. These include necrosis of the scalp and intracranial haemorrhage, but both are less common than they are with forceps and are usually due to the prolonged and repeated application of the extractor. Occasionally, a large confluent haematoma beneath the scalp may be so extensive as to exsanguinate the child and may even make transfusion necessary.

Apparatus. As shown in Figure 43 the instrument consists of a metal cup which can be applied to the baby's head. Several sizes of cup are supplied, but only one is shown in this figure. To the inside of one of these cups a vacuum is applied by means of a rubber tube, a pump and a vacuum bottle. This vacuum inside the cup causes it to fill with caput and so stick to the baby's scalp, but, as it is not possible to pull on a simple rubber tube, a chain is passed inside it and anchored at one end to a metal plate inside the cup, and, at the other, to a handle on which traction can be exerted. To secure this handle to the chain and allow for varying lengths of tube, a pin is passed through this handle to secure it. On each of the two larger cups is a knob which can be used to assist rotation of the head. A wire basket is supplied with which to support and protect the vacuum bottle.

Method: Vacuum extraction.

Have the apparatus including the rubber tube B (Figure 43, upper diagram) boiled or autoclaved in a drum or paper covered bundle so that it is always ready for use. Some form of

anaesthetic is needed, but pudendal block will provide sufficient anaesthesia in almost all cases, especially if combined with 50 mg. of pethidine or better, Pethilorphan (30:1) intravenously.

Insert the largest suitable cup into the vagina as if it were a pessary, and apply it to the presenting part of the scalp. Make quite sure that no vaginal or cervical tissue lies between the cup and the scalp. Using the pump, reduce the pressure slowly by 0.2 kg. per cm.^{2} stages each two minutes until a maximum of 0.6 to 0.8 kg. per cm.^{2} is reached. If a vacuum is applied more rapidly than this, little caput will be formed, adhesion will be poor, and the cup will come off when pulled on. A vacuum in excess of 0.8 kg. per cm.^{2} may injure the scalp.

Pull on the handle in the axis of the pelvis perpendicular to the cup. Pull for short periods only, and time them to coincide with labour pains, relaxing tension each time the uterus relaxes. When the head lies high in the pelvis, a preliminary episiotomy may be required if traction is to remain truly axial.

As the head descends through the pelvis, the line of traction will advance, until finally, as the head is crowned, it will be directed up towards the pubis and finally over the abdomen as the head is disengaged. The direction in which traction should take place is clearly illustrated in Figure 44.

As soon as the head is disengaged, lower the pressure, and detach the cup.

Don't apply the cup for longer than 20 minutes and don't pull continuously.

Symphysiotomy

19:8 **The indications for symphysiotomy.** The usefulness of the vacuum extractor can be considerably extended by the use of symphysiotomy, for, by cutting the symphysis pubis, the two halves of the pelvic girdle are able to separate as much as 3 cm. and so provide more room for the passage of the foetus. Symphysiotomy thus enables cases to be delivered by forceps or vacuum extraction where this would otherwise be impossible, or carry an unreasonably high risk to the foetus. It is of particular value in the shallow generally contracted pelvis that is characteristic of some Bantu races.

Two features greatly recommend it: it reduces the incidence of Caesarian section with its attendant risk of subsequent rupture of the uterus, and it produces a permanent increase in the brim area of the pelvis which improves the likelihood of normal delivery in later pregnancies.

44. **THE USE OF THE VACUUM EXTRACTOR.**

1. Traction downwards when the head is high.

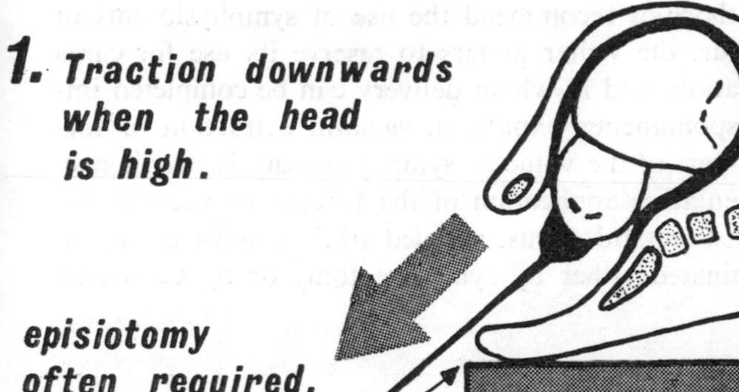

episiotomy often required.

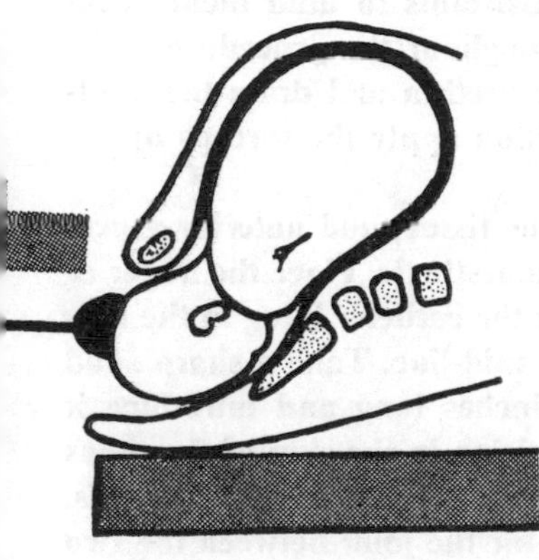

2. Traction horizontal when the head is mid way in the pelvic cavity.

Don't use a vacuum of more than 0·8 $Kg.cm^2$.

. Traction upwards as the head crowns.

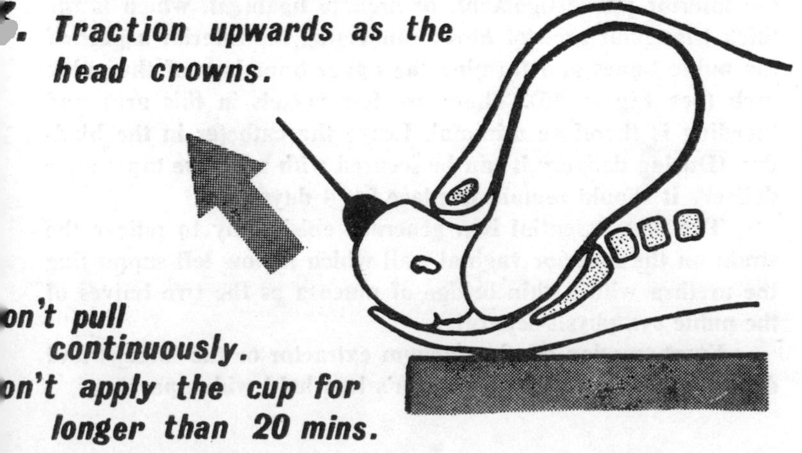

on't pull continuously.

on't apply the cup for longer than 20 mins.

Careful selection of cases is vital for success, and, while those cases where the head remains high above the brim are unsuitable, experience will enable an increasing number of patients with fairly severe disproportion to be delivered with the help of symphysiotomy.

While certain authorities recommend the use of symphysiotomy in the first stage of labour, the writer prefers to reserve its use for cases which reach full dilatation, and in whom delivery can be completed immediately, either by spontaneous expulsion, vacuum extraction or forceps delivery. Indeed, part of the value of symphysiotomy is that it may be employed where tentative application of the forceps or vacuum extractor has proved unsuccessful. Thus, a failed trial of assisted vaginal delivery may be terminated either by symphysiotomy or by Caesarian section.

Method: Symphysiotomy.

Place the patient in the lithotomy position. Don't support her legs in stirrups, but get two assistants to hold them at an angle of 80° to the horizontal throughout the procedure.

Place a rubber catheter in the urethra and drain the bladder. With this catheter still in position apply the forceps or the vacuum extractor.

Infiltrate the skin, subcutaneous tissue, and anterior aspect of the pubic symphysis with local anaesthetic. Place the finger of the left hand in the vagina, feel for the catheter lying in the urethra and push it to one side of the mid-line. Take a sharp solid scalpel with a blade at least 2½ inches long and introduce it through the smallest convenient incision in the skin of the mons pubis at the level of the superior aspect of the symphysis pubis. With the point of the knife search for the joint between the two halves of the symphysis, and divide it down but not including the inferior pelvic ligament, or arcuate ligament, which is the thick triangular arch of fibres connecting the inferior aspect of the pubic bones and forming the upper boundary of the pubic arch (See Figure 45). There are few vessels in this area and bleeding is therefore minimal. Leave the catheter in the bladder. (During delivery it can be secured with adhesive tape; after delivery it should remain in place for 4 days.)

The next essential is a generous episiotomy to relieve the strain on the anterior vaginal wall which is now left supporting the urethra with a thin bridge of mucosa as the two halves of the pubic symphysis separate.

Exert traction on the vacuum extractor or the forceps and deliver the baby with the mother's legs held wide apart.

After delivery bring the legs together, close the skin incision with a single stitch and bind the pelvis together with a bandage. A light bandage is usually placed round the ankles for the first 48 hours to limit movement.

The patient is usually happy to get out of bed on the 5th day and painless mobility is usual by the 10th day. Occasionally, this period may have to be extended but persistent pain is very uncommon and it is noticeable that much more pain is experienced by the rare cases which undergo spontaneous separation of the symphysis after normal delivery. The main danger of the procedure, accidental incision of the bladder or the urethra, should never occur if a catheter placed in the urethra is pushed out of the line of the incision as described here and care taken to cut as far as the arcuate ligament, but no further.

Success depends upon the careful selection of cases. Tears in the anterior vaginal wall will be avoided if the patients legs are supported throughout the operation and if a wide episiotomy is always performed. Don't attempt to separate the two halves of the pubic symphysis more than 3 cm.

Transvaginal Pudendal Block

9 **Surgical anatomy.** The dangers to both mother and foetus from inhalation anaesthesia during labour have been repeatedly stressed in the literature. Pudendal block provides a simple safe and cheap alternative to general anaesthesia that is suitable for the great majority of cases of assisted vaginal delivery. Anaesthesia is rapid, easy to achieve and the patient remains conscious and co-operative throughout her delivery. There is no danger of vomiting, the baby's respiration is not depressed and there is no unconcious patient to need careful nursing in the ward afterwards.

The classical approach to the pudendal nerve is through the perineum, but there are several advantages to approaching it through the vagina, and blocking it as it crosses the sacrospinous ligament close to the ischial spine (Figure 45). At this level all its branches are anaesthetized, as also is the posterior femoral cutaneous nerve, branches of which supply the skin over and lateral to the ischial tuberosities (not shown in the figure). There is no trauma to the perineum, a wide zone of anaesthesia is produced, relaxation of the levator ani muscles is more complete and less local anaesthetic is required.

Indications. Most manipulations that are vaginal rather than uterine may be performed under pudendal block and include both forceps delivery and vacuum extraction. It is also the ideal anaesthetic for breech delivery. Although certain writers extend these uses, it is not our practice

Fig.45. **THE TRANSVAGINAL PUDENDAL BLOCK.**

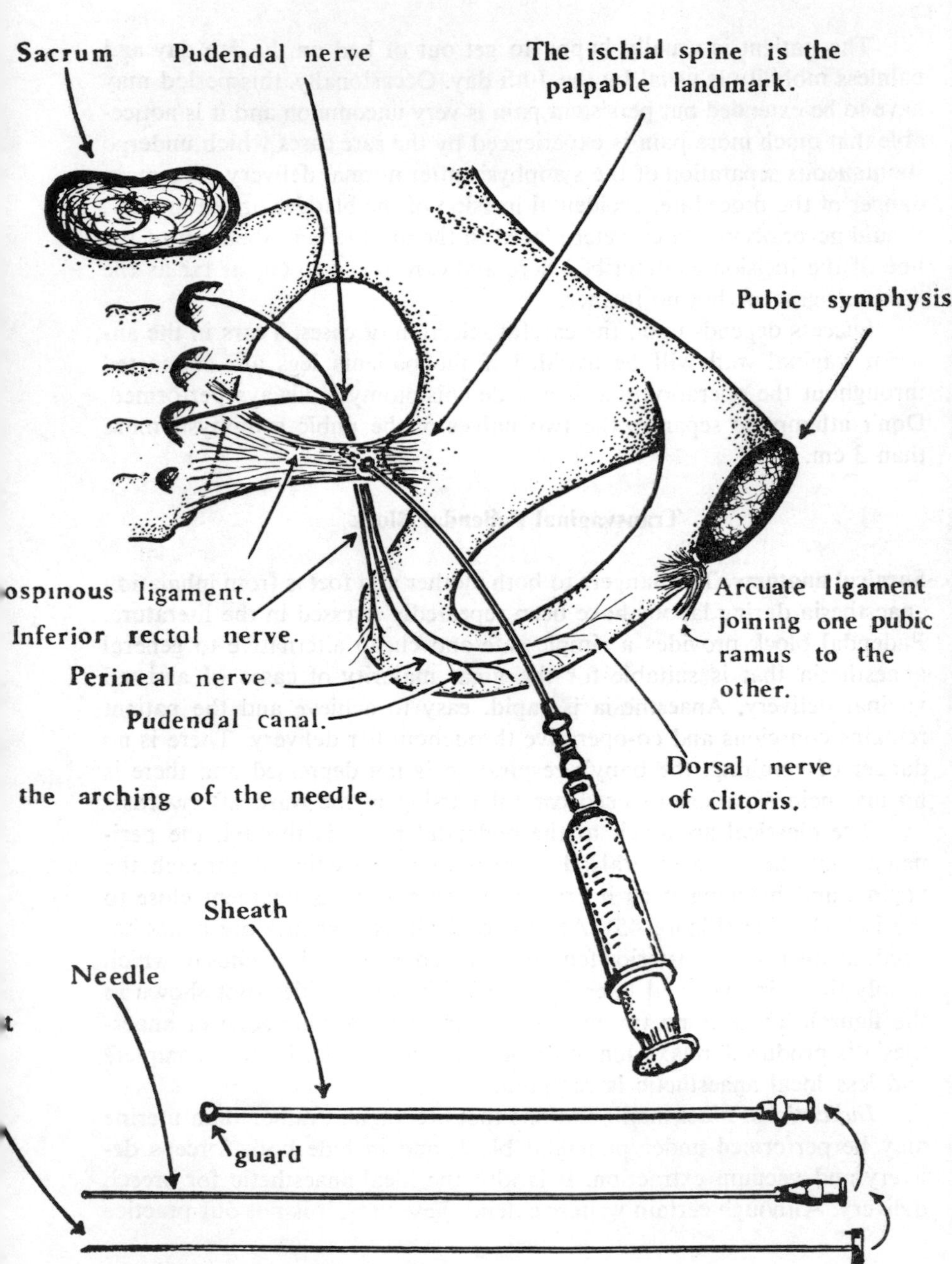

to use it for such intrauterine manoeuvres as manual removal of the placenta.

Apparatus. An ordinary strong, flexible 15 cm. (6 inch) 17 gauge spinal needle can be used, but a special needle with a small bulbous guard is well worth acquiring (DOW) for this automatically positions its tip in the correct tissue plane. This device is drawn in Figure 45 and is made in three parts. There is a central stylet which fits inside the needle proper; this needle then goes inside a sheath which bears the bulbous guard at its tip. The length of the needle protruding beyond the bulbous guard can be varied at will by sliding it up and down the sheath. Most obstetricians prefer to use the needle at the limit to which it will protrude.

Use a 20 ml. syringe filled with 1% lignocaine which produces a good block within a minute or two and lasts for at least 30 minutes, 10 ml. of this solution being required for each pudendal nerve. $1\frac{1}{2}$% procaine, either plain or with added hyalase is almost as satisfactory.

Method: Transvaginal pudendal block.

Put the patient into the lithotomy position and see that she is swabbed, draped and catheterized. To block the right pudendal nerve, hold the barrel of the syringe in the left hand. Guide the end of the needle into the vagina up to the tip of the right ischial spine with the right index finger. Hold the right thumb flexed so that the ball of the thumb is resting against the shaft of the needle. The tip of the ischial spine will be felt with the end of the right index finger. Advance needle point 0.5 cm. ($\frac{1}{4}$ inch) beyond the tip of the ischial spine over the sacrospinous ligament (see Figure 45). Arch the end of the needle by bending its point over with the end of the index finger and penetrate the vaginal mucosa — only occasionally will the patient complain of pain when this is being done. Advance the point of the spinal needle into the sacrospinous ligament until resistance is felt to give (about 1.0 cm.) indicating that its tip must now be through the ligament and lie close to the pudendal nerve. (The special needle with its bulbous guard can be advanced up *to the limit of this guard).* **Aspirate to make sure that the point of the needle does not lie in a blood vessel, and then inject 10 ml. of the anaesthetic agent.**

To block the left pudendal nerve. Change hands and repeat the procedure on the left side.

See if satisfactory block has been obtained by pricking the perinuem with a needle and asking the patient if she can feel it, and by asking her to draw in her anus. Her inability to do this means that her levator muscles are paralysed. When a block is effective the vaginal introitus gapes open. It seldom takes longer than five minutes to block both sides, and, because of the small volume of local anaesthetic used, a repeat block can safely be undertaken if required. Pudendal block is possible even when the perineum is distended by a vertex or breech. Should the ischial spines be difficult to locate, the upper border of the sacrospinous ligament is a convenient landmark which can be followed to its attachment to the spine.

Chapter Twenty

THE VILLAGE OF ARO

Professor Adeoye Lambo

20:1 **The history of Aro.** Outside Abeokuta, close to Ibadan, lie four villages, the largest of which is Aro. In 1948 Aro was chosen as the site for a mental hospital to be associated with the University of Ibadan. Work started in 1950, and in 1954 the hospital was incorporated into an 'Experimental Community Mental Health Scheme'. Aro thus provided the first real opportunity to study mental illness in Africa south of the Sahara, and, though much has been learnt since its foundation, two aspects of its work will be of particular interest to those seing the mentally sick in similar circumstances. The first is the psychiatric day hospital in its African setting, the second is the use of the 'traditional practitioner' or 'native healer' (3:10).

Aro is not the first day hospital of its kind; there have been others before it, notably that at Gheel in Belgium, but they have never been popular in industrial countries and it is to the peasant communities of the younger nations that they are so excellently suited.

The decision to provide a psychiatric day hospital can only be taken at a high administrative level, and is thus outside the scope of most of those for whom this symposium is intended. Nevertheless, the more who know about this kind of psychiatric care, the more likely it is that this way of looking after the mentally sick will spread to other developing countries.

20:2 **The psychiatric day hospital.** The purpose of a psychiatric day hospital is to enable the therapeutic techniques of an ordinary mental hospital to be applied to patients who remain in their own social environment. This is of particular benefit to the African peasant, because not only does he find a hospital ward a strange and disturbing place, but his own close knit society has exceptionally strong social and human resources which promote his mental health. Among these resources are the natural flexibility and tolerance of village communities, the therapeutic value of traditional cults, and the confessions, dances and rituals that play so large a part in peasant life. Acting together they all provide strong natural psychotherapy. It is the possibility of combining all these natural therapeutic resources with psychiatric methods of Western medicine that is of such great value to the African villager when he is mentally ill.

The hospital itself has the facilities of any up-to-date mental hospital of 200 beds and includes electroplexy, modified insulin therapy and abreactive techniques as well as modern drug medication. These will however be of less interest to the reader, and are often of less importance to the patient, than is the benefit he derives from being a member of the community at Aro.

20:3 **Family loyalty is essential for success.** Aro serves a large part of Western Nigeria, and indeed patients come to it from many other parts of West Africa. This means that very few patients can be treated from their own homes and that most of them have to be boarded out in a village household near the hospital. Every patient who is to be treated in a therapeutic community of this kind must have at least one devoted relative who will stay with him in his lodgings, look after him, and bring him to the hospital each day. This relative is a very important person; his role must be clearly defined and his co-operation sought at all times. Above all, he has to be devoted to the patient. This means that care of this kind is only possible where families are very closely knit, and there is a real sense of the mutual obligations of their members one to another. A psychiatric day hospital is only possible in Africa because most African communities still have this deep sense of family responsibility with its well defined traditional roles and duties.

Though strong family loyalty is the absolute prerequisite without which no psychiatric day hospital will work, its success depends almost as much on the details of its daily administration. Though these will vary slightly from region to region the experience gained at Aro may prove useful.

20:4 **Administering the village.** Patients are accompanied by one relative who stays with them at all times and brings them up to the outpatient department daily. When formal treatment is over, patients are given occupational therapy and return with their relatives to their village lodging late in the afternoon.

A nurse is always on duty in the village to reassure its inhabitants and to deal with insomnia or any other troublesome symptoms that may arise. She is assisted in her tasks by a guide who also looks after the relatives of patients who come from far away.

Households who volunteer to take in patients and their relatives are paid 10/- ($1.40) each month for their services, and building loans are provided so that more accommodation shall be available. There is, however, a maximum to the number of patients that a village can hold, and no more than two patients are allowed for every three of its inhabitants. Following these services to the mentally sick, many benefits have accrued to the villagers. They now have a piped water supply, a clinic, a mosquito eradication squad and pit latrines. Their economic level has also risen now that some of them are able to find work as porters or gardens in the hospital itself.

The closest co-operation has to be maintained between the medical staff of the hospital and the village community. To make this easier, chiefs from the village are represented on the governing body of the hospital, and likewise, the physicians from the hospital interest themselves in the public health and administration of the village.

It might be thought that only the most socially adapted patients could be treated in this way. In practice this is not so, and even violent cases have been successfully treated in the village. Some patients who have exhibited aggressive or anti-social tendencies in their own homes have become quite manageable once they settled at Aro.

Not every case is cured and we have been faced with the problem of how to dispose of those patients who fail to recover, even at a social level; a problem which is now being aggravated by the cultural and economic changes taking place in Nigeria. Even the most devoted relative who accompanies a patient can only stay for a comparatively short time, and, when an illness becomes protracted, none can afford the financial sacrifice of staying in the village indefinitely. The answer to the challenge of the chronic patient lies in a new experiment — the 'Aro hospital village farm'.

5 **The Aro hospital village farm.** Agricultural work is that best suited to the chronic psychiatric patient. We have therefore been fortunate in finding several big farms in the vicinity whose owners sympathize with our endeavours, and are prepared to adopt our chronic patients as labourers, even though they are still being treated.

Such patients continue to be supervised by the hospital authorities, and their relatives, who usually return home, are still able to visit them regularly. Many patients have even built their own huts on these farms as an indication of their willingness to settle in the area permanently. There is thus every sign that these long-stay farms will become a useful supplement to Aro itself, and help to complete the system of psychiatric care in Nigeria.

20:6 **The traditional practitioner.** One of the unusual features of our care of the mentally ill in Nigeria is our unorthodox collaboration with traditional healers. We have discovered, through long practice in Africa, that in understanding the African patient in his social environment, it is essential to work in close collaboration with other disciplines, and even to establish some form of inter-professional relationship with those who, by Western standards, are not strictly regarded as 'professional'. My Sudanese colleague Dr. Tijani El Mahi and I, have for a number of years made use of the services of African traditional healers, whom we have specially chosen to help us in social psychiatry — an indefensible practice by Western standards (Second axiom 1:9). With their help we have enriched our knowledge of the natural history of the mental disorders in our communities. Without them we would have been at a loss in searching for the psychological causes of the neuroses that are so common in African communities undergoing rapid social change. Most of the traditional healers with whom we have to co-operate have had long experience in managing African patients and are thus able to supervise and direct many group activities among the patients at Aro. They work under strict supervision and many participate in our epidemiological surveys as 'contact men'.

20:7 **Conclusions:** It may be helpful to summarize some of the advantages and limitations of the psychiatric day hospital as it is seen at Aro. Among its advantages are:

It secures for the mentally sick the full benefit of the dynamic resources promoting mental health that are present in the patient's own communal environment.

When mental patients are treated in a community, the social attitudes towards them and towards mental disease become more relaxed and better adapted. This is especially true of the patient's relatives; the social stigma attached to psychiatric disturbance is greatly reduced.

A patient's adaptation to society — his degree of 'social competence' — can be judged more readily when he is a member of a normal community than it can in the artificial environment of a mental hospital.

All kinds of mental illness can be treated in a psychiatric day hospital, provided always that there are a few psychiatric beds for emergency use close by.

The psychiatric day hospital deploys meagre human and material resources to the best advantage; it is economical to the medical authority, to the patient and to his relatives (Third axiom 1:10).

This kind of mental care is ideally suited to the closely knit pre-industrial, agrarian societies of Africa and Asia with their high thresholds of community tolerance.

The psychiatric day hospital has the following disadvantages:

The psychiatric day hospital is seldom possible in the loose-knit, critical, 'success oriented' societies of industrial countries and it will probably not long survive the advent of social change in developing nations.

Hitherto it has only been achieved on a substantial scale that includes a specialized mental hospital and a whole village.

Nobody has yet been able to get occasional patients from a general hospital looked after in an ordinary village.

Really sympathetic administration and good public relations are critical to its success.

Chapter Twenty-one

TUBERCULOSIS

For authorship see 21:28

21:1 **Introduction.** The ubiquity of the tubercle bacillus is well known — approximately half the population of the world are infected. Three factors, which are often present together in varying degree, convert infection into disease. They are individual susceptibility, stress, and the magnitude of the initial infection.

In general, people in developing countries have a high individual susceptibility, stress is linked to living standards and nutritional levels, and the magnitude of the initial infection is largely associated with housing and ventilation patterns. In many developing countries these three factors are responsible for a prevalence of active pulmonary tuberculosis of the order of 1 per cent — ten thousand cases for every million people. This high prevalence is the most striking difference between the tuberculosis situation in poor as compared with rich countries. Another is the relatively advanced stage of the disease at the time of its initial diagnosis. This is due to a number of factors, among them being the insidious nature of the symptoms and a general lack of health consciousness on the part of the people.

DIAGNOSIS

21:2 **The clinical history.** In adults the classical symptoms are cough, lassitude, loss of weight and anorexia. Staining of the sputum and frank haemoptysis heighten suspicion, but do not clinch a diagnosis. A query should always be made for a history of contact with a known tuberculous patient, and particularly for a history of deaths in the family. Tuberculosis is highly infectious in the dying, who usually cough up tubercle bacilli in very large numbers.

The earlier a tuberculosis patient can be diagnosed and treated the fewer people will he infect, and the more certain will be his own response to treatment. There are two approaches to early diagnosis. The first is by means of mass surveys relying largely on radiography, but these are only occasionally practicable on account of their cost. The second is by paying particular attention to two especially vulnerable groups of people. Thus tuberculosis is five to ten times more prevalent among household contacts of sputum-positive patients than it is among the general population. It is also far more common among people suffering from a chronic cough, that is, one of a month's duration or more, than it is among the symptomless. Case-finding efforts directed towards these two groups are thus the first practical steps towards early diagnosis. The more intense this effort can be, the greater will be the yield.

Though a patient may well be diagnosed after one, or perhaps two visits, he should not be discharged as being free from tuberculosis until he has been seen three times according to the following scheme. It is primarily intended for the contacts of sputum positive cases, but, with minor modifications, it applies to the patient suspected of tuberculosis who is seen in the course of an outpatient clinic.

Method: The diagnosis of tuberculosis

First attendance. **Examine the patient, weigh him, do a Heaf test, collect a specimen of sputum and instruct him to return in a week's time.**

Second attendance. **Read the Heaf test, collect a second sputum specimen and ask him to return again three months later.**

Third attendance. **Check the symptoms, weigh the patient again and collect a third sputum specimen. Examine the sputa by direct microscopy (24:14) and if possible send them away for culture. Also, where possible, X-ray the patient the first and third time he comes up, or at his second and third attendances.**

The more correct the diagnosis in suspected cases, the more economic is the use of the effort and money expended, and therefore the wider the ground that can be covered for the same cost.

3 **The Heaf test.** When an individual is infected by the tubercle bacillus his skin becomes hypersensitive to tuberculo-protein. The tuberculin test determines whether or not his skin is hypersensitive to tuberculo-protein. The test's great importance depends on two facts. The first is that a negative reaction excludes tuberculosis in the majority of instances. The second is that, whereas a positive test in an adult usually indicates sub-

clinical infection, and is thus of comparatively little importance, a positive test in infancy or early childhood indicates not merely infection but *present active disease.* Both these facts require elaboration.

As regards the first: occasionally, the tuberculin test is negative, despite the presence of active tuberculosis. This happens in cases where the patient's hypersensitivity response is depressed, as it may be if he is moribund or cachectic, if he is suffering from kwashiorkor (14:12) or measles, if his tuberculosis is miliary or meningitic, or if he is under treatment with corticosteroid drugs.

As regards the second: **in a child under two years old, or under six if he is a household contact of a tuberculous patient, a positive tuberculin test indicates active disease requiring treatment.** This is true even in the absence of positive clinical, radiological or bacteriological findings. The only exception is, of course, the child who has been given BCG.

Never omit to do the tuberculin test in a case of suspected or even of diagnosed tuberculosis — no matter how apparently unequivocal the laboratory or X-ray findings may be. AFB in the sputum may be leprosy bacilli from the nasal secretions, atypical mycobacteria from the mouth, or 'false positives' of one kind or another from the laboratory. Radiological abnormalities mimicking tuberculosis are also legion.

There are several different ways of doing the tuberculin test, the two most popular being the intradermal Mantoux test and the multiple puncture Heaf test. Whatever may be the merits of the Mantoux test in the hands of trained staff, the Heaf test is so much better suited to partly trained auxiliaries that it will be the only method described here. The gun is robust, no skill is required in using it, the results of the test are easily read, and its use is not resented by children — it can even be given to a sleeping infant without waking him. For these reasons it should replace the Mantoux test in routine use.

The 'Heaf gun' itself is shown in Figure 46 and costs £5 ($14). Several versions are available, the one advised having a magnetic head which retains a detachable metal plate bearing six needle points (A & H). This has the great advantage that when the points are blunt, and sharp points are important, the plate can be replaced for as little as -/45 ($0.06). Such detachable plates also enable the gun to be used for other purposes, such as immunization with BCG and vaccinia (17:7, 17:10).

Method: The Heaf test.

Sterilizing the gun.

i) When using the traditional type of gun with fixed points. Sterilize the end of it between patients by pressing its needles on the spirit-soaked cotton wool held in a small screw-capped jar and then rapidly passing it through a flame. Don't actually

Fig.46.

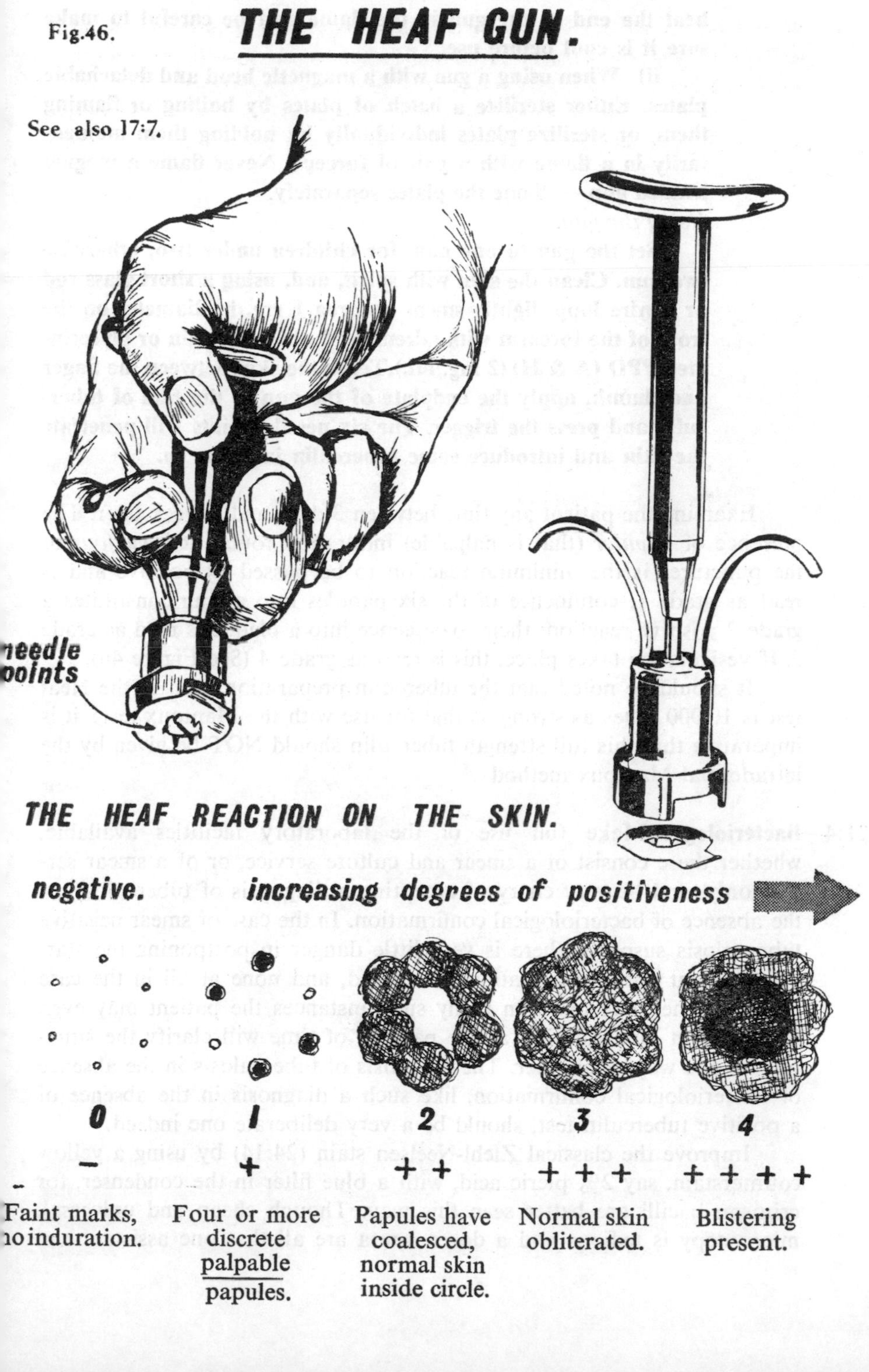

THE HEAF GUN.

See also 17:7.

needle points

THE HEAF REACTION ON THE SKIN.

negative. increasing degrees of positiveness

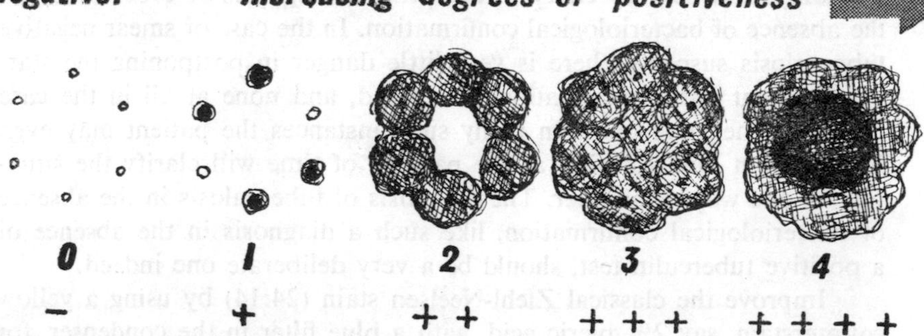

Faint marks, no induration.

Four or more discrete palpable papules.

Papules have coalesced, normal skin inside circle.

Normal skin obliterated.

Blistering present.

heat the end of the gun in the flame and be careful to make sure it is cool before use.

ii) When using a gun with a magnetic head and detachable plates. Either sterilize a batch of plates by boiling or flaming them, or sterilize plates individually by holding them momentarily in a flame with a pair of forceps. Never flame a magnet headed gun — flame the plates separately.

Using the gun.

Set the gun to one mm. for children under two, otherwise two mm. Clean the skin with spirit, and, using a short glass rod or a wire loop, lightly smear an area 1 cm. in diameter on the front of the forearm with adrenalised old tuberculin or glycerinated PPD (A & H) (2 mg./ml.).Tense the skin between the finger and thumb, apply the endplate of the gun to the film of tuberculin and press the trigger. The six needle points will penetrate the skin and introduce some tuberculin in doing so.

Examine the patient any time between 3 days and a week later. The presence of *papular* (that is palpable) induration round at least *four* of the punctures is the minimum reaction to be passed as positive and is read as grade 1; confluence of the six papules into a ring constitutes a grade 2 positive reaction; their coalescence into a plaque is read as grade 3. If vesiculation takes place, this is read as grade 4 (See Figure 46).

It should be noted that the tuberculin preparation used in the Heaf test is 10,000 times as strong as that for use with the Mantoux test: it is imperative that this full strength tuberculin should NOT be given by the intradermal Mantoux method.

21:4 **Bacteriology.** Make full use of the laboratory facilities available, whether these consist of a smear and culture service, or of a smear service only, and be very chary of accepting a diagnosis of tuberculosis in the absence of bacteriological confirmation. In the case of smear negative tuberculosis suspects, there is very little danger in postponing the start of treatment until confirmation is to hand, and none at all in the case of culture negative ones. In many such instances the patient may even benefit from this restraint, as the passage of time will clarify the situation in one way or another. The diagnosis of tuberculosis in the absence of bacteriological confirmation, like such a diagnosis in the absence of a positive tuberculin test, should be a very deliberate one indeed.

Improve the classical Ziehl-Neelsen stain (24:14) by using a yellow counterstain, say 2% picric acid, with a blue filter in the condenser, for crimson bacilli are better seen this way. Though cheap and universal, microscopy is tedious and a dozen sputa are all that one assistant can do without a break. Large numbers of bacilli imply active disease, and 'AFB scanty' on a report should prompt further specimens — a single negative is never sufficient, and three are the least number which reasonably exclude the disease. Send six if possible.

:5 **Radiology**. Radiological facilities are highly desirable in the management of tuberculosis, but without them it is still possible to manage most cases fairly satisfactorily. In the smaller hospital not only do the operator, the machine and the reader have severe limitations, but cost is prohibitive — an initial chest series at 10/- ($1.4) costs more than a year's outpatient treatment with thiacetazone or INH. Furthermore, X-rays are of little help in the clinically dubious case — their real value is to demonstrate miliary tubercles when physical signs are equivocal, and to diagnose primary tuberculosis once infancy is past. Apart from cases of primary and miliary tuberculosis, gross radiological lesions in the lungs are seldom due to untreated tuberculosis when the smear is negative. Lesser radiological lesions, although they may well be of other origin, should prompt further search for tubercle bacilli.

Although in theory X-rays can be dispensed with in some cases of tuberculosis where the diagnosis has already been made, for example, in sputum positive patients who are responding to treatment satisfactorily, it is always desirable to have an initial chest X-ray. A second X-ray picture is also indicated after a few months of treatment if the response is unsatisfactory and a change of drug regime is being considered, or after 12 to 18 months of apparently successful treatment when the time has come to consider stopping it altogether.

6 **Diagnostic difficulty.** A therapeutic trial can be valuable when tuberculosis is suspected but the diagnosis still in doubt, despite use of all the available aids. But it is only justified if streptomycin is excluded from the tentative treatment. This tentative treatment should be directed towards the alternative disease. Thus, if an aspiration pneumonia is one of the differential diagnosis in a difficult case, a course of penicillin might be given. If this succeeds, well and good, for tuberculosis is now rendered very unlikely, while if it does not, little is lost. Use the time provided by such a therapeutic trial to examine the patient's sputum again several times, for bacilli may well be found and the diagnosis thus confirmed. If this procedure does not establish the diagnosis one way or the other within a week or two, starting anti-tuberculosis treatment and carefully assessing the response may do so two or three weeks later.

Another cause of confusion is the cough of incipient cardiac failure with a negative chest X-ray. However, the improvement of such cases on rest and diuretics alone usually excludes tuberculosis.

TREATMENT

21:7 **Drug treatment.** With the coming of the great anti-tuberculous drugs, adequate treatment has come to mean adequate drug treatment. This means taking these drugs in such a way and for such a time as effectively to free the body from tubercle bacilli, in effect it is to achieve 'stable bacteriological negativity'. Subject to what is said below, this typically means eighteen months treatment with the outpatient drugs isonicotinic acid hydrazide, — 'INH' or 'INAH' and, *either* para-amino-salicylic-acid — 'PAS', *or* thiacatazone — 'TB 1', combined if practicable with daily streptomycin ('SM') injections for the first two months of treatment. If patients cannot attend daily, these streptomycin injections require his admission to self-care facilities (9:1). This then is a typical course of treatment; it is subject to many modifications as circumstances dictate. The more important of these are discussed in the remaining part of this section, *which relates entirely to patients whose bacilli are fully drug sensitive at the start of the regime.*

Hitherto INH and PAS have been the standard outpatient drugs. Recently, however, after trials in East Africa, TB 1 is coming into general use and promises to be a great advance. Not only is it cheap, but it is a fraction of the bulk of PAS, it does not cause nausea and it is well tolerated by children. In some other parts of the world the combination of TB 1 with INH is now also well established as a substitute for PAS and INH. The safety and effectiveness of TB 1 is now being investigated elsewhere, but is not advised for general use until the results of these trials are complete. The following account is based on experience in East Africa where TB 1 is of proved effectiveness.

TABLE 11

THE ROUTINE ANTI-TUBERCULOUS DRUGS

Drug	*Abbreviation*	*Standard adult daily dose*	*Cost per year*
Isoniazid	INH or INAH	300 mg.	6/50 ($ 0.90)
Streptomycin	SM	1 g.	126/00 ($17.25)
Para-aminosalicylic acid	PAS	10 g.	67/50 ($9.25)
Thiacetazone	TB 1	150 mg.	7/30 ($1.00)

Four major factors govern the use of antituberculous drugs; they are efficacy, cost, toxicity and ease of administration. Table 11 lists the main drugs in order of their effectiveness and gives their dosages and their annual cost. In using them the following points must be borne in mind.

Firstly, the SM dose should be reduced by 25% in patients over 40. Secondly, the dose of PAS should be increased by 50% when used in the dual PAS/SM regime. Thirdly, TB 1 is only effective when used in conjunction with the INH. Fourthly, the efficacy of the anti-tuberculous drugs is related to their peak blood levels; the day's drugs should therefore be given in a single dose.

The dual drug regimes commonly employed on a long term basis are INH/PAS or INH/TB 1. Either will result in success rates of the order of 80 per cent; success meaning the achievement and maintenance of sputum culture negativity in initially sputum positive cases of extensive pulmonary tuberculosis. The addition of daily SM to these regimes for the first two to four months of treatment can be expected to improve success rates to between 90 and 100 per cent.

Treatment with 'INH only' gives but a 30 per cent success rate on the criteria above. Dual or triple drug treatment to the point of sputum culture negativity followed by 'INH only' treatment gives a success rate very similar to that of the dual or triple regime itself. Further discussion of 'INH only' treatment is deferred to section 21:11.

The importance of the efficacy of the INH/TB 1 regime is not only its relatively low cost and acceptability, but also the fact that, should it fail, the SM/PAS regime is still available. This regime is however both expensive and difficult to administer because it involves daily injections of SM.

At the start of treatment correct any anaemia present, and treat any intestinal parasitic infection that may be found.

Whichever regime is decided upon, **continue treatment for eighteen months if treatment was confirmed bacteriologically and for twelve months if it was not.**

:8 **Drug resistance.** Drug resistance is important both to the patient and to the community, and in considering it two facts must be borne in mind.

The first is that a patient with bacilli graded as being drug sensitive by the standard laboratory tests always harbours a tiny proportion of bacilli resistant to each drug. It is this which makes dual regimes so necessary, for if only one drug is used this tiny proportion of resistant bacilli will multiply in the patient.

The second fact is that different groups of patients have different patterns of pre-treatment drug resistance. These patterns determine the success rates to be expected from various regimes and are shown for several countries in Table 12; they are derived from investigations done between 1957 and 1960 (27).

Resistance to TB 1 is at present being investigated, but the evidence available to date (1965) suggests that in Europe and Africa the figure is under 5 per cent. whereas in Asia it may well be considerably higher.

It is fortunate that a high proportion, perhaps 50 per cent. or more,

TABLE 12

PATTERNS OF PRE-TREATMENT DRUG RESISTANCE (27)

Patient-population	*No. tested*	*Percentage of patients with bacilli resistant to:* INH	SM	PAS
England and Wales	1338	1	2	1
France (Paris)	123	9	9	1
America (New York)	428	14	5	2
India (Madras)	522	5	2	—
East Africa	172	10	2	4
W. Africa (Ashanti)	342	9	9	6

of patients whose bacilli show pre-treatment resistance to a particular drug respond to a regime containing that drug in the same manner as do those patients whose bacilli are fully sensitive.

The pre-treatment drug resistance pattern of a population group considered together with cost determines the choice of a drug regime for routine use.

21:9a **Side effects.** These are of two kinds, toxicity and hypersensitivity; both are usually seen within the first few weeks of starting treatment. Toxic effects are specific for each drug, hypersensitivity reactions are similar for all four. INH produces side effects of one kind or another in 1 per cent. of patients, the other three drugs, in about 5 per cent. Toxic effects are more common with INH and SM, hypersensitivity is more common with PAS and TB 1.

21:9b **Toxicity.** INH toxicity presents as a peripheral neuritis or pellagra, especially in the presence of vitamin B deficiency, and responds to pyridoxine (5-10 mg. daily) or to a vitamin B complex. It is not serious, and it may even not be necessary to stop the INH treatment to cure it.

SM toxicity is usually seen in patients over 40, and in those with renal impairment. It injures the eighth nerve producing deafness or vertigo. Whenever these symptoms occur the drug should be stopped immediately.

With PAS and TB 1 the really dangerous toxicities are agranulocytosis and hepatitis. Fortunately both are rare. Both drugs must be stopped at once.

21:9c **Hypersensitivity**. This is manifest as fever and an irritative rash. Treatment must be stopped as soon as hypersensitivity is suspected because serious liver damage or the Stevens-Johnson syndrome may result. This is the name given to the association of erythema multiforme, fever, lesions on the mucous membranes and various visceral manifestations which may end fatally.

If, on the cessation of treatment, symptoms subside, *small* test doses of each of the drugs used can be given in turn, the dose used being inversely proportional to the severity of the presenting rash (0.01g of SM should be given if the reaction is severe). Recurrence of the symptoms within a few hours of giving the test dose proves the association between them and the drug. Sometimes, the hypersensitivity is multiple. The patient may be desensitized to hypersensitivity reactions, but not of course to toxic ones, by giving gradually increasing doses of the offending drug at 12 hourly or daily intervals; if necessary under corticosteroid cover should this be available.

Various minor side effects have been ascribed to each of the four drugs. The only one of importance is the gastro-intestinal disturbance sometimes associated with TB 1 or PAS in the early stage of a drug regimen. It responds to symptomatic treatment — giving the offending drug in divided doses for a few days, giving it with or after meals, or in conjunction with a simple kaolin mixture.

10 **Hospital treatment?** Studies in Madras have shown that, provided patients took their drugs as prescribed, success rates were similar irrespective of whether they were treated in hospital or at home. And this was in spite of the fact that hospital treatment was combined with enforced bed rest, and a diet much better than the grossly inadequate ones that most patients received at home, where they also led partly or fully active lives. This means that intermediate care (9:1) is required only for patients who are physically too ill to be able to be up and about, for patients with complications and emergencies, or for others with concomitant disease. Relatively few tuberculosis beds are therefore required. If the main purpose of a patient's admission is to give him streptomycin, self-care facilities are all he needs.

Such beds as are wanted are best sited in general hospitals — not in separate sanatoria. When cared for in this way patients are segregated, but remain in their own region, the awe and horror of the disease are reduced, staff and hospital services are always available and treatment is cheaper than it would be otherwise. Such wards should be somewhat apart from the main building, but need not be cubicled.

The Madras studies also showed that *most patients had already infected their household contacts by the time they were diagnosed.* This means that, by the time patients present themselves for treatment, they will have already infected most of those of their families who are going to catch tuberculosis from them: there is thus little further danger in keeping them up and about as outpatients.

Because the addition of daily SM to the first two months of the INH/TB 1 or the INH/PAS regimens is so beneficial, many recommend the erection near the hospital of a 'tuberculosis hostel' or a group of huts. These huts amount to a 'T.B. village' where self-care patients from a distance may live and attend daily for injections. Such a village is especially useful in that it prevents patients staying with their relatives nearby and thus infecting a fresh set of contacts.

It is fortunate that *continued hospitalization is of little proved benefit to the average patient,* because capital costs alone would rule it out. More than one calculation has shown that it is possible to put up a chest clinic capable of handling 1,000-1,500 new patients a year for the price of only 10-25 sanatorium beds. Much the same is true for running costs, because 15-20 ambulant patients can be treated for the price of every one in a sanatorium.

What of those countries which have already invested large sums in sanatoria? They might be able to expand their services by actually *closing down these sanatorium beds* so as to free finances for the outpatient treatment of a larger number of cases. What of the hospital which already has extensive tuberculosis wards? It too might be well advised to reconsider its treatment policy and think about the possibility of using some of these wards for other purposes.

No mention of the hospital treatment of tuberculosis would be complete without mention of the importance of Heaf testing the nurses and giving the negative ones BCG.

21:11 **INH Alone?** Reference was made in section 21:7 to two aspects of 'INH only' treatment — that it could achieve only a 30 per cent. success rate, and that, if treatment was started with a dual or triple drug regimen, the success rate of that regimen was little influenced by substituting for it at the point of sputum culture negativity an 'INH only' regimen for the remainder of the 18 months. As to the first of these aspects, it must be mentioned in justice to such a regimen that although the survivors among the 70 per cent. who are treatment failures remain sputum positive, their bacilli have been modified in the direction of reduced virulence. This represents at least a partial success among these failures in that the patient's expectation of life is greater than it would be had he received no treatment at all.

For the reasons outlined above it is sometimes considered that 'INH only' treatment is justified under certain circumstances, either from the beginning, or as a continuation treatment. The financial savings occurring from adoption of such a policy must be weighed against the disadvantages of widespread distribution of 'INH only' tablets throughout the country, and with their potential effect on the pre-treatment bacillary drug resistance pattern in general. It should also be remembered that these savings will be comparatively small in relation to the cost of the overall antituberculosis effort itself. In addition, 'INH only' as a continuation treatment complicates routine treatment procedures and calls for increased bacteriological services.

2 **Reserve drugs.** The reserve drugs, such as pyrazinamide, ethionamide, cycloserine and several others are less effective than the routine ones, they are more toxic and they are also extremely expensive. In view of these and other considerations it is recommended that, where they are used, the swallowing of each daily dose should be medically supervised. Thus they have only a very limited role in treating tuberculosis in developing countries.

ORGANIZATION

13 **Documentation.** The tuberculous patient needs treatment for some 12 to 18 months and *subsequent surveillance for at least as long again.* An adequate system of documentation is thus essential. Five documents are required. Each district has a **'Tuberculosis Register'.** Each clinic keeps a **'Tuberculosis Envelope'** or file and a **'Tuberculosis Treatment Card'** for each of its patients; it also has a **'Tuberculosis Appointment Diary'.** Each patient keeps personally his own **'TB Card'.**

14 **The Tuberculosis Register.** This should be a hard-backed book, the pages of which are divided into five columns headed 'TB Registration No.' — 'Patient's Name' — 'Detailed Address' — 'Remarks' — 'Disposal'. The TB Registration No. consists of three components: a short lettered prefix indicating the area or district to which the register refers — say EST for East Subtopia; a serial number beginning afresh at '1' each year; and the two digits indicating the year of diagnosis. Each patient as he is registered is thus automatically allocated his TB Registration No. — e.g. EST/1/65 or EST/275/65. This number should be used as a reference or identifying number on all documents and correspondence concerning the patient. In areas where tuberculosis is being diagnosed and treated at several different hospitals and clinics, each of these should be allocated a block of serial numbers in advance according to their estimated requirements — clinic A being allocated serial numbers 1 to 200 and clinic B, 201 to 300 etc. This allocation of blocks of numbers permits each clinic to maintain its Tuberculosis Envelopes in serial order, and thus to keep track of them and their patients more easily. The address entered in the register should be sufficiently detailed to allow of the patient's being traced if he defaults. The most useful note that can be made in the 'remarks' column is one which will help to trace the patient in the event of default — e.g. father employed as school teacher at such-and-such a pri-

mary school. No entry is made in the disposal column as long as the patient is under treatment; entries are then made for death 'D', transfer to another clinic 'T', lost sight of 'L', or, when the treatment is successfully completed and the patient placed on surveillance 'S'.

21:15 **The Tuberculosis Envelope and Tuberculosis Treatment Card.** The Envelope contains the patient's Tuberculosis Treatment Card, his X-ray films and any correspondence relating to him. The Tuberculosis Treatment Card should record brief clinical notes including the patient's monthly weight and details of his laboratory reports. These should include the laboratory reference number of any reports, especially incomplete reports, e.g. of smear reports where culture reports are expected later. Precise details of treatment given should also be recorded, e.g. for an outpatient 'TBI/INH, 150/300 x 28 days', and the date of next attendance.

21:16 **The TB Card.** This is a small card, preferably of a distinct colour, at the top of which is entered the patient's name, his TB Registration No. and the name of the clinic from which his treatment is supervised. The rest of the card is divided into two date columns — 'Date of Attendance', and 'Date of next Attendance'. *The patient keeps this card,* preferably in a polythene envelope. When he produces it at a clinic his Tuberculosis Envelope and its contents can be found at once, and, if he produces it at another clinic, this file can then be sent for. The patient should be told to produce his TB Card whenever he is admitted to hospital for any reason — it is disconcerting to treat a fractured femur for three months and then be asked by the patient 'Doctor, what shall I do about my tuberculosis?'

Some clinics make the TB Card of firm quarto cardboard printed on both sides with a year's dose regime. This the patient himself keeps in a polythene envelope and a duplicate is kept in his tuberculosis envelope. A continuation card can be used for the second year if needed. The virtue of this system is that the patient can see himself working through his card visit by visit, eventually to complete his course one or two years hence. When a quarto sized card is being used, provide a space for each attendance and a box where each injection and every sputum and urine test can be recorded. Such a card means of course that the regime must be standard, but this is a great convenience on a hospital scale, and even on a national one, for a patient's position in the treatment regime is visible at a glance. Should drug resistance occur and the regime have to be altered, the card will no longer fit, but this happens seldom enough for a printed card to be much more useful than a plain one. These cards are also a good site for some educational slogans such as the vernacular for

'Tuberculosis can be treated', or, 'Your sputum is dangerous to your children'.

:17 **The Tuberculosis Diary.** Each clinic has an ordinary diary. When a patient is being told when he should come up again, his TB registration number is entered in this diary on the appropriate page for that day. When the time for this clinic comes round each patient attending is crossed off the list of numbers for that date. In this way any remaining numbers automatically belong to the defaulters who can then be chased up by any of the procedures available, such as contacting the village headman, etc.

18a **Chest clinic practice.** In populous urban areas tuberculosis is best treated from special chest clinics. In rural areas it has to be treated from out-patient departments, health centres and mobile clinics. At these peripheral centres it is best for the local clinician, be he doctor or medical assistant, to set aside for the tuberculosis clinic one special day each month, or one special afternoon each week, according to the work load. He should of course, attend to patients who come on the 'wrong day', but should do his best to keep these to a minimum.

Patients should remain at work the whole time, or return to it as soon as possible after discharge, for work is a valuable therapeutic measure; it relieves the mind, and feeds both the patient and his family. The only exceptions to this rule are those who might particularly endanger others — the school teacher and the nurse.

18b **Follow-up methods.** The really helpful follow-up methods are not the ESR and the X-ray, but the weighing machine and the microscope. The ESR, traditionally so important in following up the tuberculous, is so wont to be affected by other tropical conditions, and so liable to error as to be useless — limited laboratory staff are much better employed looking at the sputum.

At some clinics patients have their sputum tested at every visit. If this is practicable well and good; if not, it should be tested at the intervals suggested in section 21:24.

18c **Prepacked drugs**. The monthly clinic attendance has become standard practice. A four-week month should be aimed at for it ensures that the clinics are always held on the same day of the week. Moreover, and more important still, drugs can be obtained pre-packed in envelopes to cover four weeks exactly.

It is essential that the routine drugs be immediately available on the clinician's table, packed and ready to give to the patient (11:3b). He may well have had a long journey to the clinic on foot, followed by a long wait to see the clinician. The return journey home lies ahead of him, and he may perhaps have a once-a-day bus to catch. To give him a prescription, and expect him to wait in a second queue, is to encourage his subsequent default. It is for this reason that routine drugs should be supplied to him by his doctor or medical assistant conveniently packed in small plastic envelopes. Those made by one firm (SNP) contain 28 tablets, a four weeks' supply at the rate of one tablet a day. Each of these tablets contains 50 mg. of TB 1 and 100 mg. of INH. For small patients (21-50 lbs., 10-25 kg.), one tablet a day is enough, so one envelope is issued. Medium sized patients (51-80 lbs., 25-40 kg.) need two tablets daily, so they get two envelopes. Large patients (over 80 lbs. or 40 kg.) need three tablets daily, and so they get given three envelopes. The average adult thus gets given three envelopes to last him a month. Another formulation of tablet is also available containing 133 mg. of INH and 50 mg. of TB 1. These were prepared when the standard adult dose of INH was considered to be 400 mg. daily, and not 300 mg. as is now advised. They will in due course be superceded by the tablets mentioned above containing only 100 mg. of INH.

The PAS/INH ('Pycamisan' (SNP)) envelope linked to the same patient-weights contains 98 grams PAS/INH powder in the approximate proportions of 100/3. One, two, or three envelopes are given according to the weights above. The daily dose is one, two or three, 3½ gram scoops, each scoop containing 3.4 grams of PAS and 100 mg. of INH. The ordinary beer bottle cap can be used as an improvised scoop, but first measure out 3½ grams and see what it looks like in the cap, so that patients can be taught accordingly.

It is most important that, for routine use, TB 1/INM or PAS/INH be given in a combined form, because this prevents the patient from taking one drug without the other, a natural human tendency.

The real difficulty is to ensure that the patient actually takes the drugs given to him, and the important rules to follow are these. Firstly, ensure that he understands precisely what he is to do and that he realizes the consequences, both for himself and for his family, if he does not do what he is told. Secondly, make it as easy as possible for him to carry out the directions he has been given. It is pointless to tell a patient living 30 miles away to attend a clinic regularly at 10 a.m. and not to be late. The approach has to be one of sympathetic common sense, flavoured by a very occasional bit of bullying as the occasion demands. Always remember that the patient is a sick person to whom *you* have a personal obligation to cure.

21:18d **Urine testing.** Urine testing for the presence of drugs can be used as a clinic routine, but it tends to lose its value as patients soon learn that they must take their drugs on their clinic attendance day, and this is no guarantee that they have done so in-between. It can also be used at surprise home visits, a tedious procedure when one considers the journey involved, the collection of the specimen in the patient's home and the later testing of it at the clinic, the recording of results and the linking of these to the patient at his next attendance. It would seem that the most effective use to which urine tests can be put is to use it to estimate the extent to which the patients as a group are taking their drugs. This means testing the urines of all patients attending at some clinics each year, combined with some surprise tests on samples taken at home visits. Not only are a number of tests done at one time well suited to the needs of the clinic, but they also suit the tests described in section 24:39 and 24:40. The test for PAS could hardly be easier, but the test for INH involving freshly made up solutions of cyanide and chloramine T is best done on a number of specimens, after which the remaining reagents should be thrown away. There is no simple test for TB 1, but if this drug is always used with INH in a compound tablet, there is no need for one.

NON-RESPIRATORY TUBERCULOSIS

19 **Incidence, diagnosis and treatment.** Non-respiratory tuberculosis usually accounts for some 15 per cent. of the total annual incidence of tuberculosis. In a considerable proportion of instances a lung lesion is also present. What has been written in earlier paragraphs in regard to diagnosis and treatment of pulmonary tuberculosis can be applied, with suitable modification, to non-respiratory tuberculosis disease also. Possibly the most important thing that can be said in this section is that patients with this form of the disease should be attached to chest or tuberculosis clinics for the supervision of their treatment.

TUBERCULOSIS IN CHILDREN

20 **Diagnosis and treatment.** *Tuberculosis in young children is a completely different disease from the tuberculosis of older children and adults*: its clinical pattern is different, and there are management problems peculiar to the young child. Signs and symptoms are indefinite and non-specific. Sometimes it presents as loss of weight, even in the absence of malnutrition, sometimes it is the cause of a chronic pyrexia or a broncho-peumonia which fails to clear — 'chronic broncho-pneumonia'. Often, the onset of tuberculosis in children is masked by malnutrition or an acute infection, especially measles.

Because tuberculosis is not easy to diagnose in children and is easily missed, **all admissions to the children's ward must be routinely Heaf tested and the Heaf gun must be in active use in the outpatient department.**

It is of great value in ailing children, in the contacts of infectious cases, and as a check on all children who have had a cough for more than two weeks. The significance of a positive Heaf in childhood, and the importance of considering all Heaf positive children under two, and in certain circumstances under six, as suffering from active disease requiring treatment has been mentioned in an earlier section — 21:3. So also has the possibility of the Heaf test being negative in PCM (14:12), measles and advanced tuberculosis, especially the miliary or meningitic form. Measles vaccination may have the same effect as measles, and both can produce false negatives which persist for as long as 6-8 weeks. It may also take 6-8 weeks for the Heaf test to become positive after an initial tuberculous infection. When a child is suspected to be gravely ill with advanced tuberculosis, and yet turns out to be Heaf negative, he should be put on antituberculous treatment and retested some weeks later.

No sputum can be obtained from young children because they swallow it, and, if facilities for culturing the tubercle bacillus are available, material for culture should be obtained by gastric lavage and sent away in the appropriate buffer (Appendix D). This prevents the bacilli being killed by the gastric acid.

Method: Gastric lavage in young children.

Fast the child overnight.

Pass a tube.

Withdraw the contents and place it in one of the buffer containing universal containers specified in Appendix D.

If insufficient material can be obtained to fill the container at least half full, introduce a little water into the child's stomach, suck this back and place this in the universal container.

Dispatch the container to the laboratory with as little delay as possible.

Mild cases of tuberculosis can be treated as outpatients, but moderate and severe cases should be admitted to the wards for streptomycin treatment, preferably for three months, though 4-6 weeks is usually as long as is practicable. In hospital they should be given intramuscular streptomycin once daily and INH and TB 1 (or PAS if this is being used instead of TB 1) by mouth, also once daily. Thereafter these children should be treated as outpatients on INH and TB 1 (or PAS) for a year. If they have been severely ill some would advise that this treatment be continued for two years.

Drug dosages are given in Appendix I. As has been mentioned above (21:18c), compound TB 1 & INH tablets are available, the older one with a 50 mgm/133 mgm. formulation and the newer one with a formulation of 50 mgm./100 mgm. Neither of these are convenient in children who require about four times as much INH as they do TB 1, instead of only twice as much which is the adult proportion. Until some enterprising manufacturer makes a compound tablet with, say, 25 mg. of TB 1 and 100 mg. of INH, children will have to be issued with separate tablets of each of these drugs.

PUBLIC HEALTH

.1 **Household contacts.** Do not forget the community in caring for the patient. In particular, never omit to examine the family and the household contacts (21:2) — Heaf test them all.

Heaf positive contacts. If possible, X-ray all Heaf positive contacts, and, if they are producing sputum, see that this is examined. Heaf positive contacts under six years old should be given 6-12 months of anti-tuberculous treatment (21:3).

Heaf negative contacts. Ideally, and especially in those under six years of age, Heaf negative contacts should be separated from the index case of eight weeks, and then given BCG only if they are still Heaf negative. *Alternatively,* such Heaf negative contacts can be given INH, as an infection prophylactic, in a single daily dose of 10 mg./kg. (5 mg./lb.) (maximum dose 300 mg. daily) until such time as the index case becomes sputum negative and then BCG. Neither of these two alternatives may be very easy to arrange in practice, and the most satisfactory course of action under many circumstances may be to give all Heaf negative contacts BCG and follow them up carefully.

The newborn child of a sputum positive mother is a special case. Do not separate him from his mother — to do this in a developing country is usually to save him from tuberculosis only to ensure his death from nutritional marasmus. Treat the mother vigorously and give the baby INH for a minimum period of six months. If she can be persuaded to wear a mask while feeding him, then so much the better. If at the end of six months she is sputum negative, Heaf test him, and if he is Heaf negative give him BCG. If at the end of six months she is still sputum positive, continue giving him INH until she becomes sputum negative and, if he is still Heaf negative, give him BCG.

The ideal way of treating these children is probably to use INH resistant BCG (GLA) which enables INH to be given prophylactically at the same time, without its killing the BCG.

THE ROLE OF A TUBERCULOSIS LABORATORY

21:22 **The work of a tuberculosis laboratory.** Apart from very special procedures, this consists of examining smears, culturing the tubercle bacillus and testing its sensitivity to drugs.

The purpose of a smear and culture examination is threefold:

i) To confirm the diagnosis of an individual patient.
ii) To assess the response to treatment of the confirmed case.
iii) As a case finding procedure to detect pulmonary tuberculosis in the pre-symptomatic stage among the general population.

The purpose of drug sensitivity testing is twofold:

i) To establish the pre-treatment drug sensitivity pattern for a community, so that suitable drug regimes can be prescribed without it being necessary to test the sensitivity of the bacilli from each individual patient.
ii) To determine the sensitivity pattern of the bacilli isolated from a sputum positive case so that it can be guaranteed that the drug regime prescribed will prove effective.

Very relevant to the use of these procedures in developing countries is the fact that a smear report can be available the day the specimen arrives at the laboratory, a culture report takes one or two months, and a drug sensitivity report is only available a month after that. Also relevant to their use are the relative costs of the different procedures. The culture of a single specimen costs about ten times more than a smear examination. A sensitivity test for the four routine drugs costs of the order of fifty to a hundred times as much as a smear examination.

21:23 **Sputum examination by smear and culture.** The relative efficiency of these two procedures is best considered in relation to their purpose.

From the point of view of the individual patient the advantage lies with the smear if his sputum contains many bacilli, because both smear and culture give the same result and the smear report is available much earlier. When there are few bacilli in the sputum the advantage lies with the culture because this is the more sensitive test. But the advantage is less than it might appear because by the time the culture report is available further smear examinations may well have become positive. When there are no bacilli present both procedures give the same negative answer, the smear earlier, but the culture with greater certainty.

In assessing the response of the individual patient to treatment there is very little to chose between the two procedures. If progress is satisfactory, the sputum rapidly becomes free of bacilli. At the three month point the smear examination is, paradoxically, owing to its relative insensitivity, the more helpful test. At the six month point and later the results of smear and culture usually coincide. In the small group of patients who become sputum negative and later relapse culture will often demonstrate the return of the bacilli a little earlier if serial tests are put up at monthly intervals.

For case-finding culture of the sputum is twice as efficient as examining it by smear. However, the patients who are the greatest danger to the community, those with very many bacilli in their sputum, are revealed equally readily by both methods. Even so, use culture facilities where possible in addition to examining smears. They are more effective, and, even though they are ten times as costly, laboratory costs are only a fraction of the total cost of the case-finding effort.

4 **The use of facilities for smear and culture: the diagnosis and management of drug resistance.** The facts that have just been related make it economic to use facilities for smear and culture in the following way.

In diagnosis reserve culture facilities for those smear negative patients who are suspected to be tuberculous.

In assessing the response to treatment rely primarily on smear facilities. A satisfactory procedure would consist of smear examination at the six month point, the same treatment being continued whether it is positive or negative, but, if it is positive, a specimen is put up for culture. When the report of culture and sensitivity is to hand, proceed as follows. If the culture is negative, continue the same treatment. If the culture is positive, repeat the smear examination. If this is now negative continue the treatment unchanged. But if the smear is positive change treatment in accordance with the sensitivity report. Examine more smears at the 12 and 18 month points.

What if no culture and sensitivity tests are available? How should the case be managed then? Provided the patient is taking his drugs, and failure to take these drugs is much the most important cause of failure to free the sputum of bacilli, then initial drug resistance is probable when the sputum fails to clear in six months — most sensitive cases clear in two or three. Secondary resistance is probable when a case, once regularly sputum negative, becomes consistently sputum positive again. *Provided reliance is placed on multiple smears and the patient really is taking his drugs,* such repeated smear examinations are a fairly satisfactory substitute for sensitivity tests.

5 **Drug sensitivity testing.** To have pre-treatment drug sensitivity testing done in the case of the individual patient is a grave abuse of this facility unless steps are taken to ensure that treatment is governed by the test result. This means that drug sensitivity tests should *not* be done unless the physician is prepared:

i) *either* (a) to withhold all treatment for two to three months until the result is to hand,
or (b) to treat the patient with at least three drugs for the duration of this period; AND

ii) to treat the patient for a total period of 18 months with *any* two of the drugs in the event of his bacilli being resistant to the third.

When it is a question of the individual patient, and when cost is a major consideration, drug sensitivity testing should be restricted to treatment failures, or suspected treatment failures, as described at the end of the preceding paragraph. A common instance is the sputum positive patient who, at the time of initially seeking medical advice, admits to previous treatment with several of the anti-tuberculosis drugs — or where this situation is suspected.

The importance of establishing the pre-treatment bacilliary drug sensitivity pattern of a community has already been stressed. This is the earliest priority for drug sensitivity testing in a developing country.

21:26 **Organization of tuberculosis laboratory services.** It will be appreciated from what has already been said that, where diagnosis and control of treatment are concerned, an efficient smear service is the first essential. This service must be of a high technical standard and must be readily available at peripheral hospitals and clinics. Fluorescence microscopy should replace the Ziehl-Neelsen method for routine use wherever there are more than 40 direct smears to be examined each day and some skilled supervision is available. Fluorescence microscopy is twice as rapid, and the extra equipment required is less expensive than the additional microscope needed to examine the same number of specimens by the Ziehl-Neelsen method. The cost of replacing the vapour lamps is less than the salary of the technician whose time is saved. In the hands of the unsupervised laboratory attendant the Ziehl-Neelsen method is still the best.

Of equal priority to the smear service is the establishment of the bacillary pre-treatment drug sensitivity pattern for the country in general. Once this has been done further drug-sensitivity testing is of a considerably lower priority.

The second essential in order of priority is the development of culture facilities, primarily for use in case-finding procedures, but including the diagnosis of smear negative patients where tuberculosis is suspected. Since, in case-finding procedures in general, only one half of 1 per cent of all specimens are likely to prove smear negative but culture positive, and, since in developing countries the lines of communication between the periphery and the capital tend to be two-stage through regional centres, it is preferable that laboratory culture facilities be organized on a regional basis. Such laboratory facilities will require supervision and the supply of culture medium from a central laboratory.

The third stage in the organization of laboratory facilities should be the provision in the main central laboratory of drug-sensitivity testing procedures for use, in the first instance, in connection with patients whose primary drug regimen has — or is suspected to have — failed. It is only when this stage is successfully passed that the application of drug-sensitivity testing, and all that that implies, should be contemplated in the case of the individual patient.

27 **Conclusion.** Tuberculosis is chosen as an example in the section on health education (6 : 12), but a point which is not made there is that, right at the start patients must be instilled with the fact that it is going to take them at least one year to get well, and that curing tuberculosis is not just a matter of a few injections. The delinquent patient is a danger to himself, a menace to his community and no credit to the medical service — his defection is so often simply due to his being neglected — both in hospital and in the clinic.

Finally, it cannot be stated too strongly that, now that drugs and the methods of diagnosis are both comparatively cheap and reliable, **the challenge in treating tuberculosis has become one of 'training, organizing and supervising auxiliaries' to diagnose the disease and administer the drugs to the millions who need them.** Scientifically, the problems are mostly solved, the challenge has passed to the district medical officer and his assistants to make this knowledge available — everywhere.

28 **Acknowledgement.** This chapter is based on a talk by Dr. Murray Short, but it owes much to Dr. Pierce Kent, Dr. Wallace Fox (17), Dr. John Billinghurst and Professor D. B. Jelliffe.

Chapter Twenty-Two

ANAESTHETICS

For authorship see 22:19

22:1 **Anaesthesia in developing countries.** A safe anaesthetic can be taken for granted when there is a qualified anaesthetist there to give it. But such specialists are never available in the smaller hospitals of the developing countries. Here most anaesthetics have to be given by medical assistants or nursing sisters, and staff are sometimes so short that even the theatre cleaner may find himself called to this task! Not only is there a shortage of trained staff, but equipment is limited, only the cheapest drugs can be used and there are often many poor risk patients who have delayed coming to hospital until their disease is far advanced. It is under these circumstances that doctors, nurses and medical assistants must understand the fundamental principles of anaesthesia, become familiar with a few simple safe and inexpensive techniques, and know something of the pharmacology of a limited range of drugs.

The principles they must understand are comparatively straightforward and include the pre-operative assessment of the patient, the signs and stages of anaesthesia, the maintenance of a perfect airway and the prevention and treatment of inhaled vomit.

The techniques with which they should be familiar are, open ether, its induction with thiopentone, chloroform, or ethyl chloride: the use of the 'EMO' apparatus, spinal anaesthesia, endotracheal intubation and intravenous local anaesthesia. Some, such as open ether, and intubation, are best mastered by practical instruction from an expert at a regional centre, but the others can well be learnt from a book.

Opinions differ on the place of muscle relaxants in the rural hospital. Some hold that they have no place; others, however, consider their use to be an important skill that both doctors and medical assistants should master. One thing is certain — neither should attempt to use them without a period of expert instruction.

The drugs suitable for routine use include ether, ethyl chloride, chloroform, thiopentone, cinchocaine, procaine, lignocaine, adrenalin and atropine.

There is one item of equipment that no rural hospital should be without; this is the 'Epstein-Macintosh-Oxford' or EMO inhaler (LON), the unique feature of which is that it enables a measured concentration of ether to be given, regardless of both the ambient temperature, and the respiratory pattern. The EMO thus makes it possible to give ether in a more certain and regular manner than has ever been possible hitherto. It is simply constructed and portable, and, at £100 ($280) it is also comparatively cheap. The EMO was specially designed for the rural hospital, for it can be handed to an assistant, leaving the surgeon confident that his patient is getting a preselected concentration of ether. Like intravenous local anaesthesia the EMO is a recent innovation, and, as no substantial account of either appears in the standard textbooks, both are described here. If the reader wants to know more about the EMO he should write to the makers for their pamphlet.

No description is given of ordinary local or regional anaesthesia, for, though they are in some ways suited to the single handed, they require so much skill that general or spinal anaesthesia is usually the wiser choice. The novice is therefore cautioned away from them — if he wants to use them he should acquire a special book /104/.

Space is severely limited and this chapter cannot be comprehensive; all it can do is to describe a few limited techniques in some detail. One device is particularly commended to the reader, this is the Ambu suction pump (BOC) which is illustrated in Figure 47 and costs £17 ($48). A sucker is an essential item of theatre equipment, this is the best foot operated one. If more than one can be afforded, there should be one in the labour ward and another in the children's ward.

INTRAVENOUS LOCAL ANAESTHESIA

2 **The principle of intravenous local anaesthesia.** Local anaesthesia can be produced in a limb distal to an arterial tourniquet by injecting $\frac{1}{2}$% lignocaine *without* adrenalin into a vein, and letting this diffuse through the vessels of the isolated region — the addition of adrenalin to the lignocaine may cause gangrene. A critical feature of this form of anaesthesia is that the tourniquet must be tight enough to seal off the circulation completely in the distal part of the limb, and so retain the lignocaine in the isolated area.

Such analgesia can be used for any operation on the hand, forearm, leg or foot though in practice it is more satisfactory on the arm than the leg. It must *not* be used if the patient carries gene for haemoglobin 'S',

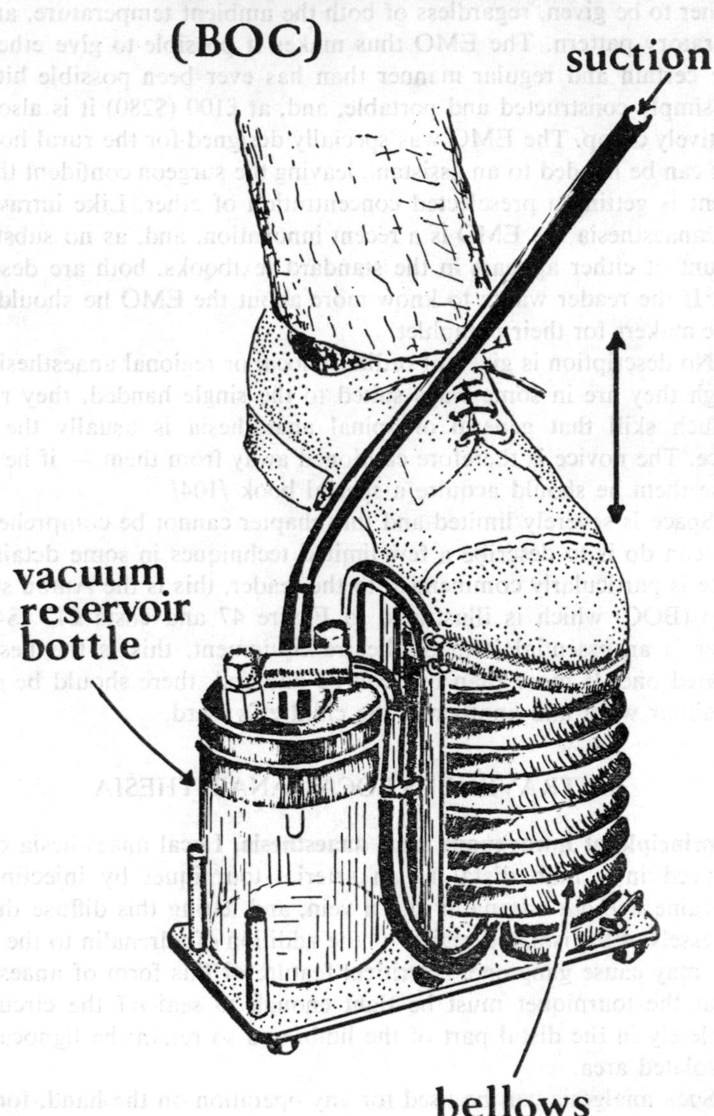
Fig.47.
THE AMBU
SUCTION PUMP.
(BOC)
suction
vacuum
reservoir
bottle
bellows

for if he does, the application of a tourniquet alone may cause gangrene from the 'tangles' of sickle cells that form and obstruct the vessels. In the hands of laboratory assistants the sickle cell test (24:22) is probably not to be relied upon absolutely to exclude the presence of haemoglobin 'S', so this method is therefore not advised in areas where sickle cell anaemia is seen.

Method: Intravenous local anaesthesia.

Measure the systolic blood pressure in the limb, let down the sphygmomanometer cuff and insert a self-sealing needle into a convenient vein. Secure this needle with strapping, raise the arm for five minutes to drain off any surplus blood. Inflate the cuff to 30 mm. Hg. above the systolic pressure and then lower the arm.

Through the self-sealing needle inject 20-30 ml. of ½% lignocaine for a hand, or 30-40 ml. for a forearm or foot. Leave the limb for ten minutes keeping the cuff inflated the whole time, both before the operation and during it, so making sure that the anaesthetic is not diluted by incoming blood. Watch the sphygmomanometer cuff very closely and don't use one which leaks.

Lignocaine is slowly broken down by the tissues, and at the end of an operation lasting half an hour such as remains usually produces little effect when released into the general circulation. If, however, a deflated cuff lets a large quantity into the circulation suddenly, the patient may convulse. But despite the fact that most of the drug will have been broken down by the tissues during the operation, it is advisable to watch the patient for 15 minutes post-operatively, for untoward results occasionally follow the arrival of even the remains of the drug in the general circulation. To make sure that the drug reaches the circulation at a safe rate, it is also advised that the cuff be blown up again for five minutes or so as soon as reactive hyperaemia develops.

If the cuff becomes painful, apply a second one distal to the first; inflate this to the same pressure and then remove the first one. Because of the danger of the limb becoming gangrenous, don't leave a tourniquet on for more than two hours before restoring the circulation.

SPINAL ANAESTHESIA

3 **Principle.** If a local anaesthetic agent is introduced into the cerebrospinal fluid it will anaesthetize the spinal nerves and render part of the body anaesthetic. The position and extent of the area of anaesthesia will

depend upon the specific gravity of the drug, that is whether it rises or falls in the CSF, the dose of the anaesthetic agent introduced, and above all the position in which the patient is placed immediately the anaesthetic has been given. In the anaesthetic area the sensation of pain will be abolished and profound muscular relaxation produced.

Certain anatomical points have an important bearing on the practice of spinal anaesthesia.

Fig. 48. **THE ANATOMY OF SPINAL ANAESTHESIA.**

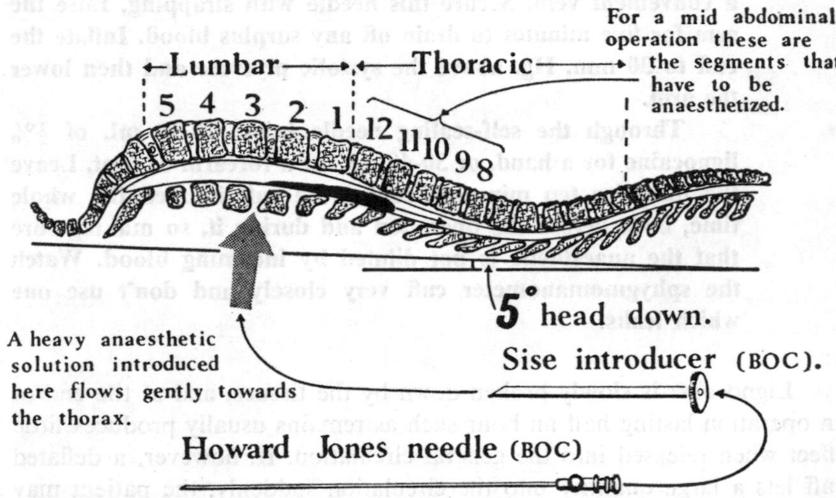
←Lumbar→
←Thoracic→
5 4 3 2 1 12 11 10 9 8
For a mid abdominal operation these are the segments that have to be anaesthetized.
5° head down.
A heavy anaesthetic solution introduced here flows gently towards the thorax.
Sise introducer (BOC).
Howard Jones needle (BOC)

22:4 **Anaesthetic anatomy.** An important anatomical point is the fact that, when a patient lies on his back, his thoracic spine is concave upwards, the bottom of the concavity being T6, but his lumbar spine is convex upwards, the summit of the convexity being L3, the site of the lumbar puncture — see Figure 48. Thus, if a heavy anaesthetic solution is introduced at this site and the patient turned flat on his back, the solution will flow down both sides of the lumbar spine, some proceeding towards the sacrum and some towards the thorax. For an abdominal operation, that flowing towards the sacrum is wasted, for it is anaesthesia of the lower thoracic segments that is wanted — T6 supplies the xiphisternum, T10 the umbilicus and L1 the inguinal region. For an abdominal operation the table is therefore given a SLIGHT head-down tilt, so that when the patient is turned on his back after the anaesthetic has been given, the anaesthetic solution is encouraged to flow towards the thorax. Unless the lower thoracic segments are anaesthetized in this way, the anaesthetic will fail.

To ensure proper anaesthesia of these lower thoracic segments, the patient is laid on his back with his knees flexed, and the table is tilted 5° head down for ten minutes immediately after the anaesthetic has been given. At the end of this period the anaesthetic will have been 'fixed' to the nerve roots, and the patient can now be turned into any position — including the Trendelenberg.

:5 **Indications.** In the fit patient spinal anaesthesia provides admirable conditions for abdominal surgery, for the operative field is remarkably bloodless, the gut is well contracted and there is perfect muscular relaxation. Unfortunately however, if complications do arise, they are apt to be serious, and the operating time is limited by the duration of the drug's action.

Spinal anaesthesia is particularly useful when there is no trained anaesthetist available, for the surgeon can first give the anaesthetic and then perform the operation. It is also valuable when the patient has recently eaten yet operation is urgent, and where there is some definite contraindication to general anaesthesia, such as a respiratory infection, or a deformed airway.

:6 **Contraindications.** Spinal anaesthetics are not suitable for children, or for cases of heart disease. They are contraindicated by sepsis anywhere on the back, nor is it advisable to give them if there is a colostomy or even a suprapubic cystotomy. Some hold them to be contraindicated for Caesarian section, but though not ideal, they may well be the best anaesthetic for the purpose in a district hospital. A standard spinal anaesthetic may well prove lethal in any unfit patient with a low blood volume who is maintaining his blood pressure only by general vasoconstriction. In such patients, the paralysis by the drug of the sympathetic vasoconstrictor fibres leaving the cord between T1 and L2 or L3 produces a widespread vasodilation that results in a grave and often disastrous lowering of the blood pressure. Many anaesthetists consider a spinal anaesthetic contraindicated unless the patient is generally fit.

:7 **Drugs.** Use cinchocaine (nupercaine) without adrenalin. This produces two or three hours of anaesthesia and is sold in 3 ml. (15 mgm.) ampoules of a 1/200 solution 'heavy' with 6% glucose. Procaine can be used but its action is too short for safety and convenience — only 45-60 minutes. Oxygen should be available as well as a vasopressor drug such as Vasoxine or Methedrine.

Use the following volumes of heavy cinchocaine: —

All upper abdominal operations. 2 ml.

Lower abdominal and leg operations,
e.g. herniorrhaphy, appendicectomy. 1.5 ml.
Anal, vesical, urethral operations and
'low spinals', e.g. haemorrhoidectomy,
cystoscopy, urethrotomy. 1 ml.

22:8 **Apparatus.** A 'Sise introducer' (A & H) is a useful accessory. It is a short stout needle with a stylet that can be pushed part of the way into the patient and so enable a fine spinal needle to be passed down it into the subarachnoid space. The use of a fine spinal needle is desirable because it reduces CSF leakage through the dura. The Howard Jones, or Harris needles (A&H), are the ones recommended. A Sise introducer is also said to diminish the risk of sepsis. Without such an introducer the spinal needle has to be thicker, for it will have to reach the theca unassisted. The skin should be nicked with a scalpel to assist its passage.

Besides the Sise introducer obtain two 2 ml. syringes, a fine 15 cm. needle, a stout 5 cm. needle for drawing up the anaesthetic, and two fine 22 SWG 10 cm. spinal puncture needles with steep 45° bevels and stylets to fit.

Pack this equipment into the pockets of a cloth roll with ampoules of anaesthetic agent, ampoule files, a swab holder, 2 bundles of swabs and a gallipot. Such a roll is best autoclaved together with some sterile towels inside a drum, but they can be wrapped in several layers of paper instead. Several such bundles or drums should be kept ready in the theatre, the date of autoclaving marked on the seal and each bundle or drum reautoclaved every week (30:8). Cinchocaine can be autoclaved many times without losing its potency, but the glucose in it chars in time and discoloured solutions are best discarded.

Method: Standard spinal anaesthesia.

Wash, shave and sedate the patient; wrap a stethoscope and a spygmomanometer cuff round his arm and secure an indwelling needle in one of his veins with strapping. Measure and record his blood pressure.

Lie him on his side on the table, or on a tilting trolley — slightly head downwards — 5°.

Swab the lumbar region with iodine 3 times using a fresh swab each time. Repeat the process with the lumbar spines only, being careful that no iodine falls on to the equipment on the trolley.

While taking great care not to touch the patient in the process, place two sterile towels horizontally across him and an-

other two vertically, so as to leave only a square of skin in his lumbar region uncovered. Push the lower towel under him with the swabholder to prevent it being dislodged. A better system is to use a single large towel with a 'window' in it, because if several separate towels are used they are apt to fall off. (Such towels with windows are also useful for marrow biopsy and lumbar puncture settings (24:27 and 24:56)).

Fill one of the syringes with a little cinchocaine, with which to anaesthetize the skin and fit a fine needle to it; fill the other with the full dose needed for the anaesthetic itself.

Sit on a low stool so that the puncture site is at eye level, and ask the nurse to place one hand behind the patient's neck and the other behind his knees. Get her to arch his back as much as possible so as to open up the intervertebral spaces. Choose the widest space between two spines, provided it is below L2. To identify the spines place one hand on the highest point of the iliac crest, which can be felt through the sterile towels, and follow a vertical line downwards from it. This line passes over the spine of L4 or through the space between L3 and L4.

Having chosen the site for the puncture, make a small intradermal wheal there with the fine needle. This wheal may be made mid-way between two spines, so that the introducer can be directed straight forwards, or just cephalic the lower one so that it can be directed slightly towards the head while aiming at the umbilicus. In either case, always keep the introducer at right angles to the skin in the vertical plane.

Push the Sise introducer through this wheal; in most patients it reaches as far as the ligamentum flavum. Pass the spinal needle through it holding it by the hub, and position it so that the bevel of the needle will divide rather than cut through the longitudinal fibres of the dura when it reaches them. A distinct loss of resistance will usually be felt as the spinal needle passes through the ligamentum flavum. *Take care never to touch the point or shaft of a spinal needle with the hand.* If by chance it has to be held, as when no Sise introducer is used, support the shaft with a sterile swab.

Once through this ligament remove the stylet and advance the needle very slowly through the dura, which may be felt as a very slight loss of resistance. At this point CSF should flow out of the needle. But, if it does not, rotate the needle once, reinsert the stylet and remove it again, holding the hub firmly with the other hand meanwhile. If still unsuccessful, get the

patient to strain so as to raise his CSF pressure.

If bone is struck withdraw the spinal needle into the introducer and check its direction; it may not be in the mid-line, it may be pointing too high or too low, or the patient's back not be flexed enough. Advance the lumbar puncture needle again until it passes the ligamentum flavum, but, before changing its direction, even a little draw it back into the introducer. After two or three failures try another space, further failure being an indication for giving a general anaesthetic.

As soon as CSF flows, reinsert the stylet and leave the needle and the introducer in situ. Inject the cinchocaine, then remove the spinal needle and the introducer.

For middle abdominal surgery lie the patient on his back with knees flexed for 10 minutes — the table will already be tilting 5° head down. For one sided operations such as herniorrhaphy leave him on the desired side for 5-10 minutes after the anaesthetic has been given. For leg operations the patient lies on the affected side and the table is not tilted.

22:9 **The course of anaesthesia.** In a standard spinal the cinchocaine flows towards the thorax while the patient lies on his back after the injection. In doing so, it becomes fixed to the nerves and is absorbed by the veins, any excess pooling in the thoracic concavity at T4-5.

The block will not extend any higher unless either an excessive amount of anaesthetic is given, or the table is tipped too steeply. Should it perchance extend to higher segments, extreme hypotension and respiratory depression may result.

Five or ten minutes after the anaesthetic has been given the patient can be turned into any position, but if it is required to have him sitting up during a spinal anaesthetic, his blood pressure should be checked before he is brought into the sitting position.

Before starting to operate test the success of the block by pricking the boundaries of the operative field with a needle to see if the patient feels anything. If the block is not completely successful after a further period of waiting, and operation is imperative, give the patient a general anaesthetic, but be *very* cautious in using thiopentone (Pentothal) after a spinal.

When the block extends above the umbilicus, it is highly desirable, though perhaps not absolutely essential, to give oxygen during the operation, preferably by BLB mask or Polymask, for the lower intercostal muscles will be paralysed and respiration weakened. If there is a large abdominal tumour, this may splint the diaphragm, and there is a grave danger of anoxia unless oxygen is given.

Record the blood pressure every five minutes and, should the systolic pressure fall below 80 mm. Hg., give a small dose of a vasopressor drug intravenously, e.g. Vasoxine 4 mgm. or Methedrine 5 mgm., together with twice this quantity intramuscularly for its sustained action. After a high spinal the response to vasopressors is poor, while after a perineal one they should not be needed for no sympathetic nerves are paralysed.

Low spinal or perineal anaesthesia. Good anaesthesia for such operations as cystoscopy, urethrotomy and haemorrhoidectomy can be produced by anaesthetizing the sacral segments only. The injection is made in the sitting position so that the heavy anaesthetic agent can fall to the bottom of the spinal theca.

Because it does not extend high enough to involve the sympathetic nerves, a low spinal block for perineal anaesthesia may be given to any patient, provided he is well enough to sit up.

Method: Low spinal block for perineal anaesthesia.

Sit the patient on the table or a trolley, his feet on a stool and his head forward to obtain the maximum flexion of his lumbar spine. Paint his back in the usual way and put a sterile towel under his buttocks. Inject 1 ml. of cinchocaine into his spinal theca and keep him sitting up for the next five minutes. After this he can be turned into any position and operated upon.

Post-operative care (both types of spinal). Nurse the patient flat on his back for the first six hours, give him one pillow only and raise the foot of his bed. For the next six hours keep him flat with his bed horizontal. Over a further six hours he may sit up gradually, one pillow at a time. Explain to him that at no time during this period must he sit up suddenly, and that these are measures to diminish the leakage of spinal fluid and thus reduce the chances of his having a headache.

Complications. Prevent headache by using a fine needle and insisting on the postoperative regime described above. Minimize the danger of a septic meningitis or an extradural abscess by scrupulous aseptic technique.

Avoid the risk of cardiac arrest and grave hypotension by not giving spinals to patients with a low circulating volume, and refrain if possible from giving a spinal anaesthetic to any patient who is generally unfit from whatever cause. Reduce the danger of respiratory arrest from too high a block by not exceeding the dose of cinchocaine advised, and not giving the table too steep an initial head-down tilt.

Fig. 49.

THE STRUCTURE OF THE EMO.

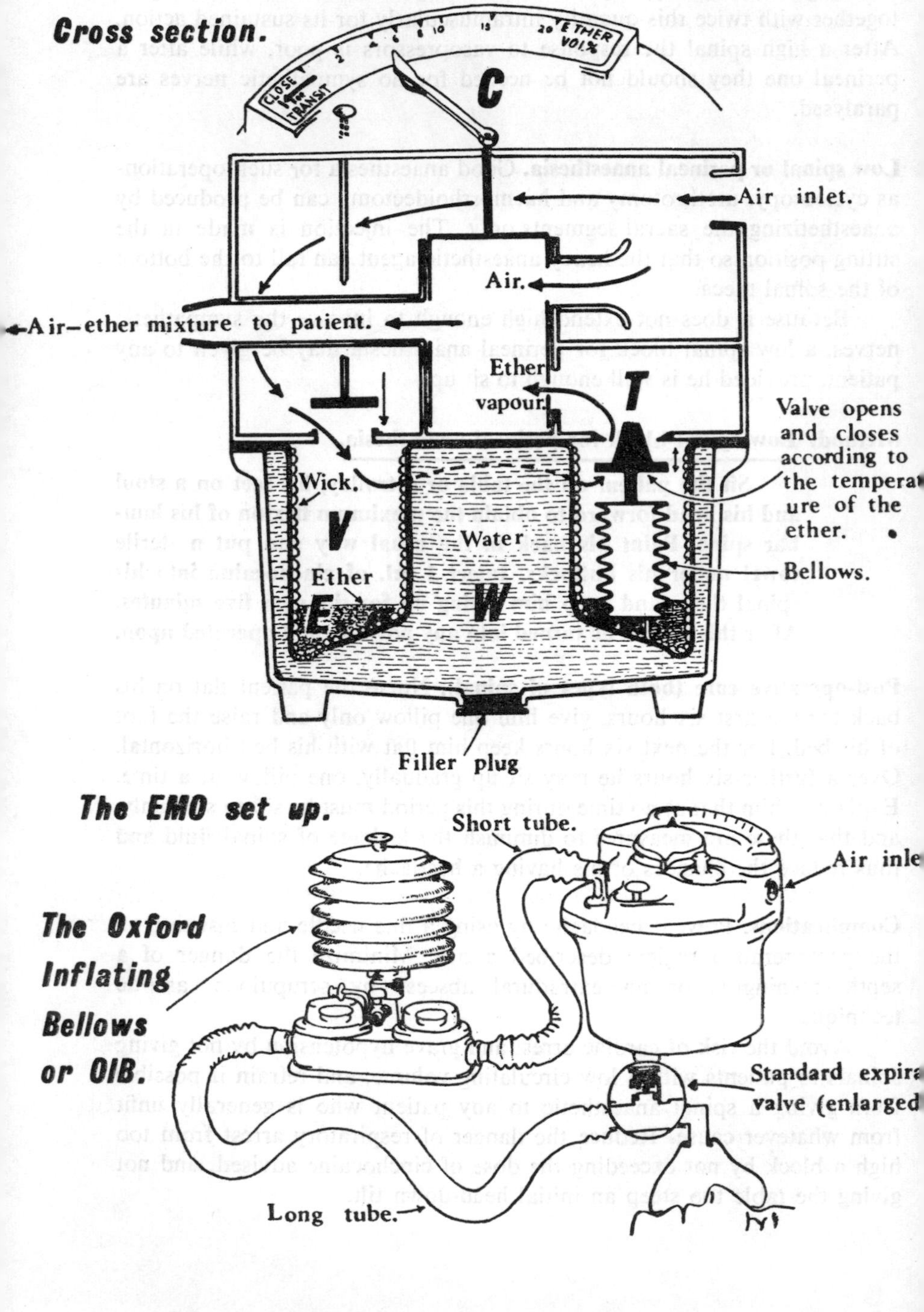

Cross section.

ETHER VOL%
2 4 6 8 10 15 20
CLOSE FOR TRANSIT
C
Air inlet.
Air.
Air–ether mixture to patient.
Ether vapour.
T
Valve opens and closes according to the temperature of the ether.
Wick.
V
Water
Ether
E
W
Bellows.
Filler plug

The EMO set up.

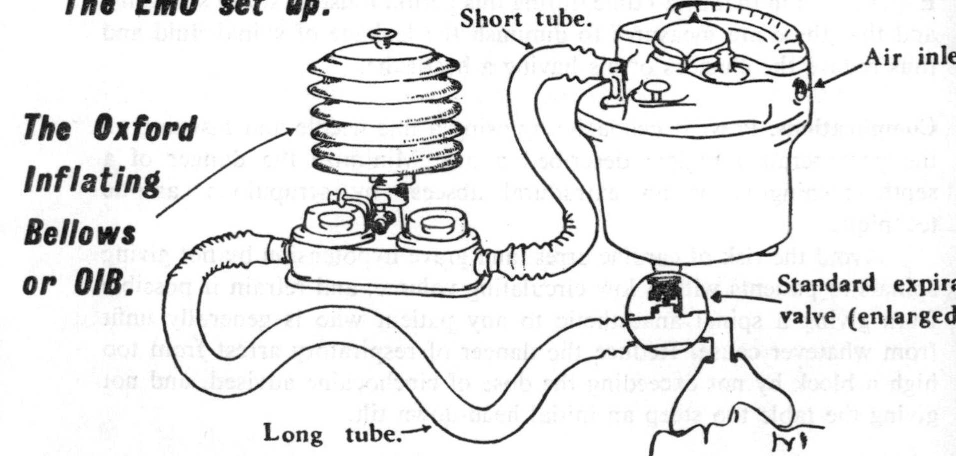

THE EMO INHALER

13 **Description.** The inhaler is illustrated in Figure 49. A vapourising chamber (V) is surrounded by a water jacket (W) which acts as a buffer against extreme changes in the temperature of the surrounding air. An automatic thermo-compensator (T) regulates the volume of ether vapour leaving the vaporizing chamber of the machine according to the temperature of the liquid ether (E). This allows more ether vapour to be added to the anaesthetic gases as the ether cools, and thus ensures that the vapour concentration reaching the patient is independent of temperature. When air is drawn through the EMO inhaler, some, depending upon the concentration control setting (C), passes through the ether chamber (V) and then mixes again with air which has bypassed this chamber, the machine being designed so that the concentration of ether reaching the patient is independent of the rate of flow through it.

The EMO inhaler is connected in series with the Oxford Inflating Bellows, or 'OIB' and together they form a unit suitable for almost all types of surgery. Essentially, OIB is a spring loaded concertina bellows with non-return valves either side of it — these valves provide unidirectional flow and eliminate rebreathing. The combination of the OIB and the EMO has many advantages, for during induction, the bellows may be used to blow a low concentration of ether vapour over the patient's nose and mouth, while the mask is held a little way from his face. Once anaesthesia has been established, the bellows form *some* guide to the volume of respiration. The bellows are, of course, only a measure of inspiration, because, while the patient is expiring, the non-return valve closes off the bellows from the patient who expires through the expiratory valve by the face piece. During this time the bellows, under the power of its spring, fills with air and ether vapour from the EMO. If the bellows are to form a true guide of expiration and inspiration, their expiratory valve can be immobilized by the magnet. This must be *for a few breaths only* because no CO_2 will be eliminated during this period.

Artificial respiration is also possible with the EMO-OIB combination, provided the face mask is lifted off the patient's face to allow him to expire. Because this procedure requires much skill, the use of a Reuben valve is advised, for it is easier and makes immediate artificial respiration possible, during an anaesthetic for example.

Apart from its use in conjunction with the EMO, these bellows form a portable unit to be used whenever artificial respiration is required. They may thus prove life saving in cases of poliomyelitis and narcotic poisoning, and ventilation can even be maintained while a patient is in transit. In hospital, a simple mechanical pump can be used to drive the bellows indefinitely.

22:14 **The preparation of the EMO.**

Fill the water jacket. When first obtained, fill the water jacket. Set the concentration control lever to the 'transit' position, turn the machine upside down; unscrew the water filler plug, and remove it as far to the side as the retaining chain will allow. Pour in slowly about 1250 ml. of water at room temperature and replace the plug.

Check the water level every few months to make sure that it is still full.

Fill with ether. Depress the 'filler' knob and pour in ether. (In earlier models pull the ether filler knob upwards and rotate it slightly to lock it in this position). About 150 ml. of liquid will be required to saturate the wicks, after which the ether level indicator will begin to rise, and about 300 ml. will be required to fill it completely, by which time the red disc of the indicator will have moved from 'E' (empty) to 'F' (full). There is no need to fill the EMO completely, but the end disc of the indicator must always be between 'E' and 'F'. Do not over-fill the inhaler by pouring in more ether after the indicator has reached the 'F' position, for if it is too full, the wrong concentration of ether vapour will be delivered to the patient.

After filling, release the filler knob — it will spring back into a closed position. If left open, a dangerously high concentration of ether may reach the patient.

Check the temperature compensator indicator. The temperature compensating mechanism must work correctly as shown by the indicator — a metal rod with a black and red band surmounted by a metal cap (In some models of the EMO, a plastic cover is fitted over the indicator which must be removed in order to inspect it). The rod and the cap must be visible — if they are not the apparatus is too cold. When the black band alone shows, the EMO is at the right working temperature; if the red band is also visible the EMO is too hot.

If the EMO is too cold, either place it in a warm room for some time, or empty the water jacket and refill it with water at 25°C. If the indicator still fails to appear, the apparatus is faulty and it must not be used.

If the EMO is too hot, as may happen with room temperatures above 32°C, cool it, either by filling the jacket with water below the room temperature, or by forcing the ether to evaporate for a few minutes. To do this set the concentration control at 20%, hold the ether filler open, and, with the OIB connected, pump the bellows vigorously for a short time.

After this, not only will the ether temperature be lower, but the piping will be full of very strong ether vapour. To remove this set the concentration control to '0', close the filler knob and give the bellows a few more pumps. Finally, only the black band of the indicator should be visible, signifying that the EMO is now at the right temperature.

15 **The Oxford Inflating Bellows (OIB).** A press stud inside the concertina keeps the bellows closed; release it by a sideways twist of the knob at the top. Two unidirectional valves are visible under the plastic domes, while near them is a small red horse-shoe magnet and a stopcock. *Use this magnet ONLY when it is desired to immobilize the unidirectional valve on the outlet side of the bellows (Figure 50B) — do not do this when using a standard expiratory valve at the facepiece, or rebreathing will take place into the bellows.*

Only immobilize the outlet valve of the OIB when using an automatic inflating valve (e.g. the Reuben valve) instead of the standard expiratory valve. For this purpose attach the magnet to the metal bracket above the plastic dome on the outlet side of the OIB. In this position it draws up the valve and renders it immobile as shown in Figure 50B.

Administer oxygen by opening the stopcock and attaching the tube from an oxygen cylinder and flowmeter to the nipple.

16 **Setting up the complete unit.** This is done as in Figure 49B. The OIB is between the EMO and the patient, the shorter corrugated tube being between the EMO and the bellows, and the longer one joining the bellows to the patient. With this arrangement, the spring inside the bellows draws air containing ether vapour from the inhaler into the concertina. This is then inhaled by the patient from the concertina at his next breath. As the patient expires, the outlet valve of the OIB prevents any return of air through the breathing tube, so that all the expired gasses are forced out through the expiratory valve. Meanwhile, the concertina will have refilled itself from the EMO by virtue of its internal spring.

After use, set the concentration control pointer to the 'transit' position, but the water need not be emptied while any ether remaining in the inhaler may be kept for the next anaesthetic.

METHODS OF ANAESTHESIA IN ADULTS

17 **A simple technique.** Atropine is the only essential drug for premedication, but in a resistant patient the judicial use of morphine or omnopon and scopolamine (10 mgm. /0.22 mgm.) will facilitate smooth induction. On the other hand too large a dose of morphine will lead to respiratory depression and thus slow the uptake of ether. It is sometimes difficult to get busy nursing staff to give the premedication in the way they should, and it may be convenient to do this in the theatre by giving an adult 0.6 mg. of atropine intravenously. Ether can be given ten minutes later when the mouth is dry.

Fig. 50. **TWO FURTHER WAYS OF USING THE EMO.**

A. Both employ intermittent positive pressure respiration, one uses finger occlusion,

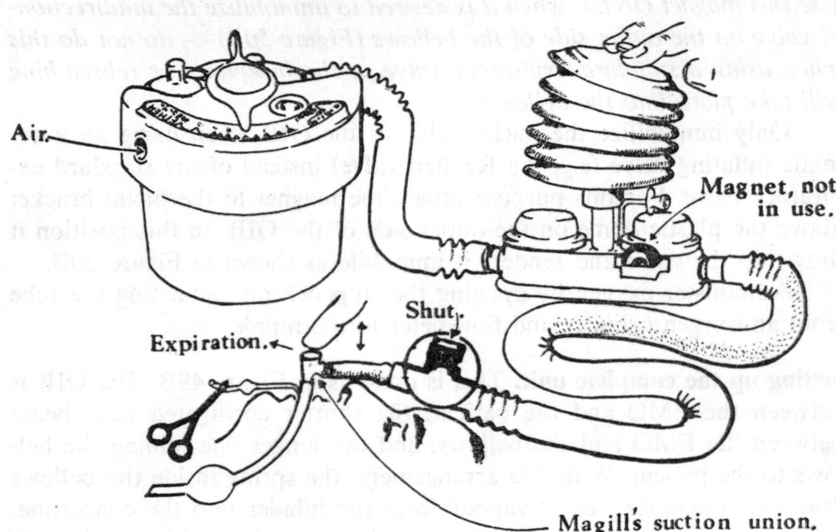

B. the other a Reuben valve.

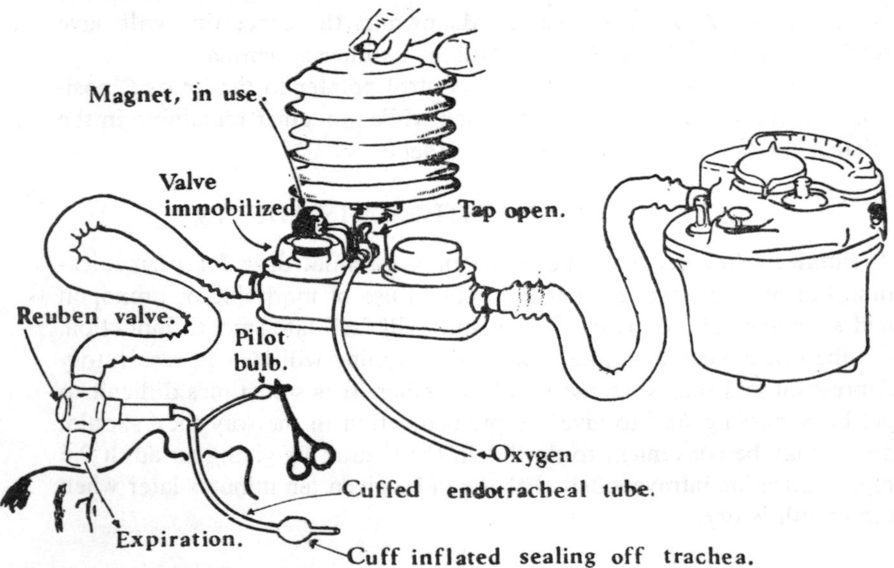

Method: Ether induction with the EMO.

Hold the mask about six inches above the patient's face, and slowly raise and lower the bellows with the concentration control set at 4% — some patients object to this, if they do try 2%. Lower the mask gradually on to the nose and mouth while slowly increasing the concentration to 6%. Once the mask is firmly applied the patient's own respirations will move the bellows, so stop pumping. Steadily increase the concentration of ether to 15% (20% in a robust adult) over the course of the next ten minutes — don't increase the concentration suddenly, because ether is irritant and the patient will cough. However, with reasonable care a very much smoother induction can be achieved with the EMO than with the 'open' method. It is a good rule to wait until the patient has taken six clear breaths (without swallowing or breath-holding) before slightly increasing the concentration.

After breathing 15% ether vapour in air for 10 minutes, the patient will be ready for the surgeon to operate. As anaesthesia proceeds, reduce the concentration to a maintenance level of 6 to 8%. This is enough for surgery that does not require muscular relaxation, and the patient's recovery at the end of anaesthesia will be relatively rapid.

For intra-abdominal surgery, particularly in robust individuals, use concentrations of 15 to 20% to secure muscular relaxation, but, with these higher concentrations respiratory depression may be marked and recovery of consciousness will be delayed.

3 **Induction with intravenous barbiturate.** The slowness and unpleasantness of ether-air induction can be avoided by use of a rapidly acting intravenous barbiturate — thiopentone (Pentothal). Use this drug in 2.5% solution — it is just as effective as the formerly popular 5% solution, and much less dangerous.

Although thiopentone is an easy drug to administer, it is exceptionally dangerous in inexperienced hands, and over-dosage can be rapidly fatal. 0.5 gm., that is 20 ml. of 2.5% solution should be regarded as the maximum induction dose — this should never be exceeded in ordinary circumstances. Aim to give only just enough to produce sleep, more depresses respiration.

Method: Thiopentone induction with the EMO.

Use any vein on the forearm or back of the hand, but avoid the medial side of the antecubital fossa because of the danger

of intra-arterial injection, and the gangrene that follows the injection of thiopentone into an artery. To avoid this, watch out for aberrant arteries, feel for pulsation both before applying a tourniquet to distend the veins, and on releasing it prior to injection. Inject the drug slowly and pause after 2 to 3 ml. have been given to ask the patient whether his arm is quite comfortable. If the reply is 'Yes' continue injecting until gentle stroking of the patient's eyelashes elicits no response — by this time 10 to 12 ml. will usually have been given. Support the patient's jaw if signs of respiratory obstruction appear during the injection. Thiopentone is a powerful respiratory depressant; a momentary cessation of respiration is common during the injection — stop the injection until breathing recommences. If necessary assist the patient's respiration with the OIB.

If a self-sealing needle is available, leave it in a vein on the back of the hand, so that supplementary injections of thiopentone can be given if necessary. When using an ordinary needle, take it out of the vein after the patient has become anaesthetised, apply the face mask as quickly as possible and set the ether concentration at 3 to 4 %. Allow a few breaths, just to ensure that the patient will not object to this concentration, and then proceed as described above — it will usually be possible to begin with a higher ether concentration than when no thiopentone is used.

22:19 **Acknowledgements.** Based on material kindly provided by Dr. J. Farman and Dr. R. M. A. McClelland, and prepared with the assistance of Drs. Brenda Vaughan and Felicity Reynolds of Mulago Hospital.

Chapter Twenty-Three

BLOOD TRANSFUSION

Otto Walter

3:1 **The ultimate objective.** There is a wide gap between the highly organized transfusion services of the industrial countries, and the absence of any tradition of blood donation among developing nations. Their goal must be the eventual creation of the kind of facility shown to such perfection by the National Blood Transfusion Service of the United Kingdom, and some of its peers in a few other fortunate countries. The main features of this service are that blood is given free by the donor. Transfusion is organized without profit on a national scale, and run from regional centres by specialist staff. The service aims to send blood of any group, anywhere in the kingdom, at any hour, and to supply it always in the volume in which it is wanted. But, though this is a great ideal, it is remarkable how closely it is attained in practice.

This section describes the first steps in setting up a transfusion service that will make blood available to the smaller hospitals remote from a national or regional transfusion centre.

RECRUITING DONORS

:2 **'Cross-cultural conflict'.** The first stages in setting up a transfusion service can be very difficult indeed, because, before the populace have become accustomed to it, they almost invariably misunderstand the motives for which transfusion is done. Many cultures impart a mystical significance to blood, and the uneducated often fail to realize that blood shed or donated is quickly replaced by the body. Some donors need reassuring that blood donation will not impair their fertility, or their potency, or give the patient who has received their blood some magical power over them. Because these beliefs and attitudes are of such critical importance, it is essential to enquire just what the local community think about blood transfusion before starting a drive to recruit donors. This is just one example of the usefulness of the cross-cultural outlook described in Chapter Four.

Donor recruitment can thus be a formidable challenge in health education, but it is one to be tackled just like any other task in this field and should be approached along the lines discussed in Chapter Six.

23:3 **Donation by the patient and his family.** The patient himself can be a useful source of blood. This depends on the fact that a pint of blood can be stored three weeks, but in a much shorter time than this most of its constituents will have been restored to the donor's circulation. It may thus be useful to ask patients, on whom some elective surgery is to be performed, to donate a pint of blood two weeks before their operation, so that it can be used later in the theatre should the need arise. No cross-matching is required for such an auto-transfusion, and, apart from the minor hazards of storage, it is perfectly safe, while, should it not be wanted, this is a pint for the blood bank. Failing this, a patient can be told that no elective surgery is possible, unless one of his relatives will donate blood on his behalf, but not necessarily for him specifically. This practice can also be extended to the antenatal clinic, where mothers can be booked for hospital delivery, only on the understanding that some member of the family becomes a blood donor.

Such routine donation by the family to a bank is better than the desperate attempt to find the relatives of particular cases needing blood in a hurry, often in the middle of the night. But it is only the first stage in building a transfusion service, and no more than a temporary stop-gap while the tradition of blood donation is established in the whole community. 'Family donation' has one very important limitation. This is that if a woman is transfused with her husband's blood, she may develop anti-bodies to his blood group antigens which may endanger her children in future pregnancies. Thus, no woman should ever be given her husband's blood.

23:4 **The community.** The secondary schools are often the most convenient source of donors. They should be visited in turn by arrangement with their headmasters, and a short talk given to the whole student body after which time must be allowed for questions. The apparatus should be shown to the audience, and, at the end of the talk, a demonstration should be given of how blood is actually taken; a volunteer can, if necessary, be brought along for the purpose. If the talk and the demonstration are well done plenty of volunteers will usually come forward. Some should be bled immediately, either in the sickbay or in a dormitory, and, if some of the masters themselves become donors, this will be a great encouragement to their pupils. Sixteen is usually the minimum age, but size is more important. On one occasion enthusiasm was so great that two little girls, disappointed by being told that they were too small, asked if they could share a transfusion bottle and fill it up between them — not of course that this is allowed!

There are other sources of blood besides the schools, and having exhausted them, the next institutions to try are the churches, the chiefs and headmen, the police and the prisons. Last of all come government departments and industrial firms. These are often difficult administratively and the response is apt to be poor. Though some employers will produce their staff for a talk just before a pay parade, it is often difficult to get a satisfactory audience. Institutions do not like being troubled too often and should be worked through in a regular six monthly cycle, the most senior person being thanked for the privilege after each visit. If the donors can be bled on the premises, then so much the better, otherwise they will have to be taken back to the hospital and bled there. With all institutions the aim must be to build up a regular tradition of blood donation by continued encouragement.

In the early stages of a transfusion service it will not be possible to summon donors by postcard or telephone. This is however the ultimate ideal, and it is worth making a start by sending out printed cards summoning to regular bleeding sessions all who have once been donors and who are not more conveniently dealt with through the institutions to which they belong. Few will come at first, but these cards are good blood donor education none the less. Newspapers and posters also have a part to play in the educational process and the wider newspaper cover the better.

The tradition of free donation is a priceless asset to any community. Once payment has been started, it may be difficult to stop. Donors should not therefore be paid, however difficult it may be to find them, even if there is money available for the purpose. If the patient has to be charged, it should be made clear to him that this charge is one for apparatus and services only, and that the blood itself is a present to him from the donor.

Though hospitals vary widely in the volume of blood they use, it can be taken as a general guide that each hospital bed will require about 1500 ml. (3 pints) of blood each year. Only when this level of donation is achieved, can a transfusion service be considered to have reached a satisfactory level of development.

5 **Records and badges.** Blood donor badges (GAU) are often treasured by their possessors, besides being a good advertisement for the transfusion service. Each donor should therefore be sent one with his card as soon

as his first pint has been grouped. Ideally, these cards should be printed on a nation-wide scale with spaces to insert the name of the hospital, the name of the donor, his group, and the laboratory record number; there should also be space enough to record the date and signature for a dozen donations. These cards should be desirable possessions, they should be folded in half to make a little booklet, be small enough to fit inside a wallet and be variously coloured for the four main blood groups. Because colours reduce the chance of clerical error, they should distinguish all transfusion stationery; blue for group O, yellow for group A, pink for group B, and white for group AB. Coloured stationery of this kind becomes increasingly important as a service grows, and the number of cards and forms printed must reflect the blood group frequency of the population they are intended for.

If booklets seem a luxury, donors can be given a simple card printed with the outline of several empty transfusion bottles. Each time a donation is made the outline of one of these bottles is filled in with red chalk to indicate that it is now full — a useful device with an unsophisticated community.

In the hospital itself each donor needs a card. These are conveniently made 20 cms. x 12 cms. (8″ x 5″), the smallest size that most duplicating machines will handle, and stencilled with boxes for the donor's name, his address, his blood group, and the laboratory data. They are usually better filed by institution than by blood group and are more convenient than a ledger.

23:6 **The transfusionist.** Blood transfusion is time-consuming. Who is to do it? Early on it has to be done by a doctor, because the effort to get a bank going and to secure the good will of the schools requires drive and personality beyond that of the average assistant. Right from the start, however, a doctor must be assisted by someone who will later be able to take over the routine work, and the training of such a 'transfusionist', must be an early priority. Though highly responsible, blood transfusion is not only monotonous and technical, but to most doctors it is tedious beyond measure. Furthermore, in developing countries doctors are too valuable to use like this, and anyway someone with only a secondary education can be taught to do this work very well. School leavers are best trained in special courses, but, when it is not possible to find someone trained in this way, a suitable recruit will have to be trained from scratch 'in service', or some existing member of the hospital staff will have to be adapted to this role. A trainee will need to be taught how to take blood from donors and how to group, store and cross-match it. He will be even more useful if he can also learn to set up a transfusion. Because a trainee transfusionist will probably have to start work when still only partly trained, an important safety measure must be to insist that he shows every cross-match he does to a second observer for verification, and continues to do this until he is really reliable.

Until the bank handles about 25 pints a week the work of a transfusionist will be part time only and he should be able to assist with other duties also. Transfusionists need to be of some personality, if they are to be effective in recruiting blood donors, and will be more useful if they can also drive a small van.

Auxiliaries of this kind make transfusion services possible, but, though these will not be perfect, they will be better than those now existing in many places, and which amount in effect to nothing. The consequences of error are no greater in blood transfusion than they are in anaesthesia, and partly trained anaesthetic assistants have been common for a long time. There have been and there will be anaesthetic deaths, and there have been and there will be some very occasional transfusion deaths also, but the lives lost will be a tiny fraction of those saved in the operating theatre, or rescued by blood transfusion. Like an anaesthetic or a surgical operation, any blood transfusion is a calculated risk. The risks will be greater in blood banks run by auxiliaries and the indications for transfusion will be different, but the risks of not giving blood may well be certain death. The only attitude must be to reduce them as much as humanly possible, weigh them up and proceed accordingly.

MATERIALS AND METHODS.

7 **Apparatus.** There is a choice between disposable and reusable equipment. A disposable giving and taking set together costs about 7/- ($1) (CIP) (POV), reusable ones just under 10/6 ($1.5). Because most of the equipment in a reusable set lasts indefinitely, sets of this kind will prove more economical where labour is cheap. The type that is advised is that developed by the Medical Research Council of the United Kingdom (the 'MRC'). This is shown in Figure 51 and described in Table 13. Its parts fit into a special tin, but neither this nor the band which fits in the groove on the base of the bottle are shown in this figure. This equipment can be obtained from a single supplier (TUR). The great advantage of reusable equipment of this kind is its economy in the giving of salines, formulas for these and for 'acid-citrate-dextrose' for blood transfusion being given in section 30:2. These sets require careful cleaning and assembly in the following way.

Method: Cleaning MRC blood transfusion apparatus.

Soak the drip sets in water immediately after use, take them to pieces completely, scrub the gauze well with a nail brush,

wash through with large volumes of tap water, follow this if possible with plenty of distilled water, reassemble them cutting off the ends of the tubing if this fits loosely, wrap them in paper and sterilize them in a tin. Use silicone tubing for most of the set, but keep a short rubber section for injections into the drip — silicone tubing leaks if pierced with a needle. Use fresh rubber closures each time, because bacteria may enter through a pierced cap.

TABLE 13

SPECIFICATIONS AND SUPPLIERS FOR MRC BLOOD TRANSFUSION APPARATUS

Description

1. Cap, metal, screw thread with 14 mm. hole for transfusion bottle.
2. Rubber disc, for metal screw cap.
3. Viscap, white opaque, size 6 cut down to $2\frac{1}{4}''$ for use on transfusion bottle also supplied by (VDC).
4. Needle transfusion, giving 1.5 x 35 mm. Olive tubing mount.
5. MRC pattern I.V. cannula 37.5 mm. x 15 BWG.
6. Adaptor male metal olive tubing mount.
7. Tubing blood transfusion red rubber $\frac{3}{16}''$ bore x $\frac{1}{16}''$ wall.
8. Tubing, blood transfusion silicone $\frac{3}{16}''$ bore x $\frac{1}{16}''$ wall.
9. Drip counter, glass, MRC type.
10. Clamp, regulating MRC pattern
11. Tube, glass $9\frac{1}{2}''$ for MRC giving set.
12. Bung rubber with two holes MRC type.
13. Filter, gauze, metal MRC type.
14. Tubing, polyvinyl chloride 4 mm. bore.

15a. Needle blood taking 1.9 x 40 mm.

15b. Needle, blood transfusion closure piercing 2.1 x 37 mm.

16. Transfusion bottle, 540 ml. capacity, straight sided flint glass.
17. Tube, glass $2\frac{1}{2}''$ for MRC type giving set.

23:8 **Bleeding donors.** A transfusionist soon becomes better at doing this than most doctors. If the local community recognize jaundice, donors who have had it should be turned away: the anaemic should also be excluded by one of the methods described in Chapter Twenty-Four. Transfusion bottles can either be filled by the vacuum method or by gravity. The 'taking set' used is pictured in Figure 51.

Method: Blood donation.

Tie a luggage label on to the bottle, label it with the donor's name, his blood group and the date, and write in also the date when the blood will expire exactly three weeks later.

Lie the patient on a couch, examine both his arms and select the best vein. Inspect the bottle carefully, especially if it is locally made, to make sure that the anticoagulant is perfectly clear and uninfected. Apply a sphygmomanometer cuff to the

Fig. 51. **M.R.C. BLOOD TRANSFUSION APPARATUS.**

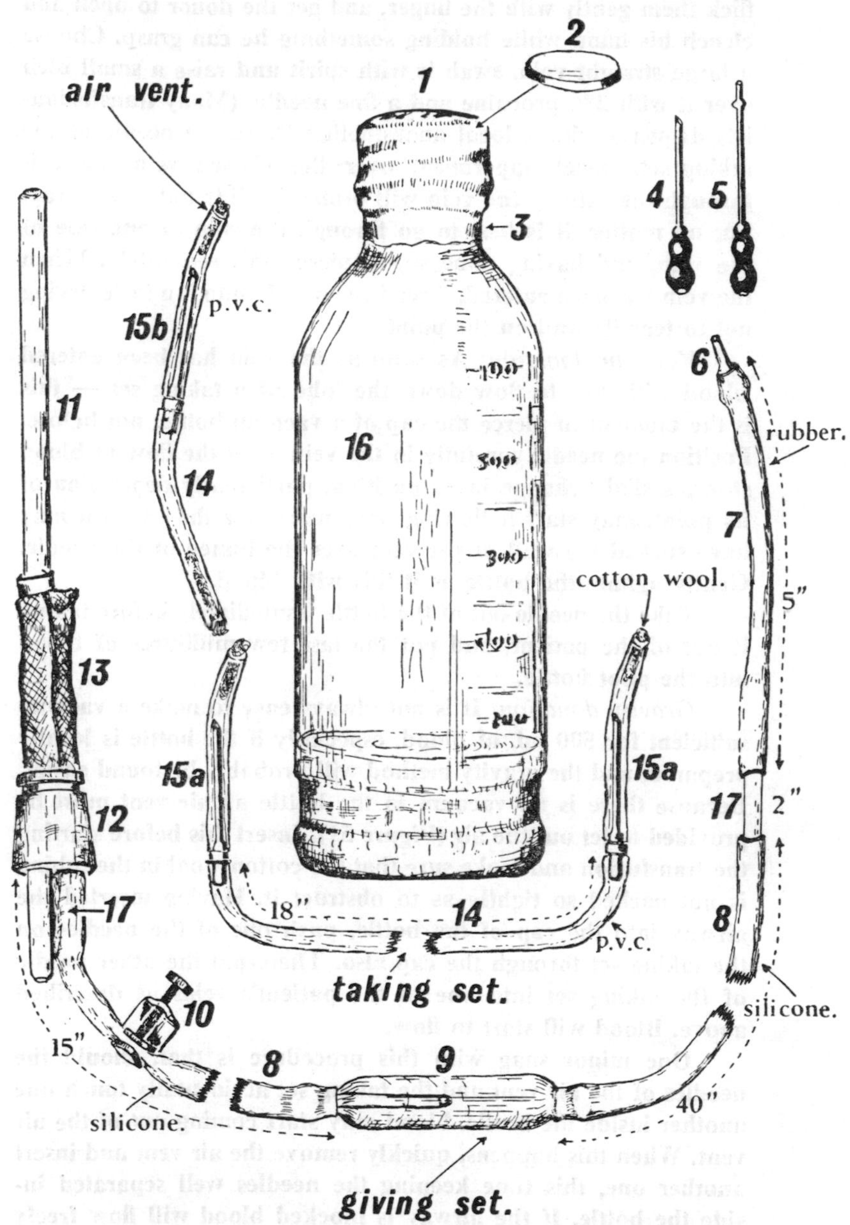

(SEE TABLE 13 FOR DETAILS.)

upper arm and inflate it to 50-60 mm. Hg. — not more. Put a hand round the donor's forearm and squeeze the blood up towards his elbow — this dilates the veins: if they are still small flick them gently with the finger, and get the donor to open and clench his hand while holding something he can grasp. Choose a large straight vein, swab it with spirit and raise a small bleb over it with 2% procaine and a fine needle. (Many transfusionists dispense with a local anaesthetic.) Place the needle of the taking set, bevel uppermost, over the chosen vein, push it through the skin — the vein will probably slide out of the way, but no matter, it is best to go through the skin to one side of the vein, and having done so, to pierce this separately. When the vein has been entered, thread the needle into it a little, trying not to tear its wall on the point.

Vacuum donation. As soon as the vein has been entered blood will start to flow down the tube of a taking set — this is the moment to pierce the cap of a vacuum bottle, not before. Position the needle carefully in the vein — if the flow of blood stops, a slight change in its position, particularly depression of its point, may start it flowing once more, for the vacuum may have sucked the wall of the vein over the lumen of the needle. Gently agitate the bottle as it fills with blood.

Take the needle out of the bottle immediately before taking it out of the patient, and put the last few millilitres of blood into the pilot bottle.

Gravity donation. It is not always easy to make a vacuum sufficient for 500 ml. of blood, especially if the bottle is locally prepared, and the gravity method will probably be found easier. Because there is no vacuum in the bottle an air vent must be provided to let out the air (Figure 51). Insert this before starting the transfusion and make sure that the cotton wool in the tubing is not packed so tightly as to obstruct it. Having inserted the airway into the cap of the bottle, push one of the needles on the taking set through the cap also. Then, put the other needle of the taking set into one of the patient's veins as described above. Blood will start to flow.

One minor snag with this procedure is that, should the needles of the air vent and the taking set accidentally touch one another inside the bottle, blood may start coming out of the air vent. When this happens, quickly remove the air vent and insert another one, this time keeping the needles well separated inside the bottle. If the airway is blocked blood will flow freely at first and then stop.

Be careful not to lower the pressure in the sphygmomanometer while the bottle is filling, because the air in the bottle may be under sufficient positive pressure to flow back up the tube and into the veins of the patient. Make sure therefore that the pressure in the sphymomanometer is never lowered without first clamping the tube on the taking set. Keep a pair of artery forceps for the purpose.

Keep all donors lying down for ten minutes after they have given blood, for they sometimes faint if they stand up quickly after a donation. Don't bleed them again for at least three, and preferably not for six months.

23:9 **The blood bank.** No rule can be defined as to when it is worth supplementing a donor panel — 'a walking blood bank' — by a continuously maintained stock of refrigerated blood. This will depend upon the number of transfusions given, the ease with which donors can be called in a hurry, the number of cases likely to want blood urgently and the reliability of the refrigerator itself. However, when more than four pints of blood are given each week it will probably be worth keeping a blood bank, and, anyway, it is always useful to have a refrigerator set carefully at 4°C so that the occasional bottle of blood can be held a few days if need be.

When calls for blood are infrequent a panel of donors is enough, but some of them must be close at hand so that they are easily called in an emergency. Though the hospital staff themselves form the most accessible panel, there is a temptation to call on them too often, and they should only be used as a last resort.

Small refrigerator units are made which are admirably suited to the needs of the smaller blood bank (FRI), but in default of one of these a domestic refrigerator can be used instead. The electrical compressor variety maintain a more even temperature than the absorption type running on paraffin or gas, but neither are really satisfactory for the prolonged storage of blood, and the sooner a special one is obtained the better.

A clockwork recording thermometer (BRI) is the best way of recording temperature, but a mercury and alcohol maximum and minimum thermometer is an effective substitute. This should be kept in a transfusion filled with water for bottles of blood will follow the same temperature changes. The best temperature is 4°C, though a range from plus 6°C down to minus 0.5°C is just permissible. Blood must never be stored in the freezing compartment of a refrigerator, and discarded immediately it freezes — such blood is lethal. Check the temperature of the refrigerator frequently.

Blood should not be used unless there is a clear line of demarcation between the sedimented cells and supernatant plasma; this should be straw coloured and free from visible signs of haemolysis. Haemolysis is shown by a reddish purple discoloration in the plasma immediately above the cell layer, which gradually spreads upwards. Fat may collect as a white layer on the surface of the plasma in some bottles: this is not a contraindication to the use of the blood. Haemolysis is easily seen but the changes of infection are more subtle. However, provided it has been taken with reasonable skill, and not opened meanwhile, the chances of infection are slight — in case of doubt tip the bottle down the sink.

Gross clotting is another cause of waste and is due to layering of blood in a bottle or plastic bag as it is taken from the donor. This prevents it being properly mixed with the anticoagulant, and can be prevented by agitating the container as it is filled from the donor.

Some waste cannot be helped, but if in a small bank as little as a quarter is eventually thrown away, the hospital is lucky. Blood is better thrown away when there is the slightest doubt as to its safety, for wasted blood is better than a dead patient.

23:10 **The 'Eldon Card'** (NOR). These are cards with a smooth waterproof surface printed with several panels on two of which anti A and anti B sera have been dried. These antisera are reconstituted with a drop of tap water after which capillary blood is added to them. The mixtures of blood and reconstituted serum are then stirred with a special rod whereupon agglutination occurs and is visible to the naked eye. Cards are also prepared which enable rhesus testing to be undertaken.

Detailed instructions are provided with every card so they will not be repeated here: the important fact about them is that they must be followed *exactly* and only the special droppers and stirring sticks provided with the cards used for the procedures described. Cards can be left to dry out and stored, but false agglutinations may occur as the panels dry, so they are best not used as a permanent record. Heavy rouleaux formation (see below) sometimes makes grouping impossible, agglutination being seen in all squares including the control. When this happens, and also when the patient is very anaemic, his cells should be washed in saline (again see below) and concentrated to approximately the strength of normal blood before being used on a card.

The Eldon card is a useful way of blood grouping but it is a poor way of cross matching, particularly in the tropics where abnormal serum globulin patterns are common. Patients grouped on Eldon cards must therefore be cross matched by one of the methods which follow.

A serious disadvantage of Eldon cards is their cost, and at 2/- ($0.28) each they become expensive when a blood bank grows to any size. When this happens liquid sera should be obtained and used by the technique about to be described. For the occasional user Eldon cards are the best method of blood grouping; they are also the best way of determining the occasional rhesus group. Thus, the hospital which is starting its transfusion service, and that which is starting to undertake rhesus grouping, is advised to begin by laying in a stock of these cards, and to change to the use of liquid sera as its experience grows.

11 **ABO grouping.** Liquid anti A and anti B sera should be prepared from local donors and distributed by a central blood transfusion laboratory. When they are not available from this source sera can be obtained, either freeze dried or in liquid form, from a commercial supplier (POV). Dried serum must be reconstituted carefully with distilled water and all liquid sera must be stored in a refrigerator, preferably frozen solid. This will minimize the danger of their deteriorating and so losing their effectiveness; it will also lessen the danger of their becoming infected, as also will their preservation with 0.1% sodium azide. Such preservation is usually done by the manufacturers, and should be a routine measure with all sera issued for use by small blood banks. Nevertheless every new batch of sera used must be tested against controls of A and B cells; sera should also be retested if they have been stored for more than a day or two. Many experienced workers advise the setting up of controls *every* time a blood sample is grouped. Suitable cell samples for testing can be taken by pricking the ear or finger of members of the staff whose group is known. Better still, some control cells can be kept refrigerated in a little sterile acid-citrate-dextrose and renewed from time to time. The practice of colouring anti A serum blue or green and anti B serum yellow is highly commended, for, like coloured cards, it reduces error.

In order to avoid false positive reactions, cells for grouping and cross matching must first be 'washed'. By washing is meant centrifuging them in at least twenty times their volume of saline so as to remove any serum present. This is particularly important in the tropics, where the incidence of abnormal serum globulins that might cause confusion is higher than it is elsewhere.

The methods to be used both for grouping and cross matching are depicted in Figure 52. Here, it is assumed that a bottle of blood has been taken from a donor and is being grouped by the procedures at the top of the figure. In the lower part of the page this blood is then cross matched against the serum of a patient who has previously been grouped. For pictorial convenience he is found to be of the same group as the bottle in the diagram. Two different methods of cross matching are shown, one (continuous line) is the saline cross match; the other (interrupted line) is the albumen cross match.

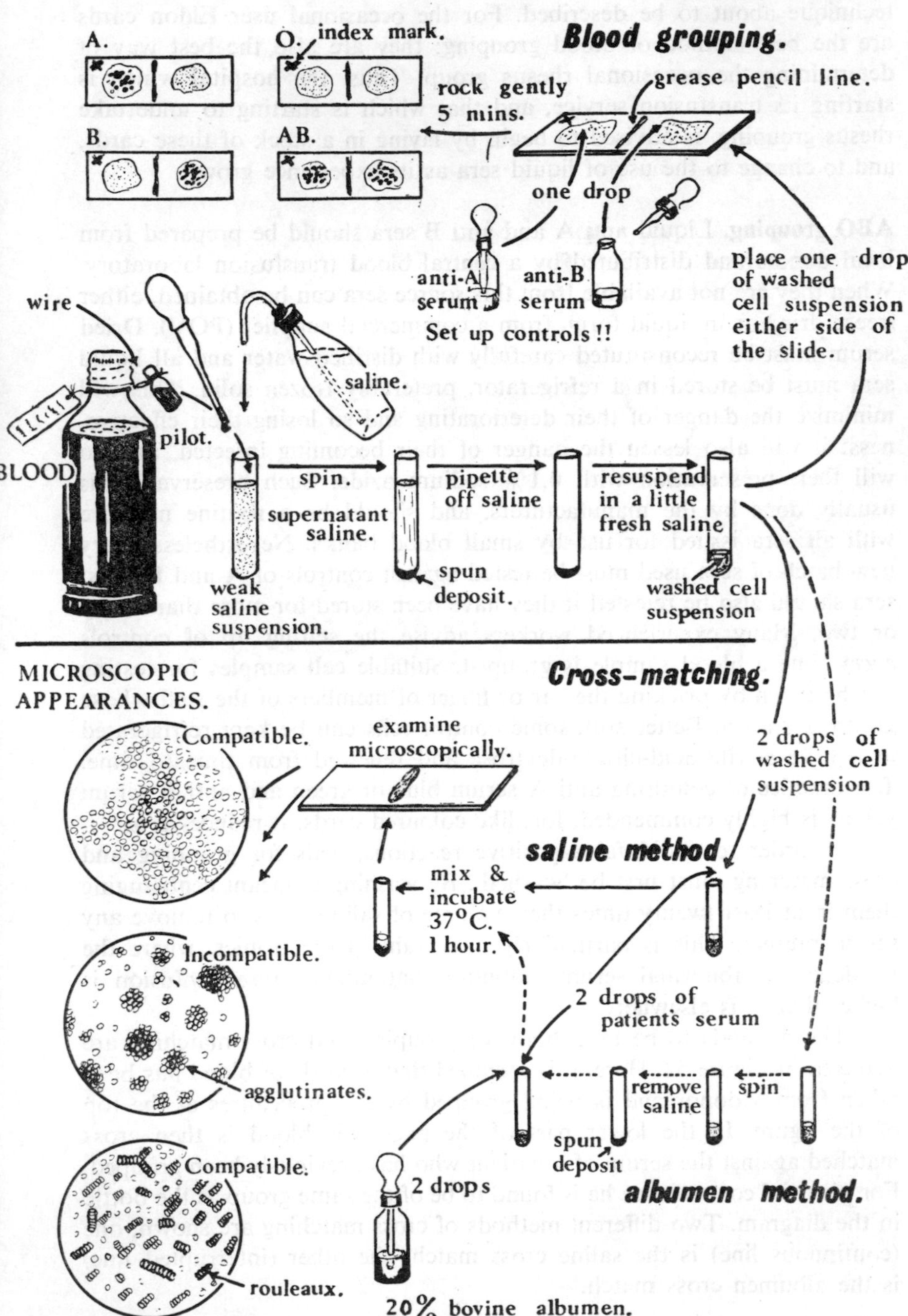
Fig. 52. AN AID TO BLOOD GROUPING & CROSS-MATCHING.
Blood grouping.
A.
O.
index mark.
B.
AB.
rock gently 5 mins.
grease pencil line.
one drop
anti-A serum
anti-B serum
Set up controls !!
place one drop of washed cell suspension either side of the slide.
wire
saline.
pilot.
BLOOD
spin.
supernatant saline.
weak saline suspension.
pipette off saline
spun deposit.
resuspend in a little fresh saline
washed cell suspension
MICROSCOPIC APPEARANCES.
Cross-matching.
Compatible.
examine microscopically.
2 drops of washed cell suspension
saline method
mix & incubate 37°C. 1 hour.
Incompatible.
agglutinates.
2 drops of patients serum
remove saline
spin
spun deposit
Compatible.
2 drops
albumen method.
rouleaux.
20% bovine albumen.

Method: ABO grouping on a slide or tile.

Fill a plastic cup with clean saline and put an empty one next to it into which to rinse the pipette. Fill a Kahn tube (24:7) with saline from a wash bottle, and, using a Pasteur pipette and teat, add to it about five drops of citrated blood from a pilot bottle, or a little clot from a clotted specimen. Mix, and make sure that any clot is well broken up. Spin (centrifuge) the suspension, pipette off the supernatant, resuspend the cells in just enough saline to make about 5% suspension — judge this with practice and don't make it too weak.

Divide a slide in half with a grease pencil, and make a cross or index mark in its top left hand corner to prevent it being turned round by mistake. Put a drop of suspension on each half of the slide. Add a drop of anti A to the left hand drop and anti B to the right, rock the slide gently back and forth. Observe the agglutination which will be readily seen as clumps of cells visible to the naked eye.

Sometimes fresh serum may lyse rather than agglutinate the cells to which it is added; this is due to the complement it contains and is to be read as a *positive* **reaction, with the same significance as agglutination.**

If there is doubt about the potency of sera used for slide grouping in this way, leave two drops of the washed cells and two of antiserum in a small tube, preferably for two hours, and then examine the mixture microscopically. At the same time, test the patient's serum, and the grouping serum, with known samples of A cells and B cells in the same way.

Rinse out the pipette well between all samples, particularly after it has contained grouping serum. If the pipette is difficult to empty, blow out the last drops with its end held against the side of the cup.

A white builder's tile or a piece of plastic sheet can also be used for grouping, and is often more convenient as it enables several specimens to be tested at the same time.

2 **Cross matching.** *All blood should be cross matched,* exceptions being permissible in only the direst emergencies. This is done by incubating the serum of the recipient with the cells of the donor for one hour at 37°C. A waterbath to maintain this temperature is therefore essential equipment (HEA) (GRA). **Only if there is no agglutination when the mixture is examined microscopically at the end of this time is the blood fit for transfusion.** Of the two methods described, the albumen (POV) method is much the best.

Method: The saline cross match.

Prepare a washed 5% cell suspension of the donor's blood as described above. Put two drops of this and two drops of the patient's serum in a clean 2 x ¼ inch tube. Mix, incubate for one hour at 37°C in a waterbath. Gently remove the cells with a Pasteur pipette, lay them across a slide and look for agglutinates microscopically. If no agglutinates are seen the blood is safe for transfusion.

Method: The albumen cross match.

Put two drops of washed 5% donor's cells in a clean 2 x ¼ inch tube, spin and carefully remove the supernatant with a *fine* **Pasteur pipette taking care not to disturb the cells at the bottom of the tube. To the nearly dry button of cells, add two drops of patient's serum and two drops of 20% albumen (keep the albumen in a dropping bottle; some prefer 30%). Mix by flicking the bottom of the tube and incubate at 37°C for an hour. Spin the tube** *very gently* **for a minute (not shown in Figure 52) and examine the deposited cells microscopically as above.**

'Rouleaux formation' is a common cause of confusion: it is due to a property possessed by some sera containing abnormal globulins that makes all red cells with which they are in contact lie together like piles of coins (Figure 52). These piles or columns of cells are different from the random adhesion of agglutination and are without significance. Rouleaux formation may be seen combined with agglutination, and there are occasions when it may not be easy to distinguish them by methods within the scope of this chapter. When in doubt the blood is best not given. Dextran and other 'plasma expanders' produce conspicuous rouleaux formation, so, to avoid the confusion that this might cause, blood must be taken for cross matching before any of these substances are given.

In grave emergency a cross match can be shortened to 15 minutes. If curtailed like this, the saline as well as the albumen type of cross match should be spun gently before being examined.

23:13 **Rhesus grouping.** In the rural hospitals with which this symposium is concerned the importance of rhesus grouping is disputed; however, one thing is certain — it is better to transfuse on the basis of the ABO group alone, than not to transfuse at all. Little difficulty would be expected from the low percentage of rhesus negative individuals in many tropical communities, and in the tropical new-born severe jaundice is probably more often due to prematurity and infection than it is to erythroblastosis.

Added to the comparative difficulty of the technique itself, the cost of commercial rhesus antiserum is likely to be prohibitive, and those wanting to be able to undertake occasional rhesus testing are advised to use Eldon cards. If blood transfusion has to be started from scratch under very difficult circumstances, it is best to begin by ABO grouping and to resolve to commence rhesus grouping as soon as possible.

If rhesus serum is obtained, it may be of the saline type, in which case it should be used in small tubes with a saline suspension of cells incubated at 37°C for an hour, or it may be of the so-called albumen variety, in which case it should be used just as if an albumen cross-match were done, except that this serum is used and not that of the patient. With both types of sera, small drops of both serum and cells should be used so as to conserve this expensive reagent. *Some* rhesus sera are so potent that they can be used on a slide; if this is so, instructions will be supplied with the serum.

4 **Safety measures.** Besides cross matching in all but the very gravest emergencies, another useful routine precaution is to check on a tile the ABO group of all blood taken from the bank, especially if it has to be given in a hurry. This is rapidly done, and is a very valuable additional precaution, particularly when the transfusionist is only partly trained.

The great danger is an ABO mis-matched transfusion, which is a much more likely cause of disaster than the subtle antibodies that would only be detected by more refined methods of cross matching than those described here. Besides the scrupulous checking of names on all occasions, there are certain other precautions to be taken.

One is to wire, with a pair of pliers, a 'pilot bottle' to every bottle of blood (Figure 52). These are conveniently 'Bijou bottles' (24:9) containing 1 ml. of acid-citrate dextrose, into which are put the last few drops of the donor's blood, when the main bottle itself is full. Cells for grouping and cross matching are taken from this pilot bottle and *never* because of the danger of infection, from the main bottle itself. To avoid confusion, the pilot bottle must *never* leave the main bottle, to which it is wired, until they are both eventually washed up when the transfusion is successfully completed.

No pilot bottle is required if disposable plastic taking sets are used, because the tube forming the taking set is merely knotted in several places, and one of these knotted sections is simply cut off and the cells inside it removed.

Transfusion reactions. There is no way to tell if a mild fever is simply the response to an unimportant pyrogen, or heralds a major transfusion reaction. A blood transfusion should therefore always be stopped in cases of doubt, particularly if the patient has rigors, or feels pain in the back or chest.

Method: The measures to be taken in a transfusion reaction.

When incompatibility is suspected, recheck the group of the blood sent to the laboratory, that in the bottle and that of the patient. If blood is still required, do not hesitate to give further compatible blood or dextran. Warm the patient and give him morphia. Measure the urine output, and, while anuria lasts supply fluid to cover this and the insensible loss (1500 ml. daily in a tropical climate — more if the patient is sweating profusely) but give no electrolytes until urine is passing again. Be careful about giving drugs that are excreted by the kidneys, lest toxic quantities accumulate in the body, and transfer anuric cases to a large institution as soon as possible.

23:16 **Plasma and packed cells.** Two useful blood fractions are easily prepared, they are plasma and packed cells. When a pint of blood is left undisturbed in the refrigerator, the cells pack, or sediment, to the bottom, and the supernatant plasma can be removed for storage in another bottle. The separation of plasma and cells should be a common procedure, because both chronic anaemias needing packed cells, and burnt patients needing plasma will probably be common.

Method: The preparation of plasma and packed cells.

To one end of an eight inch length of rubber tubing, attach the same length of glass tube; to the other end attach a large needle. Wrap the whole in paper and autoclave it.

Autoclave a clean empty bottle with its lid on loosely, taking care to discharge the air in the autoclave in the correct manner. When autoclaving is over and the pressure in the autoclave has reached atmospheric once more, take out the bottle and immediately screw its lid down tight — the condensing steam will leave a vacuum behind it.

Introduce the end of the glass tube aseptically below the surface of the plasma of a well sedimented bottle of blood, push the needle through the cap of the vacuum bottle whereupon the plasma will run over leaving packed cells behind.

If this equipment is not available, put a drip set in a well sedimented bottle of blood and slowly invert it. Keep it still and transfuse only the packed cells in its lower half.

Use both plasma and packed cells within 24 hours, unless the plasma can be frozen solid in the freezing compartment of a

very cold refrigerator. Here, provided it stays frozen solid, it will probably keep several weeks.

17 **Some minor points.** The intravenous route is the common one by which transfusions are given. In adults this is usually easy, but it may be difficult to give children blood this way, though the use of a scalp vein may make matters easier (15:11). As an alternative, the intraperitoneal route (15:10) has much to commend it when treating chronic anaemia in children, and no immediate increase in blood volume is required. By this route there is a detectable rise in haemoglobin 24 hours after a transfusion, and improvement continues for as long as a week. In such diseases as thalassaemia and chronic hookworm anaemia, this is thus a very useful as well as a very easy procedure (13:7).

Blood in the peritoneal cavity is important in quite another way — as a complication of ectopic gestation. Here it should be collected at operation in a small basin, filtered through a funnel containing some gauze to remove the clots, and returned to the circulation through an intravenous drip. Blood up to three days old is usually well tolerated, and it has been given when a week old without mishap.

In an endemic area no account need be taken of malaria in blood donors, for transfusion does not compare in importance with the mosquito in the transmission of this parasite. Microfilaria transferred by transfusion do not develop further and are thus harmless. If it is not possible to exclude syphilis serologically, either let the spirochetes die out by storing the blood three days, or give 2 ml. of procaine penicillin (600,000 units) at the same time as the transfusion.

A mother's serum can be used for cross matching blood for her child only in the first three months of his life, and it is usually also safe to give him her blood during this period. The important exception is erythroblastosis foetalis, which may not be easy to diagnose in the absence of a Coombs' test. However, an icteric and anaemic neonate is probably suffering from erythroblastosis if numerous nucleated red cells can be found in its peripheral blood film (24:17).

Chapter Twenty-Four

THE LABORATORY

Maurice King

THE LABORATORY IN GENERAL

24:1 **A laboratory for the laboratory assistant.** Laboratory technicians are scarce, but, although increasing numbers of them are now being trained, there will long be hospitals where laboratory assistants (7:2) have to do most of the work. Such assistants are frequently poorly trained and are often given too much to do, but it is not this that usually makes their laboratories so inadequate; it is rather the little interest that is wont to be taken in them, combined with a lack of knowledge of the methods they should be using and the equipment that these require.

One of the purposes of this chapter is to remedy these last two deficiencies by giving a detailed account of the methods suited to laboratories of this kind, which is closely integrated with appendices on apparatus and reagents. Together, they form an outfit which has been selected so as to make a wide range of methods possible on a very limited budget. This outfit is to be looked upon as forming the *minimum* laboratory. Readers whose laboratories are less than this, are advised to check what they have against appendices E and F, and order what they lack as soon as possible. As with drugs in the dispensary (8:9), the newcomer to a hospital is advised to look round the laboratory as soon as he arrives, consult the appendices and to set about obtaining the essential reagents and minor equipment that may be missing. So often, the real hindrance to a reasonable service is not having the right minor equipment. This is so comparatively inexpensive that cost hardly applies (8:9) (12:9).

These laboratory methods can only be used if stores departments are prepared to stock and issue the equipment listed in the appendices: such lists will be of great advantage and some medical stores are already using them. It must be stressed that together this equipment forms an 'outfit', and one item is often useless without another. Thus, the writer found that one stores department had ordered and issued the Lovibond blood sugar discs without the comparator or the reagents going with them. Alone, these discs were completely useless.

But this chapter has other purposes; it is the basis of the clinical pathology teaching here at Makerere, for these are also the methods with which all doctors practising in the tropics must be familiar. They are also the routine methods for the student and houseman in the ward side rooms, for the doctor in the up-country hospital and for the general practitioner in his clinic. Many of them are also suited for use by auxiliaries at health centres. Although the tests are described in sufficient detail for a doctor to be able to carry them out himself, and teach an auxiliary, there is insufficient space to describe them in a way which will make them self-explanatory to a laboratory assistant. In the near future therefore, it is proposed to expand the descriptions, to add many more illustrations, and so produce 'A Manual of Clinical Pathology for Developing Countries' based on the same apparatus and techniques.

Though they are not usually considered laboratory techniques, biopsy of the marrow and liver are important diagnostic procedures in the tropics, and it has been found convenient to include an account of them here. This has also been found to be the best place to discuss the rational management of anaemia based on the methods this chapter describes.

4:2 **Making the most of the laboratory.** A doctor's time is too valuable for him to spend much of it in the laboratory, but he will find it very useful to know how to do the tests described here. Many of them can be done so rapidly, that it is quicker for a doctor to do them himself, than it would be for him to call in an assistant after working hours. The time spent becoming really 'slick' at these tests is thus likely to be well repaid. A working knowledge of laboratory procedures also enables a doctor to supervise and, if need be, teach his assistants, who are more likely to be conscientious if they know that their work can be checked. Regular visits to the laboratory do much for the morale of its staff, and all particularly urgent or exacting work is better taken to the laboratory in person. Those who send in specimens often get the answers they deserve, and courtesy in dealing with a laboratory is always well rewarded. It is also a great help if specimens reach a laboratory early in the day.

When the reliability of a laboratory is in doubt, a useful check is to divide an occasional specimen in half and send in both under different names. Another is to ask a central laboratory to send round control samples.

Laboratories are almost invariably overloaded, for the better a laboratory becomes the more is asked of it, the final equilibrium too often being overworked staff and mediocre service. Some of the tests asked for may not be necessary; for example, in a hyperendemic area, *routine* thick films for malaria are not required, and it is usually better to give the patient chloroquine and use scarce laboratory facilities in other ways. Nor, in the kind of laboratory considered here, is there any place for that tedious and inaccurate investigation, the red cell count — measure the haemoglobin instead. If a critical examination of the requests fails to cut them to the capacity of a laboratory, the only alternative may be a 'points system' to limit the amount of work done each day.

Some tests are frequently asked for while others, such as the blood sugar, are less commonly needed, but, nevertheless, when they are wanted, they may be wanted very badly and the result must be reliable. It is too much to ask a laboratory assistant to do an uncommon test correctly every time, so he should be kept in practice by being asked to do all the tests of which he is capable sufficiently often to keep him familiar with them.

24:3 **Layout, heating and lighting**. The best way for specimens to reach a laboratory is through a hatch. This should open on to a bench inside the room, and on to a shelf in the passage outside where specimens can be left after hours. The benching must be wide enough (65 cms., 26 ins.), some being at standing height (75 cms., 30 ins.) and the rest at a convenient height to sit at (65 cms., 26 ins.). If it has to be of softwood, this should be treated with Stitt's black (Appendix D), and liberally treated with paraffin wax. Benches easily become cluttered with equipment, so plenty of shelving will be needed. Immediately above the bench, this should be narrow, but higher up the wall it can well be wider. Because glare makes microscopy more difficult and fatigues the microscopist, the microscope should be in a dark corner as far as possible from bright windows.

When there is no other continuous source of electricity, a twelve volt car battery can be used and charged in any convenient vehicle. This will necessitate making a special housing for it, and providing a single-pole double-throw switch to cut out the vehicle's own battery, and connect up the one to be charged, once the engine has started. Twelve volt centrifuges can be obtained (ADL), and twelve volts are also suitable for a microscope lamp, or a 'Grey wedge photometer'. Suitable tappings from it can also be used to run an EEL colorimeter. When used like this a battery is said to need charging only about once a week under average conditions, so there is no need for any laboratory to be without electricity where there is a vehicle available to recharge a battery. A trickle charger can also be used to charge the laboratory's battery if the hospital has mains electricity for part of the day. The battery of any stationery vehicle can also be tapped directly, and the ubiquitous Land Rover has a dashboard socket for this very purpose.

Bottled gas is usually the best source of heat, but it has to be used with a special kind of burner. Pasteur pipettes are essential equipment, and, though they can be made on a Primus stove, they are more easily made on a plumber's blowlamp in default of a Bunsen burner. When a Primus stove is being used this should be of the 'loud' rather than the 'silent' type, the length of glass tube being held at one edge of its flame. A water bath for blood transfusion work is another vital item of equipment, and models can be obtained that can be heated by either oil or gas (HEA); these have fluid-filled metal capsules specific for the altitude as well as the temperature at which they operate; both these variables must therefore be specified when ordering equipment of this kind.

Records. Rubber stamps save much useless writing; they are cheap, universally available and are easily made to suit the exact needs of a laboratory. They must be carefully adapted to the report slips which should be small, both in the interests of cheapness and of saving space in the patients' case records. These records should be designed so that the report slips can be pasted on so as to overlap one another, and, where this is so, the name of the test should be at the bottom of the stamp rather than at the top. This is also the place for the date to be stamped where it will be readily visible beneath the bottom edge of the succeeding form. The same stamp can serve several purposes, thus all the common blood investigations can be reported with the same one.

The endless time that is often wasted keeping laboratory records will be reduced if an identical report slip is pinned to that reaching the laboratory with each specimen, and both these slips are immediately rubber stamped and dated appropriately. Work is then done on the specimen and the results recorded in the appropriate spaces in the rubber stampings on both these slips. One slip is returned to the ward, while the other is filled alphabetically in a box made for the purpose. Cardboard dividers will be required between one letter and the next in these boxes, but only two boxes will be needed, one for 'this month' and one for 'last month'. Apart from records of blood groups, which should be kept in a separate book, there will be little call for the results of tests further back, the slips for which can be bundled up and stored away just in case they are wanted. The only data that needs entering in a ledger for every specimen is the patient's name, the type of specimen and the ward. Such an arrangement does everything required of a laboratory record system and is highly economical in time. A paging numerator set to repeat three times (on both forms and in the ledger) is a useful addition, but is far from essential.

24:5 **The microscope.** Many of the microscopes at present in use are quite unserviceable, and as new ones can be purchased for as little as £19 ($57) (OLY), defective instruments should be replaced if possible. When new ones are bought spring loaded objectives should be specified, for this does much to preserve them in the hands of inexperienced assistants. A X 6 eyepiece will be wanted, and likewise 'low power' (X 10), 'high power' (X 40), and oil immersion objectives (X 100). If a binocular instrument can be afforded, this is likely to lead to improved results when many films have to be searched.

When assessing an existing instrument, check the mechanical parts, examine the surface lenses of the objectives with a magnifying glass — some are grossly pitted. Make sure also that the upper surfaces of objective lenses are clean — remove dust with a paint brush. If the field of view is not perfectly clear, rotate the top and bottom lenses of the eyepiece separately when movement will locate the site of the foreign matter. The life of a microscope will be prolonged if there is always lens tissue available in handy booklets, and if xylol or petrol but *never* alcohol is used to clean its lenses. When moulds grow on the surface of a lens they can often be removed by gently wiping with tissue and saliva.

24:6 **Measuring instruments.** The haemoglobin, the blood sugar and the blood urea all require a measuring instrument. There are three possible ones to choose from with a fourth late in the process of development. They are the 'Lovibond Comparator' (TIN) the 'Grey wedge photometer' (KEE) and the 'EEL colorimeter' (EEL). The haemoglobin is adequately estimated with the Lovibond, and well estimated with the other two instruments. The CSF protein is very easily estimated with the Grey wedge, but is so comparatively difficult to measure with either of the others that a set of proteinometer standards for 100/- ($14) (GAL) has also to be purchased when these are the only instruments available. The blood urea method described here is best suited to the Lovibond; the blood sugar is measured equally well on all three instruments.

The Lovibond comparator. This is a plastic box containing a number of interchangeable plastic discs, each with a series of coloured glass standards round its edge. The disc is rotated until a standard is found which matches the liquid under test; the value for this is then read directly from a figure on the disc. The comparator itself costs only 65/- ($9), but one and often two further discs are required for each additional test, each disc costing about 80/- ($11).

The Grey wedge photometer. The British Medical Research Council Grey wedge photometer costs £42 ($118) complete for several tests, and replaces the numerous glass standards of the Lovibond comparator by a ring shaped grey optical wedge and three coloured glass filters. The test

Fig. 53. THREE MEASURING INSTRUMENTS.

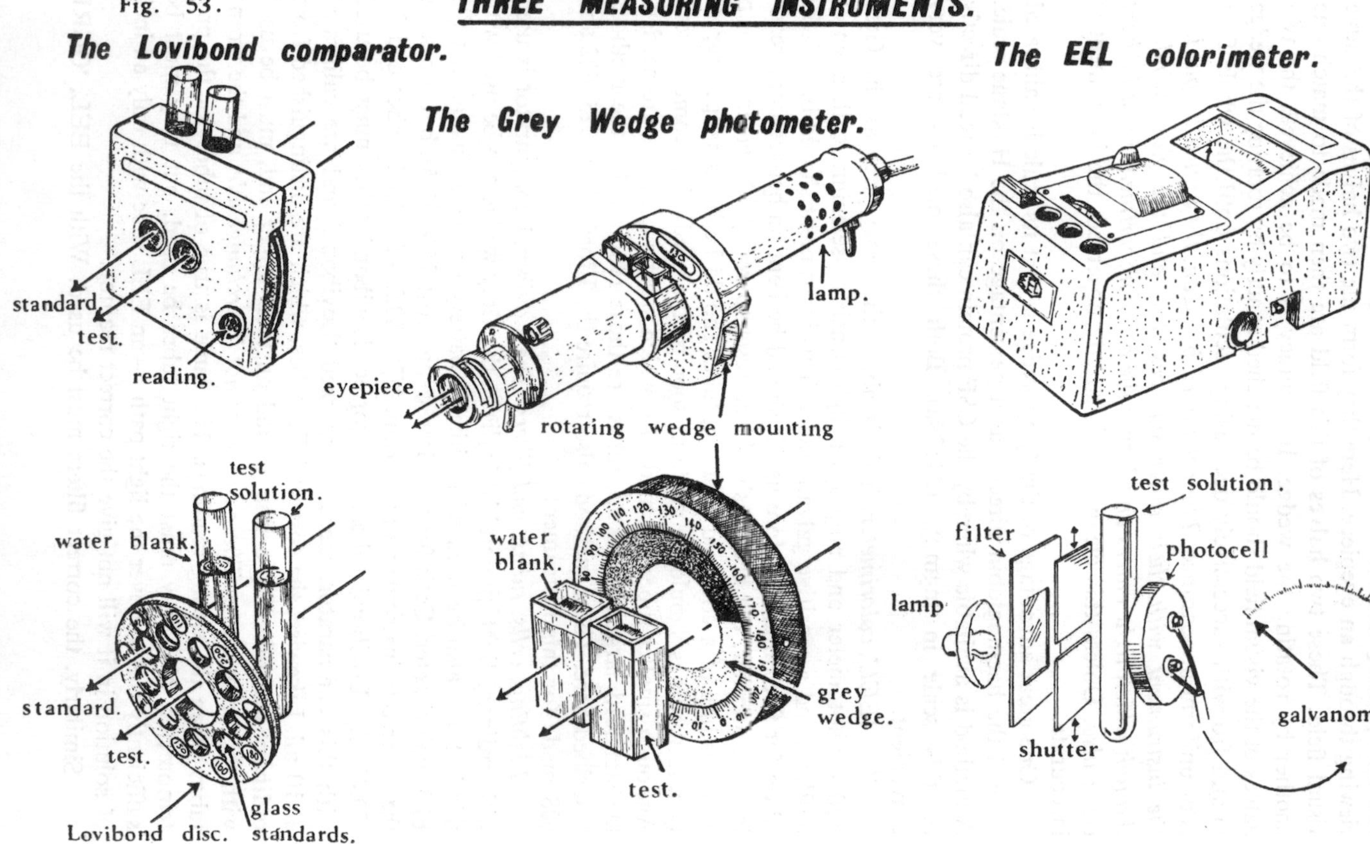

solution is placed in a glass cell, and the beam of light passing through it and that passing through the wedge are brought together by prisms for viewing through an eyepiece. Here they form the two halves of the same visual field. These two halves of this field are then made to match one another by rotating the wedge. If accuracy is to be achieved, the two halves of the visual field should be matched exactly by rotating the wedge to and fro with successively decreasing oscillations until the whole field is of uniform appearance. *The cells must be clean, they must be put into the instrument with their outer surfaces dry, and the glass windows through which light enters and leaves the cell compartment must be kept clean also.* Unless this cleanliness is strictly observed, the instrument is inaccurate.

One great advantage of the Grey wedge is that its scale is calibrated to read the haemoglobin directly as a percentage on the Haldane scale. A method is available whereby the CSF protein can also be read directly on this scale in mgm.% (24:29a). Both these methods are very convenient.

The 'EEL' colorimeter. This is about the same price as the Grey wedge photometer and employs a light-sensitive selenium cell, a series of filters and a sensitive galvanometer. This instrument should be switched on for five minutes before use, it should be kept on between one reading and another, the needle should be reset to zero with water between each reading of a coloured solution, tubes should be interchanged rapidly, and readings should be made as soon as the needle has come to rest. Although smaller tubes are made, for which special adaptors are needed, the standard large size 10 ml. tubes are those required for the methods described here. These methods also require the Ilford filters 625, 622 and 608 made for this instrument.

Lighting, cells, tubes, and filters. The Lovibond comparator is used with ordinary light, preferably daylight, the Grey wedge can be used with this but can also be used with either a battery or the mains, as can the EEL colorimeter. Cells for the Grey wedge cost 25/- ($3.5), but tubes for the other two instruments are cheap, 1/70 ($0.23) for EEL tubes and 3/- ($0.42) for Lovibond tubes. The correct Lovibond tubes must be used with this comparator, these are marked 'Lovibond' and are calibrated at 10 ml. Likewise, the correct EEL tubes, which are distinguished from ordinary test tubes by a line ground on their upper end, must be used with this colorimeter. *These tubes are not interchangeable,* and the wrong tubes mean the wrong readings. The same is true of tubes for the proteinometer. Not only must the right tubes be used, but they must be sufficiently full to cover the light path — an EEL tube with only an inch of solution in it will not give the correct reading.

Similarly, the correct filters must be used. With the EEL, 'OGRI' will *not* replace '625', even though both are green; with the Grey wedge, No. 2 will not replace No 3, even though both these are also green.

'Thompson's grey'. No standard solutions are required with the Lovibond comparator, but it is usual to use them with both the other instruments. They can however be dispensed with for the Grey wedge which has its own internal standard (the wedge), and the scale in Figure 55 enables a blood urea or a blood sugar prepared according to the Lovibond methods described here to be read on this instrument. The EEL has no such internal standard, but it is possible to use 'Thompson's grey solution' instead. This is complex inorganic solution which lasts indefinitely and has a known optical density. Using the methods described here, this solution has been found equivalent to a serum urea of 135 mgm.% (Ilford 622), a blood sugar of 145 mgm.% (Ilford 608); and is made equivalent to a haemoglobin of 14.6 g.% (Ilford 625). Thompson's grey solution can be bought ready prepared (KEE), and sealed into EEL tubes with 'Araldite' as described in section 24:17, but the makers of the EEL now market this solution already sealed in tubes.

The choice of an instrument. All three instruments are accurate enough. The Lovibond comparator is virtually foolproof, but the EEL colorimeter is somewhat temperamental and spare cells, bulbs, and, ideally, a spare galvanometer should be available.

The conversion scales described here for the blood sugar and the blood urea make the Grey wedge the instrument of choice; it is slightly

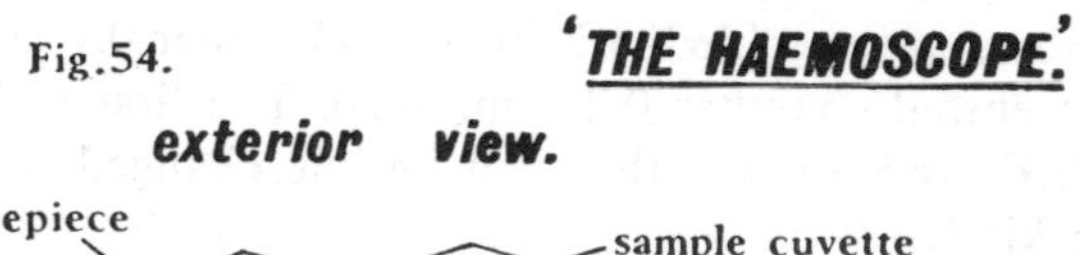

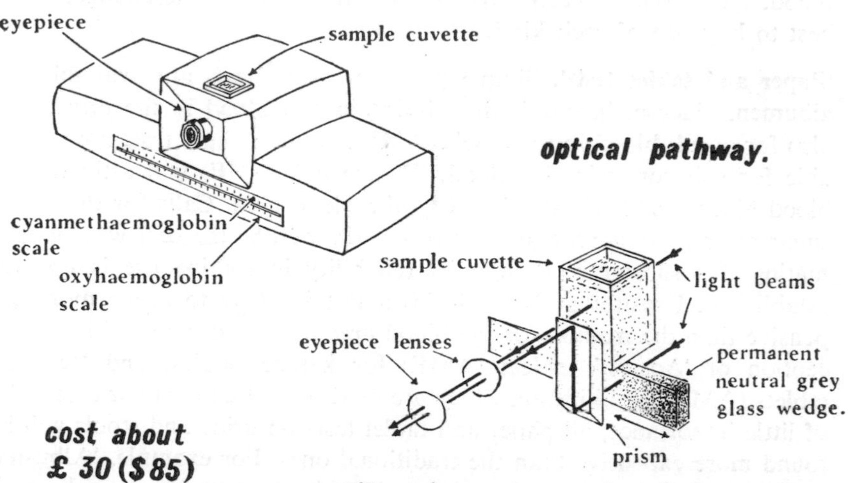

This wedge can be moved to & fro until the two halves of the visual field in the eyepiece match one another.

more expensive than the Lovibond comparator and the discs that go with it, but it is more versatile. Where there is a little more money available and someone capable of supervising the use of an EEL, this and either a set of proteinometer standards, or better still, a Grey wedge photometer, would be the ideal combination.

The 'Haemoscope'. A fourth instrument has now been developed; this is the 'Haemoscope' (KEE). Its place in the rural laboratory cannot yet be assessed, but it will probably be similar to the Grey wedge photometer, but cheaper at £25 ($70). It may well be the perfect instrument under these conditions.

24:7 **Minor equipment.** A wide range of plastic equipment is specified in appendix F and replaces much fragile glassware, the polythene dropping bottles in particular are a great advance on the older type of glass ones (Figure 55). A special test tube block is also shown in Figure 55 and is designed to hold the three sizes of tube that the laboratory will find it convenient to use. These are the ordinary 16 mm. (5/8 in.) test tube, the 12 mm. ($\frac{1}{2}$ in.) Kahn tube and the 5 mm. ($\frac{1}{4}$ in.) tube. These latter two are mainly used for blood transfusion work.

An inexpensive £11 ($30) centrifuge is listed (MSE), but, if the standard type capable of 3,000 revolutions per minute can be afforded, the packed cell volume can be estimated. From this and the haemoglobin a very useful value, the 'mean corpuscular haemoglobin concentration', or 'MCHC' can be calculated (24:68).

Two counting chambers are specified, a Neubauer chamber 0.1 mm. deep, and the Fuchs Rosenthal chamber 0.2 mm. deep. The first is for blood, the second for CSF, and, though they can be interchanged, it is best to buy one of each kind.

24:8 **'Paper and tablet tests'.** Simple paper or tablet tests are available for albumen, glucose, ketone bodies, bilirubin and blood in the urine, and also for occult blood in the stools (AME). Among paper tests now available for substances in the blood, 'Dextrostix' (AME) will estimate the blood glucose and 'Urastrat' (WCL) the blood urea. Calls for the blood sugar are not common and Dextrostix may well be the best way of estimating this substance, though its reliability in routine use is not yet established. Urastrat at 1/80 ($0.25) a test is likely to prove more expensive than the method for the blood urea described here. With the exception of 'Acetest' tablets (AME) for ketone bodies, and 'Ictotest' tablets (AME) for bilirubin, which are used so seldom for their cost to be of little importance, all paper and tablet tests on urine and stools will be found more expensive than the traditional ones. For example, 'Albustix' (AME) is ten times more expensive than the reagent for the salicylsulphonic acid method of testing the urine for protein.

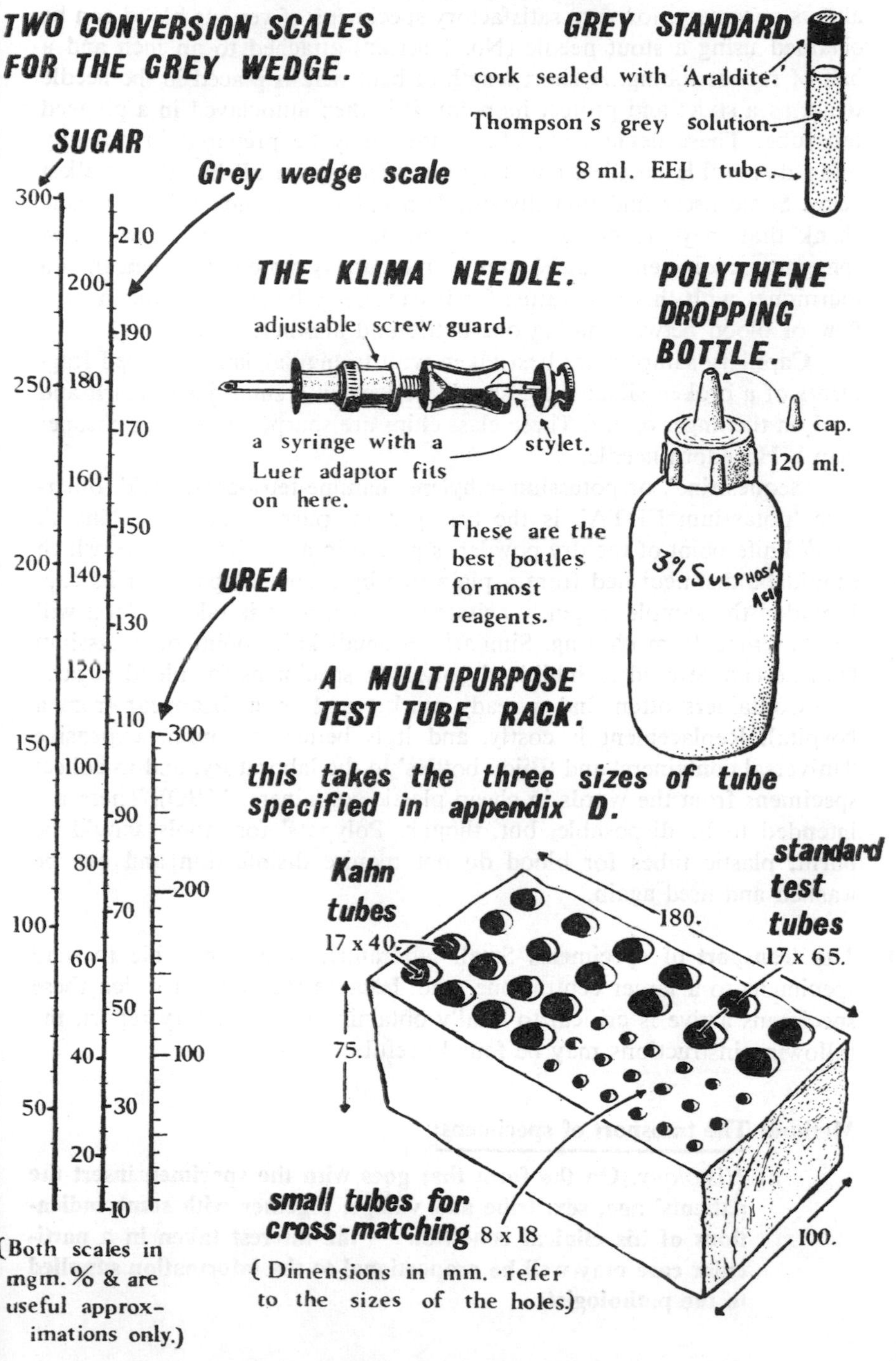
Fig. 55.
SOME MINOR EQUIPMENT.
TWO CONVERSION SCALES FOR THE GREY WEDGE.
SUGAR
Grey wedge scale
300
250
200
150
100
50
210
200
190
180
170
160
150
140
130
120
110
100
90
80
70
60
50
40
30
20
10
UREA
300
200
100
(Both scales in mgm. % & are useful approximations only.)
GREY STANDARD
cork sealed with 'Araldite.'
Thompson's grey solution.
8 ml. EEL tube.
THE KLIMA NEEDLE.
adjustable screw guard.
a syringe with a Luer adaptor fits on here.
stylet.
POLYTHENE DROPPING BOTTLE.
cap.
120 ml.
These are the best bottles for most reagents.
3% SULPHOSA ACID
A MULTIPURPOSE TEST TUBE RACK.
this takes the three sizes of tube specified in appendix D.
Kahn tubes
17 x 40.
standard test tubes
17 x 65.
180.
75.
100.
small tubes for cross-matching 8 x 18
(Dimensions in mm. refer to the sizes of the holes.)

24:9 **The collection of specimens.** Syringes are often scarce, nor are they always necessary, for very satisfactory specimens of venous blood can be obtained using a stout needle (No. 1 serum) attached to an inch and a half of rubber tubing. A short length of bent wire is placed in the needle to act as a stylet and protect its point; it is then autoclaved in a plugged test tube. These devices are cheap, they may be prepared in quantity using disposable needles, and they are effective on all but the smallest veins. Some users find that disposable needles have such a large plastic shank that they are easily held and no length of tubing is needed. A sphygmomanometer set at 20 mm. of mercury is more convenient than a tourniquet with this apparatus, for it can easily be used to shut off the flow of blood between filling one bottle and another.

Capillary samples are best taken with triangular lancet-shaped fragments of a broken slide; these should be kept in a small jar of spirit and used on the finger or ear. These glass chips are sharper, safer and cheaper than a Hagedorn needle.

'Sequestrine', or potassium-ethylene-diamine-tetra-acetic-acid, otherwise 'potassium EDTA', is the best general purpose anticoagulant. A *small* knife point of the dry powder is placed in a specimen bottle, which should be distinguished from a plain one by a spot of paint on its cap. Provided the sample is gently agitated as soon as it is taken, blood will be prevented from clotting. Similarly, a small knife point of potassium fluoride can be used to inhibit glycolysis in specimens for blood sugar.

Containers often find a ready market and soon disappear from a hospital. Replacement is costly, and it is better to confine expensive 'Universal containers' and 'Bijou bottles' to the laboratory, and to collect specimens from the wards in cheap plastic containers (MBO). These are intended to be disposable, but, though 'Polypots' for stools should be burnt, plastic tubes for blood do not require disinfection and can be washed and used again.

24:10 **The transport of specimens.** Small laboratories are often able to send specimens to a larger central one, and, because the state in which these specimens arrive is critical to finally obtaining a satisfactory report, the following instructions may be found useful.

Method: The transport of specimens:

a) *Histology*. **On the form that goes with the specimen insert the patients' age, sex, tribe and village, together with some indications of his clinical condition — the interest taken in a particular case may well be proportional to the information supplied to the pathologist.**

All tissue must be fixed at least in five times its volume of formol-saline for long enough to ensure adequate fixation. Fluid must also be able to reach the middle of any large mass. The time needed for this varies with size of the specimen, small shreds will fix in twelve hours, but large specimens take much longer. Put pieces of an inch cube into formol-saline directly, but, if a large specimen such as a big tumour mass is to be examined, blocks must either be cut from it, or the whole mass must be fixed. Usually, it is best to cut blocks, but choose them carefully. Cut them 1½ x 1 x ½ inch, one being enough if the specimen is uniform, but, if it is not, cut several from different areas and supply a drawing or even a photograph to show where they came from.

If the whole mass must be sent, cut it into slices about an inch thick, but leave them joined together at one edge. Put the slices together again as far as possible, tie them loosely with string if need be, and fix the whole in a bucket of formol-saline — ideally in the cool of a refrigerator. A covered bucket of formol-saline is useful, for several large specimens can be put in at once, their labels hanging on by a string leading outside the bucket.

Send small specimens in small, watertight, screw capped bottles — Universal containers travel adequately when packed in strong envelopes. Large screw topped jars break and leak in the post, so, if a big specimen must be sent whole, cut and fix it a week in the manner described, fold it several times round in a polythene bag, seal this with adhesive tape — not staples — and pack the bundle in a cardboard box. Such a bag keeps large specimens moist, and, though small specimens can also be sent wrapped like this, it is wise to pack a little formalin-soaked cottonwool in with them.

Sealed polythene bags are even better, and can be made from a roll of 'layflat' polythene tube sealed with a hand sealing machine (30:5). Pack blocks of tissue or the whole of small specimens in such a bag with a little formalin — the 'sachet' formed preserves them perfectly for transport.

A very satisfactory system is for the central pathological laboratory to supply outlying hospitals with labelled wooden blocks, each holding a universal container filled with formalin. These have a square lid which pivots on a nail and are merely fastened up with 'Sellotape' and dispatched.

b) *Serology.* **Ideally, take sterile blood samples into screw capped bottles, and send them to the central laboratory packed on ice**

in a vacuum flask. This is usually impossible, but, if taken aseptically into sterile bottles and sent 'on the clot', most serological samples travel well. If the delay is too great, separate the serum and add sodium azide (POISON) to a final concentration of 0.1% — a minute amount of the dry powder being judged by eye or one drop of a 2% solution being added to each ml. of serum. Renew such a solution monthly and store it in a refrigerator because it may deteriorate on keeping. Azide affects some tests, so state on the request form that it has been added.

c) *Bacteriology.* **Many bacteriological specimens travel satisfactorily, particularly those for the culture of the tubercle bacillus. Special transport media have been developed for some purposes and the central laboratory should be consulted about their use. Blood cultures must be well sealed in a tin — the hazards of a broken typhoid blood culture bottle are only too obvious.**

d) *Haematology.***The haemoglobin can still be measured on blood many days after it has been taken, but films are valueless on samples older than a few hours. Therefore, prepare films from blood or marrow, and fix them immediately by pouring a little methanol over them, and letting this evaporate. Label them in pencil across the heal of the film, state that they have been fixed and despatch them by post. Send thick films for parasitological investigation unfixed.**

e) *Biochemistry.* **With the exception of samples for the estimation of the serum calcium and total and differential serum proteins, for which 1 ml. of clear serum are required, most biochemical specimens travel badly.**

f) *Parasitology.* **(Other than blood). Preserve large parasites in formol saline, and faeces in two or three times their volume of the same solution.**

g) *Virology.* **Send serum for serology, or material for the isolation of virus, or both.**

For the isolation of virus. **Send 10-20ml. of clotted blood taken in the acute febrile period during the first three days of the disease. Make sure it is taken into a sterile container and dispatch it rapidly in a Thermos flask on ice.**
During an outbreak take as many samples as possible. Faeces, CSF, pharyngeal washings or autopsy material may also be sent, but on most occasions serum taken in the acute febrile stage is the important specimen.

A one gallon Thermos container is better than the smaller kind, place plenty of ice in it, wrap the containers in cotton wool, pack the Thermos with shavings or wadding etc., so that there is no free movement, and, if the Thermos flask is going to have a rough journey, pack it in a four gallon petrol tin with shavings. Give full clinical details and label it well. Place the accompanying letter outside the flask attached to it with 'Sellotape'.

For virus serology. **Send paired sera taken with rigid aseptic precautions; one sample taken early in the disease, the other ten days later. This enables a rising titre of antibody to be demonstrated. Send the samples unseparated in a Thermos flask on ice.**

TECHNICAL METHODS

11 **Some general details.** All the reageants mentioned in the following section are described in Appendix B.

Method: General detail.

Many methods need Pasteur pipettes. Glass tubing for them is specified in Appendix F, they are cheap, they can be reused many times and assistants must be taught to make them so they can be available in adequate numbers. If their tips break off, two can be fixed together in the flame and new tips pulled with very little loss of length.

When measured quantities of blood are required, say, 0.05 or 0.1 ml., see that the specimen bottle is well mixed first, that the outside of the pipette is wiped clean before the blood sample is added to whatever diluent is being used, and that the pipette is finally rinsed out once or twice in this diluent.

When searching a slide for, say, trypanosomes, choose the lowest power of the microscope under which the organism can be seen, start at what appears to be the top left hand corner of the area to be searched, move across to the top right hand corner, move exactly one field down and then proceed to the left again. Proceed in like manner until the whole area has been searched.

Get assistants into the habit of using the plus notation in 26:11.

Finally, test tubes must be clean — wash them out immediately after use.

STAINING METHODS

24:12 **Leishman's stain.** With a little skill and experience this technique provides much valuable information, and can be used on the sternal marrow as easily as it can be on blood. The examination of such a film should be thought of in the same way as that of a chest X-ray; as something that is prepared by an assistant but examined by a doctor. The information that can be elicited from a blood film can be so useful that a regular visit to the laboratory at the end of a ward round to have a look at the films of perplexing cases can be time well spent. Among important 'clinical signs' in the blood film are, leucocytosis, leucopenia, hypochromia, polychromasia, anisocytosis, leptocytosis, target cells, nucleated red cells, immature white cells, and thrombocytopenia — quite apart from the many parasites that may be seen.

To be worth looking at a Leishman film must be well made; this means careful attention to detail.

Method: The preparation of the Leishman stained blood film.

Wash slides well in a detergent, store them in a jar of spirit and flame them before use to remove the grease. The slide used as a spreader needs a really smooth edge, so, having found a good one, keep it for this purpose alone. Put a small drop of blood at the end of a slide, draw the spreader backwards at an angle towards it, and, as soon as contact has been made, and blood has flowed across the slide, push the spreader steadily forwards, leaving a thin film behind (Figure 56). Dry it rapidly by waving it a few moments in the air, and label it in lead pencil to include the date as well as the patient's name. Place it across two rods laid over a sink or tin having first seen that these are level. Drop on to the film 'one volume' of stain, measured either as a certain number of drops, or from an arbitrary mark on the pipette. Provided the whole film is covered with stain the quantity used is unimportant. The methanol in the stain will fix the film. Add 'two volumes' of dilute Leishman buffer, measured in a similar way, drop by drop over the slide. Draw the liquid on the slide in and out of the buffer pipette a few times to make sure it is well mixed. Leave it for five minutes, tip off the liquid, flood the film with a stream of buffer from a wash bottle. Leave some of the buffer on the slide for a minute or two or until it has become a good pink. Finally, drain it and leave it to dry.

There are many points to be considered in making a good film. The greater the haemoglobin, the steeper the spreader and the faster it travels, the thicker will be the film. A good film

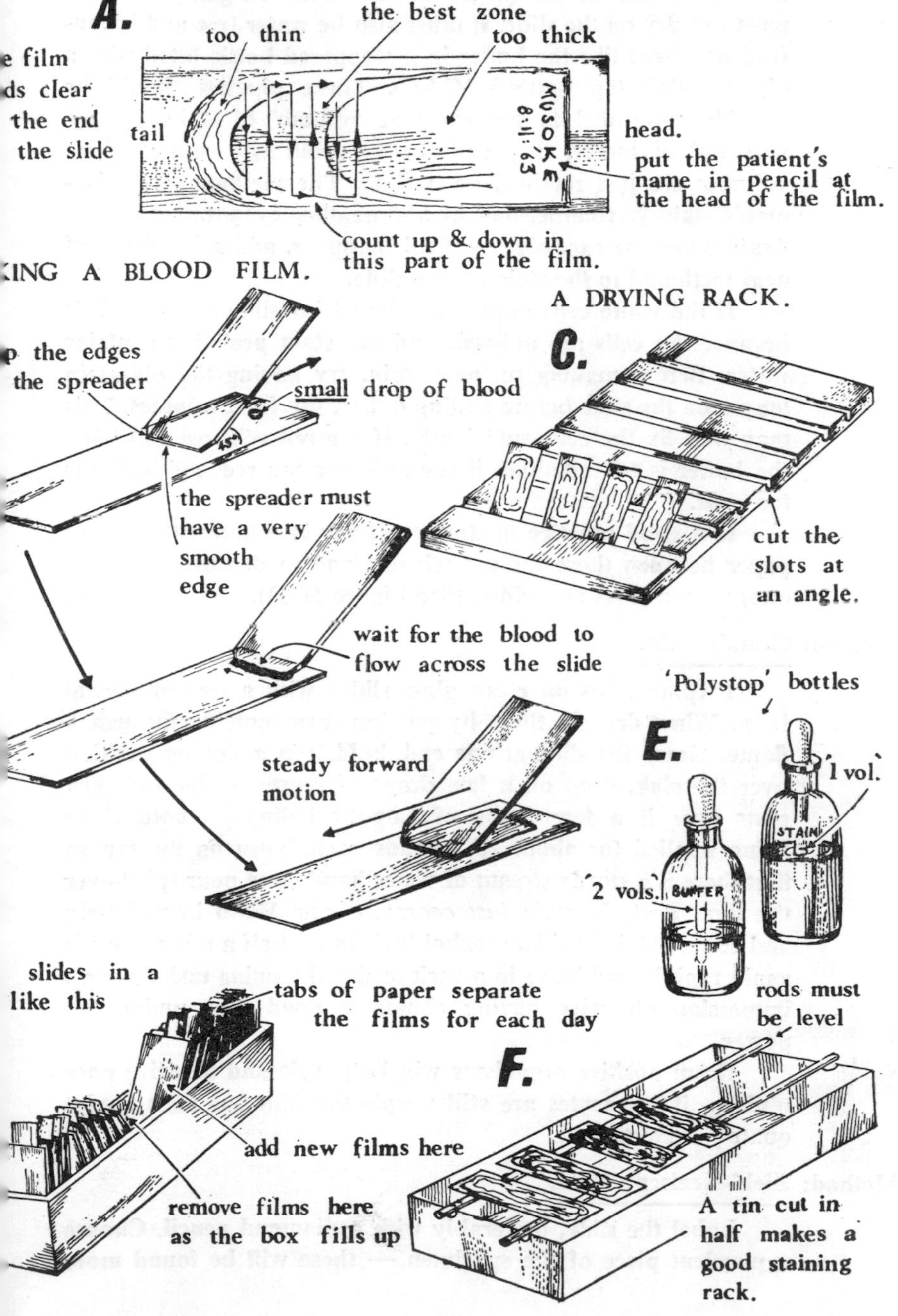
Fig.56.
THE LEISHMAN BLOOD FILM.
A.
the best zone
too thin
too thick
e film
ds clear
the end
the slide
tail
head.
MUSOKE
8:1:'63
put the patient's name in pencil at the head of the film.
count up & down in this part of the film.
KING A BLOOD FILM.
p the edges
the spreader
small drop of blood
45°
the spreader must have a very smooth edge
wait for the blood to flow across the slide
steady forward motion
A DRYING RACK.
C.
cut the slots at an angle.
'Polystop' bottles
E.
1 vol.
STAIN
2 vols.
BUFFER
slides in a
like this
tabs of paper separate the films for each day
add new films here
remove films here as the box fills up
rods must be level
F.
A tin cut in half makes a good staining rack.

fills three quarters of the slide, does not quite reach its edges, has few tails, and should be even with the minimum of cell overlap in the useful third quarter of its length. The stain must not dry on the slide. It must also be water free and is conveniently kept like the buffer in a stoppered bottle fitted with a pipette (Polystop bottles) (GAL). These pipettes should be roughly calibrated to contain 'one volume' of stain or 'two volumes' of buffer, they are chosen arbitrarily so that three volumes are just retained on a slide. The methanol in Leishman's stain is volatile, and in hot weather evaporation during fixation may be excessive — if this happens, add a few drops of neat methanol to the stain on the slide.

If the white cells appear as almost invisible shadows, it is because the cells are unfixed, and the stain probably contains water. Before making up new stain, try having the old stain longer on the slide before adding buffer, say for 2 minutes. This may well fix the cells sufficiently. If the red cells are too blue, the buffer is too alkaline; if the cells are too red, the buffer is too acid.

It is good practice to store the films in a box with slips of paper between those taken each day and to discard the oldest ones as new ones are added (See Figure 56 D).

4:13 **Method: Gram's stain.**

Prepare films on clean glass slides with a bacteriological loop. When dry, fix them by passing them quickly through a flame. Grasp the slide at one end, hold it in a sloping position over the sink, drop on a few drops of crystal violet and then pour over it a few drops of Lugol's iodine — both these being applied for about 15 seconds each. Turn on the tap so that there is a steady stream of water handy and pour spirit over the film *until the stain just ceases to run.* Wash immediately and counterstain in *dilute* carbol fuchsin for half a minute; wash again rapidly and leave in a rack to dry. Examine under the oil immersion objective having chosen a good area under low power.

Gram positive organisms will be purple and negative ones pink — if leucocytes are still purple the film has been inadequately decolourized.

4:14 **Method: Ziehl-Neelsen's stain.**

Label the slide, preferably with a diamond pencil. Choose a purulent piece of the specimen — these will be found more

readily in wide-mouthed cardboard or polythene cups, and if in a narrow bottle, pour the sputum into a Petri dish. Sputum is often tenacious, so use two loops to tease out the specimens and make an even smear, one of them of wire twisted double on itself for greater strength. The key to a good film is to take a small purulent portion, to tease it out very thinly — if the specimen is very tough squash it between two slides, and to be sure it is quite dry before staining.

Fix the film by passing it rapidly once or twice through a flame and lay it flat on the rack. Pour on strong (not dilute) carbol fuchsin till the slide will hold no more without the stain running off. Heat it gently for five minutes — *the stain must steam gently but not boil or go dry.* **Use a spirit lamp, a bunsen burner, or a wire handled asbestos wool swab soaked in spirit — those sold for paraffin pressure lamps serve very well. Wash in a stream of water, drain, lay the film flat in the rack and cover it with acid-alcohol — 3% for** *Myco. tuberculosis* **and 0.5% for** *Myco. leprae* **— 5 minutes for** *Myco. tuberculosis* **and somewhat less for** *Myco. leprae.* **The thinner parts of the film should be almost colourless at the end of this stage, if not, decolourize it further. Wash rapidly, drain, and counterstain momentarily with malachite green, though some prefer a yellow stain and use 2% picric acid. Wash rapidly again and leave to dry. Under the low power choose a suitably cellular area for scrutiny under the oil immersion objective — search until crimson bacilli are seen, or for not less than five minutes.**

A common mistake is to let the stain boil — it should only just steam. As soon as the steam starts to rise from the slide take away the source of heat and apply it again only when steaming stops. Boiling precipitates stain on the slide which is difficult to remove. Another error is to decolourize insufficiently. The background of the finished film should be a *pale* **clear green.**

The method is insensitive and thus false negatives are inevitable, but false positive ones are due to bad technique and must be avoided. There are several reasons for them: used slides from previous positive specimens may have been inadequately washed and bacilli may remain on the slide — avoid this by breaking up all positive ones: stained bacilli may become detached from a positive slide and carried to a negative one in the oil on the microscope objective — avoid this by wiping the objective with lens tissue after every positive specimen: bacilli may be transferred from slide to slide on the rod of the oil bottle — avoid this by letting oil drop on to the surface of the slide. Finally, never use staining jars, for these readily get contaminated with bacilli, and discriminate carefully as to what constitutes an acid fast bacillus and what does not — red stained objects in the midst of hyaline material may be imperfectly decolourized and a false positive reported.

24:15 **Field's stain.** With Field's stain the red cells in a thick layer of blood are haemolysed by a hypotonic solution, the parasites inside them are liberated and most of the haemoglobin is washed away. At the same time, both any parasites present and the leucocytes are stained purple or blue.

Method: Field's stain for plasmodia, borelia and microfilaria.

In the middle of a grease free slide make a film the size of a postage stamp, and of such a thickness that print or the hands of a watch can just be seen through it. *A common fault is not to make the film thick enough.* **Let it dry — its degree of dessication is critical. A night in an incubator is best, but failing this five minutes on top of a microscope lamp will serve — if too wet it washes off while if too dry it flakes off. Use three wide-mouthed screw capped jars that can be closed after use. In the first place the blue stain A, in the second dilute Leishman buffer, and in the third the red stain B. Wave the film gently to and fro for 1-2 seconds in A, drain it momentarily on the edge of the jar, repeat the process in the buffer, then in stain B, and finally back in the buffer once more. Leave it to dry in a rack, scan it under low power, and, having found a good area, search this under oil — an area with several leucocytes per high power field is about right. If the right field is found, malaria parasites or trypanosomes will be seen staining blue and purple against a clear orange background, which is thick enough to show obvious cracks under the oil immersion objective.**

The staining times are very short indeed, the film being held in the buffer only until the blue stain ceases to run. Before being examined it must be dry and a domestic hair dryer will be found very useful. Be careful to distinguish platelets from the young trophozoites of *P. falciparum;* **the chromatin dot and the ring of cytoplasm serve to distinguish them.**

The stains last several weeks if kept in closed jars, but renew them when they discolour. Because microfilaria are so comparatively large, when looking for them, first smear the whole film with oil and examine it under low power. Make sure that film has been well stained in stain A.

:16 **Demonstrating fungi.** Though not strictly a stain this is the most convenient section in which to describe the alkali clearing method for demonstrating fungi.

Method: The demonstration of fungi by clearing in strong alkali.

Put a drop of 20% sodium hydroxide on a slide, add the specimen which may be a skin scraping, pus, hair or a nail clipping. Leave it a few minutes, then examine microscopically with the condenser racked well down.

The alkali will clear the material and enable mycelial filaments, or yeast cells to be seen, but, if the material is very dense, the slide may have to be heated gently and examined again. Potassium hydroxide is traditionally used for this technique and may be better if it is available.

METHODS FOR BLOOD

:17 **Haemoglobin.** Three methods are described. The Lovibond method is ideally suited to health centres and outpatient departments. The great disadvantage of the EEL colorimeter is that it has to be used with a liquid standard. The one most suitable for tropical use is Thompson's grey (24:6) (KEE).

Method: Haemoglobin.

a) using the EEL colorimeter.

1) *Preparing the standard.* **Obtain some Thompson's grey solution, fill one of the large (10 ml.) EEL test tubes to within 2 cms. of the top. Make sure the inside of the top of the tube is dry, obtain a cork that fits this tube, smear it with 'Araldite' glue and fix it in the tube. Cut the cork off flush with the top of the tube. Smear the top of the cork with more Araldite. (Commercially prepared standards are available (EEL)).**

Place an Ilford 625 filter in the EEL, zero the instrument with a tube of water, read the scale reading given by the grey standard — this is equivalent to 14.6 g.% of haemoglobin (100% Haldane). On the abscissa (horizontal scale) of a graph draw a scale 0-100 for the scale reading of the instrument, on the ordinate (vertical scale) draw a scale 0-20 for the grams % of haemoglobin in the sample. Join the point given by the standard to the zero point on the graph. Read the haemoglobin of test samples from this line. Cover the graph with clear X-ray film as described in section 13:7. Check the value of the standard daily and alter the graph if a significant deviation appears.

2) *The test itself.* **Measure 10 ml. of haemoglobin diluting fluid into a universal container, add 50 cu.mm. (0.05 ml.) of blood, mix, pour the mixture into a large EEL tube. Using an Ilford 625 filter zero the instrument with a tube of water, determine the scale reading for the sample, and use the graph described above to obtain the haemoglobin value.**

Provided the standard is correctly prepared and checked with the graph at frequent intervals, this is the most satisfactory and the most consistent routine haemoglobin method of the three described here.

b) Using the Grey wedge. **Dilute 20 cu.mm. of blood in 4 ml. of haemoglobin diluting fluid, or 50 cu.mm. (0.05 ml.) in 10 ml. Pour the solution into the right hand cell of the instrument, fill the left with distilled water. Using the green No. 2 eyepiece (not No. 3), rotate the disc until both halves of the field match one another exactly. Read the Haldane haemoglobin percentage directly from the scale provided.**

c) Using the Lovibond oxyhaemoglobin disc 5/37. **Fill a Lovibond tube to the 10 ml. mark with haemoglobin diluting liquid. Add to it 0.05 ml. (50 cu.mm.) of blood. Place the tube in the right hand compartment of the comparator. Put a tube of water in the left hand compartment. Match against the standard on the disc holding the comparator against the sky where possible. Read the haemoglobin content of the sample in the indicator window in the bottom right hand corner of the comparator.**

The disc only reads down to 8 grams % of haemoglobin. When the haemoglobin is suspected to be less than this, take two samples of 50 cu.mm. (0.05 ml.) or one of 0.1 ml. (100 cu.mm.) and halve the final reading. If the patient is very anaemic indeed, three samples may be needed, the final reading being divided by three.

4:18 **Total leucocyte count.** A small glass pipette with a bulb in it is still the instrument most often used to count the leucocytes in the blood, but these are expensive, difficult to clean and inaccurate. It is time that they were replaced by straight 50 cu.mm. (0.05 ml.) pipettes and this volume of blood diluted with 1 ml. of diluting fluid in a small bottle. Pipettes can be purchased calibrated to contain 100 cu.mm. (0.1 ml.) and 50 cu.mm. (0.05 ml.), and can be used for other purposes also (EMI) (Figure 57).

Method: The total leucocyte count.

Fill the 50 cu.mm. pipette to the mark from ear, finger or sequestrine bottle. Wipe the outside, add the contents to 1 ml.

of diluting fluid in a small tube or Bijou bottle. Rinse the pipette out once or twice, put the cap on the bottle, agitate for 15 seconds, and fill the counting chamber evenly with a Pasteur pipette, taking care that no fluid runs into the troughs alongside the ruled area. When the chamber is full count the cells as shown in Figure 57.

Make sure that the venous blood is well mixed before the sample is taken, and likewise that the dilution bottle is well agitated before the chamber is filled.

9 **Method: The differential leucocyte count.**

Prepare a blood film and stain it with Leishman's stain (24:12). Count a hundred cells (better 200), and mark them off in blocks of five on a piece of paper. Follow a course on the slide that includes as many fields on the edge of the film where polymorphonuclear leucocytes predominate as it does in the centre where lymphocytes are more numerous (Figure 56A).

0 **The erythrocyte sedimentation rate or 'ESR'.** Traditionally, the main reason for estimating the erythrocyte sedimentation rate has been in following the progress of cases of pulmonary tuberculosis, but there are better ways of doing this (21:18b). The Westergren method is generally considered the best and in the modification described here the tubes hang from a hook and so are always vertical, but in the absence of a stand a row of cup hooks serves just as well.

Method: The Westergren ESR.

Add 2 ml. of blood from the vein or a sequestrine bottle to 0.5 ml. of 3.8% sodium citrate. Fill a Westergren tube to the zero mark and read the position of the top of the red cell column an hour later.

The dilution must be reasonably accurate. The appendix lists special hangers for these tubes and rubber cups ('policemen') to close their lower ends, but both can be improvised; the hanger with a paper clip and a split pin, and the rubber cap by a short length of plastic tubing, the end of which has been softened in a flame and pinched tight with a pair of pliers. The column of blood will be less disturbed as these are fitted if a small hole is pierced near their upper end with a red hot needle. A water pump makes it easier to clean the tubes which must be dry.

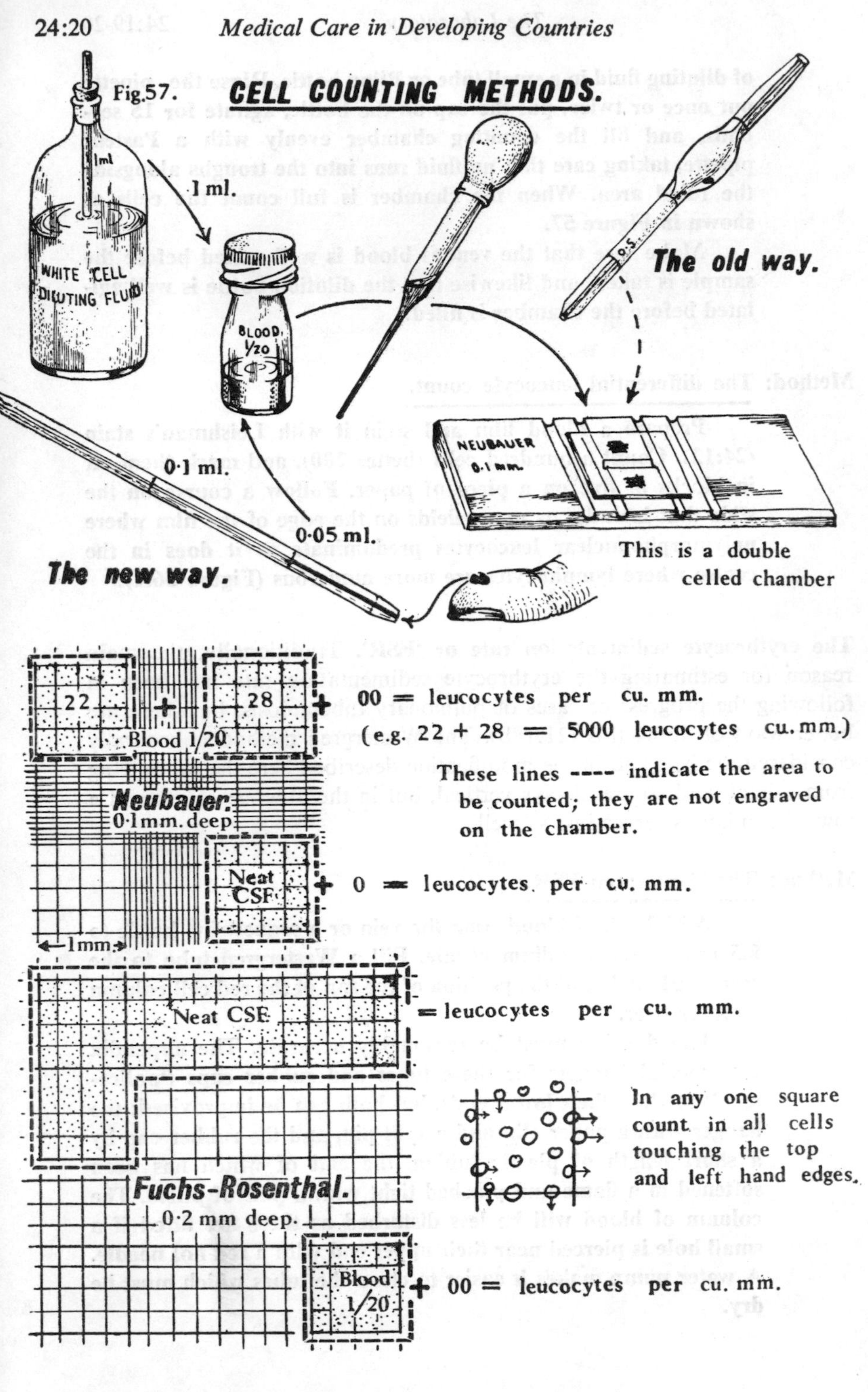

Fig.57.
CELL COUNTING METHODS.
1ml
1 ml.
WHITE CELL DILUTING FLUID
BLOOD 1/20
0.5
The old way.
NEUBAUER 0·1 mm.
0·1 ml.
0·05 ml.
The new way.
This is a double celled chamber
22
+
28
Blood 1/20
+ 00 = leucocytes per cu. mm.
(e.g. 22 + 28 = 5000 leucocytes cu. mm.)
These lines ---- indicate the area to be counted; they are not engraved on the chamber.
Neubauer.
0·1mm. deep
Neat CSF
+ 0 = leucocytes. per cu. mm.
←1mm.→
Neat CSF
= leucocytes per cu. mm.
In any one square count in all cells touching the top and left hand edges.
Fuchs-Rosenthal.
0·2 mm deep.
Blood 1/20
+ 00 = leucocytes per cu. mm.

The Formol Gel Test. The following is a simple and entirely non-specific test for a very high gamma globulin. It is positive in many chronic infections of sufficient severity and duration, and particularly in visceral leishmaniasis.

Method: The Formol Gel test.

Add a drop of formalin (not formol saline) to a millilitre of the patient's serum, mix gently and let the mixture stand. If strongly positive (++++) it will gel and become opaque in 20 minutes; if weakly positive (+) gelling will be delayed 24 hours.

A combined test for sickle cells and reticulocytes. Tests to demonstrate the sickling phenomenon have to be done on a wet preparation and reticulocytes can also be looked for this way. As both are common and important tests in the management of anaemia, a combined method which enables both to be examined on the same slide will be found very convenient (Figure 58). The method about to be described uses solid sodium metabisulphite which does not have to be weighed out or made up fresh each day. Because it has only been tried out on a limited scale at the time of going to press, an account of the standard method also is given.

If a suspension of blood in saline is placed under a coverslip, some powdered sodium metabisulphite placed at one edge and the preparation sealed, the powder will dissolve and slowly diffuse through the diluted blood. Somewhere on the diffusion gradient it will be present at the optimum concentration for sickling to take place. Thus, close to the powder itself the concentration will be too high and may even cause haemolysis, further away there will be a zone of unhaemolysed normal-looking cells and outside this again a zone where sickling takes place. Further on still where no reagent will yet have diffused no sickling will be seen. If the preparation is first examined near the powder and then progressively further away from it the band of sickling will be readily found. The preparation is sealed with a vaseline paraffin wax mixture which both excludes the air from the sickling preparation and anchors the coverslip. The saline must not be hypertonic.

Unfortunately, because brilliant cresyl blue seems to inhibit sickling, it is not possible to add it to the sickle preparation directly and search for reticulocytes and sickle cells in the same field. A double preparation must therefore be made in the following way.

Method: The combined sickling and reticulocyte test.

Divide a slide in half with a broad grease pencil line right across it. Place two large drops of saline close to either side of

Fig. 58.

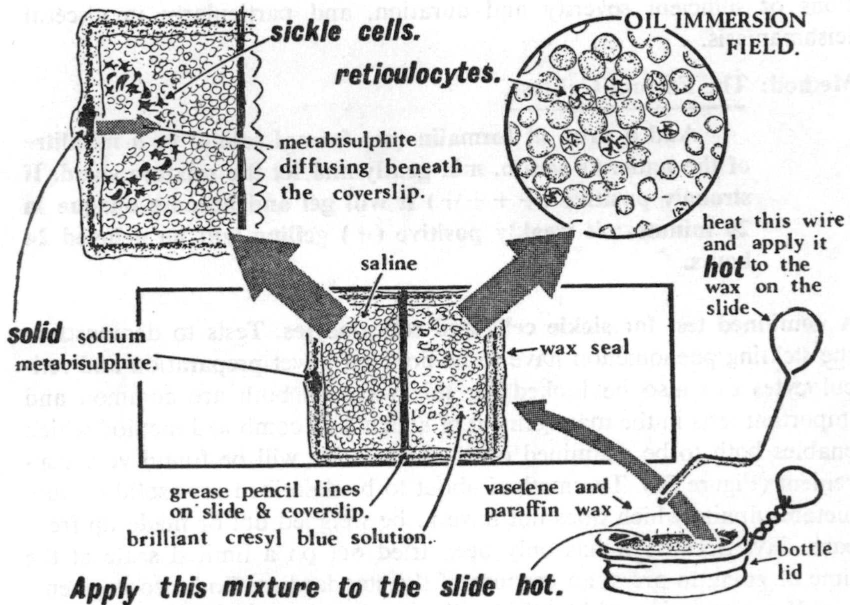

this line. To the right hand drop only, add a loopful of 1/500 brilliant cresyl blue solution. Take a loopful of blood in any anticoagulant, mix it in the left hand drop and transfer a loopful of this diluted suspension to the right hand drop.

Divide a coverslip in half with a grease pencil line, place it on top of the two drops on the slide such that the line drawn on it lies over the line on the slide. The grease will prevent the two drops mixing.

Place a small knife point of finely powdered sodium metabisulphite half way down the left hand margin of the coverslip. Gently tap the coverslip adjacent to the reagent once or twice; this will draw a little of the dissolving metabisulphite inside the preparation. Blow away the excess powder.

Seal the coverslip with equal parts of melted vaseline and paraffin wax (candle grease), heating the mixture in a deep tin lid with a wire handle and applying the hot liquid mixture with a stout wire (welding rod) bent as shown. Cover the undissolved metabisulphite with the sealing compound. Heat the wire in the flame and apply it hot to the mixture on the edge of the coverslip; this melts the mixture, promotes even sealing, and makes sure that the wax seal is not so high as to make it

difficult to examine the edge of the coverslip with an oil immersion lens.

The reticulocyte preparation can be examined immediately under the oil immersion objective, whereupon reticulocytes will be seen containing a network of tiny dense purple particles. By the time that the reticulocytes have been examined sickling may well have started; but if it has not, examine the preparation after it has been standing 20 minutes and again an hour later. Look first of all at the cells close to the sodium metabisulphite and work outwards from it.

The test is both simple and rapid; but one point to watch is the size of the drops of saline; these should not be too small, for when the coverslip is in place the cell suspension should just exude from its edges and so provide a little liquid in which the dry powder can dissolve. Another point is the importance of distinguishing sickled from crenated cells — sickle cells have long sharp points sticking out of them; the projections on crenated cells are rounded. Set up controls until thoroughly familiar with the method. The concentration of the brilliant cresyl blue is not critical, if the preparation is well sealed with wax the cells should not move about, and if reticulocytes are to be counted it will be helpful if the cell suspension is dilute and there are comparatively few cells in the field.

3 **Method: The standard sickling test.**

Place a small drop of blood on the centre of a clean microscope slide. Add two drops of 2% sodium metabisulphite, freshly prepared that day from powder that has been stored dry. Stir with the corner of a slide. Apply a coverslip. Let it stand 20 minutes. Rack down the condenser. Look for sickled cells; these are said to be most easily seen along the edge of the coverslip. It is advised that controls be set up every time.

4 **Method: A concentration method for trypanosomes and microfilaria.**

Take blood into citrate solution as for the Westergren ESR. Centrifuge it immediately for ten minutes — for trypanosomes at the maximum speed — for microfilaria slowly at 1,000 revolutions per minute. This is as much as a hand centrifuge will do, and about a third the maximum speed of most electric ones. The blood will separate into a layer of plasma, a narrow vague greyish layer of leucocytes (the 'buffy coat') and a layer of red cells. For trypanosomes examine the leucocyte layer, but when

looking for microfilaria take some of the red cell layer as well.

This is best done by removing the plasma with a Pasteur pipette before using the same pipette to transfer the leucocyte layer to a slide for examination beneath a coverslip.

Search the *whole* area of the coverslip, look for motile organisms using a medium or low power objective, depending upon whether trypanosomes or microfilaria are being looked for, and above all, examine fresh blood quickly (24:11).

A rapidly moving snake or fish-like object is likely to be either a trypanosome or a microfilaria; trypanosomes are of the same order of size as red cells, microfilariae are as long as, say, a hundred red cells.

Because trypanosomes often appear in the blood in a cyclical manner they may be missed unless the blood is examined daily for at least ten days.

24:25 **The blood sugar.** Though Dextrostix (AME) may well replace it, the Lovibond adaptation of Folin and Wu's technique is described here. Though adapted for the Lovibond comparator, the conversion scales in Figure 55 enable the method to be used with the Grey wedge photometer, while Thompson's grey enables it to be used with the EEL colorimeter (24:6). There are two closely similar Lovibond methods for the blood sugar: the one described here uses Lovibond discs 5/2A and 5/2B — these discs are not interchangeable with any others.

The principle of the method is that the blood proteins are precipitated with tungstic acid made by mixing equal volumes of solutions of sulphuric acid and sodium tungstate. Some of the clear protein-free filtrate is then heated under carefully controlled conditions with a solution of alkaline copper whereupon the glucose reduces part of the copper present. A blue colour is then generated with this reduced copper by adding phosphomolybdic acid to the mixture. Ready made solutions (BDH) can be purchased, but they are better prepared and distributed by a central laboratory.

Method: The blood sugar.

Measure 3.5 ml. of distilled water into the bottom of a standard test tube, not a centrifuge tube. Add 0.1 ml. of the blood sample. Add 0.2 ml. of 10% sodium tungstate. Mix by inversion with the thumb held over the top of the tube. Add 0.2 ml. of $\frac{2}{3}$N sulphuric acid. Mix again. Let stand for ten minutes while the protein clumps, then either filter the mixture through a *small* filter paper or centrifuge it. (A 7 cm. Whatman 41 paper is best but a Whatman No. 1 will do). Take 2 ml. of

the filtrate, add 2 ml. of alkaline copper, mix well by careful agitation, plug the tube loosely with cotton wool, and place it in a *vigorously boiling water bath for exactly six minutes,* **making quite sure that the mixture in the test tube is beneath the level of the boiling water. Cool a minute or two only under the tap, add 2 ml. of phosphomolybdic acid, add 6.5 ml. of water, mix, and rotate briskly to get rid of the bubbles of carbon dioxide.**

a) Use the Lovibond comparator directly.

b) With the red filter in the eyepiece of the 'Grey wedge, match the solution with the wedge and convert the reading on the disc to the blood sugar using the conversion scale in Figure 55.

c) Use the red Ilford filter No. 608 in the EEL colorimeter, zero the instrument with water, read the scale value for the Thompson's grey standard, read the scale value for the test solution and calculate according to this formula:

$$\textbf{Blood sugar} = \frac{\textbf{Reading of Test}}{\textbf{Reading of grey Standard}} \times 145 \text{ mg.\%}$$

It is convenient to add the sodium tungstate and the sulphuric acid as a measured number of drops from pipettes with tips of the same sizes kept in dropping bottles. The quantity used is of less importance than the equality of the volumes added. To ensure this, not only must the pipettes be of the same size but they must be held vertically. The size of the tips of these pipettes can be compared by seeing how they fit into any convenient small hole. The actual number of drops needed to make 0.2 ml. can be calculated from the number required to fill 1 ml. in a graduated centrifuge tube. The plugged test tube described here is an improvement on the expensive and fragile Folin tube usually used. With all three measuring instruments the cells or tubes must be substantially free of bubbles, or false results will be obtained. If the final solution is so intensely blue that it is beyond the scale of the instrument, repeat the test using 50 cu.mm. (0.05 ml.) of blood and doubling the result obtained. Otherwise, and less satisfactorily, dilute the deep blue solution with an equal quantity of water, take the reading and double the answer.

6 **The serum area.** This is an incorporation by the editor of the Lovibond urease Nesslerisation method and a modification suggested by Lile (25). Though unpublished elsewhere, it has proved highly satisfactory in emergency use in Mulago Hospital.

The serum urea closely approaches the blood urea, and is very easily estimated using a preparation of urease in glycerol to hydrolyse the urea to ammonia followed by the addition of Nessler's solution which forms a brown colour with this substance.

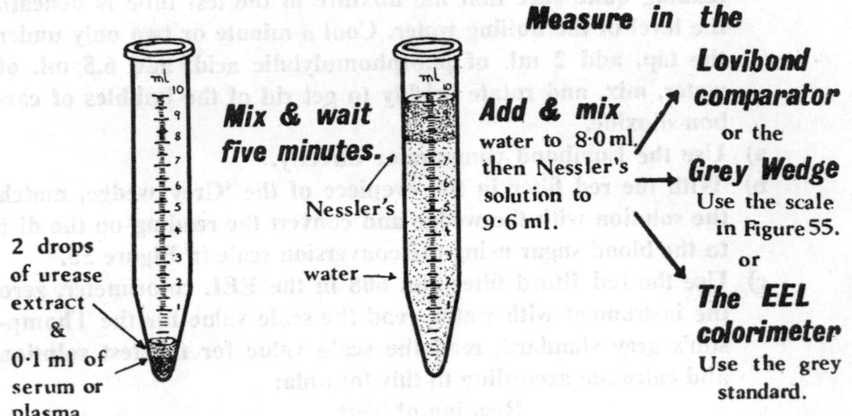
Fig. 59.
THE SERUM UREA.
Measure in the
Lovibond
comparator
or the
Grey Wedge
Use the scale
in Figure 55.
or
The EEL
colorimeter
Use the grey
standard.
Mix & wait
five minutes.
Add & mix
water to 8·0 ml.
then Nessler's
solution to
9·6 ml.
Nessler's
water
2 drops
of urease
extract
&
0·1 ml of
serum or
plasma.

Method: The serum urea.

In the bottom of a conical centrifuge tube graduated in 0.1 ml. divisions place 0.1 ml. of clear serum or plasma (citrated or sequestrinated but NOT oxalated plasma). This should be measured with a 0.1 ml. pipette, but some estimate of the urea can be obtained merely by using the first 0.1 ml. graduation at the bottom of the tube. Add two drops glycerol urease extract and mix well by flicking the tube. Leave to stand on the bench for five minutes, then, using a Pasteur pipette for the final adjustment, fill to precisely the 8 ml. mark with distilled water. Mix by inversion with the thumb over the end of the tube. Add Nessler's solution to exactly the 9.6 ml. mark and mix again.

a) Use the Lovibond comparator directly.

b) With the green No. 3 filter in the eyepiece of the Grey wedge match the solution as above and convert the reading on the disc to the blood urea with the conversion scale in Figure 55.

c) Use the blue Ilford filter No. 622, zero the instrument with water, read the scale value for the Thompson's grey solution, read the scale value for the test solution and calculate according to this formula:

$$\text{Serum Urea} = \frac{\text{Reading of Test}}{\text{Reading of grey Standard}} \times 135 \text{ mg.\%.}$$

The distilled water must be free from ammonia and if there is doubt about this, set up a 'blank' with water instead of serum — there should be no perceptible colour — a minor degree of discoloration can be compensated for by putting this 'blank' tube on the left hand side of the Lovibond or the Grey wedge and by using it to 'zero' the EEL.

If, with the EEL, the reading is beyond the scale of the instrument, repeat the test using 0.05 ml. (50 cu.mm.) of blood and doubling the value obtained. In practice very little trouble has resulted from the solution becoming turbid. Because the eye corrects for minor degrees of turbidity whereas an instrument cannot, this method is particularly well suited to the Lovibond comparator. Because of the compactness of the scale reading, the Grey wedge is the least satisfactory instrument to use.

METHODS FOR THE CEREBROSPINAL FLUID — 'CSF'.

7 **Specimens.** It is good practice to make a habit of taking two specimens and doing as many investigations as possible on the second one. If puncture has not been easy, this is the one that will be less contaminated with blood.

The first step in examining CSF should always be to hold it up to the light and observe its turbidity — this is just appreciable when 100 cells per cu. mm. are present. When counting cells blood is diluted 1/20, but CSF is either examined as it is ('neat'), or diluted with an equal volume of white cell diluting fluid. If the CSF is obviously purulent, a Gram-stained film may provide all the information needed.

8 **Method: The CSF cell count.**

Fill one side of a double Fuchs-Rosenthal chamber with neat CSF and the other with CSF diluted with an equal quantity of white cell diluting fluid. Count according to the diagram in Figure 57, and, if the CSF has been diluted with an equal quantity of white cell diluting fluid, double the final answer.

A single chamber can be used, as can a Neubauer one, but a double Fuchs-Rosenthal chamber is much the best.

9 **Method: CSF protein.**

a) *Using the Grey wedge.* **With a Pasteur pipette, measure 1.0 ml. of CSF into a graduated centrifuge tube, add 3 ml. of 3% sulphosalicylic acid, mix, wait five minutes, not more, then pour the mixture into the right hand cell of the instrument. With the green No. 2 filter in place and a water blank in the left hand cell, read off the CSF protein in mgm.% direct from the scale. (Normal less than 35 mgm.%).**

b) *Using proteinometer standards.* **Dilute the CSF with sulphosalicylic acid exactly as above. Five minutes after mixing compare its turbidity with a set of proteinometer standards (GAL) using the tube supplied for the purpose.**

c) *Using Pandy's test.* **Add a few drops of CSF to a few ml. of Pandy's reagent. There is no cloudiness with normal CSF and increasing cloudiness with increased protein. This test is usually reported as measuring 'increased globulin', but in practice a positive Pandy's test closely parallels the total protein. Below 25 mg.% of protein no CSF gives a positive Pandy's test, above 35 mg.% they all do. The test is thus a very useful indication of an abnormal CSF protein.**

24:30 **Method: THE CSF sugar.**

Proceed exactly as for a blood sugar except that four times as much CSF (0.4 ml.) as blood should be used and the answer divided by four. 60 mgm.% is the normal value; below 40 mgm.% the case is likely to be tuberculous, unless the case is one of suppurative meningitis when the sugar will be very low indeed (13:10b). If the examination is delayed, inhibit glycolysis in the sample with a tiny knife point of potassium fluoride.

24:31 **Method: Trypanosomes in the CSF.**

Spin several ml. of fresh CSF as fast as possible for ten minutes. Carefully pipette off the supernatant from the tiny bit of white precipitate that will probably be all that will be seen. *Suspend this in the least possible quantity of CSF,* **place it under a coverslip and search all of it in an orderly manner for moving organisms, using the medium power objective of the microscope (24:11).**

The following routine saves time, and though described as if cultural methods are possible, this part of the procedure can easily be cut out.

24:32 **Method: CSF general routine.**

Place a coverslip on a double Fuchs-Rosenthal chamber. In a test tube block a small blood grouping tube, an unsterile, graduated centrifuge tube, a sterile plugged centrifuge tube, and a Kahn tube filled with Pandy's reagent. With a sterile Pasteur

pipette take CSF from the second of the two specimen bottles, place 3-4 ml. in the sterile plugged centrifuge tube, add exactly 2 drops to the small tube, put a few drops in the Pandy's reagent and fill one side of the counting chamber, (this process should be aseptic until the plugged tube has been filled). Empty the pipette, add two drops of white cell diluting fluid to the small tube, empty the pipette again, mix the contents of this tube and with it fill the other side of the chamber.

Spin the plugged tube and count the cells while the tube is spinning. After five minutes at the fastest speed that the centrifuge will allow, remove the plugged tube and with a second sterile Pasteur pipette transfer 1 ml. of the supernatant to the graduated centrifuge tube for the estimation of protein, discard all the rest except for the smallest drop at the bottom. Suspend the deposit in this, transfer a drop of it to Petri dishes of media for culture and make a film of the remainder; stain it by Gram's method. The procedure should be aseptic until the film is made.

Prepare a gram-stained film whenever the CSF has come from a gravely ill patient for bacteria may sometimes be present, even though there is little increase in cells or protein. In other cases a film is only required if cells or protein are increased. Acid fast bacilli can be found in CSF from cases of tuberculous meningitis, but this is a very time consuming and skilled technique.

If the tap is bloody, it may be useful to remember that, when blood contaminates the CSF, its constituents are added in approximately the proportion of one leucocyte per cu.mm., five mgm.% of protein and 1,000 red cells per cu.mm.

METHODS FOR URINE

3 **General.** There are several very rapid chemical tests for substances in the urine. All are standard with the exception of the test for INH (10). This is for the acetylated derivative that is excreted in the urine, it will not work therefore with a solution of INH tablets. The test employs Chloramine T and has the disadvantage that only some batches of this substance will work — that made by Eastman Kodak (EAS) is specified. A further disadvantage is that the test employs the deadly poison, potassium cyanide. This makes it potentially dangerous in the hands of auxiliary staff to whom its dangers must be explained. Bottles of cyanide must be marked 'POISON', it should never be pipetted by mouth, and no strong acid should ever be added to any cyanide compound or a deadly gas may be evolved. Lastly, the tests should be done in a well ventilated place.

24:34 **Method: Urine protein.**

Mix 1 ml. of clear urine — filtered if necessary — with 3 ml. 3% sulphosalicylic acid solution. A turbidity or precipitate indicates the presence of protein. Some prefer to add a few drops of 25 % sulphosalicylic acid to the urine.

24:35 **Method: Urine reducing substances.**

Mix 8 drops of urine and 5 ml. of Benedict's qualitative reagent. Hold the tube in a sheet of paper folded into a narrow strip. Boil the mixture hard for two minutes, agitating meanwhile to prevent it bumping out of the tube. Let it stand a few minutes and examine for turbidity. A grey precipitate is negative, but with increasing quantities of reducing substance, its colour changes from green (+), through yellow (+ +) and orange (+ + +) finally to become brick red (+ + + +).

The time of heating and the proportions of urine and reagent are important. A convenient way of measuring the proportions approximately is to fill a tube, say ⅓ full of urine, to pour it rapidly into another one where it can be used for the protein test and then put the first one back in the rack. Enough urine will remain in this tube to form the right proportions for testing if an inch (2.5 cm.) of Benedict's solution is now added. Several sugars give a positive reaction, particularly lactose, but only glucose is positive with the 'Clinstix' test.

24:36 **Method: Urine acetone bodies.**

Fill a test tube with half an inch of dry powdered Rothera's reagent, pour on urine so that this is just covered and mix gently — most of the reagent will dissolve. Add an inch of concentrated ammonia. If negative the tube remains pale pink, if acetone bodies are present, it changes through red (+) to the deepest purple (+ + + +). Users will probably find 'Acetest' tablets (AME) more convenient.

24:37 **Method: Urine bilirubin.**

Add one volume of 10% barium chloride to two volumes of urine, filter the turbid mixture through a small paper. As soon as the urine has flowed through remove the paper, put it in the sink and add a drop or two of Fouchet's reagent to the precipitate — if this goes blue bilirubin is present. 'Ictotest' tablets (AME) can be used instead.

8 **Method: Urine urobilinogen — Ehrlich's test.**

To 5 ml. of *fresh* urine add an equal quantity of Ehrlich's reagent, let it stand for 10 minutes, add 10 ml. of saturated sodium acetate. If urobilinogen or porphobilinogen is present in abnormal amount the mixture goes pink or red.

9 **Method: Urine 'PAS'.**

Dip one of the strips described in Appendix D into the urine. PAS or any other salicylate (e.g. aspirin) turns them blue — a light blue in low concentrations, a darker blue in higher ones.

0 **Method: Urine 'INH'.**

Use a porcelain or plastic plate with circular wells. (See Appendix F 'Haemagglutination Tray'). If the plastic is transparent place a sheet of white paper behind it.

Place four drops of urine in a well, then add four drops of 10% potassium cyanide (POISON) solution. After this add nine drops of chloramine T solution. When INH has been ingested up to 12 hours previously a red colour of varying intensity develops within one minute. For the following 12 hours INH is only present in the urine in trace amounts and the urine only goes pink. Negative urines remain yellow. The exact number of drops used is critical as is the sequence in which the reagents are added and the brand of chloramine T used (see 24:33). Do not shake the plate between the addition of reagents.

1 **Method: Urine spun deposit.**

Place 10 ml. of urine in a centrifuge tube, spin hard for five minutes, carefully pipette off the supernatant urine and examine the deposit under a coverslip. When looking for the ova of *S. haematobium* search the whole area of the coverslip in a regular manner (24:11).

2 **Method: Urine pus cell count.**

If the cells have had time to settle mix the urine well. Fill a Fuchs-Rosenthal counting chamber with neat urine and count the cells after the manner of Figure 57. Normal people have less than 10 cells cu.mm. A count higher than this is often due to a urethritis or a vaginal discharge. Only if those two causes are excluded can an abnormal pus cell count be attributed to disease of the kidneys or bladder.

A METHOD FOR THE GASTRIC JUICE

Though it will seldom be wanted this is a very simple method for testing for the presence of free acid in the gastric juice.

24:43 **Method: Free acid in the gastric juice.**

Give a fasting patient 100 mg. of mepyramine ('Anthisan') intramuscularly. Half an hour later give him 0.04 mg./kg. of histamine subcutaneously. Half an hour after that pass a gastric tube and test the material aspirated with congo red paper. If 'free acid' is present this paper will turn blue; in this it is unlike litmus paper which goes red in the presence of acid.

VAGINAL AND URETHRAL DISCHARGES

It is so easy to examine for the presence of *T. vaginalis* that a microscope should be readily available in every outpatient department. Because trichomonads die so readily this is much more satisfactory than sending specimens to a laboratory. Urethral discharges in which no presumptive gonococci can be found by Gram's method should also be examined for this parasite (For treatment see 30:1).

24:44 **Method: Finding T. vaginalis**

Using a clean pipette transfer some vaginal or urethral discharge to a slide and immediately examine it under a coverslip. In these situations any motile protozan is almost certainly *T. vaginalis.*

METHODS FOR STOOLS

24:45 **General.** The only chemical method described here is the orthotolidine-barium peroxide method for occult blood; this should supersede the use of benzidine which is carcinogenic. Two concentration methods are described; the formol ether method is a general purpose procedure, and the AMS III method, which closely resembles it, is the best way to demonstrate the ova of *S. mansoni* in the stool. Under most circumstances these are methods to be used for the occasional perplexing case. Though ether is specified for both methods, preliminary experiments indicate that petrol may be equally effective.

24:46 **Method: Occult blood in the stools.**

Dissolve 200 mg. of orthotolidine-barium peroxide mixture in 5 ml. of glacial acetic acid — the solution will go green.

Smear a faecal sample over the corner of a piece of filter paper, place it in the sink, and pour some of the test reagent over it. A deep greenish-blue colour within 15 seconds is strongly positive (+ +); a greenish colour appearing after 30 seconds is weakly positive (+); if no colour appears in 30 seconds the test is negative.

This test is only positive if 3 ml. or more of blood are lost each day — a useful degree of sensitivity: the only dietary restriction should be the avoidance of blood, black pudding or large quantities of meat or liver. The reagent is stable for one day only. 200 mg. of mixture should be weighed a few times, until it can be judged by eye on the end of a knife point, or in a little scoop kept in the cork of the bottle of powdered reagent.

Faecal microscopy. The microscopy of faeces requires considerable skill, and the best way for an assistant to acquire it is by a period of apprenticeship to an experienced microscopist in a central laboratory. If they can both see the same field at the same time using a double binocular microscope (ZEI) instruction is rapid — this is much the best way to teach any form of microscopy.

Method: The saline faecal smear.

Put a drop of saline on a slide, choose a mucoid or blood stained part of the stool and emulsify it with an applicator stick. When a coverslip is applied the whole of its area should be evenly filled with an emulsion of such an opacity that newsprint can just be read through it. This is a convenient 'standard faecal sample' (see 24:65) and contains about 1/500 of a gram of solid faeces. First examine the preparation under the low power — this will demonstrate the larger ova while cysts will appear as small refractile spheres; these can then be examined under the high power objective, and if need be, under oil. If an oil immersion objective is being used seal the coverslip with vaseline paraffin wax mixture described in section 24:22. In difficult cases nuclear detail is improved if a drop of iodine is run in under one edge of the coverslip.

Method: The formol-ether concentration test.

With an applicator stick or glass rod emulsify one or two grams of faeces in 10 ml. of water in a centrifuge tube. Pour the thin suspension that results through a fine sieve into

another tube. Centrifuge, decant the supernatant, add 10 ml. of formal saline. Add to it 3 ml. of ether, preferably cold and straight from the refrigerator (For the use of petrol see 24:25). Shake it hard, centrifuge it at 2,000 revolutions per minute for two minutes. Three layers will be seen, an upper etherial one, a middle layer with much debris and a lower clearer aqueous one. Loosen the middle layer by passing an applicator stick round the inside of the tube. Carefully pour off anything except the deposit at the bottom of the tube. Clean the inside of the tube with a gauze swab. Use a fine Pasteur pipette to transfer the deposit to a slide, examine microscopically — increased numbers of ova and cysts will be found.

A plastic tea-strainer makes a good sieve, if this is not available two layers of moist gauze in a funnel will serve. 2,000 revolutions per minute should be approached gradually and attained at the end of the two minute period. This is somewhat less than most bench centrifuges will do, though about the limit of the one specified in Appendix F.

24:49 **Method: The AMS III concentration test.**

Emulsify one or two grams of faeces in 10 ml. of sodium sulphate-hydrochloric acid mixture. Pour the fine suspension that results into another tube through two layers of moist gauze or a plastic tea-strainer. Centrifuge at 2,000 revolutions per minute for two minutes. Decant the supernatant, add 10 ml. of the same mixture to the deposit. Resuspend. Centrifuge again as before. Decant the supernatant once more, add 10 ml. of the mixture plus 3 ml of cold ether and a drop of 'Teepol' or other detergent. Shake hard, centrifuge, and proceed as for method 24:48 except that the final deposit should be suspended in a drop of saline.

Don't leave these specimens on the microscope stage — the hydrochloric acid vapour will destroy the objectives.

BIOPSY TECHNIQUES

24:50 **General.** There are several biopsy techniques that should be within the scope of every doctor; the simpler ones are the rectal snip for *S. mansoni*, the skin snip for *O. volvulus*, skin smears for *Myco. leprae* and nasal smears for *Myco. leprae*. Slightly more complex methods are bone marrow aspiration and needle biopsy of the liver. Aspirated marrow can be examined in every hospital, but liver biopsy will only be practicable in areas where there is a good histology service.

51 **Method: The rectal snip for *S. mansoni.***

Pass a sigmoidoscope or proctoscope. Select a suspicious area of the mucosa. Remove a small piece of mucosa with biopsy forceps.

Put in on a slide, moisten it with saline. Place another slide on the top of it, press them together and look for the lateral spined ova of *S. mansoni* under the microscope.

52 **Method: The skin snip for *O. volvulus.***

Send the patient out into the warmth of the sun for half an hour — this improves the chances of finding the worms. Insert a sharp needle about a millimetre into the skin of the iliac crest keeping the needle in the surface plane of the skin. When the skin is impaled on the end of the needle, lift it up and raise a small fold. With a razor blade or sharp scalpel cut off a 2 mm. skin fragment from the very summit of this fold, just beneath the needle point. Put the fragment on a slide, add a drop of saline and a coverslip. Examine it under the low power of the microscope. In heavy infections the microfilariae of *O. volvulus.* will immediately be seen worming their way out of the snip but do not discard the preparation as negative until twenty minutes have passed.

53 **The laboratory diagnosis of leprosy. (By courtesy of Dr. S. G. Browne).** The laboratory diagnosis of leprosy depends upon the finding of *Myco. leprae* in smears from the skin or nasal mucosa, or upon the presence of a characteristic histological picture in the dermis. While, in the great majority of patients leprosy can be diagnosed on clinical grounds alone, and should be, the examination of material obtained from smears from the skin or nasal mucosa is frequently of value for confirmation of the diagnosis, for assessing the gravity of the infection, for classification and for prognosis.

Sites to smear. The most active part of the edge of the most active lesion; the ear-lobes; the mucosa of the nasal septum; the buttocks or thighs; the apparently unaffected skin — in that order. The nasal mucosa is almost never affected first, but it frequently remains positive longest.

The presence of Myco. leprae. In lepromatous leprosy, all the sites smeared usually contain *Myco. leprae,* either singly or in a globi containing about fifty bacilli. In tuberculoid leprosy, no *Myco. leprae* can be found by standard procedures, except during reactional phases. In cases of the intermediate kind bacilli may or may not be present. Saprophytic acid-fast organisms may be present in nasal mucus, but confusion with *Myco. leprae* should not occur if technique is good. In nasal smears *Myco. leprae* are present in globi as well as singly, and are interspersed with tissue cells.

Histology. The excision of material for histological examination differs in no way from standard methods employed in other conditions. The skin should be excised under local anaesthesia so as to include the edge of a lesion and enough of the papillary layer of the dermis for the terminal nerve fibrils to be included. This will also ensure that the cellular histology of both the deep and the superficial layers of the dermis is available for study.

Unfortunately, when the clinical features are equivocal, little help is, as a rule, to be gained from either smears or histology. If there is any atypical feature in the clinical appearance, then both take smears and remove a portion of skin for histology — surprises lie in store, even for the most experienced.

4:54 **Method: Skin smears.**

Thoroughly clean the skin with a cotton woolswab soaked in spirit, and allow it to dry. Compress a skin fold between the thumb and the forefinger of the left hand, and, with a sharp and sterile scalpel (a small Bard-Parker scalpel serves excellently), make an incision half a centimetre long *just* into the papillary layer of the dermis. If pressure with the fingers is maintained and if the incision is not too deep there should be no bleeding. Turn the blade of the scalpel through a right angle, and, with its point, firmly scrape the sides of the incision from end to end. Do this twice. Transfer the juice and pulp thus obtained to a new clean microscope slide. Try to obtain a uniform amount of material from successive sites, and try to spread this material over a uniform area of slide. Always follow the same order in transferring material from site to slide. Six to eight smears may conveniently be made on each slide, while still leaving sufficient space at the ends for marking in the patient's name with grease pencil.

To avoid false positives wipe the scalpel on a spirit soaked swab and flame it, both between one site and another, and between one patient and another. For staining see 24:14.

24:55 **Method: Nasal smears.**

A useful spud for removing material from the nasal mucosa may be made from a straightened paper clip (the stout variety), or, better still, from a bicycle spoke. Hammer out

the ends of these instruments, so that they become fusiform. The edges should be somewhat sharp — not too sharp.

Expose the septum in a good light by inserting a nasal speculum into the nostril. Remove any mucus present on the septum with a dry cotton wool swab. Firmly stroke, either the hyperaemic mucosa, or a definite nodule in it, so as to obtain a small amount of mucus membrane. A little capillary oozing is unavoidable, but blood in any quantity will make the specimen valueless. Spread the material on a microscope slide; fix and stain by the method in section 24:14.

56 **Marrow biopsy.** In large hospitals bone marrows are usually biopsied by the laboratory staff and examined by specialists, but the method itself is easy and a doctor who makes a habit of looking at marrows soon becomes familiar with them. When learning to examine them, a doctor should first examine a patient's film himself, he should then lay one aside and send the others away for a pathologist's opinion. When this comes back, and the pathologist thinks differently, the film can be examined again in the light of what has been said about it.

Among the conditions where a marrow biopsy will be found valuable are megaloblastic anaemia, visceral Leishmaniasis, and leucaemia. A detailed marrow count is seldom required, and after a little practice a rapid glance at a marrow film will produce the information required in most cases.

A method is given here for preparing a complete setting in a sterile roll, though some prefer to have the needles autoclaved separately in a large test tube and get the rest of the setting boiled up on each occasion. But complete settings can often save much time. They can also be used for liver biopsy and lumbar puncture, and, if the ward staff do not know how to make them up, they should be provided with a rough diagram of what is required.

57 **Apparatus.** Obtain a Klima marrow puncture needle (A&H). This has the advantage of possessing a screw guard that cannot slip, and so allow dangerous penetration of the needle point (Figure 55). Obtain a well fitting 10 ml. syringe with a piston that produces a good vacuum and which fits the Klima needle. Obtain also a 5 ml. syringe for the local anaesthetic, a fine hypodermic needle and a somewhat stouter intramuscular one. Make a cloth roll with separate pockets at its centre to contain the several items of this equipment and another to contain swabs. Provide a tin, and place in it a gallipot, the roll of instruments and a hand towel. Close the lid and autoclave it. When cold place a strip of adhesive plaster across the edge of the lid and write in the word 'sterile' and the

date of the autoclaving. This set will be ready at any time, it can be fetched during the course of a ward round and will enable a marrow biopsy to be undertaken at a moment's notice.

24:58 **Method: Marrow biopsy.**

Preferably sedate the patient (24:62). Lay several clean slides on the instrument trolley.

Lay the patient on his back in bed, put a pillow under his shoulders so that his head is thrown well back and his chin out of the way of his sternum.

Swab the skin of his manubrium sterni with iodine. Right in the centre of the manubrium raise a wheal in the skin with 1% procaine, or a similar anaesthetic, using the fine needle. With the stouter needle, go through this wheal to infiltrate the subcutaneous tissues and the periosteum of the manubrium with about 3 ml. of the anaesthetic agent.

Set the guard on the Klima needle so that only about 12 to 15 mm. of needle shaft protrudes. Dissipate any local anaesthetic that may be causing a swelling at the proposed site of the puncture by pressing it with a sterile swab.

With a boring motion push the needle through the skin and subcutaneous tissues into the cavity of the bone in the middle of the manubrium. The amount of force required varies, but it may have to be considerable. It is usually easy to tell when the cavity of the bone has been entered for the needle will then be firmly impaled in the manubrium. When this happens, remove the stilette, fit the 5 ml. syringe, and suck up a small quantity of marrow. If the tip of the needle is in the marrow cavity the patient usually complains of severe pain when suction is applied — a good indication that the needle is correctly in place. *Immediately marrow appears in the syringe stop sucking* **and transfer small drops of aspirate to the slides that have been put out to receive it. Prepare films in exactly the same way as when making them from blood, wave them dry in the air.**

Many workers prefer to discharge the aspirate from the syringe on to a watch glass containing a few crystals of sequestrine (potassium EDTA Appendix E) and to draw back the blood into the syringe. This leaves the larger marrow fragments behind. These are then transferred to slides with a pipette, and films made in the usual way.

Send the films along to the laboratory immediately to be stained by Leishman's method. Call and have a look at them

at the end of the ward round. Scan the film first under low power, and then choose a suitable area for scrutiny with the oil immersion objective.

The procedure is usually easy. The first cause of difficulty is failure to obtain marrow on initial aspiration with the syringe. When this happens reinsert the stylet, rotate the needle and try again. Should this fail, repeat the aspiration a few millimetres to one side of the first puncture using the same skin wound. If this again fails, the process can be repeated on one of the spinous processes or just posterior to the anterior superior iliac spine.

Dilution of the marrow with blood is sometimes unavoidable, but can be reduced by sucking with the syringe for the *minimum* time only. Blood and marrow are readily distinguished on the slide for marrow is greasy with particles of fat.

Careful technique will minimize the danger of infection, and it is good practice to autoclave needles for the procedure inside stout glass tubes in the pockets of the roll. The stylet in particular should be put back in this sterile tube between one attempt at aspiration and the next.

:59 **Needle biopsy of the liver.** Where a good histological service is available needle biopsy of the liver is a valuable diagnostic aid in distinguishing carcinoma of the liver from cirrhosis, and in diagnosing visceral Leishmaniasis, brucellosis and schistosomiasis. It also promises to be of great value in separating from the diverse group of 'tropical splenomegaly' those cases which are due to chronic malaria ('big spleen disease'), for there is increasing evidence that the livers of these patients have a characteristic type of round cell infiltration of the sinusoids, and that they respond well to antimalarial therapy.

Liver biopsy is thus of particular value in the tropics and it is fortunate that it has also been made much easier and safer by the invention of the Menghini needle (CHT) 25/- ($3.5) (Figure 60).

:60 **Contraindications.** Needle biopsy is contraindicated by deep jaundice; severe anaemia and any bleeding tendency as evidenced by petechiae, eccymoses or haemorrhages; it is also contraindicated by hydatid disease where it may lead to anaphylaxis or fatal dissemination. Needle biopsy is not justified where there are no transfusion facilities available (23:1) and it is normally advised that it should only be undertaken when the one stage prothrombin time is not more than 5 seconds longer than the control. Though ideal, this is a precaution that may be dispensed with, provided that the above contraindications are adhered to and the patient is carefully watched for 8 hours after puncture, and his pulse taken half hourly. He should also remain in bed for 24 hours afterwards.

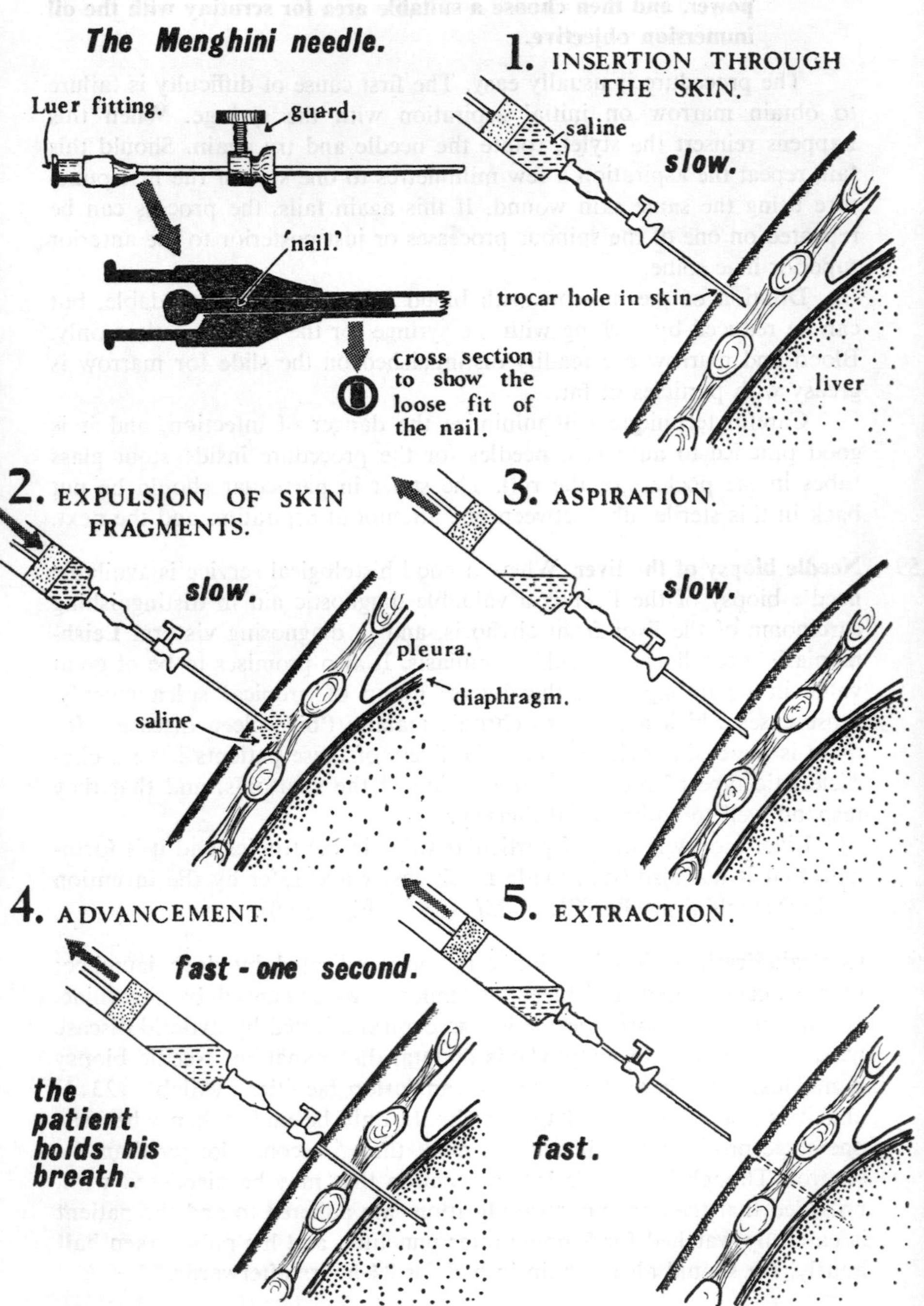
Fig.60.
LIVER BIOPSY.
The Menghini needle.
Luer fitting.
guard.
'nail.'
cross section to show the loose fit of the nail.
1. INSERTION THROUGH THE SKIN.
saline
slow.
trocar hole in skin
liver
2. EXPULSION OF SKIN FRAGMENTS.
slow.
pleura.
diaphragm.
saline
3. ASPIRATION.
slow.
4. ADVANCEMENT.
fast - one second.
the patient holds his breath.
5. EXTRACTION.
fast.

:61 **Apparatus.** The Menghini needle consists of a stout needle with a specially sharpened end, an adjustable guard, and a special loose fitting device, 'the nail', which slips inside the needle and serves to prevent the biopsy fragment falling back and fragmenting in the syringe. It is supplied in 3 sizes, 1 mm., 1.6 mm., and 2 mm. The 1.6 mm. needle is the most often used. A short sharp trocar is supplied with which to pierce the skin, and also an obturator to clear the needle — these are not shown in Figure 60.

:62 **Method: Menghini needle biopsy of the liver.**

Try out the needle by performing a biopsy on a banana and if possible practise on a cadaver first.

If there is ascites present, tap it.

Give the patient a mild sedative such as 50 mg. of pethidine, and 50 mg. of chlorpromazine ('Largactil') by mouth half an hour before puncture.

Before starting the procedure make quite sure that the patient understands what is being done, and get him to practise holding his breath. This is important, because both puncture itself and the introduction of the anaesthetic beforehand, must be undertaken while the patient holds his breath at the end of expiration. If he breathes, and so moves his liver when there is a needle inside it, a severe laceration may result.

Lie the patient on his back with his right side as near to the edge of the bed as possible, place a firm pillow against his left side in the hollow of the bed. Place his right arm behind his head, and turn his face to the left.

Choose a point in the mid or anterior axillary lines in the 8th, 9th or 10th intercostal space, but whichever place is chosen, puncture must be undertaken at the point of maximal dullness to percussion. This will vary from patient to patient.

Clean the skin with iodine or 'Hibitane', anaesthetize the chosen site with 2% procaine and pierce the anaesthetized area with the special trocar provided, or with a scalpel. While the patient holds his breath use a long (8 cm.) fine bore needle to infiltrate 5 ml. of procaine solution into the pleura, the diaphragm, the peritoneum and the capsule of the liver.

Fit the Menghini needle to a well fitting 10 ml. syringe, set the guard at about 4 cm. and draw up 3 ml. of sterile saline.

Pass the needle point through the anaesthetized track down to but not through the intercostal space. Inject 2 ml. of saline to clear the needle point of any skin fragments. (There is some difference of opinion as to the plane in which this is best

done. Menghini himself advises that saline be discharged and the needle cleared in the subcutaneous tissues. This is shown in Figure 60, drawing two, but others prefer to go through the intercostal muscles just short of the liver before clearing the needle by injecting saline. It seems that this is the better procedure).

GET THE PATIENT TO HOLD HIS BREATH IN EXPIRATION.

Start to aspirate, and, while continuing to aspirate, ***rapidly*** **push the needle into the liver perpendicular to the skin and** ***immediately pull it out again.*** **There is no need to rotate the needle. As soon as the needle has been removed apply pressure to the site of the biopsy.**

Continue aspirating until the needle point has been placed under some saline in a glass dish. Discharge the saline remaining in the syringe. The biopsy specimen will appear. Rescue it and transfer it to formol saline. Clear the needle with the obturator.

24:63 **Aftercare.** This is important because a very occasional patient bleeds. Confine the patient strictly to bed and take his pulse half hourly for eight hours. Should this rise, and his blood pressure fall, transfusion may be required.

The great advantage of this method over that of Vim-Silverman is that the needle is in the liver only for the briefest period. Though convincing statistical confirmation is lacking it is probable that the Menghini procedure is better than that of Vim-Silverman. Not only is the method safe but discomfort to the patient is minimal, and the instrument is both cheap and simple. The great disadvantage of the method is that its failure rate is high in the presence of cirrhosis, so where the liver is likely to be cirrhotic, a Vim Silverman needle may be used. Because this is not nearly such a simple procedure, and is probably not such a safe one, it is not described here.

THE LABORATORY IN THE DIAGNOSIS OF ANAEMIA.

24:64 **The diagnostic régime.** The methods at hand for investigating anaemia are strictly limited in a rural hospital, and have been described in detail in the preceding sections. But even so, when combined with the clinical findings, they enable the common anaemias to be diagnosed satisfactorily and thus make it possible to apply the therapeutic measures available in a logical way. Because these are all of them only effective when given for the right indications, correct diagnosis is clearly essential.

There are several readily available measures for the relief of anaemia and they have often to be combined. They are, 'TCE' for hookworm anaemia (13:7), anti-malarial drugs, iron as ferrous sulphate tablets or iron dextran, folic acid for the various types of megaloblastic anaemia, and cyanocobalmin (Vitamin B12) for pernicious anaemia. As well as these there are surgical operations such as hysterectomy for the cure of excessive uterine bleeding, drugs for the treatment of schistosomiasis, and blood transfusion for the relief of the gravest cases of anaemia (23:17). But how are these measures to be deployed to the best advantage, particularly in those cases where there is no obvious clinical cause for the anaemia?

Figure 61 is an attempt to answer this and shows the steps that can be taken to arrive at the right diagnosis with a limited number of tests. The thickness of the arrows is an attempt to give some idea of the importance of particular conditions, but these will have to be modified to suit local circumstances such as the existence of thalassaemia for example.

The first step is to estimate the haemoglobin (24:17) and to decide upon some arbitrary standard as to how severe an anaemia must be before it is worth investigating further. 10 grams % (70% Haldane) is the value chosen here, but it may well have to be lower and must be altered in accordance with the number of patients seeking treatment, the severity of their anaemias, and the time that can be spent investigating them. Having decided on a level, it may be found convenient to ask the laboratory assistant to proceed with the next steps in the investigation automatically.

The first of these is to make a Leishman film (24:12) and a reticulocyte-sickle cell preparation (24:22) on all those blood samples with a haemoglobin less than the agreed value. But, if it is to be useful diagnostically, the Leishman film must be well made, particularly if it is to be used to judge hypochromia. To this end detailed instructions have to be given in the text and a diagram has also been provided (Figure 56).

The first feature to examine in a blood film is the way in which the cells are filled with haemoglobin, for this enables cases of anaemia to be divided into the three broad groups shown in the figure — the macrocytic, normochromic, and hypochromic anaemias.

65 **Hypochromic anaemias.** It is convenient to discuss the hypochromic anaemias first. These are due to impaired haemoglobin production which is usually the result of iron deficiency, but in some areas it can also be due to thalassaemia (see below). In hypochromic anaemias the red cells are poorly filled with haemoglobin and so appear pale. The average size of these red cells is also smaller than normal, but this is apt to be less easy to judge than their pallor.

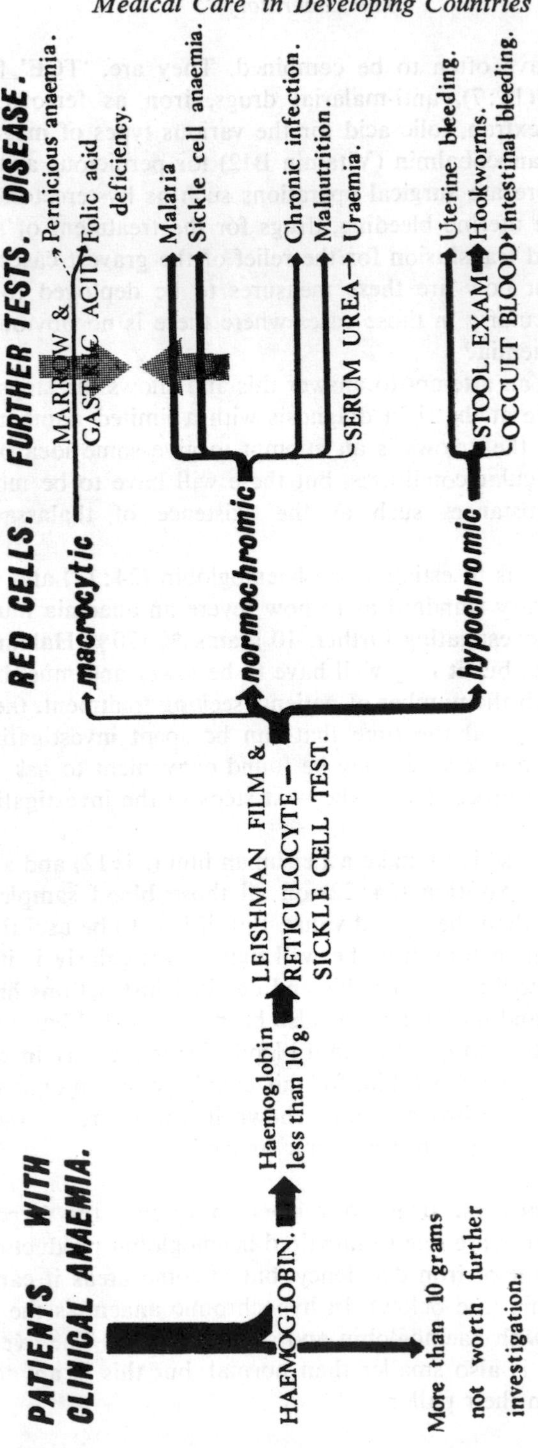

THE DIAGNOSIS OF ANAEMIA.
PATIENTS WITH CLINICAL ANAEMIA.
HAEMOGLOBIN.
More than 10 grams not worth further investigation.
Haemoglobin less than 10 g.
LEISHMAN FILM & RETICULOCYTE – SICKLE CELL TEST.
RED CELLS.
FURTHER TESTS.
DISEASE.
macrocytic
MARROW & GASTRIC ACID
Pernicious anaemia.
Folic acid deficiency.
normochromic
Malaria
Sickle cell anaemia.
Chronic infection.
Malnutrition.
SERUM UREA
Uraemia.
hypochromic
Uterine bleeding.
STOOL EXAM
Hookworms.
OCCULT BLOOD
Intestinal bleeding.
Arrows indicate those conditions where the reticulocytes are typically either increased or decreased . See 24:64.

Fig.61.

The commonest cause of hypochromic iron deficiency anaemia is likely to be hookworm infection; next comes chronic blood loss from the uterus and gastrointestinal tract, to which urinary schistosomiasis must be added in some areas. If the red cells look pale the laboratory assistant should himself ask the patient to provide a stool to be examined for hookworm ova.

In many areas most of the population will harbour some hookworms, yet few may have enough to cause significant anaemia. It is useful therefore to be able to form some idea of the severity of an infection. This can be done by making a standard faecal smear by method 24:47 and counting *all* the ova beneath a 22 x 22 mm. (7/8 x 7/8 inch.) coverslip after the manner described in section 24:11. Below 20 ova the infection can be considered mild and treatment may not be warranted. Above 20 and certainly above 40 ova the patient should be treated. There is also a general correlation between the number of ova present and the presence of occult blood in the stools (24:46). When tested by the method described here it is invariably positive (+) when more than 70 ova are present, and, when strongly positive (++), there will not be less than this number of worms present. When the occult blood test is strongly positive, and yet there are less than this number of ova present, some other cause for intestinal bleeding should be sought.

Until iron has been given the reticulocyte count of patients with hypochromic anaemia is likely to be low.

4:66 **The normochromic anaemias.** In this group the red cells are normally filled with haemoglobin and are of normal size. This is likely to be the largest group of all, and is conveniently divided into two subgroups. The first is that in which haemolysis predominates; typically the reticulocyte count is high and provides evidence that blood is being actively regenerated. The common causes are malaria, sickle cell anaemia and thalassaemia, depending upon the area. Between them, the Leishman film and the sickle cell test will already have provided evidence for both malaria and sickle cell anaemia and given some help in the diagnosis of thalassaemia. (See below, section 24:68).

In the second normochromic subgroup the reticulocytes are normal or reduced. Uraemia will be responsible for a very small proportion of these cases but most will have to be diagnosed more or less by exclusion as being due to chronic infection or malnutrition. Such cases are likely to be both common and comparatively mild.

4:67 **Macrocytic anaemia.** A macrocytic anaemia is one in which the average size of the red cells is larger than normal. A variable proportion of these cases, depending on the area, will be due to a megaloblastic change in the marrow, the important causes of this being folic acid deficiency, or, much more rarely vitamin B 12 deficiency. When the marrow is megaloblastic, careful search of the peripheral film will show not only red cells of larger than average size but also a few red cells with immature nuclei. Patients with a peripheral blood picture of this kind should therefore have a marrow biopsy (24:56), followed by a test for the presence of free acid in their gastric juice (24:43). It must be emphasized, however, that true pernicious anaemia forms such a small fraction of all cases of megaloblastic anaemia in most parts of the tropics that the routine examination of the gastric juice for the presence of free acid must be considered a council of perfection. In most areas it is justifiable to give folic acid without first excluding the achlorydria of pernicious anaemia.

Is it justifiable to give folic acid to anaemic patients whose peripheral films suggest a megaloblastic marrow without first doing a marrow biopsy? The answer is yes, though, as has been pointed out earlier, a marrow biopsy is so easy that it should be undertaken very readily.

As with iron deficiency anaemias the reticulocyte count is likely to be low until treatment is begun.

Very occasionally, the Leishman film will provide immediate evidence for the cause of anaemia and demonstrate the presence of leukaemia.

68 **Further diagnostic difficulty.** How complete is such a scheme and what are its weak points? Perhaps as many as four-fifths of all cases of gross anaemia can be diagnosed in this way. One of its weaknesses lies in the difficulty of assessing milder degrees of hypochromia and macrocytic change in a blood film. A major assistance with the first is an accurate packed cell volume, preferably obtained with a 'microhaematocrit centrifuge' (HAW) (£56, $150). The packed cell volume can be combined with haemoglobin, which incidentally must be accurate, to give the 'mean corpuscular haemoglobin concentration,' or 'MCHC', low values for which are very good evidence for the presence of iron deficiency. The MCHC is easily obtained by dividing the haemoglobin in grams by the packed cell volume as a percentage and multiplying by 100. Normally it is between 32% and 36%.

Then, there is the multiple causation of many cases of anaemia and particularly the relative folic acid deficiency that may be seen in such diseases as sickle cell anaemia, thalassaemia and chronic malaria. In these conditions the primary disease produces an increased demand for folic acid that a poor diet cannot meet. Though it may have no effect on the primary condition, folic acid may yet be of great benefit in these cases (13:12). It is fortunate therefore that folic acid is cheap (30:1). Because the folic acid in local diets varies greatly from one area to another, so also does its importance as a cause of anaemia and the value of supplying it as a supplement. Folic acid deficiency is a common cause of anaemia in parts of West Africa and India, but not apparently in Uganda.

Lastly, there is the difficulty of diagnosing thalassaemia in the areas where it is seen without more sophisticated tests. For genetic reasons the production of normal haemoglobin is impaired, abnormal types of haemoglobin are produced and the cells appear hypochromic. Though it is often possible to be fairly certain about the diagnosis of thalassaemia major from the appearance of the blood film, further consideration of it is beyond our scope here. Without the use of more sophisticated tests, even an expert cannot distinguish blood films due to thalassaemia minor from those due to iron deficiency. In the rural hospital, therefore, the diagnosis of thalassaemia major must thus rest on hypochromia and its clinical features; in the latter it resembles sickle cell anaemia in some respects. The diagnosis of thalassaemia minor has to rest very unsatisfactorily on the finding of a hypochromic anaemia which fails to respond to iron.

When an adequate diagnosis cannot be achieved in other ways a therapeutic trial can be useful, particularly if the haemoglobin can be estimated reasonably accurately, and a watch is kept for the reticulocytosis that will be maximal about seven days after giving iron or folic acid on the correct indications. Such a trial is always justified with iron, but, because folic acid may so confuse the diagnosis of pernicious anaemia, it is bad practice in temperate countries to give this substance as a therapeutic trial for a megaloblastic anaemia. Though not ideal in the tropics, because pernicious anaemia does occur here, folic acid deficiency is so much more common that a therapeutic trial of this kind is justified. It must be mentioned however that a reticulocyte response to folic acid is obtained even when folic acid is given to cases of pernicious anaemia. Thus a reticulocyte response to folic acid does not prove that the anaemia was necessarily due to folic acid deficiency.

Not only is an estimation of reticulocytosis valuable when the diagnosis is in doubt, but it is also good practice to confirm the efficiency of treatment even when diagnosis is certain by looking for a reticulocytosis routinely seven days after treatment has begun. This time interval is important, because a reticulocyte response may be missed if it is not observed fairly strictly.

Chapter Twenty-Five

X-RAY DEPARTMENT

Thomas Eddie

25:1 **General.** During the course of their training most doctors acquire a useful degree of skill in the interpretation of radiographs, without at the same time acquiring any knowledge of the way they are taken. Because this knowledge is very useful in a rural hospital, this chapter makes some attempt to supply it. These few pages will, it is hoped, give the doctor enough insight into the work of a small X-ray department to enable him to supervise it satisfactorily, and to use it to the best advantage. It will also give him some ideas on the type of plant available and its installation.

25:2 **Theory.** At its simplest an X-ray tube is an evacuated glass vessel containing two electrical conductors or electrodes, a negative electrode or cathode, and a positive electrode or anode (Figure 62A). The anode is usually a disc of tungsten set in a block of copper; the cathode is a thin wire filament heated by current of about 12 volts. When a potential difference of upwards of about 40 thousand volts — 40 kilovolts or 40 kV — is applied between these electrodes, a stream of electrons leave the hot filament (the cathode) and flow across the vacuum to hit the anode. In striking the anode these electrons produce X-rays, which are given off in all directions. Of this radiation, a small part is allowed to pass through a window in the X-ray tube and the shielding around it, and so through the patient and on to the X-ray film.

The *quality* or penetrating power of the X-rays is determined by the kV across the electrodes, the *quantity* of X-rays produced is determined by the current in milliamps — 'the mA' — flowing through the filament, and the time for which it flows.

Fig. 62. **X-RAY APPARATUS.**

A. THE X-RAY TUBE.

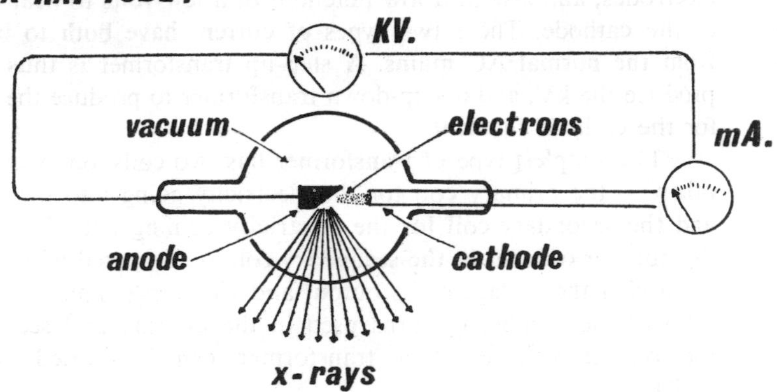

B. A SIMPLE CIRCUIT DIAGRAM.

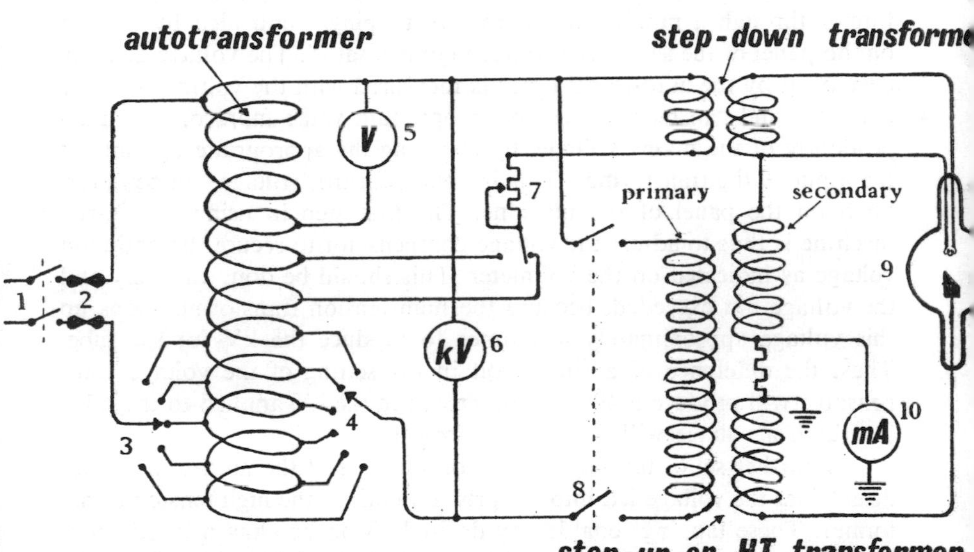

1	Double pole mains switch.	6	kV meter (pre-reading).
2	Fuses.	7	mA control.
3	Voltage compensator.	8	Exposure contactor.
4	kV selector.	9	X-ray tube.
5	Voltmeter.	10	Milleammeter.

25:3 **Circuits.** Electricity at two quite different potentials is needed to produce X-rays. It is required at a high potential of many kV across the two electrodes, and also at a low potential of a few volts to heat the filament of the cathode. These two types of current have both to be produced from the normal AC mains. A step-up transformer is thus required to produce the kV, and a step-down transformer to produce the low voltage for the cathode filament.

The simplest type of transformer has two coils, one wound over the other — the primary coil for the electricity going into the transformer, and the secondary coil for the electricity coming out of it. The greater the number of turns in the secondary coil as compared with the primary, the higher the voltage of its output and vice versa. Thus, by altering the ratio of the number of turns used in the primary and secondary coils, the output voltage of a transformer can be varied within wide limits.

The coils need not be separate and can be combined together as an 'auto-transformer'. The first transformer of an X-ray set is usually of this kind and serves several functions, one of which is to compensate for variations in mains voltage. The mains are led into such an auto-transformer through a number of alternative tappings controlled by a knob on the panel of the set — the 'voltage compensator'. The voltage actually developed by the auto-transformer is measured with the voltmeter of the machine, and can be adjusted to an optimum value more or less independently of the mains voltage, by choosing the appropriate tapping on the input of the transformer. This is done with the 'voltage compensator' knob on the panel of the machine. The first step in using any X-ray machine is thus to adjust the voltage compensator to secure the optimum voltage as indicated on the voltmeter. This should be done carefully and the voltage not exceeded, because the high tension transformer steps up this voltage approximately 400 times to produce the kV for the tube. Thus, the difference of a single volt in the setting of the voltage compensator will produce a 400 volt difference in the kV applied to the tube. Too high a voltage will, in time, destroy it.

A further set of tappings on the output side of the auto-transformer determines the voltage led into the primary coils of the high tension transformer. These tappings enable any desired kV to be chosen in advance, the knob which controls them being called the 'kV selector' — the greater the number of turns of the secondary coil included in the circuit, the greater the kV. The voltage across this part of the auto-transformer is read by another voltmeter — 'the prereading kV meter'. Because it is not easy to measure the kV directly, this voltmeter is calibrated to read as the kV that will be delivered *after* it has been stepped up in the high tension transformer. A variable resistance alters the voltage across the primary coil of the step-down transformer which supplies current to heat the filament (cathode).

So far all current has been alternating, this means that the electrodes in the X-ray tube are continually changing polarity; the cathode is continually changing from negative to positive and vice versa. As the tube will only work when the cathode is negatively charged, such a tube only operates at half its potential efficiency with an alternating current. Larger X-ray plants therefore incorporate some means of rectifying this AC current in the high tension circuit — such refinements are not shown in the circuit diagram here.

5:4 **Machines and their installation.** Many firms produce a small X-ray unit with a maximum capacity of 20 mA and 90 kV (PHI). At much greater expense larger units offer higher mA — 500 and more, and somewhat greater kV — 125 kV and upwards. The advantage of larger machines is, that by using higher mA and kV the time of exposure can be shortened and thus the disadvantages of movement can be greatly reduced. Small sets of the 20 mA — 90 kV type enable limbs to be X-rayed and fairly satisfactory straight chest films to be taken. Views of the skull, the spine, the pregnant uterus, etc. are normally taken using a stationary grid (see below), and require such long exposures with these machines that they are usually unsuitable for these purposes, except on very co-operative patients.

All X-ray plant requires alternating current, the smallest sets requiring 18 amps at 220 volts (4 kVA). However, because this current is required for such a short time only, such sets can be operated with safety from a 13 amp mains socket.

The short heavy load drawn by an X-ray plant imposes severe demands on a small generator on which it acts as a sudden break. Unless the generator has been specially designed for X-ray plants, and equipped with a very heavy flywheel to enable it to cope with this sudden load, the output of the generator should be at least twice that demanded by the X-ray plant. A special petrol generator delivering 5.5 kVA is available (PHI) which will run small X-ray plants requiring 4 kVA, as well as supplying electricity for such purposes as dark room illumination.

Altitude should also be considered in specifying the output required for the generator of an X-ray plant, for the output of an internal combustion engine falls 5 per cent. with each increasing 1,000 feet (300 metres) of altitude above sea level.

The generator should be near the X-ray department, for they have to be joined by a heavy copper cable, the size of this cable being determined, not by its current carrying capacity, for which a much smaller cable would do, but by the necessity for it to have a very low resistance.

25:5 **The X-ray exposure.** Besides the X-ray machine and the film, it is usual to use two other pieces of apparatus each time an exposure is made. One is an intensifying screen and the other is a grid. An intensifying screen is a thin piece of cardboard that is normally coated with calcium tungstate and is placed inside the cassette close against the film itself. A screen of this kind converts some of the X-rays reaching it into light to which the emulsion is more sensitive than it is to X-rays. An intensifying screen therefore makes possible a considerable reduction in the exposure required.

When X-rays strike tissue some of them are scattered and impair the quality of the radiograph. It is therefore usual to cut down these scattered rays by interposing a grid between the part to be X-rayed and the plate. A stationary grid is composed of fine alternating strips of opaque and translucent material, but though it improves the definition of the film, it covers it with a series of fine lines. The only way to remove these lines is to cause the grid to move slightly during the course of the exposure — such a moving grid is called a Bucky diaphragm, or more simply, a 'Bucky', and is an invariable fitting on bigger machines. An equally important method of ensuring radiographs of the best possible quality is to restrict the area irradiated to the minimum practicable, by the use of a series of interchangeable metal cones attached to the X-ray tube.

An intensifying screen decreases the exposure required and a grid increases it, but these are only two of many factors which influence the quality of a radiograph.

When films are processed in a standard manner the quality of a radiograph depends on the following variables:

1) The time of exposure — long exposures tend to be associated with poor definition due to movement of the patient and/or the X-ray tube.
2) The kV used — the higher the kV, the greater the penetrating power of the X-rays but also the poorer the soft tissue contrast.
3) The mA — the greater the mA the larger the quantity of X-rays produced and in consequence the shorter the time needed for an exposure. Thus, if the mA are doubled the time can be halved.
4) The focus-film distance — the greater the distance the sharper the detail, but a longer exposure is required. The distance factor is a powerful one, for the intensity of the radiation falling on the film decreases with the square of the focus-film distance.
5) The sensitivity of the film; 'slow', 'medium' and 'fast' films are made. Fast films mean a loss in detail and poorer keeping qualities, but they make shorter exposures possible.

6) The intensifying factor of the intensifying screen, 'slow', 'medium' and 'fast' screens are available — again fast screens mean poorer detail.
7) The 'grid factor' — this is a measure of the radiological opacity of the grid or Bucky.
8) The thickness and density of the part being X-rayed.
9) A factor dependent on the efficiency of the machine itself.

All these nine variables must be considered when taking any radiograph. How are they all to be balanced against one another? No neat formulae are available and radiography is something of an art — experience is the only answer. However, it is usual to use medium speed intensifying screens, except for thin parts like the hand, for which paper wrapped film can be used without grids or intensifying screens. This leaves only the following variables, time mA, kV, focus-film distance and the part to be X-rayed. Tables are supplied with most machines to relate these variables: these give suggested exposure times for every part at given values for mA, kV and focus-film distance. Experience of local conditions may show however that some modifications need to be made to these average figures.

Low mA can be compensated for by increased time and vice versa. It is therefore usual to consider these together as milliamp-seconds or mAS. It is a useful rule that if the kV increases by ten in the range 40-90 kV, the mAS can be halved.

Radiographic assistants soon get to know the standard exposures for their machine, but when posted to a new plant they are advised to take a postero-anterior chest film of an average man at the standard 2 metres (6ft.) at 6 mAS and 72 kV. This film when developed under standard conditions will give them some idea of the efficiency of their plant and they can adjust their other exposures accordingly.

When money is scarce screening may appear to offer a substantial economy in the use of X-ray film. However, a special screening plant is needed before patients can be safely screened and the usefulness of a low powered plant for barium studies of the stomach and colon is very limited. No radiographic assistant is competent to screen — this must be done by a doctor wearing lead gloves and a lead apron.

When a radiographic assistant has been properly trained he should take the correct precautions against exposure to radiation as a matter of course. Many radiographic assistants have not been so trained and even trained ones sometimes become slipshod in this matter. They must stand behind the X-ray machine when an exposure is taken and wherever possible behind a lead screen, should one be available. An X-ray tube should always be pointed away from other people, that is at the floor, or a wall.

25:6 **Economics.** The smallest machine costs £600 ($1,700) including the cost of installation, lasts about ten years and may require a new tube costing about £100 ($280) every three years or so. A radiographic assistant is usually paid about £25 ($70) a month, twelve monthly changes of developer and fixer add up to about £15 ($42) and bring the total annual expense of the smallest department to about £505 ($1,400) inclusive of depreciation on the equipment but exclusive of the salaries of a darkroom assistant — and films. The cost of electricity is negligible provided it is not produced for the X-ray plant alone. A 'chest film' costs about 4/- ($0.55) and smaller ones are proportionately cheaper.

25:7 **Practical points.** Check the darkroom safelight by ascertaining that the safelight filter is the one recommended by the X-ray film manufacturer, and that the lamp used in the safelight is of the correct wattage. In order to test the safelight illumination, all lights in the darkroom should be put out except the safelight under test. A film is then placed at the working distance and upon it is placed a row of coins. A piece of black paper is placed over the film and then withdrawn by uncovering a section surrounding one coin at a time. In this way the film is exposed for varying times. After processing the film is inspected for traces of fog showing in contrast to the unexposed portions which were underneath the coins during exposure. The longest exposure which produces no visible fog is equivalent to the longest time that the film may be handled with safety under the existing conditions of lamp wattage and distance.

Insist that the strict times and temperatures specified by the makers of the developer are adhered to by the assistant — under development is *not* a remedy for over exposure.

Change the solutions regularly each month and, if possible, employ stainless steel developing tanks. If using plastic ones, box them strongly in wood because the pressure of the liquid inside them makes them bulge in time.

X-ray plant is harmed by water, so a damp cloth is all that should be used for cleaning, and on no account should the X-ray department ever be sluiced out with buckets of water.

Chapter Twenty-Six

MEDICAL RECORDS

David Morley

1 **The importance of good records.** To many readers, the title 'Medical Records' will probably bring to mind visions of inky fingered clerks covering in an infinitely laboured hand page after laborious page of a dog-eared ledger; of outpatient forms so grubby, porous and ephemeral that they almost melt in the hand; of queues interminable and of cardboard cartons stuffed record-full lying dusty under tables. Such a state of affairs is highly unsatisfactory for the loss of a record can on occasion mean the loss of a life. At one clinic in Mulago Hospital no less than a third of the patients were considered as 'new cases' merely because their little slips of paper had gone astray. Well adapted records thus require as much careful thought as does any other part of a hospital's work.

There are two sides to a record system. On the one hand, are the patients' own records, which are a summary of their clinical condition to enable the staff to make out at a glance the essentials of an illness; on the other, there are the files and ledgers which record the work of the hospital as a whole, both for its own use and for that of the State. In considering them here frequent reference will be made to the practice of the Wesley Guild Hospital at Ilesha and the records introduced there by Doctor Andrew Pearson and the writer, with the help in one instance of Glaxo laboratories.

2 **Making the most of the record number.** On all hospital records, after a patient's age, sex, tribe and village there comes his number. This is usually a six or seven figure serial that started when the hospital first opened. Such a number has its uses, but the writer would like to suggest, though he has never yet had the opportunity to try it out, that this num-

ber might be made more useful by making it carry further information — by making it do more 'work'. As well as performing its present task of distinguishing one patient from all others, it could with little extra trouble, be made to contain his birth date and therefore his age. Thus, the first two figures of the number might denote the date, the next, a letter could denote the month; this could then be followed by two more figures signifying the year and finally it could end with a serial number different for each patient born on that day. It would be convenient if every month of the year began with a different initial letter, but as they do not, another would sometimes have to be used, and the third could be chosen whenever the first repeats. The code would thus become JFMAYNLGSTVD for the months from January to December. As an example, the ninety-ninth person registered as born on the 11th August 1964 would be given the number 11G6499. Such a system would mean that the hospital would have to keep daily a list of those born, and give to each of them a different final serial, but this however is easily done.

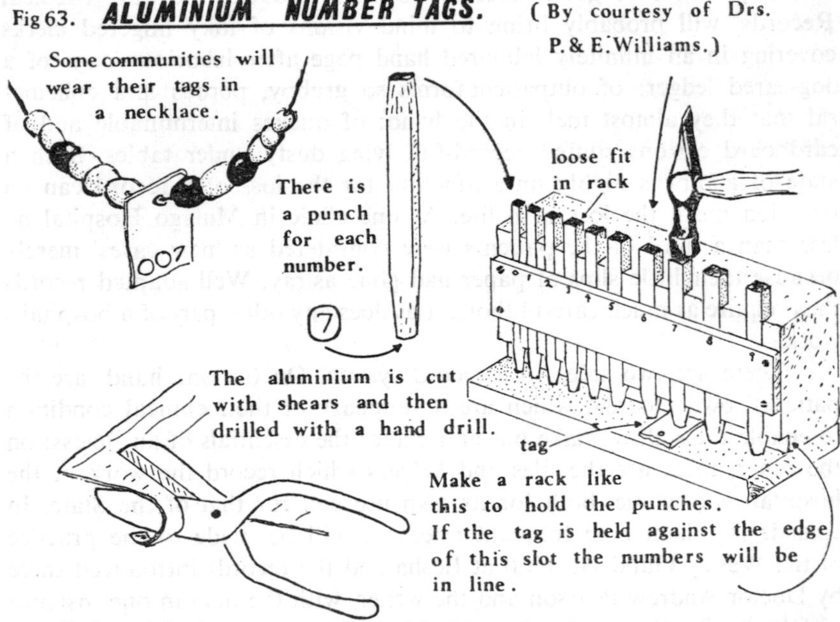
Fig 63. ALUMINIUM NUMBER TAGS. (By courtesy of Drs. P. & E. Williams.)
Some communities will wear their tags in a necklace.
007
There is a punch for each number.
7
loose fit in rack
The aluminium is cut with shears and then drilled with a hand drill.
tag
Make a rack like this to hold the punches. If the tag is held against the edge of this slot the numbers will be in line.

It is critical to a system of this kind that it records the date of a patient's birth and not merely the day he first registers. This is often a matter of difficulty in a rural community, for villagers often do not know the exact date of their birth. It is possible therefore, when a patient does not know his birth date and yet it is required for the records, for the hospital to make a good guess and invent one for him. Under the age of three, it is usually possible for a child's mother to guess it to the nearest week by relating his birth to some fixed event, so all the hospital staff need do is to choose some day within this week.

When a number starts with the birth date, records file automatically in 'cohorts', that is to say, in groups of patients of the same age — a great statistical convenience. Best of all however, a number is easily found if a patient knows his birthday, for the search through final serials is rapid, as only two hundred patients register each day for every million of the population.

Some hospitals use a code for the name of the patient's village and file the record cards by this. But, though such a system is useful epidemiologically, and convenient to the health visitor, who then has all the cards for one village in the same drawer, in Nigeria at least it has one important snag. Here patients are wont to give a fictitious urban address of 'high status', rather than their correct one which may well be in a small hamlet.

A number can also be used which combines both the birth date and the birthplace, but this is cumbersome, and one or other of these two items of information is about all a number will conveniently carry. The point to be made, however, is that a good opportunity is wasted if records are not filed by something more useful than a meaningless serial.

Were a system of national numbering ever possible, this might be worth the effort it would entail, for such a number could then serve for health purposes, taxation, insurance and the many other needs of the twentieth century, besides assisting cross-analysis. In the older countries this is now very difficult but in the younger ones it would be a valuable innovation.

:3 **Number-tags.** So much for the number itself but how are patients to remember it? Numbered cards can be issued and some patients will keep them, but in other cultures a metal number tag may be more practical. These can be cut by the record clerks from sheet aluminium, they cost almost nothing and can be stamped with hand punches (B&H). Clerks will find them easier to make if they use the simple wooden punch holder drawn in Figure 63.

Patients paying fees can be charged for the loss of their cards, and the sale of a card to the patient can also be used as a simple form of health insurance. By making such cards valid for a year only, some hospitals are able to raise a useful fraction of their expenses, with the minimum of hardship to the patients (2:10) (1:19).

:4 **The value of cardboard**. Hospital records have a hard life for they pass through many fingers, and may have to be extracted from the files many times. Records should therefore be made of cardboard, especially as a particular card is much more easily found in a row of others than is a flimsy sheet of paper among a pile of many. No record clerk is therefore to be blamed who cannot locate a flimsy paper from among hundreds of similar ones.

Card may be a little more expensive than paper, but both sides can be both printed and written on, and it lasts much longer. The use of colour helps the illiterate, assists sorting and brightens life generally. Its additional cost is marginal. But colours need to be chosen carefully, for in some societies they have a particular, and even a dreadful significance. Small cards are both economical and easily stored, so records should be made as small as is convenient. Eight inches by five inches (20 cm. x 13 cm.) is a suitable size for outpatient record cards, but before deciding on a size, the printers should be consulted, so as to make sure that the size chosen cuts economically from the standard sheets of card they stock.

26:5 **The weight chart for the under-fives clinic.** This is illustrated in Figures 64 and 33 (16:7), and is the most recent version of that devised for this clinic. These charts are now coming into use both in Sierra Leone and elsewhere, and more than a quarter of a million of them have now been printed. They are integral with the whole practice of the clinic, for they provide at a glance the child's weight curve in graphic form, a record of his inoculations, some details of his family history and space on which to record such major events as 'coming off the breast' or an attack of measles. Coloured, and printed on stiff card so that they will withstand five years' hard use, they are ten inches by just under twelve (26 cm. x 30 cm.) and fold in three to form a firm narrow package 4 inches (10 cm.) wide. This fits a special polythene envelope and both together cost less than -/40 ($0.06). Such an envelope is essential, for a mother can keep the chart without soiling; it becomes proof against being carried almost anywhere on the person and is rendered immune to the ubiquitous palm oil, so pervasive in the Nigerian household.

The care of this chart is still being hotly debated. Is it to be kept by the mother, or shall it be stored by the clinic? At Ilesha the chart is sold to a mother for a small charge and always remains in her keeping — a practice which is now being followed increasingly elsewhere. By making her pay for it, and leaving it with her, a mother becomes in some additional way responsible for the health of her child and, as has already been said, this is fundamental to health education (6:1). But there are more practical reasons for mothers keeping these charts: mothers lose about one chart in every hundred, while clerks are wont to lose five times as many. The charts remain with mothers wherever they go and Nigerian women travel much. None of their precious time is wasted as clerks search for weight charts every time they visit a clinic. When mothers keep these charts, health visitors and doctors have no need to search them out of the files before they visit patients in the villages. And, as

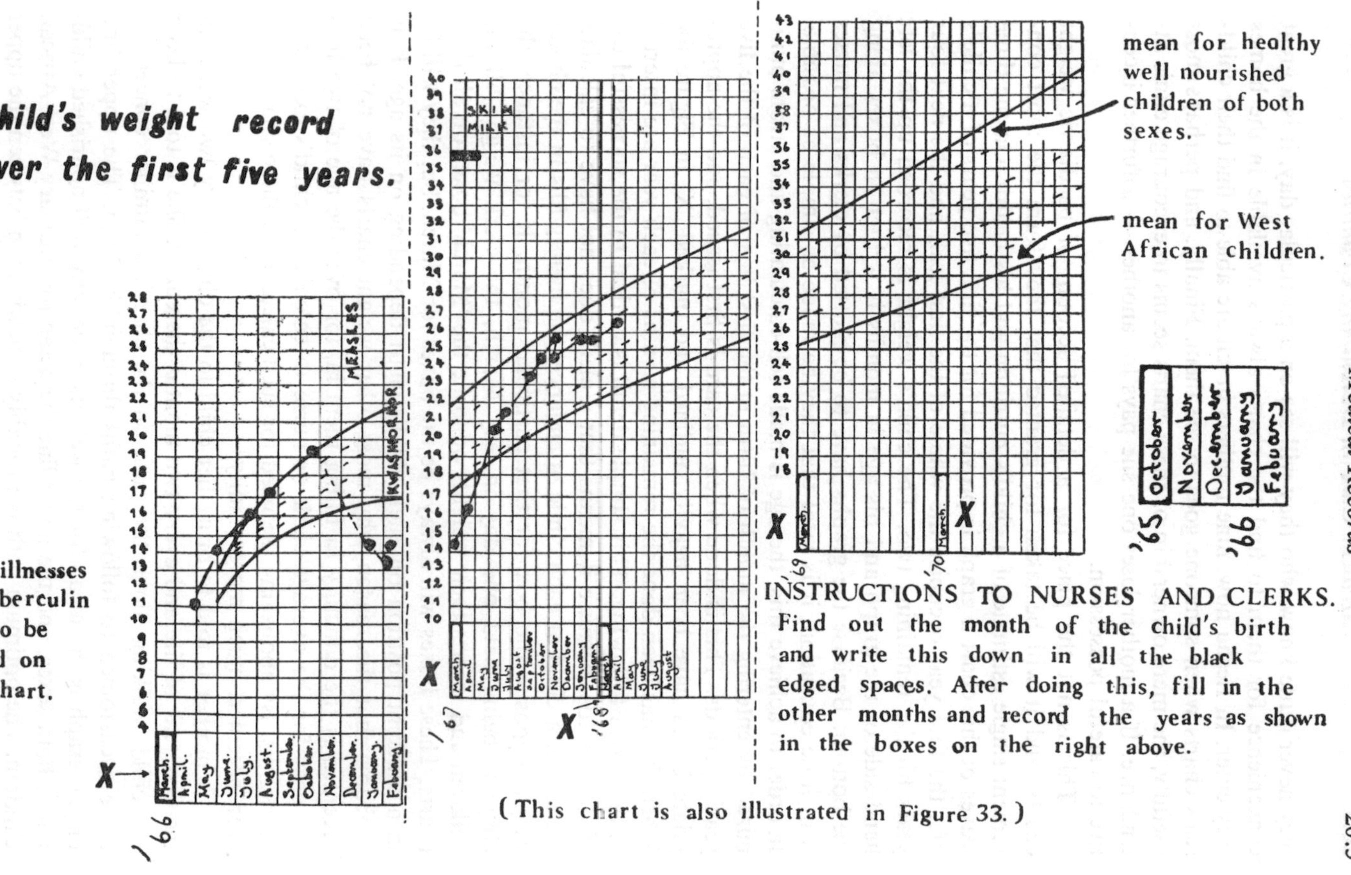
Child's weight record over the first five years.
Major illnesses and tuberculin state to be entered on this chart.
MEASLES
KWASHIORKOR
SKIM MILK
March. April. May. June. July. August. September. October. November. December. January. February.
mean for healthy well nourished children of both sexes.
mean for West African children.
October
November
December
January
Febuary
INSTRUCTIONS TO NURSES AND CLERKS.
Find out the month of the child's birth and write this down in all the black edged spaces. After doing this, fill in the other months and record the years as shown in the boxes on the right above.

(This chart is also illustrated in Figure 33.)

they never quite know who they will see on a particular day, it is a great convenience for them to find the charts always available in the homes they enter. In Ilesha now, nine mothers in ten are able to find their children's charts when someone goes to see them. Finally, and perhaps most usefully, the mere ownership of these charts seems to encourage clinic attendance. If a mother loses one she pays for another — a further incentive to careful possession.

This is not the place for a detailed account of paediatric weight charts, and it will be taken for granted that they form the most convenient single estimate of a child's nutrition and his health. On the three leaves of this chart a graph is provided for the first five years of a child's life; the first year occupies the whole of the first leaf, and the next four years fill the remaining two. The child's weight is recorded up the left hand side of the graph and his age in months is written in boxes along the bottom. Because the graphs have to be plotted by clerks and nurses with little education, it is vital that they be made as simple as possible. In order to achieve this, the age is made self-calculating and errors minimized by entering the month of birth in the first box of each of the five yearly periods. This is done when the card is first issued, and the appropriate boxes have been heavily outlined and marked 'X' in Figure 64. When this has been done the remaining months of each year are inserted in the boxes following. This simple detail is critical to the successful use of these cards, because it means that a clerk does not have to calculate the age of a child at each clinic attendance: he merely fills in the child's weight opposite the box for that particular month. If for instance, the clinic is being held one day in, say March, the clerk weighs all the children and inserts their weights opposite the 'March' boxes on all their charts. These boxes will always be the boxes for March, but they will be in a different position on each child's chart depending on its age. It is probable that the reason why most other weight charts have not been accepted is the difficulty in filling them in, for over the age of two it is not easy for the average clerk or nurse to calculate a child's exact age in months. By abolishing the need for such calculation, these charts have been accepted much more readily.

A mother is told to bring her child to the clinic every two weeks in the first year of life and every two months thereafter. She is told to keep her child 'walking along the path on the chart', a familiar concept to those accustomed to following paths through the bush. The upper line on the graph is the mean for the weights of healthy well nourished children of both sexes, and the lower line the mean for ordinary West African children. The optimum path is probably somewhere in between the upper and lower lines, for the upper one may well represent the 'hypernutrition and obesity of more privileged communities. Apart from such extremes of mankind as the Watusi giants of Rwanda or the pygmy dwarfs of the Ituri forest, such graphs apply to most societies, for it is now becoming increasingly clear that well nourished infants of most human groups follow the same curve in early life. It has now been shown that when well nourished the Nigerian child does so too.

In practice, the position of a child's weight curve on the chart matters much less than the change in his weight, thus if a child continues to gain steadily, he may be flourishing even though his weight is low, while a heavier child who loses weight is likely to be in a worse position and needs examining carefully. The use of these charts makes it possible to see that normal growth is maintained and malnutrition prevented. For example, supplementary feeding, such as the issue of the milk packets advised in section 14:14, can be started when a child fails to gain weight as he should. These charts make a positive approach to health possible, which is much to be preferred to merely treating malnutrition after it has occurred.

There is also space on the charts to record a child's tuberculin state and his major illnesses, there being neither time or need for any more detailed records. Because these illnesses often cause dramatic and characteristic changes in the curve, its very shape will often bring a child to mind in a busy clinic, more readily than will his face.

On the back of the card are boxes for the names of a child's father and mother, the date of his birth, the date he was first seen, as well as the name of the house where the family live (Figure 33 (16:7)). Under this is a space for the merest outline of the fate of his brothers and sisters, and overleaf there is a list of the months for the five years of the card's life. These months are ticked off each time the monthly pyrimethamine tablet is given and so form a useful record of a child's malarial suppression. On this leaf there is also a space to record inoculations with smallpox, triple-vaccine, BCG and any other immunizations that may be given. Finally, there is room for some educational slogans.

The successful introduction of these charts into an existing clinic requires careful education of both the mothers and the staff, as well as some additional help in the early stages. This, members of the Red Cross or a woman's voluntary organization may sometimes be able to provide. Both helpers and mothers will have to be taught, and to make this easier a flannelgraph of the weight chart is available for £2 ($5.6) (MOR). As for the charts themselves, it is understood that UNICEF intend to print these on a large scale. Those wanting them should write to their area representative.

6 **Cards for schoolchildren and adults.** What happens when the five years are done? This is the time that fortunate children go to school, and a

school record card should ideally take over when the clinic card is complete. Height as well as weight needs to be recorded, and, though it has been tried out so extensively, samples of a school record card can be obtained from the writer (MOR).

At Ilesha the adult outpatient record is a simple printed card, eight inches by five, that is filed in the outpatient department, but, unlike those for the under-fives, these cards remain there, because an adult attends hospital so much less frequently that this is the only practical way to keep them. Such cards take little space and can be filed in drawers.

26:7 **Inpatient records.** The quality of a hospital's inpatient records is a good measure of its efficiency. At their simplest they consist of the temperature chart, a card or sheet of paper on which to write the patients' history, and another on which to prescribe his drugs. The many sheets which accumulate are inconvenient in use, and soon become both bulky and difficult to file without a comparatively expensive envelope or folder. In order to promote cheapness combined with ease of writing, data correlation and filing, Dr. Willis of Canada has invented what he calls 'Columnized Medical Charting'.

As used at Ilesha this system of medical charting consists of a quarto card, and a quarto sheet of paper, which are printed on both sides, pasted together along their edges, and folded over after the manner shown in Figure 65. It will be seen that the temperature chart goes down the card rather than across it. Opposite the temperature chart for the day, and going right across both the card and the paper sheet, are spaces to record the patient's pulse, respiration, bowels, and fluid balance, his laboratory reports, the doctor's orders the progress notes and finally the bill.

Nurses quickly get used to charting the temperature down a chart, instead of across it. The time of the observation is left for her to fill in, so, when changing from twice-daily to 4-hourly, or even hourly observations, the same chart can continue. Laboratory investigations are ordered in the laboratory column, the request going to the laboratory on a small coloured slip, six inches by two (15 cm x 5 cm), with space on it at the top for the investigations required, and at the bottom for the result. When these come back from the laboratory, they are folded in half, and stuck to the chart in the laboratory column opposite the day when the test was done (these are not shown in Figure 65). The doctor's orders are divided into 'stat.' or 's.o.s.' orders, which are for one occasion only, with a space for the nurse to insert the time a drug was given, and standing, or 'p.r.n.' orders, which are to be continued until countermanded. This section is subdivided by dotted lines into several columns. Each standing order begins in a new column, and the time a drug is given is inserted by the nurse in these columns. When the drug is to be discon-

Fig. 65.

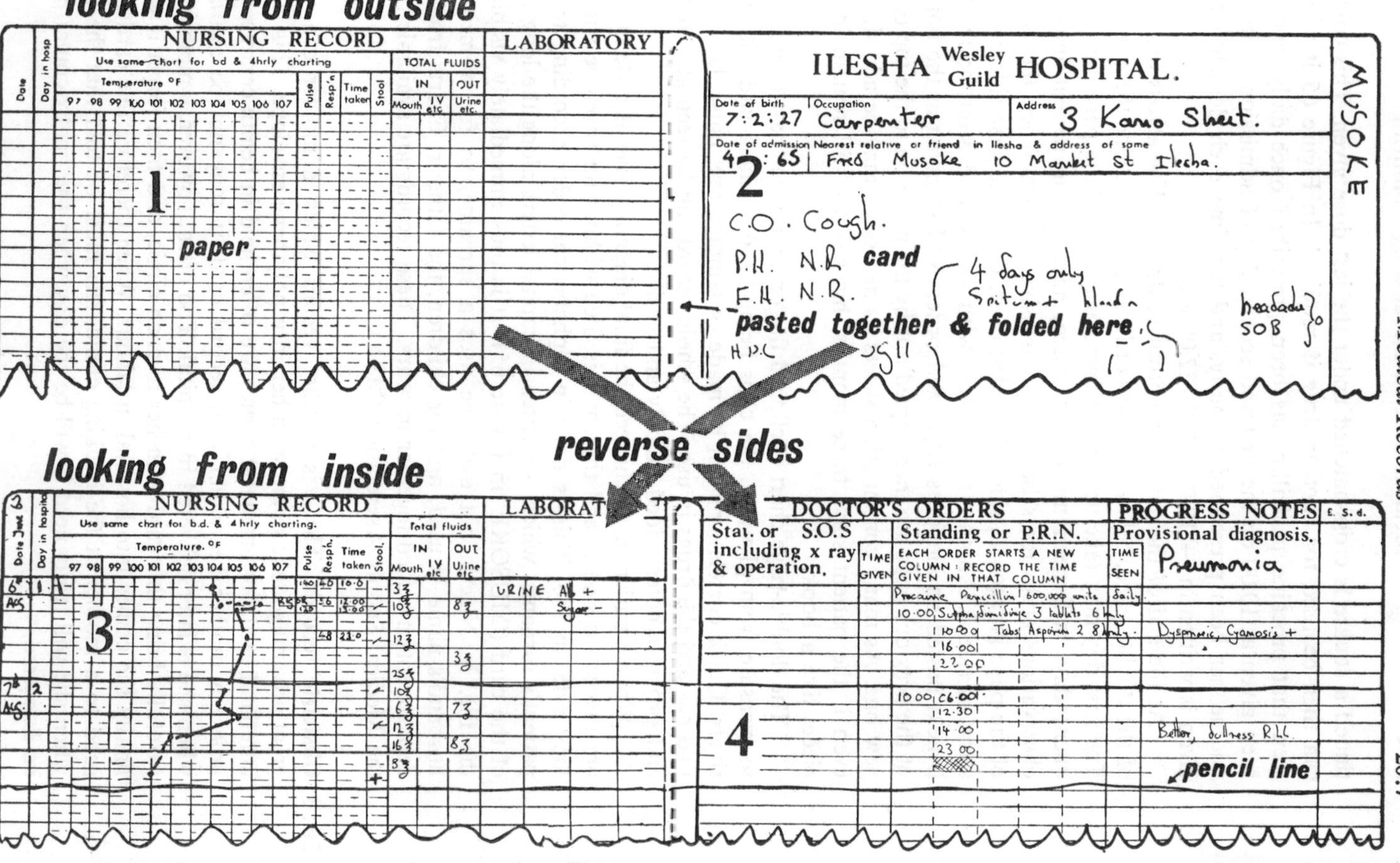
THE ILESHA INPATIENT RECORDS.
looking from outside
NURSING RECORD
Use same chart for bd & 4hrly charting
Temperature °F
Pulse
Resp'n
Time taken
Stool
TOTAL FLUIDS
IN
OUT
LABORATORY
1
paper
ILESHA Wesley Guild HOSPITAL.
Date of birth 7:2:27
Occupation Carpenter
Address 3 Kano Street.
Date of admission 4:2:65
Nearest relative or friend in Ilesha & address of same Fred Musoke 10 Market St Ilesha.
MUSOKE
2
C.O. Cough.
P.H. N.R.
F.H. N.R.
card
pasted together & folded here
reverse sides
looking from inside
NURSING RECORD
3
URINE Alb +
Sugar −
DOCTOR'S ORDERS
Stat. or S.O.S including x ray & operation.
Standing or P.R.N.
EACH ORDER STARTS A NEW COLUMN: RECORD THE TIME GIVEN IN THAT COLUMN
PROGRESS NOTES
Provisional diagnosis.
Pneumonia
Dyspnoeic, Cyanosis +
4
pencil line

tinued a square is cross-hatched under the last dose given. This column can then be used for another drug if required. In Figure 65 it will be seen that procaine penicillin has been prescribed once daily, and has been given at 10.00 on the first and second day of admission. Sulphadimidine has been prescribed 6-hourly, and the time each dose has been given is written in — 10.00, 16.00, 22.00 etc.

At the end of the day the night-nurse draws a line across the whole of the double page, below whatever orders or observations there may be. The first day may take up several lines, or even half the page, but subsequent days will need much less space, and, as the patient improves observations and orders become progressively fewer. When the bottom of the page is reached, side 4 is folded over. On the reverse side, it is the same as side 3. Another paper sheet with side 4 (and 3 on the reverse) is next pasted on along its edge, and orders still standing at the bottom of the previous page are then copied out by the nurse on to the top of the new one. As many continuation sheets as necessary may be added, and, even if the patient stays three months, his records still remain in one piece, like a book.

The double-page chart is clipped flat on to a wide chart-board made to measure from plywood, the clips being fixed to the board with split rivets. Quick correlations can be made of temperature, pulse, laboratory findings and the drugs in use. The whole record can be seen at a glance, and progress notes added quickly and easily.

When a patient is discharged the final diagnosis and its code number are placed on side 2, and the chart is filed without an envelope with its long side on top. This is done in alphabetical order according to the patient's surname, which is written in capital letters along the long edge of the card ('MUSOKE' in Figure 65). It is thus immediately visible in the file. In Nigeria not everyone uses a surname, so for women the husband's name is used, and for children, the father's. Charts from all departments are filed together in years. These records are available from the Medical Supply Association (MSA).

26:8 **Obstetric records.** There is another record which a mother can with great advantage take home with her in a polythene envelope. This is her antenatal card, for antenatal clinics are often held in health centres, and, unless a mother keeps her own record card, it may not be available when she is later delivered in hospital. Too often, however, a mother will carefully bring this card with her to each clinic, and then forget it when finally she comes into hospital in labour. When therefore this card is issued to a mother at the booking clinic, she must be told that the time when she will really need it will be the day when she finally comes in to be delivered.

At Ilesha each antenatal patient is issued with two cards when she first books in. The first is the 'Maternity Record Card', which records her past obstetric history and all permanent factors which may influence, or be of importance in a subsequent pregnancy. These include her height, blood group, and such medical or obstetric factors as hypertension or pelvic deformity. This card is not limited to the present pregnancy and is kept by the mother, although a duplicate is sometimes also kept in the hospital files. The second card is the 'Antenatal Record Card' which records observations on the current pregnancy only. While she is pregnant, a mother carries this with her 'Maternity Record Card' in the polythene envelope, and brings it with her to all antenatal clinics and also when she comes in to be delivered. After delivery the essential information from the 'Antenatal Record Card' is transferred to the 'Maternity Record Card'. The 'Antenatal Record Card' is then either disposed of, or filed with the inpatient records. When a mother returns to hospital for her second and subsequent pregnancies she is given a new 'Antenatal Record Card', but the original 'Maternity Record Card' is retained, so her previous obstetric history does not have to be written out again. A great advantage of this system is that a mother holds her own 'Maternity Record Card' on which an accurate obstetric history is built up unencumbered by excessive detail. If she travels to another part of the country, this valuable record goes with her.

:9 **Hospital data.** There is comparatively little to say about the second side of the system — the ledgers and files that record the work of the hospital. It is however worth looking at that dog-eared ledger and the laborious clerk who fills it (26:1). Just what is he recording? Is it worth while? At some hospitals clerks merely write down the patient's identification number and use the time saved more profitably. Many hospitals are however beset by daily, monthly or yearly returns and the complex forms that they are required to send in. Much valuable time is wasted recording this information which is mostly useless, and a more rational and economical system is often required. It should be a duty to educate those who demand such forms to make them simpler and at the same time more valuable. There is an excellent manual on this subject /82/.

Ministries of health need to know the prevalence of diseases in a country, but much of the data sent into them in the form of hospital outpatient returns is valueless. They would obtain more correct information, if they were to depute some competent person to examine a random sample of those attending an outpatient department — say one patient in every twenty. A full examination, including X-rays and laboratory investigations, could then be done on this limited number and the data obtained would be of much greater value.

When the diseases to be reported have code numbers it may be found useful for the clerks to have a board with numbered nails corresponding, and for paper slips to be impaled upon them for counting at the end of the week — foolproof perhaps, but time consuming.

26:10 **Disease notification.** This is often a farce, as was proved at one hospital when more cases of measles were found in one town than were notified during a similar period from a population of nearly twenty million. If notification is to be done, it is worth doing properly, and in the under-fives clinic or general outpatient department it may be found useful for nurses or medical assistants to have duplicated sheets on their tables with boxes in which to mark off the notifiable cases they see. If particular information is required, such as the age or address of the patient, these duplicated sheets can be designed with special boxes so as to make this information easy to collect. Each week these sheets can be collected for analysis and will provide some of the information required for making the community diagnosis (5:1). Epidemiologic tables can be constructed and the relevant information entered on maps of the defined area (5:5). (Samples of these sheets can be obtained from the writer (MOR)).

26:11 **Taking notes and the use of shorthand.** (Written by the editor). Well designed stationery makes good records possible, but the notes that are written on it are what really matter. This final section is therefore devoted to certain ideas on record taking that deserve wider use. But, before discussing them further, there is an important principle to be made clear as to the occasions on which clinical records are made, and the notes appropriate to them.

The classical approach to a clinical diagnosis requires a lengthy history, a detailed physical examination, some tests on the urine, and the ordering of further investigations, the complete process taking about three-quarters of an hour. At the other end of the scale are cases in which experience enables a snap diagnosis to be made and treatment prescribed in a minute or two. The classical approach is that by which students are trained, but the method of snap diagnosis is the one which doctors in developing countries have inevitably to use for most of the patients they see. The classical method requires extensive notes, the snap diagnosis almost none. It might seem therefore that to discuss any form of complete clinical record is unjustified, when there is so little time to spend on each patient. The point to be made, however, is that a detailed history and examination on a limited number of cases is of great value in maintaining and developing a doctor's clinical skills. Occasional cases should therefore be examined completely, and for this purpose as well as for student use, some rational system of note taking and 'clinical shorthand' is required. Most doctors employ some form of shorthand and, though a few symbols are more or less standard, practice varies from one school to another and differs even more from country to country. Because clinical shorthand is not private to the writer but has to be interpreted both by other doctors and by the nursing staff, some standardization is clearly desirable. A recognized list of abbreviations will also be useful to doctors trained on the continent of Europe when they come to practice in developing countries whose medicine is based on the English pattern.

TABLE 14
SOME CLINICAL SHORTHAND

OE	On examination.
CO	Complaining of.
PH	Previous history.
FH	Family history.
SH	Social history.
HPC	History of present complaint.
POGH	Previous obstetric and gynaecological history.
CNS	Central nervous system.
URT	Upper respiratory tract.
RS	Respiratory system.
CVS	Cardiovascular system.
GIT	Gastro-intestinal tract.
UGT	Urogenital tract.
KJ	Knee jerks.
AJ	Ankle jerks.
AB	Apex beat.
MCL	Mid-clavicular line.
JVP	Jugular venous pressure.
HS	Heart sounds.
BP	Blood pressure.
RVH	Right ventricular hypertrophy.
LVH	Left ventricular hypertrophy.
SOB	Short of breath
PN	Percussion note.
VR	Vocal resonance.
VF	Vocal fremitus.
BS	Breath sounds.
RUL	Right upper lobe.
RLL	Right lower lobe.
MCH	Maternal and child health.
ROA	Right occipito-anterior.
LOP	Left occipito-posterior.
FHH	Foetal heart heard.
FHS	Foetal heart sounds.
FTND	Full term normal delivery.
FTNL	Full term normal labour.
BBA	Born before arrival.
BID	Brought in dead.
PM	Post mortem.
TCU	To come up.
TCA	To come again.
PR	Per rectum.
PV	Per vaginam.
PU	Per urethram.
IV	Intravenously.
IM	Intramuscularly.
SC	Subcutaneously
PCM	Protein calorie malnutrition.
SBE	Subacute bacterial endocarditis.
PTB	Pulmonary tuberculosis.
PA	Pernicious anaemia.
PUO	Pyrexia of unknown origi
URI	Upper respiratory infection.
GC	Gonorrhoea.
CA	Cancer.
NG	New growth.
CCF	Congestive cardiac failure.
LVF	Left ventricular failure.
RVF	Right ventricular failure.
MS	Mitral stenosis.
MI	Mitral incompetence.
POP	Plaster of Paris cast.
SPC	Suprapubic cystotomy.
EUA	Examination under anaesthesia.
DSM	Dried skim milk.
FCM	Full cream milk.
EBM	Expressed breast milk.
PAM	Penicillin alluminium monostearate.
PPF	Procaine penicillin forte.
SM	Streptomycin.
INH	Iso-nicotinic acid hydrazide.
PAS	Para-amino-salicylic acid.
TB 1	Thiacetazone.
TCE	Tetrachlorethylene.
ATS	Antitetanus serum.
WBC	White blood count.
ESR	Erythrocyte sedimentation rate.
HB	Hæmoglobin.
BS	Blood slide.
AAFB	Acid and alcohol fast bacilli.
HW	Hookworm.
MT	Malignant tertian.
BT	Benign tertian.
CSU	Catheter specimen of urine.
ECG	Electrocardiogram
NR	Not relevant.
NAD	Nil ad demonstrandum, 'nothing to show'.
b.d.	*Bis die*, twice daily.
t.i.d.	*Ter in die*, thrice daily.

Before proposing a table of abbreviations there is one convention that could be used more often. This is the 'plus notation'. It runs like this: '—' negative, '±' doubtful, '+' mild, '++' moderate '+++' severe, '++++' gross. This notation is often applicable, whether it be the size of the spleen that is being described, the degree of a patient's anaemia, the amount of albumen in his urine or the number of acid fast bacilli in his sputum. It is better than the vague adjectives that are usually the only other alternative. Thus, 'Pus cells +' is preferable to 'scanty pus cells' and avoids the use of such terms as 'a few', 'some', or 'present'. '+ and '++++' are easily defined, '+' meaning definitely positive but minimally so, and '++++' meaning maximal, 'it could hardly be larger' or 'there could scarcely be any more'. '±' meaning doubtful is also straightforward. The symbols '++' and '+++' are less easily defined, but represent useful degrees in between '+' and '++++'.

Figure 66 largely explains itself but there are certain points in it which are worthy of note. One is the use of a larger bracket like those after 'cough' or 'pain', in which all the features distinguishing a symptom or sign can be grouped together. Another is the practice of putting all the symptoms and signs that have been inquired after, or searched for and found absent, in brackets on the extreme right of the page with the symbol 'o' after them. The convention of putting the presenting symptom in capitals is a good one; as is that of underlining other symptoms that have been volunteered by the patient. Symptoms that have to be elicited by direct questioning are distinguished by being written in small letters without underlining.

At the bottom of Figure 66B a prescription is shown for penicillin which was started on March 6th and stopped on March 10th. It is cancelled with a large 'Z' which is dated and signed, a practice that is to be commended because it makes the subsequent analysis of case notes very much easier.

26:12 **The analysis of data with punch cards.** (Written by the editor.) There are two common types of punch cards. One of these has holes punched round its edge (Figure 67B), and a pack of these can be sorted by simply pushing a knitting needle through the required hole and letting those cards, from which the margin of the hole has previously been removed with a special punch, fall by gravity from the pack. Such cards are simple, the information that a particular hole records can be printed on the card adjacent to it, and there are standard printings for many purposes (COP). These cards are convenient for small runs, but they become hopelessly cumbersome when over 500 cards or much information has to be sorted.

Under these circumstances another kind of punched card is used; this is the standard computer card (Figure 67A) which can be punched over its whole surface with a series of small rectangular holes and is capable of storing very much more information than the simple edge-punch-

Fig. 66.

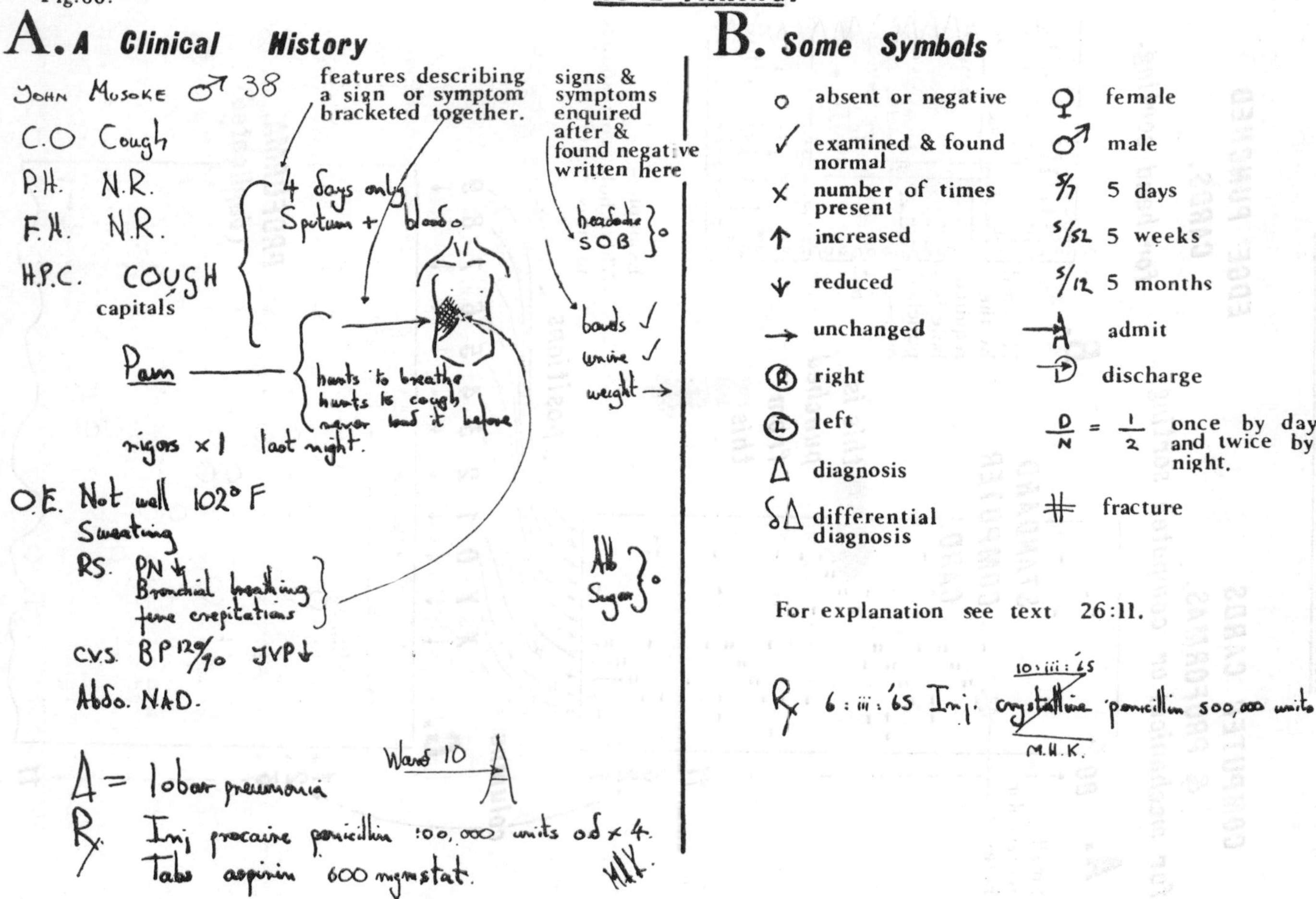
NOTE TAKING.
A. A Clinical History
John Musoke ♂ 38
C.O Cough
P.H. N.R.
F.H. N.R.
H.P.C. COUGH
capitals
features describing a sign or symptom bracketed together.
4 days only
Sputum + blood o
Pain
hurts to breathe
hurts to cough
never had it before
rigors × 1 last night.
signs & symptoms enquired after & found negative written here
headache
SOB
bowels ✓
urine ✓
weight →
O.E. Not well 102° F
Sweating
RS. PN ↓
Bronchial breathing
fine crepitations
Alb
Sugar
C.V.S. BP 120/90 JVP ↓
Abdo. NAD.
Δ = lobar pneumonia
Ward 10
Rx Inj procaine penicillin 100,000 units od × 4.
Tabs aspirin 600 mgm stat.
B. Some Symbols
o absent or negative
✓ examined & found normal
× number of times present
↑ increased
↓ reduced
→ unchanged
Ⓡ right
Ⓛ left
Δ diagnosis
δΔ differential diagnosis
♀ female
♂ male
5/7 5 days
5/52 5 weeks
5/12 5 months
admit
discharge
D/N = 1/2 once by day and twice by night.
fracture
For explanation see text 26:11.
Rx 6 : iii : '65 Inj. crystalline penicillin 500,000 units b.d.
10 : iii : '65
M.H.K.

Fig. 67. **RECORDS FOR PUNCHED CARDS.**

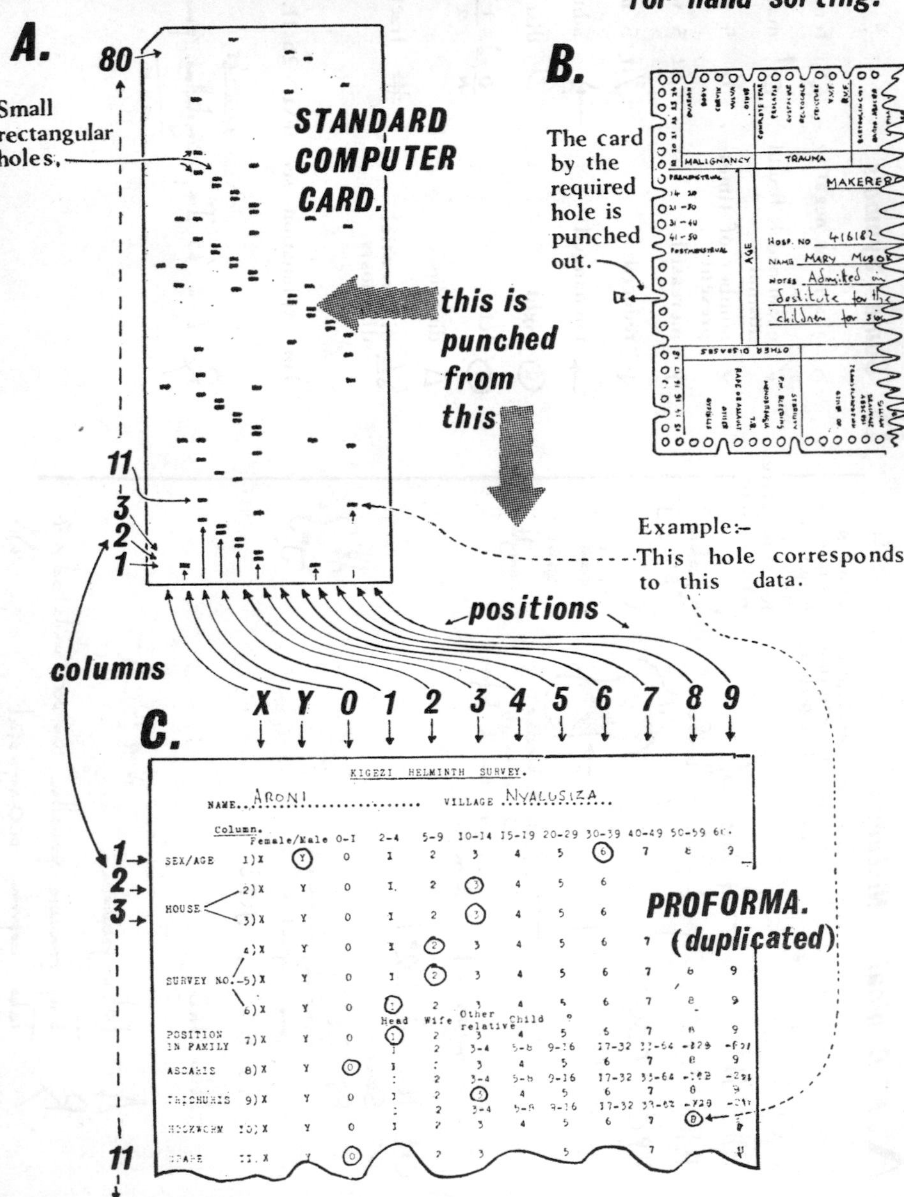

ed cards that have just been mentioned. Computer cards can either be sorted and counted mechanically in a 'counter sorter' or, as their name implies, they can be analysed with a computer. They differ from the edge-punched cards in one very important respect; it is that the information to be stored on them has initially to be recorded on a proforma (Figure 67C) and then transferred to them by a special operator who punches the holes using a machine with a series of numbered keys like an adding machine. Card sorting machines are now comparatively widely available in government finance departments, in universities and in large commercial offices, and computers are starting to become available, even in developing countries. *The purpose of this section is to encourage those who gather data on duplicated proformas to design them in such a way that this data can, if necessary, be punched on to computer cards directly without further tedious, expensive, and possibly erroneous transcription on to yet a further proforma.* It is often difficult to decide at the start of an investigation how much information is going to be collected, or how difficult it is going to be to analyse, but, if it is recorded in such a way as to make its mechanical or computer analysis easy, this may save much trouble later. If carefully designed, these proformas can often be filled in by auxiliaries, and their adaptation to punch cards does not make them any more difficult to analyse by hand.

The design of a suitable code for data collection depends upon understanding the standard computer card. This measures about $7\frac{1}{2}$ x $3\frac{1}{4}$ inches, and has 80 columns in which holes can be punched in positions, X, Y, 0, 1, 2, 3, 4, 5, 6, 7, 8 and 9. Positions 'X' and 'Y' differ little from the others, and are best looked upon as merely two extra positions in which information can be stored. Any position can be made to mean anything that the investigator wishes. Thus, in Figure 67C the first position 'X' in the first column represents female, the second position 'Y', male, and the numbers 0 to 9 in this column represent the subject's age in years, in suitable age groups after the manner shown. The next two columns stand for the number of his house, the following three his number in the survey, and the next his position in the family. After this comes information about the number of ova found in his stools. In this example the subject is a male aged between 30 and 39, living in house 33; he is number 221 in the survey, is head of the family and has no *Ascaris,* 3 or 4 *Trichuris* and between 64 and 128 hookworm ova in the quantitative stool sample examined. Position 0 in column 11 was used during the course of the survey to indicate clinical anaemia.

When the data are being collected, the investigator, or one of his assistants, takes with him a pile of empty proformas and circles the position corresponding to the item of information he wishes to record. Completed proformas are handed to a punch card operator for punching. Instructions are then given to the operator on the sorting machine to sort, say, all cards into male and female as in Figure 67 (X and Y in column one) and then all males into age groups, and then the age groups by their worm burden. Ideally, the investigator should be with the sorting machine operator as he sorts, so that he can ask for additional cross classifications that earlier analyses show might be interesting. Very often, it is not possible to know which particular cross classifications or 'sorts' are going to be useful, and it is thus quite justified to collect data with only vague ideas or 'hunches' in mind; most will be valueless, some may be illuminating.

There are many sophistications, such as the punching of X or Y, X and Y, and neither X nor Y to give four alternative meanings to each of the positions 0 to 9 that follow, and so increase the amount of data that a column as a whole can contain. In recording age for example, X might signify the age in the 0-9 decade, Y age in the 10-19 decade, X and Y age in the 20-29 decade, and neither X nor Y age in the 30-39 decade. This is not the place to analyse these elaborations further, but it is convenient to summarize some practical points as follows:—

Method: Recording data for punch card analysis.

Edge punch cards. **If it is not possible to have edge punch cards specially printed use plain ones. So as to be sure what each hole means in a plain one, place an empty card in the middle of a much larger one, draw round it and write in the meaning of each hole in the surrounding margin. If an arrow points from the writing to the site of the hole it will not be confused. For filling in, or for subsequent reading, merely place the cards on this 'master'. Mark the edges of the holes in pencil, and punch them all later with a special punch (COP) (7/-).**

Computer cards and proformas. **Make arrangements with a government department, business firm or university to do the punching and sorting and agree on prices; they will also supply the computer cards. Duplicate the proforma on foolscap, give each column a single line,** *make sure that each position is directly over the corresponding one in the column below* **and draw clear boxes that will be easy to fill in (Figure 67C is deliberately compressed for ease of illustration). Number all columns and type in the meaning of each position on the stencil.**

Where possible leave a '?' position to be filled in when a particular item of information is not available, has not been filled in or is in doubt. In Figure 67C this has only been done in column 7 (position 5), it should have been done in the other

columns also. Leave some spare columns on the proforma to be given such additional meanings as the investigation may later require. Don't worry about unfilled positions, and try not to use 'X' and 'Y' for small categories.

A way of designing proformas that is very useful when coding the answers to questionaires is to make a list of the several possible answers to a given question and number them. The person filling it in merely selects the answer he desires and enters the appropriate number in a box at the right of the form. This box is printed with the column number, the subject's answer merely denoting the position.

Where the number of columns permit, use each for a different purpose and try not to combine the same one for two purposes, as is done in column one here. Sorting machines have no difficulty in handling cards punched with several holes in the same column, but some computers only deal satisfactorily with cards with a single hole and do not readily handle X and Y.

Encircle the relevant positions on the proforma with something that is readily visible such as a red pen.

Treat computer cards with great care; if bent, dog-eared, or soiled in any way, they will jam on the sorting machine.

Make a habit of recording all suitable information in this manner, whether or not it is intended for immediate mechanical analysis.

Remember, the validity of the final statistics can never be greater than that of the observations from which they were drawn.

This was the way in which the data for the economic survey in Chapter Twelve were analysed, and where the attendance/distance relationship was initially quite unsuspected (2:7). Edge-punched cards are likely to be the most convenient way in which data for the community diagnosis in section 5:1 can be analysed, and computer cards combined with suitable proformas would be the best way of analysing outpatient data obtained in the manner suggested in section nine of this chapter. Studies are now being done at Makerere to design an outpatient attendance form that is printed in the manner advocated here. If such a form were designed and used on carefully examined samples of patients on a nationwide basis, say the first 100 outpatients attending each health centre each month, a computer programme could readily be designed to abstract from them with the minimum of trouble the data for the annual returns needed by a Ministry of Health.

Card sorting machines are comparatively commonplace, and there are, or shortly will be, computers in Nairobi, Kampala and Lusaka and doubtless in other capital cities also; this is one good use to which they can be put.

Chapter Twenty-Seven

TEACHING AND TEACHING AIDS

Arthur French

27:1 **Teaching methods.** The teaching that must go on in a hospital has often been stressed by the contributors to this symposium. Doctors and sisters have a duty to teach the rest of the staff, and all the staff have some part to play in teaching the patients (7:7) (8:3). Although the main purpose of this chapter is to provide detailed advice on teaching aids, it would be unbalanced if something is not first said about teaching methods.

Method: Some general rules on teaching.

First decide what your aim is. Set out in some detail what you want your class to know, or what you want them to be able to do at the end of your lesson, or series of lessons.

When you first meet your class, find out what they already know on your subject.

Develop their knowledge in a systematic way.

The first ten to twenty minutes of a lesson are the important ones. People cannot give concentrated attention to a talk for longer than this. If there is plenty of illustration or demonstration, interest will be held longer.

Bring the class into your teaching. Let them help with demonstrations. Whenever appropriate, let them practise what they are taught ('If I do it, I know', 6:8).

Ask questions, and encourage the class to ask them. Use repetition, revision and summaries. Do not assume that something said once is known or understood.

Test the class frequently, in writing, orally, or by practical work, and compare the results of these tests with your teaching aim.

Use praise and encouragement freely. They are more effective than criticism.

Inexperienced teachers should plan their lessons carefully in advance giving more attention to aim and variety of method than to the words to be used. Include in this plan the choice, preparation and use of teaching aids, such as those in the sections following.

27:2 **Teaching aids.** Formal group instruction succeeds best if good use is made of teaching aids, for verbal teaching alone will not relate new facts to the experience of the audience to the best advantage. These aids, particularly the more complex ones, require an outlay of both the money and the time needed to prepare them. As these commodities are likely to be in short supply, teaching aids are easily passed over as not being worth the effort. This is a short-sighted policy, for once prepared they greatly improve teaching efficiency and constitute a stock that will need only minor modification from year to year. Teaching aids are thus an investment that can pay large dividends. In their use a point to be remembered is that, if other members of the staff are to use them, the doctor should set the example and use them himself. In this way these aids acquire a 'status' that they would not have otherwise.

It must be remembered that many aids use pictorial conventions which have to be both learned and taught, a fact that was discussed in some detail when the use of posters in health education was described in section 6:7. These conventions should therefore be kept as simple as possible and their efficiency checked by frequent questioning.

The blackboard is still often the best teaching aid; drawing should be rapid and simple and full use made of coloured chalks. Next to this, the most useful aid is the projector with 35 mm. (2″ x 2″) transparencies which can be made in the hospital itself. An expensive camera is not necessary, for simple ones costing as little as 70/- ($10) including a flash attachment and a close-up lens can produce good colour slides under a wide range of conditions. Cameras taking square pictures on 127 film will also produce slides which fit these projectors. A camera is invaluable because pictures showing local people are far more effective than professionally made slides from another country. By using locally made ones teaching can be intimately adapted to the local culture (Twelfth axiom 1:19). The great virtue of these transparencies is the extreme ease with which they can be prepared.

With an ordinary projector, colour slides and film strips may be shown at night or in a darkened room, the outpatient department in section 11:4 and Figure 22C being specially designed for this purpose. But, although the need for darkness limits the value of an ordinary projector,

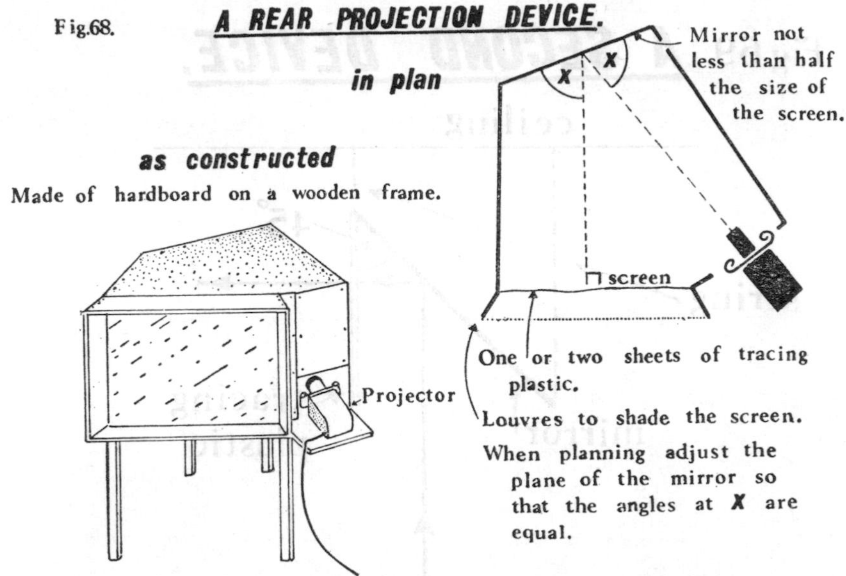
Fig.68.
A REAR PROJECTION DEVICE.
in plan
as constructed
Made of hardboard on a wooden frame.
Projector
X
X
Mirror not less than half the size of the screen.
screen
One or two sheets of tracing plastic.
Louvres to shade the screen.
When planning adjust the plane of the mirror so that the angles at X are equal.

the use of a rear projection screen greatly extends the usefulness of transparencies. Though the equipment can be purchased (EFV), it is cheaper if locally made, and there should be sufficient information in Figure 68 for this to be possible. Exact dimensions are not given for they are not critical and will vary with the projector used. The device is merely a box, the front of which is formed by a sheet of translucent tracing plastic such as 'Ethulon' (M&B). Some brands of this material are so thin that two sheets may have to be used together. The back of the box is formed by a mirror set at an angle and at one of the front corners a ledge is provided which will support the projector. The whole is built of hardboard or other suitable material and supported on legs so the bottom of the screen is at the eye level of a seated audience. The instructor stands at one side of the the device and is able to face the class and change the transparencies at the same time. It can be used whenever the ambient illumination is not too bright, but the screen itself should be shaded with the projecting ledges shown.

There is an alternative form of this device which is shown in Figure 69. A mirror hangs permanently from the ceiling in the manner shown, and it is reported to be effective, even in quite a brightly lit room. Like all rear projection devices it suffers from the disadvantage of rather a narrow viewing angle within which the audience must be seated. (Figure 69 was kindly supplied by Mr. K. Bale of OVAC.)

27:3 **Film strips.** Many slide projectors can be equipped with a film strip attachment. Several firms (KAY) will prepare film strips from a customer's

Fig.69. **A SECOND DEVICE.**

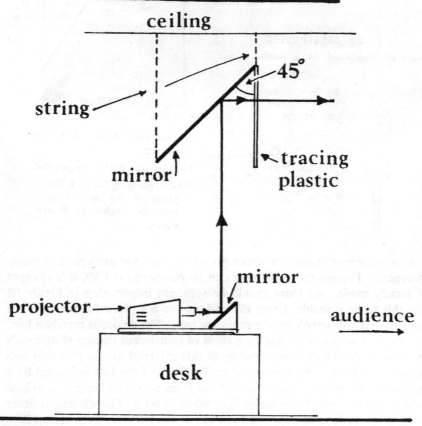

ceiling

45°

string

mirror

tracing plastic

mirror

projector

audience

desk

This is the device that holds the projector in the diagram above

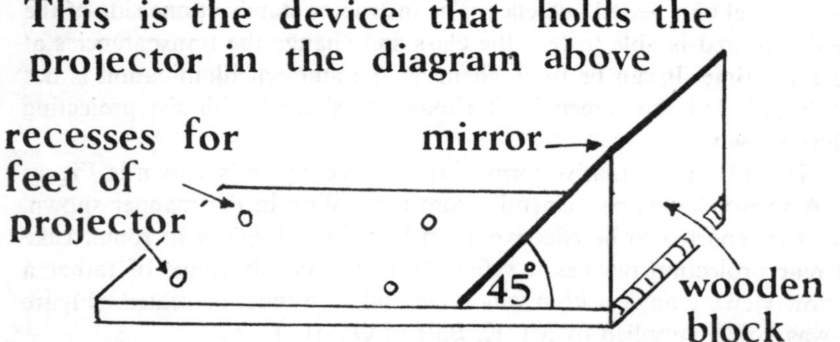

material and charge very little for doing it. Now that film strip and slide projectors are available for as little as £16 ($45) and can be adapted to run from a 12 volt car battery (CAB) (24:3), the film strip has become a really versatile aid with many advantages. Among them are colour, novelty in the eyes of a villager, the ease with which local material can be incorporated and a speed of presentation which can be adapted to match the understanding of the audience. The author of a well-made strip can sometimes sell many copies, and the cost per copy can thus be kept low.

Method: Making film strips.

Put all material on cards of the same size. These can either be on cards of proportion 3:4 (the 'single frame' or 'cine size'), in which case the long axis of the picture goes across the strip, or it can be on cards of proportion 2:3 (the double frame or 'Leica size') where the long axis of the picture runs the length of the strip. Choose one proportion and stick to it. Cards 15 cm. x 20 cm. (6 in. x 8 in.) are a convenient 3:4 proportion but, unless the film projector has a rotating film carriage, see that all the frames are the same way up. Some projectors will take the 'single frame' size only.

Use either black-and-white or colour; employ photographic prints, drawings or paintings, colour slides or transparencies, but avoid half-tone printing, or the 'dots' of which the picture is composed will appear on the screen. Trim all material so that the cards are filled as nearly as possible. Retouch, and cut away the background if required. When figures are required try cutting them out of coloured paper. Black and white diagrams are best done with black and white poster paint on grey paper, for plain white will seem too glaring on the screen. Letter by hand, stencil, 'Letraset' (LET) or typing, but don't make letters smaller than ½ cm. (¼ inch) on a 15 x 20 cm. card. Number all cards a little clear of their corners, and, if using photographs, stick the numbers on with rubber solution.

Below 20 frames the strip will not be economical, above 60 it will be cumbersome.

27:4 **The flannelgraph.** This is a good device for teaching simple villagers and one that health educators should make the most of. It is a vivid way of putting simple pictures and instructions before a class.

Method: Flannelgraphs.

Pin a green cloth with a good pile (OVA) to a board the size of the blackboard. If the right material is not available

flannelette, a 'market blanket' or lint will serve. Put this board in front of the class so that it slopes backwards very slightly. If cards, to the back of which flannel or any fluffy or rough material such as sandpaper has been pasted, are now placed on this board they will stay in any position and can be moved about or taken down at will. Make cards of a suitable colour and shape to depict any object required. Use large printed or written words and employ drawings, newspaper cuttings, or photographs. Most effective of all are bold simple symbols cut from stiff brightly coloured material such as felt (DRY). Posters can also be 'dissected' to make flannelgraphs. Once made, an outfit of cards can be kept from one class to another and when well used form a very effective aid indeed. It has been said of the flannelgraph that a good one does these things:

It tells a story in which you can see things happen.

It has strong colours that you can see well.

It has pictures that are big enough to be seen from a little way off.

It looks like the things that people are used to seeing.

It makes the people who see it talk about it and ask questions.

It lets some of the people help the teacher to tell the story and in this way promotes the interest of the class.

27:5 **The 'flip-chart.'** This is a very effective aid with more sophisticated audiences.

Method: Preparing 'flip-charts'.

Obtain large sheets of newsprint from a stationer, say 100 cm. (40 inches) by 50 cm. (20 inches), but, if these are not available a newspaper office will often give away free the ends of their newsprint rolls. Use felt-tip pens with coloured ink to make bold drawings or instructions on these sheets and attach several of them to the top of a blackboard with large paper clips. As soon as one is finished with, it can be 'flipped' over the top of the board to expose the next. A series of vigorous, cheap, easily made drawings can thus be presented to a class in rapid succession. Afterwards, they can be rolled up, stored and used another time. When the 'felt pens' dry up moisten their contents with the special inks made for them.

27:6 **Tape recorders.** These are now cheap, reliable and widely available. Portable battery models can be used anywhere. The great merit of tape in health education is that it can record material in the local vernacular which can even include a musical accompaniment on the local instruments. Members of the hospital staff can record a 'programme' which can be repeated at will any number of times, and with little training the machines can be operated by nursing staff in the wards or clinics. A film can also be given a 'sound track' in the local vernacular. One of the difficulties in the use of tape recorders is to provide circumstances sufficiently free of distraction in which the patients can listen with sufficient attention to what is being said. Some workers have used an extra loudspeaker so that a large number of waiting patients can hear. But despite this difficulty, the time spent in devising and recording such health education programmes can be well repaid.

27:7 **OVAC.** The Overseas Visual Aids Centre (OVAC) in London exists to further the dissemination of information about visual aids of all kinds and issues catalogues of books, charts, posters, diagrams, films, film strips, slides, 'flash cards', flannelgraphs and models — it is well worth a visit by those fortunate enough to be in London. OVAC also run courses lasting 3-10 days which have a very good reputation.

Chapter Twenty-Eight

SUPPORTING SERVICES

Lester Eshleman

Those accustomed to work in large, well run hospitals are tempted to take many important services for granted, and only realize how critical these are when they find them missing or inadequate in some small and struggling district hospital. Among these services are the laundry, the workshop and the transport section. A few principles on the management of these services are therefore gathered here for the benefit of those who may be called upon to run them.

28:1 **The laundry.** The laundry is a common source of trouble. When the entire process has to be done by hand the following rules may be helpful. Many items need not be boiled, though it is better if they are, common exceptions that always need boiling being bandages, nappies and theatre towels.

Method: Rules for a hand laundry.

Basic procedure.

1) **Separate the foul linen, sluice it, soak it separately for 3-12 hours.**
2) **Transfer to hot water. Agitate hard for 15 minutes. Wash 12 sheets or their equivalent in 25 gallons of water containing about half a pint of soap powder — the quantity needed depends on the hardness of the water.**
3) **Rinse, preferably three times.**
4) **If possible boil for 15 minutes in clean water with soap as in 2) Agitate during boiling.**
5) **Rinse three times.**

6) **Wring out.**
7) **Dry as quickly as possible.**

Soak blood and meconium stained articles 12 hours in saline then treat as above. If badly stained, insert a bleaching process between soaking and washing as follows:

Bleaching process. **Mix 3 tablespoonfuls of chloride of lime in a gallon of water. Tip this into a fifteen gallon tub of hot water. Mix well, add the linen item by item, agitate for five minutes. Remove the linen, rinse, and transfer it to stage 2) above. The operator should use rubber (post-mortem) gloves. Too long in too strong a bleach will spoil the linen.**

General points. **Arrange a convenient line-of-flow, with separate tubs for the stages 1), 2), 3), 4) and 5) above. This enables several batches to be dealt with at once. Put tubs close together to minimize the effort of moving heavy wet linen. Failing the standard type of tub, use petrol drums cut in half and painted inside with roof paint which will serve all purposes except boiling. If wooden tubs are used, keep them wet. Provide large rapid water inlets (a 2 inch pipe, with a 10 foot head of water) and outlets (a 3 inch or preferably a 4 inch pipe). If water is short, three rinses with a little water is better than one with much.**

The first stage to mechanize is the washing itself, and for this a large petrol driven domestic pattern washing machine (MAY) may be found useful by those hospitals without electricity. For those with some electric power there is an admirable series of machines which are all electrically driven but which can be heated by either electricity, gas, coal, wood, oil or steam (MIE). They consist of a large horizontal perforated drum with a door at one side through which the laundry is inserted. This drum is rotated until the liner is clean in a bath of hot water to which a detergent has been added. The smallest model costs £260 ($740), holds 12 kg. (25 lbs) of dry linen and is ideally suited to the laundry of a small hospital.

For those with sufficient electric power to heat the water, there is a machine which is substantially cheaper than the above (£143) ($400) and acts as both a washing machine and a hydro-extractor (VAB).

The wringing process is the next stage to be mechanised. A spin-drier or hydro-extractor, removes the excess water in the linen after washing by spinning it round at a high speed in a vertical perforated cylinder. The smallest spin-drier for laundry as opposed to domestic use costs about £120 ($335) and will spin the equivalent of 8 kg. (17½ lbs.) of dry laundry (MIE).

After spin drying linen is still too moist to be ironed immediately and it must either be dried on a line or in a drying machine or, better still, in a vacuum tumbler-drier. At £210 ($600) (MIE) these machines are expensive and most hospitals will have to rely on the traditional washing line. Such lines are a great temptation to thieves and it may be necessary to erect a cage of netting round them. Where rain makes it difficult to dry clothes out of doors on a line, it is possible to make a drying room using the hot air from the radiator of the diesel-electric generator which lights the hospital. This hot air can either be taken from the radiator to the drying room in a duct, or the radiator itself can be built into the wall of the drying room and its fan reversed so as to blow in hot air directly, but, whichever method is used, this is a fine way of drying wet laundry in rainy weather.

Ironing is the last stage to be mechanized; for this the simplest machine costs £500 ($1,370) (MIE), but although ironed sheets may seem a luxury, they are reputed to stay clean longer.

Care should be taken not to order machines that will overload the mains and to plan a laundry to match the growth of a hospital. There is no easy way of matching machines to beds, because the laundry produced per bed varies so widely, but, if the weight of laundry can be estimated, machines can be ordered to suit it. They are quoted as capable of dealing with a certain weight of dry laundry in each load. As a very rough estimate each bed can be estimated to produce 2 lbs. (1 kg.) of dry laundry daily. As a basis for planning allow at least three if not six wash days a week, give the washing machines five loads in an eight hour day and a hydro-extractor four loads an hour. Two smaller machines are usually better than one very big one, because laundry is apt to arrive continuously throughout the day and a large machine may have to stand idle while waiting to be filled.

Though linen is best washed in hot water it can be washed cold, and for this purpose some detergents are said to be better than others (UNI). The routine use of a bleach such as 'Chloram' (ICI) costs very little and makes a great difference to the whiteness of the linen.

Those wanting to install a steam supply for laundry and sterilization purposes are advised to consider the possibility of an oil fired steam generator (KAR) which is much cheaper than the standard pattern of boiler.

Before ordering laundry machinery the prices of two firms (VAB) and (MIE) should be compared. The interested reader is advised to write for a manual, *Planning a Machine Equipped Laundry* produced by the former firm.

28:2 **The workshop.** A hospital without a workshop hardly seems possible, yet some there are without one. When the building of a hospital was discussed it was pointed out that its fabric is in a continual state of change and parts of it are always wearing out (10:1). This will be particularly important, if, as was so strongly urged in sections 1:10b, 10:6, and 12:3, cheap methods of construction are used which require more maintenance. The need for maintenance applies not only to whole buildings, but also to furniture and fittings as well, so that unless someone is continually making small repairs a hospital soon becomes a very difficult place to work in. Alteration and manufacture are needed as well as repairs, for minor changes in such things as shelving and cupboards are continually wanted and there is steady demand for the furniture and simple equipment that a clever workman can make. Such a person is a great economy as well as a great convenience, and to illustrate this one hospital superintendent calculated that the cost of having a basin fitted by the public works department would have paid such a workman's wages for no less than three months.

The hospital workman must have both the tools and the materials for the jobs he will be required to do, and needs stocks of timber, piping, cement, paint, bricks and sand, as well as a multitude of nails, screws, bolts and minor ironmongery. His tools should enable him to function in the humbler capacities of carpenter, tinsmith, builder, electrician, mechanic and instrument maker, but, should it be thought that such a genius is not to be had, it can only be said that some hospitals do indeed have such a person. If a suitable man cannot be found ready trained, a careful selection should be made among primary or early secondary school leavers, and the right trainee sent to learn his trades under an expert in another hospital or else apprenticed in some other way. Such a man soon becomes indispensable, but if he is to be retained, he may later have to be well paid. Clearly, his salary is likely to be money well spent.

Not only will a workman need the right tools and materials, but he will also need a suitable shop in which to work. If hard physical labour is expected of him in the heat of the tropics, at least two sides of his workshop should be open to the breeze and screened with coarse netting against thieves.

When the book was planned it was the original intention to include several pages of detailed drawings of hospital equipment for local manufacture, but as it grew and matured there was seen to be insufficient space for them. Two items are however included in Figure 70; one is a labour room bed that was much preferred by the midwives using it to an alternative one of commercial manufacture. The other item is a drip stand, but these are only two of many pieces of equipment that can be made locally with great economy. The editor will be pleased to supply readers with such further drawings as he has, and will in turn be grate-

Fig.70 **TWO ITEMS FOR THE WORKSHOP.**

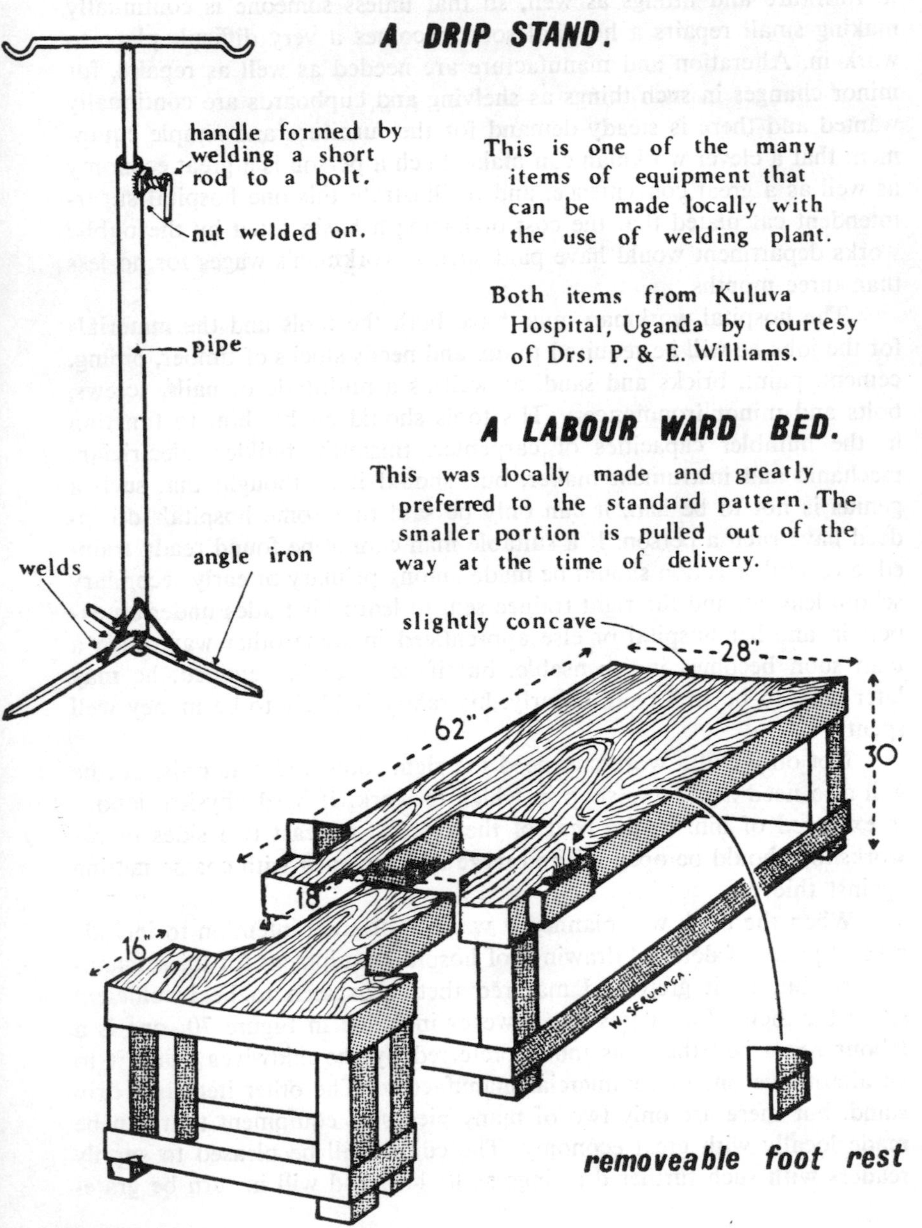
A DRIP STAND.
handle formed by welding a short rod to a bolt.
nut welded on.
pipe
welds
angle iron
This is one of the many items of equipment that can be made locally with the use of welding plant.
Both items from Kuluva Hospital, Uganda by courtesy of Drs. P. & E. Williams.
A LABOUR WARD BED.
This was locally made and greatly preferred to the standard pattern. The smaller portion is pulled out of the way at the time of delivery.
slightly concave
28"
62"
30"
18"
16"
W. SERUMAGA
removeable foot rest

ful if they will send him drawings of equipment that they have and think other hospitals might like to make. If the supply of ideas and the demand for them warrant it, the editor intends to produce a manual of hospital equipment for local manufacture.

Fig. 71. **TWO ADAPTATIONS OF THE BICYCLE.**

A locally made wheel chair.

Designed by Mr S.W. Eaves.

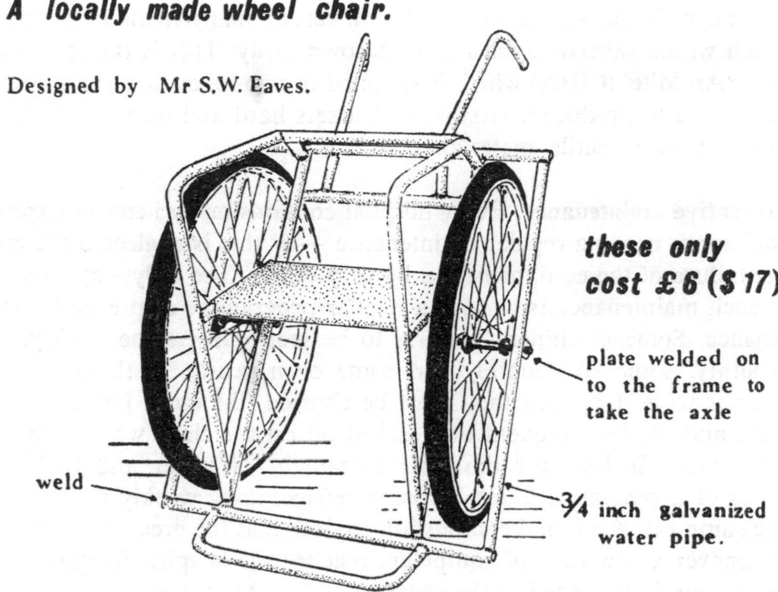

A factory made bicycle ambulance.

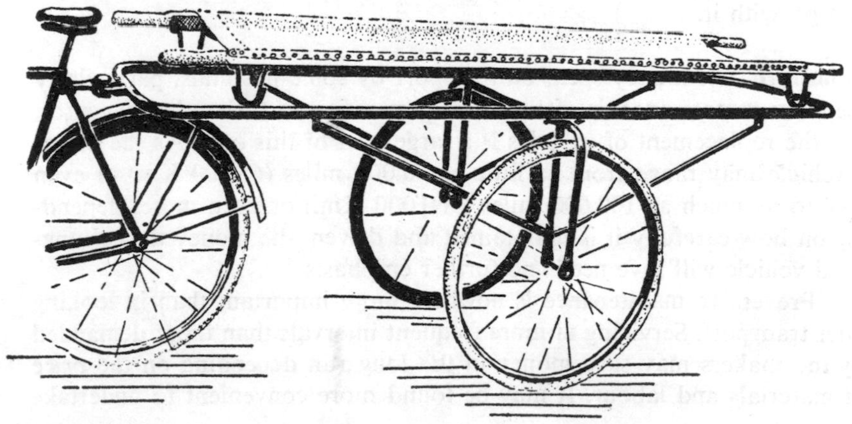

Mild steel tubing is readily available in most parts of the world and welding plant is universal wherever there are motor cars. It is thus possible to make many items of steel hospital furniture at a fraction of the cost of the imported ones. It is therefore no longer excusable to order such things as drip stands, instrument trolleys or wheel chairs from abroad (Figure 71). Ideally such hospital equipment should be made in a central workshop, but some hospitals may find it economic to own their own welding plant.

There is one substance which will rescue many items of equipment which would otherwise have to be thrown away. This is the epoxy resin glue, 'Araldite' (CIBA) which is supplied in two tubes that are mixed just before use to produce a mixture which sets hard and resists boiling; it is thus a very versatile material.

28:3 **Preventive maintenance.** Every hospital contains many items of expensive equipment needing regular maintenance — if this is neglected the resulting failure of the equipment can be very costly. The only way to be sure of such maintenance is to have a regular programme of preventive maintenance. Some machinery requires to be seen daily, some weekly, some monthly, some six monthly and some even yearly. If these servicings are not to be forgotten they must be charted, the chart pinned up on a wall, and the less frequent ones ticked off on the chart when completed. Such tasks include the daily replenishment of water and fuel in the tanks of a generator, filling kerosene refrigerators, weekly inspections of the sump oil of internal combustion engines and the greasing of bearings. Whenever a new item of equipment reaches the hospital its maintenance needs should be added to the chart.

Preventive maintenance includes the holding of spares, particularly such things as gaskets for autoclaves. These should be held in the workshop or store, and no new equipment ordered without the spare parts that go with it.

28:4 **Transport.** The money spent on transport by some hospitals, particularly the more remote ones, is often out of proportion to their other expenses, and the replacement of vehicles is a large part of this cost. As the life of a vehicle may range from as little as 40,000 miles (65,000 Km) or even less, to as much as 100,000 miles (160,000 Km.) or even more, depending on how carefully it is maintained and driven, the money that a long-lived vehicle will save needs no further emphasis.

Preventive maintenance is nowhere more important than in looking after transport. Servicing at more frequent intervals than those demanded by the makers may save money in the long run depending on the price of materials and labour. It may be found more convenient to undertake a number of servicing procedures together at intervals of say 1,000, 3,000, 5,000 and 10,000 miles rather than carry out a few at a time at less convenient intervals. Here again, a maintenance chart should be on the wall of every garage where a driver is expected to service his own vehicles, and in every log book where he is not.

If vehicles have to be serviced and repaired in the hospital, the makers' workshop and spare parts manuals are indispensable and the right tools must be available. Essential among these are a set of combination open ended and ring spanners to fit the vehicle, and a set of box spanners with their attachments.

The smaller the vehicle, the cheaper it will be to replace and run, and a cheap, light runabout car may prove a good investment, while a motorized bicycle or scooter may enable an itinerant midwife to make visits which would otherwise be too expensive (3:12). It may be argued that it is essential to have a vehicle with four wheel drive. So it is in many areas for several months of the year at least, but there are numerous regions where the roads are passable to a cheaper, lighter vehicle for three-quarters of the year and more. In practice there may be a choice between not providing mobile services at all, or providing them in a cheap light vehicle during the dry season only. The latter is likely to be much the best option and some services, immunization for example, are likely to be little hindered by being compressed into part of the year only.

The Landrover deserves its 'go-anywhere' reputation, but it is expensive to buy, costly to run and maintain, and unless carefully looked after its life is short. A cheaper, lighter vehicle with a good record of service in the developing countries is the Renault 4L, and a newer alternative is the British Motor Company 'Mini-Moke', which is the utility version of its well known 'Mini-Minor'. This is half the price of a Landrover, it uses about a third as much petrol, and, like the Renault 4L, in service it may well cost well under half as much to run. Light vehicles such as these have a big part to play in making mobile services economical enough to be practicable (2:10) (3:12) (12:7).

Another matter of considerable importance in determining the economy of a vehicle's use is its driver, particularly his training, the ease with which it is possible to fire him if he neglects his vehicle, and the possibility of giving him a salary bonus if he makes it last a long time. Reckoning that a £1,000 vehicle lasts five years and depreciates at the rate of £200 annually, depreciation will be seen to be of the same order as its driver's salary. Thus the driver who can get an extra year's life out of his vehicle deserves a very substantial bonus indeed — an employer would not lose out on such a bonus until it exceeded the man's salary. A much smaller bonus would be a sufficient inducement, and the employer would thus be left with a clear profit. This does of course mean linking one man to one vehicle, but so great are transport expenses, that it may well be worth the extra trouble and waste of the driver's time that this involves. But, in a developing country, it is vehicles that are in short supply, not drivers.

The bicycle must not be forgotten in the drive for economy and there is even a place for the bicycle ambulance shown in Figure 71 (W. A. Pashley Ltd., Chester St., Aston, Birmingham 6, U.K.). One hospital in Uganda keeps an ambulance of this kind and lends it to relatives who want to bring in sick patients. The family is thus saved the cost of a taxi, and the hospital the expense of a motor vehicle. In view of what has been said about the money patients spend on transport in section 12:7 a bicycle ambulance may be a useful asset.

Chapter Twenty-Nine

THE LIBRARY

Maurice King

29:1 **The general position.** The correct books contribute greatly to the medical standards of a hospital. They include those in its library as well as those in the personal possession of the staff, especially its auxiliaries. Because bookshops are remote from the places where many doctors work, an attempt has been made to list and evaluate some of the books that may be useful to them. They are referred to briefly here, full details and prices being given in Appendix C. Although they may be obtained from other booksellers, readers may find it convenient to purchase them from H. K. Lewis and Co. (LEW), who publish two very convenient catalogues, one on medicine and the other on nursing.

Cheap paperback textbooks are becoming increasingly common and those of the English Language Book Society are highly commended. Davidson's textbook of medicine /51/, for instance, is much cheaper in this series than it is in the standard hard covered edition. An increasing number of cheap English textbooks are now being produced by this society specifically for the needs of developing countries.

29:2 **Books for auxiliaries**. Few books are of more importance than those given to auxiliary staff and no class of book is on the whole so poorly adapted to the needs of its readers. When the number of English-speaking auxiliaries is considered, and the quality of the knowledge that they need to be taught, the deficiency of really suitable books is indeed tragic. Such books need to be intimately related to the specific needs of the auxiliary, closely related to his comprehension, and particularly to his vocabulary, and liberally and clearly illustrated. They should, where relevant, be related to the particular community where the auxiliary works, no new word should be introduced without an explanation in the text and nothing included that is not strictly necessary.

Books for auxiliaries are of two kinds, those which he should possess and study constantly, and those which should be on the shelves of the training school where he works. *The first group he must take with him when he leaves as the nucleus of his own personal library,* but it matters little how he comes to possess them, whether by gift, by the use of a book grant, or by subsidized purchase. The books that should be in the library of an auxiliary training school include both those on the wider aspects of the subjects being taught, and those which will increase the student's general knowledge. Some books of both kinds are suggested in Appendix C.

New books of particular value to auxiliaries appear from time to time, Jelliffe's *Child Health in the Tropics* /86/ is a recent example, and, when they do a medical service must see that they reach the hands of all the auxiliaries who will profit by them. Their cost is trivial compared with the benefit they confer, and, because auxiliaries have no means of knowing of their existence, their issue should be the responsibility of the medical administration.

The richness of the English language and the complexity of medical terms make dictionaries essential. The enrolled nurse, for instance, needs both a pocket dictionary /113/ and a nurse's dictionary /16/ for her personal possession. The library of the training school should contain a larger English dictionary /43/ and a more substantial medical one /26/.

Certain books need special comment. The first are the Oxford series for medical auxiliaries /111 a. b, c, d/ which contains books on medicine, surgery and midwifery, and is shortly to contain one on anaesthetics, and it is hoped also one on laboratory procedures (24:1). Another is the *Tropical Dispensary Handbook* by Chesterman /39/, now in its 7th edition and 27 years in print. Although a classic, it contains so much archaic information that it has probably reached the limit of its useful life. A book that has already been mentioned and which readers will find invaluable is *Child Health in the Tropics* /86/, a pocket sized, hard covered book that is up to date and full of relevant, concise and highly practical information. This should be in every tropical children's ward and in the pocket of every medical assistant.

At present the test book for the laboratory assistant is that by Baker /18/ and for the transfusion assistant that by Farr /60/. Those teaching physiology to auxiliaries will probably find the books by McNaught & Callender useful, especially the cheap paperback version /99/.

There are a large number of books on nursing to choose from, almost all of them based on English or American practice. Some of those which have been found useful in Kenya and Uganda are listed in Appendix C. In this Appendix Balliéres 'Aids' series figure prominently. These are now being republished in slightly larger format as further editions are required in the form of 'Concise Medical Textbooks', many of which are suitable for auxiliaries.

Compared with the very many hospitals who are, or should be, training enrolled nurses or instructing their dressers and wardmaids, there will be comparatively few who will be training auxiliaries of other kinds. Only one suggested book list based on Kenyan experience will therefore be given here. This is for the enrolled public health nurse or comprehensive nurse (3:4), who acts as the nurse, midwife and health-visitor, who is trained for both hospital and health centre work, and who is needed in very large numbers.

A personal library for the enrolled public health nurse. /10/, /15/, /16/, /63/, /77/, /79/, /86/, /101/, /111a/, /113/, /138/. About £5 ($14) in all.

Some books for the library of training schools for enrolled public health nurses. /8/, /13/, /27/, /33/, /34/, /35/, /43/, /62/, /64/, /70/, /71/, /75/, /78/, /97/, /98/, /108/, /111b/ (40), (43), (44), (45), (46), (49), (50). About £25 ($70) in all. The latter books, or rather pamphlets, are mainly for the benefit of the teachers.

Finally, it must be emphasized that the correct books for auxiliaries can give an excellent return for the money spent on them. All those reading this section and responsible for auxiliaries are therefore advised to ask their staff what books they have, so that deficiencies can be brought to light and remedied rapidly, where possible by the free issue or the heavily subsidized sale of the books required.

29:3 **A library for the district hospital.** The most suitable standard textbook of moderate price is that by Davidson /51/ and the most concise account of tropical medicine the supplement to it which is bound in with the paperback edition. The best book specifically devoted to clinical tropical medicine is that by Adams and Maegraith /3/. *Non-infective disease in Africa* by Trowell /131/ is an invaluable source of information and one which should be on the bookshelf of every hospital.

Either Dunlop's *Textbook of Medical Treatment* /54/ or Conn's *Current Therapy* /45/ are essential, and many would not be without Birch's *Emergencies in Medical Practice* /24/. As a formulary for use in the tropics the 1965 revision of the Ugandan formulary /134/ is commended to the reader; it contains a list of the common therapeutic procedures and is well suited to the use of medical assistants.

There is an admirable paperback by Vaughan on opthalmology /135/ a useful atlas of skin disease in the African by Clarke /41/ but it needs to be supplemented by a standard textbook such as that by Roxburgh /120/. Any hospital treating much leprosy should possess the standard work by Cochrane /42/.

A textbook of emergency surgery is essential and there are two to choose from, either that by Hamilton Bailey /12/, or the slightly cheaper one by Farquharson /58/. As a general textbook that by Bailey and Love /12/ is the best and for the simpler surgical procedures that by Pye (Vols. I and II) is indispensable /116/, and well suited to the more able auxiliary.

A book dealing specifically with problems in Africa is that by Bowesman /29/ which contains the fruit of much experience that is to be found nowhere else. Another work in this field is *The Companion to Surgery in Africa,* edited by Davey from Ibadan /50/.

The two books by Adams, one on orthopaedics /4/ and the other on fractures /5/ are the most convenient ones of their kind at the time of writing. They will, however, shortly be supplemented and should probably be replaced by two by Huckstep, one called *A Simple Guide to Fractures* /83/ and the other *The Rehabilitation of Poliomyelitis in Developing Countries* /84/. Both of them are copiously illustrated in this author's best style, are based on experience in Uganda and have been tried out as experimental editions; they are well suited to orthopaedic assistants — see (7:5). As a short book on diseases of the ear nose and throat, that by Reading is advised /117/. A useful textbook of anaesthetics is that by Wylie and Churchill-Davidson /144/ and one specifically devoted to regional and local anaesthetics that by Moore /104/.

As a standard textbook on obstetrics that by Baird /17/ is as good as any, while that by Donald /53/ on practical obstetric problems will be of great interest to all who deal with the day to day problems in this field. By the time this book is available Messrs. Arnold will have published *Obstetrics and Gynaecology in the Tropics* by Professor T. B. Lawson from Ibadan and Professor Stewart from Jamaica. This will be the first specifically tropical work in this field /89/.

Child health in the tropics /86/ has already been mentioned twice. The standard and more expensive work in this field is however, that by Trowell and Jelliffe /132/. The WHO monograph on the assessment of nutrition, also by Jelliffe /87/ will interest many readers (14:1), and the paperback by Welbourn /138/ is highly commended as essential reading for auxiliaries as well as doctors.

Those who have purchased an EEL colorimeter and want to extend the range of techniques they can undertake are advised to buy the standard work in this field by Wootton /142/. If they wish to undertake more bacteriology, the book to buy is that by Cruickshank /47/ while further haematological techniques are to be found in the volume by Dacie /49/. Further information on blood transfusion may be obtained from Mollison /103/

The first and only book on tropical health education is that by Holmes which gives a very useful account of the subject /75/. Of particular interest also is his pamphlet /76/ on the interpretation of visual symbols. This must be considered essential reading for anyone preparing pictorial material for health education.

There are an admirable series of cheap 'do-it-yourself' manuals by Alcock intended for the West African villager — the 'How to build' series /6/. A book which the amateur builder will find very useful is *Field Engineering* by Longland, even though it is somewhat dated /94/.

29:4 **A library list.** It is suggested that the minimum district hospital library for the use of doctors should contain the following books: Davidson's Medicine /51/ (Shs. 25/-), Adams and Maegraith /3/ (Shs. 63/-), Trowell's *Non-Infective Disease in Africa* /131/ (Shs. 70/-), 'Dunlop' /54/ (Shs. 65/-), 'Vaughan's opthalmology' /135/ (Shs. 42/-), 'Roxburgh's skin diseases' /120/ (Shs. 50/-), 'Farquharson's operative surgery' /58/ (Shs. 120/-), 'Bailey & Love' /12/ (Shs. 84/-), Pye (both volumes) /116/ (Shs. 80/-), the two books by Adams /4/ (Shs. 37/50) and /5/ (Shs. 30/-) pending the issue of those by Huckstep /83/ and /84/, Reading /117/ (Shs. 24/-) Wylie's anaesthetics /144/ (Shs???), Baird /17/ (Shs. 105/-), Donald /53/ (Shs. 70/-), Jelliffe's recent book /86/ (Shs. 15/-), that he wrote with Trowell /132/ (Shs. 105/-), also Holmes' book on health education /75/ (Shs. 21/-). This or its close equivalent should be looked upon as the minimum list, it adds up to about £55 ($150). In addition books will also be required for the personal possession of the auxiliaries and may possibly involve the expenditure of as much money again.

Chapter Thirty

MISCELLANEOUS

Maurice King

When twenty-nine chapters have been set in order some useful material still remains, but it is in fragments too small to merit whole chapters to themselves. It has therefore been gathered here and includes such diverse information as the comparative costs of drugs, the preparation of intravenous solutions, the use of plastics, central sterile supply services and a table on the use of rabies vaccine.

THE DISPENSARY

0:1a **The cost of drugs.** As has been pointed out in Chapter Twelve, drugs do not form a large fraction of the total hospital budget. Nevertheless, there are some useful economies that can be made, and there are some preparations which, though they may be more expensive than others, are yet so much more convenient in use as to be well worth the extra cost.

The approximate comparative costs of a variety of drugs are set out in Table 15. Costs are continually changing, so these figures should be interpreted with caution.

In this table it will be seen that tabs. Codein Co. are five times the cost of aspirin without it being certain that they are any more effective. 'Pethilorphan' (ROC), a combination of pethidine with levallorphan to allay its depressant action, is more than twice the cost of plain pethidine, but its value in obstetrics makes it well worth the extra expense.

Digoxin is about three times the price of the equivalent quantity of prepared digitalis. Tolbutamide and insulin are approximately equal in cost at equivalent dosage. The absence of the need for injections thus makes tolbutamide a very practical substitute for insulin in suitable cases.

'Ergorondase' (EVA), a preparation of ergometrine and hyaluroni-

TABLE 15

THE COMPARATIVE COST OF SOME IMPORTANT DRUGS

All costs from the 1962 Uganda Government Medical Stores List or E.A. wholesale prices in E.A. shillings and cents. Significant comparisons are grouped together. (One cent E.A. = $0.0014)

Drug	*Cost per unit in cents E.A.*	*Cost over a Period or Course for an Adult*
Tab. Aspirin 0.3 g.	0.4	
Tab. Codeine Co.	2.0	
Tab. Phenobarb 8 mg.	0.4	
Tab. Chlorpromazine 25 mg.	8.0	
Inj. Pethidine 50 mg.	14.0	
Inj. 'Pethilorphan' 50 mg.	35.0	
Tab. Digoxin 0.25 mg.	3.0	
Tab. Digitalis preparata 25 mg. (1 gr.)	1.0	
		per month
Soluble Insulin 40 units	100.0	30/- (40 units daily)
Tolbutamide 0.5 g.	23.0	27/- (2 g. daily)
Inj. Ergometrine	20.0	
Inj. Ergometrine + hyaluronidase ('Ergorondase')	200.0	
Tab. Fer. Sulph. 200 mg.	0.2	
Inj. Iron Dextran ('Imferon') (2 ml. 100 mg. Fe) (intramuscular)	181.0	
Inj. Saccharated oxide of iron ('Ferrivenin') (5 ml. 100 mg. Fe) (intravenous)	181.0	
Tab. Yeast	0.3	
Tab. 'Multivite'	1.2	
Tab. Folic acid 5 mg.	1.0	
Inj. Cyanocobalmin 50 micrograms	20.0	
Inj. Chloroquine 80 mg.	20.0	**per month—prophylactic use**
Tab. Mepacrine 100 mg.	1.5	-/45 (30 tabs.)
Tab. Chloroquine sulphate 200 mg.	3.6	-/29 (8 tabs.)
Tab. Pyrimethamine ('Daraprim') 25 mg.	12.0	-/48 (4 tabs.)
Tab. Proguanil 100 mg.	3.6	1/08 (30 tabs.)
Emulsion of Benzyl Benzoate 100 ml.	40.0	
Tetmosol 5 per cent in rubbing oil 100 ml.	15.0	
Tetrachlorethylene 5 ml.	5.0	
Bephenium ('Alcopar') one sachet	110.0	
Tab. Piperazine adipate 300 mg.	1.0	**per course**
'Stovarsol vaginal compound' 4 gr.	4.0	3/80
Tab. Metronidazole 0.25 g.	86.0	18/-
		per week
Tab. Sulphathiazole 0.5 g.	1.2	1/00 (6 g. daily)
Tab. Sulphadimidine 0.5 g.	1.6	1/35 (6 g. daily)
nj. Procaine penicillin 300,000 units ml.	16.0	1/12 (1 ml. daily)
nj. Procaine penicillin Forte 400,000 units ml.	22.0	1/54 (1 ml. daily)
Inj. 'Triplopen' 1.4 mega units	72.0	1/44 (2 injections)
Caps. Chloramphenicol 250 mg.	10.0	2/80 (1 g. daily)
Caps. Tetracycline 250 mg.	27.0	7/50 (1 g. daily)
Snake antivenine 10 ml.	1400.0	
Anti-tetanus serum 1500 units	100.0	

dase, acts almost as rapidly by the intramuscular route as does plain ergometrine when given intravenously. It is thus very valuable in the hands of those midwives who are unable to give an intravenous injection, but at ten times the price of plain ergometrine many users will have to save it for emergencies only.

The small cost of oral as compared with intravenous and intramuscular iron is well shown. A yeast tablet costs half as much as one of 'Multivite'. The cheapness of folic acid is fortunate in view of the prevalence of anaemias which respond to it, particularly the folic acid deficiency anaemias of pregnancy; it is also widely needed as a long-term supplement in sickle cell anaemia (13:12).

Mepacrine is half the price of chloroquine, but, though slightly less effective as a schizontocide, it is a cheaper and equally satisfactory as a way of treating the milder 'fever' though it is not advised for children. For malarial prophylaxis chloroquine is significantly cheaper than pyrimethamine when both these tablets are given weekly. However, when pyrimethamine is given monthly as a semi-supressant as advised (16:10), it is cheaper than chloroquine at the standard weekly dose, and has been proved effective.

Tetmosol in rubbing oil, is a third the price of benzyl benzoate for treating scabies. Tetrachlorethylene is a twentieth the price of bephenium for treating hookworm. Metronidazole ('Flagyl') has revolutionized the treatment of trichomoniasis, but at 18/- ($2.5) a course, it might seem to be beyond the range of almost all tropical patients, particularly as the husband should also be treated. However, the condition is so troublesome that some poorer patients are prepared to pay for it if the situation is carefully explained to them.

Sulphathiazole is the cheapest sulphonamide, but the slightly more expensive sulphadimidine is more satisfactory in routine use — the latter is however slightly more expensive than penicillin, there being no significant difference in cost between the procaine and crystalline varieties. In comparing the costs of penicillin and the sulphonamides no account is taken here of the cost of syringes, nor of the cost of actually giving the injection.

The convenience of such long acting penicillin preparations as 'Triplopen' (GLA), which is a mixture of benethamine procaine and crystalline penicillin, has been described in section 13:5. Unit for unit 'Triplopen' and 'procaine penicillin forte' or 'PPF' differ little in cost, a megaunit of the former costing -/60 and one of the latter -/55.

Chloramphenicol is almost a third the price of the next cheapest broad spectrum antibiotic — tetracycline. Antisera will be seen to be by far the most expensive drugs on the list.

1b **A hospital drug bill.** The drug bill for Mulago Hospital is instructive. About 40 per cent. of it is accounted for by antibiotics, half of this being penicillin. 7½ per cent. of the total is spent equally on insulin and tolbutamide, another 7½ per cent. on disinfectants, and about 5 per cent. on each of the following analgesics (mostly aspirin and codeine), antimalarials, sulpha drugs, antihistamines, hypotensive agents and anaesthetic agents. Intramuscular iron and dextran for infusion each account for 2½ per cent., a final 10 per cent. being miscellaneous items.

If economies have to be made, they are likely to be easiest to make by a comparatively small percentage economy in the use of those items which from the largest fraction of the drug bill. Another possibility is to withdraw expensive, but not normally life saving drugs, such as griseofulvin for instance, from routine use altogether. When drugs are sold to the patients, a certain profit on the common drugs are what will make pharmacy pay its way.

0:2 **The preparation of intravenous solutions.** Commercial intravenous solutions are too expensive for many hospitals and transport makes it difficult for others to obtain them from a regional medical store. There may thus be no alternative to going without, but to prepare such solutions locally, possibly under less than perfect conditions.

The British Pharmacopoeia requires that solutions containing sodium lactate be prepared by the titration of lactic acid against sodium hydroxide. This is unlikely to be practicable, but sodium lactate 70 per cent. (HOW), a faintly brown heavy syrup, is a satisfactory substitute. There is no B.P. specification for this substance, but the other materials should be of B.P. quality.

Ideally, these solutions should be made up from carefully prepared distilled water filtered through a sintered glass filter (MAT), but a still may not be available (MAN), nor a filter either. However, rain-water can be used, preferably that caught off an aluminium roof. Discard first catchings after a dry spell and likewise the first fraction of the distillate from a still, but, whichever kind is employed, water for intravenous solutions must be fresh. Ideally it should be used on the day it is prepared for pyrogens may appear overnight.

In Table 16 quantities are given for five litres, the volume contained in a bucket, but it is convenient to purchase a polythene 10 litre carboy with a tap and make up larger quantities.

If the acid citrate dextrose is wanted in smaller quantities its percentage composition is trisodium citrate 1.32%, citric acid 0.48% glucose (dextrose) 1.47%.

TABLE 16

THE PREPARATION OF INTRAVENOUS SOLUTION TO MAKE 5,000 ml

(All quantities in grams or millilitres)

	'Normal' Saline	*5% glucose*	*'Normal' saline in 5% glucose*	*⅓ normal saline in 5% glucose*	*Full strength Darrow's solution*	*Half strength Darrow's in 2.5% glucose*	*1/6 Molar Lactate*	*Acid Citrate Dextrose 'ACD'*
Glucose (Dextrose BP)	—	250	250	250	—	125	—	73.5
Sodium Chloride BP	45	—	45	15	20	10	—	—
Potassium Chloride BP	—	—	—	—	13	6.5	—	—
Sodium Lactate 70%	—	—	—	—	32	16	100	—
Tri-Sodium citrate (dihydric)	—	—	—	—	—	—	—	66
Citric acid BP	—	—	—	—	—	—	—	24
Water	to 5,000 ml.							

Method: The preparation of intravenous solutions.

Prepare these solutions in the standard MRC bottles (Figure 51) and see that they are used to no other purpose. Discard all caps that have once been pierced with the needle of a taking set, for bacteria can enter through the hole that a needle has made. Wash all bottles and caps well with soap and water, scrub them out with a stiff bottle brush, rinse them well with plenty of tap water and then give them a final wash in distilled water.

Dissolve the ingredients in the quantities specified, distribute the solution in 500 ml. quantities (110 ml. for acid citrate dextrose) and autoclave it at 15 lbs for 15 minutes. When cold, either cap the bottles with 'Viscaps' (VDC) or else use a strip of adhesive plaster marked 'Sterile' which extends from the cap of the bottle across to its neck — this is removed when the cap is taken off and never put on again. *Before using them inspect all solutions carefully for cloudiness lest bacteria have grown, particularly those containing glucose.*

The preparation of these solutions is a responsible task, and if grossly wrong quantities are weighed out, particularly the wrong quantity of potassium chloride, they will be dangerous. Careful autoclaving is essential as sterility tests may not be practicable. Solutions containing glucose or sodium lactate may be slightly brown after autoclaving, this is due to caramelization of the glucose and does not matter.

0:3 **The preparation and packaging of dried skim milk.** In the outpatient department dried skim milk can be used in two ways, either plain or reinforced with edible oil and sugar to provide additional calories — 'reinforced dried skim milk' (14:6). At Mulago Hospital reinforced dried skim milk is prepared in 87 gram packets which are the equivalent of a pint of ordinary milk, and plain dried skim milk is put in larger 900 gram packets. There is, however, no reason why other quantities should not be packed.

If the local children are short of calories as well as protein, use reinforced milk packets rather than plain dried skim milk, but, whichever kind is used, some convenient form of protein supplement must be available in every outpatient department, health centre and under-fives clinic where PCM is seen.

Reinforced milk packets. The following directions describe the preparation of reinforced milk packets on a small scale and on a medium scale. Other quantities can be obtained from Table 3 (14:6).

Method: Reinforced milk — small scale.

Mix 450 grams (1 lb.) of dried skim milk and 100 grams (3½ oz.) of sugar, add in 160 ml. (5½ fl. oz., 4½ oz.) of any edible oil. Stir for five minutes and store the mixture in a closed container: it will make 4½ litres (8 pints) of reconstituted milk at the rate of 87 grams (3 oz.) of the dry mixture to 570 ml. (1 pint approximately) of cold clean boiled water.

Make polythene bags from 5 inch lengths of 3 inch wide 250 gauge 'Diothene Layflat tubing' (MBO) which have been sealed at one end with a heat sealing machine (AUD). Fill the bags with 87 grams of the basic mixture using a 1½ inch diameter metal icing gun without its nozzle and seal them up. 87 grams are easily judged with practice but occasional packets should be check weighed.

Method: Reinforced milk — medium scale.

Put 3.54 kilograms (7 lb. 13 oz.) of dried skim milk, 720 grams (1 lb. 9 oz.) of sugar and one litre of oil (2 lb.) in the bowl of an electric mixer (HOB) and mix for two minutes. This will make 60 packets of 87 grams (3 oz.) sufficient for 34 litres (60 pints) of reconstituted milk.

Fill the same packets with an electric filler (GDM), and seal them with a semi-automatic electric sealer (PAC).

Plain milk packets. These larger packets enable dried skim milk to be handed out in a very convenient form.

Method: Plain milk packets.

Cut 33 cm. (13 in.) wide Diothene Layflat tubing into 20 cm. (8 in.) lengths. Seal one end with a heat sealer. Deliver 900 grams (2.2 lb.) of dried skim milk into the bottom of the bag

through a wide funnel, taking care to keep the inside of the top of the bag free from milk powder. Seal the top of the bag.

One of the difficulties of sealing milk powder inside a bag is that of keeping the line of the seal free from powder, for this reduces the efficiency of closure. These bags should if possible be printed with educational instructions like those in Figure 28 (14:14). If it is not technically possible to print the polythene bag itself, enclose a printed paper 'handout' with the powdered milk.

30:4 **An electrolyte mixture for protein-calorie malnutrition — 'PCM mixture'**. The following mixture contains the equivalent of 1.6 g. of sodium and 1.6 g. of potassium chlorides and 0.15 grams of magnesium hydroxide in 15 ml. (½ ounce).

Method: PCM Mixture.

Add 106 grams of sodium chloride, 106 grams of potassium chloride and 10 g. of magnesium hydroxide to a litre of water. Label, and colour as convenient.

Add 15 ml. (½ oz.), of this mixture to each pint (570 ml.) of 'milk' feed, especially to those based on calcium caseinate. SHAKE WELL BEFORE USE.

PLASTICS

30:5 **Plastics in the service of the hospital.** Plastics in the form of tubing, sheeting, and apparatus of various kinds (POR) have made several new techniques possible and many others cheaper and more convenient. In one form or another they have so much to offer that it is important to make the most of them. They exist in such confusing variety and have such diverse qualities that a description of the method of sterilizing some of the commoner ones may be useful.

'PVC' (Polyvinyl chloride). This varies according to the method of its manufacture, some formulations are destroyed by boiling, others withstand autoclaving, but, PVC should always be handled with care while hot.

Standard polythene. This may be boiled but not autoclaved. Boiling is, however, generally unsatisfactory and must be for the shortest possible time only (1 minute). Like PVC standard polythene becomes soft when hot and thus needs handling with care.

High density polythene. This can be boiled without harm but not autoclaved.

Nylon and polypropylene. These can both be boiled repeatedly and autoclaved with impunity.

Plastic film is available as sheets or, more conveniently, as wide thin walled tubing, termed 'Layflat tubing', which is purchased packed flat as a continued roll (POR) (MBO). Short lengths of such a roll can be sealed with a heat sealer to make watertight packets that are useful for many purposes. Among them are envelopes for weight charts and records (26:5), sachets for histological specimens (24:10). They can also be used for prepacked tablets (11:2, 21:18c) and for the issue of dried skim milk as described above.

A confusing number of gauges and sizes are available. Use a stout one for record cards and histological specimens (0.004″ or 0.1 mm) and the cheapest, thinnest one for prepacked tablets.

Fig.72. **A SEALING MACHINE FOR PLASTIC FILM.** (AUD)

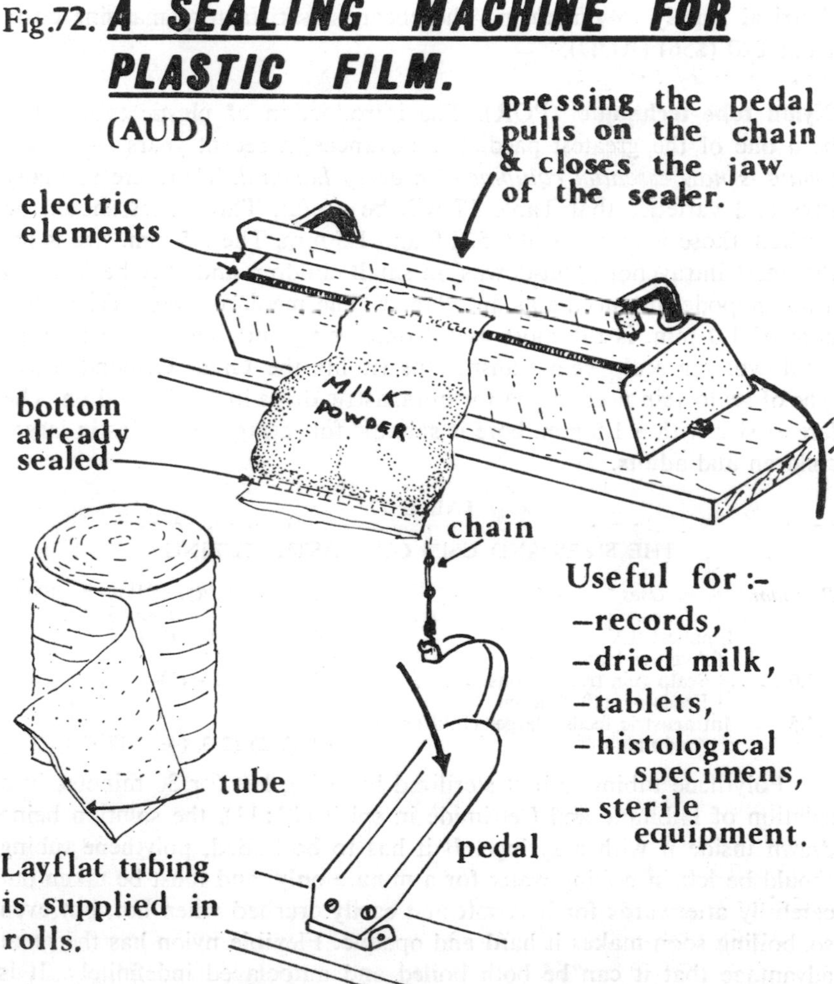
pressing the pedal pulls on the chain & closes the jaw of the sealer.
electric elements
MILK POWDER
bottom already sealed
chain
Useful for :-
–records,
–dried milk,
–tablets,
–histological specimens,
–sterile equipment.
tube
pedal
Layflat tubing is supplied in rolls.

None of these requires autoclaving, so the cheaper polythene film can be used, but, for sterile apparatus and dressings of all kinds, very handy sterile packs can be made from nylon film which will withstand the temperature of an autoclave. Because this film is permeable to steam but not to bacteria satisfactory sterilization is possible. It is available (POR) as flat tubing in rolls from 1.3 cm. (½ in.) to 76 cm. (30 in.) wide and is comparatively inexpensive. If no heat sealing machine is available it can be sealed with a special tape (POR) that can be autoclaved and which changes colour on heating and so provides certain evidence that a particular pack has been sterilized.

Heat sealing machines are so convenient that these devices must now be considered essential items of equipment in any hospital with an electrical supply to run them. The cheapest satisfactory machine costs about £20 ($56) (AUD).

30:6 **'Nylon tube technique'** (POR). The introduction of plastic tubing has been one of the greatest paediatric advances in recent years — *plastic tubing is now essential equipment in every hospital.* There are so many sizes and varieties that Table 17 will be useful. Three sizes should be stocked, those with bores of 0.5, 1.0 and 1.5 mm. The 0.5 mm. size is for the finest intravenous 'cut-downs' in small children and may be fitted to a fine hypodermic needle as an adapter. The medium sized tube with a bore of 1.0 mm. is the most useful one, being suitable for the average cut-down, for scalp vein transfusions (it fits the Great Ormond Street type of scalp vein needle) and for intragastric drips in small children. The largest size with a 1.5 mm. bore is suitable for intragastric drips in larger children and adults.

TABLE 17

THE SIZES AND USES OF PLASTIC TUBING

Bore mm.	*Uses*	*Cat. No. (POR) and Price per 100 ft.* *Polythene*		*Flexible Nylon*	
0.5	Smallest 'I.V. cut-down'	(PP.30)	7/9	(00)	9/9
1.0	Average 'cut-down' Scalp vein transfusions Feeds—small children	(PP. 120)	12/-	(3)	14/6
1.5	Intragastric feeds—larger children and adults	(PP.202)	12/3	(4)	17/-

Polythene tubing is best sterilized by being left for 30 minutes in a solution of Hibitane and Cetrimide in spirit (18:11), the solution being drawn inside it with a syringe. *If* it has to be boiled, polythene tubing should be left in boiling water for a minute only, and must be taken out carefully afterwards for it is soft and easily crushed when hot, but even so, boiling soon makes it hard and opaque. Flexible nylon has the great advantage that it can be both boiled and autoclaved indefinitely. It is slightly less supple than polythene but its greater resistance to heat and its longer life make *nylon the tubing of choice, even though it costs a little more than polythene*.

30:7 **'Tube feeding'.** The invention of plastic tubing has made it possible to tube feed babies and children. This is a procedure of great value in protein-calorie malnutrition, for it overcomes the anorexia which is such a feature of this condition.

Method: Tube feeding.

Estimate the length of the tube required by doubling the distance between the top of a child's forehead and his xiphisternum, and smooth the end of a new tube by holding it a moment in match flame. Lubricate it with oil, pass it through a nostril, hold it in place with strapping, and, if need be, it can stay as long as a week, but, before using it test it first with a little water just to make quite sure it is in the stomach — it is apt to curl up at the back of the nose.

The way in which the tube is strapped in place is critical to its success. Use a length of half inch strapping which stretches across the face just above the upper lip. It should extend from the cheek on one side, to just in front of the ear on the other and must lie close to but not occlude the nostrils. The tube must lie underneath this strapping and only come free near the ear.

Teach the nurse to renew the strapping whenever it comes loose round the nose or when the child hooks his fingers in and pulls it out. If the tube is properly strapped in place it should not be necessary to tie the child's hands, or to splint his arms.

Feeds can be given continuously by attaching the tube to a 'drip set', but see that someone stays with the child, and in hot weather change the bottle six hourly lest it sour. If a continuous drip is inconvenient, give three-hourly feeds slowly down the tube with a syringe. Some prefer to use a douche can instead of a transfusion bottle to hold the milk.

STERILE SUPPLIES

30:8 **Central sterile supply — prepacked settings.** Even to mention this may seem entirely unrealistic to many readers. But, though the fully developed central sterile supply unit is likely to be quite impossible, *elementary central sterile supply services and particularly prepacked sterile settings can be made available wherever there is an autoclave*. Packing sterile equipment should present no problem for it can be wrapped in several layers of newspaper (stout brown kraft paper is better), and tied with string. Syringes, cut-down sets and even settings for such tasks as Caesarian section can be prepared and kept in readiness in this way. Larger settings need an outer covering of cloth to keep them together and are conveniently packed in an enamel bowl or dish. Cloth should not be relied on entirely and at least one layer of paper should be placed inside it. Nylon film sealed with a heat sealer or with special tape is the ideal way of preparing settings of this kind and has been described above.

Another alternative is to take a large theatre towel and make a series of pockets in it for the equipment or dressings needed for a lumbar puncture, a cut-down or a marrow biopsy. The apparatus required for the setting is placed in the pockets, the towel is then rolled up and either autoclaved in a tin with a mask and gallipot, or else tied up with paper and string. Whichever method is preferred, a piece of plaster should be put across the join in a bundle, or across the edge of the lid of a tin, and the date of autoclaving written on it — only packs or tins with an unbroken 'seal' should be used. Unused packs should be resterilized each fortnight.

If packs and syringes are prepared in the theatre and exchanged 'one-for-one' with the wards, a central sterile supply service will have been created. It demands a stock or 'float' of equipment which some hospitals may not be able to provide, however, in the theatre especially, *prepacked sterile settings enable major economies to be made in the use of the time of skilled staff.* There need be no waiting about while equipment is boiled up.

When autoclaving make quite sure that the operator understands the importance of discharging the air from the autoclave before raising the steam pressure. Make a practice of testing the autoclave regularly either with 'Brown's tubes' (BRO), which change colour when the required temperature has been maintained for the necessary length of time, or, if there are bacteriological facilities available, with spore strips (OXO). Cheaper than either, though less satisfactory as an indicator of effective sterilization, is the special autoclave tape (POR), which changes colour when a package has been through the autoclave, and which has already been mentioned. If sterilization procedures are giving trouble, write and ask the makers of Brown's tubes (BRO) for their pamphlet.

RABIES

30:9 **The indications for giving rabies vaccine.** Two main kinds of rabies vaccine are available, one, the newer type made from duck embryos, and the other, the traditional type of vaccine made from sheep's brain. Although the risk of complications is less with the newer vaccines, it is still necessary to weigh up the risks from the vaccine with the risks from the

Table 18. THE TREATMENT OF RABIES.

A. Local Treatment of Wounds Involving Possible Exposure to Rabies

(1) Recommended in all exposures

(a) First-aid treatment

Immediate washing and flushing with soap and water, detergent or water alone (recommended procedure in all bite wounds including those unrelated to possible exposure to rabies).

(b) Treatment by or under direction of a physician

(i) Adequate cleansing of the wound.
(ii) Thorough treatment with 20% soap solution and/or the application of a quaternary ammonium compound or other substance of proven lethal effect on the rabies virus.[1]
(iii) Topical application of antirabies serum or its liquid or powdered globulin preparation (optional).
(iv) Administration, where indicated, of antitetanus procedures and of antibiotics and drugs to control infections other than rabies.
(v) Suturing of wound not advised.

(2) Additional local treatment for severe exposures only

(a) Topical application of antirabies serum or its liquid or powdered globulin preparation.
(b) Infiltration of antirabies serum around the wound.

---

[1] Where soap has been used to clean wounds, all traces of it should be removed before the application of quaternary ammonium compounds because soap neutralizes the activity of such compounds.

Benzalkonium chloride, in a 1% concentration, has been demonstrated to be effective in the local treatment of wounds in guinea pigs infected with rabies virus. It should be noted that at this concentration quaternary ammonium compounds may exert a deleterious effect on tissues.

Compounds that have been demonstrated to have a specific lethal effect on rabies virus *in vitro* (different assay systems in mice) include the following:

Quaternary ammonium compounds

0.1% (1 : 1000) benzalkonium chloride = mixture of alkylbenzyldimethylammonium chlorides
0.1% (1 : 1000) cetrimonium bromide = hexadecyltrimethylammonium bromide
1.0% (1 : 100) Hyamine 2389 = mixture containing 40% of methyldodecylbenzyltrimethylammonium chloride and 10% of methyldodecylxylylene bis(trimethylammonium chloride)
1.0% (1 : 100) methyl benzethonium chloride = benzyldimethyl{2-{2-[*p*-(1,1,3,3-tetramethylbutyl)tolyloxy]ethoxy}ethyl}ammonium chloride
1.0% (1 : 100) benzethonium chloride = benzyldimethyl{2-[2-(*p*-1,1,3,3,-tetramethylbutylphenoxy)ethoxy]ethyl}ammonium chloride
1.0% (1 : 100) SKF 11831 = *p*-phenylphenacylhexamethylenetetrammonium bromide.

Other substances

43–70% ethanol; tincture of thiomersal; tincture of iodine and up to 0.01% (1 : 10000) aqueous solutions of iodine; 1% to 2% soap solutions.

B. Specific Systemic Treatment

Nature of exposure	Status of biting animal (irrespective of whether vaccinated or not)		Recommended treatment
	At time of exposure	During observation period of ten days	
I No lesions: indirect contact	Rabid	—	None
II. Licks:			
(1) unabraded skin	Rabid	—	None
(2) abraded skin, scratches and unabraded or abraded mucosa	*(a)* healthy	Clinical signs of rabies or proven rabid (laboratory)	Start vaccine[1] at first signs of rabies in the biting animal
	(b) signs suggestive of rabies	Healthy	Start vaccine[1] immediately; stop treatment if animal is normal on fifth day after exposure
	(c) rabid, escaped, killed or unknown	—	Start vaccine[1] immediately
III. Bites:			
(1) mild exposure	*(a)* healthy	Clinical signs of rabies or proven rabid (laboratory)	Start vaccine[1, 2] at first signs of rabies in the biting animal
	(b) signs suggestive of rabies	Healthy	Start vaccine[1] immediately; stop treatment if animal is normal on fifth day after exposure
	(c) rabid, escaped, killed or unknown	—	Start vaccine.[1, 2] immediately
	(d) wild (wolf, jackal, fox, bat, etc.)	—	Serum[2] immediately, followed by a course of vaccine[1]
(2) severe exposure (multiple, or face, head, finger or neck bites)	(a) healthy	Clinical signs of rabies or proven rabid (laboratory)	Serum[2] immediately; start vaccine[1] at first sign of rabies in the biting animal
	(b) signs suggestive of rabies	Healthy	Serum[2] immediately, followed by vaccine; vaccine may be stopped if animal is normal on fifth day after exposure
	(c) rabid, escaped, killed or unknown *(d)* wild (wolf, jackal, pariah dog, fox, bat, etc.)	—	Serum[2] immediately, followed by vaccine[1]

[1] Practice varies concerning the volume of vaccine per dose and the number of doses recommended in a given situation. In general, the equivalent of at least 2 ml of a 5% tissue emulsion should be given subcutaneously daily for 14 consecutive days. Many laboratories use 20 to 30 doses in severe exposures. To ensure the production and maintenance of high levels of serum-neutralizing antibodies, booster doses should be given at 10 days and at 20 or more days following the last daily dose of vaccine in *all* cases. This is especially important if antirabies serum has been used, in order to overcome the interference effect.

[2] In all severe exposures and in all cases of unprovoked wild animal bites, antirabies serum or its globulin fractions together with vaccine should be employed. This is considered by the Committee as the *best* specific treatment available for the post-exposure prophylaxis of rabies in man. Although experience indicates that vaccine alone is sufficient for mild exposures, there is no doubt that here also the combined serum-vaccine treatment will give the best protection. However, both the serum and the vaccine can cause deleterious reactions. Moreover, the combined therapy is more expensive; its use in mild exposures is therefore considered optional. As with vaccine alone, it is important to start combined serum and vaccine treatment as early as possible after exposure, but serum should still be used no matter what the time interval. Serum should be given in a single dose (40 IU per kg of body weight) and the first dose of vaccine inoculated at the same time. Sensitivity to the serum must be determined before its administration.

disease, and not to embark upon the tedious course of vaccination unless this is warranted. It is not easy to weigh up these risks and for this reason the advice given by the World Health Organization is recorded here as Table 18 (48).

There are several important principles to be followed. Always impound the dog for ten days, and, if another animal was responsible, try to impound this also. Don't wait for a laboratory report, and be prepared in some circumstances to treat the patient, even if the report is negative. Don't neglect local treatment to the wound and where indicated apply anti-rabies serum locally. In cases of severe exposure give anti-rabies serum *and* vaccine, and don't forget the booster doses of vaccine 10 and 20 days later.

The World Health Organization advise the reader as follows:

> **'The recommendations in Table 18 are intended only as a guide. It is recognized that in special situations modifications of the procedures laid down may be warranted. Such special situations include exposure of young children and other circumstances where a reliable history cannot be obtained, particularly in areas where rabies is known to be enzootic even though the animal is considered to be healthy at the time of exposure. Such cases justify immediate treatment, but of a modified nature, for example local treatment of the wound as described in Table 18 followed by administration of a single dose of serum or three doses of vaccine daily; provided that the animal stays healthy for 10 days following exposure, no further vaccine need be given. Modification of the recommended procedures would also be indicated in a rabies-free area where animal bites are frequently encountered. In areas where rabies is endemic, adequate laboratory and field experience indicating no infection in the species involved may justify local health authorities in recommending no specific anti-rabies treatment.'**

APPENDIX A

A LIST OF SUPPLIERS

Please quote this manual in all correspondence with these firms.

The following firms supply the equipment mentioned in this book. Firms have been specified in many parts of the world but firms in the United Kingdom predominate. The editor would be very pleased to hear of those making cheaper alternative equipment so that their names can be inserted in subsequent editions, should these be required.

Two institutions are listed which supply a wide range of equipment to missionaries — (MIS) and (MMS). If mission hospitals do not already know of these firms they are advised to write for catalogues.

(A&H) Messrs. Allen and Hanbury Ltd., London E.2. (Surgical equipment). (ABV) A.B. Vacuum-extractor, Drotlingen 13, Gothenburg C, Sweden. (The vacuum extractor). (ADL) Messrs. Adler Staal N.V., Stadhonderskaade 35, Amsterdam, Holland. (12 volt centrifuges). (AME) Ames Company (London) Ltd., Nuffield House, London, W.1. (Paper and tablet tests). (ARH) Arnold R. Horwell, 17 Cricklewood Broadway, London N.W.2. (Laboratory equipment). (AUD) Audion Elektro, Groenburgwal 31, Amsterdam. (Plastic sealing machines). (B&H) Buck and Hickman Ltd., 2-8 Whitechapel Road, London. (Tools and ironmongery). (BOC) British Oxygen Co., Hammersmith House, London, W.6. (BRI) The Bristol Instrument Co. Ltd., Century Works, Lewisham, London S.E.13. (Recording thermometers). (BRO) Albert Brown Ltd., Chancery St., Leicester, U.K. (Brown's tubes for autoclaves) (BTL) Baird and Tatlock, Freshwater Road, Chadwell Heath, Essex. (Scientific equipment). (BUR) Burroughs Wellcome Ltd., Wellcome Building, Euston Road, London N.W.1. (Vaccines). (CAB) Sunlight Industrial Co. Ltd., Fudosom Kaikan Buildings, No. 5, Yolsuya, 3 Chome Shinzuku-Ku, Tokyo, Japan. (12 volt projectors). (CHE) Chevrolet Motors Ltd. (Pickup trucks with side opening cabinets). (CHT) Charles Thackeray, 38, Welbeck St., London W.1. (Surgical equipment). (CIP) 'CIPAC', Via Imperia 27, Milan, Italy. (Disposable transfusion equipment). (CMO) C. Morgan and Co., 18, Campden High Street, London N.W.1. (Weighing scales). (COP) Copeland Chatterson Co., Gateway House, Watling Street, London E.C.4. (COS) Coseley Buildings Ltd., Lanesfield, Wolverhampton. (Prefabricated buildings). (CRO) The Crown Agents 4, Millbank, London S.W.1. (Exporters of equipment to Commonwealth countries). (DOW) Down Brothers, Church Path, Mitcham, Surrey. (Surgical instruments). (DRY) Dryad Ltd., Leicester. (Materials for flannelgraphs). (EAS) Eastman Kodak Co., Rochester, New York. (Chemicals). (EEL)

Evans Electroselenium Ltd., 10 St. Andrews Works, Halstead, Essex. (Colorimeters). (EFV) Educational Foundation for Visual Aids, 33, Queen Ane St., London W.1. (Film strips). (ELD) Nordisk Insulinalaboratorium, Gentofte, Denmark. (Eldon cards). (EMI) 'E-Mil', H. J. Elliot Ltd., Treforest Industrial Estate, Pontypridd, Glam., U.K. (Volumetric glasware). (EVA) Evans Medical Ltd., Speke, Liverpool 24. (Drugs). (FRI) The Frigidaire Division of General Motors, Stag Lane, London, N.W.9. (Blood banks). (C&G) Griffin and George (Sales) Ltd., Ealing Road, Alperton, Wembley, Middlesex, England. (Scientific equipment). (GAL) A. Gallenkamp & Co. Ltd., Technico House, Sun Street, London E.C. 2. (Scientific equipment). (GAU) J. R. Gaunt & Son Ltd., 5, Warwick St., Regent St., London W.1. (Blood donor and other badges). (GDM) G. Diel Mateer Co., Stafford Wayne, P.A., U.S.A. (Mateer electric filler with Curtis Air Compressor — see 30:3). (GLA) Glaxo Ltd., Greenford, Middlesex. (Drugs etc.). (GRA) Grant Instruments Ltd., Barrington Road, Cambridge. (Electric waterbaths). (GUR) Edward Gurr Ltd., 42, Upper Richmond Road West, London S.W.14. (Stains and reagents for microscopy). (HEA) Charles Hearson, 68 Willow Walk, London, S.E.1. (Oil and gas operated incubators and water baths). (HAR) The Hartman Leddon Company, 60th Avenue. Philadelphia, U.S.A. (Glycerol Urease reagent). (HAW) Hawksley and Sons Ltd., Lancing, Sussex. (Micro-haematocrit centrifuges). (HOB) Hobart Ltd., Hobart Corner, New Southgate, London N.11. (Hobart electric mixer, model AE 200, bowl of 20 American quart capacity is the model required for section 30:3). (HOH) Hohabe Inc., 333 Henderson Avenue, Kenmore, N.Y. 14217., U.S.A. (Lippes Loops). (HOW) Howards Ltd., Ilford, London. (Fine chemicals). (IPP) The International Planned Parenthood Federation, 64, Sloane St., London S.W.1. (Family planning information). (KAR) Alfred Karcher, 7057 Winnenden, Wurtembourg, Germany. (Steam raising plant). (KAY) Kays Filmstrip Studios, 3, Greek Street, Londo W.1. (Will prepare filmstrips from customers' materials). (KEE) C. Davis Keeler Ltd., 47, Wigmore Street, London W.1. (The M.R.C. 'Grey wedge photometer'). (KEY) The Kenyan Ministry of Health, Box 30016 Nairobi. (Health Centre plans). (LET) Letraset Export Ltd., St. Georges House, 195/203 Waterloo Road, London S.E.1. (Dry lettering transfers). (LEW) H.K. Lewis and Co., 136, Gower Street, London W.C.1. (Booksellers). (LON) The Longworth Scientific Instrument Co., Radley Road, Abingdon, Berks. (The EMO Inhaler). (M&B) May and Baker Ltd., Dagenham, Essex. (Drugs and chemicals). (MAN) Mannesty Machines Ltd., Liverpool, 24. (Stills). (MAT) Matburn, 20-24, Emerald St., London W.C.1. (Medical equipment). (MAY) Maytag Washing machines. American Steel Export Co., 292 Madison Avenue, New York, N.Y. 10017. (Petrol driven washing machines). (MBO) The Metal Box Co.,

(Overseas), 37, Baker St., London W.1. (Plastic specimen containers etc.). (MIE) Mielewerke G.m.b.H. Guttersloh, Westfalia, Germany. (Laundry equipment). (MIR) Miromit Sun-Heaters Ltd., Box 6004, Tel Aviv, Israel. (Solar heaters). (MIS) Missionary Equipment Service, 210, West Chestnut St., Chicago 10, Illinois, U.S.A. (Medical equipment for missionaries). (MMS) Missionary Medical Supply, 110, East 13th St., New York 3, New York, U.S.A. (Medical equipment for missionaries). (MOR) Flannelgraphs of the weight chart of the under-fives clinic can be obtained from Dr. David Morley, The London School of Hygiene and Tropical Medicine, Gower St., London W.C.1. (MSA) The Medical Supply Association, 95 Wimpole Street, London W.1. (MSE) Measuring and Scientific Instruments Ltd., 25-28 Buckingham Gate, London S.W.1. (Centrifuges). (NRP) National Fund for Research into Poliomyelitis, Vincent House, Vincent Square, London S.W.1. (A periodical etc.) (OLY) Olympus Optical Company, 73-Chome, Kanda Ogawamachi Chiyoda-Ku, Tokyo, Japan. (Microscopes). (OVA) Overseas Visual Aids Centre, 'OVAC'. 31, Tavistock Square, London W.C.1. (Visual aids) (OXO) Oxoid Division, Oxo Ltd., Southwark Bridge Road, London S.E.1. (Media, spore strips for autoclaves). (PAC) 'Pac-Rite' Sealing Machines, Milwaukee, U.S.A. (Sealing machines). (PAF) The Pathfinder Fund, 73, Adams St., Milton 87, MASS., U.S.A. (Charitable foundation). (PHI) Phillips Ltd., Eindhoven, Holland. (X-ray plant). (PIL) Pilchers (Merton) Ltd., 314, Kingston Road, Wimbledon, London S.W.2. (Land Rover mobile dispensary conversion). (POR) Portland Plastics Ltd. ('Portex'). Basset House, Hythe, Kent. (Plastic medical equipment). (POV) Poviet Production N.V. Mauritskade 14, Amsterdam, Holland. (Blood transfusion materials, sera and sets). (PRE) Messrs. Prestware Ltd., Southdown Works, Kingston Road, London S.W.2. (Plastic trays). (ROC) Roche Products Ltd., Welwyn Garden City, England. (Drugs). (SCH) Schuco International Ltd., 46, Ravensdale Avenue, London N.12. ('Dermojet') (SCI) Scientific Equipment Mfg. Corp., 20, North Avenue, Larchmont N.W. ('Ped-o-jet'). (SNP) Smith and Nephew, Pharmaceuticals, Welwyn Garden City, Herts. UK. (Drugs and dressings). (TIN) The Tintometer Co. Ltd., Waterloo Road, Salisbury, England. (Lovibond equipment). (TUR) R.B. Turner and Co., Church Lane, East Finchley, London N.2. (MRC Blood transfusion equipment). (UNI) Unilever Export Ltd., Port Sunlight, Cheshire. (Detergents). (VAB) V.A.B. Calor. Box 11005, Bromma 11, Sweden. (Laundry machinery). (VDC) Viscose Development Co., 40, Chancery Lane, London W.C.2. ('Viscaps' for blood transfusion bottles). (WCL) Warner-Chilcott Laboratories, Morris Plains, New Jersey, U.S.A. (Rapid clinico-pathological tests). (WRI) F.H. Wright, Industrial Estate, Kingsway West, Dundee, Scotland, ('Dermojet'). (XLO) Xlon Products Ltd., 323a, Kennington Road, London, S.E.11. (Plastic equipment). (ZEI) Carl Zeiss, Oberkochen, Wurthembourg, Germany. (Double binocular microscope).

APPENDIX B

REFERENCES

(1) Bennett, F.J., Hall, S.A. Lutwama, J.S., Rado, E. (1965). *East Afr. Med. J. 42*: 149. 'Medical Manpower in East Africa — Prospects and Problems'.

(2) Blacker, J.G.C., (1963) in *The Natural Resources of East Africa* Ed. E.W. Russell, Nairobi.

(3) Bull, G. M., (1960). *West Afr. med. J. 9*: 139. 'Impressions of a medical tour of Eastern and Western Regions of Nigeria.'

(4) Burgess, H.J.L., Burgess, Anne P., (1962). *East Afr. med. J. 39*: 417. 'Reinforced Milk for the Treatment of Malnutrition'. See also the same authors in the 1966 volume of this journal.

(5) Caddell, J.L., (1965) *J. Paediat. 66*: 392. 'Magnesium in the Therapy of Protein-Calorie Malnutrition in Childhood'.

(6) Cannon, D.S.H., Hartfield, V.J. (1964) *J. Obst. Gyn. Brit. Cwlth.* 71: 940. 'Obstetrics in a Developing Country'.

(6b) Cooper, C., et al., (1966). *Lancet* i, 1076 'Administration of Measles vaccine by Dermojet'.

(7) Dean, R.F.A., (1962). *East Afr. med. J. 39*: 425. 'Reinforced Milk for the Treatment of Malnutrition'.

(8) *Daily Express* of Nigeria, April 6th, 1962, quoted by (6).

(9) Edwards, E.O. Unpublished paper.

(10) Eidus, L., Hamilton, E.J., (1964). *Am. Rev. resp. Dis. 89*: 587. 'A new Method for the Determination of N-acetyl isoniazide in the Urine of Ambulatory Patients'.

(11) Fendall, N.R.E., (1963). *J. trop. med. Hyg. 66*: 219. 'Health Centres; a Basis for a Rural Health Service'.

(12) Fendall, N.R.E., Killen, O.H., Southgate, B.A., (1963). *East Afr. med. J. 40*: 118. 'A National Reference Health Centre for Kenya'.

(13) Fendall, N.R.E., (1963) *Public Health Rep. 78*: 977. 'Planning Health Services in Developing Countries'.

(14) Fendall, N.R.E., (1965). *J. trop. Med. Hyg. 68*: 12 'Medical Planning and the Training of Personnel in Kenya'.

(15) Fendall, N.R.E., (1965). Personal communication.

(16) Ferrand, G., (1960). 'Le Centre Medical Rural'. *Sociétié Etudes de constructions hospitaliers* 171, Rue de la Pompe. Paris XXI.

(17) Fox, W., (1964). *Brit. med. J. 1*: 135. 'Realistic Chemotherapeutic Policies for Tuberculosis in the Developing Countries'.

(18) Frederiksen, H., (1964). Duplicated Report WHO/Mal/429. 'Maintenance of Malaria Eradication'.

(19) Griffiths, Margaret I. et al., (1965). *Brit. med. J. 2*: 399. 'Intrademal B.C.G. vaccination by jet injection'.

(20a) Hamilton, P.J.S., Anderson, A., (1965). Privately circulated document on the admission of patients to Mulago Hospital.

(20b) Harland, P.S.E.G., *J. trop. Paed.*, (in the press) 'The Mulanda Project.'

(21) 'The Harar Report' (1959). 'Recommendations for Strengthening Science and Technology in Selected Areas of Africa South of the Sahara'. International Co-operation Administration (National Academy of Sciences — National Research Council Washington, D.C. Quoted in *The Lancet* (1965) i: 307.)

(22) Huntingford, P.J., (1959). *J. Obst. & Gyn. Brit. Emp. 66*: 26. 'Pundendal Nerve Block'.

(23) Jelliffe, D.B., Dean, R.F.A., (1959). *J. trop. Paed. 5*: 96. 'Protein Calorie Malnutrition in Early Childhood'.

(24) Lawless, J., Lawless, M., (1963). *Lancet 2*: 972. 'Kwashiorkor, the Result of Cold Injury a Malnourished Child'.

(25) Lile, E.C., et al., (1957). *J. Amer. med. Ass. 164*: 277.

(26) Morley, D.C. (1963). Trans. *R. Soc. trop. Med. Hyg. 57*: 79 and 392. 'A Medical Service for Children under Five Years of Age in W. Africa'.

(27) Scadding, J.G., (1962). Transactions of the Health and Tuberculosis Conference, Nigeria.

(28) Schaffer, R.D., The East African Medical and Research Foundation, Nairobi, personal communication.

(29) Seale, J.R., (1960). i: 1399. 'Assumptions of Health Service Finance'.

(30) Sen, B.R., (1963). FAO Third World Food Survey.

(31) Sherman, D.H., (1963). *Centr. Afr. J. Med. 9*: 344.

(32) Titmuss, R. M. et al., (1964), *The Health Services of Tanganyika*. Pitman, London.

(33) Uganda General African Census 1959.

(34) U.N.O. Demographic Yearbook, 1963.

(35) Waddy, B.B., (1963). *Trans. R. Soc. trop. med. Hyg. 57*: 384. 'Rural Health Services in the Tropics and the Training of Medical Auxiliaries for them'.

(36) Waddy, B.B., (1964). Personal communication.

(37) Welbourn, H.F., De Beer, G., (1964). *J. trop. med. Hyg.*, 'Trial of a Kit for Feeding in Tropical Village Homes'.

(38) Wilkinson, J.L., (1964). *West Afr. med. J. 13*: 9. 'Ecology and Prevention of Child Malnutrition in a Rural Community'.

(39a) Wilkinson, J.L., (1965). *J. trop. med. Hyg., 68:* 167. 'Measurement and control of mortality among children in Sierra Leone and other West African countries'.

(39b) World Health Organization, Second Report on the World Health Situation, No. 122.

The following World Health Organization, Technical Report Series:

(40) 24 Expert Committee on Nursing.

(41) 55 Expert Committee on Public Health Administration.

(42) 60 Working Conference on Nursing Education.

(43) 91 Expert Committee on Nursing Education.

(44) 93 Expert Committee on Midwifery Training.

(45) 115 Administration of Maternal and Child Health Services.

(46) 167 Public Health Nursing.

(47) 194 Local Health Service.

(48) 321 Expert Committee on Rabies 5th Report.

(49) 212 The Use and Training of Auxiliary Personnel.

(50) 215 Planning Public Health Services.

(51) 290 Expert Committee on Tuberculosis.

APPENDIX C

BOOKS

The list of books below are mostly those discussed in Chapter Twenty-Nine on the library; some have been referred to in the text as references in this form '/1/'; others receive no further mention in these pages but are included here as having been found of value in the training of auxiliary staff, particularly for training school libraries. They may all be obtained from Lewis's (LEW). Especially recommended books have been given an asterisk.

1. Abel-Smith, B., *History of the Nursing Profession,* 1960, Heineman. 30/-.

*2. Adams, A.R.D., and Maegraith, B.G., *Tropical Medicine for Nurses,* 1963, 2nd Ed. 42/-.

*3. Adams, A.R.D., and Maegraith, B.G., *Clinical Tropical Diseases,* 3rd Ed., Blackwell, 63/-.

4. Adams, J.C., *An Outline of Orthopaedics,* 1964, 5th Ed., Livingstone. 37/50.

5. Adams, J.C., *An Outline of Fractures,* 1964, 4th Ed., Livingstone. 30/-.

*6. Alcock, A.E.S., 'How to Build', a series of five manuals.
How to Build to Size and Shape, Reading Plans,
How to Build for Climate, How to Plan your Market,
How to Plan your Village, Longmans.

7. Altschul, A., *Aids to Psychiatric Nursing,* 2nd Ed., 1964, Bailliere. 12/50 paper.

8. Altschul, A., *Aids to Psychology for Nurses,* 1962, Bailliere. 10/50 paper.

9. Appleton, A.B. and others, *Surface and Radiological Anatomy,* 1958, 4th Ed., Heffer, Cambridge. 50/-.

10. Armstrong, K.F., and Jamieson, N., *Aids to Surgical Nursing,* 1961, 7th Ed., Bailliere. 12/50 paper.

*11. Bailey, H., *Emergency Surgery,* 8th Ed., 1965 (in preparation), Wright, Bristol. 189/-.

*12. Bailey, H., and Love, R.J.McN., *A Short Practice of Surgery,* 1965, 13th Ed., Lewis's. 84/-.

13. Bailey, R. E., *Aids to Pharmacology for Nurses,* 1964, Bailliere. 10/50 paper.

14. Bailliere's *Aids to Ear, Nose and Throat Nursing,* 1962, 3rd Ed. 10/50 paper.

15. Bailliere's *Midwives Dictionary,* 1962, 4th Ed. 7/50.

16. Bailliere's *Nurse's Dictionary,* 1961, 15th Ed. 7/50.
17. Baird, Sir D., *Combined Textbook of Obstetrics and Gynaecology,* 1962, 7th Ed., Livingstone. 105/-.
*18. Baker, F.J., et al. *An Introduction to Medical Laboratory Technology,* 1962, 3rd Ed. Butterworths. 35/-.
*19. Barber, Renata, *Igbo-Ora, a Town in Transition,* Oxford.
20. Bellack, L., *A Handbook of Community Psychiatry and Community Mental Health,* 1964. 102/-.
21. Bendall, E.R.D. and Raybould, E., *Basic Nursing,* 1963. 17/50 paper.
*22. Best, C.H., and Taylor, N.B., *The Living Body,* 1959, 4th Ed. Chapman and Hall. 50/-.
*23. Biggam, Sir A., and Wright, F.J., *Tropical Diseases,* Livingstone. Supplement to *Principles and Practice of Medicine* by Davidson. 10/60 paper. This supplement is bound into the English Language Book Society paperback edition of /51/.
24. Birch, C.A., *Emergencies in Medical Practice,* 1963, 7th Ed. 50/-.
25. *Birth Atlas,* Maternity Centres Association, New York. 84/-. (English edition of smaller page area 30/-).
26. Black's Medical Dictionary, 1963, 25th Ed. Bailliere. 40/-.
27. Bocock, E.Y., and Armstrong, K.F., *Aids to Bacteriology for Nurses,* 1962, 2nd Ed. Balliere. 10/50 paper.
28. Bordicks, K.J., *The Nursing Care of Patients having Chest Surgery.* 1962, Lewis, 25/-.
29. Bowesman, C., *Surgery and Clinical Pathology in the Tropics,* Livingstone. 110/-.
30. Bowlby, J., *Child Care and the Growth of Love,* 1953 Pelican. 3/50 paper.
31. Breen, G.E., *Fevers for Nurses,* 7/50.
32. Brigden, R.J., *Operating Theatre Technique,* 1962, Livingstone. 7/50.
33. Brockington, C.F., *A Short History of Public Health.* Churchill.
34. Brockington, C.F., *The Health of the Community.* Churchill.
35. Browne, F.J., and J.C.McC, *Antenatal and Postnatal Care,* Churchill. 45/-.
36. Calder, Jean McK., *The Story of Nursing,* 1963, 4th Ed. Lewis. 15/-.
37. Caplan, G., *An Approach to Community Mental Health,* 1961, Tavistock. 44/-.
38. Chamberlain, E.N., *Symptoms and Signs in Clinical Medicine,* 1961, 7th Ed. 45/-.

39. Chesterman, C.C., *Tropical Dispensary Handbook,* 1960, 7th Ed. Lutterworth. 21/-.

*40. Clark, K.C., *Positioning in Radiography,* 8th Ed., published for Ilford Ltd., by Heinemann. 126/50.

41. Clarke, G.H.V., *Skin Diseases in the African,* 1959, Lewis. 84/-.

*42. Cochrane, R.G., and Davey, T.F., (1964), *Leprosy in Theory and Practice,* 2nd Ed. Bristol, Wright.

43. *Concise Oxford Dictionary,* Clarendon.

44. *Conybeare's Textbook of Medicine,* 1964, 14th Ed. Livingstone. 63/-.

45. Conn, R.B., et al., *Current Therapy,* Saunders, 91/-. This work is revised annually.

46. *Control of Communicable Disease in Man,* The United States Public Health Association, 1960, 9th Ed. 7/50 paper.

47. Cruikshank, R., *Medical Microbiology,* 11th Ed., Livingstone. 55/-, (formerly Mackie & McCartney: *Handbook of Bacteriology.* An English Language Book Society paperback edition is also available).

48. Curran, D., and Partridge, M., *Psychological Medicine — an Introduction to Psychiatry,* 1963, 5th Ed. Livingstone. 30/-.

49. Dacie, J.V., and Lewis, J.M., *Practical Haematology,* 3rd Ed. Churchill. 40/-.

*50. Davey, W., (1965). *A Companion to Surgery in Africa,* Ready 1966? Livingstone.

*51. Davidson, Sir S., *The Principles and Practice of Medicine,* 1964 7th Ed. Livingstone, 25/- paper. (English Language Book Society edition which includes /23/.)

52. Davies, P.M., *Medical Terminology for Radiographers,* 2nd Ed. Heinemann.

*53. Donald, I., *Practical Obsteric Problems,* 3rd Ed. Lloyd-Luke. 70/-.

*54. Dunlop, Sir D.M., et al., *Textbook of Medical Treatment,* 1964, 9th Ed. Livingstone. 65/-.

55. Ellis, N.R., *Handbook of Mental Deficiency,* 1963, 116/-.

56. Ewatt, J.R. and Farnsworth, D.L., *Textbook of Psychiatry,* 1963. 74/-.

57. Falconer, M.W., et. al., *Drug, Nurse, Patient,* 1962, 2nd Ed. Sauders Philadelphia. 49/-.

*58. Farquharson, E.L., *Textbook of Operative Surgery,* 1962, 2nd Ed. Livingstone. 120/-.

59. Fash, B., *Body Mechanics in Nursing Arts,* McGraw Hill.

60. Farr, A.D., *A Laboratory Handbook of Blood Transfusion Techniques,* Heinemann. 17/50.

61. Fiddler, G.S., and Fiddler, J.W., *Occupational Therapy: A Communication Process in Psychiatry,* 1963, 2nd Ed. 36/-.
62. Fream, W.C., *Aids to Arithmetic in Nursing,* 1964, 3rd Ed. 8/50 paper.
*63. Fream, W.C., *Aids to Tropical Hygiene and Nursing,* 1964, 5th Ed. Balliere. 10/50 paper.
64. Fream, W.C., *Applied Human Biology for Nurses,* 1964, Balliere. 25/-.
65. Goodman, N.M., *International Health Organisations and their Work.*
*66. Goodwin, L., and Duggan, A.J., *A New Tropical Hygiene,* 1960, Allen and Unwin. 5/50 paper.
67. Hare, R., *Bacteriology and Immunity for Nurses,* 1961, Balliere. 18/50.
68. Harlow, F.W., *Modern Surgery for Nurses,* 1963, 6th Ed. 35/-.
69. Harmer, Bertha, and Henderson, Virginia, *Textbook of the Principles and Practices of Nursing,* Macmillan.
*70. Hector, W., and Bourne, G., *Modern Gynaecology with Obstetrics for Nurses,* 1963, 3rd Ed. 17/50.
*71. Hector, W., *Modern Nursing Theory and Practice,* 1962, 2nd Ed. Heinemann. 30/-.
73. Hill, H. and Dodsworth, E., *Food Inspection Notes,* 1965, 6th Ed. Lewis. 15/-.
74. Hoffling, C.K., and Leininger, M.M., *Basic Psychiatric concepts in Nursing,* 1960. 50/-.
*75. Holmes, A.C., *Health Education in Developing Countries,* Nelson 21/-.
*76. Holmes, A.C., (1963). *A Study of Understanding Visual Symbols in Kenya.* Overseas Visual Aids Centre (OVAC publication No. 10). 5/-.
*77. Houghton, M., *Aids to Practical Nursing,* 1960, 9th Ed. Balliere. 8/50 paper.
*78. Houghton, M., *Pocketbook of Ward Information,* 1961, 10th Ed. Balliere. 6/50.
*79. Houghton, M., and Whitton, M., *Aids to Medical Nursing,* 1962, 6th Ed. Bailliere. 12/6 paper.
80. Houliston, M., *The Practice of Mental Nursing,* 1961, 3rd Ed. Livingstone. 10/-.
81. Houston, J. C., and Stockdale, M. G., *Principles of Medicine and Medical Nursing,* 1958. 7/50 paper.
82. H. M. S. O., *The Design of Forms in Government Departments.* 20/-.

*83. Huckstep, R. L., *A Simple Guide to Fractures,* Livingstone ready 1967.

*84. Huckstep, R. L., *Poliomyelitis, A Guide for Developing Countries,* Heinemann, ready 1967.

85. Illingworth, Sir C. P. W., *Short Textbook of Surgery,* 1965, 8th Ed. Churchill.

*86. Jelliffe, D.B., *Child Health in the Tropics,* 1965, 2nd Ed. Arnold. 15/-.

87. Jelliffe, D. B., *The Assessment of the Nutritional Status of the Community,* 1966, WHO Monograph Series.

88. Jordan, H., *Tropical Hygiene and Sanitation,* 1965, 3rd Ed. Bailliere 12/6.

*89. Lawson, J.B., and Stewart, *Obstetrics and Gynaecology in the Tropics,* 1966, Arnold.

90. Keller, H., *The Story of my Life,* Longmans.

91. Kershaw, J. D., *Handicapped Children,* 1965, 2nd Ed. Lewis.

92. Kimball, L., *Psychiatric Nursing: Syllabus and Workbook for Student Nurses,* 1962, Ed. Mosley. 24/50 paper.

93. Korkis, F. B., *Ear, Nose and Throat Nursing,* 1955, Churchill 12/6.

93a. Lewis, O., *Children of Sanchez.* Penguin 8/-.

*94. Longland, F., *Field Engineering,* printed by the Government Printer, Dar es Salaam. 10/-.

95. Marshall, J., *Neurological Nursing, a Practical Guide,* 1956 Blackwell Oxford. 18/50.

*96. Mead, M., *Coming of Age in Samoa, Growing up in New Guinea, Male and Female,* Pelican books each about 6/-.

97. McEwan, M., *Health Visiting,* 1962, 4th Ed. Faber. 28/-.

98. McLetchie, J. L., and O'Neill, *Handbook for Dispensary Attendants,* 1956, Oxford. 7/6.

*99. McNaught, A. B., and Callender, R., *Nurse's Illustrated Physiology,* 1964, 7/50 paper.

*100. McNaught, A. B., and Callendar, R., *Illustrated Physiology.* 30/-.

101. McNiven, J. N., and Warne, B. E. M., *Aids to Gynaeological and Obstetric Nursing,* 1964, 7th Ed. Bailliere. 10/50 paper.

102. Micks, R. H., *The Essentials of Materia Medica Pharmacology and Therapeutics,* 1965, 9th Ed. 40/-.

103. Mollison, P. L., *Blood Transfusion in Clinical Medicine,* 1961, 3rd Ed. Blackwell Oxford. 72/6.

104. Moore, D. C., *Regional Block,* 1961, 3rd Ed. 100/-.

105. Moroney, J., *Surgery for Nurses,* 1964, 9th Ed. 37/50.

106. Myles, M. F., *Textbook for Midwives,* 1964, 5th Ed. Livingstone.

107. Munro, J. M., *Pre-nursing Course in Science,* Bailliere. 12/50.
108. Nash, D. F. E., *Principles and Practice of Surgical Nursing,* 1961 2nd Ed. Arnold. 42/-.
109. Nicholls, L., *Tropical Nutrition and Dietetics,* 1961, 4th Ed. Balliere. 50/-.
110. Norris, W., and Campbell, D., *A Nurse's Guide of Anaesthetics, Resucitation and Intensive Care.* 1964, Bailliere. 20/-.
*111. Oxford Handbook for Medical Auxiliaries. Oxford University Press.
    a) *Medicine*: Wright, F. J., and Gould, J. C. (21/-).
    b) *Surgery*: Kerr, W. G.
    c) *Midwifery*: Fensom, M., (5/50).
    d) *Anaesthetics*: Vaughan, J., (in preparation).
112. Pare, C. M. B., *Practical Introduction to Psychiatry,* 1964, Churchill. 25/-.
113. *Pocket Oxford Dictionary,* (clear type).
114. *Practical First Aid Handbook*: British Red Cross Society.
115. Priest, H. A., *Modern Textbook of Personal and Communal Health.* 15/-.
*116. Pye, W., *Surgical Handicraft,* Vols, I & II 1962, 18th Ed. Bristol, Wright. 40/- each.
117. Reading, P., *Common Diseases of Ear, Nose and Throat,* 1961, 3rd Ed. Churchill. 24/-.
118. Roaf, R., and Hodkinson, L. J., *The Oswestry Textbook for Orthopaedic Nurses,* 1963, Lewis. 35/-.
119. Ross, J. S., and Wilson, K. J. W., *Foundations of Anatomy and Physiology,* Livingstone. 30/-.
120. *Roxburgh's Common Skin Diseases,* 1961, 12th Ed. Lewis. 50/-.
121. Sawyer, J. R., *Nursing Care of Patients having Urologic Diseases,* 1963, Lewis. 58/-.
122. Seward, C., *Bedside Diagnosis,* 1962, 6th Ed. Livingstone. 30/-.
123. Smout, C. E. V., *Basic Anatomy and Physiology,* Arnold. 12/50.
*124. Southall, A. W., and Gutkind, R. C. W., *Townsmen in the Making,* 1957, East African Institute for Social Research, Box 16022, Kampala, Uganda. 6/-.
*125. *Swire's Handbook for the Enrolled Nurse,* 1964, 5th Ed. Bailliere. 17/50.
126. Taylor, S. F., and Worrall, O., *Principles of Surgery and Surgical Nursing,* 1961. 7/50 paper.
127. Ten Teachers, *Diseases of Women,* 1964, 11th Ed. Arnold. 50/-.
128. Thornton, H., *The Inspection of Food,* Bailliere.
129. Toohey, M., *Medicine for Nurses,* 1963, Livingstone. 32/-.

*131. Trowell, H. C., *Non-Infective Diseases in Africa,* 1960, Arnold. 70/-.

*132. Trowell, H. C., and Jelliffe, D. B., *Diseases of Children in the Subtropics and Tropics,* 1958, Arnold. 105/-.

133. Tudor Hart, B., *Learning to Live: Understanding the Child from Birth to Adolesence.* 25/-.

134. *Ugandan Formulary,* The Government Printer, Box 33, Entebbe, Uganda.

135. Vaughan, E., et al., *General Opthalmology,* 1962, 3rd Ed. 42/-. paper.

136. Warwick, C. K., *Anatomy and Physiology for Radiographers,* 2nd Ed. Butterworths. 52/50.

137. Welbourn, H. F., and Tredgold, N., *Health in the Home,* East African Literature Bureau.

*138. Welbourn, H. F., *Nutrition in Tropical Countries,* 1963. Oxford. 4/50 paper.

139. Wilson, T. E., *Surgical Nursing and After Treatment,* 1960, 11th Ed. Churchill. 30/-.

140. Whillis's *Elementary Anatomy and Physiology,* 1961, 5th Ed. Churchill. 24/-.

141. Wilson, F., *The Nursing Care of the Anaesthetised Patient,* 1962, Bailliere. 10/50.

142. Wootton, I. D. P., *Micro-Analysis in Medicdl Biochemistry.* 1964, 4th Ed. Churchill. 30/-.

143. Wulfsohn, N. L., *Aids to Pre and Post-Operative Nursing,* 1963, 2nd Ed. 12/50.

144. Wylie, W. D., and Churchill-Davidson, H. C., *A Practice of Anaesthesia,* 1965, 2nd Ed. Lloyd Luke. Price ?

APPENDIX D
LABORATORY REAGENTS

The items marked with an asterisk are all better made up centrally, or bought ready prepared. Phosphomolybdic acid solution, alkaline copper, Nessler's solution, sodium tungstate and 2/3 N sulphuric acid all require to be made up with some care; the rest are not so critical.

Acid alcohol 3% — *Myco. tuberculosis.* Dilute 3 ml. of concentrated hydrochloric acid to 100 ml. with spirit. Use in a polythene wash bottle.

Acid alcohol 0.5% — *Myco. leprae.* Dilute 0.5 ml. of concentrated hydrochloric acid to 100 ml. with spirit. Use in a polythene wash bottle.

***Alkaline copper** (Folin and Wu). Dissolve 40 g. of anhydrous sodium carbonate in about 400 ml. of water and transfer to a 1,000 ml. flask. Add. 7.5 g. of tartaric acid and wait till this dissolved. Then transfer quantitatively to this flask 4.5 g. of crystalline copper sulphate which has been dissolved in about 100 ml. of water. Mix, and make up to 1,000 ml. A sediment often forms in time, in which case decant the clear supernatant solution.

Barium chloride 10%. Make 10 g. of barium chloride up to 100 ml. with distilled water.

Benedict's reagent — qualitative. Dissolve 17.3 grams of copper sulphate in about 100 ml. of water. And, while solution is taking place weigh out 173 grams of sodium citrate and 100 grams of anhydrous sodium carbonate. To them add 600 ml. of water and stir to dissolve. When solution is complete add the copper sulphate solution a little at a time — a precipitate may form but it will rapidly redissolve on further stirring. When all the copper sulphate solution has been added transfer the mixture to a litre cylinder and make up the volume to 1,000 ml. Keep some for immediate use in a polythene wash bottle.

Brilliant cresyl blue solution 1/500 in saline. Dissolve 200 mg. of brilliant cresyl blue in 100 ml. of saline. Keep some in a small screw capped bottle.

Buffer for gastric lavage specimens (21:20). Add 20g. of anhydrous disodium hydrogen phosphate Na_2HPO_4 (*or* 25g. of $Na_2HPO_4.2H_2O$, *or* 52g. $Na_2HPO_4.12H_2O$) to 30 ml. of distilled water, heating gently to dissolve. Cool, transfer to a measuring cylinder and make up to 50 ml. Place 0.5 ml. of this solution in a series of universal containers and autoclave (15 lbs. for 15 mins.) with the lid screwed on loosely. Cool overnight and screw the lid down tight. Prepare a number of bottles in this way and keep them for use as required.

Buffer for Leishman's and Field's stains. Buffer tablets can be bought for this purpose (GUR), but it is cheaper to make up a 0.2M pH6.8 phosphate buffer in the following way. Two types of sodium phosphate are required, one the *disodium* hydrogen phosphate, and the other the sodium *dihydrogen* phosphate. These are available in the anhydrous state and in various degrees of hydration, but it is immaterial which is used, provided the correct quantity is weighed out.

Weigh out, *either* Na_2HPO_4 anhydrous 13.9 g., *or* $Na_2HPO_4.2H_2O$ 17.6 g., *or* $Na_2HPO_4.12H_2O$ 35.5 g.

Add to it *either* NaH_2PO_4 anhydrous 12.2 g., *or* $NaH_2PO_4.2H_2O$ 15.9 g.

Dissolve the two salts and make up to 1.000 ml. Label 'Concentrated Leishman Buffer'. For use dilute 2ml. of this solution to 100 ml. for Leishman's and Field's staining methods.

Carbol fuchsin (*Strong*). Weigh 25 g. of phenol into a litre flask (an enamel basin will do), add 5 g. of basic fuchsin, let them dissolve by *gentle* heat over a flame or by immersion of the flask in boiling water for about five minutes. When solution is complete, cool the mixture by holding the flask under a tap, add 50 ml. of spirit, and 500 ml. of distilled water, mix well, filter, and the stain is ready for use.

Carbol fuchsin (*dilute*). 6.0 ml. of the strong stain are made up to 100 ml. with water.

Chloramine T 10%. Make 1 g. of chloramine T up to 10 ml. with water. The chloramine T must be the brand specified (EAS), see 24:33. It is better made up fresh in small quantities each time it is wanted.

Chromic acid cleaning fluid. Any laboratory using small blood pipettes must have this available for, if they choke with blood, this is likely to be the only thing that will free them; it is highly corrosive and is best kept in an ungraduated litre cylinder into which long pipettes can be put. If beakers or other objects are to be cleaned it can be poured into a polythene bowl while for short pipettes a little can be kept in a test tube. It will corrode metal and rot rubber, and, while most plastics are resistant, new apparatus should be exposed to it with caution. 100 ml. of concentrated sulphuric acid, it is added very cautiously to 900 ml. of water, a little at a time. 20 g. of technical potassium dichromate are dissolved in the solution. This is somewhat weaker than is often used and, though not quite so effective, is safer in the hands of partly trained staff. Discard it when it goes green.

Crystal violet (*Gram*). Dissolve 0.5 g. of crystal violet in 100 ml. of distilled water. Store in a polythene dropping bottle. Filter when prepared and again if it has stood a long time.

Ehrlich's reagent. Dissolve 0.7 g. of para-dimethylaminobenzaldehyde in a mixture of 150 ml. of concentrated hydrochloric acid and 100 ml. of water.

Field's stain A. Dissolve 2.5 g. of powdered Field's stain A (BDH) in 100 ml. of water.

Field's stain B. Dissolve 2.5 g. of powdered Field's stain B (BDH) in 100 ml. of water.
Formol saline. Place 100 ml. of 'Formaldehyde solution' or 'Liquor Formaldehyde B.P.' in a litre cylinder, add 8.5 g. of any grade of sodium chloride (even cooking salt) and dilute to a litre. Large quantities will be needed.
Fouchet's reagent. Dissolve 1 g. of ferric chloride in 10 ml. of water, while solution is taking place dissolve 25 g. trichloracetic in about 50 ml. of water in a 100 ml. cylinder. When solution of the acid is complete, tip in the ferric chloride and dilute the solution to 100 ml. Store in a polythene dropping bottle with a slow stopper that allows the exit of single drops.
***Glycerol urease solution.** This can be purchased ready made (HAR) but is easily prepared. Take 5 g. of jack beans or else the same quantity of jack bean meal. Powder the beans very finely in a pestle and mortar. Mix the meal or the powdered beans well with 100 ml. of 70% glycerol in distilled water, stand overnight, centrifuge the suspension and store the supernatant in a refrigerator — it remains active for many months.
Haemoglobin diluting fluid (for oxy-haemoglobin methods, Grey wedge and EEL). Add 0.4 ml. of strong ammonia (0.910) to a litre of water.
Hydrochloric Acid — sodium sulphate mixture for the AMS III technique. Place 225 ml. of concentrated hydrochloric acid in a measuring cylinder, add 53 g. of anhydrous sodium sulphate or 118g. of hydrated sodium sulphate (Glauber's salt). Dissolve and make up to a litre with water — its specific gravity should be 1.080.
Iodine, Lugol's. Dissolve 1.0 g. of iodine and 2 g. of potassium iodide in 100 ml. of water.
Leishman's stain. Weigh 0.2 g. of powdered Leishman's stain into a clean dry bottle, add 100 ml. of 'Methanol special quality BDH for the preparation of Leishman's and other stains', replace the stopper, shake well at intervals and leave overnight. Decant the following morning and the stain will be ready for use; however, it improves on standing, so keep a batch in hand to mature. The grade of methanol specified is important, for, though more expensive grades work just as well, this is often the cheapest satisfactory one. *Both the stock methanol and all vessels used to prepare the stain and store it must be absolutely dry,* and, as it is very volatile, all containers should be tightly stoppered. Keep the stain for use in a 'Polystop' bottle.
***Nessler's reagent.**

(a) *Double iodide solution.* Dissolve 75 g. of potassium iodide in 50 ml. distilled water. Add 100 g. of mercuric iodide, HgI_2 and wait till solution is complete. Then dilute to 500 ml. with distilled water and filter. Dilute the filtrate to 1,000 ml.

(b) *10% sodium hydroxide.* Prepare a saturated solution of sodium hydroxide (about 55%) by adding an excess of NaOH to about 200 ml. water and stopper securely. After two or three days decant the clear supernatant fluid, and dilute with distilled water to 10%. (Add 45 ml. of water to each of 10 ml. of supernatant fluid). Check the concentration by further diluting 10 ml. to 25 ml., with distilled water, and titrating 10 ml. of supposed 4% NaOH with N/1 acid. If the concentration differs from the theoretical by more than ± 5% (i.e. if in the titration 10 ml. of sodium hydroxide requires more than 10.5 ml. or less than 9.5 ml. of N/1 acid) it must be adjusted.

(c) *To prepare Nessler's reagent from the above solutions.* Mix 350 ml. of the 10% sodium hydroxide, 75 ml. of the double iodide and 75 ml. of distilled water. *Store the mixture in a dark bottle.* A precipitate may form in time — this is of no importance, but take care not to disturb it and use only the clear supernatant.

Occult blood reagent. Mix 2.0 g. of ortho-tolidine with 16 g. of barium peroxide. Try not to keep the mixture too long.

Pandy's reagent. Fill a screw capped bottle one-third full of phenol and then to the neck with water, shake and let stand overnight. Decant the aqueous upper layer which is the reagent — a saturated solution of phenol — and replenish the bottle with water for further occasions.

PAS test strips. Soak strips of filter paper in 5% ferric chloride and leave them to dry.

***Phosphomolybdic acid solution.** Dissolve 35 g. of molybdic acid, and 5 g. of sodium tungstate in 200 ml. of 10% NaOH plus 200 ml. of water in a litre beaker. Boil vigorously for twenty to forty minutes so as to remove as completely as possible the ammonia present in the molybdic acid — test this by smelling the steam from the beaker. Cool, and transfer to a 500 ml. volumetric flask, washing in with sufficient water to make the volume 350 ml. Add 125ml. of 89% w/w phosphoric acid (S.G. 1.75) and make up to 500 ml.

Potassium cyanide 10%. Make 1 g. of potassium cyanide (POISON) up to 10 ml. with distilled water. Store in a dark bottle with a pipette and teat. Potassium cyanide is a **deadly poison;** solutions must NEVER be pipetted by mouth and bottles containing it must be marked 'POISON'.

Rothera's reagent. Grind a crystal of sodium nitroprusside in a mortar with some ammonium sulphate, a little at first and then more later, until and even *pale* pink powder results.

Saline, 'normal' or physiological. Dissolve two 40 grain solution-tablets BPC of sodium chloride in 564 ml. (1 pint) of water. These tablets are much the most convenient way to make up saline for routine purposes. Otherwise, dissolve 85 g. of sodium chloride to 1,000 ml. of water. Label 'x 10 normal saline' and dilute 100 ml. to a litre for use.

Sodium acetate — saturated. Fill a bottle half full with sodium acetate, fill it with water, shake until no more will dissolve and pour off the supernatant for use.

Sodium citrate solution for the Westergren ESR. Dissolve 1.9 g. of sodium citrate in 50 ml. of water and distribute in 0.5 ml. quantities in Bijou bottles, either storing them in the refrigerator or autoclaving them to prevent the rapid growth of moulds.

Sodium hydroxide 20%. Make 20 g. of sodium hydroxide pellets up to 100 ml. with water. Store in a polythene dropping bottle.

***Sodium tungstate 10%.** Make up 10 g. of sodium tungstate to 100 ml. with water.

Stitts black. Stain new benches immediately they are put up with this mixture. Otherwise scrape and scrub the surfaces of old ones thoroughly. Dissolve copper sulphate 20 g. and potassium permanganate 40 g. in 500 ml. of water. Apply two coats of this at 12 hour intervals. Follow this with two further coats of aniline 60 ml. and concentrated HC1 90 ml., again dissolve in 500 ml. of water (Chemicals not in Appendix E).

Sulphosalicylic acid solution 3%. Make 3 grams of sulphosalicylic acid up to 100 ml. with water.

***Sulphuric acid $\frac{2}{3}$ N.** Dilute 2 ml. of concentrated sulphuric acid with 100 ml. of water; ideally this reagent should be prepared centrally under circumstances where it can be titrated against standard alkali and concentration adjusted to the required value.

Thompson's grey solution, This is the permanent liquid standard for use with the EEL colorimeter and, though it can be prepared, it is much better bought ready-made, either in a bottle (KEE), or, better still, sealed into an EEL-tube ready for use. See 24:6 and 24:17 (EEL).

White-blood-cell diluting fluid. Dilute 2.0 ml. of glacial acetic acid to 100 ml. with distilled water, add two or three drops of Gram's stain to colour the solution a pale violet. Store in a bottle with a 1 ml. pipette passing through the cork.

Malachite green. Dissolve 0.3g. of malachite green in 100 ml. of distilled water.

APPENDIX E
LABORATORY CHEMICALS

Chemicals are listed in the quantities appropriate to an initial order for a district hospital. Items marked with an asterisk are for making up reagents that are better bought ready prepared or prepared in a central laboratory — see Appendix D.

Chemicals containing mercury and iodine are comparatively expensive, all the rest are cheap. Except where specified chemicals should be of 'General purpose reagent' or 'GPR', quality: analytical or 'AR' grades are not required. Sodium azide, barium peroxide and potassium cyanide are very poisonous; the dangers of their use must be explained to the assistants, their solutions NEVER pipetted and all solutions containing them marked 'POISON'.

Solid chemicals. *Acid, molybdic, 500g.: Acid, sulphosalicylic, 500 g.: *Acid, tartaric, 500 g.: Acid, trichloracetic, 25 g.: Ammonium sulphate, 500 g.: Barium chloride, 100 g.: Barium peroxide, 100 g.: Chloramine T, 100 g. (EAS): Copper sulphate crystalline, 500 g.: p-dimethylaminobenzaldehyde 25 g.: Ferric chloride, 100 g.: Iodine, 100 g.: *Jack bean meal, 100 g.: *Mercuric iodide, 500 g.: Ortho-tolidine 25 g.: Phenol, 500 g.: Potassium cyanide, 100 g.: Potassium ethylene-diamine-tetra-acetic acid (Potassium EDTA), 100 g.: Potassium dichromate, technical, 1,000 g.: Potassium fluoride, 100 g.: Potassium iodide, 250 g.: Sodium acetate, 500 g.: Sodium azide, 10 g.: Sodium carbonate anhydrous, 1,000 g.: BPC Solution-tablets of sodium chloride 40 grains, 500 g.: Sodium chloride, 1,000 g.: Tri-sodium citrate, 500 g.: Sodium hydroxide pellets, 1,000 g.: Sodium metabisulphite, 250 g.: Sodium nitro-prusside, 50 g.: Dihydrogen sodium phosphate $NaH_2PO_4.2H_2O$, 250 g.: Disodium hydrogen phosphate, $Na_2HPO_4.2H_2O$ 250 g.: Sodium sulphate hydrated 1,000 g.: Sodium tungstate, 100g.

Liquid chemicals. All required in quantities of 2½ litres except where stated. Acid, acetic, glacial: Acid, hydrochloric, concentrated: *Acid, orthophosphoric, 89% (S.G. 175) 500 ml.: Acid, sulphuric, concentrated: Ammonia solution, concentrated, S.G. 0.91: Ether: *Glycerol, 500 ml.: Microscope immersion oil, 100 ml.: Liquor formaldehyde B.P.: 'Teepol' (SHE), 100 ml.: Methanol, 'special quality BDH for Leishman's stain etc.': Spirit, rectified: Xylol.

Dry microscopic stains. Basic fuchsin, 50 g.: Brilliant cresyl blue, 10 g.: Crystal violet, 50 g.: Field's stain A, 100 g.: Field's stain B, 100 g.: Leishman's stain, 50 g.: Malachite green 10 g.

Test papers. Congo red (H&W): Litmus red and blue.

Biologicals. Anti A and Anti B sera (POV) Bovine albumen (POV).

APPENDIX F
LABORATORY APPARATUS

This list of equipment is suited for a hospital laboratory staffed by a laboratory assistant. With minor modifications it is also the equipment required by a health centre. The apparatus required will depend in part on which measuring instrument is to be used. For convenience only the Lovibond equipment has been specified, so this should be omitted if it is decided to use an EEL colorimeter (EEL) or a Grey wedge photometer (KEE). The Grey wedge photometer is supplied complete with three filters and two cells but extra cells and spare bulbs should be ordered. Ilford filters No. 625 (yellow-green), No. 622 (blue) and No. 608 (red) will be required for use with the EEL, also spare tubes (10 ml. size), spare bulbs and a spare selenium cell. When the Grey wedge is being ordered the Gallenkamp proteinometer will not be needed.

Catalogue numbers are given for convenience and to avoid confusion, but apart from Lovibond equipment for which there is no alternative supplier, equivalent equipment from other sources is likely to be equally satisfactory. One item of each kind should be ordered except where specified in the last bracket for each item before the colon. A bunsen burner for butane gas ('Bottogas', 'Calor gas' etc.) has been included, as has a 220 volt centrifuge. If a 12 volt centrifuge is required this will have to be obtained from another supplier (ADL). If no electricity is available and a water bath is being ordered (HEA), specify whether it is for gas or kerosene. The haemaglutination trays are for testing the urine for INH — see 24:40. The 10 ml. graduated centrifuge tubes specified (BTL C6/0102) are fragile and should thus be replaced by plastic ones as soon as these become available in mid-1966. Plastic replacements for this item are to be made in poly-carbonate (water clear but harmed by organic solvents) and polypropylene (translucent but solvent resistant) It is likely that the latter will prove the most satisfactory (XLO).

The approximate total cost of the apparatus is about £100.

BALANCE, Griffin Minor (C&G) S13-236: BLOCK for test tubes, locally made, see diagram Fig. 55: BLOOD SEDIMENTATION TUBE, Westergren, (GAL) MC-670 (6): HANGER for the former (GAL) MC-676 (6): RUBBER CAPS (policemen) for the former (GAL) RV-180, int. diam. $\frac{1}{4}$ in. (6): BOTTLES, dropping, polythene, 4 oz., (BTL) B15/0650, (24): BOTTLES, dropping glass, with plastic stopper and vinyl teat 60 ml. (Polystop bottles) (GAL) BS-157 (2): BOTTLES, polythene, wash, 250 ml., (BTL) B15/1360 (4): BOTTLES, narrow mouth, polythene, 1,000 ml., (GAL) BS-345 (12): 'Canada Balsam bottle' (for immersion oil) (G&G) S16-270: BURNER, bunsen, for use with butane gas,

(BTL) B18/1150 $\frac{3}{8}$in.: Centrifuge 'MSE MINETTE', complete with dual purpose four place head, 'on-off' switch, and four buckets, (MSE) 7604-A: COMPARATOR, Lovibond, (LOV) AF201: DISC, Lovibond, for oxhyhaemoglobin, (LOV) 5/37: DISCS, Lovibond, for blood sugar, (LOV) 5/2A and 5/2B: DISCS, Lovibond, for blood urea, (LOV) 5/9A and 5/9B: COUNTING CHAMBER, double cell improved Neubauer, (G&G) S52-672 Type No. 10: COUNTING CHAMBER, double cell Fuchs-Rosenthal, (G&G) S52-672 Type No. 20: COVERGLASSES paired for double counting chamber (BTL) D3/0051 (6 pairs): CUPS, polythene, multicoloured, domestic (3) (in lieu of glass beakers): CYLINDERS, graduated polythene with spout (BTL) B41/1150 1,000 ml. one, 100 ml. one, 10 ml. one: CYLINDER, ungraduated, polythene, 1,000 ml., (ARH) (for dichromate cleaning fluid): FILTER PAPER circles, 7 cm., Whatman, No. 1 (BTL) B34/0290 (3 boxes): FUNNELS, polythene, flexible, $2\frac{1}{2}$ in. diam., (BTL) B37/0200 (4): FILTER PUMP, black plastic, (BTL) B35/0400: HAEMAGLUTINATION TRAYS, disposable, opaque 96 cavities, 5.18 x 12.34 (PRE) (2): HOLDER for platinum wire, (BTL) B12/0360 (2): LENS TISSUE, (BTL) C15/0036 (10 booklets): PENCILS, 'Chinagraph' assorted colours (BTL) B52/0110 (24): PIPETTE calibrated at 0.1 and 0.05 ml. (EMI), G. 5091 (3): PIPETTE, graduated, (BTL) B41/2330 1 ml. (3), 2 ml. (3), 5 ml. (3), 10 ml. (3): PROTEINOMETER, standard set, (GAL) ME-450, (£6): SLIDES, microscope, 3 x 1 in. cheapest, gross (6): SPATULA, nickel with spoon, 120 mm., (BTL) B60/0140: TILES, white glazed, builders, (3): TRIPOD stand (BTL) B61/1300: TUBES TEST: 'Pyrex glass', standard rimless, 125 x 16 mm., (BTL) B67/0050, (gross): TUBES TEST, soda glass, standard rimless, 2 in. x $\frac{1}{4}$ in., (BTL) B67/0035, (gross): TUBES TEST, 'Khan', 75 x 12 mm. (BTL) D3/0470, (gross): TUBES CENTRIFUGE, graduated conical, 10 ml., 'Pyrex' (BTL) C6/0102 (10): TUBES CENTRIFUGE, plain conical, 15 ml., polythene, (BTL) C6/0105 (12): TUBES, Lovibond, 10 ml., (LOV) AF217, (10): TUBING, flexible metalic, 5 ft. length, (BTL) B75/0260: TUBING, soda glass, ext. diam. 6-7 mm., (BTL) B75/0060, 10 lb. bundle: TEATS, red rubber, size 2, (BTL) B57/0040, (12): WATER BATH, electrical, 'Junior Thermostatic', 12 x 5 x 4 in. int. (GRA) JB 1, state voltage, £12, or Junior Water bath, gas heated (HEA) H1030: WEIGHTS, 10 mg. — 100 g., (G&G) S14-080: WEIGHING SCOOP, 6 ml., (EMI), G3227: WIRE, nickel chrome 22 SWG, (BTL) B77/0030, yard:

APPENDIX H

The Protein Composition of some Important Foods (14:4)

The following list gives the number of pounds (or fractions of a pound) and grams of various foods required to yield the same quantity of protein, the quantity chosen being 100 g. or 3½ oz. It will enable readers to work out the comparative costs of their foods in terms of their protein content. In this list 'EP' means the edible portion of the food only. The list starts with the most protein rich foods, those with 100 g. of protein in the smallest weight of food, and progresses to the poorer foods. The editor is grateful to Miss Ingrid Rutishauser for preparing it.

Dried fish (EP) 0.4 lb. or 180 g.: dried skim milk 0.6 lb. or 270 g.: shelled ground nuts 0.8 lb. or 365 g.: hard cheese 0.9 lb. or 410 g.: kidney beans 0.9lb. or 410 g.: chick peas 1.1 lb. or 500 g.: liver 1.1 lbs. 500 g.: fresh fish (EP) 1.2 lb. or 550 g.: chicken 1.2 lbs. or 550 g.: moderately fatty beef (EP) 1.4 lbs. or 640 g.: moderately fatty mutton (EP) 1.7 lbs. or 770 g.: hen's eggs 1.9 lbs. or 860 g.: wheat flour 2.0 lbs. or 910 g.: whole sorghum grain 2.1 lbs. or 930 g.: termites (EP) 2.2 lbs. or 1,000 g.: refined maize meal 2.8 lbs. or 1,300 g.: polished rice 3.1 lbs. or 1,450 g.: whole grain finger millet 3.7 lbs. or 1,700 g.

To use this list, inquire in the local market for the prices per lb. of these foods or those similar to them, and multiply the value found by the fraction of a pound containing 100 g. of protein. Thus, if fish costs 5/- a pound locally, 5/- x 0.4, or 2/- worth will contain 100 g. of protein. Cow's milk is not shown on the list: 100 g. of protein is contained in about 5½ pints (3,000 ml.) of milk. The very high protein content of peas and beans is clearly shown in this table, and they are likely to be the cheapest protein source. The importance of persuading mothers to mix at least a little animal protein with the vegetable protein they give their children has been emphasized in section 14:4.

APPENDIX I

DRUG DOSAGE IN CHILDREN

This list is intended as a rough guide for drug dosage for young children. Local variation in dosage may be necessary, and the strength of available tablets and mixtures must be known.

Aspirin. 0—1 yr. 150 mgm. (2½ grains)/dose
Over 1—4 yr. 300 mgm. (5 grains)/dose.
Over 4—10 yr. 600 mgm. (10 grains)/dose.

Chloral hydrate. For light anaesthesia: 60 mgm./kgm./dose (½ grain/lb./dose).
For sedation: 30 mgm./kgm./dose (¼ grain/lb./dose).

Chloramphenicol. 50—200 mgm./kgm./day (25—100 mgm./lb./day). (Divided into 3 doses 8-hourly or 4 doses 6-hourly.) *Caution is needed with dosage for the newborn* (25 mgm./lb./day), especially for the premature (12.5 mgm./ lb.day). 1 capsule contains 250 mgm. chloramphenicol.)

Chloroquine.
Intramuscular or subcutaneous: 5 mgm./kgm./dose (2½ mgm.lb./dose). Doses are calculated on the base content of the tablet.

By mouth: 0—1 yr. ¼ tablet/day for 3 days
Over 1—5 yr. ½ " " " " "
Over 5—10 yr. 1 " " " " "
Over 10 yr. 2 " " " " "
(1 tablet usually contains 150 mgm. chloroquine base.)

Dichlorophen ('Antiphen'). 4—6 gm. (single dose).

Isoniazid (INH or INAH). 10—20 mgm./kgm./day (5—10 mgm./lb./day), divided into 1—2 doses/day. Max. dose 300 mgm./day (1 tablet contains 50 mgm. INH).

Iron dextran ('Imferon') See Figure 25 (13:7).

Mepacrine. (1) *Giardiasis.* 0—2 yr. 25 mgm./dose.
Over 2—5 yr. 50 mgm./dose.
(Two doses twice daily for 5 days.)
(2) *Tapeworms* 2—5 yr. 400 mgm., over 5—10 yr. 600 mgm., over 10 yr. 800 mgm.
(1 tablet contains 100 mgm. mepacrine.)

Paraldehyde. Intramuscular. 0.3 c.c./kgm./dose (0.15 c.c./lb.dose).
By mouth or rectum. 0.6 c.c./kgm./dose (0.3 c.c./lb./dose).

Para-aminosalicylic acid (P.A.S.) 250 mgm./kgm./day (125 mgm.lb./day). (Divided into 3 doses daily.)

Phenobarbitone. 3 mgm./kgm./day ($\frac{1}{14}$ grain/lb.day).
(Divided into 3 doses daily.)

Piperazine. Up to 2 yr. 2 gm.; 2—5 yr. 3 gm.; over 5 yr. 4 gm.

Promethazine. ('Phenergan').
1 mgm./kgm./dose ($\frac{1}{2}$ mgm./lb./dose).
2—4 doses daily. (1 tablet contains 25 mgm.)

Sulphonamides. 250 mgm./kgm./day (125 mgm./lb./day).
(Divided into 4 doses 6-hourly.) (1 tablet contains 0.5 gm.)

Streptomycin. 40 mgm./kgm./day (20 mgm./lb./day) intramuscularly. (Single daily dose in tuberculosis; divided into 2 doses in respiratory and neonatal infections.)

Tetrachlorethylene. 0.1 c.c./kgm./dose ($\frac{3}{4}$ minim/lb./dose).
(Given as a single dose.) Maximum 5 c.c.

Tetracyclines. ('Aureomycin', 'Terramycin', 'Achromycin').
20—50 mgm./kgm./day (10—25 mgm./lb./day).
(Divided into 3 doses 8-hourly or 4 doses 6-hourly.)
(1 capsule contains 250 mgm.)

Thiacetazone. (Tb. 1.) Below 20 lb.—25 mgm./day; 20—40 lb.—50 mgm./ day; 40—80 lb.—100 mgm./day; over 80 lbs.—150 mgm./day.

APPENDIX J
A LIST OF DRUGS

This list is to help those who want to make sure that their hospital contains the drugs necessary to the practice of medicine in tropical countries. It is shorter than most 'standard lists' and is to be looked upon as a basic selection which will be adequate for ordinary purposes. The list contains about 140 drugs and is intended to be handed to a dispensary assistant with the words 'Just look and make sure we have got these things, and make me out a list of what we lack' — see 8:9.

Some attempt has been made to distinguish those drugs which are required for occasional use from those which are wanted routinely; drugs for occasional use are marked with an asterisk and only a small stock will be required. Where quantities are specified, these usually refer to the size of the common tablet, or to the quantity contained in a 1 ml. in a vial or ampoule. They are no indication as to dose and are included for assistance in ordering.

Drugs acting on the cardiovascular system.

Aminophylline, inj. amps.
Adrenaline tartarate, inj amps.
*Nor-Adrenaline, inj. 4 mg. amps.
Methyl amphetamine ('Methedrine') inj. 30 mg. amps.
Prepared digitalis, 65 mg. tabs.
Digoxin, 0.25 mg. tabs.
Digoxin, inj. 0.5 mg. amps.
*Heparin, inj. 5,000 units per ml. vials.
*Protamine sulphate inj. 1% vials (Heparin antidote).

Drugs acting on the nervous system.

Acetylsalicylic acid, 300 mg. tabs.
Ergotamine, 1 mg. tabs.
Morphine sulphate, inj. amps. 15 mg.
Phenobarbitone, 30 mg. tabs.
Pethidine 50 mg. tabs.
Pethidine hydrochloride, inj. 50 mg. amps.
Amylobarbitone sodium ('Amytal'), 65 mg. caps.
Phenobarbitone 30 mg. tabs.
Sodium phenobarbitone, inj. 200 mg. amps.
Paraldehyde, inj. 10 ml. amps.
Epanutin, 100 mg. caps.
Chlorpromazine ('Largactil') 25 mg. tabs.
Chlorpromazine, inj. 50 mg. amps.
Chloral hydrate crystals.

Lignocaine without adrenaline. 2% vials.
Dental lignocaine with adrenalin, 2% cartridges.
Procaine, inj. 2% vials.
Omnopon and scopolamine, inj. 20 mg. plus 0.4 mg. amps.
Sodium thiopentone ('Pentothal'), inj. amps. 0.5 g.
Anaesthetic ether, cans.
Ethyl chloride, tubes.
Drugs acting on the uterus.
Ergometrine maleate, inj. 0.5 mg. amps.
Synthetic oxytocin ('Syntocinon'), inj. 0.5 ml. amps.
Pethidine with levallorphan ('Pethilorphan'), inj. 50 mg. amps.
Drugs acting on the respiratory system.
Ephedrine, 30 mg. tabs.
Nikethamide, 2 ml. amps.
Antihistamines.
Chlorpheniramine ('Piriton'), 4 mg. tabs.
Promethazine ('Phenegan'), 25 mg. tabs.
Promethazine, 10 mg. in 4 ml. elixir.
Antiparasitic agents.
Penicillin, crystalline, inj. vials.
Penicillin, procaine with aluminium monostearate, inj. vials.
Penicillin, procaine fortified ('PPF'), inj. vials.
'Triplopen' — see 13:5 and 30:1.
Chloramphenicol, 250 mg. caps.
Chloramphenicol suspension, 125 mg. in 5 ml. bottle.
Tetracycline, 250 mg. caps.
Tetracycline suspension, 125 mg. in 5 ml. bottle.
Tetracycline, inj. 250 mg. amps.
Streptomycin sulphate, 1 g. vials.
Sulphadiazine, 0.5 g. tabs.
Sulphadimidine, 0.5 g. tabs.
Isoniazid (100 mg.) and TB 1 (thiacetazone) (50 mg.) compound tablet (SNP) see 21:18c.
Paraminosalicylic acid ('PAS'), powder.
Dapsone, 100 mg. tabs.
Chloroquine phosphate, 250 mg. tabs.
Chloroquine, inj. 40 mg. amps.
*Quinine hydrochloride, inj. amps. 300 mg. (13:6).
Primaquin, 7.5 mg. base tabs.
Emetine hydrochloride, inj. 60 mg. amps. (amoebiasis).
Diloxamide furoate ('Furamide'), 0.5 g. tabs. (amoebiasis).
Pentamidine isethionate, inj. 200 mg. amps. (trypanosomiasis).
Tryparsamside, 3 g. amps. (trypanosomiasis).

Mel B. 5 ml. amps. (trypanosomiasis).
Stibophen, inj. vials (*Schistosoma haematobium*).
'Astiban', inj. 2 g. amps. (*Schistosoma mansoni*).
Diethyl carbamazine ('Hetrazan'), 50 mg. tabs. (filariasis).
Piperazine adipate, 300 mg. tabs. (ascariasis).
Dichlorophen, 0.5 g. tabs. (taeniasis).
Tetrachlorethylene ('TCE'), liquid.
Acetarsol pessaries 250 mg. (trichomoniasis).
Metronidazole ('Flagyl') 200 mg. tabs. (trichomoniasis) (30:1).
'Tetmosol', liquid (scabies).
DDT application (lice).

Hormones.

Soluble insulin, inj. 40 units ml. vials.
Insulin zinc suspension ('IZS') inj. 40 units. ml. vials.
Tolbutamide, 0.5 gm. tabs.
*Hydrocortisone sodium succinate, inj. 100 mg. amps.
Prednisone, 5 mg. tabs.

Minerals and Vitamins.

Ferrous sulphate, 300 mg. tabs.
Iron dextran ('Imferon') inj. 2 and 5 ml. amps.
Folic acid, 5 mg. tabs.
'Multivite', tabs.
Vitamin A concentrated liquid, 50,000 units ml.
Vitamin D concentrated liquid, 10,000 units ml.
Menapthone sodium bisulphite (Vitamin K), 10 mg. amps.
Cyanocobalmin (Vitamin B_{12}) inj. 50 μg. amps.

Drugs acting on the gut.

Magnesium trisilicate powder.
Liquid paraffin.
Cascara sagrada, 125 mg. tabs.

Drugs acting on the kidney.

Mersalyl, inj. 2 ml. amps.
Bendrofluazide ('Aprinox'), 5 mg. tabs.

Intravenous solutions.

Acid citrate dextrose for blood transfusion (23:7) (30:2).
Half strength Darrow's solution with 2.5% glucose (30:2) (15:4).
Physiological saline. (30:2).
Glucose 5%.

Antidotes for poisoning.

*Dimercaprol, inj. 5% amps. (anti-heavy metals).
*Bemegride ('Megimide'), amps. (anti-barbiturate).
*Nalorphine ('Nalline'), 10 mg. and 1 mg. per ml., 5 ml. amps. (anti-morphia).

Vaccines, antigens and antibodies (all with expiry dates).
Glycerinated PPD (A & H) (Heaf test).
BCG vaccine (GLA).
Vaccine lymph.
Triple vaccine (Diptheria, pertussis, tetanus).
*Rabies vaccine.
*Rabies hyperimmune serum.
*Antitoxins for diphtheria, tetanus and gas gangrene.
Eye preparations.
Fluorescine, 2% eye drops.
Cocaine 4% with homatropine 2% eye drops.
Esserine ½%.
Tetracyline, 1% eye ointment.
Sulphacetamide ('Albucid'), 10% eye drops.
Ear preparations.
Chloramphenicol ear drops 5%.
Glycerine and phenol ear drops.
Boric acid and spirit ear drops.
Skin preparations.
Emulsifying ointment (a basic ointment).
Aqueous emulsifying ointment (washable and can be used on the hair).
2% salicylic acid in emulsifying ointment (useful for many scaly lesions).
Gentian violet 0.5% aqueous (Sepsis).
Potassium permanganate crystals (use as a dilute (1/8,000) wash for widespread sepsis).
Ammoniated mercury ointment with tar (6%) and salicylic acid (2%) (psoriasis).
Calamine lotion (itchy lesions).
Calamine lotion with 2% phenol (itchy lesions).
Calamine liniment (eczemas).
Calamine liniment with 2% sulphur (acne).
Hydrocortisone cream (if possible, expensive; for infantile eczema).
Antiseptics and disinfectants.
Hibitane.
Cetrimide.
Lysol.
Spirit.
Iodine.

APPENDIX K
ACKNOWLEDGEMENTS

Very many people have given of their knowledge and experience to this symposium. Some have provided the material from which whole chapters were written, others bright ideas; many were present at the conference held at Makerere on 'Hospitals and Health Centres in Africa' out of which this book was built, and some have been kind enough to read and criticize the manuscript in the many stages through which it passed. Such virtue as may be accorded to these pages thus stands to their credit.

Dr. G. Ambrosoli, Kalongo Catholic Hospital, Lira, Uganda.
Dr. F. J. Bennett, Reader in Preventive Medicine, Makerere.
Dr. J. R. Billinghurst, Lecturer in Medicine, Makerere.
Dr. C. B. S. Bosa, Deputy Chief Medical Officer, Buganda.
Dr. D. J. Bradley, Lecturer in Microbiology, Makerere.
Dr. R. Brown, Rockefeller Fellow in Paediatrics, Makerere.
Dr. & Mrs. Leslie Burgess, Adviser in Nutrition, The World Health Organization, Dar es Salaam.
Dr. G. Busato, St. Luke's Hospital, Angal, Uganda.
Dr. D. B. Byarhuanga, The Ugandan Ministry of Health.
Mr. D. E. Church, A.R.I.B.A., Kampala, Uganda.
Miss J. M. Cocker, Principal Matron, The Ugandan Ministry of Health.
Dr. Robert Cook, Ankole Pre-school Protection Programme, Mbarara, Uganda.
Dr. Christine A. Cooper, Consultant Paediatrician, The Medical Service, Sierra Leone.
Dr. P. Corti, St. Mary's Hospital, Lacor, Uganda.
Dr. P. S. V. Cox, The B.C.M.S. Hospital, Amudat, Uganda.
Dr. Mary A. Doyle, St. Joseph's Hospital, Masaka, Uganda.
Mr. S. W. Eaves, Instrument Technician, University College Hospital, Ibadan.
Mr. T. Eddie, Senior Radiographer, Mulago Hospital.
Dr. J. L. Eshleman, Shrati Mennonite Mission Hospital, Tanzania.
Dr. J. V. Farman, Consultant Anaesthetist, Addenbrookes Hospital, Cambridge.
Dr. N. R. E. Fendall, lately Director of Medical Services, Kenya, presently with the Rockefeller Foundation.
Professor W. D. Foster, Professor of Microbiology, Makerere.
Dr. W. Fox, the M.R.C. Tuberculosis Research Unit, London.
Mr. A. French, Senior Lecturer in Education, Makerere.
Dr. D. P. Ghai, Special Lecturer in Economics, Makerere.

Dr. P. J. S. Hamilton, Lecturer in Medicine, Makerere.
Dr. P. S. E. G. Harland, The M.R.C. Infantile Malnutrition Research Unit, Kampala.
Dr. Pauline Haswell, St. Anne's Hospital, Liuli, Tanzania.
Miss Faith Hodgson, Public Health Nurse Adviser, WHO, Kenya.
Mr. A. C. Holmes, Health Education Adviser, The African Medical and Research Foundation, Kenya.
Professor M. S. R. Hutt, Professor of Pathology, Makerere.
Dr. H. Haigh, The Methodist Hospital, Ituk Mbang, Nigeria.
Dr. Jean T. Holland, Uganda Blood Transfusion Service.
Professor D. B. Jelliffe, F.R.C.P., UNICEF Professor of Child Health, Makerere.
Mr. R. Jolly, Lecturer in Applied Economics, Cambridge University.
Dr. F. Kamunvi, The Bugandan Medical Service.
Professor S. Kark, Visiting Professor of Social and Preventive Medicine, Hadassa University, Jerusalem.
Dr. O. Killen, Public Health Advisor, WHO, Kenya.
Professor A. Lambo, Professor of Psychiatry, University College, Ibadan.
Mr. M. Linton, Laboratory Technician, Mvumi Hospital, Dodoma, Tanzania.
Dr. J. M. Maitland, The Freda Carr Hospital, Ngora, Uganda.
Dr. R. Manché, The Ugandan Medical Service.
Dr. T. C. H. Matthews, The Kenyan Medical Service.
Dr. Gertrude Mayer, Bumbuli Hospital, Soni, Tanzania.
Dr. R. M. A. McClelland, Senior Lecturer in Anaesthetics, Welsh National School of Medicine.
Sister M. Mechtilde, Nsambya Catholic Hospital, Kampala.
Dr. R. Mol, Medical Officer, WHO, Butare, Rwanda.
Dr. D. C. Morley, Senior Lecturer in Human Nutrition, The London School of Hygiene and Tropical Medicine.
Dr. S. A. Mwankemwa, The Tanzanian Ministry of Health.
Dr. M. B. Ngirwamungu, The Tanzanian Ministry of Health.
Dr. H. Bernadette O'Brien, The Medical Missionaries of Mary.
Dr. A. P. Oomen, The Catholic Hospital, Sengerema, Tanzania.
Dr. E. M. Poulton, MCH Adviser, WHO, Uganda.
Dr. E. R. Rado, Lecturer in Economics, Glasgow University.
Dr. J. Rawes, St. Francis Hospital, Katete, Zambia.
Dr. J. Richmond, Senior Lecturer in Haematology, Edinburgh University.
Dr. & Mrs. G. A. Saxton, Lecturer in Preventive Medicine, Makerere.
Dr. I. Schneideman, WHO Lecturer in Paediatrics, Makerere.
Dr. C. Sezi, The Ugandan Medical Service.

Dr. R. D. Shaffer, The African Medical and Research Foundation, Nairobi.
Dr. A. G. Shaper, Reader in Medicine, Makerere.
Dr. J. L. H. Sharp, Kisiizi Hospital, Uganda.
Dr. G. M. Short, lately Tuberculosis Officer, The Ugandan Medical Service.
Dr. Imgen C. Snow, The Nordic Tanzanian Centre.
Dr. J. P. Stanfield, Lecturer in Paediatrics, Makerere.
Professor R. R. Trussell, Professor of Obstetrics, Makerere.
Dr. J. Taylor, Mvumi Hospital, Dodoma, Tanzania.
Dr. W. Holmes Taylor, The Ankole Mission Hospital, Uganda.
Dr. A. Brenda Vaughan, Reader in Anaesthetics, Makerere.
Dr. O. Walter, Bumbuli Hospital, Soni, Tanzania.
Dr. A. Warley, WHO Lecturer in Paediatrics, Makerere.
Dr. Aileen Williams, Nabusanke Catholic Hospital, Uganda.
Drs. E. H. and P. H. Williams, Kuluva Hospital, Arua, Uganda.

Epilogue

THE EVALUATION OF CARE—THE NEED FOR ACTION

Maurice King

The evaluation of care. This symposium is largely intended for students, and the opening paragraphs of the epilogue are for them. The practising doctor, already heavy eyed from hard work and lack of sleep, is therefore asked to skip them and pass on.

It is three o'clock on a Sunday morning; there is a tap at the window and the yellow light from a paraffin lantern shines into the room. It is the night dresser from the outpatient department to say that the medical assistant on duty wants the doctor to come and see a woman they have just admitted straight to ward four. It has been a hard day; to turn over, to go to sleep and to see her in the morning, or to get up and go along now, which is it to be?

Whatever has been said in the chapters preceding about medical care, the answer to this question is the final criterion of it. Without the attitude of mind that gets up and goes, all that has been said in these pages has been said in vain, for it is actions such as this, and countless others like them in the care of common man as a person that finally determines the quality of the medical endeavour.

But, granted that this attitude of mind is the ultimate standard, what more tangible if lesser ones are there whereby good medical care is to be distinguished from that not so good? How, for instance, are a Minister of Health, or a foreign visitor to judge the quality of care provided when they visit immaculate white corridors and see the glistening chromium plate of one hospital, or are shown the humble 'mud-wattle-and-white-wash' of another?

There were once two distinguished visitors who were wont to be shown round many hospitals and who used to judge them by asking to see first hospital's library and then its laboratory. Both these requests were apt to produce such consternation in their hosts that these visitors used to take it in turns to ask them. Both are good criteria, particularly the library, but there are others, and among the questions they might have asked are these:

How much time is spent teaching the junior staff? (8:3). What teaching aids are used? (27:2). Have they got such manuals as might help them? (29:2).

How many pints of blood does the hospital manage to raise for each of its beds each year? (23:4).

What does the hospital know about the incidence of disease in the community it serves? Has any attempt been made to make a community diagnosis? (5:10).

What is the place of mothers in the children's ward? (13:3).

What provision is made for intensive care? (9:5).

How much health education is done? (6:2).

Are the local schoolmasters doing their best to impart the necessary health knowledge? (6:6c).

Have the humbler members of the hospital staff been instructed in their role in health education? (6:6).

How many auxiliaries are capable of setting up a scalp vein transfusion, doing a lumbar puncture or applying a plaster cast? (7:5).

What proportion of the children round about are immunized, and what with? (17:1).

Has any attempt been made to co-operate with and teach the indigenous midwives? (19:2).

How actively is outpatient care taken to the people? (2:10).

What proportion of the tuberculous patients complete their course of treatment? (21:18a).

Is an oral repair fluid readily available, such as 'saline mixture'? (15:8).

Is the most made of the advantages offered by tube feeding? (30:7).

Has any attempt been made to make even a rudimentary central sterile supply service? (30:8).

Does the hospital own a vacuum extractor? (19:7).

Is family planning an integral part of the MCH service? (18:6).

Are milk packets available in the outpatient department for malnourished children? (14:14).

Has the hospital a 'master plan'? (10:1). Are there copies of it in the ministerial headquarters?

If the visitor is in authority in the territory, he in his turn might be asked the following questions:

What priority is accorded to health centre services? (3:1).

How closely is the development of the service adapted to the economic realities of the country? (1:11).

How vigorously are training programmes being instituted for medical auxiliaries and particularly for medical assistants? (1:16).

Is there a 'service newsletter' which keeps the directorate in touch with its officers, and its officers with one another on matters technical, administrative and social?

How often are conferences, seminars and refresher courses organized in the larger centres for doctors, medical assistants, midwives and nurses? (1:17a).

Has it been possible to reduce the restless posting that upsets so many services by letting a few doctors act as locums, with a financial inducement if need be, so that many shall enjoy the security and opportunity of being in the same place as long as they want to?

How does the service look upon creativity, zeal and dedication? Is it recognized, encouraged and where possible rewarded? As some evidence for it what have members of the service published during the past few years? (1:15).

What is the morale of the service? Is it a service to which all its members from the top to the bottom are proud to belong? If not, what is being done to make it so? (8:2a).

What is the career structure for medical assistants? What is their morale? At the height of their career can they ever earn as much as the newly qualified doctor?

The need to act. In the early pages of the preface the editor saw himself as but a merchant for the ideas of others, merely as a provider of paper and ink. Thirty chapters and eleven appendices later he has no reason to change his mind, and this holds for his own chapters also. But, when the time comes to sum up, this provides a usefully objective vantage point. He would like to use it to do two things, one of which follows from the other.

The first is to exhort the reader, and especially the student, to be critical about what has been said. It is unlikely that several hundred pages contain only ideas that require no further qualification, and only information that is minutely correct, whatever pains may have been taken to make it so. This then is not a book to be swallowed whole, but one to be studied, criticized and examined, for to be critical implies having thought about what has been said.

If, when this critical analysis is complete, there remain ideas that seem excellent and want following up, then the reader is exhorted to do something about them. What he can do will depend upon who he is.

If he is a student this is easy, for he will know that he is likely to be examined on health centres and will be expected to be able to cross-match blood for transfusion.

It is the reader who is a doctor already in rural practice in a developing country who will best be able to put the ideas here into practice. He is urged to look back through the book, take paper and pencil, and list the items that promise to be useful together with the steps needed to put them into practice. If progressive patient care promises to be valuable, then what must be done to start it going? If certain simple pieces of equipment or reagents are missing from the laboratory, then these need listing. Knowing what should be done is one thing, *but the ability to get it done is quite another.*

If the reader is a student in an industrial country and a period of service abroad seems a good idea, then he is urged to make the decision, take the necessary steps, and come.

Perhaps the reader is merely the citizen of an industrial country, who has remembered the first section of Chapter One and the footnote under it recording the fact that the level of aid from the industrial to the developing nations is something of the order of less than 1 per cent. of their Gross National Products, and is falling, even from this low level. If so, he is urged to do all he can to see the level of aid increased, both in men and money, so that the most can be made of the vast human potential of the developing countries, which now lies dormant lacking sufficient food, education, employment and medical care. It is to the common man in these countries that this book is dedicated. It is in his care both medically and otherwise, both globally and as 'a village mother', that the command to care for one's neighbour, the humanistic ideal to make the most of mankind, and the biological common sense not to let the infinite potential of our species lie wasted, all unite in one final and compelling imperative — do all you can — *ACT*.

The figure overleaf is a spare copy. Cut it out carefully, cover it with clear x-ray film and pin it up on the ward notice board.

Note. If the ward staff have difficulty in using figures 27 and 30, get them to take a piece of paper, to put its top right hand corner on the diagonal line of the graph to be followed, and to find the child's weight with its right hand margin. Its top will then tell them where to read the vertical scale. If they cannot keep the paper straight, rule a few vertical and horizontal lines to help them.

Fig. 25 **A NOMOGRAM FOR THE USE OF INTRAMUSCULAR IRON**

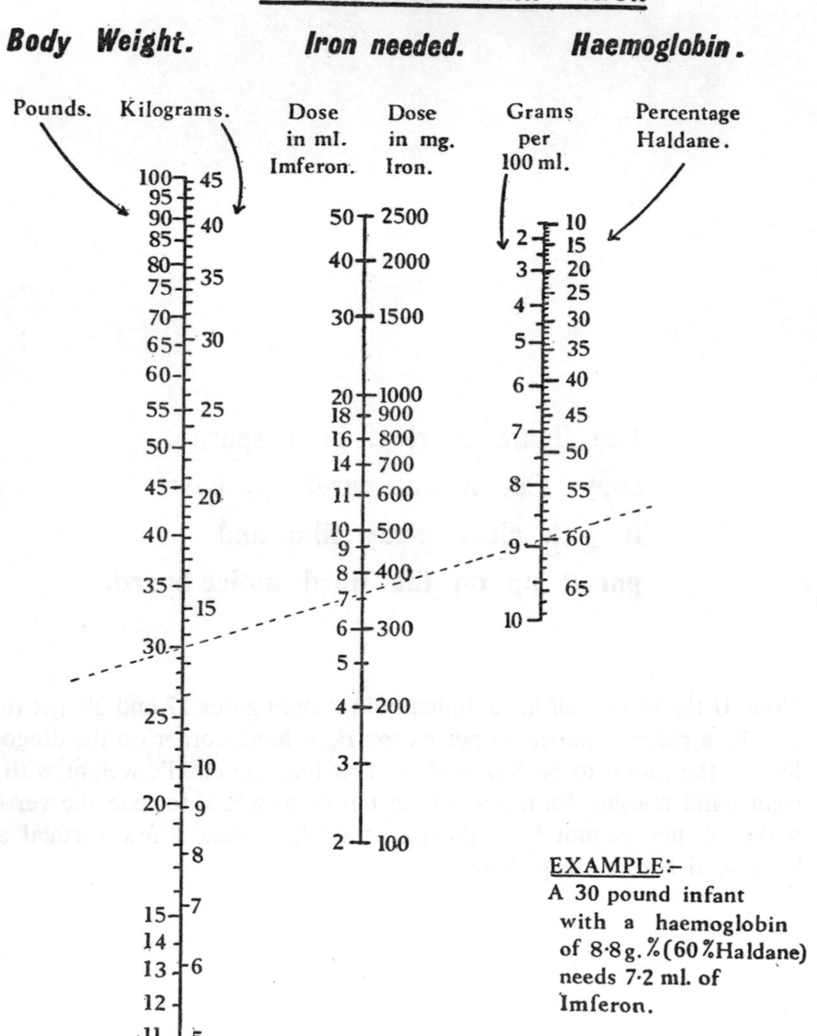

Weigh the child & measure his haemoglobin. Find these values on the scales & join them up with a ruler. The point where it cuts the central scale gives the dose of iron required. The dose in ml. refers ONLY to those iron solutions containing 50 mg. of iron in each ml., Imferon for example.

The figure overleaf is a spare copy. Cut it out carefully, cover it with clear x-ray film and pin it up on the ward notice board.

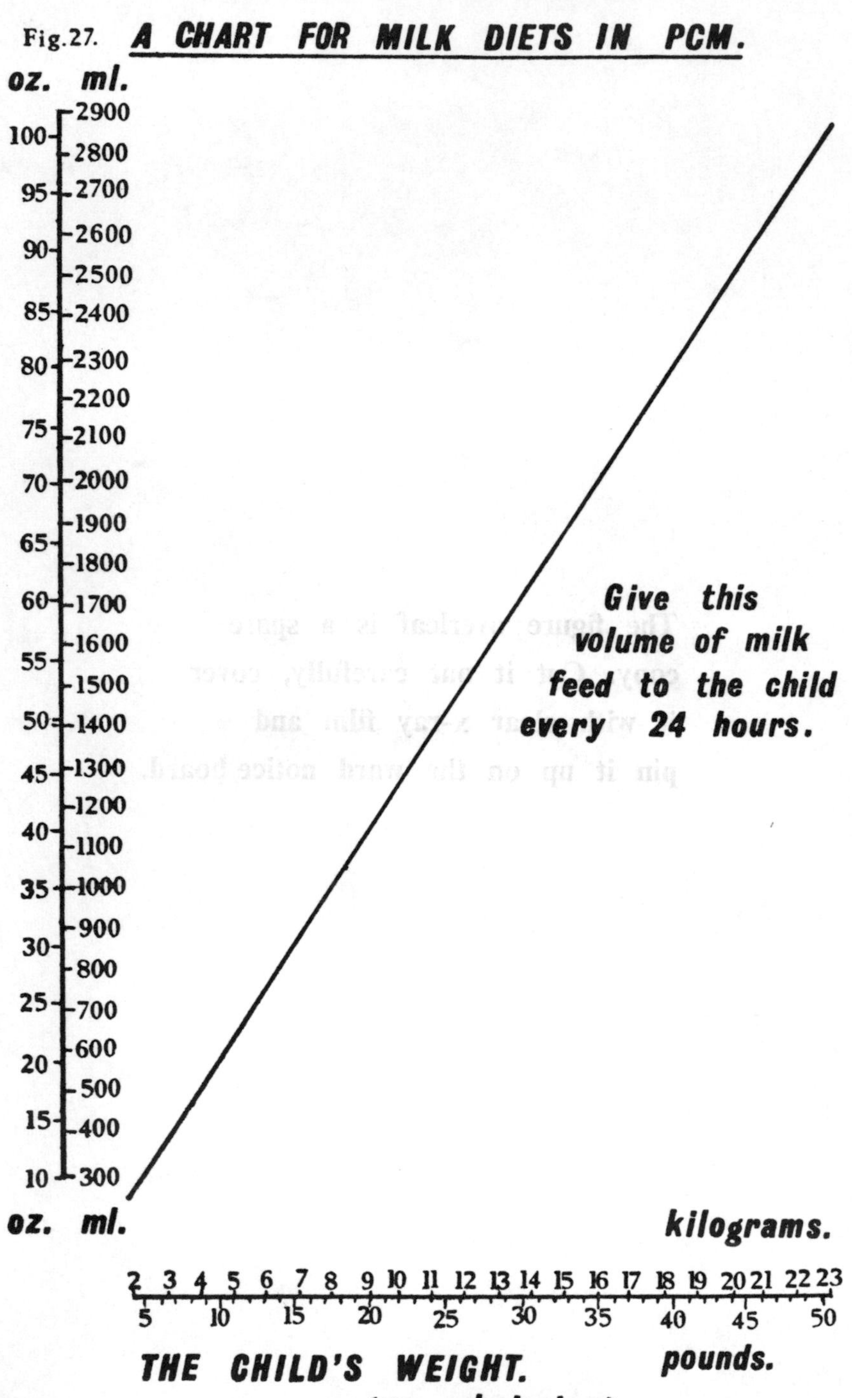
Fig.27. A CHART FOR MILK DIETS IN PCM.
oz. ml.
100 95 90 85 80 75 70 65 60 55 50 45 40 35 30 25 20 15 10
2900 2800 2700 2600 2500 2400 2300 2200 2100 2000 1900 1800 1700 1600 1500 1400 1300 1200 1100 1000 900 800 700 600 500 400 300
Give this volume of milk feed to the child every 24 hours.
oz. ml.
kilograms.
2 3 4 5 6 7 8 9 10 11 12 13 14 15 16 17 18 19 20 21 22 23
5 10 15 20 25 30 35 40 45 50
pounds.
THE CHILD'S WEIGHT.
(on admission)

The figure overleaf is a spare copy. Cut it out carefully, cover it with clear x-ray film and pin it up on the ward notice board.

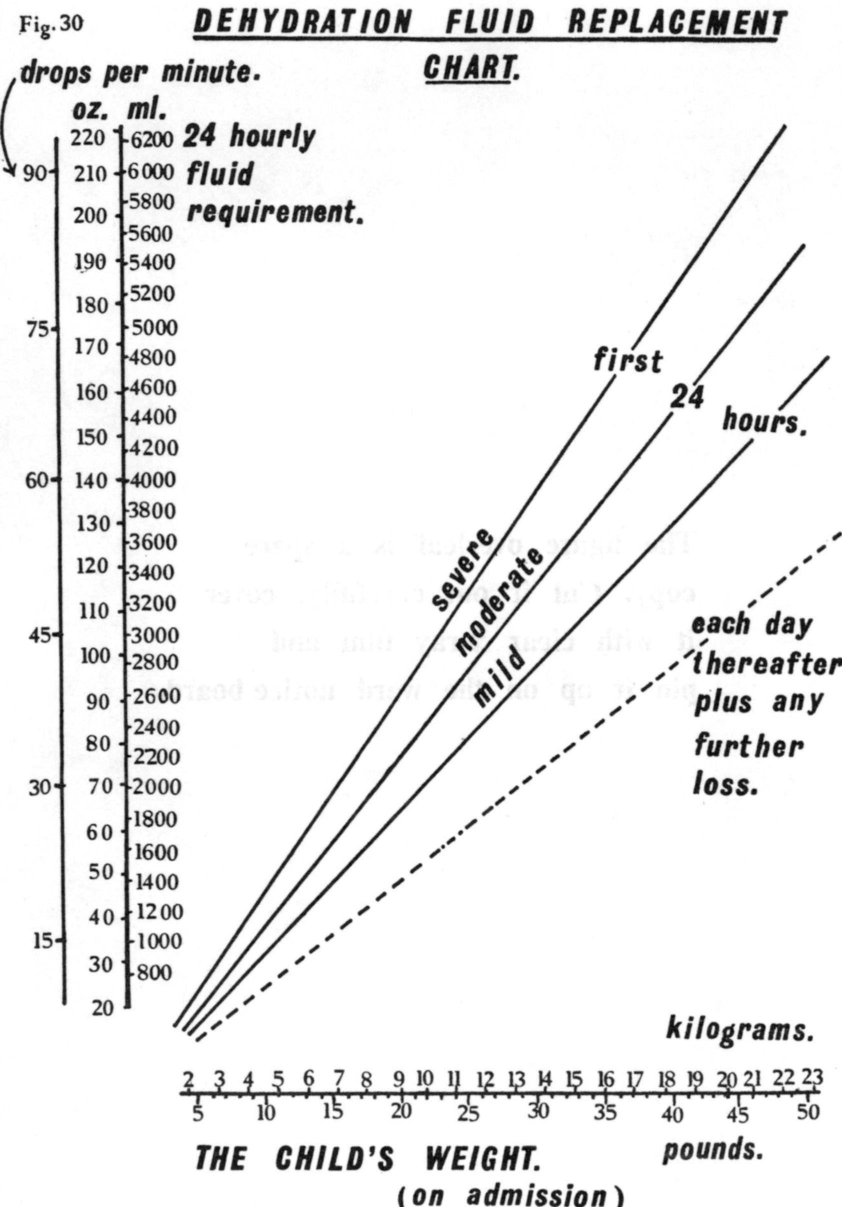
Fig. 30
DEHYDRATION FLUID REPLACEMENT CHART.
drops per minute.
oz. ml.
24 hourly fluid requirement.
90
75
60
45
30
15
220
210
200
190
180
170
160
150
140
130
120
110
100
90
80
70
60
50
40
30
20
6200
6000
5800
5600
5400
5200
5000
4800
4600
4400
4200
4000
3800
3600
3400
3200
3000
2800
2600
2400
2200
2000
1800
1600
1400
1200
1000
800
first 24 hours.
severe
moderate
mild
each day thereafter plus any further loss.
kilograms.
2 3 4 5 6 7 8 9 10 11 12 13 14 15 16 17 18 19 20 21 22 23
5 10 15 20 25 30 35 40 45 50
pounds.
THE CHILD'S WEIGHT.
(on admission)

INDEX